BENJAMIN RAND

# THE LIFE, UNPUBLISHED LETTERS
### AND
## PHILOSOPHICAL REGIMEN
### OF
## ANTONY, EARL OF SHAFTESBURY

Elibron Classics
www.elibron.com

ANTHONY, EARL OF SHAFTESBURY.

The Right Honorable Anthony Ashley
Cooper Earl of Shaftesbury, Baron Ashley of
Wintourn S.ᵗ Giles, & Lord Cooper of Pawlett.

P. Westerman Pinx.                                     Sim: Gribelin sculp.

W.S. Pells. Ph. Sc.

# THE LIFE, UNPUBLISHED LETTERS,

### AND

## PHILOSOPHICAL REGIMEN

### OF

# ANTHONY, EARL OF SHAFTESBURY

AUTHOR OF THE "CHARACTERISTICS"

EDITED BY

## BENJAMIN RAND, Ph.D.

*Harvard University*

LONDON

SWAN SONNENSCHEIN & CO. LIM.

NEW YORK: THE MACMILLAN CO.

1900.

# PREFATORY INTRODUCTION.

The present volume consists of a sketch of the life, of the unpublished letters, and of the philosophical regimen of that most fascinating English moralist, the third Earl of Shaftesbury. The entire material for the work, apart from the letters addressed to Locke, has been obtained from the Shaftesbury Papers, which are now deposited in the Record Office in London. Mr. Thomas Fowler in his "Shaftesbury and Hutcheson[1]" expressed the belief that these papers would well repay a more careful investigation than he was able to give them in the preparation of his book. Such research has been made and the results of it appear in the present work. The perusal of it will not only fully confirm the favourable forecast as to the probable worth of the manuscripts for the life of Shaftesbury, but will also reveal, I believe, that they contained from his pen one of the most remarkable unpublished contributions of modern times in the domain of philosophic thought.

The sketch of the life of the third Earl, which forms the first division of this book, was written by his son, the fourth Earl of Shaftesbury. Its contents have been essentially printed by Thomas Birch in the General Dictionary (1734—41) of Bayle, without any due acknowledgment of their source, although apparently by permission (British Museum, Birch MSS., No. 4318). But this is the first time for the Life to be published under the name of its real author, and with the exception of a necessary change in the order of paragraphs to conform with known events, almost precisely as it exists in the original manuscript. Various clauses and paragraphs of interest have also been inserted as footnotes, which have been taken from a rough draft of the life in manuscript that undoubtedly served as the basis for the copy here followed in the text. In addition, moreover, to the value of this sketch as

---

[1] Thomas Fowler, Shaftesbury and Hutcheson, Lond., 1882.

an original and heretofore comparatively inaccessible source of information for the life of the third Earl, its publication here affords in a compact and narrative form the various events in his career necessary to be known by the reader in order to obtain a clear and ready understanding of the contents of the letters which immediately follow in the work.

The second division of this book comprises, with a few indicated exceptions, the unpublished letters of Shaftesbury. These begin in 1689, when he was eighteen years of age, and continue for the most part with desirable regularity, until the time of his death in 1713. The social position, political activity, and philosophical renown of the writer accord to them an unwonted value. The events of his personal life, and the character of the times in which he lived, are here revealed with a naturalness and sincerity which impart to the correspondence a charm often lacking in similar productions too evidently intended for posthumous publication. All these letters have been arranged in their chronological order. Certain characteristic series of them may, however, very properly be mentioned.

Scattered throughout the work is a succession of letters which relate to the personal and family affairs of the third Earl. A small volume of such letters, chiefly in reference to his first unsuccessful love affair and subsequent marriage to another, was published in 1721, by John Toland. These were printed during the lifetime of the two ladies concerned, and naturally evoked the indignation of the fourth Earl. Shaftesbury's engagement to a lady whom he had never seen does not conform, it is true, with modern standards and procedure. Nevertheless the choice is not difficult to make between a courtship that might largely have preceded marriage and the continued and deepening devotion which the third Earl bestowed on his wife throughout their wedded life. There is nothing that demands concealment in his career, whatever his mistakes or shortcomings; the more closely one presses home upon the inner motives and exalted purpose of his life the richer and more ennobling does his character appear. Without any attempt at perversion, therefore, much new material here awaits the reader from Shaftesbury's correspondence with relatives, household officers, and life-long friends.

The letters of this volume which perhaps most strikingly disclose the benevolent disposition of Shaftesbury are those written to or concerning young men. This gracious trait was first made known by a small collection of his letters printed in 1716, entitled "Several Letters written by a Noble Lord to a Young Man at the University." These were addressed by Shaftesbury to Michael Ainsworth, a student taken by him from his own household and sent to University College, Oxford. The originals of most of these letters, as well as of several additional to "Good Michael," as he is generally styled in them, are among the Shaftesbury papers. Only such of them as are of marked value or have been tampered with in the printed book are here reproduced. The letters of this volume will be found to exhibit a much broader range of Shaftesbury's philanthropic efforts. They disclose a constant and unvarying helpfulness to numerous aspiring youths maintained throughout his entire life. Whether the protégés succeeded or failed his active goodness suffered no diminution or restraint. A most typical instance of this benevolence may be mentioned in the fact that the only reward he sought for many years of political service was a civil position, not for himself or any of his relatives, but for his deserving young friend Micklethwayte. Various letters in this work, moreover, show that he insisted upon the fulfilment of this claim with unyielding persistency amid changing political factions until at length he won. It is this generous and self-sacrificing spirit so frequently displayed in the interests of others which proves the third Earl to have been a most worthy predecessor to the noble and philanthropic seventh Earl of Shaftesbury.

Historical interest will chiefly centre in the political letters from the pen of Shaftesbury which this work contains. He played either an active part or tendered when in retirement fruitful advice during the prolonged critical period in English national affairs when the Stuart dynasty gradually gave place to the present ruling house of Guelph. Throughout the reign of William of Orange, and in that of his successor Queen Anne, Shaftesbury was loyal to the maintenance of a Protestant succession. During his entire parliamentary career, moreover, he ever exercised a "passion for true liberty." The political measures which he most strongly supported at home were those which had for their aim the protection of the rights and liberty

of the individual. In foreign affairs he resisted to the end of
his life every doubtful compromise on the part of England with
Louis XIV. of France, whose desire for universal monarchy
he deemed the most threatening and direful evil of his time.
His true compatriots were thus discovered among the
liberty-loving spirits of the Netherlands, whom he thrice
visited, and with whom he was in constant communication.
Considerable political material from this source by Shaftesbury
has already been made public in the "Original Letters," [1]
addressed by him to Benjamin Furly, the English Quaker
merchant at Rotterdam. The manuscripts of these are now in
the Record Office, and they have here occasionally been used to
give proper continuity to the political career of Shaftesbury.
The fresh and additional value of the present volume consists in
heretofore unpublished correspondence, which clearly reveals for
the first time his direct personal relations with the chief military
and parliamentary leaders of his time. Of the former class this
work contains letters to General Stanhope, to the family of Lord
Peterborough, and to the great Duke of Marlborough; and of the
latter class among others to Lord Godolphin, to Lord Sunderland,
and to the noble Lord Somers. The numerous letters to John
Molesworth, a foreign envoy, have, moreover, throughout a
political character.

Inasmuch as Shaftesbury's reputation has heretofore chiefly
rested on his authorship of "The Characteristics," correspondence
of a philosophical import would naturally by many be most
eagerly sought. Among the earliest letters in this volume are
a considerable number written by Shaftesbury to John Locke.
They afford the much desired information as to the personal
correspondence of the two philosophers. These letters were
originally included among the manuscripts bequeathed in 1704
by Locke to his near relative and sole executor, Sir Peter King,
who afterwards became Lord Chancellor of England. They are
now the property of this Chancellor's lineal descendant, the
Hon. Captain Lionel Fortescue King Noel, second son of the
first Earl of Lovelace. To the courtesy of the present owner of

[1] Original letters of Locke, Algernon Sidney, and Anthony Lord
Shaftesbury, edited by Thomas Forster. Lond., 1830; second edition,
1847.

this Lovelace collection, which has here been so fittingly
exhibited in the cause of learning by the grandson of Lord
Peter King, to whom we owe a "Life of Locke," the readers of
this work are indebted for their present publication. In
connection with these letters to Locke, mention must also be
made of two additional letters of Shaftesbury in this work
relating to that philosopher. In the one dated December, 1704,
written to a young friend, Locke's farewell charge to Anthony
Collins receives from Shaftesbury a very remarkable counter-
charge; and in the other, dated November 9th, 1709, addressed
to General Stanhope, Shaftesbury reveals his secret opinion
of Locke's philosophy, inasmuch as he writes in it to his
philosophical disciple: "I have thus ventured to make you the
greatest confidence in the world, which is that of my philosophy
against my old tutor and governour." The letters to Pierre
Coste, Jean Le Clerc, and Des Maizeauz, which here appear,
are all of philosophical interest, as they make known to us
Shaftesbury's connection with these contemporary philosophical
writers. Especially valuable are the references which those
to Coste contain of Shaftesbury's relations to Leibnitz. The
entire series of letters to Lord Somers, above mentioned, have
moreover a unique philosophical importance. As is well known,
Shaftesbury's "Letter concerning Design," which was included
in "The Characteristics" for the first time in the edition of 1732,
was written to accompany a gift of his "Treatise on the Judgment of Hercules" to Lord Somers. But every preceding treatise
of Shaftesbury was in like manner presented to Lord Somers
with a similar accompaniment of a letter. This remarkable series
of letters of presentation now appears for the first time in print.
In the letters to Thomas Micklethwayte will be found the interpretation of the mythical illustrations and an account of the
numerous changes in the second edition of "The Characteristics."
The kindness of Shaftesbury to this young man was well repaid
by his undertaking the publication of that revised work during
the author's last illness in Italy. The philosophy of Horace, as
it may justly be termed, is contained in a letter of October 1st,
1706, written by Shaftesbury to Pierre Coste. The study,
indeed, of the ancient classics, and more especially of the works
of Horace, Epictetus, and Marcus Aurelius, had the profoundest
bearing upon Shaftesbury's own philosophy.

The third division of this work consists of the Philosophical Regimen of Shaftesbury. This is a most natural supplement to the sketch of his life and to the preceding letters, inasmuch as it is a revelation both of the inmost purpose and of the outward procedure of his life. The manuscript material of this portion is to be found in two note-books among the Shaftesbury Papers of the London Record Office. The earliest writing in these books is dated Holland, 1698, and the latest, Naples, 1712. Their contents thus cover almost the entire period of the author's literary· activity, but centre chiefly, however, about his two "retreats" into Holland, the one in 1698 and the other in 1703-4. The form in which the work is written is that of a series of reflections upon various philosophical subjects. These include such topics, among others, as natural affections, deity, good and ill, human affairs, self, passions, pleasure and pain, fancy, character, nature, life, and philosophy. The reflections on the different subjects are intermingled among one another in the note-books, but are brought together under their several themes in this printed reproduction of them.

Shaftesbury entitles the reflections Ἀσκήματα (exercises). The title of Philosophical Regimen is, however, here employed both because the term regimen is frequently used by him in reference to the reflections, and also because it best reflects their true meaning and character. Many passages throughout the work may be discovered which thus clearly indicate the purport of the reflections in the mind of Shaftesbury. The real key, however, to their interpretation is contained under the subject Improvement. " Memorandums," he here writes, " for what ? About what ? A small concern perhaps, a trifle, for what else can it be ? Neither estate, nor money, nor policy, nor history, nor learning, nor private affairs, nor public. These are great things. In these are great improvements. How many memorandums, how many common-place books about these ? Who would think of any other memorandums ? Would one think of making any for *Life*. Would one think that this were a business to improve in ? What if this should be the thing of all others chosen out for a pocket-book and memorandums? But so it is . . . Begin therefore and work upon this subject. Collect, digest, methodize, abstract. How many codes, how many volumes, how much labour, and what compiling in the study of

other laws ? But in the law of life how ? They who seek not
any such in life, nor think that there is any rule, what are they
better than vulgar ?" The reflections of Shaftesbury printed in
this work thus embody the attempt made by him to ascertain
the correct principles of life and to map out the rules of their
practical application in his own conduct. They are a veritable
Philosophical Regimen.

To discover a law and a code of life Shaftesbury pursued,
especially during his retreats in Holland, the study of classical
authors among the ancients. " Perhaps no modern," says Toland
in his introduction to the Shaftesbury letters, " ever turned the
ancients more into sap and blood, as they say, than he. Their
doctrines he understood as well as themselves, and their virtues
he practiced better." If this statement be limited to the Stoics
it is most accurate. It was with the works of Epictetus and
Marcus Aurelius that Shaftesbury was most thoroughly conversant. From them he draws most of the topics and their
maxims in the Regimen. He reproduces not only their thought
but also to a considerable extent their technical language. It
would be difficult indeed to find any author with quotations in
every instance so apt as those which Shaftesbury makes from
these writers. With their philosophy, moreover, he was most
thoroughly saturated. " Nor were there indeed," he writes,
" any more than two real distinct philosophies, the one derived
from Socrates and passing into the old academic, peripatetic and
stoic; the other derived in reality from Democritus and passing
into the Cyrenaic and Epicurean. The first, therefore, of these
two philosophers recommended action, concernment in civil
affairs, religion, &c., the second derided all this and advised
inaction and retreat. And with good reason, for the first maintained that society, right and wrong were founded in nature, and
that nature had a meaning, and was herself, that is to say, in her
wits, well-governed and administered by one simple and perfect
intelligence. The second derided this and made Providence and
dame nature not so sensible as a doting old woman. The first,
therefore, of these philosophies is to be called the civil, social,
theistic ; the second, the contrary." Almost every page of the
Regimen demonstrates that the philosophy of Shaftesbury
belongs to what in this passage he calls the civil, social and
theistic, derivable from the Stoics. The real sources of his

philosophy are to be sought in particular in Epictetus and Marcus Aurelius.

Although the philosophy of Shaftesbury is thus founded on stoicism, this Philosophical Regimen is a new and brilliant presentation of that moral system. The discourses of Epictetus were uttered, it is believed, extempore. They have a popular form, but often lack in continuity of expression. The thoughts of Marcus Aurelius, on the other hand, were written down merely for personal use. They bear the evidence of private honesty, but are stated in short paragraphs which are often obscure. The merits rather than the defects of these two works are combined in the Philosophical Regimen of Shaftesbury. It is written in a style that can at all times be readily understood, and it likewise possesses all the sincerity of personal writing where the purpose is " only to improve by these, not publish, profess, or teach them." The eloquence of the utterance is frequently such as could only have proceeded from Shaftesbury, whose method of philosophical rhapsody so captivated his contemporary Leibnitz. The permanent strength of this Regimen, however, consists in the fact that it is one of the most consistent and thorough-going attempts ever made to transform a philosophy into a life. Just as Spinoza was "God-intoxicated," so Shaftesbury was " intoxicated with the idea of virtue." He is the greatest Stoic of modern times. Into his own life he wrought the stoical virtue for virtue's sake. This exalted purpose he sought to attain by means of this Regimen. It thus embodies a philosophy which must compel a renewed and critical study from the stoical standpoint of his " Characteristics." Indeed, it may be said, we believe, with perfect truth that there has been no such strong expression of stoicism since the days of Epictetus and Marcus Aurelius as that contained in the Philosophical Regimen of Shaftesbury. The Greek slave, the Roman emperor, and the English nobleman must abide the three great exponents of stoical philosophy.

BENJAMIN RAND.

HARVARD UNIVERSITY.

# CONTENTS.

PREFATORY INTRODUCTION... ... ... ... ... ... ... ... ... ... ... ... ... ... ... ... **PAGE** v.

SKETCH OF THE LIFE OF THE THIRD EARL OF SHAFTESBURY: BY HIS SON, THE FOURTH EARL ... ... ... ... ... ... ... ... ... ... ... ... ... ... xvii.

## I.—THE PHILOSOPHICAL REGIMEN.

NATURAL AFFECTION ... ... ... ... ... 1
DEITY ... ... ... ... ... ... ... ... 13
PROVIDENCE ... ... ... ... ... ... ... 40
THE END ... ... ... ... ... ... ... 48
GOOD AND ILL ... ... ... ... ... ... 53
SHAME ... ... ... ... ... ... ... ... 60
REPUTATION ... ... ... ... ... ... ... 64
HUMAN AFFAIRS ... ... ... ... ... ... 70
NECESSITY ... ... ... ... ... ... ... 90
POLITICAL AFFAIRS ... ... ... ... ... 100
FRIENDS ... ... ... ... ... ... ... 104
SMALL POSSESSIONS ... ... ... ... ... 109
SELF ... ... ... ... ... ... ... ... 112
ARTIFICIAL OR ECONOMICAL SELF ... 124
NATURAL SELF ... ... ... ... ... ... 133
FAMILIARITY ... ... ... ... ... ... ... 140
THE BODY ... ... ... ... ... ... ... 147

PASSIONS ... ... ... ... ... ... ... ... 151
PLEASURE AND PAIN ... ... ... ... ... 161
FANCIES OR APPEARANCES ... ... ... 164
SIMPLICITY ... ... ... ... ... ... ... 179
NATURE ... ... ... ... ... ... ... ... 184
CHARACTER AND CONDUCT ... ... ... 189
CHARACTER ... ... ... ... ... ... ... 192
FANCY AND JUDGMENT ... ... ... ... 207
THE ASCENTS OF THE JUDGMENT ... ... 209
NATURAL CONCEPTS ... ... ... ... ... 214
OPINION AND PRECEPTS ... ... ... ... 221
MAXIMS ... ... ... ... ... ... ... ... 224
ATTENTION AND RELAXATION ... ... ... 231
IMPROVEMENT ... ... ... ... ... ... ... 239
THE BEAUTIFUL ... ... ... ... ... ... 244
LIFE ... ... ... ... ... ... ... ... ... 253
PHILOSOPHY ... ... ... ... ... ... ... 267

## II.—LETTERS OF SHAFTESBURY.

To John Locke, December 1st, 1687 ... 273
„ John Locke, December 22nd, 1687 ... 274
„ his Father, May 3rd, old style [1689] ... 275
„ his Father, July, 1689 ... ... ... ... 280
„ Mr. Taylor, of Weymouth, February 16th, 1689-90 ... ... ... ... ... ... 285
„ John Locke, January 21st, 1692 ... ... 287
„ John Locke, March 3rd, 1692 ... ... 288
„ John Locke, March 26th, 1691-2 ... 289
„ John Locke, July 7th, 1692 ... ... ... 291
„ John Locke, (?) 6th, 1693 ... ... ... 294
„ John Locke, May 28th, 1694 ... ... 294
„ John Locke, September 8th, 1694 ... 296
„ John Locke, November 29th, 1694 ... 299
„ Thomas Stringer, February 15th, 1695 ... ... ... ... ... ... ... ... 300
„ his Mother, beginning of 1696 ... ... 301
„ Lord Rutland, April, 1696 ... ... ... 302

To his Mother, October 10th, 1696 ... ... 303
„ his Mother, November 14th, 1696 ... 305
„ John Locke, April 9th, 1698 ... ... 306
„ M. Des Maizaux, August 5th, 1701 ... 307
„ Mr. Bennett, November 15th, 1701 ... 308
„ Benjamin Furley, November 29th, 1701 ... ... ... ... ... ... ... ... 309
„ Lord Marlborough, April 10th, 1702 ... 310
„ Benjamin Furley, November 4th, 1702 ... ... ... ... ... ... ... ... 312
„ M. Des Maizaux, November 2nd, 1703 ... ... ... ... ... ... ... ... 313
„ John Wheelock, November 6th, 1703.. 314
„ John Wheelock, November 16th, 1703. 315
„ Lord Sunderland, November 9th. 1703 ... ... ... ... ... ... ... ... 317
„ Sir Rowland Gwinn, January 23rd, 1704 ... ... ... ... ... ... ... ... 318

PAGE

To the Bishop of Sarum, February 5th, 1704 ... ... ... ... ... ... ... 320

,, his Sister Frances, March 18th, 1704... 321

,, Sir Rowland Gwinn, April 19th, 1704 ... .. ... ... ... ... ... 322

,, John Locke, September 7th, 1704 ... 323

,, Dr. Burgess, January (?), 1704-5 ... 324

,, Peter King, January, 1704-5 ... ... 325

,, Jean Le Clerc, January 13th, 1705 ... 326

,, Jean Le Clerc, February 8th, 1705 ... 328

,, Sir Rowland Gwinn, February 24th, 1704-5 ... ... ... ... ... ... 334

,, Lord Somers, October 20th, 1705 ... 336

,, Lady Peterborough, October (?), 1705 . 341

,, Lord Cowper, December 2nd, 1705 ... 344

,, a Friend, December 2nd, 1704-5... ... 344

,, Mr. Van Twedde, January 17th, 1705-6. 347

,, Jean Le Clerc, March 6th, 1705-6 ... 352

,, Mr. Stephens, July 17th, 1706 ... ... 354

,, Pierre Coste, October 1st, 1706 ... ... 355

,, Teresias, November 29th, 1706 ... ... 366

,, Lord Sunderland, December 7th, 1706 ... ... ... ... ... ... ... 369

,, the Duke of Marlborough, December 7th, 1706 ... ... .. ... ... ... 371

,, Lord Somers, January, 1706-7 ... ... 371

,, M. Basnage, January 21st, 1706-7 ... 372

,, Joseph Micklethwayte, January 11th, 1706-7 ... ... ... ... ... .. ... 378

,, Joseph Micklethwayte, February 26th, 1706-7 ... ... ... ... ... ... ... 379

,, Michael Ainsworth, October 3rd, 1707 381

,, Maurice Ashley, October 21st, 1707... 382

,, Maurice Ashley, November 5th, 1707... 383

,, Robert Molesworth, December 13th, 1707 ... ... ... ... ... ... ... 383

,, Mr. Darby, February 2nd, 1708 ... ... 385

,, Lord Somers, July 12th, 1708 ... ... 386

,, Benjamin Furley, July 22nd, 1708 ... 387

,, Robert Molesworth, September 30th, 1708 ... ... ... ... ... ... ... 389

,, Robert Molesworth, October 23rd, 1708 ... ... ... ... ... ... ... 391

,, Lord Somers, December 10th, 1708 ... 394

,, Lord Halifax, December 16th, 1708... 395

,, Pierre Coste, February 19th, 1708-9... 396

,, Lord Townsend, May 28th, 1709 ... 399

,, Lord Somers, June 2nd, 1709 ... ... 400

,, Michael Ainsworth, June 3rd, 1709 ... 403

,, John Wheelock, July 9th, 1709 ... ... 405

,, John Wheelock, August 8th, 1709 ... 406

,, Lady Russell, August 24th, 1709... ... 408

,, Maurice Ashley, August 24th, 1709 ... 409

,, James Eyre, August 26th, 1709 ... ... 409

,, Jean Le Clerc, November 6th, 1709 ... 411

PAGE

To General Stanhope, November 7th, 1709 ... ... ... ... ... ... ... 413

,, Arent Furley, November 7th, 1709 ... 417

,, Thomas Walker, April 23rd, 1710 ... 418

,, Bishop Burnet, May 23rd, 1710 ... ... 419

,, Lord Somers, May 26th, 1710 ... ... 420

,, Michael Ainsworth, July 10th, 1710 ... 421

,, Jean Le Clerc, July 19th, 1710 ... ... 422

,, Sir John Cropley, July 24th, 1710 ... 425

,, Lord Godolphin, January 29th, 1710-11 426

,, Lord Dartmouth, January 29th, 1710-11 427

,, Lord Halifax, February 23rd, 1710-11 . 428

,, Lord Howe, March 26th, 1711 ... ... 429

,, Lord Somers, March 30th, 1711 ... ... 430

,, Lady Waldegrave, May 4th, 1711 ... 433

,, Michael Ainsworth, May 11th, 1711 ... 434

,, Lord Godolphin, May 27th 1711 ... ... 435

,, Sir John Cropley, July 2nd, 1711 ... 435

,, Sir John Cropley, August 11th, 1711... 436

,, Thomas Micklethwayte, August 11th, 1711 ... ... ... ... ... ... ... 438

,, the Duke of Berwick, August 28th, 1711 ... ... ... ... ... ... ... 441

,, the Duke of Berwick, September 5th, 1711 ... ... ... ... ... ... ... 442

,, Pierre Coste, October 3rd, 1711 ... ... 442

,, John Molesworth, September 7th, 1711 ... ... ... ... ... ... ... 444

,, John Wheelock, November 6th, 1711 . 445

,, Mr. Chetwynd, November 17th, 1711 .. 446

,, Pierre Coste, November 23rd, 1711 ... 447

,, Thomas Micklethwaite (?) ... 448

,, Thomas Micklethwait, December 8th, 1711 ... ... ... ... ... ... ... 449

,, John Molesworth, December 15th, 1711 ... ... ... ... ... ... ... 452

,, Sir John Cropley, December 29th, 1711 ... ... ... ... ... ... ... 453

,, Thomas Micklethwaite, December 29th, 1711 ... ... ... ... ... ... 455

,, Pierre Coste, January 12th, 1712 ... 459

,, John Molesworth, January 19th, 1712. 461

,, Thomas Micklethwaite, January 19th, 1712 ... ... ... ... ... ... ... 462

,, The Rev. Dr. Fagan, January 23rd, 1711-2 ... ... ... ... ... ... ... 466

,, Sir John Cropley, February 16th, 1712 ... ... ... ... ... ... ... 468

,, John Wheelock, February 23rd, 1712 . 470

,, Thomas Micklethwait, February 23rd, 1712 ... ... ... ... ... ... ... 472

,, Sir John Cropley, March 1st, 1712 ... 475

,, Thomas Micklethwaite, March 9th, 1712 ... ... ... ... ... ... ... 477

,, John Molesworth, March 29th, 1712 ... 480

# Contents.

| | PAGE |
|---|---|
| To Sir John Cropley, March 29th, 1712 ... | 481 |
| ,, Mr. Chetwynd, April 5th, 1712 ... ... | 482 |
| ,, Thomas Micklethwait, April 12th, 1712 ... ... ... ... ... ... ... | 484 |
| ,, Sir John Cropley, April 12th, 1712 ... | 487 |
| ,, Abbé Farely, May 3rd, 1712 ... ... | 488 |
| ,, John Molesworth, May 17th, 1712 ... | 490 |
| ,, The Rev. Dr. Fagan, May 21st, 1712... | 491 |
| ,, Pierre Coste, June 5th, 1712 ... ... | 492 |
| ,, Sir John Cropley, June 7th, 1712 ...' | 495 |
| ,, Thomas Micklethwaite, June 28th, 1712 ... ... ... ... ... ... ... | 496 |
| ,, John Wheelock, July 12th, 1712... ... | 498 |
| ,, Thomas Micklethwaite, July 19th, 1712 ... ... ... ... ... ... ... | 499 |
| ,, Pierre Coste, July 25th, 1712 ... ... | 502 |
| ,, Thomas Micklethwaite, August 2nd, 1712 ... ... ... ... ... ... ... | 505 |
| ,, John Molesworth, August 2nd, 1712 ... | 508 |
| ,, Sir John Cropley, August 9th, 1712 ... | 510 |
| ,, Benjamin Furley, August 9th, 1712 ... | 510 |
| ,, John Molesworth, August 30th, 1712 ... | 511 |
| ,, Thomas Micklethwaite, August 30th, 1712 ... ... ... ... ... ... ... | 514 |

| | PAGE |
|---|---|
| To Sir John Cropley, October 11th, 1712 ... ... ... ... ... ... ... | 517 |
| ,, Benjamin Furly, October 18th, 1712 ... | 519 |
| ,, John Molesworth, October 25th, 1712 ... ... ... ... ... ... ... | 520 |
| ,, Thomas Micklethwaite, November 22nd, 1712 ... ... ... ... ... | 522 |
| ,, Pierre Coste, November 22nd, 1712 ... | 523 |
| ,, Sir John Cropley, November 22nd, 1712 ... ... ... ... ... ... | 524 |
| ,, Thomas Micklethwaite, December 20th, 1712 ... ... ... ... ... | 527 |
| ,, Thomas Micklethwaite, December 27th, 1712 ... ... ... ... ... ... | 529 |
| ,, Thomas Micklethwaite, January 3rd, 1713 ... ... ... ... ... ... | 529 |
| ,, Sir John Cropley, January 10th, 1713 ... ... ... ... ... ... ... | 531 |
| ,, Thomas Micklethwaite, January 10th, 1712 ... ... ... ... ... ... | 532 |
| ,, John Wheelock, January 10th, 1713 ... ... ... ... ... ... ... | 533 |
| Mr. Crell to John Wheelock, February 21st, 1713 ... ... ... ... ... ... | 535 |

.

# A SKETCH OF THE LIFE

OF THE

# THIRD EARL OF SHAFTESBURY,

## BY HIS SON, THE FOURTH EARL.

The following sketch of my father's life was once intended to have been prefixed to the new edition of the *Characteristics*, though upon considering further on it that thought was laid aside; for the lives of persons who spend most of their time in study and retirement can never afford matter to enliven a narrative; that probably the expectations of the generality of the world might be raised to conceive, they should find something which neither the capacity of the writer nor the nature of the subject would admit. The single end proposed in these few sheets is, by giving the character and sentiments of the author of the *Characteristics*, as they really were, to take off some ill impressions which well-meaning persons may possibly have received from many calumnies which have been cast on him. I am sensible the works themselves must be tried by their own merit and not by the absurd comments of envy or error. And as some of these inquisitors have descended so low as even to quote passages from my father's private letters to maintain their charge against him, I hope I shall not be thought impertinent in quoting some others of his private writings, which are in a great measure necessary to mention in going through the account of his life, and which may possibly be a means to explain those passages in the *Characteristics* which have by some been greatly misapprehended.

I hope I need not make any apology for prefixing the following relation of my father's life to this edition of the

B

*Characteristics.* Some sketch of an author's life is generally pleasing to the curious. A just representation of his character must be agreeable to the candid. And as this short account will give a view of his real opinion of our national church and religion, it may possibly be a means to explain those passages in his writings, which have by some been greatly misapprehended.

My father was born the 26th of February, 1670-1, at Exeter House, in London (where his grandfather[1] lived) who, from the time of his birth, conceived so great an affection for him that he undertook the care of his education, and who, being sensible of the great advantages which accrue from a good share of literature,

[1] The first Earl of Shaftesbury, one of the foremost statesmen of his time, was born 22nd July, 1621. He married (1) Margaret, third daughter of Thomas, Lord of Coventry, February 25th, 1639, who died July 11th, 1649 ; (2) Lady Frances Cecil, daughter of David, third Earl of Exeter, April 25th, 1650, by whom he had one son, Anthony ; and (3) Margaret, sixth daughter of William, second Lord Spencer, of Worthington. The first Earl died January 31st, 1683, in Holland. Anthony, his only son and successor (father of the third earl), born 16th January, 1651-2, married September 22nd, 1669, Dorothy, third daughter of John, eighth Earl of Rutland, by whom he had issue of three sons—Anthony, John, Maurice ; and four daughters—Lady Frances, married to Francis Stonehouse, Esq., of Hungerford Parks, in Co. Berkshire ; Lady Elizabeth, wife of James Harris, Esq., of Salisbury ; and Lady Dorothy, espoused to Edward Hooper, Esq., of Hurn Court, in Co. Hampshire ; and died in 1749 ; Gertrude, the other daughter, died unmarried. His Lordship dying 10th November, 1699, was succeeded by Anthony (third Earl) ; the second son, John, died before him in his 21st year, or 1693 ; Maurice lived till 1726. He was many years in the House of Commons, and in the 13th of King William was chosen from Wiltshire. The second Earl died November 10th, 1699. (Memorandum in Shaftesbury MSS.) Anthony, third Earl of Shaftesbury, author of "The Characteristics," was born on 26th February, 1671, married Jane, daughter of Thomas Ewer, Esq., of Bushey Hall, Lea, county Hertford, August 29th, 1709 (died November 23rd, 1751), and had issue of one son, Anthony (the fourth Earl). The third Earl died February 15th, 1713, in Naples. Anthony, the fourth Earl, was born February 9th, 1711, married (1) Lady Susannah Noel in 1725, (2) Mary, daughter of Jacob, Viscount Folkestone, 22nd March, 1759, and had issue, Anthony, born September, 1761. The fourth Earl died May 29th, 1771.

thought that necessary work could not be begun too early. That his grandson, therefore, might make the quickest dispatch, he chose a method of instilling (as it were) the ancient languages into him by placing a person* about him who was so thoroughly versed in the Greek and Latin tongues that she could speak either of them with the greatest fluency. By this person's instructions my father made so good a progress in his learning that he could read with ease both the Latin and Greek tongues when eleven years old. At this age his grandfather sent him to a private school, where he remained till after his grandfather's death. In the end of the summer following, viz., 1683, his father carried him to Winchester, where he was treated very indifferently by all except the schoolmaster (Dr. Harris), being often insulted on his grandfather's account, whose memory was very odious to the zealots for despotic power. His ill-usage there made Winchester very irksome to him, and therefore he prevailed with his father to take him from thence and consent to his desire of seeing foreign countries. He began his travels in 1686. The person who attended him as tutor[1] was a very ingenious, honest man, and every way qualified for the employment. Sir John Cropley too (with whom my father continued in the closest friendship to the end of his life) accompanied him everywhere, together with Mr. Thomas Sclater Bacon. My father spent a considerable time in Italy, where he acquired a great knowledge in the polite arts.[2] That he had a sound judgment in painting, the treatises he wrote on that subject plainly evince. He understood sculpture also extremely well, and could himself design to some degree of perfection. Of the rudiments of music too he was not ignorant, and his thoughts concerning it have been approved by the greatest masters in that science. He made it his endeavour while abroad to apply himself as much as possible to the improving in those accomplishments, and for that reason did not

* "Mrs. Elizabeth Birch, daughter of a schoolmaster of Oxford or Berkshire." Rough Draft of the Life in Shaftesbury's MSS.

[1] Rough Draft : "Mr. Daniel Denoue, a Scotchman."

[2] Rough Draft : "Such that he might very properly be called a virtuoso."

greatly seek the conversation of other English young gentlemen on their travels (which as he had friends along with him he had the less occasion to desire). But whenever it happened that this could not conveniently be avoided, it was observed his discourse was principally directed to the young gentlemen's tutors, from whom he might either learn something or at least converse on such topics as were most agreeable to his genius. He spoke French so readily, and with so good an accent, that in France he was often taken for a native; and the ease and agility he showed in performing those exercises in which that nation excel, contributed to the leading them into that opinion.

My father, after three years' stay abroad, returned to England (in 1689) and was offered a seat in Parliament from some of those boroughs where the family had held an interest. But there were several reasons which induced him not to accept their offer at that particular time; and what prevailed more strongly with him than anything was the resolution he had taken of applying himself entirely to study, and to increasing his knowledge in those subjects with which it is of consequence to be acquainted.[1] In these he happily succeeded, and his learning, though very extensive, was that of an ingenious gentleman. My father continued his strict course of study nearly five years, till on Sir John Trenchard's[2] death he was elected a burgess for Pool. Soon after his coming into Parliament he had an opportunity given him of expressing that spirit of liberty which he maintained to the end of his life, and by which he always directed his public conduct. It was the bringing in the Treason Act[3] which appeared to

[1] *Quod aeque pauperibus prodest, locupletibus aeque. Aeque neglectum pueris senibusque nocebit.* ["Which is of equal benefit to the poor and to the rich; which neglected will be of equal detriment to young and old."]—*Horace Epist.* II., 1, 25-26.

[2] Sir John Trenchard (1640-1695) was a prominent opponent of the Stuart Dynasty. He became Secretary of State after the accession to the throne of King William.

[3] The Parliament which met on the 22nd of November, 1695, passed early in its first session the famous Act for regulating trials in case of treason, in which there was a special provision that a person indicted for treason should be granted the benefit of counsel.

him the more necessary, as his family at the end of King Charles's reign had been in great danger for want of such a law. He was determined, therefore, to contribute all his endeavours towards the passing of what he thought requisite to secure the life of the subject, which might be taken away almost at the pleasure of the crown. The removing of this defect in our constitution was by most friends to liberty looked on as a matter of the last importance. To this end my father prepared a speech, which those, to whom he showed it, thought a very proper one upon the occasion. But when he stood up to speak it in the House of Commons the great audience so intimidated him that he lost all memory, and could not utter a syllable of what he intended, by which he found how true Mr. Locke's caution to him had been, not to engage at first setting out in an undertaking of difficulty, but to rise to it gradually. The House, after giving him a little time to recover, called loudly for him to go on, when he proceeded to this effect :—" If I, sir, who rise only to speak my opinion on the Bill now depending, am so confounded that I am unable to express the least of what I proposed to say, what must the condition of that man be who is pleading for his life without any assistance and under apprehensions of being deprived of it ? " The sudden turn of thought (which by some was imagined to have been premeditated, though it really was as I mention it) pleased the house extremely; and it is generally believed, carried a greater weight with it than any of the arguments which were offered in favour of the bill [1] which was sent to the Lords and passed accordingly. My father during this and the other sessions he continued in the House persevered in the same way of acting, always heartily concurring in every motion for the further securing of liberty; and though these motions very frequently came from people who were of a differently-denominated party in politics, yet he was never for refusing any proposal that he apprehended to be beneficial to his

[1] This story is also related of Charles Montague, subsequently Earl of Halifax, in his Memoirs (p. 30), published in 1715. The minuteness of detail in the present account would however tend to confirm its application to Lord Ashley.

country, and was always for improving the present opportunity, forming his judgment of things by their own merit, and not by the quarter from whence they came. This independent manner of acting which my father observed himself, he also strove to increase in others to the utmost of his power, as he was sensible that independency is the essence of freedom.[1] The fatigues of attending regularly upon the service of the House (which in those active times generally sat long) as well as upon committees at night, in a few years so impaired my father's health, who was not of a robust constitution, that he was obliged to decline coming again into Parliament after the dissolution in 1698.

My father, being released from the confinement of the House, was at liberty to spend his time wherever it was most agreeable to him. He went directly into Holland, where he became acquainted with several learned and ingenious men[2] who resided in that country, which induced him to continue there about a twelve-month. Being determined not to be interrupted in what he principally went thither to follow, viz., studying, and that in the most private manner, he concealed his name, pretending to be only a student in physic, and in that character became acquainted with the celebrated Mr. Bayle,[3] with whom he soon grew intimate. A little before his return to England, being willing to be made known to him by his real name, he contrived to have Mr. Bayle invited to dinner by a friend, where he was told he was to meet my Lord Shaftesbury. Mr. Bayle, accidentally calling upon my father that morning, was pressed by him to stay. " I can by no means," said Mr. Bayle,

[1] Rough Draft : "Several gentlemen in the House of Commons who were of the same sentiments with my father formed a little society by the name of the Independent Club, of which he was a member, and had a chief hand in setting up, but the club was of no long duration."

[2] Amongst the " learned and ingenious men " were undoubtedly Joh. Le Clerc, editor of the *Bibliothèque Universelle* ; Phillipe van Limborch, the celebrated Dutch theologian ; Benjamin Furly, an English quaker merchant, the correspondent alike of Shaftesbury and of Locke ; and Pierre Bayle, subsequently the author of the *Dictionnaire Universelle.*

[3] Benjamin Furly, at whose house Locke had resided during his stay in Rotterdam.

"for I must be punctual to an engagement where I am to meet my Lord Shaftesbury."[1] The second interview, as may be imagined, caused some mirth, and their intimacy was rather increased than lessened after the discovery[2], for they never ceased a correspondence after my father's return, till Mr. Bayle's death.

During my father's stay in Holland an imperfect edition[3] of his *Inquiry after Virtue* was printed, surreptitiously taken from a rough draft, sketched when he was but twenty years of age. He was greatly chagrined at this, and immediately bought up the whole impression before many of the books were sold, and set about completing the Treatise which he published[4] himself not long after. The person who treated him so unhandsomely he soon discovered to be Mr. John Toland, who made this ungrateful return for the many favours he had received from him. Indeed my father then allowed him (at his earnest importunity) an annual stipend, though he never had any great opinion

[1] Properly Lord Ashley, as this was his title while his father lived.

[2] In the MS. of this life the Fourth Earl gives the account of the acquaintance of the Third Earl with Bayle, and also of the surreptitious publication of the *Inquiry*, which immediately follows, in connection with his father's visit to Holland in 1703-04. Both incidents have here been transferred to the earlier visit of 1698-99. This change has been made not only in accord with the example of Birch in The General Dictionary, whose publication was revised by the Fourth Earl, but more particularly because there is direct evidence from the letters of Shaftesbury that he was acquainted with Bayle prior to 1704. In a letter, for instance, to Furly (dated January 30th, 1702) he expressly states : "I received lately a present from Mr. Bayle of his *Dictionary*, for which pray return him my humble thanks. I shall do it myself in a post or two." The publication of the Inquiry, moreover, belonged with certainty to the earlier visit.

[3] Shaftesbury himself, in a letter dated June the 3rd, 1709 (p. 403) also styles this edition "an imperfect thing, brought into the world many years since contrary to the author's design, in his absence beyond sea and in a disguised disordered style. It may one day perhaps be set right, since other things have made it to be inquired after."

[4] The *Inquiry*, as completed, was printed in second volume of the first edition of the *Characteristics*, where it is described as "printed first in 1699," and "formerly printed from an imperfect copy ; now corrected and published entire."

of him. In this manner he also frequently bestowed pensions on men of learning who stood in need of such assistance, and gave sums of money besides to those, whom by experience, he found deserving.

Soon after my father returned to England in November, 1699, he became Earl of Shaftesbury. The multiplicity of business in which he was necessarily involved by the taking possession of his estate so fully employed him (as he was always so prudent as to inspect his affairs with a proper care) that he was prevented from attending the House of Lords the first session after he came to the Peerage; nor did he appear there the next till his friend, my Lord Somers, sent a messenger to acquaint him with the business which the Parliament then had under consideration, viz., the Partition Treaty in February, 1700-1. Immediately upon this notice he went post to London, and though when Lord Somers' letter was brought to him he was in Somersetshire, yet he made such despatch as to be present in the House of Lords the day following. So great a fatigue to one in his infirm state of health was enough to endanger even his life. But he was willing to hazard that or whatever he was possessed of when he thought the doing of it was for the service of his country. He attended the House the remainder of the session as much as his health would permit, being earnest to support King William's measures, who was at that time projecting the Grand Alliance. In my father's judgment nothing could assist that glorious undertaking more effectually than the choice of a good Parliament. He therefore did his utmost upon the dissolution of this, to contribute to that design; and was so successful (the parties being then near an equality) that the King told him he had turned the scale; and my father after this was so well approved of by the King that he had the offer of the place of Secretary of State. This, however, his declining constitution would not allow him to accept. But, although he was disabled from engaging in such a course of business, he was not prevented from giving the King his advice, who frequently consulted him on matters of the highest importance; and it is pretty well known that he had the greatest share in composing that celebrated last speech of King William, December 31st, 1701. On the Accession of Queen Anne to the throne, he returned again to his retired manner of living, being no longer advised with concerning the public, and was at this time removed from the Vice-Admiralty of Dorset, which had been in the family for three successive generations. This slight, though it was a matter of no sort of consequence to my father, was the only one that could be shown him, as it was the single thing he held under the Crown, and was imagined to have been advised by some of those who resented my father's services to the other party in the late reign.

My father made a second journey to Holland in the beginning of the year 1703, and returned again to England at the end of the year 1704. Soon afterwards the French Prophets[1] vented their enthusiastic extravagancies which made a great deal of noise throughout the kingdom. There were different opinions as to the method of suppressing this distraction, or at least of stopping its progress, and some advised a prosecution. But my father, who had thoroughly considered the matter, and abhorred any step that looked like persecution, apprehended that such measures tended rather to inflame than cure the disease. This occasioned his *Letter concerning Enthusiasm*[2] which he sent to Lord Somers, then President of

[1] The French Prophets arose among the poor peasants of the Cevennes who were driven from their homes by the Edict of Nantes.

[2] " It was published in August, 1708, at London, in 8vo. under this title, ' A Letter Concerning Enthusiasm to my Lord . . .,' and was attacked in October following in a pamphlet in 8vo., entitled, ' Remarks upon a Letter to a Lord concerning Enthusiasm, not written in raillery but good humour '; and in another, published in May, 1709, in 8vo., under the title of ' Bart'lemy Fair, or an enquiry after wit, in which due respect is had to a Letter concerning Enthusiasm to my Lord . . . ,' by Mr. Wotton ; and in a third piece entitled ' Reflections upon a Letter Concerning Enthusiasm to my Lord . . . In another letter to a Lord,' London, 1709, in 8vo. A French translation of the ' Letter Concerning Enthusiasm,' by Monsieur Samson, was printed at the Hague in 1708, in 8vo. . . . Monsieur Leibnitz also wrote some *Remarks* in French on the ' Letter Concerning Enthusiasm,' which are published by Des Marizeaux in the second volume of ' Reiueil de diverses Pieces sur la Philosophie, la Religion Naturelle, l'Histoire les Mathematiques,' &c., par Messieurs. Leibnitz, Clarke, Newton et autresautheurs cólebres printed at Amster-

the Council, and which being well approved by him and others to whom he showed it, my father made public, though without his name or that of the person to whom it was addressed. The Letter gave offence to some who thought he treated the subject in too ludicrous a manner, considering the affinity it bears to the most serious ones. But when we consider the occasion on which it was written we shall see things in another light; for where he is pointing out ridicule as the most proper and surest way to suppress such vain and idle delusions, with what propriety could he himself have been serious. He derides not religion. Let its sacred name be reverenced, but not the false appearance of it. My father had perhaps greater antipathy to enthusiasm than most persons, having seen many of the fatal consequences attending this deception in some people with whom he was particularly acquainted. He wrote a little treatise upon the subject some years before the *Letter of Enthusiasm* which he addressed to his brother, and which has never been made public. The great freedom of thought expressed in this and all his writings has given some people such a dislike to him that they have not only questioned his regard for the Church of England, but even his belief of revealed religion. But to a considering person freedom of thought will never appear dangerous to religion, for free thinking in its proper sense is the examining into things carefully by the standard of unprejudiced reason in order to form a judgment upon mature deliberation and impartial inquiry. This far from staggering us will certainly confirm us in our religion, whose truth always prevails when tried by this test. Some men indeed who, having raised themselves above the ignorance of the mere vulgar, conceited with their imagined elevation, contemptuously look down upon the rest of mankind as wandering in the paths of error, and though they are really enemies to everything sacred would shelter themselves under the appellation of free-thinkers. But is not such a superficial examination under the specious pretence of free-thinking to banish thought from the world ? In order to show my father's

dam in 1720."—Birch. Shaftesbury's own remarks upon the replies to this treatise may be found in a letter dated May 5th, 1709, which is one of those he addressed to a student in the University.

sentiments on our religion, I shall quote a passage from the treatise I mentioned where he speaks of himself and his brother, with whom he had no reserve: " Being risen both of us pretty late in the morning which was Sunday, we went (you know) to church for the first time this New Year. Thither I never went with truer zeal, in a better disposition or with wholesomer reflections. And what satisfied me still the more, it was by appointment that we were that day to receive the Sacrament together, having had no opportunity of a long time. Here we both joined in blessing that good Providence which had by reason and education separated us from the impure and horrid superstitions, monstrous enthusiasms, and wild fanaticisms of those blasphemous visionaries we saw abounding in the world, and which had given us on the contrary side such established rites of worship as were so decent, chaste, innocent, pure; and had placed us in a religion and church where in respect of the moderate party and far greater part the principle of charity was really more extensive than in any Christian or Protestant church besides in the world; where zeal was not frensy and enthusiasm; prayer and devotion not rage and fits of loose extravagance; religious discourses not cant and unintelligible nonsense; nor the character of a Saint resembling that of their inspired and godly men or women leaders; but where a good and virtuous life, with a hearty endeavour of service to one's country and to mankind, joined with a religious performance of all sacred duties and a conformity with the established rites, was enough to answer the highest character of religion, and where all other pretences to gifts or supernatural endowments beyond these moral and Christian perfections were justly suspected and treated as villainy, cheat, imposture, and madness." My father was very constant in his attendance at church and in receiving the Communion when his asthma would permit. He had also a great respect for many of the writings of our best Divines, particularly those of Dr. Whichcote, since by his means two volumes of sermons were published from copies, which had been taken down in shorthand as that great man delivered them.

To return to the thread of my father's life in the year 1709, he was married to Miss Jane Ewer, youngest daughter of Thomas Ewer, Esq., of the Lee, in Hertfordshire, to whom he was related.  A year or two afterwards, finding his health still declining, he was advised to seek assistance from a warmer climate.  Before he left England he took leave by letter of several of his acquaintances, and among that number of the Earl of Oxford, who was then just promoted to that title.  As this letter is not in the usual strain of those addressed to Ministers of State, I shall for that reason insert it.

" Reygate, May 29th, 1711.

" My Lord,—The honour you have done me in many kind enquiries after my health, and the favour you have shown me lately, in forwarding the only means I have left for my recovery by trying the air of a warmer climate, obliges me ere I leave England to return your Lordship my most humble thanks and acknowledgments in this manner, since I am unable to do it in a better.

"I might, perhaps, my lord, do injustice to myself, having had no opportunity of late years to pay my particular respects to you, if I should attempt any otherwise to compliment your lordship on the late honours you have received, than by appealing to the early acquaintance and strict correspondence I had once the honour to maintain with you and your family, for which I had been bred almost from my infancy to have the highest regard.  Your lordship well knows my principles and behaviour from the first hour I engaged in any public concern, and with what zeal I spent some years of my life in supporting your interest, which I thought of greater moment to the public than my own or family's could ever be.  What the natural effects are of private friendship so founded, and what the consequences of different opinions intervening, your lordship, who is so good a judge of men and things, can better resolve with yourself than I can possibly suggest.  And being so knowing in friends (of whom your lordship has acquired so many), you can recollect how those ties or obligations have been hitherto preserved towards you, and whose friendships, affections and principles you may for the future best depend upon in all circumstances and variations public and private.  For my own part, I shall say only, that I very sincerely wish you all happiness, and can with no man living congratulate more heartily, on what I account a real honour and prosperity. Your conduct of the public will be the just earnest and insurance of your greatness and power. And I shall then chiefly congratulate with your Lordship on your merited honours and advancement, when by the happy effects it appears evidently in the service of what cause and for the advantage of what interest they were acquired and employed. Had I been to wish by what hands the public should have been served, the honour of the first part (your Lordship well knows) had fallen to you long since. If others from whom I least hoped have done greatly and as became them, I hope, if possible, you will still exceed all they have performed, and accomplish the great work so gloriously begun and carried on for the rescue of liberty and the deliverance of Europe and mankind. And in this presumption I cannot but remain with the same zeal and sincerity as ever, my lord, &c."

My father set out for Naples in July, 1711, and pursuing his journey through France, was obliged to pass through the Duke of Berwick's camp, who at that time lay with the army under his command encamped near the borders of Piedmont. He was entertained by the Duke in the most friendly and polite manner, and was by his care conducted safe to the Duke of Savoy's dominions. He lived nearly two years after his arrival at Naples[1], dying there the 4th February (O.S.) 1712-13. The only pieces which he finished after he came to Naples were the *Judgment of Hercules* and the *Letter concerning Design*, which last was first published in the edition of the *Characteristics* of 1732, but till then unaccountably suppressed by his executors,

[1] Rough Draft: "My father lived two years after he came to Naples, which was a long time considering the severe illness he was afflicted with and which nothing but the excellence of the air in Italy and the uncommon care of my mother in attending him, could have preserved so long." And again the Fourth Earl writes: "His life would probably have been much longer if he had not worn it out by great fatigues of body and mind, which was owing to his eager desire after knowledge, as well to his zeal to serve his country. For he was so intent upon pursuing his studies that he frequently spent not only the whole day, but the great part of the night besides in severe application, which confirmed the truth of Mr. Locke's observation on him that the sword was too sharp for the scabbard."

though it was his express direction to have it printed. The rest of his time he employed in ordering his writings for publication, which he placed in the order they now stand. The several prints then first interspersed in the work were all designed by himself, and each device bears an exact affinity to the passage to which it refers.[1] That no mistake might be committed, he did not leave to any other hand, even so much as the drudgery or correcting the press. In the three volumes of the *Characteristics* he completed the whole of his writings which he intended should be made public,[2] though some people have, however, in a very ungenerous manner, without any application to his family, or even their knowledge, published several of his letters,[3] and those too of a private nature, many of which were written in so hasty and careless a manner, that he did not so much as take copies of them. A little before his death he had laid a scheme of writing a "Discourse on the Arts of Painting, Sculpture, &c," which, had he lived to have completed, would have been a very

[1] See letters of the year 1712, in this volume.

[2] Shaftesbury's *Characteristics of Men, Manners, Opinions, and Times,* was published at London in its first edition in 1711. It consisted of the *Inquiry Concerning Virtue,* which was surreptitiously issued in 1699 ; the *Letter Concerning Enthusiasm,* printed separately, by himself, in 1708 ; the *Moralists : A Philosophical Rhapsody,* which first appeared in January, 1709 ; the *Sensus Communis,* an *Essay upon the Freedom of Wit and Humour,* likewise printed in May of the same year ; the *Soliloquy,* or *Advice to an Author,* dated 1710 ; and the *Miscellaneous Reflections,* the only treatise not published previously to this collected edition of his works. The second and corrected edition, here mentioned in the context, which included the *Judgment of Hercules,* was not published until 1714, immediately after his death. The third edition was published in 1723 ; the fourth edition in 1727 ; the fifth edition, with the *Letter Concerning Design,* in 1732 ; the excellent Baskerville edition in 1773 ; and a single volume of an edition, undertaken by the Rev. William M. Hatch, in 1871. At the present time, therefore, a new and complete edition of this celebrated work is a desideratum.

[3] Toland's *Letters from the late Earl of Shaftesbury to Robert Molesworth, Esq.,* which were published in 1721, during the life time of parties therein mentioned.

pleasing and useful work; but his death prevented his making any great progress in it.

What has been here said may suffice for the characterising of him, since what shall appear from the judgment of reason, on the perusal of plain matters of fact, is far more likely to be a proper one, than the too general method of working out a character from the conceptions of a heated imagination.

# THE PHILOSOPHICAL REGIMEN

## (ἈΣΚΉΜΑΤΑ).

## NATURAL AFFECTION.

"ΕΣῃ ποτὲ ἆρ', ὦ ψυχή, ἀγαθή, καὶ ἁπλῆ, καὶ μία, καὶ γυμνὴ, φανερωτέρα τοῦ περικειμένου σοι σώματος; γεύσῃ ποτὲ ἆρα τῆς φιλητικῆς καὶ σρερητικῆς διαθέσεως [" Wilt thou then, my soul, never be good and simple and one and naked, more manifest than the body which surrounds thee ? Wilt thou never enjoy an affectionate and contented disposition?"—*Marcus Aurelius Antoninus, Meditations,* Bk. X., § 1.]

What is it to have Natural Affection ? Not that which is only towards relations, but towards all mankind; to be truly φιλάνθρωπος [a lover of men], neither to scoff, nor hate, nor be impatient with them, nor abominate them, nor overlook them ; and to pity in a manner and love those that are the greatest miscreants, those that are most furious against thyself in particular, and at the time when they are most furious?—How is it in a mother, or a nurse towards sickly children ? How often is that seen in children themselves and in good-natured people towards other creatures ? And how kindly are several species of creatures entertained by us, so as that to use any of these harshly and cruelly is ill looked upon, as, on the contrary, to be kind and favourable towards them is recommending ? What is more amiable than such affection ? And is it not most of all amiable towards men ? When is it, therefore, that thou shalt become, as it were, a common father of mankind ? So as to say, whatever wretch or whatever number of such thou seest, whether of the most prosperous or most dejected, whether of one country or another, whether of the simplest or of those that are thought wise : " These are they whom, though they have no care of themselves; no, none amongst them truly affected or concerned for them; though they are animated against one

c

another, and can least of all endure one that would take this care of them; yet these are they whom I make to be my care and charge; whom I foster and do good to, against their wills, and shall ever do so, as long as they are *men,* and I am of their kind." [1]

When shall this happy disposition be fixed, that I may feel it perpetually, as now but seldom? When shall I be entirely thus affected and feel this as my part grown natural to me? It shall then be, when thou no longer seekest for anything they seek, when thou no longer wantest anything from them, or canst be worked by anything that may happen to thee from them. In short, it is then only that thou canst truly love them, when thou expectest neither thy good nor thy ill from them. Whilst that expectation is, we must of necessity be jealous of and suspect them, flatter and court them, be one while in great familiarity with them, at another time in open enmity, to-day in favour, to-morrow in disgrace, this moment warm and affectionate, the next, cold and indifferent, ashamed of what we just before were proud, and sick of those we before so highly relished. Let this therefore be remembered, when we see the children play and content, when they have their nuts and their apples to divide, and are busied about their childish affairs. We look upon them with pleasure and are kind to them, without anger, without concern, always benign, gentle and mild towards them, with sincere affection and love; nor are we provoked by them, if froward or unruly towards us, but doing what is necessary to amend the fault, we pass it by; never imagining ourselves hurt, never meditating revenge against the child though he were ever so perverse, but thinking only how to cure and set him aright. And by virtue of what is it that all this is performed?—By this. Because the nuts and apples do not concern us; because those things which they esteem as children we despise as men; and because it is never considered what the children say of us amongst themselves; whether they are angry or pleased, whether they thank us for our pains, or so much as think of us or remember us; but whether this that we

[1] Homo sum, humani nihil a me alienum puto.—*Terence, Heaut.*, Act I., line 25.

do be for the children's good, be fit or not fit in their case; and whether this be done with the due skill of one who has the care and charge of children. But, if he who has the charge should want to play himself, if he should fall in love with the apples and nuts, and think it his good to have a name amongst the children, where would his authority be? And what else must follow, but that from the moment this begins, he must begin also to hate and torment the children, and no longer be their tutor, but their tyrant? Consider then as to mankind. Thou wouldst love men. But in what way is this possible? They love riches, they love pleasure, they love honour, preferments, power; therefore, they will have it for themselves. Give it them, be unconcerned, and thus thou mayst love them and take care of them. But thou wilt be concerned thyself. Thou must have thy share. Go in, then, and fight for it; make court, solicit, and lay wait; digest repulses if thou canst; bear with thy rivals and competitors, and be patient when others carry it from thee; but expect not any more to stand in that other station towards mankind. Think not any more of loving these as men, for true affection cannot be except where true liberty is.

To have natural affection is to affect according to nature or the design and will of nature. For without respect to a design and will of nature, nothing can be said to affect naturally, or have natural affection. Is it natural for a parent to love the offspring, or for a creature of any kind to affect more particularly his own species or kind? If this be called natural, what else is understood but that the preservation and support of such a certain species is designed by nature, after this manner, and by these means? This therefore is the design and will of nature, that by the natural and good affection of creatures towards their own species the species should be preserved and be prosperous. Now either this design of nature is an excellent wise and good design, and it is my good to follow it, or otherwise what have I to do but to throw off this that is called natural affection and live after some other rule? If there be a better rule, let us see what that is, let us see how it is with men that lose these natural affections; how it is even with beasts and the common creatures. Which are the happiest, or in the best state, those that live orderly and obey these affections, or those that are hardened against nature and have all of this kind unnatural and in disorder? Of this there has been enough said elsewhere. Nor is anything more evidently demonstratable than this, that the only means and rule of happiness (even amongst these other creatures, as far as they are capable of happiness) is *to follow nature*, and whether knowingly or unknowingly, to act in pursuance of this design, and under the power of such affections as these.

Thus much as to all human and other creatures, being either wholly irrational, or considered only in such a use of reason as is common; but not such as contemplates nature, and considers of *the whole;* what it is; how governed; by what laws; whether it be one and simple, fixed and constant, equal to itself, knowing, wise and good. Let us consider, therefore, how the matter stands with a creature who is after this other manner and in this higher degree, rational.

Either this which we call natural affection and this that we have shown of the order of nature in particular, is notwithstanding wholly and solely from chance, and not properly designed; or, it is from a limited and imperfect design; or, it is from an all-powerful, wise and perfect design.

If the first or second be supposed we must consider other matters, and how either of these opinions can stand; but if the latter be allowed it will follow that besides that relation to a species, there is a further relation which every creature has, viz., to the whole of things as administered by that supreme will or law which regulates all things according to the highest good. If it be thus, it follows that a creature who is in that higher degree rational, and can consider the good of the whole, and consider himself as related to the whole, must withal consider himself as under an obligation to the interest and good of the whole, preferably to the interest of his private species: and this is the ground of a new and superior affection. Now if it has been made the good and happiness even of unknowing and irrational creatures to follow that private and inferior affection which is only towards a species and part of the whole, how can it but be much more the good of every knowing and rational creature to live according to that affection which is the highest and most perfect? Nature has made this the reward of every creature, even unknowingly and unconsciously pursuing her intention and design; that by this very pursuit the creature preserves itself in its most perfect state. And shall the same nature and sovereign wisdom of the whole have made it less the happiness and good of a knowing and rational creature, to have a right and deserving affection towards nature and the whole? What is it, therefore, that we call a right and a deserving affection? Let us consider what this is, and to what this supposed relation, if it be true, obliges us.

If a father be in danger of his life, if his safety or interest call for it, we are to expose ourselves willingly. Labour, pain, and even death (if necessary) are to be suffered without murmuring, without complaining, cheerfully, generously. This is according to nature. This is natural affection. This, if it be lost or wanting in any creature, the creature is vile, degenerate, imperfect, wretched.

If friends are in danger, and their interest call for it, our part also is to expose ourselves freely and voluntarily: if our city or country, much more. These are the relations, these the affections. Now, let us see how this is elsewhere and in another degree.

If there be a supreme parent, a common father of men and all other beings, and if all things happen according to the will of this first parent, it follows that everything is to be kindly and well accepted ; no murmuring, no complaining. If all things in the universe are for the good of one another, all united and conspiring to one end, all alike subject to one wise and perfect rule, all alike produced from one original and fountain : it follows that I must in a certain manner be reconciled to all things, love all things, and absolutely hate or abhor nothing whatsoever that has being in the world. If the universe be as one city, and the laws of that city perfect and just, it follows that whatsoever happens, according to the laws of that city, must be accepted and esteemed. And since there is nothing but what is according to those laws, there is nothing that happens but what I ought highly to applaud, and to accompany with my mind and sincerest affection. And if I do otherwise I am impious, unjust, unnatural, ungrateful, an apostate from reason, and vicious in a higher order and degree.

Here, then, is that new relation. Here it is that that other affection arises, and this is the *natural affection* of a rational creature, capable of knowing nature and of considering the good and interest of the whole.

Now, how is this affection preserved? How made consistent with those other affections, or rather those others with this? If every other affection of that lower order (however natural any such may be) be not entirely subordinate to this superior affection, this is wrong. If a relation be beloved; if a friend; if it be thy city, thy native country; if all this be not freely, willingly, readily, resigned, what is this but disobedience? What else but this can be called apostacy? If there be any reluctancy, any murmuring or grieving, any abhorrence, any aversion, what is this but rebellion, impiety, resistance?

Thus are all other affections to be subdued. This is the new order, the new economy which belongs to another degree. This is the province of the truly wise man who is conscious of things human and divine : to learn how to submit all of his affections to the rule and government of the whole; how to accompany with his whole mind that supreme and perfect mind and reason of the universe. *This is to live according to Nature, to follow Nature, and to own and obey Deity.* If I have friends, I act the part of a friend; if I am a father, the part of a father. If I have a city or country, I study its good and interest; I cherish it as I ought; I hazard myself and do all for it that in me lies. If I must no longer be a father; if children or friends are taken from me; if He who gave me a country and a nation take it back, and either by war or any other means cause it to cease or perish, all is well. I am free and unconcerned, so that I have done my part for my country; so that I have not been wanting to my friend; so that I have acted the part of a father. But shall I not bemoan my child? Shall I be thus indifferent and unconcerned? Shall I have no more natural affection? Wretch! consider what it is thou callest natural affection. In what way canst thou have natural affection whilst this thou callest so is still retained? In what way freely and readily resign both children and family when any higher duty calls or thy country is to be served? In what way resign alike country, children, mankind and all else in this world when He who placed thee calls thee from hence? In what way canst thou accompany

Him, or applaud all that He does? How act or suffer as becomes thee, as becomes a man, and one that is free, generous, disinterested? How can this be whilst thou retainest this other sort of affection? Now if it be thus even with respect to such subjects as these, what must it be towards those other matters such as riches, honours and the rest? What must that degeneracy be which detains us by any affections towards things of such inferior kind?

Be it so. But where is the good or happiness of having this natural affection? Where is the ill of having that which is falsely called so? This it is. If thy affection be such either towards friends, relations, countrymen, or whatever else is engaging or delightful, it must happen that when anything here succeeds amiss thou must be at a loss and disturbed within thyself, wholly dissatisfied with Providence and the order of things, impatient, angry, full of complaint, bitterness, vexation, discontent. Nor is this any more consistent with true affection than with happiness. For in what way can the affections of such a one be preserved in due order? in what way preserve a mind in the midst of such convulsions and disorder? and how maintain those subordinate affections in their several degrees, if this supreme affection be thus shaken and overturned? On the other hand, if we stand affected towards these things as we ought, if our affections are such as can immediately give way and without struggle or hindrance readily close with what happens ever so contrary, if our will be in conformity to the supreme will, and ready to receive whatever happens and is appointed: this only can afford us happiness and content; bestow peace, serenity, calm; make us to live in friendship with men and with due acknowledgment and reverence and piety towards God. Nor can those several relations, offices, duties, parts, be any otherwise preserved but after this manner. It is in vain to think of being virtuous, just, or pious but upon this foundation. It is on this that integrity, faith, honour, generosity, magnanimity, and everything of that kind depends. Now, how is it that this is accomplished? in what way can we arrive at this natural affection? in what way affect and disaffect, as we ought to do, and according to nature?

*Of things that are, some are of our own power and juris-*

*diction: some not.* ¹Τῶν ὄντων τὰ μέν ἐστιν ἐφ᾽ ἡμῖν, τὰ δὲ οὐκ
ἐφ᾽ ἡμῖν, &c. This is all, this is the whole concern, and nothing
but this. Here all depends; here the labour, pains, employment,
and this is the sum of all. Καταφρόνησις τῶν οὐκ ἐφ᾽ ἡμῖν.
["Despise the things which are not within our power."—*Epict.
Ench.*, c. xix., § 2.]

Remember, therefore, henceforward not to think any more
of natural affection in the imperfect and vulgar sense, but
according to the just sense and meaning of the word and what
it imports.

Is my appetition,* seeking, aversation, right and natural?
am I not frustrated? am I not at a loss, hindered, disturbed?
do I affect safely, on sure ground, and with certainty of success?
Is it not merely chance that has made me hitherto prosperous in
my desire, aim and wish? and is it not merely that and nothing
else, which now at this time is the occasion of my present ease
and satisfaction? How is it that I am affected towards a change
in any of these outward circumstances? how towards the conclusion of all and the finishing of my part? how towards the
loss of friends, companions, relations, children, country? Is it
here that I can prove my affection natural? Can nothing of this
kind separate me from nature, or hinder me from joining with it
and accompanying it? Is it no longer in the power of any chance
whatsoever to raise any contrary affection or to interrupt the
course of that which carries me with the whole of things and
makes me to be unanimous with Deity? If it be otherwise, it is
in vain to plead nature and say, I lament and grieve; but I am
natural. This is the part of a father.—Wretch! consider what
art thou thyself and whence? where dost thou inhabit? in whose
city? under what administration? whence dost thou draw thy
breath? at whose will and by whose donation has thou received
this being, and art now at this moment sustained? Dost thou
not consider that by thus deserting Him, by thus opposing and
(as much as in thee lies) impugning and destroying His rule and
administration, thou art not only far from being (as thou
sayest) a father; but art thyself, an unnatural son, an ill-subject,
an ill-creature? What hast thou to do with nature? what

---

¹ *Epictetus, Enchiridion*, c. i., § 1.          * ὄρεξις, ὁρμή, ἔκκλισις.

pretence of being natural ? What other relation, what part dost thou tell us of, after such a part as this, after having thrown off this relation, this highest duty and obligation, upon which the rest depends?—But all other creatures are thus affected towards their young.—And are all other creatures therefore sensible of that other relation? were they made to consider nature as thou dost? were they brought into the world to contemplate the order of it and recognise the author and supreme, to join themselves to him, and assist in his administration and rule? were they made free, unhinderable, invincible, irrefragable, as to that inward part? Had they any means or natural accommodations, instructions, or faculties given them towards justice, faith, piety, magnanimity? If not; what should they follow but that other affection, which with respect to them is natural? But if thou also wouldst act thus and still be natural, divest thyself in the first place, of that other part; be no longer a man; and then we will grant it, that thou dost act naturally, and according to thy constitution and end.

All affection carries with it an inclining or declining, so that if this inclining and declining be right and natural, the affection is right and natural; else not. If all that nature produces be natural, *i.e.*, orderly and good, to incline or decline contrary to nature, or to what nature produces, must (with respect to the particular mind) be unnatural and ill. But to repine, to grieve, to be mean, or lament, is to decline contrary to nature, and is therefore unnatural affection.

Every affection is natural which affects the preservation and good of that which nature has assigned to it. Thus the natural affection of a part or member is to work for the preservation of the body. Thus the natural affection of a father is to love his children. Thus the natural affection of a man, a rational creature and citizen of the universe, is to love whatsoever happens according to those laws by which the universe is upheld. See how duly these parts are preserved. Does not the finger or hand, of its own accord, carefully decline every touch that may be hurtful; but when the head is in danger, does it not as readily expose itself of its own accord, and without waiting the order or dictate of the mind? Is not the care of the whole body and private person set aside when the part or duty of a parent calls?

Are not relations, children, and all of this kind forgotten when the part of a citizen comes on ?   How is it that we honour and praise the severity of those Romans, deaf to all entreaties, inflexible, immovable, and with an equal temper and unaltered countenance, performing the part of the magistrate in the sentence and execution of their beloved children ?

And is this part thus readily found and thus preserved and obeyed everywhere else in nature, and shall it only be wanting towards nature itself ?   If therefore the highest and most natural part be that which is towards nature, consider what it is to be wanting in due affection here, and for the sake of a member, a body, children, friends, city, or anything of this kind, to be divided from nature, to accuse nature, and to disaffect that which the supreme and sovereign will decrees for the good and preservation of the whole.

Either nature which has given the several subjects of affection, is itself a subject of affection to a rational creature capable of considering nature, or it is not so.   If it be not so, we can no longer say we affect any duty or part because assigned to us by nature ; and thus nothing can be properly called natural. If, on the contrary, I adhere to that which is natural, and for that reason because it is natural, then nature is to me a subject of affection.   If nature be at all a subject, what can it be but the highest subject ?   If it be the highest subject, then, to be wanting in affection towards it, is to be most of all unnatural. Now everything that happens is from the same nature (the nature of the whole), and, therefore, to be dissatisfied with what happens, is to be dissatisfied with nature.   Now to grieve, bemoan, and repine is to be dissatisfied with what happens and to throw off our affection to nature.   Therefore to affect anything, so as on account of it, to grieve, bemoan, or repine, must of necessity be wrong and unnatural affection.

To consider of natural affection, and is it to examine and measure the affection due to every particular, as nature has appointed ?   What is the subject ?   Is it (for example) a finger, or a hand ?   Preserve it, cherish it as a member.   But if the whole body come in question, expose it freely, slight it, abandon it, give it up ; for, this is due to the interest of the whole.   Thus if I have friends, relations, children, city, I prize and cherish

these. In what way? As given me by nature, thus to love and
to take care of. But if the interest of nature call, I forsake
everything else and follow nature, without murmuring, without
complaint. In what way, therefore, shall I love my children or
relations? As strongly and affectionately as is possible for me
to love them, but so as that nature may be accused; so as that,
whatever happens, I may still adhere to nature and accept and
embrace whatsoever nature sends. This is the foundation. This
is all. Consider this, and it will be easy to find the true measure
of all affection, and what discipline and rules must be followed
to reduce our affection to nature and to affect as becomes a
rational creature.

A mind that refuses its consent to what is acted in the
whole and for the good of the whole, is the same as a hand that
should refuse to act for the body. What is a hand? A single
part made for the use and convenience of the body. What am
I? A man. But how a man? As an Athenian? As a Roman?
As a European? And is this all? No, but *as a citizen of the
world.* This is to be a man. This the nature of man signifies.
How is it then that I preserve the part of a man? How am I a
Roman?—when I prefer the interest of Rome. How a man?—
when I prefer the interest of the world. Now in what way
prefer the interest of the world and yet be angry or dissatisfied
at what happens in the world? Consider, therefore, what is it
that makes me averse to anything of this kind? What is the
occasion of reluctancy? For whatever affection this be, whether
towards a body, or towards friends, or towards a son, or towards
a city, this is that which makes me be unnatural; this, in me,
is the opposite to natural affection.

Love thy friends, relations, companions, but thy country
better. Love thy country as thou art an Englishman, but thy
country as a man much better. Who can be said to love his
country who grieves at what is for its good and what is
necessary for its establishment and safety? Now consider!
Hast thou any country as a man or not? Are the laws of that
country wise and just? Is the public good, and welfare aimed at
and successfully carried on? Is there order, rule, intelligence and
a mind? If so, what is that happens, or can happen, but according to that wise economy and perfect will? Now if that economy

were changed or interrupted; if that will were controlled or disobeyed; all must perish, and that first and ancient commonwealth be overturned and destroyed. Therefore, whatsoever happens in the economy of the whole is necessary for the happiness, perfection, and establishment of the whole, that it should have been; and to have annulled this (if it had been possible) must have been to have annulled and made void that economy of the whole by which its happiness and perfection are maintained. Now see of what a nature it is to repine at anything that happens. What is the loss that thus affects? Is it of a limb? wilt thou not give it up, τοις ὁλοις? Is it of thy relations? wilt thou not remember thy other relation? Is it of thy country? wilt thou not remember another country, state, polity, government, law?

Therefore remember on any approaching misfortune or calamity to say: "this is for the good of my country; this is according to the constitution, law, custom, of my native country." If such a one be to die: "it is the laws of my country that decree it." If such a one fail and prove vicious: "the same laws have ordered it so." If this which I commonly call my country be sinking; what is this still but "the laws of my real country." See therefore how it is thou cherishest, lovest, embracest those laws, and accordingly thou mayest say thou either hast or wantest *Natural Affection.*

# DEITY.

Ἐν σοὶ μέν τις κόσμος ὑφίϛτασθαι δύναται, ἐν δὲ τῷ παντὶ ἀκοσμία; ["Can a certain order subsist in thee, and disorder in the All?"—*Mar. Aurel., Med.*, Bk. IV., § 27].

The elements are combined, united, and have a mutual dependence one upon another. All things in this world are united, for as the branch is united and is as one with the tree, so is the tree with the earth, air, and water which feed it, and with the flies, worms, and insects which it feeds. For these are made to it, and as much as the mould is fitted to the tree, as much as the strong and upright trunk of the oak or elm is fitted to the twining and clinging branches of the vine or ivy, so much are the leaves, the seeds, the fruits of these trees fitted to other animals, and they, again, to one another. All hold to one stock. Go farther : and view the system of the bigger world. See the mutual dependence, the relation of one thing to another; the sun to the earth; the earth and planets to the sun ; the order, symmetry, regularity, union, and coherence of the whole.

It follows, therefore, that as the plant or tree has a nature, the world or universe must have a nature, and here arises the question, *What sort of a nature should this be?* There are in this world three sorts : a vegetative, a sensitive, and a rational. Should the nature of the universe, which contains and brings forth all other natures, be itself merely vegetative and plastic, like that of a tree or of a fœtus ? or, should it be only a degree further, and be sensitive, as an animal ? or should it be yet further, and be rational, but imperfectly so, as man ? Or, if this seem still utterly mean and absurd, should not the nature of the universe, which exhibits reason in all that we see; which practises reason by a consummate art and prudence in the organisation and structure of things; and (what is more) which produces principles of reason and raises up intelligences and perceptions of several degrees in the beings that are but of a

moment's duration, that start out of it, as it were, and sink into
it immediately; should not this sovereign nature of the whole
be a principle itself of much greater understanding and capacity
than any else? Should not the most extensive sight or knowledge with which we are acquainted and the highest wisdom
which we admire, be as nothing in comparison with that original
one from whom all is derived? And should not that affection,
which we see in all natures towards their offspring and productions, towards what is more remotely united to them, or what
is strictly any part of themselves, be much inferior to that
affection of the Supreme Nature towards all and to what is
produced and administered by it, as everything is? And what is
this, in one word, but that God is; that He is one and simple,
infinitely wise and perfectly good?

Things are finite or infinite. If infinite, that which we call
the whole is infinite; if finite, still that which exists is the whole.
But next of what kind or nature is this whole? Is it like
that of a stone or of scattered pieces of sand? Then that had
remained for ever its nature, and it could never have given rise to
other natures or principles that unite and conspire together, as
plants, vegetables, animal-bodies and the like. Is it, therefore,
only a vegetative nature? Then that had remained its nature;
it might have flourished and grown and thriven as those other
natures, and might have borne its fruit and varied itself a
thousand ways. But in what way could such a nature have produced reason? In what way could it bring perception out of itself
if it were not in itself? Therefore the nature of the universe
is intelligent. Therefore, says one, there is indeed intelligence
in things, or in the nature of things, and as eternally belonging
to them. But the whole, says he, is not united as you suppose.
So that there is not, therefore, *one* intelligence. Let us hear,
then. Are not the small fibres of this root conspiring together
and united? They are; but, with what? With the plant; and
the plant with what? With the earth and other plants. And
the earth and other plants with what? With air, water, animals
and other things around; the animals themselves with one
another and the elements in which they live and to which they
are fitted, as either by wings for the air, by fins for the water, and
other things of that kind. In short, all these conspire together,

and so all other things, whatever they may be, in this world. And is it not the same with the world itself in respect of the sun and the planets? How then? Is there beyond this anything or nothing? If nothing, then is this the whole, and then the whole is as one and has one nature. But there is more beyond this.—Undoubtedly there is so. And shall that and this have no relation nor mutual dependence? Shall not the coherence and union be the same, to the infinite? Or shall we come at last to something in the whole which has no relation to the rest of things and is independent? It remains, therefore, that all things cohere and conspire; all things are in one, and are comprehended in the nature of the universe. This nature is either merely vegetative, and then it could have produced only things of the same species; or if there be in the universe beings of another kind, that is to say, such as have perception and intelligence, by what should they be produced unless by a like nature? But there is no other nature to produce anything except the nature of the universe; therefore the nature of the universe is intelligent, and therefore there is a universal intelligent and provident principle.

If it be not yielded that the universe is one, or has one nature, so as to conspire together and to one end, it will not be denied, however, that this is proper to the stalk of grass. If the stalk of grass has it, then (by what has been said before) the whole earth has it, and not only the earth, but the whole system of the bigger world, as far as we know of anything. Either, therefore, this system, with all that exists besides, holds together, is still one whole, and is united; or (what is strange to imagine), though there be such perfect coherence in this apparent whole, yet there is incoherence in that *great whole*, and in what remains besides of things. If the latter, there are no other such worlds, and what is besides is disorder and confusion; or if there are such worlds, they are independent. If it be the first, it will still remain that this world is one and must (as has been shown) be intelligent. For either it has its intelligence elsewhere, and then there is elsewhere in the universe a principle on which this world depends; or, it had it from itself, and then it was eternally a principle of intelligence to itself: since nothing can be more certain than that what is intelligent cannot be produced out of what is not intelligent, and that what was never produced but was eternal, must remain eternal. Accordingly it will still remain as to this world, that in as far as it has a nature by which it is one and united as a plant or animal body (this nature being utterly different from disorder and confusion) and in as far as it has sense, perception, and intelligence (which if it have not received from a principle of that kind it must be a principle of that kind itself), it must be said that it has a nature or soul not merely vegetative, but knowing and intelligent. Hence there is in this respect a supreme eternal mind or intelligent principle belonging to this whole; and this is Deity.

If there are more such worlds, and independent of one another, they are still so many intelligences, and must be eternal principles of that kind. But since it is unreasonable and unaccountable thus to multiply principles, as, for instance, to say that of the motion that is in the world, there should not be one and the same principle, but several; so with respect to what is intelligent, it must be unreasonable to think that there is any more than one common principle of intelligence, or that there should be intelligences and thinking beings of several kinds produced anywhere by one such principle, and that there should not be one common one to all of that kind. Either the whole, therefore, is not united like this which we see, and then, however, there must be either one intelligent eternal principle or several such; or else the whole or infinite of things is united and is one, and then it follows that there is one common principle of intelligence and wisdom—one eternal and infinite mind.

Either this that we see is order, proportion, harmony, or it is not so. If this be not so, and if neither the frame of the heavens nor the body of man demonstrate order, what else is order? If it be order, and consequently of quite a different nature from disorder, then how could that which was of quite a different nature and even its contrary, have produced it? If it never was produced by disorder, then it must be a principle in things, or be proper and natural to things. If it be natural for some things to correspond and unite, then surely to all things. Or say why natural to some things, if not as well to all? If to all things, then all things are united and have one nature. If there be a nature of the whole, it must be a nature more perfect than that of particulars contained in the whole ; and if so, it is a wise and intelligent nature. If so then, it must order everything for its own good, and since that which is best for the universe is both the wisest and justest, it follows that the supreme nature is perfectly wise and just.

All things stand together or exist together by one necessity, one reason, one law : therefore there is one nature of all things, or common to all. Nothing is out of the whole, nor nothing happens but according to the laws of the whole. Now every particular nature certainly and constantly produces what is good to itself, unless something foreign molest and hinder it, either by overpowering and corrupting it within, or by violence from without. Thus nature in the patient struggles to the last and strives to throw off the distemper. Thus even in plants and seeds every particular nature thrives and attains its perfection if nothing from without obstruct and if nothing foreign to its nature has already impaired and wounded it; and even then it does its utmost to redeem itself. What are all weaknesses, distortions, sicknesses, imperfect births and seeming contradictions or crossnesses of nature, but merely this ? And how ignorant must one be of all natural operations who thinks that any of these things happen by a miscarriage of the particular nature, and not by the force of some foreign nature that overpowers it ? Thus, therefore, every nature is constantly and never-failingly true to itself, and certain to produce only what is good to itself and to its own right state. And if every particular nature do this, shall not the nature of the whole do it ? or shall that alone miscarry and fail ? or is there anything foreign that shall do violence to it, or force it out of its way ? If not, then all that it produces is for its own good, the good of all in general; and that which is for the good of all in general is just and good. If so, then rest satisfied, and not only rest satisfied, but be pleased and rejoiced with what happens, knowing from whence it comes and to what it contributes.

*To sympathize*, what is it ?—To feel together, or be united in one sense or feeling.—The fibres of the plant sympathize, the members of the animal sympathize, and do not the heavenly bodies sympathize ? Why not ?—Because we are not conscious of this feeling.—No more are we conscious of the feeling or

D

sympathizing of the plant; neither can we be conscious of any other in the world besides that of our own. If, however, it be true that these others sympathize, then the world and the heavenly bodies (more united and more harmoniously conspiring together than either the plant or animal body) must also sympathize. If there be a sympathizing of the whole, there is one perception, one intelligence of the whole. If that, then all things are perceived by that intelligence. If so, then there is one all-knowing and all-intelligent nature.

This we know. We ourselves have a mind, because we are conscious of it. But we cannot be conscious of any other mind, or that there is any such thing as a mind besides our own. If, therefore, we will believe in no other mind, there is an end, and we can go no further. If we presume or believe there is anywhere a mind out of ourselves, or that there are anywhere perceptions, intelligencies, or natures such as perceive and act; by what is it are we induced to believe this? Is it only because we speak and converse with such? If so, then we cannot speak and converse but with our own kind, nor believe any such thing but in our own kind; so there is an end, and we can go no further. But if we can have cause to believe it from any other grounds, then what is it that is sufficient to make us believe of anything that it perceives and acts? It must be this, or nothing: When there is a consent and harmony of parts, a regular conduct for the good of the whole, a steady management suitable to one end and design. Now, here the question arises. The system of things we see, and with it the whole of things, is thus, or it is not thus. If it be thus, it bears the marks and has a mind. If it be not thus, show in what it is otherwise, and it will appear either that the objection, whatever it be, is from gross inequality and partiality, by referring all things to ourselves, and to the good or interest of one small and inconsiderable part of things; or, that it is mere ignorance, the same as his who, being ignorant in anatomy, would find fault with the glands, as useless and superfluous, or with the pores, as inconvenient and the occasion of receiving harm.

Where the principle or cause is chance the product and effect must be disorder and madness. Where the cause is design and a mind, the effects must be order and harmony. Which of these is the case ?

If there be an economy of the whole and a mind, is it such as that thou shouldst expect to see it, as thou seest a man, for example ?—Certainly not. What is it, then, that thou wouldst see to satisfy thee of this mind ?—the effects of such a mind. And what must those be ?—What else but order, agreement, sympathy, unity, subserviency of inferior things to superior, proper affections of subjects making them to operate correspondingly towards a general good, a conversion of everything into use, a renovation of all things by changes and successions; nothing idle, nothing vacant, nothing superfluous, nothing abrupt. See, therefore, if all be not thus, and whether it be not ignorance and short-sightedness, or an ill-temper and wrong affection, which makes things to appear otherwise.

Yesterday thou wert entertained with the contemplation of several natural things. The order of the heavens was wise and wonderful; the anatomy of man most complete and perfect. It was a wonder with thee how the orbs should be preserved and steadily hold those courses; how the wisest Providence could have contrived so well for the support of such a body as thy own. These were thy thoughts yesterday. To-day it was an earthquake; or not so much, a storm only that destroyed some corn; a slight infection of the air which hurt some cattle, or which affected thyself. And what follows ? Why Providence is arraigned. The world is become a new thing, all is wrong; all is disorder. But was not all this owned possible, and even natural, but yesterday ?—It was.—Which is it, then, that is wrong and disordered ? the world, or thyself ? What is this but temper ?

View the heavens. See the vast design, the mighty revolutions that are performed. Think, in the midst of this ocean of being, what the earth and a little part of its surface is; and what a few animals are, which there have being. Embrace, as it were, with thy imagination all those spacious orbs, and place thyself in the midst of the Divine architecture. Consider other orders of beings, other schemes, other designs, other executions, other faces of things, other respects, other proportions and harmony. Be deep in this imagination and feeling, so as to enter into what is done, so as to admire that grace and majesty of things so great and noble, and so as to accompany with thy mind that order, and those concurrent interests of things glorious and immense. For here, surely, if anywhere, there is majesty, beauty and glory. Bring thyself as oft as thou canst into this sense and apprehension; not like the children, admiring only what belongs to their play; but considering and admiring what is chiefly beautiful splendid and great in things. And now, in this disposition, and in this situation of mind, see if for a cut-finger, or what is all one, for the distemper and ails of a few animals, thou canst accuse the universe.

*That the Deity is present with all things, knows all things, and is provident over all.*—Where is the difficulty of this? How is this hard of conception? Could a plant or tree reason, and were to answer to the question how it was possible for it to perceive the approach or neighbourhood of some other fellow-plant, it would answer by the touch. But what if not touched, how then? It were impossible it should know anything.

Thus the plant, and though I should again and again aver that without touching the leaves or boughs of another plant it could have notice of their motions and feel, as it were, when they were agitated, and how; this in all likelihood would be a paradox till the sense of hearing was added. But this being added, let us again ask in what way a grove, being placed at a distance from it, the trees could be perceived in their situation, distance from one another, in their different shapes, growths, as also in their very healths, sicknesses, age and youth, by any other notion than that which arises from a perceptible alteration of figure? Would not this be a new and yet greater paradox? I perceive yonder, afar off, that the leaf of that tree is withering and in decay. Does it seem shattered or broken? No, but as to shape and fashion perfectly entire. What is it then that gives the intimation? Something from the surface. What something? Is it rough or smooth, even or uneven? Does there anything grow upon the surface? Are they regular figures or irregular — triangles, globules, lines? I know not. What are they, then? Colours.

This to the plant must be unintelligible, and not only unintelligible but (if the plant be not a wise plant) incredible. But how is it with thyself? Wilt thou be as dull and stupid as that plant would be, and reason in the same manner? Is there nothing in the universe beyond hearing and sight, because thy wretched body has nothing better than an ear and eye? But why need I mention the Deity, who is infinite? Suppose merely that creature of His, the sun, to be intelligent, to what distances does he convey himself? how noble a part of the universe receives influence from him? What are the earth and other planets who perpetually receive from him both light and heat? Now what should the sense of such a creature be (if such a one I may call a creature) compared with this earthly kind? this that is confined to such wretched and perishing bodies? this that is admitted and supported by such poor organs in common to us with other fellow-animals? Yet this still supposes something exterior, whereas, with respect to the Deity, what is there or can there be exterior? Does not He contain all within Himself. Is there anything foreign to the universe? anything beyond the extent of that mind which resides in it? Shall all other things be thus disposed and governed by it; and shall that which is of the same nature and kind have no communication with it? Shall all other motion be subordinate; and shall the motions of minds, shall thoughts, sentiments, or whatsoever is of that kind, be independent, separated, and hid?

Remember, therefore, in what a Presence thou actest, and instead of an assembly of men, instead of Greece, instead of Rome, instead of thy city, friends, country, instead of a full concourse (if it were possible) both of moderns and ancients; remember that One, who is more than all. Thus contemplating Him, how is it possible thou shouldst either act or think anything mean, abject, or servile?

Which is more shameful? to think of Providence as those do who count themselves naturalists; or thinking of Providence as thou dost, to be no otherwise affected than as thou art? Which of the two is the more absurd? to have the faith of Epicurus, and believe in atoms; or, being conscious of Deity, to be no otherwise moved by His Presence than if He were not, or had no inspection of our thought or action? This is in the same manner, to live without Deity, and perhaps this last may be esteemed the greater impiety.

Either atoms or Deity; if the latter, consider what is

consequent; who it is that is present; how and in what manner. Dost thou, like one of those visionaries, expect to see a throne, a shining light, a court and attendance? Is this thy notion of a presence? And dost thou wait till then, to be struck and astonished as the vulgar are with such appearances and show?—Wretched folly!—But if without all this He be here, actually present, a witness of all thou dost, a spectator of all thy actions and privy to thy inmost thoughts, how comes it that thou livest not with Him, at least but as with a friend? Who is there whom thou wouldst thus treat? whose presence, whose testimony, whose opinion dost thou ever slight thus? Who is there that passes with thee so for little? What wretch ever so mean? Is this living so much as with a friend? Is this living with a benefactor? a father? a superior, who is more than magistrate, more than people, more than friends, relations, country, mankind, world? Is this thy conception and belief of a Deity? Art thou still with thyself, as if alone? This is, in effect, to believe and not believe.

The foundation of all those seeming strange things taught us by a certain philosophy is solely this: *That there is a God.*\* And having once this notion, am I to rest here?—Impossible. For, being concerned as I am in this general administration of things, it behooves me of necessity, if I believe such a ruler, to enquire what His rule and government is; what His laws, what His nature; what I myself am, how related to Him. This the vulgar think they see, and on this account worship Him, pray to Him, and do whatsoever else they think is acceptable to Him. Why?—That they may receive good from him; avoid ill. What good?—Life, health, estate, children, &c. What ill? —Death, poverty, losses, disgrace. These are the pursuits and endeavours, these the aversions and declinings. If I cannot satisfy my lust, I grieve and repine. If I meet with evils and afflictions, I murmur and complain, if I dare do so, if I may have leave, if not, and that I am withheld by fear, what do I still but murmur and repine? What is it that can make me

---

\* ὅτι ἔστι θεός . . . .ἡμεῖς δέ, τίνες ὄντες ὑπ᾿ αὐτοῦ γεγόναμεν καὶ πρὸς τί ἔργον; [That there is a God . . . and who are we, who were produced by him, and for what designed?—*Epict. Disc*, Bk. II., c. xiv., § 27].

praise or think well of Providence ? A command ? Impossible. Nor can anything else besides the reason of the thing, besides satisfaction, besides conviction. What conviction ?—That His administration is entirely just and good. Why then am I miserable ?—This is natural. This cannot be otherwise. Hence all those expostulations with Providence and sentiments which we endeavour to stifle but cannot. Thus the vulgar.

But he who has otherwise considered the nature of God, so as firmly to hold that opinion of Him and his administration as of what is most wise and perfect, such a one receding from the vulgar has no longer the same notions of good and ill, happy and unhappy, amiable or detestable ; but in all these things is utterly different. Men despise and condemn me.—Hast thou done anything unbecoming a man ? hast thou violated any law of the Deity ? If not, in what way can this be called disgrace ? how is this shameful ? On what is it that disgrace or honour depends ? Is it on the opinion of the wise or ignorant ? of the vulgar, or those who have reason ? of the virtuous or vicious ? Thus disgrace, infamy, contempt, is not an ill. For if real shame and disgrace depend on the judgment of the most considerable, and not of the most vile, then that which is disgrace with men, but is honourable, right, and becoming with respect to God, is either not disgrace, or the Deity not Deity. But I suffer pain, I undergo fatigue, I am exposed to dangers and death.—Where is that soldier who thinks of these in the presence of his general ? What wounds, what fatigues does he complain of ? What life is he concerned for ? And is not the cause much greater here ?

Thus are outward things despised, nor is this anything more than what is consequent from a real sense of Deity. Now let me once but be convinced, that my good is elsewhere than in outward things ; let me exercise myself in this, so as to incline and decline aright; and see how firm and undisturbed I shall remain in my thoughts of Providence and Deity ! how satisfied with administration ! how clear of doubt and scruples ! how far from any murmuring or repining, and in all respects how pious, religious, just, and good ! But otherwise than thus, this cannot be. Remember, therefore, how it is that this revolution is wrought, and how these things mutually operate on one another. For by conceiving highly of the Deity, we despise outward things; and by despising outward things we become strong and firm in the opinion and conception of Deity. But as this opinion can never be made lasting, sound or just, whilst we retain those other false and unsound opinions; so it is here chiefly that we are to labour, and to expect the fruit of this when we are further advanced. And thus it is that the same philosophy recommends to us the use of the ἔκκλισις [aversion], and to suspend for a certain season the ὄρεξις [desire]. For how can we worthily contemplate God, how raise our thoughts to things of this kind, or look steadily on all those causes, revolutions, and that order and economy of things in the universe; whilst at the same time the things that strike and astonish us are such as happen in the common course of that Providence ? *

Consider also, besides what has been said, a further reason against the use of the ὄρεξις [desire] in this place. Consider the age, vulgar religion, how thou hast been bred, and what impressions yet remaining of that sordid, shameful, nauseous idea of Deity. Consider in the case of any good motions or affections that way; what affinity they have with vulgar prayers and addresses to Deity, and what a wretched effect this has within, when anything of this kind mixes, or whilst so much as the remembrance of those other feelings remain. Therefore if thou wouldst praise, worship, and adore aright, wait till other habits are confirmed and until ideas of a certain kind are worn off, as they will be when the whole scope of life is changed ; aims, aversions, inclinings and declinings reversed, transferred ; the whole thought, mind, purpose, will, differently modelled, new. Then it is that thou mayest soundly, unaffectedly and safely sing those hymns to God which the divine man mentions.† But till such time, see how dangerous this is, and instead of being wholesome diet, how likely it is to give a surfeit and create a sort of pall and aversion, which may be of ill consequence and even fatal.

* What is said here will appear with light enough after reading *The Discourses of Epictetus,* Bk. III., c. xiii., concerning solitude, &c. : how this may be borne ; how nature contemplated ; how the Deity imitated.

† *Discourses of Epictetus,* Bk. I., c. xvi.

Again, consider whence comes that weakness and irresolution in the opinion concerning *man's being sociable by nature*; and also in that of other creatures being made serviceable to him and for his use. Whence comes this floating and hesitation, but from the inward jarring of those principles as they touch and have affinity elsewhere, as they borrow, as it were, from another system, and derive from another fountain of which they still retain something and cannot flow wholly clear and pure ? Otherwise ; what could be more absurd ?

Has the spider her web and art for no use ? And are so many species of volatiles made and framed for her proper prey, and as so many subjects of her art and faculties, and shall the understanding and reason and faculties of man, his tongue and hands and power of employing and managing these as he does, be esteemed a lesser matter, an accident, a vagary, a scape and oversight of nature, foreign to her design, and owing to blind and random chance ? Then may the whole world be so, full as well, and let us hearken to Epicurus' atoms.

What shall we say, therefore, as to all these domestic animals which are thus framed and fitted to us, some of which can scarce be imagined able to subsist without us ? Shall sheep and cattle and the rest of that kind be only accidentally man's; but properly and naturally the lion's and the tiger's ?

Are bees, ants, and even all creatures that do but herd, allowed society and man denied it ? and this, too, when he of all creatures is most impatient of solitude, most exposed in such a state, most indigent and helpless in maturity as well as infancy, and can no way subsist or be preserved without it, and neither subsist in winters without some artificial lodgment and provision of food, nor be protected against the creatures that can master and devour him ? All this is senseless and absurd, and yet see what happens ! Consider, how great must be the power of those former impressions to mar and corrupt ? and how inveterate is this evil ? Apply this, therefore, upon all occasions to the idea and contemplation of God, and remember the preceding caution.

If the writer of the Table [1] described, after such a manner, Imposture and her Cup; if the draught was such in those days,

---

[1] *Cebes, Tabula.*

what is it now? and how deeply have we drunk? Is it possible, therefore, that we should have stomachs to receive any strong or wholesome truths till we have vomited up those dregs? Can we expect anything but qualms, nauseatings, crudities, indigestions? What must we do, then? Be contented with slender diet: observe a *regimen* and course: refrain?—No, but I must follow my instinct and bent; I must eat stronger food; I must go out into the open air; I must exercise and use my limbs. Go, then, and write and think and speak high things of Deity; talk * magnificently of virtue, exhort others, imitate a man in health; act a Cato, a Thrasea, a Hebridius, a Rufus: but expect to suffer for this. Remember what will be the event, since even within, in thy own breast, these things are cautiously to be approached.

If presently after what has been said, it be lawful to venture on a strong thought of Deity, and even renew withal one of those dangerous ideas, take this single reflection. Consider a Paradise, an Eden (as in Milton), where that favourite of the Almighty was placed: how privileged: how adorned: fitted to view and contemplate the noble scene; and admitted even into a part of the administration. What sort of solitude † he passed; in what thoughts, what affections; after what manner he had communication with Deity, access, commerce, discourse, entertainment. This and more than this (for these are still low ideas) are verified in him, who having followed certain precepts, has accordingly framed himself a mind and will, and gained that situation τὸ συντάττειν ἑαυτόν τοῖς ὅλοις [where he adapts himself to all things]. This, those ancients (those only heroes) knew and were possessed of. This, the worshipper of the τὸ δαιμόνιον had; this the explorator had; this the seeming wretch, who was φίλος ἀθανατοις [dear to the immortals]; and this he who could say πᾶν μοι συναρμόζει [everything harmonizes with me.—*Marcus Aurelius Med.*, Bk. IV., § 23.]

Again, consider how it had been with thee in former days, if, according to the idea then conceived of Deity, a voice had been heard, an angel or messenger appeared. What an immediate

---

* *Discourses of Epictetus*, Book III., c. xiv., against the use of the ὄρεξις.

† *Epict., Disc.,.* Bk. III., c. xiii.

change ? how sudden a renouncing of all other things ? and how strong an application to that one affair, whatever it were that should be thus enjoined ? Consider how it is with thorough enthusiasts who are actually persuaded of some such message or resolution ? how resolute and bold in despising all other things ? and how transported with this one honour, this sole dignity ? Now is it not a thousand times more ridiculous than the merest enthusiasm of these people, to be convinced of a being infinitely more perfect than all that they conceive or think; and yet to be by so many degrees less affected than they are ? Is it not a thing monstrously preposterous to be fully and absolutely convinced that there is a Deity, and of the highest perfection; that He superintends all things, sees and knows all things, and is present everywhere; and yet at the same time to be so little affected by such a presence as to have more regard even for the commonest human eye ? What can be the meaning of this ? where does the mystery lie ? Consider, and thou mayest soon find. The vulgar have an idea of God; they have ideas also of good, of excellent, of able, admirable, sublime. Now they for their part unite these ideas and join those of this latter kind to the idea of their God. Therefore that which they count good they ascribe to him. Thus they give him a will such as their own; passions such as their own; pleasure like that of their own; revenge, as delighting in revenge; praise, as loving praise: thus attendants and a court, external pomp, splendour, and whatsoever they themselves admire. Consider now thy own idea of God; and whether thou joinest to it the ideas that thou hast of good, glorious, amiable, and excellent. Otherwise, what can such an idea produce? Is arbitrariness or revenge at any time a good with thee? If so, ascribe the same to God; imagine Him to be one that is always thus entertained and that enjoys the highest advantages of this sort. Thus thou shalt admire Him, imitate Him, conceive the highest esteem and value for Him.—What is despicable? If the things themselves are such, why dost thou admire them ? If they are of the nature of good; if they are excellent and of worth; where should they be but with the Deity? What will Deity be, when deprived of these ? what will there be left to admire or emulate ? how praise or greatly esteem such a condition ?

No wonder, therefore, if the vulgar surpass us in their opinion of Deity. No wonder if the vulgar admire and adore theirs with more sincerity than the philosopher his; if all we mean by philosophy be this. How should it happen otherwise with those of this sort? What should they be else but in a certain manner Atheists? They have discernment enough to find that such ideas as these agree not with the idea of God; but not discernment enough to find that they agree as little with the notion of good.

Ὅπου γὰρ τὸ συμφέρον, ἐκεῖ καὶ τὸ εὐσεβές. ["For where our interest is, there, also, is piety directed."—*Epict. Ench.*, c. xxxi., § 4.] Now try to philosophize after this rate and see what will happen. Correct the vulgar idea. Divest the Deity of all which we esteem happiness and good; take from Him what we reckon power, what we extol as great and mighty: and what remains? what must be the effect? Where can piety be? where adoration, reverence, or esteem? In what way can we admire or respect such a being but so much as in comparison with some great prince or dignified man? Now, where is the remedy? what cure? Nothing but this. To consider what is excellent and good, what not. For where we imagine this to exist, thither our admiration will be turned; where we think this is wanting, thither our contempt. If that which vile and wicked men possess be excellent and good, we must admire vile and wicked men; there is no help for it. If pleasure be good, we must admire those who enjoy pleasure and have the means of being voluptuous. If anything of those external things (anything besides what belongs to that perfection of a mind) be good, it follows that we must attribute either these things or something of the same kind with these things to Deity; or otherwise we must think lowly and contemptibly of such a being. In short, if we would truly own or worship Deity, if we would leave room for any true and sincere veneration, honour, admiration, or esteem, we must either ascribe those things to Him which we admire as excellent and good, or we must no longer admire as excellent or good those things which we cannot ascribe to Him.

If what has been said above be just, consider what a wretched kind that is which we call *free talking* about matters of religion, and the established rites of worship. What the effect is, when we oppose or impugn such opinions as those, especially if it be done after a certain manner, that is to say, if it be not still with a certain economy and reserve; if it be vehemently; if it be acutely, and as showing wit; if it be ridiculingly and with contempt.

Consider what the προλήψεις [preconceptions] are in this place, and that the vulgar cannot better apply them than they do; so that to disturb them in these formed opinions is to overthrow those very προλήψεις [preconceptions], lead them into greater error and render them profane and impious. They have now the right notion in general, that there is a Supreme Ruler, that He is powerful, that He is just; but they know not rightly what is power and what impotence, what is just, unjust, right or wrong. How should they know? Where have they learned to apply these notions rightly, and to accommodate them to their proper subjects? Wilt thou teach them? If not, what dost thou teach them in this other way, but impiety and atheism? Now dost thou appear to them as one sacrilegious and profane? As indeed thou art, on this very account. For what greater sacrilege is there than that which removes the notions of Deity out of the minds of men, and introduces atheism. Remember therefore to respect these rites, whatever they be, which others have within their own minds erected to the Deity, as well as those other rites which they have publicly erected and in other outward temples.

If modern superstition disturb thee be thankful it is not Indian and barbarian, that they are not human sacrifices, that they are not Druids. In the meantime imitate the chastity, decency, and sanctity of the ancients, remembering Xenophon, remembering Marcus, remembering Socrates and his last words, remembering Epictetus σπένδειν δὲ καὶ θύειν [" it is incumbent on every one to offer libations and sacrifices."—*Epict. Ench.*, c. xxxi., § 5], with what follows ὅταν μαντικῇ [" when you have recourse to divination."—*Ibid.*, c. xxxii.], and what stands at present in room of this.

All this preposterous conduct, this pressing and earnestness to correct those notions of theirs in religion, is due to an ignorance of the προλήψεις [preconceptions]; how it is that they apply them, how far they can go, and no further. Build to what-soever pitch, if these be not rightly applied and plain truth spoken out, all will tumble, all will unravel again and be as before. How should this be any otherwise? Grant but this, *that all vice is error; that all pursue their good and cannot but do so; that there is no good but a good mind, and no ill but an ill one:* immediately all is right. See how all the rest will follow; how smooth and easy the way is; how all those other matters come to nothing: offence, vengeance, anger; and those other things which presuppose these: forgiveness, mercy, favour, placability. What placability? what forgiveness? towards a mad man? towards a poor distempered wretch? Who is ever offended at such a one? where is the anger? what room for mercy? what for punishment? how is any one hurt and by what? But consider things in any other way. Suppose that a creature may do better than he does, and that he may follow something else than what appears to him his good; suppose vice to be one thing, and ill another; suppose vice itself to be an ill in the whole. See what must necessarily follow. Must not Deity be offended? must not I be so, much more? am not I hurt? must not I complain? must virtue be thus abandoned? must the things of the world be thus unequally distributed? Go and say that these things are of no moment; that they are not real goods. Persuade them that to be affronted, to be despised, to be poor or to smart, is not to suffer; that the sack or ruin of cities and destruction of mankind are not in themselves ill; and that with respect to the whole, these things are orderly, good and beautiful. Inculcate this. Make them understand it. But if this be ridiculous to think of, how much more ridiculous is it to endeavour to change their other opinions; or if they seem convinced of anything, to think that this should stand a moment, thus propped, without that other foundation?

Why thus concerned, particularly for their wrong opinion of *Deity?* Could they understand this, then all those other paradoxes would be easy. Then that also would be conceived (which is now so monstrous), that whatsoever happens in the world or to me in particular, of whatever nature it be, I should affect and love as natural, kind, sovereignly good and beneficial; as that which is nearly related to me, was designed me and fitted to me, and as that which is best both for the world in general and in particular for me. For how is this any longer a paradox?

If there be an order and economy for the good of the whole, then nothing can happen to me except from that economy which provided for me in particular the best that was possible, and had respect to my good. If I am convinced of this, I must naturally love whatever happens to me from that economy. If I would have that not to happen, which happens according to this economy, I destroy (as much as in me lies) this economy, which is for my good, and but for which the universe must live under perpetual ills, and myself be exposed to whatsoever may be imagined of ill. And of some such economy as this, even those are sensible who least think of Deity. For how is it that they say? "Nature has done her part. Nature has been kind in this and in that, in affording a passage out of life, in putting an end to misery. Nature has provided. Nature has taken care." Therefore, but for some nature or another (whatsoever that nature be) things had been worse, and my condition more miserable. Therefore, thanks be to that nature. But nature might have done better still.—Here is the question; upon this it turns. How is nature wise? How is nature thus universally good? How is nature the tender mother of all? For if this were true, who would not love nature? who not embrace her dispensations? who not adore Providence and Deity? Where, then, is the paradox, if Deity (real Deity) be believed? For, thus it will follow.

If there be Deity, there is no chance or contrary ill design. If all be from one wise and good design, then all is one and the same end, and nothing is supernumerary or unnecessary. If so, then there is a concatenation and connection; all things are related to one another, depend on one another, and everything is necessary to everything. If so, then if any one cause be removed or perish, all perishes, and I must trust to disorder and confusion.

If there be a supreme reason of the whole, then everything happens according to that reason. If anything happen contrary, the reason of the whole must cease and perish. If so, then there is nothing which can carry on the interest of that whole, or which can prevent any ill that may happen to the whole itself, or parts of the whole; if so, then ill may be infinite, and my sufferance and misery infinite.

Thus does it follow as a necessary consequence from the opinion of Deity, that whatsoever happens in the world, or whatever is appointed to me in particular, should be kindly affected, esteemed, and beloved by me, be it hardship, poverty, sickness, death. For, what else should I choose, or what else esteem and love, but that which tends to the good and perfection of the whole in which I am included? Now, if the whole be perfect, everything that happens in the whole is such.

Either the whole is perfect or imperfect. If it be an imperfect whole, how can there be Deity? If, therefore, it be a perfect whole, what is there in it besides what is just, equal, necessary, good? How can anything be altered and not the whole be rendered imperfect? See, therefore, that neither on thy own or any other account, thou desire ever to correct anything of the order of things. For, what is this but, as much as in thee lies, to destroy the perfection, happiness, and security of the whole, and consequently also thy own?

O Soul! think how noble will be thy state, when in the manner that thou art taken with other beauties, other simplicities and graces, thou shalt proportionably contemplate and admire that chief original beauty and that perfect simplicity and grace of which all other is the shadow, reflection, and resemblance. How well will it be with thee, when all those other inferior secondary objects are loved according to their order, never but last; and when the first object is loved and in its due rank antecedently to all; with an affection above all other affection, and according to real natural affection, not that which is called so towards a relation or friend. Now, see how thou art moved at the present friendly object of this kind; see the power of this inferior love. How dear those features, and all the external explications of the soul beloved. Now as the face of heaven outshines this other face; as the frame and structure of the celestial bodies surpass the goodliness and beauty of this other body; so is that soul more beautiful than this other soul; so is that love more beautiful than this other love. Why fear enthusiasm? Why shun the name? Where should I be ecstasied but here? Where enamoured but here? Is my subject true, or is it fiction? If true, how can I forsake it? How be ashamed of it? How desert * the artificer, the creator, parent, prince?

Am I ashamed to desert a vulgar friend, or disown him because of his mean appearance (if by chance he be unfashionable and in a despised garb)? Am I withheld from being discountenanced or suffering shame on his account, by another shame of a just kind? And shall nothing withhold me here? Shall I be ashamed of this other friend? Shall I be ashamed of this diviner love and of an object of love so far excelling all those objects in dignity, majesty, grace, beauty and amiableness? Is this enthusiasm? Be it: and so may I be ever an enthusiast. Happy me, if I can grow on this enthusiasm, so as to lose all those enthusiasms of every other kind and be whole towards this. Shall others willingly be accounted enthusiastic and even affect this sort of passion as virtuosos, men of wit, pleasure, politeness, each in their several ways and for their several objects (a song, a picture, a pile of stones, a human body, a shape, a face), and shalt thou be concerned at being found enthusiastic upon another subject so far excelling in itself, and which is original to all the rest?

Who would lose a moment's solid good, who would willingly be separated from the highest enjoyment and quit the amiable object that creates it? Or is that beauty, that amiableness only a chimera? Is the beatific vision enthusiasm? Or suppose it enthusiasm, is it not justifiable and of a right kind? What can be more highly reasonable? What greater folly, poorness, and misery than to be without it? Is there a rational and admired enthusiasm that belongs to architecture, painting, music, and not to this? Who is there that is not seized with admiration at the view of any of those ancient edifices, where order and proportion apparent in all the parts, and resulting from the whole, forces in a manner its effect, and is visible and striking even to vulgar

* Οὐδὲ ταῦτα ἱκανὰ κινῆσαί τινας καὶ διατρέψαι πρὸς τὸ μὴ ἀπολιπεῖν τὸν τεχνίτην; [" Is not all this sufficient to prevail on some men, and make them ashamed of leaving an artificer out of their scheme?"—*Epictetus, Discourses,* Bk. I., c. vi., § 10.]

E

eyes? Who is there that is not struck by those plain and obvious graces, the natural beauty and simplicity of a work of Raphael? Or who is there so little musical as to be unmoved by the voice of a Siphacio, or the hand of a Corelli?

Now join all these together. Remember the Pantheon, the wonderful fabric of St. Peter's, and (at once) the architecture of Michael Angelo, the sculpture and paintings of the masters, and the voice of the eunuchs with the symphonies. Does this raise an ecstasy and enthusiasm? and shall not a nobler architecture, nobler accords, and a diviner harmony be able to create it? Are there senses by which all those other graces and perfections are perceived, and is there no sense or faculty by which to comprehend or feel this other perfection and grace, so as to bring that enthusiasm hither, and transfer it from those objects to these and to the one original and comprehensive object? Now observe how it is in all those other subjects of art or science; what difficulty to be in any degree knowing, and how long ere a true taste is gained; how many things shocking, how many offensive at first, which afterwards are known and acknowledged the highest beauties. But it is not instantly that this sense is acquired and these beauties discoverable. Labour and pains are required, and time to cultivate a natural genius though ever so apt or forward. But who is there that so much as thinks of cultivating a genius this other way, or of improving the sense or faculty which nature has given of this kind? And is it a wonder we should be dull as we are, confounded and at a loss in these affairs, blind as to this higher scene, these nobler representations? In what way should we come to understand any better? in what way be knowing in these beauties? Is there study, science, and learning necessary to understand all beauties else, and for the sovereign beauty is there no skill or science required? Remember in painting the shades and masterly strokes; in architecture the rustic kind and that which they call *ferino*; in music the chromatic and skilful mixture of dissonances. And remember what there is that answers to this in the whole.

Animality what? And the tokens of it? The system, parts, economy, circulation of the blood, a liquid carrying globules round a centre. This, the microcosm. Now in the real κόσμος? A centre (heart), sun, and round it the globes moving in æther. Same circulation, same economy, numbers, time. Only these are regular, steady, permanent : the other are irregular, variable, inconstant. In one the marks of wisdom, determination, in the other of whims and conceit; in one judgment, in the other fancy ; in one will, in the other caprice ; in one truth, certainty, knowledge, in the other error, folly, madness. And yet to be convinced that there is something above which thinks, we want these latter signs ; as thinking there can be no thought but what is like our own. We sicken and grow weary with the orderly and regular course of things. Periods, and stated laws, and revolutions proportioned and accountable work not upon us, or win our admiration. A miracle is just contrary. By harmony, order, concord, we are left atheists; by irregularity and discord we are to be convinced of Deity. The world is accident if it proceed in course; but wisdom if it run mad. [1]

*That the whole is harmony, the numbers entire, the music perfect*; with what else of this kind has been so well proved, so often said.—But why in effect unsay this again so often ? Why make myself the hindrance ? Why break the order, interrupt the music, and destroy (as much as in me lies) this harmony and concord by repining, striving, resisting ? Why not adhere to this ? Why not always find this harmony ? How enjoy this harmony ? What can be the cause ? What, but the want of harmony within ?—And how attain this harmony ? how tune myself to this ? how consonant and of accord with Deity ? Hearken ! Begin. Wouldst thou be a musician ? Hast thou patience to learn the gamut, rudiments, and grammar of this music ?—Take up the lute. Touch the strings and tune them. Hearken ! Begin. Τῶν ὄντων τὰ μέν ἐστιν ἐφ᾽ ἡμῖν, τὰ δὲ οὐκ ἐφ᾽ ἡμῖν. [There are things which are within our power, and there are things which are beyond our power.] Say, how does it sound ? Ill, harsh, hollow ? Anything, or as good as nothing; nothing at all. Hold! lay down the lute. No more. Have done with philosophy, divinity, contemplation, thought, virtue, Deity. Go to common talk, common rules. Be

---

[1] cf. *Shaftesbury's Characteristics* (1711), Vol. II., pp. 337-8.

everything. Nothing. Or rather be nothing indeed, truly nothing. Go to atoms (if it be atoms), for that is better than a life where there is no better or more certain opinion of things than superstition or atoms. Happy he! whose faith in Deity, satisfaction, assurance, acquiescing, rejoicing in Providence and in the universal administration and order of things depends, not on any history, or tale, or tradition, or wonder amongst men; not on man himself, or any set of men; not on any particular schemes, or systems, or solutions, of the phenomena of the world; no, not even on that great solution by a futurity; but who, leaving the present things to be as they are, and future ones to be as they are to be, committing all this to Providence, to be or not to be, as to that seems best, knows, feels, and is satisfied that all things are for the best; nothing ill-made, nothing ill-governed, nothing but what contributes to the perfection of the whole, and to the felicity of Him who is the whole in the whole.

But how should this be? How is this brought about? How believe that all is good and nothing ill? How not be disturbed, nor shaken, nor in doubt? How not be afflicted, repine, nor grieve? How no ill Providence, dark Providence, hard fate? How no words, no secret thoughts, no inward murmurs of this kind?

No way but this (which thou knowest too well enough). If ἐν τοῖς ἐφ᾽ ἡμῖν μόνοις θῇς τὸ ἀγαθὸν καὶ τὸ κακόν [thou makest good and evil to consist in things which are within your power. —*Epict. Ench.*, c. xxxi., § 2.] If not the rest is idle, senseless, poor; flattering * God as a tyrant, not loving, following, obeying him as a father, or good prince. † "Dread Sovereign! Thou art all-powerful. And what then? Therefore thou art all-good. I am in thy hands, mighty Lord. And what then? Therefore, I complain not. Talk not why I was thus made, or why made at all if to be miserable; if to have been in fault and been a wretch.

---

* Κύριε, ἐλέησον· ἐπίτρεψόν μοι ἐξελθεῖν. ἀνδράποδον, ἄλλο γάρ τι θέλεις ἢ τὸ ἄμεινον ["Lord have mercy upon me, suffer me to come off safe. Foolish man! would you have anything but what is best?"—*Epict. Disc.*, Bk. II., c. vii., § 12.] † cf. Dr. Tillotson.

No, I am contented to be miserable. I say not so much as within myself that my lot is hard. I say not thou art unjust, arbitrary, cruel, or that thy order is ill, or amiss." Wretch! dost thou not say it? Is not this saying it? How canst thou help it, poor wretch such as thou art? How can Almightiness itself help it? Or how make this otherwise: that he who sees not goodness should believe goodness? that he who feels misery should not complain, even though he vows most holily that he complains not, nor ever will complain?

Faith in Deity: not faith in men. This not previous, and not fundamental to that. For, what a foundation!—Men witnessing for God! And who for men? Who for powers above men? who for miracles ever so great? What security against dæmons? what proof against magic? what trust to anything above or below if first not satisfied of Deity, *i.e.* goodness, order of justice in the whole? And how assured? By what but reason? what but philosophy?

Faith in Deity. That other, and this. A faith which depends on a philosophy proved by record; and a faith which depends on a philosophy that had neither education nor the weakness of nature on its side: sprung from strong conviction, without melancholy, even in youth and pleasure, in the midst of the world, and in an age just going contrary, all things fighting against it, superstition, libertinism, the fashionable learning and philosophy in vogue.

Imagine these two, not as separate but going together; and this latter as a confirmation of the former. Consider the care taken to preserve and retain that former, and take notice to bring the same diligence and care hither. A certain enemy of religion defining that which he understood by faith, called it a "premeditated and stubborn resolution of giving reason the lie." There is indeed a faith which carries with it a sort of resolution, and stubborn resolution to give everything the lie except the reason. The stubbornness of this faith is such as to contradict the very senses, the imaginations, the habitual and almost natural opinions of mankind, the report of men, the received notions of the world, the plausible and in all appearance most innocent thoughts, unexceptionable judgments, and warrantable fancies: as of what is good, what ill, what eligible, what ineligible, what indifferent and what of concern.  If by reason be understood the reason of the world, this is indeed giving reason, and (if you will too) common sense the lie.  τὰ ἐφ᾽ ἡμῖν, τὰ οὐκ ἐφ᾽ ἡμῖν. Is not this equally faith ?  Is not this equally mystery ?

Remember then, and respect those other mysteries, for all is faith, and without faith all must be Atheism

What is that which at present they call *Deism* ?  The belief of a God ?  What God ?  A mind ?  a real mind ?  universally presiding, acting ?  present everywhere ?  conscious of everything ?  even of secret thought and every intelligent act, as being infinitely intelligent and the principle of all intelligence ? Is it this they understand ?  Is it of such a Providence as this that they are persuaded in themselves ?—Be it so.  It is well. But if it be anything less than this ; if this be too high a key ; if the heart (the truest pledge of thought) discover plainly a sense and apprehension of things far short of this, far wide of such a system, far beneath so high and exalted an idea ; then let us hear what this idea is.  What Deism ?  What Deity ?  Of what is it they talk to us ?  What nature ?  (What is nature ?) What virtues or powers do they tell us of ?  What magic, charm, or spell ?  What coherence of things ?  or what jumble ?  How hanging together, put together, standing together ?  By what power, energy, force ?  For from one sort of man we have an account, such as it is, a blind account, be it ; but still it is an account, and in this they are fair.  *Atoms and void.*  A plain negative to Deity, fair and honest.  To Deism, still no pretence. So the sceptic.  *Perhaps so ; perhaps not so.*  But to Deism still no pretence.

From whence then this other pretence ?  Who are these Deists ?  How assume this name ?  By what title or pretence ? The world, the world ?  say what ?  how ?  A modified lump ? matter ? motion ?—What is all this ?  Substance what ? Who knows ?  why these evasions ?  subterfuges of words ? definitions of things never to be defined ?  structures or no foundations ?  Come to what is plain.  Be plain.  For the idea itself is plain ; the question plain ; and such as everyone has invariably some answer to which it is decisive. *Mind ? or not mind ?*  If mind, a providence, the idea perfect : a God.  If not mind, what in the place ?  For whatever it be, it cannot without absurdity be called God or Deity; nor the opinion without absurdity be called Deism.

For what is a mind in the infinite but an infinite mind? and how this, without infinite wisdom? and how this without infinite goodness, infinite power? and how this without a providence, consciousness, care, rule, order, such as has been mentioned? And what less than this is God? What opinion of a God but this opinion? what else can be called Deity, or denominate a Deist?

What is this Deism they talk of? How does it differ from mere Atheism? Is it some secret virtue (like magic) which they assign to things? Is it the plastic nature, or Epicurus' atoms? But Epicurus was more sincere, for his is only a god for the vulgar *ad populum phaleras* [trappings for the people]. But he pretends not to bring this into philosophy nor resolve anything in nature by this, or any such like principle. Neither does any one call the Atomists Deists. Of what system then are these Deists? Of Democritus' or the Epicureans they are not. Peripatetics, Platonists, Pythagoreans, Pyrrhonists? What?

*Faith in Deity,* and justly so called. For is it not indeed faith? implicit faith? implicit belief? For how always explicit? The sudden shocks, disturbances, foreign ideas, sophistry of wit, commotion in the affections : what in these cases, but faith? For the reasons being not present at these moments, or ready at call, must we not rely on those decrees and resolutions which reason at cool seasons and fit times of deliberation has so often confirmed and rendered peremptory? How else adhere to anything? how constant, stable, self-consistent, but by this faith? Strive, however, to need it the least that is possible; preserving the chain of thought and affections uninterrupted; that so it may be still the same reason, same comprehension, conviction and clear light. For what hinders that this should always be explicit? What but wrong opinions, wrong assent? Why therefore permit such? Why these beginnings? (for who knows the consequence ?) Why any suspension, relaxation, wrong attention but for a moment? For, to what does this tend except to the loss not only of reason but also of faith itself; the reserved powers of reason, the recourse, refuge, citadel, strength?

# PROVIDENCE.

Nothing can be wiser than that order of Providence : that the same things it has placed out of our power it should also have placed out of our knowledge. Would there be room for the natural affections ? What measure of affection inclining or declining in outward things, the good or ill of native country, friends, body, health ? What medium but either perfect indifference towards these, or perfect rebellion, perfect contempt and resistance of the Divine will ? But as things are ordered by that Divine will in making plain what is of real concern to me and hiding what is not, how can I be indifferent or without due concern in every relation ? I know how Providence bids me to affect and act; but I am ignorant what will be the event of my action. If I were not ignorant I must affect the event which might perhaps be contrary to that which is my present endeavour and action. Therefore I must either not act, or act without affection, or with my affection contrary to my action. For if I affect the end, how can I but affect in some manner and love the means ? and if the means, how unnatural would this be ? For in this manner I must oftentimes affect (as would seem most preposterous) my country's ruin, children's death, my own sickness, and the like, all absurdity and confusion. But in the other way and as it is regulated, how natural and easy is all ! For how is it that I affect the prosperity of my little family ? as it stands in the Great, if the Great call, farewell the little one; I give it up—to what ?—to my country—and my country to what ? To my first and greatest country. But what the good of that is I know not till my action is over. Therefore, I cease not to act still and affect according to nature, always satisfied with my having so affected as well as with the contrary effect, if it happen to prove contrary. And thus I affect both according to nature and with nature. According to nature, as willing the good of my relations, and country, primarily, chiefly, and as most eligible; but not absolutely. With nature, as yielding to

Providence, and accompanying Providence when its will is declared, having beforehand willed with this exception and reserve, and ὡς ἄν δίδωται [as it may be permitted] not ἐξ ἄπαντος [by all means]. *

This was eligible just now, before the thing was over. Now it is over, it is no more so, but contrariwise. What is yet to come may be eligible or ineligible, because not yet come. But it is certainly to come. How know I certainly? If certainly, must I not wish it so, whichever way it be? What deliberation? What room for choice or preference? Where would the eligible be, or the ineligible? What priority or precedency of things? What regard or deference to anything—friends, relations, country? Why more affect their good than their ill? Why not equally their ill, when Providence would have it then ill, when thou knowest that it is their ill and not their good that is to happen?—But this thou knowest not, and canst never know, till it be happened; and when happened, then affect, then choose. The one was eligible before, but now the other. Thus, before the event, affection and disaffection, approbation and disapprobation, inclining and declining had place; but now, after the event, no place. All is affection, no disapprobation, no disaffection, nothing ineligible. The past is ever eligible, and the best. ἀλλ᾿ ἀεὶ μᾶλλον ἐκεῖνο θέλω τὸ γινόμενον κρεῖττον. γὰρ ἡγοῦμαι ὃ ὁ Θεὸς θέλει ἢ ὃ ἐγώ. ["But am always content with that which happens, for I think what God chooses is better than what I choose."—*Epict. Disc.*, Bk. IV., c. vii., § 20.]

Such is the harmony of Providence with one who has harmony in himself, and knows wherein Providence has placed his good and ill; wherein not. Providence dispenses things unequally. What things? The things that are not my good. But the things that are my good, how? Are they not in my own power? How blame the dispensation?

Providence dispenses without regard, promiscuously and indifferently.—What? Indifferent things, but good and ill; how?—To the good and to the ill distinctly, not promiscuously. Be thou therefore one of the good and take of good what

---

* cf., *Epict. Disc.*, Bk. II., c. vi., § 9; Bk. II., c. x., § 6; Bk. III., c. xxiv.; Bk. IV., c. vii., § 4.

thou pleasest, and reject the ill. But if anything stick, if there be any good of thine which lies out of thy reach, any ill which thou canst not remove ; for this, still thank thyself, for why is such as this either thy good or ill ?

*The good of my country ; the good of mankind.* In what way my good ?—as wishing it. But happening contrary ?—my good still (the world's good). But thy wish is lost. What wish ? against the world. Was this my wish ? was this my good ?—Fool ! the wish itself was my good, in this lay all. My wish was right ; my aim, endeavour, action right. But the event was wrong. How wrong ? through me ? No. Through whom then ? Through Providence ?—And was that wrong ? has that failed ?—If, then, neither Providence be wrong nor I wrong, what wrong is there ? where is there any wrong remaining ? Is that wrong which for the universe is right, and just, and necessary ? But I know not what is so. And what need that thou shouldst know beforehand ? Know this only for certain, that *that* and only that has happened, or can ever happen. But how then can I wish ? or how wish well to anything ? How hope ? or how affect ? How, but with exception ? Not ἐξ ἅπαντος, but with reserve for this my ultimate final wish and desire, in which I never can be frustrated. And thus I may safely and without disturbance wish well to things, my country, mankind, or any part of things ; wishing still better to the whole of things, the general interest and common weal, as administered by that common mind, intelligence and wisdom, which is unerring.

This is that which saves from all solicitude and anxiety. For in this manner there needs no search, no divining, no penetrating, into what will be or is to be. Οὐ γὰρ ἐξήτει ποτὲ δόξαι τι ποιεῖν ὑπὲρ τῶν ὅλων, ἀλλ' ἐμέμνητο, ὅτι πᾶν τὸ γενόμενον ἐκεῖθέν ἐστιν ["For he was not used to inquire when he should be considered to have done anything on behalf of the whole of things, but remembered that everything that is done comes from thence."—*Epict. Discourses*, Bk. IV., c. i., § 155.] The good of this country, this world, is always ready found and at hand. Do not torment thyself, therefore, about the good of that other world, that other country ; only love it and do thy part for it, and for those in it. But how love it ? As loving this other

world, relation, and country much better : and as always preferring its prosperity and interest to any other prosperity or
any other interest.

One thing there is impossible for me to affect (were it in
Providence), and only one thing : that is my real ill. If that be
in Providence I cannot affect with it, for Providence itself has
made it impossible for me so to do. But withal Providence has
made it an impossible case, that I should have any contest with
it about my real good, or that there should be anything in the
whole course of nature to oppose my good. There is not, and
cannot be, any such thing in Providence ; for what is really my
good, Providence has placed within my power to obtain ; what
is ill, to avoid. Hence where can my difference be with
Providence ? Why not allow Providence to be free since I am
free ?

Providence has given me means ($\dot{a}\phi o\rho\mu\dot{a}s$) to know both it
and myself, and to be conscious for what and to what I was
born. If I use these I am a man, and as such Providence will
use me. If I use them not I am a mere animal (let my shape
be ever so much of a man), and as an animal Providence will use
me, even as we men use other animals, making them willingly or
unwillingly serve our purposes.

What is that which is dragged and forced ? What goes to
death unwillingly ? An animal—though a human creature—an
animal still (if it be thus), a mere animal ; for if it knows no
better what life is, it is still but the animal. The man knows
better, and will go to death like a man, not as to slaughter.
What slaughter ? Is God the butcher ? Man ! dost thou know
God, that thou thinkest thus of Him, and no better ? Can He
kill otherwise than kindly, fatherly ; for the good of everything,
and as the preserver of the whole ? Is there any harm ?—
Not if thou art a man ; thou canst not think so. For where is
the harm of death ? And if none here, what other harm ?
Where can there be any ? But if thou art an animal only
there is harm, in this alone, that what might have been a man
should remain still an animal, and no more. This is thy harm.
But that there should be animals is no harm in the whole.
When thou ceasest to be one (that is to say, when thou becomest
a man), neither will there be any harm to thee. So that if thou

complainest any more, complain (if thou wilt) of the hard case of animals, but not of men ; for, being once *a* man, thou wilt know there is no cause.

If I know Providence, I know my good and can follow it; so, no complaint.   If I know not my good, I do not in reality know Providence.   So if I complain, I complain of a spectre and not of Deity: I complain as an animal, not as a man.  For wherein lies the animal ? where the distinction ?   Go then and complain for the sake of animals and for thyself as being but an animal, when yet it lies in thee to be otherwise if thou pleasest.   See what a complaint !

Thus ignorant people sitting by a painter will needs be giving him instructions, guiding his hand, and teaching him his art. " This colour is harsh, this disagreeable and sad ; here the paint lies too thin and hardly covers the cloth, here thick, uneven, rough."   Come, take the pencil, let us see thy own performance, what ordering, what work thou art like to make.  But is this the case here ?—Man ! is it not much more the case ?  Canst thou judge of this in the piece ?  ·Seest thou the real piece ?  or a part only ? Is it the whole breadth of the cloth or only a thread or two ?  Art thou in a right light and at the due distance, to view this in the full breadth of time, the circle of generations, the compass of worlds and in the infinite extent of this design ?   Hast thou so much as thought of this ordering ?  Art thou a virtuoso here ? Hast thou any masterly knowledge or judgment ?   Let us see it, give us the proof; let us hear how thou camest by it.  Where did'st thou study for it, and how ?  or will the taste and knowledge of this kind come of itself ?  or come easier and with less study than that other taste ?   Is the high virtuous part more easy than the virtuoso's ?  How know a hand ?  how judge the master or the art ? how comprehend so  much  as  one  rule?—But  why  should there be tyrannies ?  why these dark sides upon the globe ? I would have no shade, no roughness, but all smooth; no sad colours, but all gay and light.—Pretty amusement ! ladies' talk ! the wantonness of children !  But is this for men too ?  Is this to study nature ?  is this an understanding of beauty ?  a knowledge of proportion, symmetry, or rule?—Where is the great *original ?* Or if none ; from whence these copies ? this derivation ?

What is there in the world that has more of beauty, or that

gives the idea of the τὸ καλόν more perfect and sensible than the view of an equal commonwealth, or city, founded on good laws? a well-built constitution, fenced against exterior and interior force; a legislature and a militia; a senate propounding, debating, counselling; a people resolving, electing; a majesty executing and in rotation?—And for what all this? Against what, this precaution? Whence this so fair, so comely and admirable a structure? How if no tyranny, no ambition, no irregular passions or appetites of men?

This is that Chrysippean paradox inveighed against by so many. Thus honest Plutarch.—But how can this (even this too) be otherwise or better? how more orderly or beautiful than as it is? Or, say, where would the prodigy of a Chrysippus be, his dialect, his astonishing force, if not liable withal to be thus taken by many and thus derided and inveighed against? For how explain these things to the vulgar? And what to say to those vulgar philosophers who thus set forth Providence? who need a dæmon to solve the ill phenomena, and who make thus a mere baby of the world, to dress, and dandle?—How?—as being babies themselves, and having baby-δόγματα. But till we have quitted and exchanged these for better this must be still with us a baby-world, and baby-like be thus dressed and undressed, taken to pieces, and put together, according to what our fancy tells us is pretty or not pretty.—O, pretty play! but which costs many a sigh and groan.—Leave the play then, and be in earnest. Be no more the child and there will be no need to cry or lament. All is well, excellent well, and thou mayest play too and play safely in another far better manner, if thou understandest that divine play (*Epict. Discourses*, Bk. II., c. v., and Bk. IV., c. vii.). For it is that alone that can make piety, religion, or virtue, earnest; Providence, in earnest, *Providence*, that is to say, in earnest, a government and good government; in earnest, wisdom, perfect wisdom, perfect goodness, than which nothing better can be thought or wished, for else this is not earnest, and when we praise, we lie and flatter.

In parliament, the *contents* and *not contents*. In Providence, which ever way the question go, always *a content*, though in voting *a not content* perhaps, and of the losing side. In this council the question may be often carried for the worst side; in the other, never but for the best. Which of these interests wilt thou favour? to which art thou a well-wisher?

It is long since (remember) that thou saidst *" When open thy eyes, to see that whilst thou seekest other times than these, other subject than this, all is wrong? When come thither, afraid to fall from thence. Therefore even then (supposing the then) still wrong, and anxiety still continues." — But the *then* will not be the case, therefore what is this but to court disappointment and love trouble for trouble's sake. For it is not required of thee to be troubled for a world which is already taken care of, unless, perhaps, thou art of opinion that it might be governed much better yet than God governs it.

† Particular Providence, in respect of general Providence, is as a shallow cause and narrow means in the room of a deep and eternal cause with extensive and infinite means.

Τὸ βούλημα τῆς φύσεως καταμαθεῖν ἔστιν ἐξ ὧν οὐ διαφερόμεθα. [" We may learn the will of nature from the things in which we do not differ from one another."—*Epict. Ench.*, c. xxvi.] In whatsoever we accuse Providence we contradict ourselves and so cannot without absurdity accuse. Sicknesses, diseases, deaths, in vegetables, animals, systems, worlds remote, and at a distance from ourselves, are natural. The answer is ready ὅτι τῶν γινομένων ἐστιν [these are events that will happen]. But bring it a little nearer and presently οἴμοι, τάλας ἐγώ [how wretched I am]. No one is so vulgar as not in some measure to contemplate the revolutions of things, and see at least the spring and fall with many other generations and corruptions of nature as really beautiful and pleasing. The same of nations and even worlds where self can but be abstracted. Animals may sicken and die: no harm still: it is natural. Men (foreign men) may die: it is natural; even our neighbour at the next door: it is natural still, τῶν γινομένων. But in my house! in my own family! there it is. And thus we stand not to our own judgment. We accuse ourselves, deny, contradict ourselves, when we accuse Providence: for were we all of us, in spite, to make

---

* From scrap of old date, viz., Holland, 1698.  † St. Giles, 1704-5.

a charge against it, we could not any way agree one with another, nor any one of us with ourselves.

Again, τὸ βούλημα τῆς φύσεως καταμαθεῖν. To know nature, feel a Providence, acknowledge its ways, own its course, the secret is only this: to be the same in cases that are the same. It is self only alters the case and will ever alter it, till self be right placed.

# THE END.

Either man is made with design or without design : if without design, it must follow that there is no end either in the whole or any part of man ; and then neither muscles, veins, arteries are designed, nor are they to any purpose, or can they be said to any end. If this be false, and that all these were made to an end, if they are all designed and have each of them their end, then there must be somewhere a last or ultimate end in man. If so, then that which plainly is a means only to something else cannot be itself that end. It cannot be said of an eye that it is its last end, either to be of such a certain form, or to move after a certain manner, or to feel itself in any certain pleasant affection, as when it has got out of darkness into the light, or out of too fierce a light into a softer and less dazzling one. Each of these are means : for both the shape and motions and affections particular to it are all towards one single end, which is that of sight. Neither is sight therefore the end of the man, since sight is in him only a means to other ends; thus the ear and hearing, thus the palate and tasting, and thus all the other senses, as well as that which belongs to generation. For, if those parts themselves are a means to a further end, then the affection of those parts and that peculiar sense belonging to them, *is* a means still, and not an end. If neither the pleasure or sense of tasting, nor that of venery, nor any other be the end, then in general, *pleasure* is not the end. What is it, then, that we call the end ? To eat, drink, sleep, copulate, and the pleasures which belong either to eating, drinking, sleeping, or copulating, are all of them only means, and refer to something further. If we can find nothing beyond, then all that we can say is, that the end of man is only to be in such a certain sound and perfect state of body; and such as serves to generate similar bodies. But if besides what has been mentioned, there are any certain dispositions of mind such as plainly refer to a species and society, and to the enjoyment of converse, mutual alliance,

48

and friendship, then is the end of man *society.* Therefore to be such as to serve to that end of society (which is to be good or virtuous) is that to which everything in man is lastly referred, and which is properly his end. And where his end or perfection is, there certainly must be his good.

The end or design of nature in man is society. For, wherefore are the natural affections towards children, relations, fellowship, and commerce, but to that end ? The perfection of human nature is in that which fits and accommodates to society, for he who wants those natural affections which tend thither, is imperfect and monstrous. Now, if the ultimate design and end of nature in the constitution of man be, that he be framed and fitted for society, and if it be the perfection of human nature to be thus fitted, how should not this, which is the end and perfection of human nature, be also the good of man ?

If that to which man is carried by nature (as to society he is) be not his good, then his own private end and good is to go contrary to nature, so that his end in nature and his end in himself must be utterly contrary. Therefore, if those natural affections are that which lead him from his own real good (as when they cause him to expose himself for others, to suffer pain or labour or hardship for others), it must be in his end also to extinguish those natural affections; or else it must be said to be consistent with his end, not to follow, but to forsake his good, which is absurd. If in order to his good he must extinguish those natural affections, then it must be his end to become savage, unnatural, horrid and inhuman. But if this can never be his good, but the contrary, then his end must be to follow nature and to attain the perfection of his kind.

If it be a detestable and miserable state to be wholly unnatural and void of humanity and humane affection, then is it the good of man to be socially inclined and affected ; if so, it is his greater good still to act by a more clear and perfect affection of that kind; if so, then that affection which is wholly towards virtue is that in which he finds his greatest good; if so, then it is his end, and not anything else is his end but to affect as is natural to him and as becomes him ; to will and incline as the nature of man requires; in short, to follow nature, or the

F

order and appointment of supreme reason in his particular constitution and make.

Whatever is a man's end is that which he cannot quit or depart from on account of any other thing. Now, pleasure of any kind, riches, honours, and life itself, are what anyone may very well quit on other accounts. But it is impossible to do well or happily in quitting either integrity, justice, faith, or anything which is the part of a man, as he is a man. Therefore, this only is his end and not the other.

He who follows pleasure as his end knows not what he follows, since contrary things procure it, and what pleases at one time displeases at another; neither are the things on which he depends ever in his power. He who follows virtue as his end knows what he follows, and can never be at a loss; neither are the goods he seeks ever out of his power.

What hesitation, doubt, perplexity, in him who has not ever one and the same end! who pursues that at one time as good, which at another time he despises! who chooses at one time what he rejects and is out of conceit with at another! What constancy, stability, and evenness in him who has one certain end to which he refers all his actions, and which is never out of his sight!

That is said to be the end of everything, to which the thing is ultimately referred. Thus the end of the watch is to show the hour of the day, and to move in such certain and proportionable degrees, for the service of him for whose use it is made. A person who had never seen anything of this kind, nor knew the use of such instruments as these, would, however, upon considering the watch, be satisfied soon that its principal perfection was not in the case, which served to cover and defend it; and that its ultimate end or design was not merely to move, but to move after a certain manner and in certain due proportions to which the wheels were adapted. How then as to man? Does it seem that his perfection is in the case?[1]—But the body perhaps is more than the case, and is as the wheels in the watch, which are principal and

[1] " It is unlikely that the good of the snail should be placed in the shell."—*Epict. Disc.*, Bk. I., c. xx., § 17.

essential to its operation. What is it, then, that we can understand to be the effect and operation of a man? Is it only when he eats and drinks and sleeps? Is it when the heart beats and keeps due time, and the adjacent parts about it correspond? If so, then indeed is this all one with the watch. But what if the fancy and imagination be wrong? what if the understanding be blind? what if the affections fight one with another? Is this a right effect? is this a due operation? What, therefore, is the operation and effect of a man? what does the nature of man aspire to and terminate in? Is it not this? " The use of reason? the exercise of understanding? a certain will and determination? certain affections?" What exists therefore, that is able to hinder these operations and these effects? Or what is there in the sufferance or injury of that other part, which is able to hinder me from acting as a man? from being either just, proud, virtuous, or good? from acting that which is before me with magnanimity and constancy? from acquiescing in what is present as the part assigned me and committed to me? from being benign, and beautiful towards men, composed and easy towards events, and in unanimity with the whole? This is what the nature of man imports. Or is it rather on the contrary to whine and to bemoan? to be peevish and malignant? to be effeminate and soft? impotent towards pleasure, and impatient of pain and labour or hardship? If manhood be the contrary to this; if it be in action and exercise, in reason and in a mind that this consists: then is it here that the man is either saved or lost. These are the springs and wheels, which, when impaired and hindered, the man ceases and is extinct. And as in the watch, a certain motion is the end to which all is referred; so also, here, it is a certain motion that is the end, and when this proceeds right, all is well, and nothing farther is required.

We see in many things what their end is in nature; but more particularly in our own bodies. The end of the muscle is the attraction or convenient motion of the part, such as the eyelid or eye itself. The end of the eye is sight; the end of sight, the preservation and protection of the animal; as the end of the seminal vessels and their proper affections is the propagation and increase of the animals, and the good of a whole species. The teeth, eyes, hands, and all other limbs and organs are made for one another and for the good of the whole body. The different sexes are made for one another and with respect to a kind or species. If so, then in the same manner as the several parts of the creature have their end, so the whole creature has his end in nature and serves to something beyond himself. If it be to the good of his kind, it must be to the perfection of his kind. If the perfection of his kind be society, then his end also will be society. And since the only perfection, the only tolerable state of man and that alone in which he can possibly endure or subsist, is society ; the end of man is therefore society. If it be not his good to follow this end ; then has he some other end within himself, which is contrary to that natural end or end in nature. If, on the contrary, it be his chiefest good to follow that end of nature, then is his private end and the real and only end of man to live according to nature.

Now that which is called our private or particular end, to which we ultimately refer or have respect, must be that which can yield to nothing else ; for, if it yield to anything, then that which is yielded to will be the end, and not what we first determined. If there be that which is preferable to everything else, and which can yield to nothing besides, this, if anything, must be called our end. Now, to live merely, cannot be our end ; for, then death could not at any time (as it may) be rightly preferred to it. What is there, therefore, that we can never (as they say) sacrifice to anything ? Bodily ease, soundness of limbs, health, and constitution are undoubtedly eligible and desirable. Are these, therefore, or is it pleasure that to which we may sacrifice everything else ? If so, then we may sacrifice our mind. Now it is certain that he who has a mind, or what is worthy to be called so, will never think of parting with it, on any other account. If so, then that which last remains and is preferable to everything else is a mind and resolution, will or reason, becoming a man. If so, then this is our end ; and our end in nature and our private end will be the same. And thus our end is, *to live according to nature.*

# GOOD AND ILL.

Nam quid sequar, aut quem? [For what shall I pursue,
whom follow? *Hor., Ep.,* I., Bk. I., line 76.] Why should it
disturb me that I am thought singular? and wherefore should
I not persist in following what I think is good, after I have
thought so long and chosen on such good grounds?—But this is
odd, this is out of the way, and against the general conceit.—
Whom then shall I follow? Whose judgment or opinion shall
I take concerning what is good, and what is not?

One man affects the hero and esteems it the greatest matter of
life to have seen war and to have been in action in the field.
Hence he looks upon those as wretches and altogether contemptible
who have never known anything of this kind. Another laughs
at this man, counts this stupidity and dullness, prizes his own wit
and prudence and would think it a disgrace to him to be thought
adventurous after that manner, or to have willingly at any time
engaged in danger.

One person is assiduous and indefatigable in advancing
himself to the character and repute of a man of business and of
the world. Another on the contrary thinks this impertinent,
values not his fame or character in the world, and would
willingly never come out of the stews or drinking houses where
he best likes to be, and which he accounts the highest good.

One values wealth as a means only to serve his palate and
to eat finely. Another loathes this, and aims at popularity.
One admires gardens, architecture, and the pomp of buildings.
Another has no relish this way, but thinks all those whom they
call virtuous to be distracted.

One there is who thinks all experience to be madness; and
thinks only wealth itself to be good. One plays; another
dresses and studies an equipage; another is full of heraldry, a
family and a blood. One recommends gallantry and intrigue;
another riot and debauch; another buffoonery, satire and the
common wit; another sports and the country; another a court;

53

another travelling and the sight of foreign countries ; another poetry and the fashionable literature. All these go different ways. All censure one another and are despicable in one another's eyes. What is it, then, that I am concerned for ? Whose censure do I fear ? or who is it that I shall be guided by. If I ask are riches good when only heaped up and unemployed ? One answers, they are. The rest deny. How is it then that they are to be employed in order to be good ? All disagree. All tell me different things. Since, therefore, riches are not of themselves good (as most of you say) and since there is no agreement amongst you as to the way they are made or have become good ; why may not I hold it for my opinion that they are neither of themselves good, nor in any way made good ?

If there be those who despise fame ; if of those who covet it, he who desires fame for one thing despises it for another ; and if he who seeks fame with one sort, despises it with another ; why may not I say that neither do I know how any fame can be called a good.

If those who court pleasure and admire it of one kind, contemn it of another, why may not I say that neither do I know which of these pleasures, or how pleasure in general, can be good ?

If among those who covet life ever so earnestly, that life which to one is eligible and amiable is to another despicable and vile ; why may not I say that neither do I know that life itself is necessarily good ?

In the meantime I both see and know certainly, that the necessary effect or consequence of loving and esteeming these things highly, and as essentially good, is to be envious, to repine and long, to be often disappointed and grieved, to be bitter, anxious, malignant, suspicious, and jealous of men, and fearful of events (all which is misery); and that on the other side the effect of despising these is liberty, generosity, magnanimity, self-appro-bation, consciousness of worth. And are not these really good, but uncertainly so, as the other ? A generous affection, an exercise of friendship uninterrupted, a constant kindness and benignity of disposition, a constant complacency, constant security, tranquility, equanimity : are not these ever and at all times good? Is it, then, of these that anyone can at any time nauseate or be weary? Are there any particular ages, seasons, places, circumstances, that must accompany these to make them agreeable to us? Are these variable and inconstant? Do these by being ardently beloved or sought procure any disturbance or misery? Can these be at any time over-valued? If not, then where can my good be but in them?

Wherefore is it that I act at any time? Why do I choose? Why prefer one thing to another. Is it because I conceive or fancy good in it, or because I fancy it? Am I, therefore, to follow every present fancy and imagination of good? If so, then I must follow that at one time which I do not at another; approve at one time what I disapprove at another; and be at perpetual variance with myself. But if I am not to follow all fancy alike, and if of fancies of this kind some are true, some false; then I am to examine every fancy and there is some rule or other by which to judge and determine. It was the fancy of one man to set fire to a beautiful temple in order to obtain immortal remembrance or fame. If this were a good to him, why do we wonder at him? If the fancy were wrong, in what was it wrong? Or wherefore was not this his good as he fancied? Either, therefore, that is every man's good which he fancies, and because he fancies it and is not content without it; or otherwise there is that with which the nature of man is satisfied and which alone must be his good. If that in which the nature of man is satisfied and can rest contented, be alone his good, then he is a fool who follows that as his good which a man can be without and yet be satisfied and contented, in the same manner as he is a fool who flies that which a man may endure and yet be satisfied. Now, a man may possibly not have burnt a temple (as Erostratus) and yet may be contented. In the same manner a man may be without any of those things which are commonly called goods and yet may be contented; as on the contrary he may possess them all and still be discontented and not at all happier than before. If so, then happiness is in a certain temper and disposition, in a certain mind and will. If so, why do not I seek it there?

Whatsoever is good must be alike good to all; whatsoever is ill, alike ill to all. Sorrow, trouble, dejection, honour anxiety, fear, tranquility, satisfaction, content, freedom of mind, good dispositions, good affections, and whatsoever creates or establishes, are alike good or ill to all, and therefore are of the nature of good or ill. If virtue be not necessary to produce satisfaction and content, or, if content may as well be without as with it, then virtue is not our good; if necessary, it is our good, and whatsoever is indifferent towards the procuring of content is indifferent in itself. Now, if this that my fancy represents to me, be necessary to content, it must be necessary towards every man's content. Is it fame that my fancy represents to me as necessary? But this is not necessary to every man's content (for there are those who can live as well satisfied without it), therefore it is not necessary to my content, and is not my good. Is it honour or power? The same. Is it riches? The same. Is it pleasure of whatever kind? The same. Neither do any nor all of these certainly procure satisfaction, since the mind may be as unquiet in the midst of these as at any other time. Now if that alone be good which is necessary to every man's content that it should be present, then that alone is ill which is necessary to every man's content that it should be absent. Now, that a man should be sure of living twenty years, or one year, or one hour, is not necessary to his content. Nor is it necessary to his content that he should not believe or know that he is to die the next year or next hour. Therefore, to be sure of dying the next year or next hour is indifferent; and, therefore, death is not an ill. If pain be ill, it must be alike ill to all men (for so is sorrow, affliction, honour, despair, anxiety, and all of this sort). But if there be a certain temper or resolution which can cause it to be slighted, then it is not an ill to him who has that temper or resolution, but to him who wants it, and therefore not constantly and in itself an ill.

But if pain be said to be ill, yet all pain is not so; since that which to an effeminate person is insufferable pain and trouble, is to a man laborious or warlike, a subject of delight and enjoyment. What else is that delight of sportsmen, or of those who love adventures and who engage in things hazardous and not accomplished but with pain and difficulty? What is the difference between one that is robust and manly, and one that is weak and tender, except this—that which afflicts the one is of no concern to the other? Therefore, if to some the greatest pains can be tolerable, and if to others the slightest pains are intolerable, then is not the greatest pain itself to be considered so much as that is to be considered which makes pain to be either well or ill-supported and to be tolerable or intolerable? Thus, therefore, neither is pain, nor death, nor poverty, nor obscurity considerable as ill. Nor, on the other hand, is pleasure, wealth, honour, or fame of any consideration as to our happiness or good. But as by fearing these former as ill, or pursuing and following these latter as good, there must of necessity be disturbance, disappointment, anxiety, jealousy, envy, animosity, which are and ever must be eternally ill and miserable; so on the contrary side, by a liberty from these, there must be serenity of mind, tranquility, security, an undisturbed enjoyment of all social affection, and an exercise of all virtue, which are and must be eternally good and happy.

He that affects what is not in his power, or disaffects in the same manner what he cannot hope to avoid, cannot be said to have content. He therefore who pursues a right affection, pursues his happiness, content and good. He who despises this affection, or says he can be content without it, contradicts himself, and may as well say he can be content without content.

The good of life is either in the sensations of the body, or in the motions and affections of the soul, or in the action of the mind in thought and contemplation; or, if it be not in one of these separately, it must be in some mixture of these one with another. If it be in sensuality alone, then it is in brutes that good is completed and most perfect, since they have more capacity for this, as they are more exempt from the other.

If it be in soul and mind, but in subserviency to sense, it is still the same, since if the highest good (supposed in the sense) be attained, the other is slighted, and thus still the bestial state is most perfect. If it be in a soul and mind eminently and principally, so the body is to be subservient, then it is to be considered how far this subserviency is to go. Now it is evident that as the activity of the mind and operations of the soul are the causes of the sensual pleasures being less felt, and are therefore the diminution of that other sort of good; so, on the other side, is sensuality the obstruction of this good which is in a mind.

Such is the opposition and fight of these two principles. Therefore, if the highest degree of this sort of good (viz., of a mind), be not attainable but by the loss of the other, then that other, as the meaner good must be sacrificed to this greater, and the only true and real good is the enjoyment of a soul and mind freed from the incitements, commotions, and disorders of sense.

Now if the chiefest good be in this of a soul and mind, and their operations, then consider how it is that thou exertest them; what thou makest to be the objects of their pursuit and intention. How dost thou employ them, and upon what? how is it that thy soul loves, esteems, admires, rejoices? what is it that thy mind contemplates with delight? and what are the thoughts it loves to be entertained with? See what the subjects are. For as is the worth of these so is thy worth. As the greatness and fulness is of these, so is that of the good thou enjoyest. See therefore where fulness is and where emptiness. See in what subject resides the chiefest excellence and beauty, and where it is entire, perfect, absolute; where broken, imperfect, short. View these terrestial beauties, and whatever has the appearance of excellence and is able to attract. See that which either really is or but stands in the room of the fair, beautiful, and good : * a mass of mettle; a tract of land; a number of slaves; a pile of stones; a human body of such certain lineaments and proportions. But go to what is more specious : a friend; a set or society of friends; a family; and that larger family, a city, commonwealth, and native country. Is this the highest of the kind? Is this of the first order, the first degree of beauty? May each of these be beautiful by themselves, without a beautiful world? Can beauty and perfection be there and not here? or, if here, can it be in a less degree than there? If beauty be at all in this κόσμος (the original and container of all other beauties) can it be less perfect in the whole than in the parts? Or, on the contrary, is it not impossible that it should be imperfect in the parts, and only perfect in the whole?—where all the pieces † are (in the artist's phrase) *rapportées*, matched, adjusted; where all is joined

---

* καλὸν καὶ ἀγαθόν.

† συμβαίνειν οἱ τεχνῖται λέγουσι ["they are suitable, the workmen say."—*Mar. Aurel. Med.*, Bk. V., § 8.]

and united; and in which all number, ῥυθμός, measure, and proportion are summed. See in painting, see in architecture, where it is that beauty lies. Is it in every single stroke or stone, which unitedly compose the whole design? is it in any separate narrow part, or in the whole taken together? is it (suppose) in the foot-square of the building, or the inch-square of the painting? or is it not evident that if the eye were confined to this, the chief and sovereign beauty would be lost, whatever slender graces might appear in those imperfect fragments? Now consider and apply this. Consider painting and architecture itself, consider music and harmony, a voice, a face, to what does this refer? how stands it in the larger piece? how in the whole? what part is it? of what is this the image, reflection, shadow? where is the sovereign beauty? where the sovereign good?

See, therefore, what is amiable in the first and what, but in the second and lower degree. Go to the first object. Go to the source, origin, and principle of excellence and beauty. See where perfect beauty is, for where that is, there alone can be perfect enjoyment, there alone the highest good.

# SHAME.

(1) They laugh at the habit, the posture, place, countenance. Shall this disturb ? But were it in another case (a loss of fortune, of friends, a melancholy or concern about a dying relation or a sinking public). This would be otherwise, there would be little regard to this or to anything they could say, though ever so full of mockery or satire. And why this ? Because thou wouldst be otherwise taken up, and in a greater concern, to which the rest would be as nothing. And is this, therefore, a slighter case ? Are those other things of more concern than that without which there is no being a friend, or possibility of being truly a fellow-citizen, or fellow-creature, an owner of deity, or lover of men ?—without which I must lie, dissemble, flatter; tremble and be a coward; soften in pleasure and be voluptuous and effeminate; hate and be an enemy; be unreconciled to Providence and be impious; in short, without which my whole life must be absurdity and contradiction ?

(2) Again, either this is a true shame (and then it is something vicious), or, if it be for nothing in itself ill, the shame is ill. But how to bear the reproach of a whole people ? How do robbers, debauchees, and the common women ? But these are not ashamed of ill actions. And shall they be unhurt by the report of others that are virtuous, whilst thou art inferior to the reproaches of those who are ignorant and vicious ? They are not ashamed (thou sayest) of what is base. Wherefore ? Because they think it not base. But if they thought it base, could they be otherwise than ashamed ? No. Then, wherefore is thy shame ? See what thou art forced to confess. In short, it is impossible we should be sorry for anything but because we think it ill. It is impossible we should be ashamed for anything but because we think it base. So that either thou art troubled because thou thinkest fame to be a good, or every virtuous action not honourable.

(3) Again, if a number of children deride thee, wouldst thou be concerned ?—No. If of idiots ?—The same. If of mechanics and the lowest of the vulgar ?—Still the same. But perhaps these whom thou fearest are judges of vice and virtue, and know what is good, what ill.—Not so. Then who are these but children, idiots, and mechanics, or all one with these ? and what have we to do with their judgments ? If they are wise, instead of condemning, they will praise the action. If they condemn, they are the same vulgar whom thou despisest, and who know neither thee nor themselves. Thus as to the great people. Thus as to kings and their court. Thus as to the formal part of the world and those who are called learned.

(4) Again, to remember that saying of Marcus Aurelius, "to look down as from on high," &c. :—a city ; a rumour of people a nest of mites; the swarming of insects. How, when the tree is shaken ? how many cities swallowed in one earthquake ? and how soon must all be swallowed by death, and the whole surface of the earth changed and new ? Not anything extant that now is. What if the change were sudden and before their eyes ; how would they look ? Where are the solemn brows, the important reproofs, the anger or mirth ? They divert themselves with me ; they please themselves. Be it so. But who can bear contempt ? Any one may that knows himself ; what it is that one contemns, and why ; what is contemptible and what not.*

(5) Again, these, by their contempt, disturb me. But if greater and better than these were present and applauded me I should bear up and should contemn them wholly and what they thought or said. Why, man ! Is there not a greater Presence than all this ? Is there no intelligence, no consciousness in the whole ? or is all there blindness, ignorance, and impotence ? Or is that Being a more inconsiderable spectator and less worthy thy concern ? or, if thy action be just and thy affection right, is not this that which he approves ? And what more ? Wouldst thou that this approbation should be signified to thee? Wouldst thou hear a certain sound as from men ? Or wouldst thou that they also should hear that thou art approved ? What folly ?

* cf. Περὶ τοῦ ἀγωνιᾶν, *Epictet. Disc.*, Bk. II., c. xiii.

Consider, therefore, these five. (1) An ordinary calamity, (2) robbers and the common women, (3) children and idiots commending, (4) the world and its inhabitants, (5) God.

Pudor, inquit te malus angit ["a false shame distresses thee." —*Hor.*, Sat. II., 3, 39.] This is what forces thee to confess thy meanness, lowness, and imbecility. This is what makes thee unequal in every strife, unable to stand a moment on behalf of thyself and inward character, or so much as to expostulate or parley with these antagonist appearances, those species, marks, spectres, phantoms, which carry all before them and make what ravage they please. This is that which in company moulds and twines thee after any manner ; forces thee to speak where thou shouldst be silent, be silent where thou shouldst speak ; makes thee to have whatever sort of countenance is commanded ; to smile, frown, pity, applaud, as is prescribed ; and to be, in short, whatever the company around thee is. For, should I not do thus, what would they think of me ? what would they say ? Why, man ! what is it to thee what they think or say ? Is not this their concern ? Are not they to look to this ? Is it not at their own peril ? What hast thou to do with their miseries and woes ? with their wrong opinions, ill judgments, and errors ? See that thy own opinions be right, and in particular that this opinion be so which thou conceivest concerning their praise or dispraise.

What is all this stooping and slavery, and whence but from that wretched opinion and δόγμα still remaining, *that another's praise and commendation is my good ?* Consider the sum of this. What if all these and all besides that are upon earth should conceive the highest opinion of thee, what good would this be to thee ? or, if they all thought ill, what ill ? I should be useless in the world. Retire then. Where is the harm ? What sorrow, what ill does this portend ? What else is it but death ? In the meantime, what is it to me, where my task is appointed to me, where my service is, how far it extends, how near ceasing and coming to that period to which, of its own accord, and by the course of nature, in a few years it will come ? Am I unserviceable now ? If not now, I must be so however within a little. If I stay, but till age and infirmity do their part, what signifies it whether it be one cause or another that sends me out of the world ? If I have still a part in it, I act ; if not, I bid farewell. Where is the ground for all this anxiety? What is the ground for all this anxiety? What is this stir about an outward character? Either it can be kept or not be kept. If not, either I have a part still, or no part. If none, it is well, I am discharged. How? as complaining that it should be thus soon? that I had not a longer time given me to act? that I had no better nor more considerable a part? Think what it is thou callest considerable. How? with respect to what? Is it with respect to Him who distributes the parts? Are not all alike considerable in this respect? But with respect to men—What are men? What are their interests[1], what is society or community but with respect to this superior and his appointment? If I have no concern for them, what is it to me what my part has been amongst them? If I have concern and am desirous of a part, it is because of nature; and what part would I have, for nature's sake, other than what nature has appointed me? What service would I render to the whole but what the whole has willed? What approbation is there. What glory or honour with respect to Deity, except in following and obeying.

Remember therefore to run still to the utmost, and not to stick half-way. Think always of the worst. They despise me.— Who?—These few, these two or three. Let it be the whole world and what then? See what is it that I fear? Is it my body that will suffer? This is not the question here. What is it then? Is it my mind? How, in what way, unless I will myself? What is fame? in what way does it hurt? in what way advantage? what good does it do me at best? what ill at worst? Where does the good or ill lie?—In the opinion. Set that right therefore, and all else will be right.

---

[1] Οὔτε γὰρ ἀνθρώπινόν τι ἄνευ τῆς ἐπὶ τὰ θεῖα συναναφορᾶς εὖ πράξεις ["For neither wilt thou do anything well which pertains to man without at the same time having reference to things divine."—*Mar. Aurel. Med.*, Bk. III., § 13].

# REPUTATION.

(Δοξαριον).

Besides many and weightier reasons for a good man's disregard of esteem and fame, even with those who are called the better sort, there is this good warrant on his side; that in reality a true character was never well relished or understood by the critics and nice judges of the world; no, not so much as in ancient times. Socrates and Diogenes appeared as buffoons, and the first a dangerous one. As shining as was Marcus' character and station, he was enough censured and under-valued by the refined people. An Augustus and a court like his were more after their taste. Cato was not so amiable with this sort. A Cicero, an elder Cato, or a Fabius agreed better; and to them a Pericles or Themistocles was beyond an Aristides or a Phocion. What these two latter, as well as Socrates, suffered, was from the faction of these great ones, even such as pretended to be for liberty. The people of themselves were well inclined towards them, and could not but live well with men whose manners were so simple and popular. The mere people, despicable as they are, have in truth the best insight and judgment in the matter. It is here as in the virtuous world. The half-witted and half-learned, who have only a smattering of the arts, are pragmatical, conceited, and only ingenious in choosing constantly amiss. A Le Brun, a Vanderwerf, a French or Flemish hand is charming; a Titian and a Carate are too masterly, and rather fright them. They can see nothing natural in that which is so very near nature. Yet often a very child or peasant shall find likeness and bear testimony to nature where these pretended artists are at a stand. Few indeed (as the satirist says) are so detestable as to prefer Nero to Seneca; but how many would prefer Seneca to Rufus? For see how even Tacitus himself treats this latter.

Why able to slight it easily in the whole, yet not by parts?

why so often at defiance, yet reconciled ? free unconcerned, dis-interested, yet drawn in again and engaged?—But new views, a better world (as they say), hopes of the world, a part in that world, and *a character*.—Here the deceit and folly, here the treachery, the τὰ ἐφ᾽ ἡμῖν forgot: the state of men and of their minds who know not what are ἐφ᾽ ἡμῖν, what not this and all of this kind forgot. The game turned. A new game, a character, a circumstance, the thing played for, not the play ; a play in earnest, a game begun not so easily left off; not a loser con-tentedly: so bowls, tables, and other games, when made a business of. Remember why these games forborn formerly and why not this game forborn therefore now ? Since playing at this game, thou canst less command thyself than thou couldst at those other games.—But try, let it be a game merely ; let it be play, real play, skill, exercise only ; not gain or victory. For what gain here but the action ? what victory but the action ? what played for, but good play only ? And can the play be good that aims in earnest at the praises of those who understand it not? Does it belong any more to this play to frame men's voices than to a gamester to make bowls or paint the cards ? Must not each take them as he finds them? But if that be the business to gain voices, it is another art and has a different name. This is not playing the cards or bowls; this is not play or exercise or skill, but a poor ordinary mean craft, a servile trade ; the turner and the toy-shop. Or is ambition anything more ? is it the business here *to make voices?*

What is at stake ?—a fortune, reputation, fame.—Is this then what is played for ? No: but honesty and virtue.—Play away then for those other are the cards and not the stake.

The dice run wrong—let them run. Is it my fault ? or shall I go to a conjurer for better fortune ? If play I must, what have I to do, but play well ? Or would you have me cheat ?—But you will be ruined. Man! how ruined? What is played for?—nothing but the play. Thou forgettest thyself, for here is no ruin in the case ; no loss at this game, but in the game or play only ; the things thou talkest of are the cards, the dice, wood, horn, paste-board, stuff. What are their opinions ? their voices ? what is all this to the game ? If they rail and I do well, is it not I that win, and are not they the losers ?

G

All is' lost. What? Reputation, name, esteem?—Who plays for these? Who made this to be the play? But there is no play without them. The game then is up. But thou must leave the play. Right, for why did I begin? But there is an end, then. And must there never be an end? But where is the loss all this while? Have I not my stake? Have I not got what I played for? Or had I any design upon the cards? Should I pocket the dice, and carry these off with me? What have I to do with these? or what care I who has them?

Again, then.—What was the opinion or fame in those early days, when honesty not succeeding with relations, or the party, thou gavest that matter up, and turning Epicurean (with Horace and his Odes) didst follow pleasure with air, mirth, humour? What was a rumour or a censure at that time? What was a grave judgment passed on thee by any of the solemn ones of lofty brows? What if some such account had been brought thee when dancing (suppose) or in any other of those entertainments? Sport, mere sport, and nothing else. —And shall the course in which thou art now engaged, the entertainments of these latter days, and the order of life now taken up with, be yet not so powerful, or of so much virtue as the fiddles? Shall that philosophy be more prevalent than this? Shall the vulgar, as they are considered, be more despised than now? Shall the chief good as then admired be more attractive than at present, after what thou hast experienced, and now seest, and knowest?

θεός οὓς νῦν πίθηκος.[1] To-day a prodigy, to-morrow an ass. So it will be. O admirable thing, *renown!* Wondrous *reputation!* Mighty *fame!* Say, then, how is it now?—An ass. To-morrow, then, a prodigy—a prodigy! To-morrow, then, —an ass; and soon an unaccountable wretch, a madman. But who is a madman?—Art not thou then one indeed, if thou thinkest to be accountable or live accountably to such as can give no account of themselves, their lives or manners, their end or scope, what they pursue or fly, what they love or hate, approve or disapprove, or by what rule they judge either of life or anything in life? For, as for those wise ones, the highest esteemed of our

[1] Once a god to the gods . . now an ape.—*Mar. Aurel. Med.*, Bk. IV., § 16.

days, do they not at times appear also as mad one to another? And wouldst thou appear better than the rest, thou whose madness (if it be so) is so unlike the common and more passable sort? But be not concerned, go on in the use of rules,* persist, and all will be tolerably well, in all likelihood, even here too. Thou wilt have admirers enough and perhaps more than enough.

Remember the other day walking out and reading a letter just received in which the δοξάριον [reputation] was threatened (sad speeches abroad! sad censures past! sad noises and reports!) Just· at that instant the chimes sounded.—And what are chimes? What are noises, and rumours of tongues?—Dull, sorry things, God knows; equally musical both, equally consonant; wires, hammers, or bells struck, pulled, moved just alike, from as intelligent, rational causes, as certain and as regular; and in comparison, the latter rather the more regular of the two. Is this the tune that should move thus? Is this the harmony that should draw thee, affect thee, sink and raise thee? Sad soul, indeed, if it be so! sad harmony within! But listen inwards; turn thy ear thither and thou wilt hear better sounds. Is it so? Thank Heaven that thou dost find it thus. Improve this ear, learn to have a good one in this kind and, fear not, true harmony will follow and come on apace.

Again these chimes sound. How? what? Is it a musician that strikes these notes? Are they from immediate art, skill, and masterly knowledge? No, but from an engine, a piece of clockwork. What wonder then if out of tune and dissonant? wilt thou admire this music as the common people? What of that other music? wilt thou also hear keen and stand in admiration with those same common people?—Do so then. But imagine that if a master or real judge of music stood by, he would despise thee for this attention; as justly he might. Hearken then to such as thou knowest masters. Hearken to the great master and organist, and to those that immediately derive from him, for as for these others what are they themselves but mere organs, chimes, set agoing of themselves without any inherent principle of true music, or any other than a poor wretched imitation.

* cf. *Epict. Ench.*, c. xxii.

The world says thus; the world expects; the world talks.—
Who is the world? who is it when the gossips say the world?
The town ladies, the parish wives, the servants, talking of one
another and of their masters, the neighbourhood in the country,
the farmers at the next fair or market; which of these uses not the
word, and with the same emphasis, *the world!*—But where
then is this emphatical world? what is it? or who?—Is it
the beau monde? is it the court and drawing-room? is it the
chocolate-house world? the coffee-house world? the quality
world or the common-people world? the scholar world? the
virtuoso world, or the politic, negotiating, managing, busy world?
the foreign or the home world?—For behold what passes
as a great story, a mighty affair in one of these worlds is just
nothing in another. Whom of these, then, or which am I to
consider? whom or which of these will I make the world? shall
it be the greater number, the mere people?—See who there is that
was best served or best deserved of them either now or anciently;
and see if a good rope-dancer or prize-player be not of the two
more talked of, not to say more loved. Shall it be the managers,
the men who govern the multitude; and not the multitude
themselves?—See, then, these managers, the politicians and
known actors in the state, the old stagers (as they call them),
those who are at the helm and have long dealt in state-affairs:
see this race; and say who are honestest, the governors or
those governed? Are not these worse yet by some degrees?
Are the courts or even the senates, parliaments, and public
stations, the passages to virtue and true honour, as well as
to fame, fortune, and honour of another kind?—*Vestigia nulla
retrorsum.*

If they once went in honest, how are they come out?
Where are the footsteps? What are they changed to soon when
there? Is this, then, the world? Are these such as thou
wouldst approve thyself to? Reckon them up by name, take
out from them those who mind chiefly their pleasures, or the
advancing themselves, those that act with design, private interest
or revenge, the downright corrupt and profligate, together with
the bigoted and superstitious, and see how many will be left.
Consider their lives and manners, their pursuits and aims, their
real worth and wisdom in themselves, and see whether this fine

world or that plain world be most considerable and fittest to carry that name *the world* ?

At a country-meeting, a fair, or bull-baiting, there is a greater world than here where the word astonishes, when I hear it pronounced, the world ! There are more eyes, more looking, more talk, more people to talk. But what people? Right, compare and see what difference.

The fable of the old man, boy, and ass. The censure of the passengers; and what this came to. Man ! keep on thy way, what is best for thee, thy boy, and ass. Mind the road and whither thou art going; to what place, and on what business. Let others mind the passengers that are idle or that travel only for diversion. Thou hast something else to mind. Follow those that can teach thee and that know this road ; not those that neither know the road, nor themselves, nor have any certain guide or rule for either.

Applause of virtue in the world as accidental— admiring not as admirable but as admired — such a one is commended. But see for what. Is the thing itself commended which is commendable ? Is this esteemed ? Is this beloved ? If not, what is this but chance and accident ; and does not time and a small change of circumstance show this to be accident, and depend on fortune merely ? " O wondrous *reputation !* rare thing renown ! who would not purchase thee ! who would not venture hard for thee !"—And in very truth is it not venturing hard to do anything for this, to bid for this, to step out of this kind ? Is it a small matter that is thus ventured every time ? And hast thou not thyself made this adventure at cost enough ? —Inward repetitions, and fictions of praises, self-enconiums, panegyrics :—*extraordinary ! wonderful ! nobody like him* ! The ridiculousness of this, the shame of this.

# HUMAN AFFAIRS.

Τὸ γὰρ ὅλον, κατιδεῖν ἀεὶ τὰ ανθρώπινα, ὡς ἐφήμερα καὶ εὐτελῆ.
["To conclude, always observe how ephemeral and worthless
human things are."—*Mar. Aurel. Med.*, Bk. IV., § 48.]

Consider the several ages of mankind; the revolutions of
the world, the rise, declension and extinction of nations, one after
another; after what manner the earth is peopled, sometimes in
one part and then in another; first desert, then cultivated, and
then desert again; from woods and wilderness, to cities and
culture, again into woods; one while barbarous, then civilized,
and then barbarous again; after, darkness and ignorance, arts
and sciences, and then again darkness and ignorance as before.

Now, therefore, remember whenever thou art intent and
earnest on any action that seems highly important to the
world, whenever it seems that great things are in hand,
remember to call this to mind : that all is but of a moment, all
must again decline. What though it were now an age like one
of those ancient ? What though it were Rome again ? What
though it were Greece ? How long should it last ? Must not
there be again an age of darkness ? Again Goths ? And shortly,
neither shall so much as the name of Goths be remembered, but
the modern as well as ancient Greeks and Italians be equally
forgotten.

Spartans, Athenians, Thebans, Achaians, the innumerable
cities of the continent and islands, the European and Asiatic
Greeks, the commonwealth of Rome, and in Africa, Carthage, &c.,
what were these once ! and now, what ! The Morea, Turkey, the
holy Patrimony and a Land of Priests ! Nations fighting for
Mahomet; Christians of different sects warring one with
another; doctrines, heresies, creeds, councils, synods, persecutions.
What a different face of things ! A little while hence, and this
too will be changed, and so that, and so the next; and after
many revolutions, the same over again. Nothing is new or
strange. That, that now is, after it has ceased, shall one time or

70

another be again ; and that, that is not now, shall in time be as
it was before. Vast and spreading commonwealths, as those of
ancient Greece, Italy, and through all the Western World. Vast
and spreading tyrannies of long duration, as those of Persia, India,
and the Eastern world. Rude and illiterate commonwealths, as
those of Gaul, Germany, the Scythians, Vandals, Goths. Polite
and learned commonwealths, as those of Greece and Rome.
Harmless rites and ceremonies of religion ; barbarous and
obscene rites ; peaceable and corresponding religions, uniting
and reconciling the world ; dark and horrid superstitions
covering the face of the world, causing wars and confusion.

Such is the state of mankind ; these are the revolutions.
The tree sprouts out of the ground, then grows, then flourishes
awhile ; at last decays and sinks, that others may come up.
Thus men succeed to one another. Thus names and families
die ; and thus nations and cities. What are all these changes
and successions ? What is there here but what is natural,
familiar, and orderly, and conducing to the whole ? Where is
the tragedy ? Where the surprise or astonishment ? Are not
these the leaves of the wood carried off with the winter blast,
that new ones may in the spring succeed ? Is not the whole
surface of the earth thus ? and are not all things thus ? Is
it not in these very changes that all those beauties consist
which are so admired in nature, and by which all but the grosser
sort of mankind are so sensibly moved ? The sum of all
this is, that be this what season soever of the world, be it
the very winter that thou livest in, or be it in the spring, all
is alike. Had it been in the full growth of letters, sciences,
arts, liberty, or what other perfection human nature in its best
state is capable of, or had it been in the autumn and decline of
all this that thou hadst lived, it amounts but to the same.
Were Rome or Sparta thy country, or hadst thou been thyself
Lycurgus or Valerius, and founded those governments, what
then ? What was all this but in order to their corruption ?
What is four or five hundred years' duration more than forty
or twenty ? or what would a thousand or ten thousand be,
supposing that things could last so long ? Is there anything
in this that can satisfy ?

What remains then but that the thing that is just, sociable, and in appearance tending to the good of mankind; that and that alone thou shouldst intend and that perform as far as lies in thee, without regard to what was in time past, or to what shall be in time to come, or to what is now present in this age. What if thou couldst at this present time set aright and in that order what thou desirest, it could not possibly continue, or be fixed any way, but must soon decline and have its period as those things which have been before. All this is endless and an abyss. To labour, therefore, and toil with anxiety and regret about these matters, to wish that thy country were for ever prosperous, and flourishing, and immortal : all this is stupid, and is the proper affection of one who either is a stranger in the world, and is ignorant of its revolutions and vicissitudes, or who, knowing these, repines and thinks them hard, and would correct the order of Providence. And what is such affection as this but impiety ?

To pursue or follow anything, as greatly concerned for the success; to promise ourselves great things; to rejoice at the progress of affairs as going well, and then be troubled and cast down when either they stop or go back again; to build with great joy and delight whilst the work succeeds, and when anything happens ill to be in affliction and trouble for it; to lay schemes and designs and projects of things to come, of reformations, changes, establishments, in a family, amongst friends in a public, or amongst mankind : what is all this, but to be like children making their houses of cards which they know very well cannot stand beyond the second or third storey, and yet when the structure perishes and the work fails under their hand, crying, and afterwards beginning anew. But the comparison seems too ridiculous perhaps, and is disliked.

Begin then in the first place with *thy body* and constitution. Of what nature is this ? What kind of work is it, to defend and rear, and nourish and prop this ? Dost thou promise to thyself always to keep this sound and whole ? Will any art keep this from being bruised and maimed and dis- tempered, and perpetually under some ill and accident or another; always wanting to have something, or be rid of something; always in indigence, always in distress, and under repair ? If there be no end of this, and no security ever to be obtained, where is either rest or happiness ? What is this but toil and labour in vain ? Consider next as to *a family.* Shall all here be one time or other prosperous ? Shall children, brothers, sisters, domestics, friends, be all virtuous and act as they should do ? How long shall this continue ? Or, how long is it that thou expectest to have them with thee in the world, or to have them thus orderly and virtuous, if they are thus already ? Consider as to the *public* the same. What reformations dost thou expect ? how far to extend ? for how long time to last ? and how long will it be ere that time comes when not so much as the name of this people shall remain ? If all this be doating, fond, and foolish, and if all things are in a constant flux, and alteration, always perishing and renewing, always passing, and nothing fixed or at a stay ; if the success of what thou art so earnestly doing, either for the health and support of thy body, or about a family, or in the public, be all uncertain, but the revolution, change and death of each of these be certain and inevitable ; if all this that we strive about be that which can never be accomplished, never brought to perfection, never kept at a stay, but be vile, rotten, and of no duration, inconsiderable for time, for substance, for place : what then, is all this but the houses of cards, and the passion and ardour of the children busying themselves ? Is nothing therefore to be minded ? Is there nothing that is important ? This certainly is, and this only : how in the midst of all, to preserve a sound and steady mind, a just and right affection, how to have a uniform and suitable will, how to approve and disapprove, choose and reject according to reason, how to act as becomes a man, as a creature and fellow-creature, sociably, justly, piously, and how to acquiesce and be contented.

Either that which thou art concerned for, and so much troubled and disturbed about, is merely what relates to thy body, and the satisfaction of those desires which have nothing in common with virtue, or else it is what is of a generous kind and relates to virtue and common good. If there be anything in this thy concern which relates to a body, life, a family, an estate, a name, a voluptuous course of living ; and that these are what thou regardest, then is thy interest and that of the public very opposite, and thou art yet far off from virtue or a virtuous affection. If it be purely a public good and virtue which leads thee, then surely thou hast considered of virtue, what it is, and wherefore thou pursuest it as good. If thou hast considered of virtue and the good of it, thou must have learned this: that it is in a certain disposition, affection, or will. If so, that which is not a loss, hindrance, or prejudice of this disposition, affection, or will, is not a loss of that good which arises from virtue. Now if anything happen ill in human affairs, or if it be ill with mankind, this does not alter thy disposition, affection or will, therefore, neither does it diminish thy good or happiness.

That another person's mind should be in health is no more necessary to my own mind, than it is necessary to my body that any other should have his body in the same disposition. If I am dissatisfied and troubled that any part of the world is vicious, I may as well be dissatisfied that any one person in the whole world should be so. In short, either my good is in certain outward circumstances or in a mind and affection. If I grieve that any of those around me are not as I would have them to be, then my good is in outward circumstances. If so, how is this virtue? or which way shall virtue be a good? or if not a good how followed or pursued?

To have a right affection and will is either a good or not so; if not so, then virtue is not a good to be followed. If virtue and right affection be a good, then that only is necessary to the good of virtue which is necessary to the support of that good and right affection. Now, that the world be either more or less virtuous is nothing to my affection or will, and therefore nothing to my good. How, therefore, is this that has happened an ill? It is not so, in the sense of the body; for those who regard the body are least of all concerned for this. Neither is it an ill to my mind, as placing its good in virtue and right affection.—But I cannot be satisfied unless men act thus.—If such be thy affection, it is not what virtue in any manner requires or has need of; nor is it of any good either to thyself or others. If not that, then what is this but fancy and wilfulness? For what else is wilfulness but to will positively and without reason, or, as we say, "to will, because we will."

Observe this temper and affection. "I must needs have such

an estate and such a house; I must needs have such and such to attend me." What is the difference between this and that other—"I must needs have every one to be good and virtuous?" Why may I not as well say—"I must needs have everyone live as long as I live; I must needs have mankind immortal?" All this is of the same kind; far out of true affection, far wide of nature and the right structure of a will. It is only wilfulness and a bent of mind not governed by reason, or capable of any measure or rule. For if I would be towards mankind as I ought to be; towards nature and the whole as I ought to be; it is enough that I will and affect rightly myself, and that this should be all my care and concern. But if this do not satisfy me, and if this be not my end, what is the difference between being bent on a certain constitution or structure of mankind, or on a certain building like that of wood or stones? What is the difference between the fancy of constituting a family or common-wealth, or that of modelling and disciplining an army? What is the difference between aiming at having a fine and splendid country, or a fine and splendid house?

If to affect the public good be virtue; and that the conse-quence of affecting thus, be to be disturbed and afflicted in ill-success; then is virtue its own torment and not its own reward. If it be true that virtue is its own reward, and that all that virtue seeks *is to be virtue;* what would I have more than this, that my affection be as it ought to be?

If knowing that my country is at the end of a thousand years to be extinct I refuse on that account to act for it, through discontent; I am mad and extravagant. If I can notwithstand-ing act with content, knowing that it shall not last beyond a thousand years; why not as well, though it last but for a hundred? or why not the same, though but till next year?

What though the age be illiterate or superstitious, or like to grow so more and more; how long was the last in that condition, and how many such ages must again and again pass in a few periods and in a small and inconsiderable portion of the revolutions of the world? What though the next age recover from superstition; what if virtue prevail; and that again there appear men, such as may be truly called so; how soon must this decline again, and superstition and barbarity arise as before?

Therefore when either thou art setting thyself to any work that seems considerable in the public or to the promotion of virtue; or whenever thou sittest down to read anything ancient, especially what has relation to philosophy, remember this—all was darkness, but a while since, now there is a little glimmering of light, and whether this proceed or no, in a little while all will be again dark. What though the philosophers be oddly represented, and their history imperfect, mixed and corrupted, ill written, and worse understood? what though Laelius, Cato, Thrasea, Helvidius, Agripinus and such as these be unknown? what though Socrates and Diogenes be forgotten, or most ridiculously represented? These were such as were not concerned for this themselves. Why art thou concerned? Hercules, Theseus, Cadmus, were long since become fables; though they perhaps were excellent men in their age. And now many things which were in those days, are grown wholly out of memory and are lost. So also in what relates to those others mentioned, their affairs are now in a manner grown fabulous and obsolete, and in a little time neither shall the name of Socrates, or Epictetus or Marcus, remain. Again barbarity, again Goths.

Go then, and in this disposition have recourse to the ancients and what remains of them; and make use of this gift of Providence, gratefully, thankfully, and contentedly; as having received the rules, and obtained these precepts, by which without more ado thou mayst be happy. If either these things or these men be unknown, or undervalued, or destroyed; if either now, or a while hence, or sooner, or later, there be ignorance and barbarity: all this is the same; all must revolve in this manner. And, at what revolutions of the world thou art present, how long the spaces shall be, how soon either such or such things shall again return and prevail: all this is indifferent. And now if thou canst stand thus affected towards these matters, if thou apprehendest the thing never otherwise than thus; then neither shalt thou be disturbed or shocked when anything in the public succeeds not; or when philosophy is traduced, or slighted by those that are ignorant.

Remember that as men are constituted, they cannot stand otherwise towards virtue and philosophy than as they do: that is to say, they of necessity must both curse it and praise it. Be not therefore lightly and foolishly raised by the praises of those that at another time must curse. Neither be concerned at the curses of those who, by the same necessity, must praise again, and at some other time admire.

He that is impatient and cannot bear with the world, such as it is, does not consider how often he himself is intolerable, and that if the world were to be reformed and become as perfect as he requires it to be, it were not fit that such a creature as he should live in it.

If thou art thyself such as thou shouldst be, what need is there of more? If thou art weak and unable to bear with things, why not reform thyself rather than the world, since the one is practicable, the other mere extravagance?

Remember what has been said concerning the folly and stupidity of those reasonings about the duration of things. What is it to thee whether the ancients be remembered or not? Whether their manners and government, whether liberty, generous sentiments, or philosophy be restored for a while and flourish for one age or two, as then? Is it to last for ever? Must not other things prevail and have their course? Must not superstition, barbarity, darkness and night succeed again in their turns? Is not this the order of things? Is not this *the chorus*, the seasons, the summer and winter, day and night? But I would have no winter here, no night.—See the stupidity of this. But if there must be winter, if there must be night, what is it to me, when or for how long? And what should I do but commit this to Him who has appointed the seasons of the world, as is most conducing, and as was necessary, for the safety, happiness and prosperity of the whole?

After this manner this one dogma is sufficient (and remember to have it in readiness): either the race of mankind is eternal or not eternal. If eternal, what though the intervals, instead of one age, were a thousand? If not eternal, what signifies it how soon any one thing ceases, since all of this kind must cease within a little? Either periods, and then that which is not now, will be, at some other time; and so again and again, after many changes and revolutions, and thus to perpetuity. Or else one period that puts an end to all; and if so, where is the harm? What is there more in the death of a whole race than of one single animal? Fear not, the whole is not likely to suffer. Nor canst thou suffer, if thou art towards the whole as thou oughtst to be. What is there, then, to fear? and for whom?

Whenever the fancy is strongly at work about the ancients and reviving something or other of that kind, remember that these things are already come to their period. The day is spent and only a twilight remains. Something else may arise in after ages, but that must be a new thing, and from new seeds. This stock that thou wouldst graft upon is decayed and sunk. Are not the laws, manners, customs, rites, abolished and sunk? Are not the languages dead? or how preserved? in what books? what fragments? how corrupted, and every day growing more so? Or what if the books remain a while longer; who are the readers? What has been the reason that either of the languages have been so long preserved? and what is now become of the first and noblest?

Therefore all those other thoughts are senseless.—*Romans! Greeks!* Fables, tales. obsolete stories. Tell us of some late war; the history of our kings; matches between crowns; titles, pretensions, nobility, barons, counts, dukes, palatines; church affairs, Reformations, Protestant and Papist, Turk and Christian. This is our present foundation; these are the affairs that concern the world. But, as for Greeks and Romans, what are they, and how do these names sound? Remember this as often as thou appliest to anything of the ancients and their story, and see that thou art not elevated, nor, by yielding at first, be afterwards transported and hurried away. For what is this but building a foundation for disturbance, and accusation of Providence?

If I am contented that the ancients should have been but are not; if I am contented that the ancients should have been ancients, and the moderns, moderns; if it be indifferent to me when these remaining books perish, which must perish within a very little time; if it be enough to me that I have that which serves to guide and conduct me in life, knowing that all depends upon myself: in this disposition I may safely read, otherwise I may perchance learn other matters and improve in other ways; but (what is most absurd and ridiculous) I shall unlearn that for the sake of which I read, and for which alone I have recourse to the ancients.

If it be a certain sort of pleasure that engages and ties thee to the ancients, set aside the library, for it is plain, this is but little better than romances (for these too are read for pleasure and serve for discourse and entertainment). If it be for the benefit of thy mind, and the sake of a certain philosophy, remember what that philosophy taught and what those persons themselves said of this matter, and what they would say (if now present) to one thus anxious and thus concerned for their memory and fame. Man! what is this to thee? Either thou knowest those principles to be true and art satisfied in thy own reason concerning them, or not. If not satisfied, what is it thou admirest or seekest? If satisfied, let us hear, concerning what? —That the universe is justly administered, that the things belonging to me are in my own power; the rest nothing.—But how, therefore, are these ancients a concern? They are extinct. Let them be so. Were they not to die at some time or another? Was it not necessary that they themselves should first die, and shortly after their memories? Or what if their memory die not as yet, must it not die at another time? What difference whether now or then? Where is the harm of this, or of any of those other deaths or changes? Whose opinion shall we take as to this matter? Theirs or the vulgar? What is fame, therefore, in their opinion? What are changes and successions, the decay and perishing of men, and memories of men?

Remember, therefore, either this that I have learned is an idle story, and so the ancients are nothing, or, if I am convinced of anything, it is of this: That ancients and moderns are all alike; for, this is no concern of mine, or in my power.

Remember that of Marcus applied in another way:— καθ' ἕτερον μὲν λόγον ἡμῖν ἐστιν οἰκειότατον ἄνθρωπος.—[*Meditations*, Bk. V., § 20.] In one nothing can be more near to me than men (and especially these men). But in another respect (viz.: as they are mortal, as they must yield to time, as they must give place to others that arise, as they must accomplish, destroy, and make good the laws of the universe) they are no more to me than is the sun or air; no more than are any of those things that are every day converted and changed by the sun or air, which at some other time, if so the universe requires, may also themselves be converted and changed. And what else do I require? what other economy do I favour? what interest should prevail besides the interest of the whole? Such therefore are the laws of the whole, such the establishment, such the order. Would I invade or overturn this?—God forbid.

What is it thou art thus eager after. Let us see. How wouldst thou order things, if the world were at thy disposal, and to be governed by thy fancy? Wouldst thou have the same age continue, and not give place to other ages? Wouldst thou that the same men should always live, or that in their room such others should always arise? Wherein the greatness of this character?— He obeyed the voice of the Deity, adhered to reason alone, rejected the vulgar opinions, and through the needs of ignorance, discovered truth.—But, what if there had been no preceding ignorance? where had been the greatness of the discovery? how had he been the light of the age? What if there had been no vulgar opinions; no sophists; no vicious or corrupt Athenians; no tyrranical oligarchy, nor licentious democracy; no Anytus or Melitus; no prison or poison, or death? Make us another history. Show us a Socrates without these; see what picture thou wouldst make.—But, why those shades? Remove the shades then; remove the darker colours. See how it will be, consider how in that other picture. How is it then that thou wouldst have changed this? what wouldst thou have amended of what then was? But this is gone and past. Right, how should it be otherwise? Wouldst thou have the same to happen over again? Must the same piece be acted again, to give satisfaction, and so the same things be produced again and again? See what the world would be at this rate? where would be the changes, succession, order? Who can endure so much as in a play that the same scene should come again and again, or the same parts remain? What would that theatre be, which could afford but one piece, and represented it always the same? Consider, then: what is magnanimity and what is that which occasions it, proves it, and raises it? What is it that shows the force of reason? what is the exercise and trial of a mind? What else but circumstances, these very circumstances: vice, ignorance, false opinions? What is it that makes the hero? and how was Hercules great but for the hydras, monsters, tyrannies he had to deal with ? How therefore should there be a Socrates, but no Anytus ? how* a Hercules, but no hydra ?

But I would have all men to be alike and to resemble these generous ones, these leaders, these of a distinguished make and mould. I would have all like these and the whole herd be such; not merely a single man; not a few only at one season; not so as to appear a while and then disappear again. What is this, but to say as the silly sort of people : I would have it to be always spring, no autumn, no winter ? Go into a wood, and when thou hast singled out some tall and stately tree, the chief beauty and ornament of the grove, say, I would have no shrubs nor brambles. How then should this be a wood ? In what way preserve that beauty, which is proper to a wood ? where would be that grace and comeliness of the whole ? where the comeliness and majesty of the principal tree ? How therefore wouldst thou order this in that greater whole ? how dispose the several ranks and degrees ? Should all be vegetable, no sand, no stone ? But vegetables excel mere stone and other such matter—right. Therefore let us throw these out of our picture; let all be roses, flowers, and verdure; no rock, or sand, or moss; no ancient trunk, no decayed or rotten boughs. Well, but are not sensible creatures above vegetables ?—They are. How then ? Should all therefore be sensible creatures ? no vegetables ? no forest ? Or should all be rational creatures, and no herd; or, amongst rational creatures, should all be rational to the degree of Socrates, and no vulgar, no herd ?

All this is stupid and senseless. But suppose, now, that one age was as it should be, must every age be alike, and produce a Socrates, or such as those who succeeded him ? Must not seasons also differ from one another ? Must there be nothing more eminent at one time than another ? Must the grove have still one and the same face ? Must there be no periods, no revolutions, no autumn, no winter ?—But the winter landscape is not so beautiful.—To thee perhaps not; but in some respect is it not equally so ? Is it not equally good and beautiful in the whole ? What if it be the winter of arts and sciences ? What if even the winter and decay

---

* *Epict. Disc.*, Bk. I., c vi., § 32.

H

of mankind? Is it ever winter in the whole? Is not the
universe always new and entire and flourishing? Does not
all tend to the prosperity and welfare of that? And is not
everything suitable to the perfection of that mind which
presides and governs it?—But these changes and vicissitudes do
not please me, nor can I find the beauty of them.—See, then,
what idea or apprehension thou hast of beauty and agreeableness
in other things; and whether the chiefest beauties, the chiefest
graces arise not from change and vicissitude. What is music?
What is one note prolonged? Nothing more dissonant and
odious. But seek the changes and vicissitudes, and those
too the most odd and various ones; and here it is where
harmony arises. Mix even a dissonance after a certain manner
and the music is still more excellent; and in the management
of these dissonances is the sublime of the art. What is
dance but a like succession of motions diversified, of which
not one single one would continue graceful if viewed by
itself and out of this change, but which taken as they are
joined together and depending on one another, form the
highest grace imaginable. Such, therefore, is that other chorus
and harmony; such is the dance (like what the poets feign) of
the hours and days; such are the seasons, ages, revolutions of the
world; the flourishing and decline of mankind; the nations that
arise and sink; the inventions, languages, letters, arts, sciences,
rites, mysteries, manners, customs, laws, governments; and in the
midst of this ore, sometimes a vein of purer kind, sometimes a
season of more than ordinary knowledge and light, sometimes a
more than common production: an effort of Nature (as we may
properly speak with relation to any particular nature) carrying
things to the highest pitch and producing sometimes a body
of more than ordinary stature and perfection, like that of a Milo,
so at other times a mind such as the mind of Socrates. Why is it
more unnatural that this should decline again, than that the breed
of bodies should decline? If it be ridiculous, considering the body
and make of man, to wonder that all men should not be as Milo,
and not rather that anyone of such strength as Milo should have
been known; how much more ridiculous is it, considering such
an animal as man, and what he holds of the brute, to wonder
that he should so often resemble the brute; and not rather

wonder that he should find out his other relation and be a God ?
For, what else is he, who, being conscious of the Divine Government, accompanies it and joins himself to it ? How ridiculous
is it, considering man such as he truly is, to wonder that such
and so many parts of the earth should be barbarian and savage,
and not rather that there should have been other nations so
wise, knowing, and polite ? Why wonder at the huts and cabins
of Indians, and not rather at the cities, manners, and government
of other nations ? Why at other governments more imperfect,
and not rather at the perfection of such a one as Sparta ?

Consider, therefore, for what is all this concern ? Is it for
the world, or for thyself ? If for the world, fear not, the world
will be governed as it should be, nor can anything there go
amiss. If it be for thyself this is thy own work, and in thy
own power, nor can anything here go amiss, if thou thyself
pleasest. See, therefore, that thy affection be but right, and all
is right. But, if thou wishest either for times or seasons or
places ; if thou wouldst correct the order of the world, and have
things to be other than they are ; thy affection is wrong, and in
the midst of all this reading and this pursuit of philosophy, thou
art thyself no better than an idiot.

Beware never to compound with any of those thoughts
concerning human affairs, as if likely to be more prosperous, as
if the age were to be restored, antiquity again acted ; other
Dions, other Phocions, other Catos, other Academys, another
Porch, and whatever dreams of this kind thou art used to fall
into, on reading anything ancient. Instead of this, suppose
everything the most contrary. Take always the reverse : nations
such as the Goths ; monarchies such as the Persian and other
Eastern ones ; superstitions such as Egyptian, &c. Consider all of
that other kind as extinct, and so ever to remain. For if once
the ὄρεξις [desire] be towards reviving anything of this kind ; if
once thou dost begin building and laying foundations, there is no
end. And if it happens thou art encouraged by some imaginary
success, the thing grows worse ; the right and steady views are
more and more lost, and the affairs of the world not answering
these other narrow, fond and mistaken views, nature is sure to be
accused ; many things complained of, many lamented, the world
pitied, mankind pitied, thou thyself pitied. All is full of calamity,

all wretched, poor, disastrous, ruinous; for so in reality all is, with respect to thyself, whilst thy mind is in this state, and thy thoughts such as these. In what way can this be otherwise, whilst thou affectest that which is out of thy power and not belonging to thee? whilst thou affectest otherwise than as nature affects? whilst thou thinkest anything excellent, but what the mind and wisdom of the whole judges to be so? If the wisdom of the whole would have it thus, I also would have it thus, and not otherwise. If otherwise, I am no longer free; I am no longer that generous and exalted mind, which aims at that which is excellent, at that which is best; which aims so as not to be frustrated, but always successful and prosperous; which is never constrained, never unwillingly submits to Deity, never merely submits but accompanies and applauds. But how accompany or how applaud that to which I am not perfectly reconciled? that which I think sad and dismal, severe or hard? How is it, therefore, when I esteem any of these changes severe or hard? How is it when either plagues or earthquakes, or any of those other things ruinous to mankind, appear thus? How if the loss of letters or sciences be feared, or anything of this kind which may happen in the world, be looked upon as sad and grievous, where will my freedom be? Where my applause? How shall I be pious? how generous? how unhappy? Or, if I am miserable, and tremble, and am dejected, what signifies it what the subject is? Am I less a slave? am I less mean?

Resolve, therefore, never to allow anything to such thoughts but introduce always their contraries. Consider the fall, death, extinction of the ancients; themselves long since, and now their memories; or if of this kind something still remain, it is about to perish; oblivion is at hand. Why not now, as well as a little later? But must there nothing of this kind arise again in time? —Perhaps never, or if ever, not till after many changes and revolutions; perhaps millions of ages ere the same again; first Greece, as before Socrates, then Socrates and followers. How many ages ere such a nation, such a language be formed as that of Greece? And afterwards how long amidst physiologers and sophists? How many ages ere a certain superstition sink? What if the age remain still as it is? What though it be yet worse, and that hereafter all be barbarous, as in those other nations? What though even this remain not, but that the whole earth be depopulated? But must the world, then, perish thus?—What world? Mankind. So that the world, then, is this one kind or species; if this kind be lost, the world is lost. If this animal lose its intelligence, there will be no more intelligence in the universe. How? Will there be no nature, no elements, no conversion, change or renewal of things, no new or different forms arising, nothing remaining of what was before? No sun, no planets, no heavenly bodies? Or, though these remain, shall we say, however, that there are no intelligencies or minds remaining? Are human bodies of such kind that intelligence is confined to these, and can nowhere lodge besides? What if a worm should happen to have intelligence, would he not reason better?

But I know men, and other intelligences I know nothing of. So, hadst thou been a worm, thou hadst conferred only with worms, and must it have followed that there were no wiser beings, no men, no Deities, or Supreme Deity? If it be true that there is such a supreme and sovereign mind, and that all is according to that mind, then all is right. Why talk to us of other minds? What matter is it where they reside, and how the sovereign mind has disposed them; whether in these bodies, or in the others; whether at one time rather than at another? If thou hast a mind thyself, be thankful that it has fallen to thee; make the use of it that thou shouldst do, and this is enough. What is it to thee that other portions of matter of the same form have it or have it not? That of the many other thou knowest only one particular species has it? Or that amongst these only a few have it, and this only at certain times and in certain periods? Why not lament because the beasts are sensible only and not rational? Why not because the plants are only vegetative, and neither sensible nor rational? Why not this as well as to lament that man is not otherwise rational than as nature has made him to be, and that this species seldom can afford a mind.* Is it not much it ever could afford

*Ὅτι δὲ τοιοῦτον ἐξήνεγκαν καρπὸν ἐν ἀνθρωπίνῃ ᾳιανοίᾳ. [But because they (the gods) have produced in the human mind that fruit.—*Epict. Disc.*, Bk. I., c. iv., § 32.]

one ? Is it not much that in such a body, such senses, such engagements to a low and brutal part there should be a way left to liberty, magnanimity, and a mind, such as can know its origin, and be one with that supreme mind of the whole ?

Therefore, remember thy privilege and advantage: what it is to have *a mind ;* and that as for all those thoughts, concerning what shall become of the world or of the age, all this is senseless, and to think after this manner is in reality *to be without a mind.*\*

Again.[1]—See of what nature those impressions are that are made from outward things and the circumstances of the world ! But a little while since, when thou hadst retired to thy studies, and thy thoughts were employed on those latter ages, the people and men of those times, and on the affairs of mankind and of the world in general, thou hadst little or no concern (more than what was right) for those poorer and more inconsiderable interests of home occasions, household and family businesses, town and country affairs, no not even for that which is called thy country, in the largest, vulgar sense. So little was all this, and even the whole state of Europe and of the world, as it now stands in comparison with what it once was, when learning, virtue, philosophy, flourished, and liberty was known and enjoyed. It was with respect to those more glorious times that all the regret and trouble arose. It was here the shocks were strongest. It was *philosophy, liberty, ancients.*

Of late it has happened that reading has been set aside. Other duties called : the care of a father, brother, sister, a family, servants. Now, it is here again that disturbance arises; here are the present hindrances, the crosses, disappointments, re-jolts; and from those of the other sort thou art free. Now, what can be more mean and poor ?—that thou shouldst thus be cured of one of these dispositions by the other, and yet not by reason ! Dost thou not see that thou art not only a slave to the present, but a slave in reserve too to those other things by that time thou hast broken again from these present masters, to return to those ? How comes it that all is not at present as it

\* This when in Holland, from July, 1688, to April, 1689.
[1] St. Giles, Dec., 1699.

was but some months since with relation to these affairs?
Hadst thou not a family then as now? the same friends,
relations, country, as now? and was not the care and concern
the same? But it was not an anxious care, it was then as it
ought to be. These things were little, narrow, poor, vile, and
perishing. And are they changed since then? Is it not still
barbarity, Goths. Or, what thinkest thou now at this present
of titles—nobility, barons, counts, now that thou art placed
amongst them?[1] Are they become new things? Are the
ancients out of date? Are these the only times, the only men?
Is lineage or family a concern? Is the State a concern? Was
it to have been so, though thou hadst lived even then and in
those governments? How therefore, even now and in these?
But, wilt thou not set aside the thoughts both of those and these?
Wilt thou not remember another family, in which thou art
included? Another state and magistracy, and other economy,
other laws, another birth and derivation?* What thou art worthy
of, and what are the things beneath thee?

If these things sink away in thy memory and the
impressions of those other prevail, if thou canst not be present
at once with these things and with those, it remains, then, either
that thou shouldst wholly retire, or, in the phrase of a pious
writer, be present as though not present, act as though not
acting, use as though not using: but as one concerned about
another use, the attention being still elsewhere and to other
things, firmly fixed, never suspended, never interrupted by any
attention to ought else. And if other matters cannot be carried
on upon these terms; if this lower degree of attention will not
serve for outward things; if on this account there be less ability,
less dexterity, less management (as needs must where there
is less presence of mind): be it so. Thou canst do no better,
and this is as it should be; for it is not thy design to quit
thy chief part for any other; or for the esteem of such as these,
to lose all esteem with God and with thyself.

Observe how that no sooner does the mind set itself to
reform or bring anything in order in outward affairs (a house,

---

[1] Shaftesbury became an Earl in 1699.
* cf. *Epict. Ench.*, c. xiii.

family, public, relation, friend,) but straightway an earnestness and hope arises; and a certain perfection in the thing managed (not the management) is that which is aimed at and becomes the end. This is the ὄρεξις [desire]. Here it perpetually grows. Hence frustration, loss, disturbance; and how should it be otherwise whilst this perfection is dreamt of and the bent is hitherward? Is this the perfection to be sought after? Are these the subjects of such a bent and application? Is not all this ruinous, and never to be made otherwise? Yet see what fancy makes of it when once thou settest about any of these things with any earnestness or remarkable intention? What perfections! What projects for duration and stability! What proposals! What ends!

How therefore trust thyself? how venture out to reformations, settlements, economies? See the danger of this, see what every moment occurs in the least things. Therefore begin (as* ordered) at the least things. Is it a plant thou cherishest? Remember it is a plant, the seasons must injure it; it must wither, it must die. Is it another plant (a human one), a servant, child? Is it not the same? Must not the seasons have power over it? the age, customs, manners, opinions? Must it not partake of the common distemper? Or wouldst thou κακίαν μὴ εἶα: κακίαν [have badness not to be badness, *Epict. Ench.*, c. xiv.]. If not, then what are these but πρὸς καθάρματα [suitable for outcasts]? What art thou rectifying. Opinions?—No, for they will still retain their own.—How then should they act, but according to these? what fruit should they bear but according to their stock? Is it not ridiculous to look for other? Change the stock, engraft other opinions.—I cannot.—Then suffer the plant to bear as is natural to it, and be not angry that the bramble should be the bramble and not the rose.

But why are there no more roses?—This is not the season, let that content thee. When it is good for the universe, the universe will in due season produce them again. In the meanwhile, be thou the rose, and instead of murmuring, admire that at such a season of the world, any sound opinions should have fallen to thy share, and that it should have been in thy power to produce

* *Epict. Disc.*, Bk. II., c. viii., and c. xvii., § 11.

any fruit of that kind. Μέγας ὁ θεὸς, &c.—*Epict. Disc.*, Bk. I.,
c. xvi., § 17.

Remember the aloes plant (which thou didst see in
Holland), of which not one in a hundred makes a shoot;
nor that one perhaps in a hundred years. But then, how
vast, how mighty a plant! Remember this when thou thinkest
of Socrates or any such, and say not of the age why does it not
produce oftener? For this is being angry at the aloes. Fool!
dost thou understand the nature of the aloes? or (what is far
more) dost thou understand the nature of the whole?

Observe the course of attention[1] as applied to human
affairs: how from the suspending the attention of one sort, the
other attention prevails, so as to cut off the retreat to that first;
from a small attention at first, to an earnest application with
hope and desire; from thence to a general scheme and plan of
affairs, contriving, building, setting out; and from hence an idea
of symmetry, order, perfection. In what? Ἐν τοιούτῳ οὖν ζόφῳ
καὶ ῥύπῳ καὶ τοσαύτῃ ῥύσει τῆς τε οὐσίας, &c. [In such darkness
then and dirt, and in so constant a flux.—*Mar. Aur. Med.*, Bk. V.,
§ 10]. Where is the symmetry, order or proportion, that can be
given to things of this kind? How can they take this form which
thou wouldst have them take? To seek for order or settlement
here, is it not to break (as far as in thee lies) the symmetry,
order, and disposition of the whole? Is not the course of things
contrariwise? Is not this against the habit and the constitution
of the whole? What an imperfection, what a deformity, what a
ruin (oh, profane and impious man!) wouldst thou be author of,
shouldst thou be able to bring to pass that other imaginary
perfection and draw the whole of things to thy model and
design?

Why fearful of any event? If it be not according to the
laws of thy first and greatest country; if it be not for the good
of the whole and according to the economy and order of the
whole; be sure it will never happen. If it be in accord there-
with; what else wouldst thou have happen?

---

[1] Attention is here applied in the stoical sense.

# NECESSITY.

If anything now acting or formerly acted in the world, grieve and disturb thee (as the ruin of Greece, a Lysander, an Alcibiades, a Demades, a Phillip, a Cæsar, Pharsalia, Philippi, Prætorian band, Goths, superstitions), and if thy passion and bent be to remedy and correct what is of this kind, remember:—

(1) How vain and ridiculous the thing is itself, considering the vastness of time and substance—the abyss before and after—the fleeting generations of men and other beings, waves of the sea, leaves, grass, the perpetual change and conversion of things one into another.

(2) That this was necessary, from causes necessary, and (whether Providence or atoms) could be thus only, and could not have been otherwise.

(3) That this is not only what was *necessary*, but what was *best*, since the mind or reason of the universe cannot act against itself; and what is best for itself, itself surely best knows. What I know and am assured of, is, that if it be best for the whole, it is what should have been, and is perfect, just and good,—But this is not best for men ; how knowest thou this ? Knowest thou all former ages of men and all to come ? the connection of causes and how they operate ? the relations of these to those ? the dependence and consequences ? how it shall be with mankind at one time, and how at another ?  But what if it were ill for mankind; is it therefore ill for the whole ? Or ought the interest and good of the whole to give way, be set aside, or passed, for such a creature as man and his affairs ? Are the laws of the universe on this account to be annulled, the government of the universe subverted, and the constitution destroyed ? For thus it must be, if any one cause be removed ; and thus the whole (which is one concatenation), must necessarily be rendered imperfect, and hence totally perish.

What if a Solon or Lycurgus had said *be it thus*, wouldst

thou have resisted his will ? Would thou have withstood the legislator ? Wouldst thou have broken his model for the sake of some one thing that thou perhaps mightst fancy better ? Or wouldst thou have presumed to have stopped so much as for one moment the promulgation and sanction of those laws on which the welfare of Athens or Sparta depended ?

But what is Athens or Sparta compared with this other city ? What is Solon or a Lycurgus in respect of that other law-giver ? And darest thou yet murmur ? Darest thou yet repine ? *Quicquid corrigere est nefas* [what is a crime to amend.—*Horace*, Bk. I., Ode 24.] And, knowing this, wilt thou still meditate remedies, and correct what is passed ? Now, instead of this, see what thy part, and remember the *precept given. For, were we to go back so as to act over again that which is passed, being conscious as we now are of what the ruler has willed, our part would be to will the very same and to co-operate even towards those very things which at present are against nature, and which it is our part to strive against. If I were conscious (says †Epictetus) of what was decreed me, and could be certain of what were to happen before it happened, I would will that and that only; suppose it sickness; suppose it infamy; suppose it death. At present, since I know not the utmost will of nature, I pursue the design and intention of it, as in my particular nature is shown me; I repel injury; I decline sickness; I decline untimely and violent death. But if I knew how this was to be controlled; if I knew what else was appointed : I would turn to this; and this should be the object of my aim; this I would affect, and nothing but this. But (says one) it may thus happen, that I may also will that I be wicked. Not if there were a possibility left of its being any otherwise; but if no possibility, I will however be pious and good (that is to say I will be happy) as long as is allowed me, as long as I possibly can be so. If I cannot be so the moment that follows, at least I will remain so this present moment that precedes, and will join my applause to what God has for the best decreed. For to will against that which is best, and to will

* *Epictetus Disc.*, Bk. II., c. x., § 5.
† In the words of Chrysippus, *Epict. Disc.*, Bk. II., c. vi., § 9.

what is impossible, what else were this but to be wicked and miserable? Now that every creature should seek its good and not its misery, is necessary in itself; nor can it be supposed the will of God that a creature should do otherwise than thus, for this is contradictory and consequently impossible even with God. So that my will towards virtue is irrefragable and immutable; but towards life, death, poverty, riches, and all other exterior things it is variable upon occasion. And I am ready to will any of these, not merely when necessary and unavoidable, but when it depends still upon my own will whether it shall be thus or not.

Where, therefore, is it that I place the good of man? Where else but in his will? If it be so constituted as to receive whatever is sent, all is well; if it resist, there it is that calamity arises. And thus wickedness and misery have the same foundation. But, if I separate these, and think misery one thing and vice another; if I think piety and virtue may live one way and happiness another; if I suppose either pleasure or riches, or life, or any outward thing to be my good, and find myself deprived of these, disappointed, urged, constrained, where will be my piety? In what way can I acquiesce in that which is my ill? In what way can I will against my good?

See what it is to wish earnestly against anything that is likely to happen, whatever it be (as either loss of fame, friends, family, or country). For suppose that according to the course of things, it shall happen contrary to thy wish (the scheme of nature and the universal design being perhaps contrary to thy own scheme and particular design) wouldst thou undo this if in thy power? wouldst thou wish it should otherwise happen than as supreme goodness has ordered it? *Or, is it not supreme goodness that orders?* Ask thyself but this question, and see if thou canst go on with such a head-strong desire and propensity, such an ὄρεξις [desire] or ἔκκλισις [aversion] as this. For, either thou must determine against goodness in the whole, or be an enemy to that goodness and to the prosperity of the whole, as well as to thy own prosperity, by being like one of those slavish people that refuse liberty when offered them. But, be thou as unlike such as is possible σεαυτὸν πάσης ὥρας εἰς ἐλευθερίαν, μετὰ τοῦ εὐμενῶς, και ἀπλῶς, καὶ αἰδημόνως [by forming thyself hourly

to freedom conjoined with benevolence, simplicity, and modesty.
—*Mar. Aurel., Med.,* Bk. VIII., § 51.]

Consider whether, in a wise and just commonwealth, thou
hast at any time abhorred sedition, faction, tumult, disobedience
to the laws and contempt of the law-giver and founder; whether
thou hast at any time detested insolent and rude behaviour
towards a magistracy, sullen and stubborn behaviour towards
parents. Consider if there be in nature any impiety, any
sacrilege, and then think of what a nature it is to murmur and
repine at what happens in the universe, or (what is the same)
to be concerned and tremble for what is likely to happen, and
seems stated and determined already in the order of things.

Return now, therefore, to the same thoughts as before on
the folly and stupidity of those reasonings about the duration
of things; about ancients, governments, empires, summer,
winter. How ridiculous to wish, hope, apprehend, forebode,
decline, incline variously and anxiously in these affairs, when at
the same time so far from knowing what is best. I mean not
what is universally best (for as to that there is nothing to
doubt), but what is particularly so, for this or that part of
things for which thou art so particularly concerned.

First, then, what a shame to wish against *the whole* and
against that general good and universal, highest, greatest,
noblest interest! And what folly too! Since this interest must
and will prevail, whether thou art willing or not willing, pleased
or not pleased.

In the next place, what shame and folly to wish this way
and that way, for and against things as turning and guiding
them to and again, when thou knowest not what would be the
consequence. Or if thou knewest that such or such an end would
be compassed, thou knowest not then which way to turn, or
after all couldst thyself answer that one poor question, *and what
then?*

What wouldst this empire produce? Or if not one
empire, but a balance, what would even this produce? What
did the balance of Greece produce when evenest? what did
an Athens and Sparta? Will the people be even better? Shall
we have a juster or more virtuous than the one; a politer, more
civilized, than the other? Can there come an empire of greater

power than that of Rome? or emperors better than some of those who governed successively for a certain time? And yet how was it even at that time? And what followed afterwards? —Prætorian band; empire by auction; destruction, prey, ravage; arts, letters, sciences perishing; misery, superstition, anarchy, barbarity, Goths. See on the other side Thucydides and his state of Greece, and yet what better? What more to be expected or hoped than what he represents? What better state of liberty, of letters, arts, sciences, philosophy and virtue than in that and the next succeeding age?

But be it so. I would have this age again, this situation of affairs, this face of things. And how knowest thou what that is which may soonest bring it on? or bring on what is *best* or likest to this state, the best thou knowest? How knowest thou whether the present hasty growth of the power[1] thou fearest, as universal monarchy coming on, may not be the best means of breaking it? and whether a present check may not perhaps give it a stronger though slower growth over mankind? or that this attempt so easily crushed may not give greater caution to a new attempter, and a better occasion of oppressing the world less apprehensive of such a power and thinking it time enough to confederate when it is too late? What of such a Prince as the present Suede, had he known a Xenophon, or been bred as Alexander, or Cæsar? What a use could be made of modern religion did a leader know the use of it, yet free and unentangled by it? What a foundation for military virtue, and an empire; were discipline known? How much mischief from the best causes? What uncertainties! what operations of causes! what contrariety of effects! How wish? how hope? how prescribe or dictate to Providence? what present state? what future? what change in governments? what in religion? what as to these Gothic models in either? How knowest thou how the rise or fall of a certain superstition may operate? whether it be best it should fall or not fall? in part, or altogether? whether it can stand in part, if not altogether?—How has the Greek language been preserved hitherto, and to what must it still be owing?—Destruction of letters by the Ottomans, Mahomet,

[1] France.

Believers. What from that seed scattered? What from that military and spiritual joint-power, if once a great prince or two successively? What of the Jews, if again collected?—the power of such a mark as circumcision, their numbers, other nations circumcised, a Messias conqueror, a new Cyrus, Christian or Jewish, a Tamerlane.—On the one side hierarchy, modern religion, letters; on the other, Scythians, Goths, barbarity, no letters. — From superstition, atheism; from atheism, superstition, a wilderness, abyss, darkness, perplexity, loss.— And what is all this to thee? why darkness? why perplexity, or loss, but because thou wilt thyself? What is there here but natural, most natural, good, sovereignty, good and best?

Enough, enough. Commit this to the mind that governs and knows how to govern in this other world; and govern thou thy own, govern what is committed to thee, what concerns thee, and what thou art capable of. Wouldst thou be a Phaeton, and take the reins (suppose) but for a day or two? Or, thinkest thou that thou shouldst make better work if this government were laid upon thy shoulders?—O, the Atlas! O, the Hercules! What a world should we have from thy managing wast thou to manage or bear it for a while! And wilt thou manage it? Wilt thou, then, be setting thy shoulders to it and heaving?— Bravely done; to it again; another lift and it will do. Now the age! Lean to this side and now to that. Bring it to rights. Now it runs right. *Rule! Fly!* Anon the game will be up.— Right; for so it will be. It is almost up already. The business of life is well nigh over, and thou art still at *rule* and *fly!* Man! what is all this? Away! Come to thyself and be in earnest. Be once a man yet before thou diest.

"O, the world! the world! What will become of the world? The poor world! sad world! and was there ever such a world?"—Fool! was there ever any other world? was it ever other than it is?—Where is the world going?—Nowhere, but there where it has gone a thousand and a thousand times : the earth round the sun, or the sun round the earth, annual, diurnal, eternal. Hither and thither, and hither again. Dark and then light. Winter and then summer, and then winter again. Is not this right? Would it please you, should it be otherwise?—Nay, but for the world's sake.—What world? Saturn, Jupiter, the planets

and their circles? Fear not; they will go as they stand. And
if these greater and including circles hold but their order, I
warrant thee (man!) these inward ones (the circles and revolutions of this planet of thy own) will go well enough, and as they
should go, both for the planets' sake, and for the rest of the
system. Fear then for thy own sake if thou pleasest, but for
the world there is care taken, the administration is good. Do
not thou father thy own wretched fears on it, and place thy
selfishness and low-spiritedness to so wrong an account.

The Universal Monarchy coming.[1]—Must it never come?
Has it not come already more than once or twice in a few ages?
a Cæsar, Alexander, Cyrus. And how many before Cyrus?
How many Alexanders, forgotten long since? How many Cæsars
are past? and how many more yet to come, within the same
periods of time?—But (alas! in my time!—Man! What is
thy time? Why not in thy time? Will it be worse for the world
in thy time than in any other?—But I must make my endeavour.
I would stop it.—So would I a plague or earthquake, if I knew
how. Tell me how I should stop it, but not by any means, not
at any rate, not at the loss of my integrity, my sincerity, truth,
modesty, my good will towards men, and my obedience to Deity.
For, let this other matter happen as it will, or let it come when
it will, I am resolved to be as well satisfied with Providence
then, as I am now. But, in what way this satisfaction is
brought about; in what way such a mind is acquired, and how
preserved; by what discipline and regimen; what studies, what
order of life, what rules; this thou well knowest. And
wouldst thou break these rules?—Right, and for honesty's sake
be a villain! For what is it to be a villain? What is it to
have neither faith nor conscience? A mind to which there
is no trust? A will to which the supreme will is no rule? To
hate men, and to murmur at Providence?

What wouldst thou?—That which is for the good of the
world.—Who knows what is good, what best for it? Who
should know but the Providence that looks after it? And what
is it that this Providence would have me do? Fight against

---

[1] The dread that Louis XIV. would establish a universal monarchy
is here meant.

itself ? Oppose and thwart ?—No, but accompany, applaud.—
Why act then, or why do anything against the course of things ?
—Because I know not as yet the course of things, because
Providence has not declared : for, when that has declared, I
declare with it, and am of its side ; thus I would have it to be,
and not otherwise.

Ruin is coming !—What ruin ? Of the world ? the real
world ? the whole universal world ?—No, but of my part of the
world, and that which to me is the whole world. Be it so. But
is thy world a world by itself, or is it dependent on the other
world ?—Dependent.—And by what order does the ruin come ?
By what other than that which governs the world is its support
and safety ? Let it come then, for if it did not, what would
become of the world indeed ?

Universal Monarchy !— Remember the real, universal
monarchy, the good, the wise, the just, the excellent, the divine.
What monarchy but this ? What is there that can happen out
of this ? contrary to this ? or otherwise than by the universally
advantageous salutary laws of this at once both absolute
monarchy and absolute equal and most perfect commonwealth ?

Thou wishest well to the world (thou sayest).—Why sigh
then ? why groan, repine, and mourn ? Is it for something out
of the world ?—No, but for something in the world, otherwise
than as happens according to the laws, interest, and government
of the world. This is wishing ill, not well to the world.

Thou wishest well to the world. Come on then ; let us see
the trial. Is it a tooth ? an eye ? a leg, or an arm ? Give it to
the world ; surrender it with a good heart ; resign it τοῖς ὅλοις
in favour of the constitution and laws that establish it. Is it a
relation, brother, friend ? an estate, a country ? Let us see what
country thou art of, and what thy world is : whether thou art
truly a citizen of the world, or, as they say, a mere worldling ?
Tied to a place, a corner, carcass, and things belonging.

What is it ?—A station in the public ; good.—But it goes ill
with it.—With what ? With the public, where thou hast no part
in it ? What hast thou to do then ? Or where thou hast a part :
what hast thou to do then, but mind that part ?—But that part
suffers.—How ?—A name, a reputation, an interest lost.—So are
other names lost, other interests, how many good men defamed !

I

How many reputations injured ? Memories abused ?—But this is mine.—How is it thine ? Say then, thou wretch : say the truth ; that it is because it is (as thou sayest) *thine.* This is thy trouble. This is thy concern ; for as to the public it is the same, and as to thy part the same still. For if it be to bear ignominy and reproach for the public, this is a part still, and one of the noblest of parts. " Βασιλικὸν εὖ μὲν πράττειν, κακῶς δὲ ἀκούειν." [It is royal to do good and be abused.—*Antisthenes* in *Mar. Aurel., Med.*, Bk. VII., § 36.]

What disturbs ?—The public interest.—How can the public (the real public) suffer ?—But my private interest—right. But how comes it that a name or an opinion (viz., another's opinion, not thy own) should be thy interest ? Man ! trouble not thy head. In the higher public all is well ; if not, why toil in this lower wretched one ? All is according to the interest it ought to be. And as for thy own interest : if thou wilt, it may be the same, and in the same prosperous condition ; if not, see who is in fault.

A reputation is lost—and what then ?—My service in the public—and what then ?—O that the public should have such a loss in me ! Admirable ! But say it more rightly. O that this should happen which for the good of the real public is best should happen ! O that I should lose and be a sufferer where there is no loss or sufferance ; but where, if I please, I may profit and make advantage.

Πόσους ἤδη ὁ αἰὼν Χρυσίππους, πόσους Σωκράτεις, πόσους Ἐπικτήτους καταπέπωκε ; [How many a Chrysippus, Socrates, and Epictetus have sunk in the gulf of time ?—*Mar. Aurel., Med.*, Bk. VII., § 19]. And not only such as shone like them, but how many who being as great as they, were yet never known so much as beyond their own city, or hardly perhaps in that ? How many hid even in Athens ? How many that got their living by labour, as Cleanthes ? How many in Sparta, where they could not shine or be distinguished, all being in one and the same discipline, same style ; eloquence and writing, being not in use ? Where had been even the philosophy of Athens but for the muses in the pen of Xenophon and Plato ? What had Socrates been (as to memory) but for these two ? and even by these had he ever been celebrated or mentioned but for the accident of his death, which gave such lustre ? a death which being forbidden to be spoken of, was so artfully represented and with such effect by the tragedian, so finely touched in the same way by Xenophon in his *Cyropaideia*, and so adorned and rendered so illustrious a tragedy in Phaedo. Thence the real history, memoirs, defence ? *Apology.* All from this death, so much lamented, for which Providence has been so oft questioned, for which thou thyself so often hast been disturbed. Had it not been for this where had been either the first or second memoirs ? where had been the subject, or where the spirit of his historian or poet ? the hero, author, or poet-philosopher ? the chastity, simplicity, politeness, justness of the one, or the divine enthusiasms of the other ?

Consider also amongst the Socratics how many unknown besides Æschylus and how many of the same kind contemporaries or otherwise at Thebes, Megara, Syracuse in Sicily, Rhodes, and the innumerable islands and commonwealths, as well as the other Greek colonies in Asia. Also how many truly great from the age of Marcus and in the decline of things : all swallowed in dark oblivion.

What is there that will move thee (oh, hard-hearted man !) if this will not ? viz.: What is done is ἐπὶ σωτηρίᾳ τοῦ τελείου ζῴου, τοῦ ἀγαθοῦ, καὶ δικαίου, καὶ καλοῦ. &c. [for the conservation of the one perfect living being, the good and just, and beautiful. —*Mar. Aur., Med.,* Bk. X., § 1.]

# POLITICAL AFFAIRS.

(τὰ πολιτικά.)

"Ἀλλ' ἡ πατρίς, ὅσον ἐπ' ἐμοί 'φησίν ἀβοήθητος ἔσται · πάλιν, ποίαν καὶ ταύτην βοήθειαν; ["But my country, you say, as far as it depends on me, will be without my help. I ask again, what help do you mean?"—*Epict. Ench.*, c. xxiv., § 4.]

Remember the politic, admired novelist, and esteemed patriot of former times; on every piece of news a *great thing!* and how ridiculous at last this came to be; how it appeared to thyself, even at that early time. How therefore should it appear *now?* Priamus and his kingdom destroyed—a great thing!—The city consumed, the storks' nests burnt—a great thing!—Achilles is angry, a Prince has the confederacy; Patroclus is dead, and now Achilles—great things!—But remember indeed where the great thing lies, and what is truly a Great Thing.*

To the grave legislators, orators, authors, advisers, and politic dealers, Aristotelians, Machiavellians, memoir readers or writers, Gothic or ancient modellers, or collectors; with all that din of state dogmatists, prescribers, moralizers, exhorters, praisers, censurers, such as the D——t's, the Fl——r's, M——th's, L——'s, &c. Remember ὦ φίλτατοι νομοθέται, [O, beloved legislators.—*Ep. Disc.* II., c. i., 25] and add to this fancy such an accosting as this in imagination : "Most noble physician of the state and inward man! great judge of morals! dispenser of happiness, wisdom, and sovereign health to mankind! Your hand, I entreat you, that I may once feel your pulse, for with you doubtless all is sound and well; at least you yourself know whatever is otherwise and can straightway apply the remedy.

" How now, doctor, what have we here? a fever! convulsions! and you yourself ignorant of this?—A hectic! a catarrh! an ulcer! scabs and running! and all this overlooked? Is this

---

* cf. *Epict. Discourses*, Bk. I., c. xxviii.

100

(O noble physician!) thy own bodily state? Is it thus under thy gown? within doors, thus? thus with thee in the family? thus with domestics? *Pelle decorus?* [Pers. Sat. IV., xiv.] And dost thou come abroad thus adorned, thus specious and imposing on us and on thyself? for on thy own domestics, or those who know thee, thou canst not impose. Physician cure thyself, or let us see, at least, such prescriptions as thou followest thyself. Let us see the effect of these in thyself, and then talk to us, then prescribe. Otherwise *Di te, Damasippe, Deaeque Verum ob consilium donent tonsore* ["May the gods and goddesses, Damasippus, present you with a barber for your wise counsel.".—*Hor.*, Sat. Bk. II., iii., lines 16-17.] Remember that, I for my part, have a better than Damasippus to go to. But that in this age there lives not so much as a Damasippus, a quack or empiric, in this method or of this regimen, therefore the more need of strictness.

See by experience the excellency of that rule : Μὴ περὶ ἀνθρώπων ψέγοντες ἢ ἐπαινοῦντες ἢ συγκρίνοντες [Converse not about men as blaming them or praising them or comparing them.—*Epict. Ench.*, c. xxxiii., § 2], and so οὐδένα ψέγει, οὐδένα ἐπαινεῖ [blames no one, praises no one.] For remember in Lord P——'s case (as just above a *great thing!*) How? In what? —Brave—yes, furious, foaming at mouth, a wild boar.—Wise, learned—astrology, legends and superstition beyond modern. How in the nursery? how with servants? wife? children? how formerly at a court? How many ways hast thou happened to see in this very person, what this greatness is, thou so much admirest by whiles?—But this is for the sake of virtue and my country.—See, therefore, what thou makest of thyself whilst acting thus (as thou sayst) for virtue and thy country? How subjected? how depressed? how made a slave? an admirer of men and things : things outward : play-things : nothings. Is this virtue? Is this thy service? But enough.

Be this so no more. Be but thou virtuous thyself, and go the way towards it that is shown thee. Let others go theirs : thou thy own. Let others praise the virtuous, that can praise and dispraise so cheaply, and at their ease. But for thy own part, be contented not to praise so much as virtue itself and θάρρει [courage]. Be not afraid that by this thou shalt betray virtue or seem the less a virtuous or honest man, if need be. Though what need? What besides being so? What is seeming in the case?

Remember the same busy actor in politics at every meeting, "Well! where are we?" So for many years, at last how nauseous? So at this hour that many more years are past, were he to be heard, would it not be the same still? "Well! where are we?" With what pleasure is this said by all those lovers of novelty, revolutions, changes, political schemes, and State transactions?— "Come let us sit down (now that we are by ourselves) and consider how things stand, and whereabouts we are.—How well would this be in another way? In a way not thought of, though much truer? How well would it be if he brought this delight, this curiosity, this inquiry homewards, and to a place more nearly touching us than either our country, or town, or family?—*No*. But how goes the world?—Ridiculous! How should it go? How, but as it has ever gone and ever will? Just the same, the very same. But what of that? And what though it went otherwise? Art thou the leader of it? Art thou responsible? Is it thy charge? Assigned to thee? THINE and at thy peril?—How goes the world?—No matter; but how go I? This is a matter, and the only matter. This is of concern. This mine, and at my peril.—How do I govern? The world?—No. But how do I govern MYSELF?—How do matters stand with me?— No. But how do I stand with matters? Are matters burdensome?—Thank myself. They needed not to have been so. Does the world go cross?—How cross? Should the world follow me, or I the world? Is it the world that is wrong, or am I wrong? See which!

Whither away? Hello! ho! What chase is this? What a pursuit art thou again engaged in? What madness! And is this sport? Is it the play? the game and management only? the chessmen, cards? αἱ ψῆφοι; οἱ κύβοι; [the counters, the dice.—*Epict. Disc.*, Bk. II., c. v., § 3]. Why then these pangs, these reachings? Is not this earnest? Hast thou forgotten ὅτι οὐ δεῖ προηγεῖσθαι τῶν πραγμάτων, ἀλλ' ἐπακολουθεῖν [that we ought not to lead events, but to follow them.—*Epict. Disc.*, Bk. III., c. x., § 18]. Stop therefore in this career.

Wonder not at the saying; but say often with thyself, and render it familiar: that in all this, an honest man should be as free and easy as a knave. Grant it otherwise, and see how long the honest man will hold honest. For what is knavery but narrowness?—*myself,* that is to say, *my purse against the public purse, my family against the public family,* and what difference between this, and *my nation or commonwealth against the world? my country laws against the universal laws? my fancy against the Divine decree?*

Remember how many have been and are every day knaves for their country: some of whom nothing else perhaps would have made knaves. Themistocles against an Aristides and against a Phocion; even a Phocion himself, perhaps, in some decree against the grave and good Xenocrates, his fellow-ambassador; the elder Cato as in opposition to the younger. In these latter days, the DeWitts, the disposition of a Mr. F——r, thy old acquaintance. The Dutch patriot, the English patriot, the Scotch. The contests about trade, precedency, honour, the flag, England, mistress of the world! giving laws to the world! and such like speeches. But go now and tell us of *justice, faith, honesty, the public!* The excellent public! the noble public-spirits! Remember too what Socrates says in Plato of such as these, how pleasant a mockery, and how handsomely called knaves, ὅταν κατορθῶσι λέγοντες πολλὰ . . . μηδὲν εἰδότες ὧν λέγουσιν, ["in which condition they say many grand things, not knowing what they say.—*Plato, Meno.,* 99 C.]; and also the words of Socrates in the Apology, εὖ γὰρ ἴστε, ὦ ἄνδρες Ἀθηναῖοι . . . οὐ γάρ ἐστιν ὅστις ἀνθρώπων σωθήσεται, οὔτε ὑμῖν οὔτε ἄλλῳ πλήθει οὐδενὶ γνησίως ἐναντιούμενος, &c. ["for I am certain, men of Athens, that no man who goes to war with you or any other multitude, honestly struggling against the commission of unrighteousness and wrong in the state, will save his life."—31 E.]

# FRIENDS.

Why silent? why thus reserved and deeply thoughtful? why these looks, this cloud?—Why not?—'Tis rigid, 'tis severe. Am I severe?—Nay, but to yourself.—Is it then that you pity me? Know you my case so well? Or, say, why is it that you pity? Why am I thus far a concern to you? why thus prefer my friendship?—For virtue.—Know you then how this matter stands with me, or how I came by such a thing (if such a thing I have?), on what terms and by what tenure I hold this character and quality by which it seems I hold your friendship. Or, if honesty be not indeed a quality of such great worth or rarity, why esteem me for this alone?—But we would not have it to be alone; we would have other qualities besides.—As what, for instance? As of a jester, fiddler, dancer?—No, but of a good companion.—Who are better companions than these? who are those they call good companions? and of what character? Are they indeed friends? are the men of wit, the entertainers of company, the story-tellers, the raisers of mirth, friends? or of a friendly character?—How reconcile this? How is it that these qualities shall be made to agree?

But it is sad to see this countenance, thoughtfulness, reserve. Say, then, suppose it were indeed a fiddler, but of the better sort, a Corelli perhaps, or some other master in that way, or in sculpture, or in painting. Or what if instead of a fiddler, a philosopher (as was once the way) were kept in the great family as an appurtenance, a historiographer, mathematician, rhetorician, linguist, would you expect this service from him? this entertainment? Would you expect that such a one should be company? Or would you be angry and think it strange that such a one should muse, or plod, or for the most part keep silence?

No, but on the contrary, were such a one ever so backward in company, dull, heavy, stupid (if you will), without attention to the ordinary discourse, his eyes ever and anon fixed, and his whole figure often like one half-awake or in a dream, would not this be far from strange or ill-taken ? Would it not rather be looked on as natural, in no way disagreeable, but the contrary, and in truth agreeable to such a character ? How else could you expect the genius in whatever kind ? How else the music ? the good composition ? the good ordering ? the design and masterly hand ?

So, here, in another science and mastership. How else the music ? the good ordering ? the life ? the friend ? Or is this nothing ? No art ? no science at all ? an accident ? a thing of course ? a bit of temper, education, birth ? a matter of no concern, no care ? " Forgive me, my good friends, I love you too well to hearken to you, and though but for your own sakes alone, shall take better care." Οὐ λυσιτελεῖ μοι οὐδὲ τῇ πόλει οὐδὲ τοῖς φίλοις ἀπολέσαι καὶ πολίτην ἀγαθὸν καὶ φίλον. ["It is not expedient for myself, nor my country, nor my fellow citizens, to destroy what constitutes the good citizen and the friend."]— *Epict. Disc.*, Bk. III., c. xxiv., § 49.

But, my friends! What indeed will my friends think ?— "This is below him, below his quality, not as becomes him, not as the world expected of him."—What quality ? What is the thing becoming ? What is the world ?—But they will think this poor and mean, low-spirited, sad. They will sigh for me, be ashamed for me.—Ashamed, with reason ? How so ? Be ashamed then for thyself, whether they be ashamed or not. For their shame is not the business. 'Tis thy own business now ; a very just and real one, if there be any shame, if there be really that which is shameful.—Nay, but they are unjust in their shame ; they are ashamed for no reason.—Whose is the shame, then ? Is it not first their shame, and a very great one, thus to be ashamed of an honest man, their friend ? thus to abandon virtue and think it mean ? thus to submit and yield to the scoffs of villainy and vice, to the corruption of riches and honours bestowed on villainy and vice ? and thus to strive with their utmost endeavour to make their friend yield also and sink under the same corruption ? Is this good and worthy in them ? Is this kind ? Is this generous, fair, or handsome ? But whose is the shame then ? And art thou for thy part ashamed ? For what ? If for anything for them and their case. Shame for them who can esteem and think so basely. But for thyself, if it be possible, thou canst be ashamed on thy own account for anything happened to thee as to an honest man, acting honestly and as becomes him. See what shame? See if thou art not thyself turning vile and shameful!—But how relieve my friends? How save them this shame of theirs?—Man, let them look to it themselves. Teach them virtue if thou canst; make them wise, and they will no longer be in pain for thee.—But how in the meantime?—How indeed? What remedy? For besides this there is one only way that I know, which is to set these thoughts of virtue aside and do as they would have thee. And yet even in this way it will not be long that thou canst please them; nor will they be all of one mind and all pleased alike. There will be the same shame then too as now, and thou wilt prove thyself at last a notable gainer by the bargain.—"Thy friends are ashamed of thee" (thou sayest). Then pity them; it is hard not to take them out of pain. But are they ashamed aright?—No, but they love me, however, and it is for me they are ashamed.—Go, then, and act shamefully that they may not be ashamed.

To be ashamed *for another* cannot well or properly be said, (for how is one man's shame another's?), but to be ashamed *of another:* that is to say, being sorry for and pitying in a certain manner another's misbehaviour, and discountenancing it, in as far as one has to do with the person. But to be ashamed for another's *no shame;* this is doubly false and monstrous, as it is corrupt and perfidious. Witness that shame thou once didst observe of the highly esteemed patriot and man of virtue of these times, how, when in gay company he shrunk from one of the best men living and his good friend, because of the mean habit he wore, as likewise did the friends of Socrates when he came abroad in the habit[1] of which Marcus speaks. And remember that same man's behaviour when once at an inn out of town in company with another young man of the same rank with thyself. What an example! what precepts of virtue, continence, temperance! and what passion he fell into on seeing us two so reserved and backward!— Now return to the harangues and treatises; tell me of liberty, country, mankind,

[1] *Mar. Aurel., Med.,* XI., § 28,

schemes, models; write, speak, exhort. These are the declaimers. Wilt not thou hearken and admire, concur and be led?

Remember also another gentleman of the same character and equal renown when talking of love affairs at the table of Atticus (the Atticus of this last age). How well he was reproved and ridiculed by a Lucullus and another great one of the same character that sat by. How much better these?—though these were professed Epicureans, in the secret of the sect, one of them with exquisite learning as well as wit. What are all these and all else, then, but τά πολιτικὰ ταῦτα, καὶ, ὡς ὄιεται, φιλοσόφως πρακτικὰ ἀνθρώπεια, μυξῶν μεστὰ [those persons engaged in political affairs and who imagine themselves philosophers; mere mutterers!—*Mar. Aur., Med.*, Bk. IX., § 29]. And what other conversations dost thou seek? what other discourses hope for? what other friends expect? what friends proof against these tables? what friends not turned, guided, governed by these tables and table-talks? And is it this that moves thee? Do these move thee who are themselves moved by this and such as this is?—Try, then; be once again the table-talk; make it when absent, keep it up and reign in it when present. Approve thyself anew to these table-judges and before these great tribunals that decide characters, distribute fame, reputation, praise, honour, and dishonour. Be well with these, that thy friends may hear well of thee, and not be ashamed any more on thy account, as one given over, censured, or slighted. Go in again as formerly amongst these and hear the noble and wished for sound of ἡδύς ἄνθρωπος, *O lepidum caput!*

What! lose thy friends?—What friends? Art thou to thyself a friend yet? If not, what other friend dost thou expect? Or what friend art thou like to prove to others, if not so to thyself?

All alone! As you see; for want of better company. I have a part, 'tis true, that is fit to come into company, knows company, and is known; but another part that is not so. I have a laughing, talking, entertaining part that does all with others, that admires and is ravished, wonders, praises, censures, rejoices, grieves, and takes on (as they say) with others; and I have a still, quiet, though not less active part, that does none of all this; neither admires, nor loves, nor pursues with others, is never pleased as others are pleased, is never angry but with itself and for what itself can remedy, bemoans nothing, condoles with nobody, nor has with whom to congratulate. The first of these parts is a faithless, corrupt, perfidious, mutinous, sacrilegious part. The second is an honest, friendly, just, pious part; in charity with men, and never at odds with Deity, never of different interests with the one or different will with the other. For the first of these parts, viz., the familiar, conversable, sociable part (for so it will be called), I can find companions enough, a large society; but for this latter, *the truly sociable,* where shall I find a companion, helper; or associate ?

Hitherto thou hast loved, because thou was courted and sought. Those qualities are now gone (let them go) that drew thee this esteem. Come on, let us see now if thou canst love disinterestedly.

" Thanks my good kinsman (brother, sister, friend), for giving me so generous a part, *that I can love though not beloved."*

" O apostate friend; how kind art thou in teaching me this lesson. I cannot indeed love thee more for this; but having once loved thee and made thee my associate, *my friend,* I never will take back my friendship, nor withdraw my love; but will cherish that affection which naturally and of itself inclines me to love with the same tenderness and to hold thy interest and concerns as dear as ever."

# SMALL POSSESSIONS.

## (Κτησείδιον—Δουλάριον—Οἰκάριον.)

Diminutives indeed !—But why are they not felt so ? Is it enough that they are in a certain degree diminished ? that they are not superlatives ? Shall it rest here ? Wretched objects! Wretched thee, who knowest them such, yet honourest them as thou dost ! Others know them not for such ; and therefore know them. Nor is the honour so preposterous. But in thee, what ? Obstinate evils ! How covered over ? how disguised ? what masks ?

Mask of the first (viz., κτησείδιον, δουλάριον) [a small property, a little slave]. Duty : a part, a character.

Mask of the second (viz., οἰκάριον) [a small house]. Philosophical : a way of living, neatness, nature, husbandry, garden. *Hoc erat in votis, modus agri,* &c., and *concha salis puri* [This used to be my wish, a little piece of land and a small shell of pure salt]. Off, off with these masks.

O subtle enemies ! more dangerous than all open ones. O close supplanters ! specious assassins ! bosom snakes ! whose sting goes deepest, and is never felt. Felt only in remote effects : a lingering sickness, preying disease, long operating but more sure and fatal poison.

Recover, resist, repel, strive, arm.—War ! war ! Or otherwise, what peace ?

The τὸ καλόν where ?—Not there, if here.—Rival beauties. Antagonist ideas. Order against order ; opposition. If this a κόσμος, that a chaos, and *vice-versâ.*

The idea of order here in these things. Why once admitted ? why borne with ? why endured ? What order ? and in what ? πηλὸς κομψῶς πεφυραμένος [This body is only a finer mixture of clay.—*Epict. Disc.,* Bk. I., c. i., § 11]. For how long ? and what then ? Who the admirers ? With whom in common ?

Enough, have done. Go to the contrary state ; view that.

Remember Ἐί προκόψαί θέλεις, &c. ["If you wish to improve in wisdom you must be content to be considered foolish and stupid for neglecting external things."—*Epict., Ench.*, c. xiii.]

Now see! in reality and effect that which in idea was reproved (when last retired*).—What hast thou done, O wretch? For what all this? and for whom? What time, what labour, what culture? And on what? on what bestowed?— But the pretext, a *study*, a *retreat*, &c.—Had it not been better to have been building this while, after another manner? Better, sure, to have built a mind on this idea, proof against fire, firm against storms and earthquakes; always temperate, excluding the sharp colds and scorching heats; harbouring no foulness, no entrance or space for vermin; clear, clean, sound, compact, and as a rock. These had been the arches! This the stone, iron, cement! This is the architecture that would have held and answered, been durable, practicable, accountable. This is safety, security: not that. These are proportions and numbers: not those. For what are those, and all of that kind? What proportion between those and a right mind? What between the things there and the condition of human life?

Imitation! Imitation!—See whence these wretched follies, and the disease whence caught and how. † Sight: commendation: affection: affectation: imitation.—How can this be otherwise? How avoid admiration, if forced to praise, or if viewed in company, and with a certain outward satisfaction and seeming delight, or complaisance? Therefore what need of care and strict watch? Else what follows? See! *Diruit, aedificabit mutat quadrata rotundis* [Destroy, build, and convert square into round.—*Hor.*, Epist. I., 1, 100], and thus *longos imitaris* [emulate the great.—*Hor.*, Sat. II., 3, 308].

Commendation therefore and praise ‡ and all accommodation of thyself to others in this way, whether over thy own fabrics and wretched possessions of this kind, or over others by relation, story, description: all equally dangerous.

---

* cf., Self.  † cf., The Beautiful.

‡ To this therefore apply principally that powerful chapter, the lesser warning, viz., *Epict. Disc.* IV., c. ii., Περὶ Συμπεριφορᾶς [On familiar intercourse].

What a noble praise, that of the Roman *that he never built!* For so was it said of Scipio, and esteemed as a continence equal to that other famous part in story.

Whenever these outward managements go heavily, and thou art ready to bemoan thyself that it is not with thee as with others; that the things do not prosper nor flourish as with others; that thy family suffers, thy relations suffer, thy friends, clients, dependents suffer through thy inaptness, inactiveness, and insufficiency in these matters, imagine that thou thus spokest to them (and so speak indeed, but within thyself and in thy own hearing only): "My good friends! I do for you as I can, and all I can, and would satisfy you all if so I could. I mind these concerns for you, an estate for you, and do the best I can for you and for my country. But if minding, indeed, an estate such as you would have me mind, and together with it something besides which you mind not, it happens that I succeed not so well with an estate as you who mind an estate only and nothing else, you must not wonder at, or blame me for it."

But let them wonder and blame on; 'tis natural, they must do so. As to *the thing besides an estate*, 'tis what they know nothing of, nor is it to be told them."

# SELF.

Οὐ γὰρ φιλεῖς σεαυτόν. ἐπεί τοι καὶ τὴν φύσιν ἄν σου, καὶ τὸ βούλημα ταύτης ἐφίλεις· ["For thou lovest not thyself, since if thou didst, thou wouldst love thy nature and her will."—*Mar. Aurel., Med.,* Bk. V., § 1.]

How unaccountable it is to live so as always to reprove one's self for the same things? How senseless and unreasonable always to want to be set right? How ridiculous is it to lose* the way that lies before one, and ever and anon, as if in a strange world, to ask "where am I?"

Resolve, therefore, never to forget thyself. How long is it that thou wilt continue thus to act two different parts and be two different persons? Call to mind what thou art; what thou hast resolved and entered upon; recollect thyself wholly within thyself. Be one entire and self-same man; and wander not abroad, so as to lose sight of the end; but keep that constantly in view both in the least concerns and in the greatest; in diversions, in serious affairs; in company, and alone; in the day time and at night. Let neither ceremony, nor entertainment in discourse, nor pleasantry, nor mirth amongst friends, nor anything of this kind, be the occasion of quitting that remembrance, or of losing that fixed attention. — But what will my carriage be in company? How shall I appear in conversation?— Dangerous consequences! But of what kind?—lest I be called ill-bred; a good companion. But is it not better I should deserve the name of friend? Is it not a better thing to be just, to have integrity, faith, innocency, to be a man, and † a lover of men? And on what this depends thou well knowst.

But if I suffer not myself to be at all transported, how shall I act with forwardness and concern in the public or for a friend?—If it be a part not consistent with the preservation of a character, it is never to be undertaken. If it be consistent, but

* cf. *Mar. Aurel.,* Bk. IV., § 46.　　† cf. Natural Affection.

with another person and not with thee, because thou hast less strength, why undertake a part beyond thy reach? For, first, thou art sure to act ungracefully, nauseously, affectedly, and so as to spoil what thou undertakest; and, in the next place, this is certain, that if thou forgettest *thyself*, thou wilt forget thy duty, and instead of acting for virtue, act for something else very different, as following thy own passion and irrational bent.

But this continual application is tedious and burdensome. Must there be no moments of rest, no indulgence, nor any relaxation?—It is here thou mayst truly cry out, οὐ γὰρ φιλεῖς σεαυτόν [thou lovest not thyself.—*Mar. Aur. Med.*, Bk. V., § 1]. It is here that thou mayst justly say, thou knowest not how to love thyself, or thy own good. What else is there in the world that can give content but this? What else can save from misery? And to neglect this, to be faint, to be remiss, or to give over here: what else is it but to be cruel towards thyself? See how it is with others who place their interest and good in other things. See the covetous, the vain, the ambitious, the effeminate : which of these is thus negligent and forgetful of himself? When is it that the one is weary of thinking of his wealth, the other of his credit and esteem, the other of his power and grandeur, the other of his person and what belongs to it? Take any of these in any circumstances, in any company, engaged in any affairs. It is still easy to observe that they are not so taken out of themselves, but that they still look towards their end. They join with others, they interest themselves and enter into other concerns, but still there is *a reserve*. Another thing is at the bottom, and the respect is elsewhere. Their manners show it and their actions, gesture, and tone of voice— even where they most desire to · hide it.—Nothing is more apparent to one who narrowly observes. How true and just a pattern is this, and how deserving of imitation, in another way. Shall those objects, such as they are, be able thus to allure and attract, and shall not virtue be as prevalent? Are sociable actions and a life according to nature less to be esteemed? Or are they things less beautiful in themselves? Shall he that is a virtuoso, a sculptor, a painter, a musician, an architect, or any one that truly loves his art or science, be wholly taken up with this, be wholly *this* and nothing else; and shall virtue alone be

K

that which fails its student ? Shall he that follows this be the least zealous ? and shall his art be of less moment with him, less attractive, less enchanting ? Yet what number, what proportion, what harmony, symmetry, or order is equal to that which is here ?

Know, therefore, what *thy art* is, and how it is to be adhered to; and remember that every action, even the slightest, which is not done according to it, is both wrong and tending to the destruction of the art itself.

How long wilt thou continue thus to abuse thyself ? Remember that thou hast now no longer any time given thee, but that if hereafter thou shalt again relapse, the thing cannot but prove fatal. Thou hast given way ; thou hast fallen, and repented. How often has this been ? And yet still thou hast engaged, still sallied out, and lived abroad, still prostituted thyself and committed thy mind* to chance and the next comer, so as to be treated at pleasure by every one, to receive impressions from everything, and machine-like to be moved and wrought upon, wound up and governed exteriorly, as if there were nothing that ruled within or had the least control. At length thou hast retired. Thou art again in possession of thyself, and mayest keep so, as thou art come as it were into a new world, and art free of former ties ; unless of thy own accord thou voluntarily and officiously renewest them and art willing to begin where thou didst leave off. Know, therefore, that when thou returnest to the same objects, if presently thou art tempted into the least feeling of that former commotion, then indeed all is lost, thou art overpowered, and canst no longer command thyself. Remember what thou dost carry in thy breast; remember those former inflammations and how suddenly all will take fire when once a spark gets in ; remember the fuel within and those unextinguished passions which live but as in the embers. Think of that impetuous, furious, impotent temper, and what trust is to be given to it. This, too, remember, that as in certain machines that are fastened by many wedges, though they be made ever so compact and firm by this means, yet if one wedge be loosened the whole frame shakes ; so, with

* *Epict. Ench.*, c. xxviii.

respect to the mind, it is not merely in one passion that the mischief is received, but in all ; it is not one spring that loses its accord, but all.

Thus warned and in this different situation of mind approach those things anew, and beware lest thou tread awry; μὴ τὸ ἡγεμονικὸν βλάψῃς τὸ σεαυτοῦ [take care not to injure your own ruling faculty.—*Epict. Ench.,* c. xxxviii.] But what will my friends say ? how will they find me disposed to them ? how shall I bear their altered countenances and their dislike of me ?—Go then, and be again a jester, and tell stories, act, and be industriously ridiculous, for, what is that thou callest wit or humour ? what is the whole of that sort of conversation ? Is this thy service with thy friends ? is it thus thou wouldst be felt ?—But if I enter not affectionately and with warmth into their concerns, if I feel not, so as to be in some degree animated, with what effect can I speak or act ? how assist them by admonition, by reproof, by commendation and exhorting? For without being touched and moved in a certain degree, nothing of this can be gracefully practised, or is to be undertaken.—True. Neither is this the time. Leave that for hereafter; when matters within shall be better established and right habits confirmed. The question at present is not, whether *they* shall be good; but whether *thou thyself* shalt be of any worth or not.

But, how shall I be of aid to others ? of what use shall I be ?— O, folly ! as if it were not apparent that if thou but continuest thus, and art able to persevere, thy example alone (when thou least regardest it) will be of more service than all that thou canst do whilst thou retainest thy selfishness, thy meanness, and subjection, which thou canst not otherwise shake off but by this course. Thou wouldst serve thy country. Right. But consider withal and ask thyself wouldst thou willingly be perjured, wouldst thou be false, wouldst thou lie, flatter, be debauched and dissolute to serve it ? Certainly I would not. But if I think to serve it as I am now bid, all this will necessarily follow. For I must prostitute my mind. I must grow corrupt, interested, false, and where will then be the service I shall render to my country ?— But if I have no sympathy with my friends, how shall I be sensible towards society, or feel any such thing as friendship ?— Stay therefore till thou canst feel this in another way, for this is not a genuine, social feeling; this is not friendship. The same temper which warms so much at present is that which must cool again soon after, and which as it rises must sink. Such is the vicissitude of that sort of passion, and this thou well knowest. But there is a constant, fixed, and regular joy, which carries tranquillity along with it, and which has no rejolt: and this thou knowest too. Wait therefore till this appear, for of this one single moment is better than a life passed in that other tumultuous joy.

Enough has been said. Long since hast thou been convinced and oft have these things been repeated. Remember now to keep firm and to adhere. And remember that the combat is in the smallest things and what seems to be of little moment. If thou art conqueror here, thou art safe. If in these beginnings thou failest, thou art undone and all is given up. See therefore in what a little compass this lies, and in what may be called * "slight things," but which, with respect to thee and to thy progress, instead of being slight, are in reality the only things that are important. All that is serious and solemn lies here; all other things ought to be esteemed as trifles, however grave or pompous. It is this alone that leads to true religion. On this, piety, sanctity, life, duty, happiness depend; to violate aught here is the highest impiety, the highest sacrilege. Begin, therefore, and, as a legislator to thyself, establish that economy or commonwealth within, according to those laws which thou knowest to be just; and swear never to transgress what thou hast thus solemnly decreed and appointed to thyself. Τάξον τινὰ ἤδη χαρακτῆρα σαυτῷ, &c. [Begin by prescribing some character to yourself.—*Epict. Ench.*, c. xxxiii., § 1.]

Remember the Isthmian and Olympic exercises and what resembles this within, ὅτι νῦν ὁ ἀγών, καὶ ἤδη πάρεστι τὰ Ὀλύμπια [that now is the contest, now the Olympic games.—*Ench.*, c. li., § 2.] Not merely upon great occasions that come seldom; but here, immediately, in that which every minute offers and gives opportunity, as eating, talk, story, argument, the common entertainment, mirth and laughing, voice, gesture, action, countenance: in

* Viz.: 1, σιωπή [Silence.—*Epict. Ench.*, c. xxxiii., § 2]. 2, γέλως μὴ πολὺς [Not much laughter.—*Ibid.*, c. xxxiii., § 4].

all these the trial is the same and at hand. Seek the occasion, tempt, provoke. Every victory here is great and considerable. Let not foolish fancy diminish this and make it seem little and ridiculous, but remember the end and to what this tends.

Grant it be hard to deny what seems so natural, so inviting and alluring; but remember how much more solidly pleasing, how much more satisfaction, the consciousness of such a victory. Not only this, but remember withal the agreeableness of the very exercise itself after a certain way when once a strong habit is established, and the mind in a good station, a good bent. Nor is this only proper to philosophy; but amongst the other sorts of mankind, those who can advantageously command themselves in any particular, or are used to hardiness and labour, take not a little delight in this sort of exercise and love to try their strength. How much more one who knows his good, and pursues a right end ?

It is ridiculous to admire a generous behaviour, incorruptibleness, magnanimity; and at the same time to admire any of those outward things by the contempt of which these first are framed and have being. Therefore, either these internal matters, the * ὄργια of virtue, and the † sacred recesses of the mind, are worthy of admiration or they are not. If they are not then cease to admire in this way. If they are, then seek to admire in that other. A celebrated beauty ! a palace ! seat ! gardens ! pictures ! Italy ! a feast ! a carnival !—how do these concern thee ? If thou admirest any of these, as being taken with them and wishing for them, what is become of temperance, continence, and those other virtues ? and where is that honesty, faith, justice, magnanimity grounded on them ? If thou art sound and free, and if the charm and allurement of these exterior things reach thee not, why dost thou then make of thyself one of the admirers, and imitate what thou disapprovest ? Is it for company ? is it in complaisance ? is it that thou mayst be admired as a judge ?—All this is monstrous. Forbear, therefore, wholly this kind of way. For there is here

* *Mar. Aurel. Med.*, Bk. III., § 6.
† Sanctosque recessus mentis.—Pers. Sat. II., line 73.

neither modesty, decency, nor simplicity in any degree. Nor can the mind be long safe in such a way.

Remember that it is impossible to admire with others, and to admire at the same time what thou desirest should be the chief subject of thy veneration and esteem. If those things are magnified, these presently seem little. If the affairs abroad grow entangling and considerable; the affairs at home grow awkward and wearisome. If others are courted and cultivated, self is forgot.

*How noble, magnificent, great!* When any of those outward things are thus extolled, think with thyself what those inward things are of which these carry a resemblance, and of which it may be so much more deservingly said, *how amiable! how great!* But, above all, take care not to fall into those exclamations thyself, neither of the one kind nor of the other; not of the first kind, for that were to give up all and wholly to quit the station of a proficient; and not of the second kind, for that not only is beside the character of a proficient, but as the world now stands, would be unbecoming even a philosopher himself if such a one now lived.

Let others speak magnificently of virtue, not thou. It is enough if thou act thy part silently and quietly, keeping thy rules and principles to thyself; and not hoping ever to make these understood by others. What could even Socrates or Epictetus do if now alive? And wouldst thou therefore imitate them—thou, who art so little fit? and this too, before such a world as this, when thou art convinced that they themselves would act a different part, according to the difference of times? For, suppose they had lived with children only, and not with men: what if with Moors or Barbarians, what if with Goths, or a nation of Turks?—Consider where we now are; amongst whom; what opinions; what lives; and where those are whom we can call *men*.

What need of all this reasoning against magnificent talking or declaiming on behalf of virtue? Stay but till thou hast exhorted thyself sufficiently, and it will be then time enough to consider who else thou shouldst exhort, and after what manner.

Whilst I find it to be my part in the world, to live as now, a more retired sort of life, to learn withal what I can from the ancients, I will continue in this, cheerfully and contentedly. If Greek be a help, I study Greek, and this though I were now only beginning, and at the age of the first Cato. If any better part be given me, I accept it. If all books are taken from me, I accept that too, and am contented. If he who placed me here, remove me elsewhere (let the scene change to Asia, Africa, Constantinople, or Algiers) I am contented. If there remain, there, any part for me to act, that I can act decently and as a man, 'tis well; if there be none such given, I know my summons, and leaving all other thoughts or care I bend my mind wholly towards my retreat, and this thankfully and joyfully.—This is the true disposition. These are the thoughts that should be retained and perpetually brought to mind. But in a little while some new matter will appear; something striking, astonishing, over-powering; from family and relations, from a set of friends, from the State, or some new national revolutions. Immediately as an enthusiast thou art snatched away; duty is alleged and morality pleaded. Then hindrances come and ill success, disappointments, disturbances. The mind is at a loss: Providence is accused: all within is disordered. Where is now that former disposition? Where is that benignity towards mankind, and that generous affection towards the ruler and sovereign? After this, when thou returnest again to thy former part, it appears poor and mean. "Is this all? Must I have nothing better to act?" And thus thou becomest one of those seditious and quarrelsome actors that mutiny against the master of the stage. For it is plain, whilst thou art thus affected, thy aim is towards spectators, not towards Him of whose approbation alone thou hast need, since in this respect every part is equally great and worthy if duly accepted and cheerfully, benignly, gratefully, manfully discharged. Remember him who said—ὁ μὲν χωρὶς χιτῶνος φιλοσοφεῖ, ὁ δὲ χωρὶς βιβλίου ["the one is a philosopher without a tunic, and the other without a book."—*Mar. Aurel. Med.*, Bk. IV., § 30].

Consider (wheresoever at any time thou comest to thy work heavily and with regret, as parting hardly with other matters and quitting other pursuits), which one thing of all those in life thou hast not often in some disposition or another been superior to, and a conqueror of? Is it venery and amours with women? How often hast thou detested this, even in those former

times, so as to wish firmly thou hadst neither appetite that way,
nor anything of that kind to give disturbance?—Is it a house
and seat, buildings and work of that kind? How often hast thou
sickened of it? and in those days too, what disquiets? what
disgusts? Or is it, last of all (for here I reckon the chief thing
lies), the plays, diversions, talk, story-telling, secrets, confidences,
and whatever else makes up that sort of conversation, which
thou art so fond of with a certain set of friends? Remember
here how often thou hast been ready to renounce this for good
and all; and to break off even this correspondence and way of
life, when circumstances seemed to require it, as family affairs,
public, envy of certain persons, apostacy and corruption.—Now,
if melancholy, if anger and disgust, if satiety, weariness, and
other such passions were able to make thee despise these
matters of outward dependence, so as to set thee free! how
much more ought a right disposition and consciousness to do
the same?

How shameful is it to be so laborious, active, and indefatigable in other employments of several kinds; and here alone to
faint where the concern is highest, noblest, and most generous?
If thy country were in war, and the charge of an army conferred
on thee by the people, what labour wouldst thou not undergo?
If a magistracy, the same : what application, what pains, to
acquit thyself well in it? what bent and continual attention
of the mind? how wouldst thou be animated, how affected?
Yet, notwithstanding this, see how thou behavest elsewhere;
and in the highest concern of all, how weakly, how miserably
affected! But what charge or what consulship is equal to that
charge thou hast in hand? What is the commonwealth, the
senate, or people in respect of that authority which has enjoined
this duty and given thee this trust to discharge? In the meanwhile, how are those other trusts to be discharged? how be a
friend, a brother, or any of those other relations faithfully,
entirely, incorruptly? What is fidelity? What is constancy,
integrity, incorruption? And on what do these depend?

What miserable subjects are those in which thou hast been
so long busied and taken up, and which have left such
impressions behind?—a neat house, garden, seat, apartment,
pictures, trees, fabrics, models, design, and ordering. Remember

to distinguish. Is it to please thyself, stand by, alone, look upon this, and admire it ? Or is it that others may ? What others ? Consider only *who.* Are they the common people who repine at it, and justly ? Are they the rich who are rivals in these matters, and see with envy and detraction ? Are they men of business and employment ? They have no relish for things of this kind, and admire something else which is in their own way, and what they are used to. Are they, therefore, a few friends for whom all this is reserved ? O, folly ! Is this the way of serving them ? Are these the studies on their behalf ? Remember also this : that by so much as they are better people, so much the less have they any admiration of these matters. Thus the preparation must be for the worse sort, or for none at all.

But what if all the world were to admire ? What if all of this kind were in the highest perfection with thee ? Is there not cause of shame ?—" Behold ! See these additional ornaments which are mine, and belong to me ! See these rewards of virtue ! these marks of justice, integrity, honesty, and a good mind ! Who are they that can show such ? With whom are these to be found ? Add also : Who are the fittest to procure the most of these ? what are the fittest measures both to obtain and to preserve these ? and who are the most able and the most deserving in this way ? What is the neglect and contempt of these a sign of ? and what does the love or liking of these prognosticate ?"— If such be the case, why admit this cheat and delusion ? why introduce it under specious names ?—a private retreat, a study, gardening, planting. But this is philosophical.—So is anatomy, botany, chemistry. But what sort of men are those that here excel ? What are those anatomists, physicians, chemists, and in a word all those other naturalists, that converse with nature (as they say) and study it ? What are their thoughts of nature ? What minds have they ? Are they not rather the very worst, and the furthest off from any true sense or feeling ? What was Epicurus with his garden ? And who was ever more taken with this than he ?—All this is hollow, unsound, rotten, corrupt. He who truly studies nature and lives with nature, needs not either a garden, or wood, or sea, or rocks, to contemplate and admire. A dunghill or heap of any seeming vile and horrid matter is equal, nay superior, to any of those pretended orderly structures of things forced out of their natural state. He that sees not the beauty of corruption, can see nothing in generation or growth; and he who has not always before him and can kindly and benignly view the incessant and eternal change and conversion of things one into another, will in the midst of his gardens and other artifices oftener arraign and disparage nature than applaud and accompany her. Therefore, impose no longer on thyself. These may be good employments for others; they are better than cards or dice; better than the common pastimes; better than the common useless conversations, and what they call company. Therefore, if thy choice be amongst these, take this which is rather the best of the sort. But if thou hast other employments for thy mind, if thou hast other subjects of thy affection, and if the whole force of thy will is required elsewhere, be not so rash and foolish, as to spend that force on other subjects, and thus to lose thy nerve sinews and spirit where they are so much required.

Watch strictly when the fancy runs out upon any notable design or outward piece of work. *Hoc erat in votis; modus agri*, &c. [This used to be my wish, a bit of land—*Hor.*, Sat. II., 6, 1], and *paulum silvae* [just a little wood], and merely *concha salis puri* [a shell of pure salt.—*Hor.*, Sat. I., 3, 14]. How rotten is all this. And yet how covered over. How speciously clothed and lurking under a certain mask? How hard still to detect it upon every occasion? But endeavour, notwithstanding, to bring it forth into the light, examine the idea, bring it to the test. See how it will bear. Is it virtue, or has it anything in common with virtue? Does it come under the will, or is it foreign and of another province? Is it my good as a rational creature, as a man, as a student, and as one that seeks to improve in a certain course? Is it a help and advancement in this sense, or is it a *remora*?

What is it that I am studying thus to bring into order? What am I embellishing?* Dirt, matter, dregs. Is it this I would adorn? Is it this I would beautify? Hear another

* "This body is only a finer mixture of clay."—*Epict. Dis.*, Bk. I., c. i., § 11.

person on this subject. As one (says he) delights in embellishing this thing or the other, so I in making myself still better and finding that I grow so. Remember the rival beauties and how the internal sort is acquired. Ὦ φίλε Πάν: δοίητέ μοι καλῷ γενέσθαι τἄνδοθεν, &c. ["Beloved Pan, give me beauty in the inward soul."—*Plato: Phœdrus,* 279, B.].

# ARTIFICIAL OR ECONOMICAL SELF.

Dreams, dreams.—A dark night; dead sleep; starts; disturbing visions; faint endeavours to awake.—A sick reason; labyrinth; wood; sea.—Waves tossing; billows surging; the driving of the wreck ; giddy whirlwinds ; eddies; and the overwhelming gulf.

How emerge ? When gain the port, the station, promontory ? that ἔστηκε, καὶ περὶ αὐτὴν κοιμίζεται τὰ φλεγμήναντα τοῦ ὕδατος ["stands firm and tames the fury of the water around it."—*Mar. Aurel. Med.* IV., § 49]. Awake; rouse; shake off the fetters of the enchantress; begin.

Again retired. See what Providence has bestowed on thee ! Once more in thy power to be saved, to redeem thyself, to raise thyself from this sink, these dregs, this guise of a world, to manliness, to reason and a natural life; to come again on the stage as an actor, not as a machine;—as knowing the author of the piece, as conscious of the design, to join in the performance, the disposition, the government; to be a spectator, a guest, a friend, and with the same friendship to retire and thank the inviter.—But O, these dreams ! this sleep !—No more. Die altogether, thou wretch ; not thus.—In the other death there is no harm. But how many deaths in such a life as this ? What else but this is deadly ? What else should terrify or concern ?

A little more, and mere dreams had gotten the better, and thou hadst waked no more. For see ! how hard to get out of this sleep ! how long and deep a one it has been ! how it has robbed thee of the truest and clearest waking thoughts ! how have its cheating visions, and false images supplanted those true ones, and deprived thee of those blessed views, that happy vision and enthusiasm without deceit !

Turn thy eyes inward, see there how things are left, how poor within ! how ransacked, how spoiled !—How bare has this winter left thee ! these blighting seasons, these intemperate climes, for which thou wert persuaded to quit those other happy ones, that healing sun and that eternal spring, those * islands and that fortress.

What is become of thee, now that thou hast put to sea again and left thy harbour ? How is it that the land appears, if, as yet, thou canst make land ? How faint and dim is all ! What supply of ideas, on any occasion ? What pilot, steerage, compass ? What χρῆσις φαντασίων [the use of appearances], inversion, art, or power ? How destitute ! how helpless !

Thou art returned, 'tis true, to the same country,[1] to the same distance and retreat. But is it the same country, the same field, and in the same condition as before ? Have not the tempests shaken and ravaged more than before ? Have not the seasons and time done more ? Is not everything more to disadvantage, everything more in the way, more cloudy, dark, and retarding long the appearance of those halcyon days ?

Thou art returned, 'tis true, to exercise, to arm again and fight once more. The ἁλτῆρες[2] are here at hand, but where the nerves and muscles ? The arm has been disused ; the limb has been bound up and is shrunk : no force this way at all ; no spirits, life or motion ; but benumbed, withered, dead. Meanwhile, how is it with the enemy ? How have the contrary *visa* profited and made their advantage of this cessation ? how robust, firm, vigorous, keen ! how polished and specious those images ! how lively those ideas ! what number ! what discipline ! and with what art they defend themselves and succour one another !

Remember, therefore, how fallen.—Compassion : sympathy : relations : family : public.—(What family ? and what public ?) —K. of S's. death,[3] Europe in civil commotions, France and universal monarchy ; a war, a parliament, elections, parties, engagements, contests.—How truly prophesied before ? In a little while some new matter appearing, and straightway an enthusiastic ? See this treachery. Think of the sore, inflammation, fuel, et ignes suppositos cineri doloso [and fires hidden under treacherous ashes].

---

* The islands of the happy.—*Mar. Aurel. Med.* X., 8.
[1] Holland, 1703.  [2] The halteres were gymnastic instruments.
[3] Charles I. of Spain died 1st November, 1700.

Wilt thou venture again once more in thy life and try this experiment anew ? And with such impaired constitution, plain decline, and probably short remaining time ?

If such be the case, why admit this cheat and delusion ? But thou hast admitted it. It crept on by degrees and under specious images of nature, virtue, public friends, and what not ? Then rural-makers, recommendation of country life, agreeableness of a place, seat alterations, gardens, groves. Thus the villa, foreigners, envoys, court ladies, satisfaction of the great, imitation of the great in little, a circumstance, report, character. Such a one, of such a nation, family, house, garden, retreat. So to the K., so T——d to the Q. of P., and so now again lately from H. D. and Sir R. G. at Hamb. the Electress and Q. of P. and *ce Conte de Sh*[1]——

Now see what thou hast got by thy success in this way. Hoc erat in votis [this was my wish], and so now auctius atque di melius fecere : bene est [the gods have granted me more and better : all is well,—*Hor.*, Sat. XXVI., 1, 3]. But is it so ? Propria haec mihi munera [are these gifts permanent for me] ? Are these *propria ?* * are they thine ? honestly thine ? † thy own very true and certain possessions properly belonging to thee and naturally thine ? Call an imposthume so, a goitre, a polypus, or any worse excrescence. These if thou hast them would be thine too, but such as thou shouldst be glad of parting with. And are not those others imposthumes ? and of the mind, which is far worse ? Are they not sufficient weights, encumbrances, and growths, such as eat out the best nourishment of that soil ? Think now how these sit and are still likely to sit, since thou hast taken such care to raise and to implant them, to make them thus, as it were, parts of thyself, and sticking to thee. Wretched things, such as they are, ἀσθενῆ, δοῦλα, κωλυτά, ἀλλότρια ["weak, slavish, subject to restraint, in the power of others"—*Epict. Ench.*, c. i., § 2], to which whoever is so joined may be truly said caudam trahere [to drag a tail]. Handles for every one's insult. Scope for every fling of malice and stroke of fortune. How notably

---

[1] Shaftesbury received, in 1704, through Sir Rowland Gwinn, an invitation to meet the Electress Sophia and the Queen of Prussia.

* cf. *Hor.*, II., Ep. II., l. 157.  † Ibid. lines, 172-4.

hast thou provided for thyself? How adorned? Behold, thou art become an appendix to a grange! an appurtenance to an estate and title!—" Ho! friend! To whom dost thou belong?" Should a stranger upon the road accost thee thus, peradventure thou wouldst be angry; but should one who was no stranger in this universe thus meet and question thee, couldst thou better answer than by pointing to the things and people, "See there to what and to whom?" Or couldst thou with an honest heart point to Heaven and say, "To that only; to the Universe and Him that gave me my part and station in it? See if I am belonging to anything besides. See if I own any other Superior, or am false to my origin and pedigree. Take that other pedigree and name. Seize any of those things that hang about me. See if I am concerned: see whether I am less myself; whether I am their appurtenance or they mine." —But if it be: "Alas, my poor estate! my family! the grange! Alas, the island! the hut! the hovel!" Then see under what subjection thou art brought, and whether it be not true that the better thou hast succeeded in these things the more ingenious thou hast been to thy own misery.

The shaking of the earth, a little fire, a puff of wind, the tumbling or perishing of a pile of timber, brick, or stone; the defacing of this or that structure, or of the imaginary and full as perishing structure of a character in the world, with country, kindred, friends; a breath of wind blasting the fruit, corn, or grass, and that other blast, as variable and uncertain, the rumour of people, the motion and sound of tongues: under how many cases bowed? at how many accidents trembling? How many things and persons anxiously provided for? Over how many tyrannize, and by how many tyrannized? But thank thyself. It was otherwise at a certain time, but thou didst reflect, and for fear of going too fast, didst go aside out of the road, secure of finding it again at pleasure. O wonderful wisdom that thus deliberated! O the goodness that produced this compassion, sympathy, and what followed!

As those were sharp and piercing sores by which this distemper and relapse first began, so these latter are the funguses that remain now that the other are closed up. Remember the greater and less excrescence, the warts, and wens, how they were formed, how they grew from a little, and to what size !

Thus cautioned, begin; take up the clue; continue the thread, and see that it break off no more; no more unravelling; but wind thyself up; collect thyself with all thy might within thyself. See first the natural, then artificial, economical self; the σχέσεις, symmetry, correspondence, harmony; not harmonizing in that other way; not sympathizing any more, and applauding thyself for this; covering it with those names of natural affection, and tenderness. But how economical? from what economy? From this below? Is there not a higher? Wilt thou not reopen thence? Or must it be as before? "Such a one, the son or grandson of such a one, such a name."

No more. Farewell such computations.—Begin then, and take it better. Τίς ὤν.

What am I? who? whence? whose?—And to what or whom belonging? with what or whom belonging to me, about me, under me?—Quality, rank, birth, of what sort? What character, what dignity, and what born to?—An estate, title, name, figure? With whom the figure? Where? in country? or in town?—No, but in the nation, in the world. —Excellent: but how? Is it magnitude or curiosity only? Is it a figure according to art and masterly skill? Where are the judges, the masters in this kind? Or is it a figure as in a sum? What sum? the great sum? the whole? Which is the greater figure and which the less in this sum? What is a little figure? How little or great? Or what though great? What though the biggest unit? How long before a blank, a cypher only? Or though still a figure, what difference from a cypher? In these sums what are cyphers set either before or after? How increase the figure, how add or multiply in these numbers? Consider then what are the right numbers, proportions, and arithmetic; what really makes a figure; what a figure is; what a cypher only.

Again, what am I? Simple or compound? If I can find nothing of the first kind, see at least what of the second.— A compound, a system of what? Of land?—No.—Of titles, honours, privileges?—No.—Of bones, flesh, and limbs.—And how, when I chance to lose any of these, is the system of self destroyed? Or is it divided or parted?—No.—Seek then elsewhere still for this system.—Where seek it but in that which *bids seek*, which now seeks, which determines, pronounces, judges of all, makes use of all, governs all?—What is it that now examines about this of self? And according to this then, what am I?—προαίρεσις [a will], a mind, a judgment.— And according to this of *self?* According to this then, what am I?—προαίρεσις [a will], a mind, a judgment—and according to this what is my good?—προαίρεσις ποῖα [a certain will], a certain mind and judgment in such a certain state and condition. —O, by no means!—But what?—a certain estate, body, circumstances, in such a certain state and condition.—And what if these are in ever so good a condition, and the other in bad? What if these are in ever so bad a condition, so the other be but in good?

Man! see but this; look a little this way; see thyself; be thyself; carry thyself along with thee in thy deliberations, thy comparisons. With what dost thou compare thyself? What art thou worthy of? and what are the things beneath thee? Τίνα φαντασίαν ἔχω περὶ ἐμαυτοῦ; πῶς ἐμαυτῷ χρῶμαι; [What do I imagine myself to be? How do I conduct myself?—*Epict. Disc.*, Bk. II., c. xxi., § 9].

First then, who?—A man; not (as they say) a mere earthling; not a worldling, but of the true world—a man of quality.—What quality? The herald quality? patent quality? court quality? Or from progenitors, courtiers? (worthy men!) progenitrices of the court? (worthy women!)—Noble pedigree! unquestionable pedigree! noble thoughts, life, manners, employment of time! Happy great ones! Noble and highly-privileged great ones! See to what privileged! to what entitled —This is quality; and is there no better? Is this derivation; and is there no better? Is this the breeding, education, instruction; and is there no better, no higher?—But consider then, what quality?—That which is measured from intellect and mind, or from matter and dregs? from the author and known father of minds and from his laws and constitution, or from the laws and constitutions of such inferior minds as these?—To whom then is the relation? Quality, what? By what measured? From what? In what? Lord of what?—"Lord of the region of the mind and will, understanding and judgment of thoughts,

L

affections, appetites, opinions, councils; King, Prince, and of the council of that greatest, highest Prince; willing as He wills; assisting in his administration; ever present with Him; co-operating, co-adjutant, and confederate with Him."

Whose am I then but His? Whence am I but thence? To what or whom belonging? Or with what belonging to me? —Slaves, household, acres; the Lord, an English Lord, European, Britain, Saxon, west or east: what is all this? When wilt thou cease to reckon from hence? Or if it be not that thou reckonest from hence: why astonished? or how ashamed or dashed? Why struck at any time? Why galled or pinched by these matters?—But, it is plain, thou reckonest still from hence, as merely one of these; as their appurtenance, their purchase; claimed, owned, acknowledged theirs. Or, if not theirs, whose? God's? As manumitted by Him and made thy own? Art thou then indeed God's?—O, wretch! canst thou say that word? Is there indeed such a Sovereign, such a country? Say then, let us hear for goodness' sake what is the worth of such a country? Or what is He worth who governs it? What may His utmost value be? And how far may He in truth be worth considering or taking notice of?—Am I alone and by myself? Nobody sees me.—Yes, somebody.—Who? Nobody but God. But stay, here are other eyes. Let me have a care, for what will they think of me? My dignity! My character!—Now the coaches, the benches, the robes, the dishes, and services.—What birth? what country? what quality considered?

Thus it is. Where is the man now placed? Where now the real country, nativity, pedigree? Where the lordship? and in what things? Lord of what? in what region? over what concerns? How goes it *within?* how are the provinces there? in what state or condition? Is it there, "my lord! sir! prince! your lordship! honour! excellence!" Is there due acknowledgment of the superior? is the governing part owned, respected, obeyed? is there command, mastery, rule, or disposition there? is there power? Is liberty there? is there that thing? or art thou there no better than a slave? a servile, stooping, creeping slave? How else should it be, when for thy own part being otherwise born, privileged and set free by the eternal laws of the eternal, thou hast voluntarily submitted and subdued thyself to these temporary feeble laws, and naturalized thyself in this lower world? How else when thou hast circumscribed thyself, thy character, estate, and goods within the verge of parchment, of a hedge, or of that ditch encompassing the piece of land, which (it seems) thou choosest to call thy country: denominating thyself from hence, and accordingly rating thyself by the nature and worth of such things as these?

Consider of those appellations and better titles: a creature, subject, citizen. Art thou such? Think what they import: and be them, in a better sense than that other mean one. Or shall it be only the honest citizen and the burgess? the islander, a British dweller, a subject of the Crown, a creature of the great man's, or of the creature of the great man's? For what signifies it when once thou art a creature and thus dependent whose creature thou art? See! look but into the world: how the little ones and great ones of it move together, depend on one another, govern and influence by turns; and then choose where thou wilt, and see if thou art not still a creature's creature of more than two or three removes?

A devoted and most obedient humble servant.—To whom? —To the great man or great woman.—And to God what?—An undevoted, disobedient, and most insolent one, a complaining, murmuring, discontented, rebellious one. How elsewhere devoted as thou art there? How possible there and here both? —Vile slave! thus to devote thyself to any service but that which if it were understood would be found truly to be perfect freedom, and not such as those slaves make of it when they turn this way.—But what should slaves be but slaves, wherever they turn? for till set at liberty from these sordid matters, what can we be even in religion too, but slaves? Here, therefore, learn to be indulgent, here above all, κατ᾽ οἰκονομίαν [in administration]; but to thyself no indulgence, no hanging on these affairs, no miscalling or disparaging heaven's distributions, no nick-naming of Providence—hard Providences, dark Providences, afflictions, tribulations, calamities, crosses.—What crosses to one who stands not cross to Providence? What affliction to one who wills only as that, nor ill in outward things which ever way dispensed, but rejoices in the dispensation?

This is the generous devotion. This is to be the devoted servant of a right person. This is to be indeed and in earnest, devout, pious, and withal free, divinely free; for how otherwise devout? If otherwise, cry, whine, expostulate, and wring hands; deprecate and at last submit, as they say; but see what submission, what kind of resignation this is like to prove. Praise outwardly, flatter, magnify, extol; but see if nature and thy own heart give thee not inwardly the lie.

Thus it is. Again remember this, and be indulgent to others, for how can this be otherwise? Is this to be told them? See that thou art not thyself a fool, and vainly impious.— Forbear!

# NATURAL SELF.

## —Γνῶθι Σεαυτόν—

Know but this self only and what self is indeed, and then fear not being too selfish, fear not to say ἐμοὶ παρ ἐμὲ φίλτερος οὐδεις [no one is dearer to me than myself.—*Epict. Disc.*, Bk. III., c. iv., § 10], and τοῦτο ὁ πατήρ, καὶ ἀδελφός, καὶ συγγενὴς, καὶ πατρὶς, καὶ θεός [this the father and brother, and family, and country, and God]. — For this is the only piety, the only friendship. Take it the other way, and good-bye all. With the first weary fit (if there be nothing else in the case) it will be "Stuff all, what care I ? and let it go as it will"; thus stretching, yawning, common weariness or heaviness, before so much as a sigh comes. But if something harder than usual come across, then (with sighs) "Why was I born ? What is this life ? these mortals ? this world and all this ado ? What good of all ? what justice or wisdom ? Why was I made thus ? why made at all ? why anything made ? How ? or by whom ? For what necessity ? What end ?"

—O cimmerian darkness! fatal and overcoming blindness! Epidemical contagion! universal and incurable! not to be sensible in this chief part of sense; not to see thus clear, apparent, first, fundamental truth; not to see that thing which sees, which judges, which pronounces, and which only *is!* For where could any selfishness remain, where could any ill-interest, disorder, murmur, complaint, or quarrel either with earth or heaven exist, were this but seen; and if nothing else, were seen for self, but what were truly so ? Τίς γὰρ ἀγαθός ἐστιν οὐκ εἰδὼς ὅς ἐστι ; [For who can be a good man if he knows not who he is ?—*Epict. Disc.*, Bk. III., c. xxiv., § 20].

How many are there that place this self, and root it as it were, so deeply in a body that they cannot persuade themselves but that they have something to do with that body of theirs, some concern, some interest in it, even when dead ?—The ancients and their *sit tibi terra levis* [may the sod rest lightly on thee]; the burning wholly left off amongst the Christians, and now-a-days an aversion to being opened; the care of coffin, grave, and resting (as they call it) there; how to lie, in what manner, and where; my burial; my grave; I would lie here; I would lie there:—everywhere *Me* and *I*. A property still kept in this body; a self still; an imaginary I; a secret link, union, sympathy. And what a horror (I warrant), what a heavy disturbance and sad bemoaning within, were it but foreseen that dogs were in a little while to eat the carcase. And if this be truly so much our self with us, what must the living one be? How dear and precious? how wholly and solely us, ourselves, our very true, and natural selves. No self to be heard of else; no persuading us (as they say) *out of ourselves*. And yet who is there that can be persuaded into himself or of himself? Even thou thyself how hard to be persuaded!

A wretchedly foolish and selfish human creature thinks he has to do with his body and that it is still some part of himself and belonging to him even after he is out of it. A wiser mortal thinks his body no part of himself, nor belonging to him when out of it. But a truly wise man thinks his body no part of himself nor belonging to him even whilst in it; only he takes care of it as of a lodging, an inn, a passage-boat or ship, a post horse. For all these are *his* while he uses them; and, as a good man, he will find himself obliged to take care of them, and to keep them the best he can, as long as they are in his possession and lent him.

Why this hankering after flesh? this clinging, this cleaving to a body? What art thou afraid should be taken from thee? what art thou afraid of losing? *Thyself?*—What is then lost? A tooth? Wilt thou go out for a tooth?—Go then.—A hand, a leg, a whole body, and what more? Is not this the furthest? and is not this in reality less still than the tooth? Or say: hast thou thus lost anything that thou wilt want? for, supposing this to be thyself, wilt thou miss thyself when thou art thus lost? How many thousand years wert thou thus lost, before thou wert born? And yet, no harm. But there is a real losing of self. There is that which, if lost, will be missed and sighed for. Take thou care of that loss.

If it must needs be *Me* and *I* (as they speak), whatever happens to this wretched body, let it be *I* then, in his senses, who spoke so generously to the tyrant.—" Thou shalt be thrown into prison.—Then I'll go live in prison.—Thou shalt be put to death.—Then I'll die.—Thou shalt be denied burial.—Then I'll stink." What is that *I* imprisoned, or the *I* killed, more than the *I* that stinks ? What is imprisoned ? My mind ? my will ? though willingly there ? though contentedly taken up with my own thought and proper exercise ? deep in the order of things and accompanying the administration ?—What is killed ? My resolution ? my integrity ? my principle that tells me death is nothing ?—But I will put an end to that thought, destroy that principle.—In whom ? in what ? in nature ? in the universe? in its original? Root and branch (as they say)?— This would be killing indeed. But at this rate thou must kill nature, truth, reason, God.—What folly !—Where, then, wilt thou do this murder ? where wilt thou kill this reason, and in what ? In nature ?—No, but in thee.—What thee ? Where is the thee that thou wouldst thus deprive ? Deprive what ? who ? A carcase ? Ridiculous. The real thee thou canst not deprive, for either it is not at all (and so wants not anything, nor can be deprived of anything), or it is out of thy reach and pretension.

Δύναταί τις ἐκβαλεῖν ἔξω τοῦ κόσμου ; [Can any one turn me out of the universe ?—*Epict. Discourses*, Bk. III., c. xxii., § 22].— To be despatched, made way with, sent out of the world :— terrible ! But whither ? where there is world still, or no world ? For, if there be any, it is the same still, or better; if there be none, it is no harm, and so no fear. *

Kill what ? the thought ?—No, thee.—Man ! *I* am that thought : if thou killest not that, thou canst not kill me.—But it shall be no longer with thee.—Again, with whom ? With the carcase ?—But thou thyself then, where ?—With nature, God ; where I should be and would wish to be. How many thousand ages had my being been already his, with him, in his power, and at his disposal ? The question here is about a few days only (for die I must, a little later, if not now), and shall I be

---

* cf. *Horace*, Epist. I., xvi., lines 72-75.

concerned to trust him for such a time as this, or any time to
come ?    Was I not from eternity thus exposed (if this be
exposing) ? and is the exposing greater for time to come ?—But
how exposed ? to whom ? and by whom ?—Nature exposing
her own works ! God his creatures ! Principle of ill ; exterior :
where ?    Interior : how ?    How anything a principle of ill to
itself ?   How anything beyond or besides nature ?   How anything against God, or God against anything ?   Anti-God ! God
against himself !—Folly ! weakness ! wretchedness all !

*Carior est illis homo quam sibi.*[1]  Do thou thyself but
love thyself as thou shouldst do, and trust these for their love.
Know, own, assert, *be thyself*, and there is no fear.

Count not such a certain figure thyself (for thou mayst lose
that figure), not such certain senses thyself (for thou mayst lose
one or more of those senses); but such certain judgments, such
certain opinions, and only such certain ones, for if they are not
those thou hast approved and confirmed, it is a wrong self, a
nothing, a lie.    Remember, then, whilst I am myself I
cannot be hurt.    When I think I am hurt by any of these
accidents that happen to a carcase, or to anything without my
mind and real self, I am then out of my reason, and am not
myself.

Fear nothing but losing thyself in this manner.   Fear not
what may happen to thyself, otherwise than in being not
thyself; and this moreover thou needst not fear, for it is in thy
choice.

The metaphysicians and notable reasoners about the nice
matters of identity, affirm that if memory be taken away, the
self is lost.    And what matter for memory ?   What have I to do
with that part ?   If, *whilst I am*, I am but as I should be, what
do I care more ? and thus let me lose *self* every hour, and be
twenty successive selfs, or new selfs, 'tis all one to me: so I lose
not my opinion.   If I carry that with me 'tis I ; all is well.   If
that go, memory must go too : for how one without the other ?

If thou preservest this true opinion of self (as not body)
even whilst in a body, it will not be surely less confirmed to thee
when thou shalt find thyself (if such be the case) even out of a

---

[1] Man is dearer to the Gods than to himself.—*Juv. Sat.*, X. 350.

body. If the now do not belie thee, the hereafter cannot. If the present state allow it, the future must demonstrate it; and the better surely for thee, that thou hast thus thought and begun thus with thyself whilst here.—But why these ifs? Why this conditioning? Wouldst thou bargain as others do?—What views? what fancies?—The *now*; the *now*. Mind this: in this is all.

Self: simple, or a system? If simple, not body; or if body an atom (unintelligible body). But if a system: how is body a part? how does it enter into the system? Can that enter into a system, of which any portion being lost, the system nevertheless remains the same? Or is the system of self not the same, but changed if a leg or arm be lost? Is the man a quarter less himself? a fifth, a sixth, or one bit less himself than before?

A man in armour.—Off then with the armour; is it not a man still? is it less a man?—A man in clothes. Off then with the clothes; does not the man remain?—But a limb. Let it be a limb. Off with it; is not the man the same? the self the same, the selfsame? or so much lost? so much remaining? a pound? an ounce? an inch? an ell?—Is it possible that self is measured or weighed out?—Where is this self then? where lies the man?—But the whole body. —Be it then the whole body. And what is the body (pray) when no mind acts upon it? When there is a mind, give me any shape, any figure, body, or parts whatsoever, whole or not whole, and I will show you the person, the man, whole still and entire. What have we to do then with body? why this concern about a body? or what regard to this more than to the armour? For if a cuirassier, and upon duty, I am bound to this, and must keep it as tight about me, as sound, nay, and as bright and fine too as the thing will bear, as becomes armour, and a soldier, not otherwise.

What am I?—A particular mind, an acting principle?— Over what?—Over a particular body, senses, &c.?—To what end? —To that which the general mind has appointed, and for so long as it has appointed that I should use such a body and such senses.—But they may be taken from thee.—Let them be so. —But thou art lost then thyself.—How lost? By having no longer a body and senses to take care of? If I have nothing to take care of, what is anything to me? If there be anything afterwards, I shall be concerned then as now; and all will be well. If there be nothing, all is well still; this is all. I am discharged. 'Tis well.—With the universe I know, all is, and will be well; and with myself the same, whilst I think as I do at present of that universe, know the order and serve Him who orders. If those thoughts and that purpose are taken from me, and the *I* remain, then may I indeed be said to be lost, or to have lost myself. But the order of the universe is too proportionable, just, and consequent to admit that this should ever happen, except in consequence of my own present thought and action : that is to say, that I should ever become wicked but by my own fault.

A mind is something that acts upon a body ; and not on a body only, but on the senses of a body, the appearances, fancies, and imaginations, by correcting, working, modelling these, and building out of these. Such is a mind. Such a thing I know there is in the world somewhere. Such a mind I am sure of. Let Pyrrho by the help of such a mind contradict this if he please. He and I have each of us our individual understandings. He understands for himself and I for myself.—But who for the world ?—Nobody ? Nothing ?—How is this possible ? What is the world ?—a body.—What are bodies of men ?—bodies in this body.—Fancies of men ?—fancies in this body.—And is there no mind that governs in this body, or acts upon these fancies in this body ? Has the goodly bulk, so prolific, kind, and yielding for all others, nothing left then for itself ? unhappily giving all away ?—By what chance, what rule, and how ? Whence such a distribution ?—*Nature* (say you).—And what is nature ? Understanding ? Or not understanding ?—Who then understands for her ?—No one. Every one for himself.—Right. And is not *nature a self?*— Or how are you yourself ?—by a principle uniting certain parts, and that thinks and acts for these parts.—And what is your whole a part of ? Or is it no part but a whole by itself, independent, and unrelated to anything besides ? But if on the contrary it be related, to what but to the whole and to nature ? If so, what are you yourself but a part of nature and united by nature to other parts to which by birth and many other ways you have relation ? Is there then a uniting principle in nature ? If so, how are you then a self, and nature not so ? How have you something to understand and act for you, and nature (who gave this understanding) nothing to understand for her, act for her, or help her out (poor being !) whatever need there may be ? Is such her ill-fortune amongst all others ? Are there so many uniting, governing, understanding principles in all, and yet nothing that unites, thinks, acts, or understands for all ? Nothing that distributes for all or looks after all ?—No (says a modern), for it was never more, nor is more than what you see.—No (says an Epicurean) for it was once yet less than what you see : chaos, and a play of atoms.—Believe it who can. For my own share, I have a mind, which serves, such as it is, to keep my body and the affections of it, my appetites, imaginations, fancies, and the rest in tolerable order. But the order of the universe, I am sure, is yet a much better order. Let Epicurus think his own the better, or, if he please, the only order ; and then give account how he came by it, how atoms came to be wise.

But setting atoms aside, to come to earnest. A body of the whole there is, and to this body an order, and to this order a mind : a general mind of this general body.—And the particular mind, what ?—Part of this general mind, of a piece with it, of like substance (as much as we understand of substance) ; alike active upon body, original to motion and order ; alike simple, uncompounded, ONE, *individual;* of like energy, effect, and operation ; and more like still, more resembling, more the same, if it co-operate (as it may and ought) with that general mind.

Consider, then, what am I ? what is this self ? a part of this general mind, governing a part of this general body, itself and body both, governed by the universal governing mind, which, if it willingly be, it is the same as to govern with it. It is one with it, partakes of it, and is in the highest sense related to it.

Τίς ὤν. [What am I ? Who ?] Wonderful word ! powerful question ! if but rightly applied and used,[1] not only in the first and leading sense, the natural self ; but in the economical parts, and in every relation, station, and circumstance of life.[2]

[1] cf. *Epict., Disc.,* Bk. IV., c. i.  [2] *Ibid.,* Bk. III., c. xxiv.

# FAMILIARITY.

What would I have, why seek familiarity with these? Can I make myself what they are? Can I reconcile my opinions to theirs? If not, why do I affect this intimacy? Their principles and mine are opposite as the antipodes. I have the utmost contempt for theirs, and they for mine; as far as they know anything concerning them. What correspondence can there be between such? What kind of alliance is this? Must not I conceal and hide myself? Must not I (if this familiarity be aimed at) prostitute myself in the strangest manner, and be a hypocrite in the horridest degree? Why do I affect to be beloved? Why lay this stress on their good opinion and esteem? Is it because they commend one, they do not know, and that which they praise is nothing of thy character? Show but thyself for what thou art; profess thy principles and let them see thy real self; and what will happen? Where will be their praise? What will their thoughts be of thee? How will their affection be towards thee?

Consider this well, and see if anything can be more ridiculous. Remember what they are, and what thou art. Thy firm and stated principles, thy cool thoughts and reasonings, are to them mere madness. If in reality they are not madness, but true sense, it follows of necessity that they who take these things for madness, are mad themselves, and at the bottom differ not from the most childish and ignorant. But thou hast long ago pronounced them mad, as following no certain opinions, and having no guide but unexamined and unsettled fancy. However it be, this is evident, either the one or the other must be mad.

Now consider this breach, consider the natural secretion and if nothing else, let modesty at least prevail. Think what it is, being such a one as thou art, to join thyself in this manner with them, as if thou wert in harmony with them, and of their principles. Is not this an intruding? is not this imposition? What is an abstemious man amongst drinkers? What is a plain man in company with such as dress? What is an unbelieving man amongst those who are celebrating superstitious rites? What has such a one to do there? Why appear beyond what is required and necessary? Why mix and associate? Why affect forwardness in these concerns, assume and act as willing to be thought somebody, and of some moment? Am not I a monster with respect to them? am not I of another make and form? am I not forced to hide my shape, lest I appear horrid and affrighting? What must I do then? Correct this shape. Be a human creature, and of their species. Conform to their principles and manner. Otherwise withdraw; and (as becomes thee) withdraw heartily and willingly. Or, if thou canst not in this way, withdraw then as one that pities himself, or as one deformed, and that for some natural defect would lament his own infirmity. However it be, I say withdraw; for it is insufferable to stand so towards them as thou dost, and to affect that amongst them which thou affectest.

Remember still what thou art to them, and they to thee, and how it must be when any occasion shall chance to show thy opposition. How will they like to be thus thought of? how treat the person who has these thoughts? What is this but natural enmity covered over? What is their friendship for one another? Consider what they are capable of, and what a little time is sure to bring about. If thy friendship which thou maintainest with them be proof to all this, it is genuine and right. If at the time when their opinions work in their natural way and produce those natural effects, nothing that happens be a surprise; it is well. But if it be otherwise, it is plain thy affection is more absurd and ridiculous than theirs. For they think of themselves that they have faith, sincerity, justice, friendship; and when anything contrary shows itself in a companion or acquaintance, they think the person changed, or that they were mistaken in him (as indeed they were). But thou, for thy part, canst not be mistaken; thou knowest their δόγματα and opinions, and that to expect ought else from hence is monstrous absurdity. How comes it then that thou art moved? Why pleased or displeased? Why this affection, zeal, and concern? What else is this but to will (as *Epictetus says) that vice should not be vice.

Whenever a certain fondness comes upon thee, such as invites and draws towards familiarity and intimacy, remember what has been said above; remember natural secretion, the fight, enmity, and opposition of principles, what it is that is placed as a gulf between us; remember hypocrisy, imposture, imposition, and intruding; remember who they are, and what I *myself* am, and that we now talk to one another masked and in disguise, so that I take not him for him, nor he me for me. He pleases himself with a spectre, and I myself with another spectre. We are nothing less than what we appear to one another. There can be nothing less in either the character of the one or of the other than what we thus love and prize in one another. Strip us; set us naked before one another; and see how each will share and be amazed. See how we shall then view one another. How will he bear the sight of my opinions? or how I his, when I see them barefaced and natural? How does he appear to me in his anger, in his pleasure, in his lust? how in a title, with an estate, in reputation or disgrace, in prosperity or adversity? how amongst his domestics? how in ordinary provocations? how in sickness? how in any cross or disappointment? How many ways intolerable? And am I more tolerable as I stand with him? Can my opinions, or such affection as mine, be borne with? Am not I a monster to him? What though he be one of the better sort, that seem to philosophize? What if he be a believer in a certain way? What if he be an atheist? Yet these, as different as they are amongst themselves, are yet in harmony and agreement with one another in respect of what they are towards me. Where then is my modesty? What decorum or decency is there in such a carriage? How becoming for me to insinuate myself and court their favour? Consider, that if there be any such thing as nauseous affectation; if it be nauseous in one of a dull and heavy genius to affect the conversation of men of wit; or in one of mean education to affect the manners and company of the polite sort; or in one deformed to affect amours and the effeminate ways of lovers: all of this kind, and whatever else

* *Ench.*, c. xiv.

may yet be added, will still be found not near so nauseous as is, in thee, that affectation of a certain intimacy with others.

Behold another age! (for so it may be called), another face of things, another scene, another period[1] of thy life. Go back to what it was lately, a year, or less than a year since. Are not all the views changed? Family, friends, father, brothers, sisters, some already gone out of life,[2] removed, changed; others in another manner changed, and in a way still of further change. New ages, new seasons of life, new companies, new opinions, new pursuits, new passions. All is under change; all is change. What is the substance and matter of our bodies? what the matter (if I may so speak) of our minds? What is opinion? How should it be but changeable, and most of anything changeable whilst mere opinion? And what theirs but opinion? What is thine? Is it not opinion also? Or if not opinion, but science; how should this have varied? how shouldst thou have given way? how doubted of thy rules? how been where thou now art?

Consider how it now is; how since thou saidst, "How long wilt thou abuse thyself?", since thou bidst, "Remember the fuel within, the impetuous, furious, impotent temper, the machine, wedges," &c. See whither the same impetuous, impotent temper has led thee! Was it for this thou didst retire? Is it this thou has brought home? τοῦτο γὰρ ἐφ' ὅ ἀποδεδήμηκεν οὐδέν ἐστιν [For this for which he has travelled is nothing]. Is it not of thee this is said?

Ἀλλὰ ἅλις [But enough]. Begin now. Consider thy shameful fall. See what is absolutely necessary in the case. What with these wounds, these sores? See as to the ὄρεξις [desire], the ἔκκλισις [aversion] what is enjoined. Consider all this, and come with a new resolution, οὐ δεῖ μετρίως κεκινημένον [not lay hold of them with a weak effort.—*Ench.* c. i., § 4]. Bear with the regimen, the prescription, the operation. Bear with dejection, mortification, weaning. How else the ἔκκλισις?

Remember the exchange ὅτι προῖκα οὐδὲν γίνεται [that there is nothing to be had for nothing.—*Epict. Disc.*, Bk. IV., c. ii., § 2].

---

[1] St. Giles, Dec., 1699.  [2] Shaftesbury's father died on Nov. 10th, 1699.

Remember former furies. What a creature! and that God should have called thee out to this; how wonderful! Enough, this but for a moment, and so to die. Vastly enough, and praise Him. Give thanks τῷ κεκληκότι [to the one who has called you.—*Ep. Disc.*, Bk. II., c. i., § 39], and thus[1] ἀπαλλάττου τοῦ βίου [depart from life]. Or if thou wilt, live. Begin then, and remember after what manner, sworn to what laws, proselyte to what, dedicated to whom. Remember the two precepts—σιώπα [be silent], γέλως μὴ πολὺς ἔστω [let not your laughter be much.—*Epict. Ench.*, c. xxxiii., § 4]. Cut off tenderness of a certain kind; cut off *familiarity*, and that sympathy of a wrong kind. Learn to be with self, to talk with self. Commune with thy own heart; be that thy companion. For what other is there? See what thou has got by seeking others. Is this *society*? Is it genuine and of a right kind, when it is that fond desire of company, that seeking of companionship, and that want of talk and story? Is this what prompts thee in the case? Is this the affection that draws thee to the sociable acts and commerce with mankind? What is this but sickness of a dangerous kind? In such a case, stir not out; move not a foot abroad; nor open thy mouth to say one pleasing thing. For what a disposition, what a temper is this! Mistake not. Friendship has nothing to do here. See with whom this is in common. See the nation and people that are the most insatiable in this way, and hunt after conversations, parties, engagements, secresies, confidences, and friendships of this kind with the greatest eagerness, admiration, fondness. And see in what place this reigns the most: the court, and places near the court; the polite world; the great ones. Of what characters, life, manners are commonly that sort who can never rest out of company and want ever to be communicating their secrets? Call this to mind, and remember that real friendship is not founded on such a need. Friends are not friends if thus wanted. This is imbecility, impotence, effeminacy; and such is all that ardour and vehemence in behalf of others. How is this being a friend? How possible on these terms to be a lover of mankind? How be a brother? How a father and that common father of

[1] cf. Life.

men ? How the tutor and not tormentor and tyrant of the children ?

But, be this so no more. And that thou mayest not return any more to those ardours and vehemencies, know the condition and law, however terrible it appear :—

> To take pleasure in nothing.
> To do nothing with affection.
> To promise well of nothing.
> To engage for nothing.

Remember ὅτι ἀνίκητος εἶναι δύνασαι, ἔαν εἰς μηδένα ἀγῶνα καταβαίνῃς, ὃν οὐκ ἔστιν ἐπὶ σοὶ νικῆσαι ["that you can be invincible if you enter into no contest in which it is not in your power to conquer."—*Epict. Ench.*, c. xix., § 1].

Begin, therefore, from this moment and see how thou canst hold up against those other sort of reasonings, those compoundings, extenuations, excuses, self-flatteries, self-bemoanings. *Shall I abandon all my friends ?*—See first if thou canst be a friend or not. Remember what it is to be πιστός καὶ αἰδήμων [true and modest], and then talk of friendship ; not till then. Shall I have no more natural affection ?—Shall I ever have any ? Shall I not be cruel ? Or say what is cruelty ? 'Τοῦτον οὖν τὸν τυφλὸν μὴ ἀπολλύναι καὶ τὸν κωφόν;' [Ought we not to destroy this blind and deaf man ?—*Epict. Disc.*, Bk. I., c. xviii., § 7]. Is not this cruelty ? How not be cruel, if angry ? How not be angry with them if pleased with them after this manner, if hoping good of them (that vice should not be vice), if sympathising with them, and harmonising in a wrong way ; if joining in the play and relishing the playthings ; in short, if thinking of them, loving them, conversing or being with them any other wise than as that natural secretion [1] allows.

Remember of thyself that thou art (what another said) as "one born out of season; an untimely plant; in a wrong climate, a wrong season of the year." It is winter, and there is nothing besides of this kind extant, nothing to grow up with, no shelter or support. How then ? If I can bear my fruit, well and good ; if not, why do I cumber the ground ? Why live

---

[1] cf. p. 142.

below my order and species, degenerate, worthless, productive of
nothing good, disagreeing with the rest of the field and grove, a
briar and worse than a briar, a fungus, an excrescence, a disease of
the earth ? For what else is ὅ ἐπαμφοτερίζων ? [the wavering] and
ἀμβολιεργὸς ἀνὴρ [the lazy man] ?  But if thou canst grow out
of these distempers, so as to answer thy stock, and not to be
that other bastard growth ; then wait the season out ; stay out
thy time and to just maturity, till thou fall as that olive : χάριν
εἰδυῖα τῷ φύσαντι δένδρῳ [blessing nature that produced it.—*Mar.
Aurel. Med.*, Bk. IV., § 48]

# THE BODY.

(Σωμάτιον.)

Be once persuaded that self lies not in the body; that the *I* and *me* are something else; and that *thou* art by no means *this*, but distinct and different from this. Begin it by what is easiest (though to the vulgar not so easy), taking it first in the total separation. And thus to the dunghill with it; to kites, vultures, wolves, dogs, or whatever else, as well as to fire-worms, or to a decent grave, as they say. Then consider it in the union, abstracting it at first from what even the vulgar can abstract, as from hair, nails, excrements, or the things which by transpiration and change of substance are in this instant becoming excrements.

And as from the parts of the body, so also abstract it from the whole body itself, an excrement in seed, already half being, half putrefaction, half corruption. Thus be persuaded of this: that I (the real I) am not a certain figure, nor mass, nor hair, nor nails, nor flesh, nor limbs, nor body; but mind, thought, intellect, reason; what remains but that I should say to this body and all the pompous funeral, nuptial, festival (or whatever other) rites attending it, "*This is body. These are of the body only.* The body gives life to them, exalts them, gives them their vigour, force, power, and very being."

What is the tyrant's court? who gives it force?—The body. Withdraw the body; kill that once; let it be truly body (thyself living), and see what tyrant, sword, or axes are in the way?—But change the scene. Let it be another court, that has nothing terrible, and only what charms.—Again, what are charms, and whence the charm? Is not this body?—titillation, luxury, effeminacy, wantonness, flattery, ceremony, show. Where is mind in the midst of all this? Is it not more stifled here than anywhere? More effectually despatched, made away with, killed, sunk, and buried under all this? Is it not

147

the body that lives and flourishes ? Is it not the more body-like, the more truly corpse ? What else is it that is thus applied to, thus set up, thus improved and made much of ? What is it that with all this ceremony is dressed, walked, and aired, and drawn about and shown ? Is it not so much the more a helpless, weak, impotent thing, full of wants, ills, necessities, cravings ? And when all is not as full and fortunate as this state requires, is it not presently all calamity ? Is there any ease or relief from those other matters—the apartments, the attendants, the amusements, the shows ? Can these fomentations help ?—What is all this pomp, then ? Why thus disguise the thing ? Why thus embellish the poor body and exalt the carcase so much the more by endeavouring wrongly to suppress it ? For, how suppress it ? How truly overcome it, and all the maladies arising from it ? How cleanse this sink, how make this stable pure ? By hands ?— A Hercules cannot do it.—By linen, silks, powder, perfumes ? —"In vain, O ye nice, sweet, effeminate ones ! Nature will belie your labours. You are not roses, nor your bodies amber; the vulgar labouring bodies which ye despise are healthier and sweeter far."

By what then is the carcase to be subdued ?—By what, but by coming out of it ? by not being *it*, but in it ; and only so far in it and joined to it as Nature has made me : giving me withal my reason and those suitable faculties by which I can abstract myself, find out and know *myself*, by which I can separate from this mere matter, and redeem myself from the carcase. For how else redeem myself ? Whither turn me ? What respite ? what relief ? what quarter ? How from death ? how as to pain ? how sickness ? how losses ? How shun all these ? how deal with these ? Or will they be better for not thinking of them ? will they come gentler by this means ? will they be put off thus by being put off in thought and never reflected on ? Is this the way to lighten them, heal the sting, abate the paroxysms, and cure the distemper at the root ?—Καὶ ποῦ φύγω τὸν θάνατον ; μηνύσατέ μοι τὴν χώραν, &c. [Where can I escape death ? Show me the country that death does not visit.—*Epict. Disc.*, Bk. I., c. 27, § 9.]

Now, therefore, the Δόγμα upon the whole. Nature has joined thee to such a body, such as it is. The supreme mind would have it that this should be the trial and exercise of inferior minds. It has given thee thine; not just at hand, or as when they say into one's mouth; not just in the way so as to be stumbled on by good luck; not so easily either, but so as thou mayst reach it; so as within thy power, within command. See! Here are the incumbrances. This is the condition, the bargain, terms. Is the prize worth contending for? or what will become of me if I do not contend? How if the stream carries me down? how if wholly plunged in this gulf? What will be my condition then? what, when given up to body, when all body, and not a motion, not a thought, not one generous consideration or sentiment besides?—Must it not come to this, and soon too, very soon, if this be indulged? Such then is the condition of minds. So are they lodged, so matched, so proved and exercised. The high architect of minds has thus built, equipped, and launched thee, not into a smooth lake or river, but a rough ocean, and fitted thee to bear out the storm.—Am I thus set adrift? thus plunged?—Plunged, but thou mayst emerge. Buried, but thou mayst rise from this grave. Beset, but thou mayst break through.—" Man! use thy arms, thy instruments, hands, members, natural arms and limbs. What hinders thee? Fight it out, buffet the billows, countermine. Work thyself out of earth and stand above ground, if thou canst."—Is there any other way? Can I do better? How deal else with the carcase? Whither fly? What machination? What invention? How redeem myself? How be myself? Τῶν ὄντων τὰ μέν ἐστιν ἐφ᾽ ἡμῖν, τὰ δὲ οὐκ. [Of things, some are in our power, others are not.] These are the powerful words. This is the charm. Up! Rouse, then; for here it is. No remission. No sparing. No quarter to this death; for it is death, true death, the other is nothing.

Remember this, then, and in the morning chiefly when rising to action heavily or remittedly—the gulf—river—grave —carcase. How redeem myself? How be myself? What way but this? Or is there any better? any other?

Body-coach. Body-guards. Ushers of the body.—Sensible expression! For what is there in the thing, but body?—The royal thing!—a body.—Majesty!—a body.—The impression it makes, the fear, wonder, admiration!—Body—body still. For what else but a vile servitude, a base homage and worship of this home-body is the occasion of such a prostitution to the body or bodies abroad?

In bodily fear.—Right, for what fear but for the body?—Or how shall we say? In mindly fear? Alas! my poor mind! What will they do to it? Murder this also? destroy this? wound this? if not, how *me*?—And yet there are murderers. There are, that spare not here neither (for so thou art pleased to suffer it), that torment, that murder.—What murderers, of time, thought, resolution, and everything good! Yet these are friends. No fear of these.—Oh wretch! When wilt thou have true fear. When fear for thy mind? For this fear is to purpose. It will bring security; all will be well, and all fear at an end.

It is the custom of our language to say *this body* or *that body*, for this or that man. Is a body, then, one and the same, when dead as when alive? How alive? Is it the warmth that makes a difference? Is it the moving of the blood? How if a body were to live always in sound state; would this be any body? would this be a real person? or the same person?—What is the same person, then? or what is the person, the self, but the self-knowing, the self-remembering, the self-determining part? And what is this but a mind? What has the body to do but as by accident? Why this body and that body, and not this mind and the other mind? For it is of a system of fancies, perceptions, thoughts, that we are speaking; not of a figure in flesh or wax; not of a statue, a piece of clock-work, a set of strings or wires.

Remember, then, where the system is: there the person and being, there the death, there the improvement and ruin, there the good and ill. He therefore who is wholly turned towards this; who is all this; who is himself, and nothing besides himself, has nothing to fear (for all is in his power). But he who has placed himself in that other system finds the contrary, and may by way of excellence (if he pleases) call himself some body; as making nothing of one who would be no body, and who thinks as no body.

That other propriety of our language happens to be indeed absurd. But hear how admirably our law speaks—"Bring the body of such a man"—"an assault on the body of such a man."—This is right and true. For, what else can be imprisoned or sent to death but the body? What else is assaulted but the body? Who assaults the mind but the mind itself?

# PASSIONS.

*Qua data porta ruunt* [Wherever an outlet is given, forth they rush.—*Virgil's Æn.*, Bk. I., 1. 83.] The same is true of the passions. Think often of this picture, for, though poetical, what can be more exact?—*Eurus, Notus, Boreas.*—Thus anger, ambition, desires, loves, eager and tumultuous joys, wishes, hopes, transporting fancies, extravagant mirth, airiness, humour, fantasticalness, buffoonery, drollery. When once any of these are let loose, when once they have broken their boundaries and forced a passage, what ravage and destruction are sure to follow? and what must it cost ere all be calm again within?

Remember the wedges in the machine, and how it is when but one of these by chance is loosened.

JOY.—There is one sort of joy which is fierce, eager, boisterous, impetuous, restless, which carries with it a sort of insatiableness, rage, madness, sting; and which afterwards is followed by disgust and discontent. There is another sort of joy which is soft, still, peaceable, serene, which has no mixture or alloy; of which there is no excess, but the more it is felt, the more perfect and refined it grows, the more content and satisfaction it yields through the whole of life. To the first of these a thousand things are necessary, a thousand outward and casual circumstances concurring, the least of which being removed, or ceasing, it also must cease. To the second there is nothing necessary but what depends upon ourselves.

Consider now withal which of these we should rather endeavour to give ourselves: whether that sort, in the midst of which, if any sudden chance invade us, we are instantly abashed terrified, confounded, sunk; or whether we should choose to be in that sort of disposition in which, whatever happens that is either disgraceful, calamitous, or tragical, we are not, on this account, in the least dejected or dismayed, we are not ashamed of ourselves, or contracted, nor do we feel any of those gripes and gnawings of discontent and bitter sadness, but can look up and

151

set our face against the weather, preserve a steady countenance, and meet our fate not only undauntedly, but cheerfully?

How miserable a joy is that which is founded in ignorance? and how ridiculous to see a person this moment thus transported, who if he heard the news would instantly be struck dead?

The test of a true joy is certain news, which, if it can be borne is sincere, lawful, sound; if otherwise, treacherous, corrupt, false. News is come that your estate is seized; that the enemy is master of it. You are condemned to banishment; you are condemned to death.—How is it now? How is this received within? If calmly, all is well; the joy was genuine, legitimate, fit to be indulged, and of the right sort. But if thou standest as one who is thunder-struck; if it be: "O wretch! what have I been doing? No more now of these fooleries!" then is it true indeed that these were fooleries, and nothing else. Then also is it that thou mayst truly despise both thyself and thy former joys. For they were only fit for one who was wholly ignorant, vulgar, and conscious of nothing noble, excellent, or truly rejoicing.

How long wilt thou continue to admit that unsociable, indecent, petulant, impotent, childish joy, and abandon that which is sober, grave, modest, fixed, constant, equal, which has no reverse or vicissitude, which has no alliance with shame, which is a stranger to remorse and repentance, which is humane, and sociable, and which is fitted to all human events? Remember that these are perfect enemies to each other, and at constant defiance. Whatever thou givest to one is lost from the other; and not merely that, but employed and vigorously made use of against the other.

The rack and ruin of all strict inward economy, and the rock on which it must necessarily split, is that light, airy, transported temper and elevated joy which raises high and aloft these ideas of the pleasures, diversions, serious affairs and businesses of the world. And though laughter be a passion which may be employed sometimes against this very evil, and against the pomp and ridiculous solemnity of human affairs, yet is there nothing more unsafe, or more difficult of management. This was well perhaps heretofore, and might suit with one who was yet unfixed, and only in a way towards improvement; but it must become a very different kind ere it be suitable for one who understands himself. It is enough to say that it is wholly unmanageable whilst any of that impotent sort remains, or whilst anything of this kind is in the least degree involuntary in the temper, and not perfectly under command. But what strength of mind, constancy, and firmness this implies is easy to understand.

Remember, if at any time the general fancy or idea of life be high, florid, luxuriant (which is the dissolution of all right discipline, conduct, and economy) that this is owing to that elevated temper, and the seeds of that intoxicating passion. And not only this; but when the mind is dejected, clouded, and in that other extreme, so as to relish nothing, and to be unapt towards the greater and worthier things, remember that this also is owing to nothing other than that sort of passion which before had raised it, and which is now the occasion of the fall.

See what kind of temper that is, in which it is commonly said *he's glad he's alive*; and how the vulgar can take notice of this, and, in a manner, see the thing. What can be more ridiculous?

What is it that those French people call *eveillé?* and whether such a one be most awake, or asleep. In a dream we are then nearest awake when we perceive that it is a dream. What is life else but a dream? Apparitions, vision, fancy. Think of this often, and thou art but as in a second sort of dream. Better, much better, *to dream* (as they say), than to be in that other manner, *awake* and *sprightly.*

What remedy is there against that fervour, eagerness, vehemence, but in the contrary behaviour, which will be called dulness and stupidity?

If at any time it be said, " He is changed ; he is grown dull; he has lost what he had either of wit or humour ;" θάρρει; all is well; and thou mayst rejoice as over a good sign, for such it is.

How happy had it been with thee,[1] hadst thou kept to these rules ! Now see whither a certain lightness and transport has led thee ! and what passions are grown from those wrong

[1] *St. Giles*, December, 1699.

# 154 *The Philosophical Regimen.*

indulgences in friendship! Wretch! ἴθι ἐπὶ τὰς ἀποδιοπομπήσεις [Have recourse to expiations—*Epict. Disc.*, Bk. II., c. xviii., § 20]. Consider ἴχνη τινὰ καὶ μώλωπες [There are certain bruises and blisters left in it which, if not effaced, will become sores.— *Epict. Disc.*, Bk. II., c. xviii., § 11]. If thou canst not think of these as sores, all is corruption and sore to the bottom of thy mind. Do, therefore, as becomes thee. Καὶ καλλίω θάνατον σκεψάμενος ἀπαλλάττου τοῦ βίου, &c. [Acknowledge death to be nobler than life, and depart hence.—*Plato Legg.*, 854 C.]. But it is in thy power to think of these as sores, and treat them as such. Therefore, remember after any weak seasons, as after dreams and fancies of the night, or after any overpowering encounters, after any of those high, florid, luxuriant thoughts, any of that treacherous *joy*, those desires, loves, impotent wishes, hopes, excursions, ravings—remember how this running ulcer is to be treated. Remember how it is that the purulent matter gathers, that the part inflames, that the funguses and proud flesh arise, and yet at last the part mortifies and grows insensible. Is the feeling in the meanwhile to be indulged on this occasion? Is the itch to be satisfied, or the patient allowed to appease the eagerness of it by scratching, or even by tampering and feeling? Is not the part to be bound up close and kept from the air? and when it is opened to dress, are not incisions, cauteries, and other things to be used? Is not all this patiently and even cheerfully endured through hope of the cure? How then? Wilt thou tamper with thyself? Wilt thou spare thy flesh and fly from the fire, the steel, the operations and sharper remedies? Or are the other wounds something, but these nothing? Is it no matter how it is within, or whether thou livest always with a macerated, corrupted mind? Wouldst thou willingly go out of the world because of such a body that is incurable, and not because of such a mind?

Either, therefore, thou art curable or not. But if curable, remember in what way, and what belongs to one who is a patient and under cure.

The same as in an amputation. Either (says he) you must part with this limb or die.—I part with it.—Then bear the operation.—But it will cost me pain.—Then die. For what is there else? How deal with such a passion as this? If it stay,

must it not be a worse gangrene than that other ? If it go,
can it go without pain ? Be patient, therefore, and endure what
is necessary; for thou must either bear the remedy, or the
disease, or death. But the disease here is intolerable; therefore
choose of the other two, and say which.

Ὥσπερ οἱ ἰατροὶ ἀεὶ τὰ ὄργανα, καὶ σιδήρια πρόχειρα ἔχουσι
[As physicians have always their instruments and knives ready
for emergencies.—*Mar. Aurel.*, Bk. III., § 13]. Well may the
Δόγματα [opinions] be compared to the surgeon and his instruments. Consider the wounds they are to cure; consider how it
is whenever the instruments are ever so little disused. What
inflammation, soreness, putrefaction ? And when the part is
benumbed and without feeling, how much worse is the symptom ?
How much more desperate the case ? What incisions ere the
sound flesh is come at and the wound again laid open as it
should be ? Remember, therefore, to search the wound, and that
here it is necessary to probe often. Remember to inquire
within, how is the sore ? How does it heal, or change ? How
was it in bed ? in the night ? as I slept ? as I lay awake ? how
this morning ? how at meals ? how after exercise, going abroad,
business, application, pleasure ?—Is it not thus with one who has
but a common sore ? And for fear of what ? For fear of being
lame; for fear of a deformity of person; for fear of being
offensive by an ill-smell. What solicitude ! what anxious care !
what concern and thoughtfulness ! "Who can tell me anything
that is good for me ? Where can I have the best advice ? Talk
to me of this, for what else can I hear of ? What can I mind
else in my condition?"—Is it not thus that they go from one company to another, inquiring, searching, reasoning, and all with
relation to this dreaded distemper ? But what is this distemper
in comparison with another ? Is this the only proper distemper ?
Are other sores less felt within ? Is there not a worse lameness,
a worse deformity and filth ? How then ? Is there to be less
solicitude here ? Is there good reason to look up and go about
unconcerned as one that has no wound, no ail within ? Is that
wretch excusable who wanders about melancholy, disconsolate,
and pining, as carrying that within his body which consumes;
and shall he only not be concerned who carries the same in a
more inward breast, and who is preyed upon and daily devoured

within? Or are the passions nothing? Is the other distemper real and this imaginary? If so, have done: go to the remedies no more: no more as he that has sore eyes to the spring and water: no more as to the surgeon's shop. But if it be not so, but contrariwise; if there be no real distemper of a man but the distemper of his mind; if neither lameness nor sores, nor any other distemper, nor death itself, be anything to him with whom opinion is not distempered—then remember that this is the only distemper, the only sore, which thou now labourest under. And remember that it is not thy business to show a cheerful face and walk abroad as one healthy and of a good constitution; but that thy proper carriage (if in a way of cure) is thus: περίεισι δὲ καθάπερ οἱ ἄρρωστοι, εὐλαβούμενός τι κινῆσαι τῶν καθισταμένων πρὶν πῆξιν λαβεῖν [" He goes about like a sick person, being careful not to move any of the things before they are firmly fixed."—*Epict. Ench.* 48, § 2].

Fear not. That which is now diet, confinement, physic, and the surgeon's instruments, will in a little time be wholesome food, liberty, open air, exercise of limbs, and a nobler use of instruments, the χρῆσις φαντασιῶν [use of appearances] according to nature; provided that thou continuest in this method invariably, immovably, remembering the two assistants ἐγκράτεια [self-contained] and καρτερία [patience] παρακαλοῦσιν, ἔφη, τοὺς παραγιγνομένους ἐπὶ τὸν τόπον, θαρρεῖν, καὶ μὴ ἀποδειλιᾶν· λέγουσαι, ὅτι βραχὺ ἔτι δεῖ καρτερῆσαι αὐτοὺς, εἶτα ἥξουσιν εἰς ὁδὸν καλήν [" They encourage travellers, he said, and keep them from cowardice and despair, letting them know at the same time that if they will but hold out and strive a little, they will quickly be easy and come into a good road"—*Cebes' Tabula*, lines 267-270].

And this ἀνέχου καὶ ἀπέχου [bear and forbear]. Ἐὰν οὖν διατηρεῖς σεαυτὸν ἐν τούτοις τοῖς ὀνόμασι, μὴ γλιχόμενος τοῦ ὑπ᾽ ἄλλων κατὰ ταῦτα ὀνομάζεσθαι, ἔσῃ ἕτερος, καὶ εἰς βίον εἰσελεύσῃ ἕτερον [" If, then, thou maintainest thyself in the possession of these names, *i.e.*, good, modest, rational, without desiring to be called by these names by others, thou wilt be another person and wilt enter on a new life."—*Marcus Aurel., Med.*, X., § 8].

Remember that the sovereign precept, " to cut off the ὄρεξις (desire), and to use strongly the ἔκκλισις (aversion)," is in a real sense dejection and mortification. It is the depressing, extinguishing, killing that wrong sort of joy and enlivened temper; the starving, supplanting that exuberant, luxuriant fancy; and the sapping and undermining of the passions, cutting the grass under their feet, drying up the sources that feed, cutting the fibres of the root, to intercept the nourishment. It is the introducing of a contrary disposition : the wearied, allayed, low, sunken; that which creates a mean and poor opinion of outward things, diminishes the objects and brings to view the viler but truer side of things. When this works strongly, the ἔκκλισις (aversion) works as it should do. 'Tis well. Be of good hope. When the other disposition has any footing, or creeps upon the mind, secretly, imperceptibly, in any form or specious shape (as of friendship, humanity, amicable pleasures, social joys, sympathy, natural affection, endearment, tenderness, love), remember here is the poison, here the corruption, the distortion of all. Here the ὄρεξις (desire) ranges, and has free liberty. Is this for thy state? Knowest thou yet how to use these affections? Is it for thee to take up the ὄρεξις (desire) and manage it as one that has nerves? Art thou past the first degree? Art thou no longer frustrated or hindered? Hast thou no more to do but to seek the σχέσεις [relations], being sure to act as thou pleasest, and as thou decreest? Art thou at leisure to polish? If far from this, if far from being conqueror of the first, if every day foiled and beaten, if the sores are still fresh and bleeding; what shouldst thou do but treat thyself as belongs to thy state?—not allowing stronger food; not aiming at robustness whilst in a languishing state; not venturing to add spirits to the fever, nor nerves to the convulsions. Or is it the same as if all were well? Is there not most reason for dejection when the distemper is thus forgotten? How when the relapses are repeated, and when there is every hour some breaking-out? What looks, what countenance befits such a one? But still I wait till confirmed, and then see. In the meanwhile let it be ὀφρύς [arrogance], and rejoice it is so.

What is that sort of joy, humour, airiness, but the mother of base opinion? And are mother and brat the same? Is not the first, opinion also?—As how?—As over some great matter or as in good and happy circumstances.—And when these circumstances change, how then ?—οἴμοι · τάλας ἐγώ [Woe to me, how wretched I am !—*Epict. Ench.*, c. 26].

In everything therefore that is in this manner agreeable, and steals upon the soul, in every still, peaceful moment not rightly accounted for, not well-derived, inquire, listen, and hear what is said *within*. Be it in conversation, amongst friends, or with books, or in ever so seemingly good situation or plausible a circumstance.—Is there not a voice that speaks within and begins to order and prescribe ? Is there not a subaltern power that says to the lord and master-mind, "Master ! it is good for us to be here. Let us to work and build."—Visions ! visions indeed ! mere visions ! how long wilt thou thus build and delight in these buildings ?

Know the bastard-joy from the legitimate.—How is it ?— Alive and well.—What is well ?—My body, estate ?—bastard ! My relations, friends, reputation, fame ?—bastard ! My country ?— bastard still, illegitimate, spurious, false. But let us hear again : what other joy, what is well ? A body ?—No ; but a mind, which has set me more at ease as to what relates to a body.—Rejoice then. This is legitimate.—I am the poor and merry.—Legitimate !—Dying and merry.—Legitimate !—Ill-spoken of and merry—Legitimate !—I can play the cards with indifference, and be cheerful ; play or leave off, and be cheerful.—Legitimate ! Legitimate !

COMPASSION.—To compassionate, *i.e.* to join with in passion, be passionate with.—To commiserate, *i.e.* to join with in misery, be miserable with. This in one order of life is right and good ; nothing more harmonious ; and to be without this, or not to feel this, is unnatural, horrid, immane. How else would the machine perform ? For this is meant still of the machine, or what is all one, of the mind, nature or temper, as it is when acting like a machine in the common way of life, in animals and men-animals, where there is no better rule than the speciousness of the object, nor no other force to act by but that of the πάθη [perturbations] raised thence, where the only energy is from pain and pleasure, sorrow and transport. Where men are thus light and heavy, airy and clouded, always under the power of passion, always passionate, always miserable in their own cases and about their own affairs, it would be unequal, unjust, unsociable, and hard not to be so in the affairs of others and be wretched too for company.

This as to one order of life, where this fellow-wretchedness agrees admirably and makes so great a part in the order of things, and shows us so fair a side of Nature. Hence the union of several species, their mutual relation, sympathy, life. But in another order of life, in another species, and in respect of another, a higher relation, nothing can be more dissonant than this; nothing more inconsistent with that true affection, which in a mind soundly rational is, as it were, in the place of all. To act by temper simply is, in such a one, the greatest degeneracy; a sinking down into a lower species of nature; a betraying of that higher one and of that relation into which he is assigned. To act by temper simply (though ever so good a temper), is in such a one, a loss even of simplicity, a quitting of that uniform, self-same, divine, and simple principle, for a various, manifold, compound, and changeable one, a composition, mere composition; for what else does the word temper signify?—Let tempers then be as they will. Happy they who by chance have a good temper and by chance keep it; who by chance are good as that is good, ill as that is ill, in temper, out of temper, as fortune pleases; as the scene without changes, so this scene within. Excellent happiness! Yet this is all; this is their happiness. And to be miserable also, to be wretched by whiles, this also is their dignity, their happiness. Were it otherwise they would be miserable indeed, miserable in a worse degree, perfectly miserable and unnatural.—Be it so then. Let those who commiserate themselves, commiserate others in the things in which, according to them, misery lies. Let them congratulate in this manner. But do thou for thy part remember that ὅπου γὰρ χαίρειν εὐλόγως, ἐκεῖ καὶ τὸ συγχαίρειν [wherever there is cause to rejoice there is also cause to congratulate.—*Epict. Disc.*; II., c. 5, § 23]. And only congratulate and condole according to the precept ὅταν κλάιοντα ἴδῃς τινὰ, &c. [when you see one weeping, have sympathy, but do not inwardly lament.—*Epict. Ench.*, c. 26]. In no way sympathise, or feel as they feel, when they take either this or the other event (even what is unpremeditated) for good or ill. Τὸ ἄλλου παρὰ φύσιν σοὶ κακὸν μὴ γενέσθω [Let not that which in another is contrary to nature be an evil to you.—*Epict. Disc.*, Bk. III., c. xxiv., § 1.] Be true then to thyself.

Malignity hid under humanity—[1]*Nigrae sucus loliginis ærugo mera.* Of this kind all that sort of false pity expressed for faults of others; affected sorrow; anger on the public account and for mankind; the quarrels engaged in for the commonwealth.—Remember that whole season from the first apostacy of a certain set of men to thy retirement hither to Holland the first time. See, therefore, whither does this false humanity lead. Wilt thou have more of it?

Remember of old, and lately just before this thy second retreat, how the passions stood, and how that certain involuntary motion towards bed-time and in bed, dreams, waking, sudden starts, rejolts, bangs, eagerness, agony.—How near to real madness! not so much by the violence of the immediate passion, as by reflection, repetition, revolving, searching, renewing, undoing, remedying, regretting, reinstating, revoking, in vain all, yet without intermission and to loss of mind. Thus before first retreat hither, speech in the other senate.—And on return, theod. and blood-letting.—Syrens and their victory.—Afterwards new perfections aimed at and affairs restored, then public again, and estate, economy, with that affair which continued even till the other day (Nov. 6th, 1703). Also the distractions before the second retreat. Thus frequently in other losses of mind, not knowing which way to turn when beset, when urged, when divided in opinion on family and public emergencies; and in reality thus distracted, with restless nights, throes, labours, groans.—From how much would a little simplicity have saved. Ἅπλωσον σεαυτόν [Have simplicity], and presently how soon all is still! σταθερὰ πάντα καὶ κόλπος ἀκύμων [Everything stable and a waveless harbour.—*Marc. Aurel.*, Bk. XII., § 32].

---

[1] The black juice of the cuttle-fish, unadulterated envy.—*Hor.*, Sat. I., iv., lines 100-101.

# PLEASURE AND PAIN.

Τραχέως κινεῖται τὸ σαρκίδιον, εἶτα πάλιν λείως—ἡ θύρα ἤνοικται ["This weak flesh is sometimes affected by harsh, sometimes by smooth impressions—the door is open."—*Epict. Disc.*, Bk. II., c. i., 19].

Μόνον ἀφορητόν ἐστι τὸ ἄλογον, τὸ δ' εὔλογον φορητόν ["That alone is unendurable which is unreasonable; but everything reasonable may be endured."—*Ibid.*, Bk. I., c. ii., § 1].

Τό ἀγαθὸν δεῖ εἶναι τοιοῦτον ἐφ' ᾧ θαρρεῖν ἄξιον; μή τι οὖν βέβαιον ἡ ἡδονή; ἐπὶ τῷ ἀγαθῷ ἄξιον ἐπαίρεσθαι; ἐφ' ἡδονῇ οὖν παρούσῃ ἄξιον ἐπαίρεσθαι; ["Ought the good to be something in which it is right to confide? Is pleasure then a stable thing? Is it right then to be elated by good? Is it right then to be elated by a present pleasure?"—*Ibid.*, Bk. II., c. xi., 20-22].

*Miseri quibus intentata nites!* ["Hapless they, t'whom thou untriedst seemest fair."—*Hor.*, Bk. I., Od. v.]

PAIN.—What disturbs?—Pain? the paradox? Cry of the world?—Come on. How as to pleasure? Riches, riot, fame?— The proofs in these cases.—What of death?—the injury?—the harm?—Are not all paradoxes, equal paradoxes?—This the hardest.—Postpone then, settle but the others which are so plain and have been so certainly proved, and see how easy this will be, and remember still that those who object against this are the same that object against the other; the same persons, the same reason. But in the other they move thee not. Thou art certain; thou knowest. Therefore wait a little; and thou mayst also say in this, *I know*.

As for pleasure; experience. As for pain, take it thus: what is it but *loss of mind*? For as long as the Δόγματα[1] are present, the consequent affections of the soul will be present

---

[1] καὶ τί ἔτι μοι μέλει μεταλοψύχῳ ὄντι; [What signifies to me anything that happens while my soul is above it?—*Epict. Disc.*, Bk. I., c. vi., § 29.]

also; and when these are incumbent, what is it that the soul can feel? And why are they not incumbent? Why do they fail upon occasion?—See, why!

Again. As long as there is *presence of mind, i.e.,* as long as the mind is present to itself, and in the use of its right Δόγματα; as long as it has these at command, it has its bent at command, and when it is bent, what is it can resist it? For how is it even with the common villains where it is mere bent, mere will, resoluteness, or resolution from one single Δόγμα or opinion, and that too imperfect and ill-grounded? A false species of the *decorum pulchrum,* τὸ καλόν? And what, therefore, should the true species cause?

Again, ἡ θύρα τοῦ οἴκτου [the door of the house]. What more? Or, if it be shut for a moment or two, bend but the whole force of mind hitherward and see who can shut it, and for how long—τετάσθαι τὴν διάνοιαν ἐπὶ τὸ πλοῖον [your thoughts ought to be directed towards the ship.—*Epict. Ench.,* c. vii.] and τετάσθαι τὴν ψυχὴν [direct the soul to this mark.—*Epict. Disc.,* Bk. IV., c. xii., § 15] have the same sense. Thank Nature that has opened; and laugh at him who would shut. But if the passage itself be unpleasant, if neither of the two can please, if it be hard both staying in and going out, 'tis sad indeed. But see what is in the way, and whether the rub be in the passage or in thyself.

Now at last consider from hence and make this sad, too sad, reflection; for such it is if thou wilt not wholly conform to thy known laws and rule of life. If this be the consequence of *loss* of mind at such a time, if such misery be from the absence of the right Δόγματα at serious hours, what is it then in wantonness and gaiety to allow this loss of mind, and at free and easy seasons to destroy this use, this vigour and ready presence of the Δόγματα, by relaxation and loss or remission of the Προσοχή? [attention.]

Coward flesh!—Why so? Why blame the flesh? Is not all human flesh the same—the hardy villain's, the true, brave man's, the effeminate, voluptuous man's? Is not the gout, the stone, the fire, the iron, the same to one as to the other? Is not the sensation and feeling the same? Where, then, is the difference? Is it not in another sort of feeling? And what is this sort of feeling but *opinion ?*—Say not, therefore, "coward flesh!" but "coward opinion!"

Such a one bears, but I cannot.—Why? What is it makes him bear? — Is it sturdiness, anger? (opinion!) — bravado? (opinion!)—hope, expectation? (opinion!)—fanaticism, enthusiasm?—Opinion, all opinion!—See, then, what thou hast within from thy own discipline to answer this opinion with opinion, and thou wilt find thou hast more than barely enough to answer it. Thou canst exceed it all; the thing is more accountable, every object is better, every reason surer, every thought juster, every affection, bent, possession, righter. But thou must see then to be truly possessed, and in order to be truly possessed with these things, and to have them for opinion (real opinion), thou must first be dispossessed of those other opinions, those prepossessions and prejudices which have gone before.—To work, then. Throw out the deceit of luxury; throw out pleasure; out with all of this kind. But if all be not out yet, wonder not if pain be such a business, and all of that kind so terrible and hard to bear.

PLEASURE.—Is it plain, then, that an army ever so brave, and formed on a right discipline of soldiery, is presently corrupted by pleasure? Was it thus a Capua? Is every soldier less a soldier for having taken of it or yielded to it ever so little?—for having fallen in love, caressed a mistress or a boy with fondness; for having eaten, or lain, or done those other things with too much delicacy; for having only had too pleasant quarters, enjoyed but for a while the pleasantness of a climate, breathed the soft air and sucked in the corrupting sweets? Is the seaman less a seaman, the huntsman less a huntsman, and so in every manly exercise or function—are the brave less brave, the generous less generous? And is it not in honesty and life the same?—Who, then, would bear with this? Who that is καλὸς καὶ ἀγαθός. O Pleasure! who would endure thee?

# FANCIES OR APPEARANCES.

IDEAS, VISA.—Μήτε ἐν ταῖς φαντασίαις ἀλᾶσθαι [Be not rambling in your ideas—*Mar. Aurel.*, Bk. VIII., § 51]. Of the fancies remember four sorts.

The first such as are absolutely vicious and require expiation: which remember religiously to perform.

The second of a mixed kind, and flattering by what they borrow from virtue. Against these, fight, as against chimeras, centaurs, monsters.

The third sort, such as are necessary, as concerning relations, family, friends, public. Let these be sparingly admitted, and never but in a certain disposition, *i.e.*, when they strike not deep, not closely affect: never but when the temper is allayed, and the ἔκκλισις [aversion] rightly set.

Fourthly, as for the last sort, viz., those unnecessary, wandering, uncertain ones, that haunt the mind, and busy it as in dreams; these, as no other than the excrescences and funguses of the mind, endeavour to cut wholly off, much rather than the warts or corns from off thy body, and not merely as lumber and weight, but because the fancies of this kind, like suckers, draw from the good nourishment of the mind and spend its strength. This is that matter which serves to feed a strong and luxuriant fancy, furnishes wit and sets off conversation. Perhaps, too, this is what may prepare for action and produce capacity and ability in affairs, by creating readiness of mind, where so many things are thought of and such a multitude of cases pre-supposed. But it is not thy aim either to be a noted wit or one of those busy engagers in the world; if it be, lay aside those other aims which are towards tranquillity and the possession of a mind. For these things are no ways mutually reconcilable.

Upon what does all depend? Where is there ground for hope? Where the refuge, safety and security, but in the aptness, readiness, vigour and piercingness of the right images, appearances, rules, and in the habit of the mind this way ? Now how should these be vigorous, prompt, offering themselves and crowding in upon occasion, when there is need of defence ? How should these become rendered thus familiar, native, genuine, but by being engrafted, rooted, or (if I may say so) incorporated with the mind ? And how should this be, whilst the mind vacates to other and contrary ideas ? whilst it lives and inhabits amongst *those* and only visits *these* ?—Remember, therefore, this δόγμα, and have it present in all trifling, fond, dallying, wandering, floating seasons. Remember that all this while I am tempering, sharpening, pointing the wrong and destructive *visa*; whilst for want of use the other lose their edge, grow dull, unwieldy, and unmanageable.

[1]When any idea of pleasure strikes, reason thus :—Before I had this idea, before I was thus struck, was it ill with me ?—No.—Therefore remove the idea and I am well.—But having this idea such as I have, I cannot want the thing without regret. See, therefore, which is better, either to suffer under this want till the idea be removed, or by satisfying this want confirm not only this idea but all of the same stamp ? What is this but to nourish impotence and lay a lasting ground-work of distress, misery, and growing want ?

To resist the assault of any one idea is to raise a siege. To yield, is to suffer a breach for all to enter and take possession. What contest, what combat can equal this, which is no less a matter than piety, friendship, fidelity, probity, magnanimity, peace, and tranquillity ? And in which deity, religion, laws, country, are included ? What are those other laurels, the naval or civic crowns ? What are those other victories or triumphs to this ? And yet what remissness, what deadness here !

See, whensoever any melancholy fancy occurs not to compound with it (as God forbid)—no, but not quite so bad—or, it may mend, or *non si male nunc et olim sic erit* [If there be evil to-day, there will not also be to-morrow.—*Hor.,* Od. II., x.]. but run straight to what is furthest, and suppose the worst, suppose all to have already happened that can happen. If it be

[1] cf. *Characteristics,* I., p. 311.

health that is threatened : suppose disease and death; if reputation : suppose infamy and utter disgrace; if it be an ill in family affairs or in the public : suppose both the one and the other entirely ruined and already extinct. Thus all low and mean thoughts will be removed ; all earnest engagements, pursuits, endeavours, laid aside : καὶ οὐδὲν οὐδέποτε οὔτε ταπεινὸν ἐνθυμηθήσῃ, οὔτε ἄγαν ἐπιθυμήσεις τινός [And you will never think of anything mean or desire anything extravagantly.—*Epict., Ench.,* c. xxi.]

There is nothing more useful in the management of the *visa,* or that helps to fight more strongly against the striking imaginations, than to have a sort of custom of putting them into words, making them speak out and explain themselves as it were *vivâ-voce,* and not tacitly and murmuringly, not by a whisper and indirect insinuation, imperfectly, indistinctly, and confusedly, as their common way is. For instance, I hear of a great, a prodigious estate. I find, I admire. What is it I say to myself ? What is that the imagination tells me ?—" Happy is he that can keep so many horses, so many coaches, such a table ! " For what else is it that makes an estate be admired ? Take away the dishes, the liveries, the furniture, pictures, brick, stone, grassplots, gravel, and the rest ; and what is there left even for the vulgar to admire ?

Again, I hear on the other side of some loss of fortune and estate. I am moved ; the fancy prevails ; what is it I say to myself ?—If this go on I must sell all and live privately.—Do so then, and live privately.—I shall not have a servant left.— Right, then begin and serve thyself.—But I shall want bread.— And what of that ?—I shall die.—Is there anything more ? Where is the harm ? Why not die thus, as well as any other way ? as well as of a fever, of gout, or stone, or (but a few years hence, if one live till then) of age ?—But this is shameful.—For whom ? For others perhaps it may be shameful that an honest man starves ; but how can it be shameful for him, himself ? how can it be his shame, if not his fault ? Can a man on any other occasion die as becomes a man, die generously and nobly ; and cannot he in the same manner starve as generously and nobly, and with as good a heart ? What is there that should hinder ? Say, what is generosity ? What magnanimity ? And where else can these be shown, where practised besides, if not here ?

These are the dialogues that are to be studied and dwelt upon, written, meditated, revolved. These are the discourses we should be versed in, instead of those which we affect so much with other people, to convince others of their duty and of what is fitting and just. What have I to do with others ? Let me first convince myself. Let me learn to reason and discourse thus with my own mind, that I may be no longer inconsistent with myself and my own reason, and live in perpetual disorder and perplexity. Let me examine my ideas, challenge and talk with them thus, before they be admitted to pass. "Idea ! Wait a little, stay for me, till I am ready : till I have recollected myself. Come on. Let us see. What art thou ? From whence ?"

What is the subject ? Is it riches ? or a title ? Is it a female ? Is it renown and credit ?—My name will be famous ! —Amongst whom ? in what place ? for how long ? What if it were to reach to Asia ? what if to continue a thousand years or more ? Erostratus has a name. Alexander has a name. What is this to them, now at this time ? What was it then during their life ? What is fame ?—A certain sound.—Of what kind ? of trumpets, timbrels, drums ?—No, but of tongues.—Of what tongues ? of such as are governed by reason, or that have any regular or steady motion, or that are consonant to themselves ?— No ; but on the contrary, that are irrationally governed, wild, incoherent, inconsonant. What, therefore, is fame ? What is the rustling of the wind amongst the trees ? Is this all ?—Say, then ; what is there else ? What is it that praise can confer ? What is there that is made better by it ? What is it to the diamond, or the purple ? What to a generous and worthy mind ? What is it to the sun whether he be magnified or disparaged ? whether he be thought intelligent or unintelligent, whether he be thought to move about the earth, or the earth and all the other planets to move about him, and to attend him ? Consider yet further. What is it to Deity itself, whether praised or dispraised, acknowledged, or disowned ? Whose is the hurt ? Can Deity suffer ? Is it His ill ? How can this be ? Yet see ; are there not those who blaspheme, revile, and disparage ? What do even those do, who think they praise ? How if Deity admit this; if Deity suffer not, what else can suffer? what other perfection be impaired? How canst thou be worsted or injured?

But others will suffer; others be deceived.—What is that to thee? What hast thou to do with their calamity, their ill? Why concerned for this error of theirs, more than for any other? If they disparage virtue, if they revile goodness, what matter is it in what subject, or who the person is? Whether it be in thy person, or in that of Socrates or Diogenes? Where, then, lies the ill of obloquy, unjust censure, and reproach? Where else but in the minds of those who carry it and are the authors of it?—But in my own mind, how is it an ill, and when?—When opinion makes it so.

This is the right use of ideas and appearances. This is treating them as is fitting. This is the art and method to be learnt: how to put them into words so as to reason with them; force them to speak; hear their language and return them their answer. This is the rhetoric, eloquence, and wit which we should affect; here it is we should be dexterous, expert, and ready. These are the turns and this the presence of mind which we should admire and be emulators of. And if we improved once in this way we should see the effect, and how well all would be within. Τὸ νευροσπαστοῦν ἐστίν ἐκεῖνο, τὸ ἔνδον ἐγκεκρυμμένον. ἐκεῖνο ῥητορεία, ἐκεῖνο ζωὴ, ἐκεῖνο, εἰ δεῖ εἰπεῖν, ἄνθρωπος [This which pulls the string is the thing which is hidden within; this is the power of persuasion, this is life, this, if one may so say, is man.—*Mar. Aurel., Med.*, Bk. X., § 38].

Remember that in the χρῆσις φαντασιῶν [use of appearances] one of the chief parts is the inversion, change, and transforming of the fancies or appearances, and the wresting of them from their own natural and vulgar sense into a meaning truly natural and free of all delusion and imposture. I am told that I shall be honoured.—Right, for I may vindicate to myself the highest dignity. I shall be enriched.—Right, for I may roll (as they say) in riches, if I mistake not what riches are, so as to take shells, minerals, and stones for such; if I mistake not about the place of riches, and instead of a mind suppose a trunk; if I take not ought else for riches but what makes rich and satisfies; brings plenty, affluence, ease, prosperity; renders fully contented so as to desire nothing beyond, and fully secure, so as to fear no change. In short, I may have of wealth all that I can think of, all that I can bear or carry; "if I esteem him rich only who is wise."

Thus as to the incident fancies that come in the way and offer from abroad. Consider now how to raise and excite other such, draw them out and exercise them, that so the superior part which disciplines, instructs, and manages these subjects may not lose its authority and command, may not be idle; but still at work, amending, framing, polishing, transforming, so as to give every thing an edge this way, and have wherewithal to render every appearance or idea instrumental and serviceable. If I am heavy and dull, unwilling to awake and rise; consider what it is that would soon awaken and raise thee up.—"The enemy is near and now entering." And is it not so? What do we call an enemy? What makes an enemy dreadful? What are the consequences feared?—Captivity, slavery, misery.—And is not this the question here? Is not the contest concerning liberty? Is it not concerning happiness and misery? whether there shall be enemies innumerable, and such as must often enslave and conquer; or whether there shall be no enemy, but all safe, secure, undisturbed, and happy? How comes it, therefore, I am not alarmed? Where should I be alarmed but here? If matters be right here, I may sleep sound and secure, whatever enemy or weapons stand at the door. If my sleep be of another kind; if laziness, torpor, and indolence have got hold of me, so that I no longer sleep because it is necessary, because it is what my body wants, and what I therefore think fit to allow it; if such be the case, up! rise! the enemy is at the door, and a dangerous, dreadful enemy, not like that other which can touch nothing that is thine, nothing that thou art concerned for. Here is the enemy to be feared, that has admittance where the things of only importance are kept. Here is the enemy that is to be opposed with all might and strength, and here, if thou wilt, thou mayest be sure of conquest.

Again, turn it another way, take it from any other side.—I am called.—Art thou not called? Is it because thou hearest no voice? I am commanded.—Art thou not commanded?—Is it not a command of a higher nature? from a higher person? of higher importance? Is it not the duty, a much greater duty? the law, a greater law?

These are the inversions. This is the right modelling or moulding of the *visa.* Such is that * good fire, or † stomach that can overpower and rightly convert whatever is thrown into it, and can turn the same to its use and advantage.—I am undeservingly reproached for acting well.—Be it so, then I may still be more deserving; if I act on. But I love applause with men—therefore I have higher applause elsewhere. I am thrown into solitude—therefore I am left with better company. I am not obliged to mind trifles. I am not diverted or called away from another presence and contemplation. I am all my own and entire towards Deity and that genius and companion which He has given me and which governs for Him and only waits His pleasure.—But I am no longer useful to the world; neither can I be so, more than for a certain time. Is it age that puts the period? 'Tis well, it comes apace. Is it anything before age? Then here is that that is instead of it. What would I have? Have I not seen enough? Is not ‡ the last act finished? Is not the piece complete? The curtain falls, and I go out. Would I begin anew and see the same over again, or stay after the spectacle is ceased, and nothing but the place remains? If neither of these, what have I to do but to retire cheerfully, contentedly, and thankfully? Could it be said even in an Epicurean manner—*Edisti satis atque bibisti* [Thou hast eaten and drunk enough]; and in the same manner—*Exacto contentus tempore vitae, recedat ut conviva satur* [When his allotted space of life is run let him retire satisfied, like a well-fed banqueter]—and shall not another say *Ipse deus simul atque voto me solvet* [As soon as God himself releases me from my vow]? Is not His dismission enough? What do I stay for more?—These are the considerations of moment. Thus are the appearances disposed and modelled. In this architecture all depends.

Remember that it is the same here as in an army. If the soldiers are often reviewed, disciplined, and kept in exercise and

* *Mar. Aurel.*, Bk. IV., § 1.    † *Ibid.*, Bk. X., § 31, 35.
‡ *Ibid.*, Bk. XII., § 36.

obedience, all will be orderly and well; if left to themselves, disorder, mutiny, and confusion will follow; much mischief, but no good, no succour, or defence. Thus if the principal and commanding part keep its command and preserve its subjects (the *visa* and appearances) in right discipline and exercise, all will be well, and every engagement and action successful and of advantage.

To the same art (viz., the inversion of the appearances) all those passages in *Mar. Aurel.* belong to a stranger, a * deserter or renegade, a beggar; an excrescence, wart, or wen; blindness, lameness, amputation; †an arm or leg divided from the body: a ‡ branch lopped off; a gardener and engrafting.—Thus also to rob § (not ‖ with hands but with another part: not as vindicating to ourselves what the law has made another's; but what a superior law has decreed not to belong to us and of another jurisdiction (τὰ οὐκ ἐφ᾽ ἡμῖν). Seed (not that which is thrown into the ¶ earth or matrix). A sale, bargain, exchange (nothing gratis). Quiet, ease, a sweet repose, happy retirement tranquillity (not that ** which outward things establish; not that which must be owing to others; not a †† sea shore, not rocks, not woods or caves). To ‡‡ see, to feel things (not with the eye or by the touch, but in another manner). And as in Marcus or elsewhere.

Thus §§ at last hardly can any appearance arise, hardly can there be any object ever so remote or foreign, but what the mind will accommodate to itself and turn to its own use. Let the fancy come in whatsoever shape, it immediately receives a different form, and its force is turned another way. This is just the reverse of what happens to those who are grown into the thorough buffooning habit. Everything that they see, be it ever so grave or serious, has a ridiculous appearance, and whether they will or not becomes burlesque. Everything is travestied so

* *Mar.*, *Med.*, Bk. X., § 25.          † *Ibid.*, Bk. VIII., § 34.
‡ *Ibid.*, Bk. II., § 8.          § *Ibid.*, Bk. II., § 10.
‖ *Ibid.*, Bk. X., § 13.
¶ *Ibid.*, Bk. IV., § 36, and Bk. X., § 26.
** *Ibid.*, Bk. IV., § 3.          †† *Ibid.*, Bk. X., § 15, 22, 33, and Bk. V., § 29.
‡‡ *Ibid.*, Bk. X., § 26, and Bk. III., § 15.
§§ *Rotterdam*, 1704.

as to make diversion out of it, and whatever be the face that offers, there are glasses ready that make it to be seen after a thousand ridiculous ways, and that, instead of that one real face, present a thousand masks of a grotesque and fantastic kind. So in the other way, everything light, airy, or fantastic, everything that raises any curiosity, or that employs or busies mankind, be the object what it will, it takes a new face and becomes serious. The difference here is that, as that other glass crooks and distorts the objects, so this continually straightens and redresses what is amiss, and sets everything in its due light, so as to hinder all confusion.

In the same manner, as one of those students of wit is rejoiced on account of some lucky word or expression that he has invented; as a poet is rejoiced when he has luckily versified; as a mathematician when he has made a discovery about lines and circles; as an architect when he has raised some artful pile; or a general some artful stratagem; so be thou rejoiced when, according to thy own art which thou hast learnt, it has happened to thee skilfully, and like a master, to have modelled or well fabricated some one appearance or idea. If thou hast succeeded well here, then say to thyself, " I had rather this, than the cubilo of Michael Angelo: I had rather this than the Philippics of Demosthenes or Cicero; rather than have written like Homer, or fought like Alexander." If thou dost not see why this is greater and more glorious than all that other, thou art so far yet from being a proficient, that thou knowest not what thy art is; what it promises, or to what it tends.

All other arts stand in need of something exterior, as materials, spectators, auditors : so in architecture, rhetoric, music, and the rest. This art alone carries its materials with it (for it is its own * subject), and not only its materials, but spectators; for itself contemplates itself; nor does it seek other witnesses than such as are always present., viz., Deity, and that inward genius.

All other sorts are incomplete, and aim at something beyond

---

* ὕλη τοῦ καλοῦ καὶ ἀγαθοῦ τὸ ἴδιον ἡγεμονικόν [The material for the wise and good is one's own ruling faculty.]—*Epict. Disc.*, Book III., c. iii., § 1.

(for which of these arts is for its own sake?). This art is complete in itself; for this being attained nothing further is requred, since this itself is happiness and prosperity.

All other arts require some relaxation and diversion, and are more vigorously prosecuted after such relief. This art alone admits not of any interval, and is the worse for every relaxation. How unaccountable is it to ask to be relieved of happiness, and to require a suspension of good? And is not this thy good? Where is it then? Where dost thou seek or expect it? If anywhere from abroad, see what danger thou art still in, and how little any relaxation can be borne with. Remember this on every occasion of this kind. I seek relief or respite, from what? From my good?—Impossible. From that which is not my good?—Then see in what thou placest thy good! Where are thy opinions? Where is philosophy? What hast thou been doing? Is conviction anything or nothing? Is all that is passed to go for nothing? Where wilt thou rest then? To what adhere?—Thus all is given up, for there is no acting here by halves. There is no middle way, no capitulation or compounding in the affairs of this kind. Either all is maintained or all surrendered. Every suspension is a total dismission; every receding a betraying of the whole.

Again thy art. Ἀποκρίνεσθαι τοῖς πράγμασιν [To give an answer to things.—*Epict. Disc.*, Bk. II., c. xvi., § 2]. Now make it good. Now to be firm. Now adhere. *Nunc animis opus est, nunc pectore firmo* [Now there is need of courage, now for a steadfast heart.—*Virg., Aen.* IV., 261]. No receding; no retreat. But being now returned; now once for all; for good and all; for if again retreat that also may be for good and all. Nay, must be: for what left afterwards but to retire indeed and go out?

To thy work then, thy art, thy life. The sole business, the main concern. Life itself and all that there is in the matter of living. The only real living (as the voluptuous men say of theirs), the only worthy, the only natural, according to nature, by the art nature has given us, the power of mind and of right reason—make it right then here [in living] as it is there [in nature]; make things here accord with things there; correct the lower by the higher; answer the one by the other; mere imaginations by proved ones; uncertain dictates by stated decrees; secret suggestions and whispers by plain utterance. Let us hear again those voices high up, distinct, aloud. Idea! wait a little, and so the rest. The discipline, the inversions as before. Thus manage, thus deal with fancy: or must we spare her, indulge her a little by whiles and upon occasion? Shall the judgment be left to her? Of what? Shall any the least thing be allowed her? What? wherein? and who shall judge? For if she for herself, then is she judge of everything; if not for herself, then of nothing, in nothing.—Nothing, therefore, or everything, for if anything, as well everything; if this be all "because I fancy."

1 The house turns round.—No, but my head turns, that's all. What is reason but a power of judging the fancies? Is everything as it is fancied? Are all fancies right? Then the house turns when I am giddy. But no. I know the fancy to be wrong.—Am I not out of order? Do I not dream?—Who says or can say this besides man or a creature rational like man? For if an irrational creature be moved by any such fancy, he follows it without more ado, for what has he better to correct it, set him right, or tell him that he dreams? And what is pleasure, what is conceit, what is a life of fancy but dreaming? Where is that that makes the difference?

This is that faculty, art, δοκιμαστικὴ ἢ ἀποδοκιμαστική [This moral approving or disapproving faculty.—*Epict. Disc.*, Bk. I., c. i., § 1]. And if I am without this, am I not distracted? 2 He who imagines precipices before him cries out for help; says there are mountains in his way when he walks on even ground; and when all is well, quiet, and still, cries "Fire! Deluge! Earthquake! Thunder!" Does he not rave? But one whose eyes strike fire, or whose head is only giddy from a ship, or who from a distemper in his ear, hears many sorts of noises; though all these fancies in being with him are the same and as strong as at other times when occasioned by outward things, yet he being in a way of resisting, judging, correcting these fancies, is in his senses (as they say) still, nor is he out of himself, though his senses are out.

---

1 cf. *Characteristics* I., p. 322.    2 cf. *Characteristics* I., p. 324.

How is it, therefore, as to other fancies?—A king appears —and what then? So in a play a king appears, also guards, courtiers, lords, attendants.—But this is but a play. And what is this other? When the tragedy chances to be over-moving, and the action strikes us, do not we say to ourselves instantly, "This is but a play?" Is not this the correcting, redressing, rectifying part? And how does this part carry itself in that other play—the serious one of life? How does it manage in this scene? Is it here still the same ruling, leading, commanding part? the ἡγεμονικόν? [the reason.]—A king, a real king appears. Right; it is a real king, and not a player; not one of those kings of the stage. So far I am right. So far the correcting and confirming part goes along with me, so much it allows good. But what else do I see besides a king? Here comes the trial. What is a king?—A man.—Right.—A man in power.—Right still; but in what power? In a power by which he is happy and blessed? Hold! here is a new matter. All this, and what follows upon this, is new. I am astonished.—Why?—I admire, applaud, envy, wish. My head turns round.—No, but I am right. I cannot but believe myself it must be thus.—Am I not mad? for were I giddy only, I should know it, and saying to myself that I was giddy, immediately be unconcerned.

The order is sent for my imprisonment, banishment, death. —Right. But what is imprisonment?—Staying within. What is banishment?—Removal from one place to another. Death?— An end of breathing, struggling for life, and against vice and corruption. What loss? What is death?—Misery! misery!— How? Where? Which way? Dost thou not know before-hand, art thou not sure, most undeniably sure (or what else canst thou ever be sure of?) that misery is nowhere in these things; nowhere from without; but, together with happiness, from within, only from within? So that in this place, when my fancy and I are all one, am I then myself? When the senses are by themselves, and there is no supreme sense above them, am I then in my senses? When they report, and nothing better than they take the report, have I my reason? Or if I say I have my reason, but at the same time judge by fancy, and not by reason, am I sound in my reason, or am I master of reason any sooner for this?

How is it then, after I have judged of death, disgrace, poverty, riches, honours, as I have done, sedately done, maturely, deliberately, that I should come (see!) in an instant to change thus and believe the contrary? For if I believed not, neither should I be moved. How is it that I assent? How is it that I join voices with the fancy and cry out, "Misery! misery!"— Happiness! Misery! Is not this the same as above? Fire! Earthquake! Thunder!—Seas of milk and ships of amber!

When certain inflammations, soft lambent flames, or playing sparks arise, which seem so innocent and gentle at first, then the leading part may in its turn cry, "Fire! Fire! Bring the engines, φέρε τὰς προλήψεις," &c. [Apply the recognised principles.—*Epict. Disc.*, Bk. I., c. xxv., § 6].

Οὐδεὶς δὲ δειλὸν κατάσκοπον πέμπει, &c. [No one sends a cowardly scout, who, if he only sees a shadow cries, "fly friends, the enemy are here."—*Ibid.*, Bk. I., c. xxiv., § 3-4]. Shadows indeed, and to be thus afraid is to be afraid of one's own shadow. But on the contrary hear! Οὐδείς, φησι, πολέμιος ἐγγύς ἐστι ·πάντα εἰρήνης γέμει [There is no enemy near, he says; all is peace.—*Ibid.*, Bk. I., c. xxiv., § 9].—Is there nothing then to be feared? No report to make?—There is, and a shrewd one. Enemies with a witness. φεύγετε ἔθη τὰ πρότερον [Fly from your former habits.—*Ibid.*, Bk. III., c. xvi., § 16]. Fly! Save thyself. These are no shadows.

Fancy has spoken; 'tis now my turn. "Good! is this all? have you any more to say? Let us hear all out, and then answer, but speak out; speak plain, high up, aloud; no muttering, no half words, no whispering, dumb signs, nodding, winking, and those other mysterious sly ways. Away with this. 'Tis not to be endured.—If thou hast ought to say (fancy), say it; let us hear patiently, but if from one thing to another I interrupt: 'To the point (fancy), to the point!' Is not this what you advanced just now, though you have since passed to other things, and so to other heaping, mixing, confounding? But to bring things to an issue, that we may fix somewhere: let us take it up here, let us hear distinctly. Was not this the suggestion? These the words? or thus and thus?— Said you not so or so?—These were the *words.*—Repeat them. Once again.—Again, a third time.—'Tis well. By your leave then; a word ere you depart; I must talk a little in my turn, and be familiar, very familiar: as well I may, for thy turn (fancy) has been long enough."

Τί οὖν ὧδε ποιεῖς, ὦ φαντασία; [What art thou doing here, Fancy?—*Mar. Aurel., Med.*, Bk. VII., § 17]. Thus must the persuader, the deceiver, the fair impostress, enchantress, be talked to; sometimes fairly, sometimes (as they say) roundly Or if thou talkest not thus with her; expect that she should talk with thee, on a high tone; put thee to silence, and manage thee as she pleases.

One of these two must ever be, viz., that a man has his fancies in right discipline, turning, leading, and commanding them; or they him. Either they must deal with him, take him up short (as they say), teach him manners, and make him know to whom he belongs; or, this will be his part, to teach the impostress Fancy and her train; show her what she is herself, and whom she has to deal with.

This is to be a man.

By whiles this question. Am I talked with, or do I talk? For something still there is that talks within and leads that very discourse which leads in action, and is what we call conduct. —Whence then the conduct? What leading? what control? who governs, or what?—Thus in a family: [1] Who rules in this house? Who's master?—Learn by the voices. Who speaks with a high tone? Who decides and gives judgment? Who has the talk, the last word? Is it the servants?—Then the servants are masters.—And dost thou blush at this?

How is this, man! What! Jealous for thy authority in thy mansion-house and outward family, but not in the least for thy authority within, in thy chiefest mansion, thy principal economy? Are the servants here to talk high and in what tone they please? Must theirs be the last word, their dictates the rules of action? O slave of slaves!

How necessary this counter-discourse with the presenting fancies, and how real it is or ought to be, learn by the too long experience of the other of wrong kind. What ability, promptitude, dexterity in those? As particularly in the cases

---

[1] cf. *Characteristics*, I., p. 823.

of the Δοξάριον. What they now say of me. What they will say anon.—ὦ ἄγαθος.—" Extraordinary! wonderful! nobody like him."—And often whole panegyrics devised thus and repeated extempore for other people and put into their mouths; teaching them what to say, and ridiculously saying for them. This chiefly after any little success in the world, in business, company; and as fancying to have left some mighty impressions behind.—Rare ingenuity!

And hast thou so long endured this, knowest thou the way so well, hast thou been so long good at this, so able, so expert, at this invention, to find talk and discourse within; so much entertainment with self and about self (though indeed a wrong self); and canst thou now at last be wanting in the same way, now that thou hast a better self to talk with and be concerned for; now that things go better far and turn upon another hinge? Or went it better the other way? Was it better as then; viz., and "What will they say of me?" "What does such a one think?" Or as now: "What do I say of myself?" "What does a higher One think?"

# SIMPLICITY.

Ἔσῃ ποτὲ ἆρ᾽, ὦ ψυχὴ, αγαθή, καὶ ἁπλῆ, καὶ μία, καὶ γυμνὴ, φανερωτέρα τοῦ περικειμένου σοι σώματος; [" Wilt not thou then, my soul, never be good and simple and one and naked, more manifest than the body which surrounds thee ?"—*Mar. Aurel., Med.*, Bk. X., § 1]. O, wretched blindness, not to see and admire this beauty above all beauties ! O, mean and despicable condition to see this, such as it is, and not enjoy it.

The senseless part of mankind admire gaudiness : the better sort and those who are good judges admire *simplicity*. Thus in painting, architecture, and other such things, the greatest beauties are what the vulgar despise : and thus even in furniture, habits, instruments, and arms, plainness and simplicity are the most becoming, and are the greatest perfection. For where proportion and exactness are wanting, there it is that there is need of those additional ornaments ; but, where order is preserved and the perfection of art attained, the rest only does prejudice and is an eye-sore.—All this is right, but take care lest, while thou admirest simplicity of this sort, thou forgettest another simplicity infinitely more beautiful and of more importance. Remember, therefore, what the perfection of man is, and that beyond this, to seek for anything, or aim at any other ornaments, is to lose simplicity, and become that gaudy piece of painting or architecture which he that is knowing despises.

Whenever there appears anything which, for its beauty and simplicity, is charming to the sight, though it be one of those ordinary things, such as a vessel, or urn, a sword or any other arm, a habit or a dress, remember still what it is that resembles this in life : unity of design, so as to exclude hypocrisy, falseness, mysteriousness, subtlety. But this also extends itself to carriage and behaviour, countenance, voice, jest. What are all those forms and manners which come under the notion of good breeding ? The affected smiles, the fashionable coughs, the tone of voice, and all those supple caressing and ingratiating ways—what is this else but embroidery, gilding, colouring ?

The perfection of carriage and manners is between the ruggedness of one who cares not how he gives offence, and the suppleness of one who only studies how to please. And this is simplicity ; for affectation is as well on the one side as on the other.

What care, what art, what labour, to attain the true simplicity of an action ! But when attained how pleasing and beautiful ! Nor are any pains so well bestowed. For what is there that has a worse feeling than affectation ? Who would not willingly be rid of it ? For, in the same manner as in the carriage and behaviour, nothing is easy but what is natural ; so, in the practice of the world, in conversation and life, all is uneasiness and constraint where simplicity is wanting. But to affect this ease or freedom where it is not, is to be most of all constrained and unnatural.

Those that speak knowingly in matters of behaviour and carriage talk of nothing but ease, freedom, liberty, unconsciousness ; but confess at the same time that there is nothing harder than this to attain ; and so far the thing is certain. What can be an easier, happier part than to live disinterested and unconcerned, as being loose from all those ties and little mean regards which make us to depend so much on others ? What can be more generous and of a better feeling than to go through companies, conversations, and affairs in the security and simplicity of mind ? But this happens not till the thing itself after a certain way, comes not to be thought of, and that those standing by are no longer considerable or awful. For in the same manner as in a court he who has once formed himself and knows his own faculty carries with him an assurance of not failing in anything, and is, therefore, free and easy in what relates to carriage, ceremony, and all those other affairs, so, in the whole of life, he who is secure as to the great events and is concerned but for one thing (which if he will himself, he need not miss), he, and he alone, is truly free ; and with respect to things within, is becoming, beautiful. He alone has everything orderly, still, quiet ; nothing boisterous, nothing disturbed ; but every motion, action, and expression decent, and such as is becoming that more noble and far superior character of one who in another sense is called *well bred*, with respect to a different discipline and breeding.

Imitation, gesture, and action in discourse; different tones of voice, alterations of countenance, odd and humoursome turns of speech, phrase, expressions;—all this is agreeable in company, and may set off a story, help in an argument, or make anything to be felt which one would desire should be so. But all this is utterly wrong, harsh, dissonant; out of measure and tone. All that is vehement, impetuous, turbulent must needs be so: as well as all that which in any degree borders upon mimicry, buffoonery, drollery. Consider what a mean and contemptible state the mind is in at that instant when it goes about anything of this kind. What it aims at: what its end and scope is: how it looks upon itself when it fails and is disappointed: what kind of joy it has when it succeeds: what sort of minds those are which partake with it in this way, and are the ablest in this art; and what morals, manners, life, this brings along with it.

But suppose now (what is far contrary) that by quitting this we were likely to lose the esteem of friends. Is it not better to be dull, silent, and unentertaining, but so as at the same time to be sincere, just, modest, and duly reserved? Is it not better to be *truly sociable*, retaining true simplicity and gravity, than, by being what the world calls sociable, to give up these and live a stranger to social affection?

Never fancy that thou hast acted a small or inconsiderable part in company, however small thy part has been in the discourse, if all the while thou hast preserved that temper which was due; if thou hast neither been at earnest, nor eager, nor over-concerned, nor over-joyed; if thou has neither studied to show thyself, nor hast contended, nor reproved, nor flattered, after the ordinary way; in short, if thou art come out of the conversation free, undisturbed, unlessened, and without prejudice to simplicity, integrity, or ingenuity. And on the other side, where there has been any prejudice to these, or that the least footstep here has been awry, think not, on any account, that matters have gone well, nor be contented though the success in discourse appear ever so happy, or to have been of ever so good consequence.

Remember the modern Theophrastus, who calls politeness a more refined sort of flattery. Examine, therefore, what politeness is consistent with simplicity and what not.

Remember that sort of dissimulation which is consistent with true simplicity : and besides the innocent and excellent dissimulation of the kind which Socrates used, remember that other sort (not less his) which hides what passes within, and accommodates our manners to those of our friends and of people around us, as far as this with safety can be allowed. Remember, therefore, what countenance is to be shown even then when all is grave and solemn within. So far be thou from any industrious affectation of gravity, or from seeming in the midst of company to meditate things of a high nature, and to despise what thou art about. But see that this be sincere, and not so as the struggle may appear ; for this would be a worse sort of affectation and more intolerable than the first ; and if so, what must that sort be, where without any real ground for any such struggle the appearance of it is yet affected ? How nauseous is this ! and how amiable the contrary carriage !—The first degree, therefore, is to need this dissimulation, and to be really grave and inwardly intent on other things. This next is to be willing to dissemble this, and to be satisfied without making ourselves either the burden or the admiration of others. And last of all, our business is to see that we be always sincere in this, and to take care that we do not *ill dissemble,* for it is then that this becomes what we properly call dissimulation : nor can anything be farther from true simplicity and ingenuity.

How many disturbances and torments do we endure for want of that true simplicity ? what jealousies ! what discontents and private envyings ! Yet these pass generally unnoticed, and though there cannot be more uneasy moments than those we feel on this account, yet we never reckon these, nor cast these into the scale when we weigh the good and ill of life ; and not to mention other passions, how much do we suffer in this way merely from curiosity ? But, indeed, how is it otherwise possible ? for how can we concern ourselves in outward affairs, as matters of consequence, in which we place our good and ill, and at the same time not be solicitous to hear ? or not come off dissatisfied and mortified when we are denied hearing, and are excluded from the concern ?

Remember, the true simplicity must ever be accompanied with gravity and a certain becoming reservedness, otherwise simplicity perishes. And as for that opposite character, that familiarity, inwardness, freedom, and openness of a certain kind, which thou dost term simplicity; this is not simplicity, but affectation, and nauseous affectation. Such is all that intemperate lavish talking, and of self particularly.—"*I have such and such faults?*" Keep them to thyself ; make the right use of them; mend them ; not multiply them ; not draw vanity from them, and a new ground of conceit, new matter for idleness, trifling, impertinence, looseness of tongue, and ungrateful, ill feeling, familiarity, and intimacy, which is out of all harmony, concord, time, measure.—But thou wouldst willingly declare thy faults and show simplicity.—Wait a moment, and there will be occasion given. Stay till thou art reproached for something. Stay till somebody says *he knows nothing, he is ignorant, he is little worth.* Show this to be true: show in what and why. Help the person that thus blames : and if he blames maliciously, and thinking that he has no reason ; show him that he has reason, and that he blames not without cause. Here is the occasion to speak thy faults (if thou wilt needs speak them). Here it is that simplicity may be shown. Ἐὰν τίς σοι ἀπαγγείλῃ ὅτι ὁ δεῖνά σε κακῶς λέγει, μὴ ἀπολογοῦ πρὸς τὰ λεχθέντα, ἀλλ᾽ ἀποκρίνου, &c. ["If a man has reported to you that a certain person speaks ill of you, do not make any defence to what has been told you; but reply, 'The man did not know the rest of my faults, else he would not have mentioned these only.'"—*Epict. Ench.*, c. xxxiii., § 9]. But thou art far from this simplicity ; and, therefore, what is all that other but affectation ?

To discourse with others about the work of self-improvement ; about what passes within ; what vices remain ; what remedies and application, is like that sort of pedantry which tells of distempers and physic, what water has been made, what stools. Man ! what have we to do with this ? Take thy physic, purge, vomit, that thou mayest be well and come abroad : but what have we to do with stools ? why talk to us of phlegm ? Form a good constitution : be healthy and sound : appear without ulcers, without scabs, or scurf : show the effect of the physic ; but not the drugs and operation.

# NATURE.

Μὴ θαυμάζετε εἰ τοῖς μὲν ἄλλοις ζῴοις, &c., νῦν δ᾽ ἡμεῖς
ἀφέντες ἐπὶ τούτοις εὐχαριστεῖν, &c. [" Be not surprised if other
animals have all things necessary.—But we, instead of being
thankful for this, complain of God, that there is not the same
care taken of us likewise."—*Epict. Disc.*, Bk. I., c. xvi., § 1, 6].
So has nature ordered for the other creatures; such is their
hardiness, strength, robustness, readiness.—But why not the
same for man ?—Say as well, why not wings for man ? why not
the air and all the elements of nature for man ? why not nature
itself for man, not man for nature ?—But if it be not nature for
man, but man for nature, then must man, by his good leave,
submit to the elements of nature and not the elements to him.
If in air, he falls ; for wings were not given him to fly in air.
If in water, he sinks ; for he has not what is necessary for
water. If in fire, he consumes. But upon earth he can do
well ; though not within the earth either : not in every part of
earth : but on the surface of the earth only ; and of such and
such earth ; not over-moist, as a morass ; not over-dry, as sandy
deserts ; nor over-hard or steep, as rocky mountains. For these
places may be for other creatures, but not for him. So little
even of this element of earth is after this manner *his*.

But let us suppose wings for him, to fit him for the air,
if we could imagine anything for him to do there ; how must
his make be changed ? See in a bird : is not the whole structure
made subservient to that almost single end ? Is it not in a
manner all wings ? two vast muscles that exhaust the strength
of all the other, engross the economy, and swallow up the frame.
How else could they perform a motion so vastly disproportionable
to the other motions, if not made in this disproportion superior
to the rest, and starving the other parts. And in man (according
to his present model) were the flying engines and members of
this kind to be added, must not the other members and parts
be starved to feed these new ones ? Or can the same matter

serve for one as for the other? In mechanics, the same
engines have equal force in one thing as in another, in one part
as in another, for twenty different purposes at a time as well
as for a single one?—What absurdity!—Where then should this
new anatomy be found? what new muscling for these parts?
and withal equally for those? where the animal spirits, the
blood, humour, juices, for these and for those? If this be
certainly absurd, where is the absurdity in saying the robbed
parts must starve? for can the same spirits feed equally, nourish,
supply equally, when saved as when consumed? or is there no
certain stock or proportion of spirits? Must the animal spirits
in every creature be *ad infinitum*, and not in any certain
proportion as the creature is bigger or less, or the organs fitted
to prepare more or less?—If this be absurd, what can be more
reasonable than, in the case supposed, to say the spirits cannot
be both here and there, not diverted from their parts or
members, yet equally feeding their parts or members? for in
this high-flying man will there not be parts that must suffer for
the ambition of their fellows: and while these new associates
are supplied, must not the feet, hands, stomach itself shame?
And how, pray, as to the brain? must not the brain also starve?
See how it is in man even as he now is, without any such
notable addition of new parts. How is it, in the first place,
with the stomach when the brain is over-much employed,
especially soon after eating? How is it, in the same case, with
the pores? Are those doors kept as well when forsaken by the
spirits as when guarded by them? How is it when a mathematician or other student thinks too intensely? Does not the
brain itself then starve the body and parts? And, on the
contrary, when the body and parts are chiefly minded, nourished,
exercised, as in a wrestler, racer, rider, fencer, dancer, have not
the parts their reprisals? Does the brain find itself as well
in this liberal dispensation to other parts as when the spirits
are used to flow a little more plentifully into their channels
there, and are not drawn off so much another way? And if it be
thus between man and man, how between the body of a man
and of one of those creatures? If the balance be so just and
even here, if so nicely held by nature that the least thing
breaks it, in creatures of the same frame and order, what would

it be to change the order quite, and make some essential alteration in the frame ?—What would it be indeed but monstrous ?
for what else is a monster ? or what else are our imaginations
of this kind but monsters ?

In this view then, consider what the divine man says here,
and see how ridiculous the complaint is which he so well
exposes—" Why was I not made strong as a horse, or hardy and
robust as this or that creature, or nimble and sprightly as the
other ? "—And yet when uncommon strength of body and great
things are added of that kind, even in our own species, see the
consequence, what happens.

Therefore, it were better and more modest for a person
so much in love with an athletic Milo-like constitution not to
ask, " Why was I not made strong as a horse ? " &c., but " Why
was I not made a horse ? " for that would be more suitable.

Being convinced of these follies and of the poorness of
these objections, go to those simple but Divine operations, those
simplicities of nature which for want of simplicity are so little
felt. See the Divine care and order so obvious, and, therefore,
for that very reason so unminded and disregarded, because so
obvious. See those beauties which in certain lucid intervals the
vulgar see, poets and painters declare, and the luxurious themselves confess. Only a right disposition is wanting, and simplicity
to judge of these simplicities, these only beauties, truths,
excellences. What is the rest but grotesque ? what is atheism
but *nature-grotesque ?* Nature seen thus in masquerade, dis-
figured, charged, as they say in painting, and after a kind of
caricature ? And how this grotesque *without ?* How but
from the grotesque-work *within ?* See the effect of those
masks, the buffoonery, drollery, and burlesque. — Beware ! —
Or wilt thou go again into those views ? Shall it be *nature-
travestie ?* For how is it that this happens ? how preserve the
right views ? how lose them ?—No more ! Remember then.

[1] Such is the admirable distribution of nature, its adapting
and adjusting not only of the stuff or matter to the shape and
form, and of the shape and form to the circumstance, place,
element, region ; but also of the affections, appetites, sensations,

[1] cf. *Characteristics,* II., 306.

instincts, passions, mutually to each other as well as to the matter, form, action, and all besides. All managed for the best; with perfect frugality, and just reserve; with perfect liberality too and utmost bounty. For how bountiful if profuse? How a just economy if employing in any one thing more than enough, which force might have been reserved for something else? Now what a reserve of this sort may we observe in the make of all creatures in general? nothing superfluous in all their structure. What a reserve in the particular creatures for their chief function, whatever that be? So in the instances just above, what reserve for those creatures of the air to add force to the chief part of their mechanism, and to lighten and ease the rest? what reserve in creatures made for swiftness, either to prey, or save themselves from those of prey by running only? What a reserve and management for everything that is principal in every creature? And should there be none for the brain of man? Or is not his thought and reason the thing principal in him and for which there should be reserve? Would he have his vigour to be spent rather another way? Would he have no saving for this part of the engine? Or would he have the same stuff or matter, the same instruments, organs, serve alike and full as well for different purposes, and an ounce (as they say) go as far as a pound? It cannot be. What would he have of a few ounces of blood in such a little vessel fitted for so little a part of nature? Will he not praise nature, will he not adore the artificer who has thus managed his portion for him with this happy reserve (happy indeed for him, if he knows and uses it), by which he has so much a better use of organs than any other creature? by which he holds his reason, is a man and not a beast?

But beasts have instincts, which he has not.—Right. They have perceptions, sensations, and præ-sensations (if I may use the term), which man for his part has not. And can anything more commend the order of nature than this very thing? Is not this according to that admirable economy, that wise, equal, and just *reserve*, which we have spoken of just now? The females of all creatures though young, and having never as yet borne young, have a perfect *præ-sensation* of their state to come, know what to provide and how, in what manner, and at what time; the season of the year, country, climate; the choice of place, aspect, situation, the basis of their building, materials, architecture; the method and treatment of their young; in short, the whole economy of their nursery: and all this as perfectly at first and when unexperienced as the last time of their lives.—And why not this, in human kind?— Nay: but on the contrary, why this? where was the use? where the necessity? why this sagacity for men? Have they not for their parts sagacity of another kind? Have they not reason and discourse? Does not this teach them? What need then of the other? where would be the prudent management at this rate? where the reserve?—The young of most other kinds are instantly helpful to themselves, sensible, vigorous: know how to shun danger and seek their good. A human infant is of all the most helpless, weak, senseless, and longest continues so. And wherefore should it not have been thus ordered? where is the loss by it, in the midst of such supplies? Does not this refer man yet more strongly to society, and force him to own that he is purposely and not by accident made rational and sociable, and cannot otherwise increase or subsist but in and by society? Is not conjugal affection, natural affection to parents, duty to magistrates, love of a common city, community, or country, with the other duties and social parts of life, deduced from hence and founded in these very wants? What can be happier than such a deficiency that is the occasion of so much good? What better than a want so abundantly made up and answered by so many enjoyments? Now if there are still to be found amongst mankind such as even in the midst of these wants are not ashamed to deny themselves by nature sociable, where would their shame have been had nature otherwise supplied these wants? What duty had been ever thought of? What respect or reverence of parents, magistrates, their country, or their kind? Would their full and self-sufficient state have better inclined them the sooner to have acknowledged nature, the sooner to have owned and reverenced a God?

# CHARACTER AND CONDUCT.

Τίνα φαντασίαν ἔχω περὶ ἐμαυτοῦ; πῶς ἐμαυτῷ χρῶμαι; [What do I imagine myself to be ? How do I conduct myself.—*Epict. Disc.*, Bk. II., c. xxi., § 9].

All turns upon the nature of a *Character ;* and according to what the fancy make of this, so in general the conduct will prove; and so matters in conversation succeed one way or another : for this is always what occurs at those times. What is the character I am to maintain ? How shall I act according to my character ? Who am *I ?*—Such a one ; the son of such a one ; of such a family, such a country, of such an estate; with such a title—What am I worthy of as such a one ?—an equipage, a certain dress, ceremonies, place.—What are the things beneath me ?—an ordinary habit, a mean appearance, obscurity, contempt. Thus, when at any time in company with foreigners, presently this occurs. I am an Englishman. How preserve my character ? How gain esteem to England ?—Man ! what is England to thee ? Why reckon from hence ? Why not the parish ? Why not Europe ? But, be it so, I am a native of those islands, of one of those islands, or of a part of one of those islands, as being the same government and under the same laws. I disdain to call myself of such a parish or town, which is but a part of that greater government. And is there no other government or city of which even this is still only a part, and in respect of which this is no more than a cabin or hut ? What are the laws of that city in respect of these other laws ? Which of these administrations is most just ? which of these laws the most ancient, wisest, most perfect, most durable, most inviolable ? which inferior and subservient ? By what laws, and for the sake of what city was it that I was brought into being, created a man ? From whence did I receive my organs of sense, my faculties, my understanding, my reason ? Where, then, is my native country ? where is that government or city from whence I can properly name myself, and which is not as a province or district of some

other ?   Begin now, and consider anew, who am I ?  Σκέψαι τίς
εἶ. τὸ πρῶτον ἄνφρωπος [Consider who you are.  In the first place,
a man.—*Epict. Disc.*, Bk. II., c. x., § I.]—Such a one, the son of
such a one, of such a name ?—No.—But what ?  who ?—A man, a
rational creature, of such a descent, of such a habitation ?  What,
am I worthy of as such a one ?  what are the things beneath me ?

But this is imaginary.—How imaginary ?  Was it my native
country (as I call it) that gave me my being ?  Did the commonwealth decree my birth ?  Were my parents the artificers of my
frame, or were they anything more than instruments ?  To what
do I belong therefore ?  and to whom ?  Who is the author of
my being ?  and what has He made to be my excellence and
highest perfection ?  Consider: thou art a man.   Does this
signify anything or nothing ?   If nothing, what besides is
it that thou callest honourable ?   Why all this conceit and
valuing thyself ?   Why offended if at any time thou art
meanly thought of and passest for a brute ?   Where is the
difference ?   Dost thou not say there is none ?   Is it not enough
that thou hast meat and drink and what else thou desirest of
that kind ?   Why, then, dost thou aim at anything further ?
Why value thyself on the qualities of a man if there be no
particular character nor dignity of a man ?   If there be, where
is it ?   Where, but in that by which he differs from a brute ?
What is a brute ?—Stupidity, gluttony, lechery, savageness.—
What therefore is *man* but reason and humanity, faith, friendship, justice, integrity ?   Now consider: how is this character
saved, how lost ?   When is it that I act according to my make ?
When do I preserve the dignity of my nation and birth ?   What
am I worthy of ?  and what are the things beneath me ?   Is it
not beneath me to dissemble, or flatter, or court ?   Is it
not beneath me to stoop to applause and solicit grace and
favour ?   Am not I worthy of liberty, generosity, constancy,
magnanimity ?   Why, then, do I talk of anything else as
beneath me ?   Why consider what else I am worthy of ?—But
it is beneath me to be seen in such a habit.—Procure a rich one,
and wear it ; for thou art worthy such a habit : thou art worthy
an estate, a coach, an equipage.   What shouldst thou do with
poverty or hardship, or how manage any such circumstance :
thou who wert never born to liberty, generosity, or greatness ;

or if born to it, hast renounced thy right and made thyself a slave? What shouldst thou do but fawn and stoop, where there is hope of riches or renown, or honours or advancement? For, what dost thou know that is better or higher? Remember, therefore, either thou art above these things, or not above them. If not above them, do all that is necessary in order to gain them: dissemble, flatter, court. But if this be beneath thee, how can disgrace or poverty be beneath thee? How can that be beneath me in which I can most of all show myself to be a man? How can that be unworthy of me which is my noblest talk and performance?

What is it then thou art worthy of? Resolve, either the one or the other. Either thou art worthy of constancy and magnanimity: or of that which is contrary to it, pusilanimity and meanness. Either thy worth and character is in a title, name, estate, and then liberty, constancy, magnanimity are nothing; or if thy worth and character be in this, then the rest is nothing. And remember, τίνα θέλεις καλὸν ποιεῖν . . . τί οὖν ἐξαίρετον ἔχεις; τὸ ζῷον; · · τὸ χρηστικὸν φαντασίαις; οὔ · τὸ λογικὸν ἔχεις ἐξαίρετον · τοῦτο κόσμει ["Who is it whom you would make beautiful? What then have you particularly excellent? Is it the animal part? Is it the power of using appearances? No. The excellence lies in the rational part. Adorn this."—*Epict. Disc.*, Bk. III., c. i., § 24-26].

Wilt thou never have done with that fancy of a name * and character in the world? pleasing thyself in this? referring still to this? What is this more than a face or dress? what is this but another sort of effeminacy?—a† Barrus, one that wishes to be called a beauty, a judge in clothes, a dancer, a shape. Thou fearest an ill report. Thy character will suffer; so will thy face if thou exposest it to the sun or wind.—What must I do then?— Stay within doors and be careful of thyself, as the women are; for, what should such a one do in a camp but be ridiculous?

How impossible is it to preserve any *real character*, whilst that other fancy is in existence concerning *a character in the world?*

---

* Τὸ δοξάριον.—*Mar. Aurel. Med.*, Bk. IV., § 3.
† *Horace.* Sat. I., 6, 30.

# CHARACTER.

## (Χαρακτήρ.)

If the first of the three [1] *great ones* (who had the preparatory part—*Epict.*, Bk. III., c. xxi.) involved himself as he did, and in those times, how much more thou ? and in these ? If the age then bore not a declaration, how much less now ?— Then not ripe : now rotten.

Remember, therefore, in manner and degree, the same involution, shadow, curtain, the same soft irony ; and strive to find a character in this kind according to proportion both in respect of self and times. Seek to find such a tenour as this, such a key, tone, voice, consistent with true gravity and simplicity, though accompanied with humour and a kind raillery, agreeable with a divine pleasantry.—This is a harmony indeed ! What can be sweeter, gentler, milder, more sociable, or more humane ? Away, then, with that other sociableness ; that inwardness, intimacy, openness. How false, how unfounded, how harsh in reality, and unfitted for what it is designed ; how unfitted for their good whom it is meant to serve, and for thine, in respect of thy own character, conviction, improvement ! Indeed the very reverse of all.

But truth ! truth !—Remember that truth is best preserved when those thou conversest with are made to think most truly of thee ; and this will least be when thou speakest most truly or most simply in this way, or wouldst correct, rebuke, and teach with the same simplicity. Seek, then, the true simplicity : for this thou usest with them is not so. As for gravity, used in their concerns, as hoping or expecting better of them, this is in good earnest ridiculous ; and not only that, but in another respect tyrannical and barbarous.

Firm, steady, even, upright, between these contrary blasts, efforts of humour, temper, sallies of disposition, the gay, light-

---

[1] Socrates, Diogenes, Zeno.

winged zephyrs, and the ruffling Boreas or heavy Notus.—
Colossus-like, fixed, poised with equal footing and foundation on
each side—a promontory parting two seas. These and more
images, examples, models may be taken from the highest things
to illustrate this simple and (in appearance) humble, mean,
insipid character; this middle genius, partaking neither of
hearty mirth nor seriousness. For what to do with such a one?
How borne with?—Nevertheless to persist herein; stand
firm; keep this station, tenour, harmony. This, as difficult
as it may seem, yet by attention and hearty application may
most easily be preserved, if on the one hand thou strenuously
resist what offers from the vulgar side and that facetious comic
kind, whatever it be of wit, jest, story, and the like; and if, on
the other hand, thou as strenuously resist and abstain from that
as ridiculous seriousness and solemnity in these affairs, eager
contention and striving in the concerns of others, and for the
reformation and conviction of others.—Notable reformation
without conviction! Notable conviction, as things stand with
them and with thyself!—Away then, no more.

Firm, steady, &c.—Equal between these two extremes of
different brows. Both mixed in a manner; convertible,
communicable by an easy change from one into another; not
starting, not shrinking from one another; not constituting two
different souls, two different men, differently known, differently
accessible, differently to be treated, spoken with. Ridiculous!
In humour; out of humour. Now no jest; now no earnest.
Now play, odious; now seriousness, more odious. All joy (good
news!). All sorrow (bad news again!). All this or all that; and
when one meets the other a jarring, a harshness, frightfulness.
Stay a little till I am in tune. O excellent harmony! O life!
Shall it be still thus? Wilt thou never think of any other
character? No more then. Have done with this game. No
more of these parts to act, no tragedy, no comedy (mere comedy);
no dismal, no deplorable; no dainty, delicate, pretty, sweet. Be
this liked or not liked, be it dull, be it insipid, what it will; yet
be thou constant to it, such as it is; constant in this medium,
this certain third thing; neither solemnity nor drollery; neither
seriousness nor jest.

Nor jest; nor earnest; for what jest with one who

P

considers vicissitudes, periods, the immediate changes and incessant eternal conversions, revolutions of the world? Again, what earnest with one who considers but the same?

Earnest: but not in earnest. Jest: but not really jest. For where is jest? and where earnest? In the things within is earnest. In the things *without*, what is all but jest? Now the first are never meant; the latter everywhere. How talk then of the first? How be earnest or in earnest, if thou wouldst ever so feign? But if the talk be never of the first but of the latter only, how talk of these and be serious? See then if the greatest seriousness be not a very jest. Therefore, be it jest or earnest with others, it can be neither to thyself. Their jest, their earnest: both in a manner a jest. But the use of this *jest,* a serious matter and far from jest. See then to use it right *within;* and for *without* remember the medium and find the balance as becomes thee.

Never to leave till this balance be brought right, or pretty near to an evenness: though the way to this be through such frequent changes and unevennesses, for so it must be to a beginner.—This was too light; this too heavy. Here feathers, there lead.—Why this sad tone? Why dismal? Why the tragedy? and anon again the comedy—all joy? From whence? for what? in what world? what circumstances? Art thou ready for a change? Will the reverse not be unseasonable?—Good, then. Be it so. There let it stand, the balance is right. But if the balance be not there, nor near there; make it more even; weigh, ponderate, redress, from one scale to the other; and go on thus removing, taking out and putting in, by this measure, this examen.—If pleasantry, as how pleasant? and what room for seriousness? If seriousness, as how serious? And what room for pleasantry of a certain kind? What are the kinds of each? How will they stand together? how break in easily and kindly without violence to one another? how mix without constraint? how pair, without being monstrous, or engendering anything monstrous?—

Such must be the freedom, such the easiness of this communication and transition in a free mind; free to either circumstance, either season, either way; equal as to what offers in either kind.—No hanging, changing, sticking. No wish, nor choice, nor disposition to one more than to another; not whining and then simpering, now this uppermost, now that. Nothing of all this; no delay or hindrance from temper, not a government of humour; not the ascendant mood, or prevalent fancy. Elevation and depression, rise and fall.—Good news, bad news, all alike.— Is it news indeed? News to me?—What news? Is it a concern to me?—What concern?—Away!—

Such then must be the test of this earnest jest, gravity, mirth, sorrow, joy, or whatever it be, still, much one and the same, no mighty difference. A mirth not out of the reach of what is gravest; a gravity not abhorrent to the use of that other mirth. In this balance seek a character, a personage, manner, genius, style, voice, action. Here the decency, proportion, and grace of all. This the study, performance, and music of life. Nor can this ever be obtained without a perfect and absolute check of that which now prevails and has prevailed so long, carrying thee as with the stream, beginning indeed in jest, but ending in earnest.—Miserable sympathy!

See, then, the best practice and exercise is to go by contraries, just in the teeth of temper, just opposite to humour. —Am I disposed to laugh? how disposed? what senseless disposition is this? Now check, now give the turn, now learn the true authority, command, and how to make temper obey. —Or am I disposed to lament?—Lament *what?* thyself? or the poor world?—But others are melancholy, others mourn.— Do thou mourn then, be in black; forbear eating, speaking, or whatever else, for company, and as accommodating thyself? But why mourn within?—Nay, but they are now changed. They are gay again. It is a holiday, a birthday.—Put on the birthday suit, the holiday suit. But what holiday within? what revel wouldst thou keep there?—Beware, then, and for safety's sake apply contraries (for here is the danger). Turn the edge the other way, present the point, and keep temper aloof. Thwart, cross, perplex, and break it thus, till it become manageable and the impetuous steed be softer-mouthed, easily guided, as with a thread, and governed not by his own head but by the master's hand.—Be it so. Mind but the exercise, and fear not; thou wilt soon have a good seat and appear in it as easy to others as thou wilt be really easy and unconstrained thyself.

Again : Jest ?—earnest.—Earnest ?—jest.—Where is the earnest ? The jest where ?—But see ! the earnest.—What ? Death !—Is this the earnest ? *Usque adeone mori miserumes?* Is it so dreadful to die ? [*Virg.,Æn.*XII.,646].—But infamy !—What ? with whom ? for how long ?—The town ! the world !—O jest ! Country ruined !—The storks' nests. Jest still, jest all.—But is there not something which may make this to be earnest, and does make it so, commonly, whether we will or no ?—Right. This is earnest. This is the thing. This (and this alone) is no jest ; viz., when that which should be jest is earnest with us. But why whether we will or no ? What hinders but it should be jest with us, as in itself it is ? What but wrong jest ? It is this that is in the way : jest in wrong places : mere jest, foolery, trifle ; the ordinary common pleasantry ; for if it be jest there, it will be earnest here.

The world, or philosophy, a jest : one of the two.—Which, then ? Say, and be not thou a jest thyself.

No more of that which if received as jest will make philosophy, religion, virtue, honesty, a jest, or which being taken as earnest will make life, riches, fortune, pleasure, fame, the possession or loss of these, to be earnest.

No more then. If there be, however, a facetiousness, a humour, a pleasantry of a right kind, proportionable and always in season, just, even, and spread alike through a whole character and life, sweet, gentle, mild, and withal constant, irrefragable, never inwardly disturbed whatever outward economy may require ; if there be this thing, this true, innocent, excellent jest and pleasantry ; let this be the care, how to preserve this jest and keep it the same ; how never to be false to it ; never to betray it, sacrifice it, prostitute it ; never basely to yield it up to that other vile and scurrilous jest, most incompatible with it, its bane, destruction, and extinction. Let there be no raillery of that sort, no drollery, no buffoonery, nor any thing that but borders upon it : not if a thousand companions, friends, cry out or wonder, or are displeased ; not for a thousand bribes the one way, a thousand admirations, exclamations ἡδὺς ἄνθρωπος [What an agreeable fellow], and the rest, nor for a thousand of those contrary invectives, slights, pityings, and the *quantum mutatum ab illo* ! [How changed since then !].

Remember another character, another dignity, another humour, pleasantry.—The Socratic genius, this mirth, these *jests*, these turns, and this simplicity. The chatter of the Roman comic poet and what he borrowed hence, and from his Socratic masters. But for Aristophanes, a Plautus, a modern play, modern wit, raillery, humour, away! This is earnest, Petronius earnest. *Jocus risus et cupido*, the muses and the graces of this sort; earnest, sad earnest.

And is it *earnest* still?[1]—How with the company? with relations, the table-talk, disputes, debates, news, the public, the world? Think if a Lesbius stood by, and asked the question, "Is not this earnest?"—Something like it, indeed too like it. Instead of Lesbius then, do thou thyself remember thus to ask thyself in domestic politics, at table, at play (whatever play), "Is not this earnest, or what is it?"

Since recovered[2] from thy long distemper, and now likely to live for some time, and as far as a broken constitution will permit to be active again in affairs of the public and friends; remembering the first and early cautions (more necessary and incumbent now and in this state), the laws as in Parliament, &c., with which thou must now again take up; begin as formerly, for there is need enough after neglect and so much time given to bodily affairs and weakness. Begin again as above: upon character, familiarity, &c.: remembering the natural secretion, modesty, and decorum; and remembering the deformity and nauseousness there spoken of (p. 142) as belonging to a certain openness and affectation of intimacy. For now these things are growing again, and by a prosperous state of public and friends, and a less difficult one of family and fortune, they lay hold and bring back to the same follies, and now more than ever inexcusable manners and character.

Begin then. Consider some late warm sallies and excursions in relation to public as well as family and friends.—Whence the loss of character?—first inward, then outward: for the latter must soon follow. Yet put a stop here if possible, that the former may recover; allow a breathing time. But if the first coming to sink, the latter be flung away after it, as in a kind of

---

[1] *St. Giles*, February, 1705.     [2] *St. Giles*, January, 1707.

despair; this is desperate indeed, and will bring on a real desperate game.

Be more composed and weigh this well. Let not the speciousness of simplicity and an open part deceive thee. The best simplicity is to go on in mending faults, not staying to tell or explain them. See then where the fault lies.

The overthrow of all character is from an over-promising or a desponding view of affairs administered, though originally it is from the first that all ill arises. The first leads to a sort of uncertainty, the other to a resigning: both equally wrong. Matters having a little succeeded, self-applause arises, and hence engagement and forwardness, beyond the measure and true tone of life. On the other side, matters growing ill, or succeeding a little worse than ordinary, self-disparagement arises, and thence aversion to all business, love of privacy, and violent affectation of retreat and obscurity. The latter is mere pusillanimity! as the other was rashness and mere madness.

In the former of these cases, certain schemes and plans are formed : Platonic commonwealths, reformations of states, families, and private persons, thy own labours made known, what progress already made, what more expected. Excellent explanations! And to whom all this? To the wise? Would they not deride thee? Or to the vulgar? And dost thou not deride thyself?

In the other case, account is to be given (forsooth!) why these affairs have succeeded thus ill; by what hindrance from thyself, from others, from the age, from the nature of things.— Again excellent explanations! And to whom all this? Where is the harmony of such a conduct? where the proportion of character?

Strive, therefore, against this, by all ways and means possible; and what other way but by that rule to go by contraries, just opposite to humour, just in the teeth of temper. Do things succeed well ?—Wonderful! who would have thought it ? Now, therefore, be diffident; now forebode; expect all ill. Think of what lies at the bottom, *et ignes suppositos cinero doloso* [and of fires hidden beneath treacherous ashes]. Μὴ γὰρ οὐ χείρονα καὶ χαλεπώτερα προσδέχεται τὰ παρὰ τῶν φαύλων; [Does he not prepare for worse and more grievous miseries from bad people ?—*Epict. Disc.*, Bk. IV., c. v., § 8.]

But on the other side, Do things go ill ?—What wonder ? What else did I expect ? Were not these the terms ? Now, therefore, be bold, now lively ; now confide not as the poet's hero, *spem vultu simulans* [feigning hope in fall], but heroically, indeed, and at heart, without deceit, suppressing grief and exalting the mind, so as to have it full of hope, yet without dependence, as at a game. And thus inward simplicity and outward economy may be reconciled. For what if the first motion be dejecting, it is resisted, conquered, despised. The second is the true. Let that be seen, so much of it as is proper, and at a proper season, when secure of thyself and returned again to thy own right mind and real self. Or wouldst thou discover a disordered false self, make others to take advice of the strife within, and call them to be witnesses to this thy *regimen* and treatment in thy sick state ? O wretched simplicity indeed ! O beggarly humility ! Is it for pity that these ulcers are uncovered ? or want they to be scratched ? Is not this calling to others to see, handing about the phlegm and stools ? If this so pitiful and mournful way delight thee, say, then (in a yet lower character), τί γὰρ εἰμί ; ταλαίπωροι ἀνθρωπάριον [For what am I ? a poor contemptible man.— *Epict. Disc.*, Bk. I., c. iii., § 5], for this is better than to disgrace the art which should make thee happy and show thee so to others.

Away, therefore, with this fulsome openness and deceitful simplicity. If things go wrong, rejoice with an innocent sort of malice and sportiveness, as at those plays of cards or dice, where a more than ordinary run of fortune, though against ourselves, is taken pleasantly, as comical and entertaining to ourselves and others. Not so, I confess, when any great matter is at stake. But what matter here ? What besides the play itself ? Is it any more than play, mere play ?—But it is part of the play to seem in earnest.—Right : and therefore do thou seem in earnest, and as one who in good earnest hopes and confides ; for so thou dost, though not as they perhaps may understand it. But they can understand no better. Do thou, therefore, accommodate thyself to their understanding, and do not perplex and confound them with certain views which thou wouldst never think of communicating with them if thou wert not thyself already in confusion and hurry of mind. So much more monstrous is it, at this season above all, to be open and familiar in a certain way. Here, therefore, resist equally as in the other case of success, but hide the resistance. For to show the struggle in this case is abject and mean, like one that cries for help; and to show it in the other is ostentation and insolence, like one who would show his strength, such a strength truly as nobody cares for. Who are they that can relish such severity? Where are the friends that will not complain of philosophy in this case?

Let temper, therefore, rather than principle, bear the charge. Be severe over thyself; but appear so as little as may be with safety (for this is the main). And if joy and alacrity in one case, or concern and care in the other, be thought wanting, it is better to bear the censure than to relax or apologise; better pass as extravagantly light, sullen, or mysterious for the time, than by a dangerous accommodation give way to the wrong affection; or by a foolish openness expose mysteries which will create greater mysteriousness and misunderstanding than before. But a sincere carriage without affectation may bear thee easily through all this. Nor is inward severity (in the thwarting either of joy or grief) so very hard to be hid, if honestly meant. But suffer it once to aim at appearance, let it but seem to want witnesses, and see presently how nauseous and offensive! What a character!

Therefore, consider of this ever in this double respect. Remember both the first and second resistance. As first, how pernicious the not resisting inwardly in both the fortunes; and in the next place, though this first resistance be stoutly made in both, yet how wrong not to resist also in that other sense of outward explanation. Here, therefore, as elsewhere, apply the rule, *ἀνέχου καὶ ἀπέχου* [Bear and forbear].

As the loss of inward character draws on the loss of outward, so the loss of outward helps forward that other loss. Save, therefore, what thou canst and make not things worse by endeavouring to mend them. If at any time the inward character suffer, keep at least the outward. Keep it within reach and recovery. Do not sign and seal to thy folly. If to publish thy wisdom and strength in the preservation of inward character be in truth but folly, and the very overthrowing of that character thou wouldst preserve; what must it be to proclaim folly itself, expose thy loss of character, and show thy own weakness, whether as sparing or condemning it? For this is all one, condemning in this place is but sparing: it is pitying, bemoaning, flattering. Didst thou go roundly to work and take thyself to task in good earnest, there would be none of all this, no room, no leisure for such fine speeches, such appeals, such explanations before such people. What have we to do with such confidants? Is it health and strength thou feelest? Why boast of it? To what judges? what masters of fence? Or, are they weaknesses and relapses that sit heavy? Be it so. How shall we lighten them? To what physicians commit them? To what surgeons shall we lay open such sores as these? In what company unbind such wounds? Or must it be as a spectacle or beggar-like to move pity? Beggarly indeed, and abject; if anything in the world can be so, yet is this abjectness inseparable from that other insolence. The same indulgence of grief, or the same admittance of humiliation so seemingly modest and which passes for such an expression of social feeling and humanity, is the actual cause and nourishment of that contrary impotence of temper in joy and exultation; when a small alteration happens in affairs, and elevates just so much more as the preceding state of affairs had power to depress. So effectually do these opposite dispositions co-operate and help forward one another.

What scene of affairs? What management?—Successful, prosperous! οὐκ ἔλεγόν σοι, ἀδελφέ; [Did I not tell you, brother!—*Epict. Disc.*, Bk. II., c. xvi., § 16.] Did not I tell you how I should manage?—What?—A family, a state, or, if occasion were, an army.—Wretch! manage thyself; learn there to be a rider and to have a seat and hand, for if thou hadst one there it would not be talked of here, but shown without talking. But if thou wantest a hand even there, how much more here? What wonder if thou art flung off, or trampled on? Where are now thy vaunts?—But mankind is unruly: the beast is headstrong.—Why now, more than before? Wretch! wilt not thou bear thy fall patiently, take the just reproof, put up the affront, and learn to be wiser the next time? Who bid thee

go these airs ?   What need of setting out in this career ? why
the great saddle and the trappings ?   Go : take thy pad again;
thy plain homely beast, thy mule or ass.   Manage what thou art
fit for, and hast strength to manage, and mount not where thou
art so soon liable to be thrown and made contemptible both to
others and thyself.   For were thy seat as it should be, no fall
would ever be such as to cause disgrace ; all being done that
art with strength proportionable could perform.       Beware,
therefore, of high mounting ; or if, forgetful of this, thou art
soon again dismounted, bear with it, swallow it, as they say,
keep it to thyself.   No excuses or bemoanings.   It is thyself
thou accusest, and before thyself ?   It is thyself thou hast
injured : nor art thou to make others amends, but thyself only.
Why, therefore, trouble others ?   This is pleading for *outward*
character, not labouring for that *within*.   And as just Providence
will have it, we lose even our outward character by this sacrifice.
Nothing deprives us of it more directly, no quicker way to lose
the shadow, even though the substance could remain with thee,
whilst thus greedy and dog-like as in the fable.   For what can
lessen thee more with others than to be seen dejected on the
account of outward things, as they will always esteem it, though
thy trouble be indeed of a better sort?   But if thou art concerned
at their thinking thus of thy concern, what is thy concern then
in reality but for outward things ?   Nor is it any wonder if this
dejection be the forerunner of a new presumption ?   For the
same foreign opinions, differently operating according to the
event or success of outward things, must of necessity alike
produce both that false simplicity, shameful nakedness, dejecting
humility, and also that contrary and anxious forwardness, vain
openness and temerity.   And what harmony of character these
two make together is easy to see.

     Alas ! what am I ?   An infirm creature, of body and mind ;
out of the world and practice, yet not in philosophy and the
possession of virtue, half - knowing, half - learned, pedantic
($\grave{o}\psi\iota\mu\alpha\theta\acute{\eta}\varsigma$), &c.—If this be inwardly spoken and not aloud, if
this be in the closet or study, in retiring time, and not in time
of action, if this be rather in success and after elevation (as
in the use of the cold *regimen)*, it is excellent, and to be
promoted, encouraged, aggravated.   Say not then pedantic

($\dot{o}\psi\iota\mu\alpha\theta\dot{\eta}s$) in the vulgar, but in the deepest, sense : say "one born out of season," the sores, the wounds, &c.—But if this contraction of thyself, this humiliation, be the contrary way and at another season, consider how abject, vile, and how contrary, in effect, even to that which it pretends, viz., modesty and the $\dot{a}\delta\iota\mu\nu\dot{\eta}$. For how soon again will the note be changed ? How soon a contrary tone ? Not "Alas ! what am I ?" but "Behold ! what a proficient I am, how strong and firm in mind, and if by nature or accident not altogether so in body, yet by art and care how well. In circumstances how well ; in character same. Philosophy, economy, management. —"How excellent, noble !"

These are the tides (a spring-tide indeed !), the ebbings and the flowings ; all from the same cause. And wilt thou ever be thus stranded ; left dry ashore, exposed thus pitifully, and almost fatally, not knowing which way to get off the shoals or clear of these quicksands ? Whence all this but from the bold launching out, the trust to the sky, the high top-gallant sails, the negligent pilot and merry crew ?

> *Rectius vives, Licini, neque altum*
> *Semper urgendo, &c.*

[You will live more wisely, Licinius, if you press not always out to sea.—*Hor., Od.* II., x., lines 1-2.] Turn that sense hitherward, and despise the cautious horror and tempting, betraying shore.

> *Neque dum Procellas*
> *Cautus horrescis, nimium premendo*
> *Litus miquum.*

[Nor yet, dreading the storm in your caution, keep too close to the unfriendly shore.—*Ibid.*, I., vi., 2-4.]

Timidity here proves rashness. The same rash opinion creates the evil as the good, where in reality there is neither. To sneak is but to prepare for boasting and vain conceit. As this is poor, senseless, contemptible (for why boast ? and of what ?), so is that ridiculous, and to be sported at. For why dejected ? and for what ? Why tell thy tale, why sing thy ditty (wretch !) thus mournfully ? Why tragedy ? Why a stage ? Why witnesses ?

What is this unbosoming? Wouldst thou have no bosom? no reserve? no heart for thyself? Or what heart if thus bestowed, thus prostituted, and made common? Or will this commonness not hurt it, not pollute it? Will it be more truly that *common* public, honest heart for being in this sense made *common* and laid open?—Away with this *simplicity*, if this may be so called. No more of this false humanity, sociableness, humility. No more shrinking thus (poor snail!) into thy shell; a notable refuge and security!—Hold up thy head, man! and if thou hast been a fool, see it and be wise at last. But be not a yet greater fool in seeking the applause of such whom, instead of winning, thou wilt by this means render less tractable, and make both to despise thee more and use thee worse. And where at this rate will be thy part so much insisted on? Where thy influence or service which thou pretendest to? Will not all character, both inward and outward, be thus overthrown?

*Sed verae numerosque modosque ediscere vitae* ["The harmony of life is my concern."—*Hor. Epist.*, II., ii., 144.] This is character. But if for outward ears only and the judgments abroad, what difference between this labour and that other—*Verba sequi fidibus modulanda Latinis?* [To fashion words to fit the Latin strings.—*Hor., Epist.*, II., ii., line 143]. Continue, therefore, and keep the harmony, if possible, uninterrupted; if not, restore it again as soon as possible, and dwell not on the miscarriage. No echoings, no repeatings; no running over again what is past. If anything slipped in the music, if a finger went wrong, a false string struck, a time mixed, pass it over and go on undisturbed, for this is the next perfection of art, not to interrupt, not break the symphony, not let the music sink nor the ear dwell upon what was wrong, but drown it by better play, overcome it by an easy transition and agreeableness of what succeeds.—But no, I have failed in the rule of art; I must stay and show the error. This stop was wrong, this key, tone, measure.—O Pedantry! And how in life? Must the gamut there, in the midst of play, be conned over? Must it be *sol, la, mi, fa?* Dost thou not know that, even at the best, these rules are burdensome and irksome to those who are not of the art? Was this so hardly seasonable in that very school and those days, too? and wilt thou nevertheless abroad, and in such days as these, come out with such things, suspend performance to make demonstrations and by these excuses teach thy art?—Rare pedagogue!

Mind but a certain physician of thy acquaintance, one sufficiently knowing in his art (simply understood), and see how a certain method and behaviour of his, somewhat like this last spoken of, has succeeded with him. As, first, how the thing appears in itself; with what kind of grace and accommodation; how it renders him to others whom he strives so much to instruct and convince; how towards his patients themselves; and last of all, how towards himself, and in his own temper and character. With other physicians it is generally far otherwise. Be ashamed, therefore, that such as these, in the use of common policy, and for the interest of their arts should observe so much a better economy and character than thou (wretch!) in thy own case and in behalf of thy art and practice, so superior to all other.

How long since all this was seen and noted! How long since another character was sworn to!—No apologising; no show of inward work; no hint; no glance. — The purple only. No earnest, clearings, &c., cares, mystery.—The honest irony, jest.

Return, therefore, again, as above, and remember the involution, the shadow, the veil, the curtain. To the false character here treated of (the impotence of a certain kind) apply that of *Marcus Aurel., Med.* x., 33—Μὴ προφασίζου, &c. [You will never cease to lament until you can do with enjoyment whatever is conformable to your own nature], and not in the strength of this and the chief Δόγμα: that of Homer, used by *Marcus Aurel.*, *Med.* xi., 31 —ἐμὸν δ᾽ ἐγέλασσε φιλὸν κῆρ (*Od.* ix., 413)—[and in my heart laughed].

So our Scripture (applying it to what has been heard and learnt in a better way than in common conversation). "If thou hast heard a word let it die with thee; and be bold it will not burst thee."—*Eccles.*, c. xix., v. 10.

Take therefore *the Word* in a higher sense, and as used in Scripture, for discipline, knowledge, message, εὐαγγέλιον, but *not to be preached* as that other. So again in the same Book, c. xxi., v. 26: "The heart of fools is in their mouth;

but the mouth of the wise is in their heart," and soon after the prayer, which begins at the last verse of Chapter xxii. (where the chapter is absurdly cut off from the dependent sense which follows), " Who shall set a watch before my mouth and a seal of wisdom on my lips ? " &c.

# FANCY AND JUDGMENT.

(Φαντασία καὶ Συγκατάθεσις.)

DISEASED FANCIES.—Αὕτη γὰρ γένεσις πάθους, θέλειν τι καὶ μὴ γίνεσθαι [" For the origin of perturbation is to wish for something that is not obtained."—*Epict. Disc.*, Bk. I., c. xxvii., § 10].

Οὕτως ἀμέλει καὶ τὰ ἀρρωστήματα ὑποφύεσθαι λέγουσιν οἱ φιλόσοφοι. [" In this manner, as philosophers say, also diseases of the mind grow up.—*Ibid.*, Bk. II., c. xviii., § 8.]

> *Si volnus tibi monstrata radice vel herbâ*
> *Non fieret levius, fugeres radice vel herbâ*
> *Proficiente nihil curarier.*

> [" Some root or simple you are told to use
> As panacea for a wound or bruise,
> You try them, and they fail you ; surely, then
> You'd never have recourse to them again."
> —*Hor., Ep.*, Bk. II., ii., lines 148-157.]

The prescriptions of the vulgar-wise, like those of the Empiricists. They know only the symptom : apply only to the symptom.—Man ! go to the cause, cure in the blood. Or what if the humour be checked in this part ? what if the breaking out, the heat, the swelling be struck in, goes it not to another part ?

> *ut solet, in cor*
> *Trajecto lateris miseri capitisve dolore,*
> *Ut lethargicus hic cum fit Pugil et medicum urget.*

> [" As pains fly from the side or head,
> And in the chest appear instead,
> Or, quickening some lethargic lout,
> Boxes this doctor's ears about."
> —*Hor., Sat.*, Bk. II., iii., lines 29-31.]

But a small matter will satisfy, a pretty circumstance (as they say) to make him easy.—Thus a wench, a handsome wife, a table, a coach and horses, a fine house, a garden.—Excellent prescriptions !—And how then ?—Presently nauseate.—No, but I enjoy still the same.—Wars and wars. See what will come of it : how inveterate the disease is growing . What effeminacy, tenderness, niceness. How as to fortune ? How lookest in the world ? How ordinary human infirmities and casualties ? How sickness, age ? *Natales grate numeras ?* [Do you thank heaven for each new birthday that you live ?—*Hor., Epist.,* II., 210.]— How temper ?—Spoiling, spoilt.—The child, brat, woman. The man, where ? How ?

To starve the preying fancies that starve the principal part. The same as in a stomach spoiled by variety, high food, repletion.—Retrench, abstain, and thus hope for a recovery ; cut off the sallying, roving, lowering, high-flying, ranging fancies, the ill-paired, the monstrously copulating and engendering ones, centaurs, chimeras, cockatrices, and the spawn of this kind.

This is the beginning. First purge (as the physicians say) ; evacuations ; then restoratives. Now remark. See if these be but retrenched, whether the mind will not turn itself a right way, find itself better work, and the Δύναμις χρησική τῶν φαντασιῶν [power to use appearances], and go honestly and roundly about its business. Take it once but from ill employment and see if it get not good. Spare its labour, force, and ingenuity in wrong matter ; and see if it become not ingenious in right.

But patience awhile. It is dull and heavy as yet; so it is with the ruined stomach. But let it be pinched a little, allow it but to be empty, it will come to itself. Or if in the real stomach (that of the body) it be not so, depend on it that in this other the thing cannot fail. The rule is infallible here, the regimen certain, and the medicine a specific : ἠρεμήσατε τῇ διανοίᾳ [Be tranquil.—*Epict. Disc.,* Bk. II., c. xxi., § 22].

# THE ASSENTS OF THE JUDGMENT.

(Συγκατάθεσις.)

PERSUASIVE FANCIES.—Τρεῖς τόποι . . (1) ὁ περὶ τὰς ὀρέξις
καὶ τὰς ἐκκλίσεις (2) ὁ περὶ τὰς ὁρμὰς καὶ ἀφορμὰς (3) ὁ περὶ τὰς
συγκαταθέσεις [There are three things in which a man ought to
exercise himself who would be wise and good : (1) that of
desires and aversions : (2) that of pursuits and avoidances : (3)
that of the assents (or judgment).—*Epict. Disc.*, Bk. III., c. ii., § 1].
—O that it [judgment] were here, and that it only stuck here.
Yet, as it is, it must be here in some degree.  For how the first
place without some help from this ?—But keep the order and
remember the τα πάθη [the passions] and this last (whatever is
borrowed from of it) for the first.  ἴδιον δὲ ἀνθρώπου . . . διάκρισις
τῶν πιθανῶν φαντασιῶν . . . καὶ τῇ παρούσῃ φαντασίᾳ ἐμφιλοτεχεῖν,
ἵνα μήτι ἀκατάληπτον παρεισρυῇ [It is the proper work of a man
to form a just judgment of plausible appearances—and to
scrutinise present impressions so that nothing may enter that
is not well examined.—*Mar. Aurel., Med.,* VIII., § 26, and
VII., § 54].

O sophistry ! artifice and deep laid design ! so artful as to
appear all simplicity ; so natural as to seem almost nature itself.
Τί γὰρ τούτων προσηνέστερον [for what is more agreeable than
this.—*Mar. Aurel., Med.,* v., § 9].  O imposture ! powerful,
charming, persuasive name ἡ πάντας τοὺς ἀνθρώπους πλανῶσα
[who leads all men astray.—*Cebes*].  What an offspring ? what
a brood engendered ?  what machines, hosts, giants !—Loves,
appetites, desires.—Opinion, fancy, all—all from this sophistry.
"Irresistible powers !  Gigantic forms !  Whence all your
strength, dimensions, weapons and array ?  The pointed steel,
the viper-teeth and scorpion stings.—What sting ? and whence ?
—Opinion, fancy—'Ω φαντασία.  Thine is the sting : thine all
the force : thine the dominion, power.  From thee this empire,

Q                                    209

without thee all faints, languishes, and dies. Loves, appetites, desires, all live in thee."

" To thee I come then, with thee is my concern, thee alone. 'Tis thou that must form me or I thee. Loves, appetites, desires, fears, horrors, anguishes, and all ye host of passions; stand by; retire and wait aloof the issue of this conflict. If I am overcome, the field, the place is yours: sack, pillage, plunder, ravage. But if I prevail, retire for ever; ye are nothing, nor have no pretence."

*Responsare cupidinibus* [to restrain the appetites.—*Hor. Sat.*, Bk. II., vii., line 5]. No such thing, but κρίσις φαντασίαις [examination of the fancies]. This is the thing. Here the resistance—the father (opinion) subdued, the children fall, of course.— Sampson's locks, Achilles' heel. Here strike. No dealing, but this way only vincible, penetrable, tractable. This way and in this sense *responsare cupidinibus* [to restrain the passions] ; to bear up, to be a match for them; to give them (as they say) their own, and send them back as they came.

Therefore, again, τί οὖν ὧδε ποιεῖς, ὦ φαντασία ; Ἀπέρχου τοὺς θεούς σοι ὡς ἦλθες [What art thou doing here, O fancy. Go, I entreat thee, as thou camest.—*M. Aur. Med.*, VII., § 17]. In this manner to the fancies of the first and second sort, (1) the absolutely vicious, (2) the mixed, and the rest, and in their several shapes, with language suitable, and real discourse, not making light of this, but remembering it as a thing essential, as the chief discourse, and the life of all. Thus, then, when in the worst shape. " Traitor thought : viper : false and inhuman dogma, τὸ θηρίον οὐκ ἀνθρωπικόν—enormous, monstrous, immense, begone.—Down rebel, impostor, corrupter.—Avaunt ! Aloof !— Expect no quarter here ; no refuge, sanctuary, nor entertainment in this breast ; thou sacrilegious wight, thou violator of all inward peace and harmony, all humane laws and all divine. Sink, hideous spectre, vanish back to chaos. Down in the womb of night where thou wert bred. Down, spurious thought, blind progeny of night. Down—— And thou, fair offspring of eternal truth, arise and usher day."

*Phosphore, redde diem.* [Phosphor, bring back the day.]

In another shape—" Insinuating, sly, busy fancy ! Off ! —To your distance, I beseech you. Not so familiar neither.—No whispering nor buzzing in the ear. No hugging (good, vagabond, dame !) Know your betters and who is mistress within.—Here is nothing for you (believe me), ask ever so long, or say what you please. Go to others that know you less and believe your stories. Go to your companions, your equals, your inferiors, whom ye need not beg of, but may govern with a word and make of what you please."

In another shape—" Thou dear, delicate creature ! Sweet, gentle, loving, fond idea !—Thou witty, pretty, fair one ! What would'st thou have ? To whom art thou solicitress ? And to what ? Whom is it that thou courtest ? For whom these flatteries and caresses ? Why are these charms thus lost ? thus ill bestowed, and in vain ?—It will not be. Go to, go to, thou wanton ! Wait not till thou art frighted hence. Here are things within will make thy poor weak nature shiver, and strike thee dead with fear.—But be advised, retire in time."

*Quo blandae juvenum te revocant preces.*

[" Where the soft prayer of youth recalls thee."—*Hor., Od.* I., c. xxi., line 8].

*Sirenum voces et Circes pocula nosti.*

[" The siren's song you know and Circe's bowl."—*Id., Epist.* II,, c., i., line 23].

*Mene salis placidi vultum fluctusque quietos*
*Ignorare jubes ? Mene huic confidere monstro ?*

[" Do you bid me pay no heed to the face of the calm sea and the quiet waves ? to trust to this monster ? "—*Virgil, Aen.,* V., lines 848-9].

In another shape—Enchanting, wondrous form ! mysterious, dubious !—How shall I know thee ? how discover thee, fly thee, know thee ? I must and question thee.

> " Bring with thee airs from heaven or blasts from hell,
> Thou com'st in such a questionable shape
> That I must call thee —— "

Hold ! for as yet thy name is wanting, which, when thy nature is known, shall frankly and without flattery or fear be given thee.—Oh, easy decision ! short question ! ready resolution ! (what tragedy ? what solemnity ? what emphasis needs there for this ?) Any ghost ! phantom ! air !—'Tis over. This is the charm. These are the words. Pronounce them, say them, but right, and with a good heart, and there is nothing to start at: nothing that can perplex, nothing that can haunt, astonish, terrify. 'Tis done. Alas at an end.

Again to the four sorts :—

1. The wild beasts, boars, tigers, lions, that tear, devour, and lay all waste.

2. The chimeras, sphinxes, centaurs, that haunt, delude, perplex, amaze, distract.

3. The sheep, oxen, swine, and necessary cattle, that soil, fatten, and make a stable of the mind.

4. And last of all, the playsome kind for entertainment, the parrots, apes, monkeys, and the viler sort. These, the worst of all, and most to be feared. Ἀλώπεκες, καὶ ὡς ἐν ζώοις ἀτυχήματα [Like monsters among foxes and animals.—*Epict. Disc.* I., c. iii., § 7], and hence that likeness there spoken of.—Out with this vermin, choose a nobler combat, a better chase.

*Aprum aut fulvum descendere monte Leonem* [A boar or a tawny lion comes down from the mountain]. Death: Banishment: Ignominy καὶ πάντα τὰ δεινὰ φαινόμενα [and every other thing which appears dreadful]. And in this manner οὐδὲν οὐδέποτε οὔτε ταπεινὸν ἐνθυμηθήσῃ [You will never think of anything mean.—*Epict. Ench.*, c. xxi.].

To the first part : the ravagers (nor is that the worst idea), eating canker worms, gnawers, corroders, vipers, creepers, and crawlers, such as truly cause and are the occasion of creeping and crawling, and of every base prostitution, pollution, villainy. —O cockatrices !

To the second sort, creatures of two parts; monsters preposterously composed. Go to the anatomy ; dissect, separate with the instruments that are given. Divorce the unnatural pair, divide the monster, &c.

To the third sort. To the fourth sort.

Conclusion. To all in general. Again the same still τί οὖν ὧδε ποιεῖς ὦ φαντασία ; [What art thou doing here, O fancy.— *Mar. Aur., Med.* VII., § 17].

"Perverse, obstinate Δόγμα. Thou had'st as good begone betimes, and for once bidding; thou had'st as good retire as be turned out by force. 'Tis true thou camest naturally, that is to say, the usual way, and according to the liberty that is given thee, or that thou takest with everybody. 'Tis well. Thou hast had thy time. But things are altered. Times are not now as then. Be advised and retire; if not thou shalt have a wretched life, a sad time of it; no ease, no indulgence, no rest, dunned eternally, reprimanded, lectured, schooled. Who would endure this? And to what purpose? For advance thou never shalt, never prevail. Therefore, good Δόγμα, in charity let me entreat and conjure thee; begone, torment not, nor be tormented."

# NATURAL CONCEPTS.

## (Προλήψεις.)

GENERAL PRINCIPLES.—Περὶ τῶν προλήψεων.—*Epict. Disc.*, Bk. I., c. xxii. τὸ καλὸν τὸ πρέπον [The beautiful. The fitting]. Τὸ αἰσχρὸν ψεκτόν ἐστι, τὸ δέ ψεκτὸν ἄξιόν ἐστι τοῦ ψέγεσθαι [The shameful ought to be blamed, and that which is blamable deserves to be blamed.—*Ibid.*, Bk. III., c. xxvi., § 9].

*Shameful!*—*are you not ashamed?*—and *O shame! shame!* —What? Where? Is there such a thing then? Is it the number, quality, power of those that cry shame that can make where it is not? Is it made or unmade by people's voices? or is there that which is shameful in itself, let who will say otherwise, or though it be thought ever so honourable?

To flatter the tyrant is at court no shame, and what if the whole world were a court, or thought as they think at court, would flattery be no shame?—No, for what is virtue or honour but opinion? What is vice or shame but opinion? Go on and say what is parricide, ingratitude, treachery, but opinion? And hast thou no shame that sayst this?—Yet see! There are those who very philosophically and religiously (as they think) say this, and establishing morality make virtue and vice, shame and honour, to be nothing but as custom or opinion make them. O excellent religion! admirable philosophy!

*Low, pitiful, sneaking.*—What matter, so it be not known, so it be in the dark (as they say), so that the thing be gained which was aimed at? What matter for the means? What is sneaking? What is cringing?—Smiling, bowing low, stooping, and (if occasion be) creeping, kissing hands, feet, or anything else.—Where is the harm? How does this hurt? Does it ache? or smart? or pain anyway? Does it pain to take up a handkerchief or buckle a shoe? Why not stoop as well here?—Hang it; I can't stoop. I hate sneaking, I can't sneak.—

Is sneaking really ill then?—Miserable, detestable.—Really

so.—Really.— Come on then, never fear, man. Thou mayst be wholly good and virtuous. Nay, thou must be so. It will follow of itself, for I will pawn my life of it, all vice is but sneaking, and that except in vice there is not so much as a ground for such a thing. Fear but sneaking, and thou canst fear nothing else. Love but generosity, and I will engage thou shalt all thy life have subject enough for good action, and all that is called generous and noble.—Matter shall never be wanting, nor ways nor means. Thou shalt not be less generous for want of an estate. Thou shalt not be less heroic for want of armies to conquer with or worlds to conquer. An Alexander may well sneak, for he served women, wine, fame, his own slaves. Even a Hercules may sit down and bemoan himself that he has no feats to do, no boars nor monsters to clear the world of. But a true Hercules need not fear this, that is to say, to be even as generous, great, and heroic as he pleases; for in true heroism there is no reckoning by the scene. It is not the greater or the less scene. It is not as the decorations or ornaments are. It is not in the parts, but in the action that all lies. The theatre is the same, the scene all alike. The presence the same, and as for those we call spectators and observe so much, it is rather an advance of character to have them absent, or if present disapproving, reviling, reproaching. For this is not only heroic, princely, royal, but God-like, divine βασιλικὸν μὲν εὖ πράττειν, κακῶς δὲ ἀκούειν [It is royal to do good and to be abused.—*Mar. Aurel., Med.*, vii., 36]. For how is it even with the divinity itself?

*Foul, sordid, vile, stinking.*— What stinks? Smell the metal (as a sordid prince said), does this stink? Are the courts of tyrants or the chambers of their mistresses *stinking?* Is anything politer, sweeter, fairer? Though whence all this, and how it is here, thou art very certain. Does the minion, the favourite, the delator, the betrayer of his country, the bought patriot, the minister, or so much as any under-engine of this sweet place, stink? Is anything neater, slicker, sprucer, than one of these?—Meanwhile, look yonder on the honest man, how he goes! how it is with him! is he as sweet? has he wherewithal to keep himself thus neat?—But the minion's part was foul. The tyrant is a monster. The whore vile.—Is there then inward vileness? May action possibly stink? and is there on the contrary sweet carriage, sweet action and behaviour? And what is sweet action? a sweet soul?—See then which of these stinks, which of the sweetnesses, are truest. If the honest man's be sweetness, then count these (as they are) stinkards and no better.

*Corruption, corrupt.*—But how? Does his breath smell ill? Is not his skin whole, smooth, slick, thriving?—But he is a villain; rotten within, hollow, unsound, tainted.—How? with what? Is he not heart-whole? Does his pulse beat ill? Is not his blood well coloured, well substanced, fair, and pure?—Where, then, is this poison? and why is not his heart as good as any heart? Is there such a thing then as a *sound heart* in that other sense—wholesome, true, staunch, not to be made lewd, not running riot, not taken off of its game? Has an honest heart such a game? is there any such pursuit or chase? is there anything in this huntsmanship? is there this discipline, this regimen, cure, faculty, art? Let us hear, then, what it is, on what it stands, and how brought about. Let us hear the method and rules. How shall I be trusty, faithful, staunch? how sound, entire, and incorrupt? What are the things that corrupt, and what those to be opposed to them?—And what name to give to this science, this study?

Come on; let us hear how it is said: *Ridiculous!* What? —Everything, or nothing? Ridiculous, indeed.—But something, therefore: something certain, something in nature so: and which, being wrongly applied, is itself ridiculous.

Childish, womanish, bestial, brutal.—Words! words! or are they anything more? But how then not a child? How least like woman? How far from beast? how removed and at a distance from anything of this kind? how properly *a man?* Σκόπει οὖν, τίνων κεχώρισαι κατὰ λόγον — θηρίων — προβάτων [Consider, then, from what you are distinguished by reason— from wild beasts—from cattle.—*Epict. Disc.*, Bk. II., c. x., § 2]. A man, and not a woman; effeminate, soft, delicate, supine; impotent in pleasure, in anger, talk; pusillanimous, light, changeable, &c.; but the contrary to this in each particular.— A man, and not a beast: not gluttonous as a hog, not lecherous as a goat, not savage as a lion, but sociable as the creatures that live in society and have a public.—*A man*, and not a child: not taken with trifles, not admiring shows, not playing, crying, taking on, angry and pleased again, froward, pettish, in humour, out of humour, wanton and cross, stomach, the belly and plaything, manna, nurse. The contraries : Manhood, manliness, humanity—manly, humane, masculine.

*Cowardly.*—But how ? Why not all fear alike reasonable and commendable ? If not, what fear is blamable ? And why ? —The degree ? how far and no further ? For what is fearful is and ought to be feared (else what is rashness, madness ?) Learn, therefore, what is and what is not fearful, and how a man may attain intrepidity and be justly said to be no more fearful.

*Revengeful.* Revenged ?—Of what ? Of a stone or madman ? Who is so mad ?—for a chance hurt, against thought or intention ? Who is so unjust ? Therefore there is just and unjust, or why anger ?

*Base, Mean.*—Why not ?—But others will hate me. Do others then hate what is base and mean ; and dost thou not hate thyself ?

Why are men *proud ?*—It is natural. Why poor and proud.—It is natural. Ugly and proud ? Even ignorant and proud ?—Natural still. Does he then who is thus destitute yet proud think himself base and mean ?—No ; but the contrary. Is pride then natural ; and is not the idea of base and mean (and of what is contrary) natural ? Can one be without the other ? What is pride, then ?—What but the wrong application of this πρόληψις [preconception].

*A brute, a dog*—and what then ? Why is it thought so offensive ? Why taken ill by those who would have no difference to be in nature between just and unjust, right and wrong ? Are we not all dogs, wolves ?—*Homo homini lupus* [man is a wolf to his fellow-man].—What difference then ? Wherein lies the dog which every one so much detests ? — Flattery, fawning, envying, biting, this is doggish ? How many dogs?

*Honest.*—Are you honest ?—Why angry if but so much as asked ?

The *beauté de l'ame* and *beauté du cœur* of the French libertine-authors, of the very courtesans, ladies of intrigue.—Is it so then ? Is there such a thing indeed ?—As how then ? A Messalina ? an Agrippina the younger ?—No, but an Agrippina the elder, a Livia and so to a Cornelia, a Portia, a Lucretia, an Arria. Or amongst the courtesans themselves, a Thais of Terence, the Bacchis of Hecyra; from the better sort of these creatures to modest wife and matron; from the real Thais or Phryne to an Aspatia, so to Hyparchia.

*Tranquillity, serenity, retreat, peacefulness, silence, order, beauty, majesty,* and the rest that is found in nature at those times when the temper leads that way, and seeks the romantic places, the rocks and seashores, wood, caverns, &c. Thus also in *Marcus Aurel., Med.* iv., § 3.—See at what this aims.—They aim indeed, but not rightly.

*Happiness, satisfaction, content.* Can there be any happiness without content ? Any beyond content ? Is there happiness and not content ? or content and not happiness ?—But what content ? Not without feeling, sense, perception : else we might say a stone's content. Not without understanding, thought, and reason : else we might say a beast's, a hog's content : not a heart's or mind's content. There is required therefore a rational content, and not merely a rational (as proceeding from certain and true reason). Now where is this reasonable content ? Is it a reasonable one and on sure ground that has its foundation on circumstances that change every minute, that satisfy one minute and not the next ? That are every way unstable, inconstant, capricious, never to be depended on, never what we can call *our own ?*—What is this content ? Is it the wealth of the Indies ? Is it a fine wench ? a boy ? is it a seraglio ? is it in all those things put together of which our poetess could say

> " That were our state as we would choose it
> 'T would be destroyed for fear to lose it ? "

Must every one then that is happy be a coward ? On the contrary, whoever is a coward must and ever will be miserable. How not be afraid, not shrink, nor tremble either at the approach of death or retreat of fortune, when she is upon the wing ?—*Si celeres quatit pennas resigno quae dedit* [If she spreads her quick wings, I resign what she has given.—*Hor., Od.,* III., xxix., line 54].

This is content indeed. This is a foundation.—Does she stay ? *Laudo manentem.* Content !—Does she flutter, sound

with her wings, mount and away?—*Resigno quae dedit.*
Content! What should hinder the saying *content?* Why not
content thus, to all things? To all but that which thou can'st
make sure of?—A long life? Content!—A short one? Content!
—A name? Content!—No name? Content!—A fortune,—
estate? Content!—Poverty? Content!—Death? Content!—Is
there anything more? If not, and that this can be truly said,
is it not well? What would I more? What would be more
than *content?* What is happiness, felicity, *summum bonum,*
but merely this and this alone?—See, therefore, how this is
acquired; on what it depends; and what precepts, what rule
of life, what knowledge of affairs thou hast need of, in the midst
of this whole administration, never to be a *malcontent,* for such
a one must needs be (as he deserves) miserable.

NAMES.—Ὀνόματα θέμενος σαυτῷ ταῦτα, ἀγαθὸς, αἰδήμων,
ἀληθὴς, ἔμφρων, σύμφρων, ὑπέρφρων, πρόσεχε μήποτε μετονομάζῃ
[When you have assumed these names—good, modest, true,
rational, brotherly, and magnanimous, take care that your
practice conform to your character.—*Mar. Aurel., Med.,* Bk. X.,
§ 8].

*Integrity, entire*—In limbs?—No. Skin?—No. But affections?—Affections towards what? whom? towards a kindred
and not a country? a country, and not a world, universe?—And
how is this affection broken? How entire? Ἐμποδισθήσῃ,
πενθήσεις ταραχθήσῃ [hindered, troubled, disturbed. — *Epict.
Ench.,* I., § 3], and what follows? Is this preserving it? is this
integrity? Therefore how not this?—The way Τῶν ὄντων τὰ
μὲν ἐστιν ἐφ' ἡμῖν, τὰ δὲ οὐκ ἐφ' ἡμῖν [of things some are in our
power, others not].

*Heartiness, heart-whole* — how *a heart?* Content — and
what beyond? what more?—But not a hog's content.—A man's
content, then; what and how?

*Tranquillity, serenity.*—Where, within or without? *Sweet
retreat!*—Whither? out of self into another world?—No, but
out of this.—This what? this air, sky, circuit of the world?—
No, but out of the affairs of it. Let the affairs alone, then;
and thou art out of it. Or, say better: what hinders but thou
shouldst act in necessary affairs, and yet allow them to go as
they will when thou hast done what belongs to thee? Is not

this letting them alone ? is not this the same retreat ? What
else is *tranquillity, serenity, peace ?* and where is this truly
and only to be had ?—" I affirm that tranquillity is nothing else
than the good ordering of the mind."—*Mar. Aur., Med.,* IV., § 3.

On the other side (of vices corrupt, see in Προλήψεις),
Dissolute—dissolution, of what ?—Some tie, bond, viz., modesty
(*pudor*), respect, reverence of a fellow species, of relations ;
the rules, laws, orders necessary for the preservation of these
relations and of this species—and how far these laws ? If any
at all, what and which ? How far do they extend ? If any
relaxation, where stop ? if any restraint, where stop ? And
whither will this restraint carry us ?—'Ανέχου καὶ ἀπέχου [bear,
and forbear]. Nothing less. When anything less, tone relaxed ;
nerves, sinews, tendons, fibres strained, burst, forced, broken.

Even when attention, the Προσοχή strict attention is but
suspended, what else is it ? What but *dissolution ?*—See the
effects too—all dissolution.—Instrument down, unstrung.—
Dissolution of liquors ; of the blood.—Dissolve in effeminacy.—
*Diffluere, luxu, voluptatibus, otio.*

Every loss of attention, every relaxation, every time of
the Πάθη [passion] of any kind, false joy, indulgence,
humour, spring of mirth, fancy, ebullition, wit, story, jest,
τῇ ψυχῇ συνέλκεσθαι ἢ ἐκθόρνυσθαι [The soul either depressed or
elated.—*Mar. Aurel., Med.,* Bk. VIII., § 51], leaping of the
heart, sympathising fellow-feeling in a certain way, the wrong
στοργή [affection] : all this *dissolution.*

# OPINION AND PRECEPTS.

(Ὑπόληψις καὶ Δόγματα.)

OPINION.—Ὅτι πάντα ὑπόληψις [Remember that all things are opinion.—*Mar. Aurel., Med.*, Bk. XII., § 22].—Ἐφ' ἡμῖν μὲν ὑπόληψις ὁρμή, &c. [In our power are opinion, impulse, desire, aversion.—*Epict. Ench.* I., § 1.]

Καὶ ἁπλῶς οὔτε θανατος, οὔτε φυγὴ, οὔτε πόνος, οὔτε ἄλλο τι τῶν τοιούτων αἴτιόν ἐστι τοῦ πράττειν τι, ἢ μὴ πράττειν ἡμᾶς, ἀλλ' ὑπολήψεις καὶ δόγματα. [In a word, neither death, nor exile, nor pain, nor anything of this kind is the real cause of our doing or not doing any action; but our inward opinion and beliefs. —*Epict. Disc.*, Bk. I., c. xi., § 33].

How long since is it that thou didst see the necessity of going deep into this? How long since that thou bidst "Say not in such a disposition; but such or such a fancy, such or such an opinion, and use thyself to this.—To satisfy thyself about opinion, see what those seasons of the mind are, which thou art used to express by the name of feelings, dispositions, moods, in which virtue, Deity, and such objects are faint and weak. What mood, what temper can be the occasion of this? What is this but opinion and a certain secret disturbance in the opining part, moved by dispositions. Places, objects, images joined before to like opinions, &c., now bringing back those false ones with whom they have held so ancient, strong, and almost natural alliance." Therefore remember πήξατε ὑμῶν τὰς ὑπολήψεις [Fix your opinions.—*Epict. Disc.*, Bk. III., c. xvi., § 13].

See the thing!—a sword, a pistol, not terrible; but a precipice!—Drowning itself, the ocean waves not terrible; but drowning in the cabin!—Thus with thyself. But with a silly woman, a sword terrible; yet a precipice not. She chooses this death: also the effeminate lover, the melancholy and naturally timorous tender man, the barbarian Indian. Xenophon's account of a whole people, and particularly of a youth. To how many is this easy, and to a demonstration is it not the easiest death that can be? But it likes thee not, it seems. Excellent fancy! Incomparable opinion! 'Twere pity but thou shouldst have thy will and be indulged. Where go the women and timorous people in a storm, or when the ship is near sinking? What say they? "I'll go into the cabin and there die." And what of thee? "No, but I can't bear the cabin."—Coward! Why not the cabin?—" I cannot bear to have the water come into me there and choke me. I'll to the deck and open sea."—And what is the sea to thee, whether in the cabin or out of the cabin? What difference? What is the business? A pail of water or less; a gallon or two perhaps. This is all my share. For I shall neither drink a cabin-ful nor the sea-ful.—Will any one tell me this is not fancy? Shall fancy tell me so? No, reason and truth show me otherwise. Then of torture, the scaffold, gibbet, executioner, and all that din and pomp about a matter which comes not near the colic or the stone. Even that very pomp a help rather (as animating, exciting by other objects and keeping up the bent of the mind), when once the first fancy and opinion is cured. For what a help is it to those hardy villains (being bred to out-brave it) whom it ought rather to confound, as exposing their guilt and shame before men?—But how where there is no guilt; but then at that time, and on that very occasion most of all deserving? Can this be frightful?

A *scaffold!*—right. What is a scaffold?—a place built for great sights, and to show things to a crowd—a coronation—as king and queen; a mountebank, a festival.—And why not this as well, a *festival* in honour of the Great Master, in testimony of His truth, a witness to Him, to His laws, to His privilege given to man? Can there be a nobler stage erected? Can there be a worthier, greater spectacle shown to men?

PRECEPTS (Δόγματα).—Πρὸς τὰς τῶν πραγμάτων πιθανότητας τὰς προλήψεις ἐναργεῖς ἐσμηγμένας καὶ προχείρους ἔχειν δεῖ [Against persuasive appearances we ought to have clear beliefs, purified and ready for use.—*Epict. Disc.*, Bk. I., c. xxvii., § 6].

In this place the Προλήψεις [preconceptions] stand as Δόγματα [precepts] : above (330-1) as θεωρήματα [principles]. Here, therefore, short, concise, pointed, keen; demonstration, conviction not being the case here, but action. Time of action,

and these fitted for that time. ῞Ωσπερ οἱ ἰατροι ἀεὶ τὰ ὄργανα
καὶ σιδήρια ἔχουσι . . . οὕτω τὰ δόγματα σὺ ἕτοιμα ἔχε [As
physicians have always their instruments and knives ready, so
do thou have precepts ready.—*Mar. Aurel., Med.* iii., 13], viz.,
for conversation—first, countenance ; second, gesture; thirdly,
voice; add to this fourthly, matter. When all these maxims
are away, how reduced, retrenched, epitomised, gall and venom,
vapour, bubble, froth, vomit, chyle, crudity, phlegm.—And be
ready with the right instruments to reduce presently the
excursory matters to their proper heads and principles. Bring it
to a head, as the surgeon says, but in a quicker way by
precipitation, more like chemistry than surgery. In what
appearance, in what colour did it break out ? — Generosity,
magnanimity, magnificent talk for virtue and the right ? Away !
gall, venom. But simplicity, openness ? Away ! froth, bubble ?—
Doctrine, instruction ? Away ! vomit, phlegm. This is that
reducing ; and as the work above is styled inversion, so may
this be, in term of art, reduction.

Remember therefore this plan and groundwork for Δόγματα.

In weariness, lassitude, torpor, and the dissatisfied, dejected
state of mind, this—" How redeem myself ? whither fly ?—Out
of nature ? how possible ? if not, how (otherwise) life tolerable ?
death tolerable ? and if neither what a hard case ! "

Again, some weariness, Μὴ σικχαίνειν (&c.), εἰ μὴ καταπυκνοῦταί
σοι τὸ ἀπὸ δογμάτων ὀρθῶν ἕκαστα πράσσειν [Be not disgusted if
thou dost not succeed in doing everything according to right
precepts.—*Mar. Aur., Med.* v., 9]. Remember that (of old)[1] " The
husbandman—what toil and pain ! what nights and days ! how
cheerfully ! and for what ? what hope ?—And wilt not thou as
much for thine ? But (good heaven !) what fruit ! what hope !
how great ! how excellent ! how happy !—But as in a ground that
is cultivated, the first thing kill the weed that chokes, over-runs;
then till, then manure, then expect. But all this not without
sweat, weariness, pangs, groans."

[1] From old folio papers remaining since last retreat in 1698.

# MAXIMS.

## (Νόμοι.)

*A.* SILENCE.—"Let only what is necessary be said," Τὰ ἀναγκαῖα [the necessaries] and no more, for if more, still more and more an itching raised. New fancies, starting, bubbling—froth, vapour, scum, wit, story—a laugh raised, γελωτοποιός [ridiculous], one foolery drawing on another: one levity making way for another: the mind apter: matter readier: guests, companions more prepared and excited; expecting and in a manner claiming. For having shown this excellent qualification, why not proceed? If a taste given, why not a whole entertainment out? Where stop? or when?—

Character (viz., inward), the Προσοχή [attention] when again to be resumed?—How as to outward character and the remission here? Is it not harder to resume? harder now than before? and so for every time that this happens.—Yet still venturing out, is it not harder to resume? harder now than before? and so for every time that this happens.—Yet still venturing out, and the poor mind τῷ ἀπαντήσαντι [in the power of any one you happen to meet.—*Epict. Ench.*, c. xxviii.]. Is not this spraining the foot with a witness? (*Ench.*, c. xxxviii.) And what must come of this if often repeated: since already so often?

The itch (as thy friend once called it) from sore lungs, something provoking within.—The scab of wit—foolish talk (φλυαρία), the French *flux de bouche*, mouth-flux, upper looseness, want of retention.

Cure this in the first place, and above all stop this saliva, dysentery, rheum, and in this sense τὰ ἕλκη πρῶτον θεραπεύετε, τὰ ρεύματα ἐπιστήσατε, ἠρεμήσατε τῇ διανοίᾳ, &c.—καὶ γνώσεσθε οἵαν ἰσχὺν ὁ λόγος ἔχει ["Do you first get your ulcers healed, your fluxes stopped. Quiet your mind, and then you will know what force there is in reasoning."—*Epict. Disc.*, Bk. II., c. xxi., § 22.]    224

Κἂν περὶ θεωρήματος [If there be any discussion among the uninstructed about principles generally be silent.—*Epict. Ench.*, xlvi.]. Silence about the θεωρήματα and all belonging.— If *then*; and unknown? a madness, a mere blasphemy.—And would not this indeed be madness and blasphemy thus to reserve, and silence be, above all other, and not to expose, reveal, betray.— To expose the mysteries of cures. —*Epict. Disc.*, Bk. III., c. xxi., § 13.—Detestable prostitution! Remember ἀντι ψυχρολογίας ἡσυχίαν οἵαν δεῖ [in place of idle talk what composure of mind there ought to be.—*Epict. Disc.*, IV., c. iii., § 2]. Remember ἡσυχίαν [silence].

*B.* LAUGHTER.—" Let not your laughter be excessive." Consider the thing itself; in the bottom, what? Ἐπιχαιρεκακία [malevolence]. Nothing else.—Gall, venom; but of a different kind, and more hidden. That anger; this contempt. That reproof; this reproach. See which is best borne with, which is easiest forgiven; and by this judge how sociable a thing, how humane; notwithstanding what they say of it belonging only to man.

See it in excess, see it when given way to and soundly followed. The characters it forms, the tempers, humours, morals of such as these.

How in politeness?—The well-bred people, those of a finer make, better taste, and raised above the vulgar; and the mere vulgar—porters, carmen, clowns; and to which of these most belongs the hearty laugh?—How seldom this with any of the former? What a sense of the real nature of the thing? What but a plain perception of the *decorum*? How perfectly abhorrent (in every kind) to the το κάλον? And when others leave it on this account, wilt thou have to do with it? Where is there one of those φιλοκάλοι [lovers of the beautiful] that will endure it? And wilt thou endure it?

Savageness, barbarity, humanity, brutality, tyranny.— Caligula, whose whole character was of this sort: a play, sport, a mockery of mankind; a playing with their passions, concerns, hopes, fears; their fortunes, possessions, serious businesses, and solemnities of life; a scramble, the joy of the gainers, and sorry faces of the losers; baulks, snubs, ill come-offs, strippings, whippings, executions, and all this with humour,

R

raillery, wit, a comedy. So Domitian and his dark rooms. Phalaris' bull and other sport of the same nature. For what is *sport* ?—Wry faces, shrugs, with a little pain for those that are little used; with more pain for those that are more used, and that have improved their pleasure by custom and frequent repetition of such spectacles and recreation.

Go to a prison and see the things there. Who merrier (as they say) than those jail-birds ? See Newgate and the sort of mirth there. That which is described so naturally by the Spanish Petronius, the character of the galley - slaves and common rogues. The humour of the soldiery when most of all cruel and in the very actions of cruelty, sack of the town, plunder, rapine, violence, death, and torments. Who merrier ? Where is drollery, buffoonery, jest more perfect or more thorough? Where is the laugh heartier, sounder ? Who have more of it ? deeper of it ? Who have it in more perfection, more *bona-fide*, and (as they say) from the very heart ?

Poor, mad people and naturals, how treated ? The laugh in this case, what ? and of what kind ?—the diversion of seeing Bedlam. The usual entertainment of princes and such as those : the court fool, the dwarf, man-monkey, or any such mockery of human kind.—How humane !—Yet what is better received than these jests ? What a better laugh !—See the malignity of this, and by this judge of all other laugh.

How happy would it be, therefore, to exchange this vulgar, sordid, profuse, horrid laughter for that more reserved, gentle kind, which hardly is to be called laughter, or which at least is of another species ? How happy to exchange this mischievous, insulting, petulant species for that benign, courteous, and kind ? this rustic, barbarous, immane, for that civil, polite, humane ? the noisy, boisterous, turbulent, loud, for the still, peaceful, serene, mild ?—

Think of a Xenophon, his own character, and that which he has made of his "false king," or the real one of his friend, Aegislaus, or any such other genius raised ever so little above the vulgar.

Whether better to laugh with a Xenophon and the Greek muses, or with a Michael de Cervantes and the modern wits ? Whether with a Socrates and the wits of that order, the

Socratics, and those that followed the Socratic way, down to the Roman Menander, or with him whom the moderns most resemble, and Aristophanes, and such as those?

Remember Socrates and laugh with Apollodorus in the prison.—Remember that of Demonax, which even Lucian sees, and Diogenes, which no one now sees, or understands, with the rest of that sweet kind. And remember what a happiness, improvement, enjoyment, to reserve all that is humorous and pleasant in the temper for such geniuses as those, and for that divine facetiousness [1] (if so I may call it) of the divine man's.

Therefore, remember this reserve, this saving, sparing, laying up, treasuring, enriching; and as by another sort of frugality an estate is gained, an interest, reputation, or good name; so do thou accordingly, and by this example remember to be *vir frugi* [an upright man].

That not only the thing itself should be of the *reserved* kind (μηδὲ ἀνειμ ενως) [not carelessly] but in the management of it, reserved, husbanded, and kept only for places, persons, and things such as these. And think but how vastly this must promote strength! How much vigour, what force, blood, spirits, virtue is wretchedly spent another way! How much lavished every day and miserably bestowed! How much spilt and thrown away!—Nor this all, for this is not only lost, but turns to poison. How laugh when *death?* When *news?* When storm [2]? (swallow the man)! when earthquake? (bury the whole town)! These are of the right kind. But expect not to laugh both *here* and *there.*—Ἐμὸν δ' ἐγέλασσε φίλον κῆρ [And in my heart I laughed.—*Homer, Od.*, IX., 413].

Here therefore the reverse of Maxim *B*, and this experienced first day of January 16th, 1704. This is that soliloquy.—Thus laugh alone and even at serious times, or rather then most of all. For what trust to that other season? Choose it, therefore, at contrary times, and excite to it rather than be carried to it by temper. ὄλεθρος γὰρ ὁ τόπος [for the place is death], even with self: a precipice, brink, declivity.

And remember long ago what was observed of that wrong

---

[1] *Epict.*, *Disc.*, Bk. II., c. v., § 27, and vii., § 6.
[2] *Ibid.*, Bk. II., c. xvi., §§ 22, 23.

and involuntary kind (p. 82). Rule in the use of this.—
Avoid these two, viz., *drollery, obscenity*—for, pursuing the
sense of the words closely, it is evident that to these two heads
are all the ill sort reducible. Hence the reasonableness of that
strict carriage and excess of modesty in these cases, which was
what once thou couldst not understand, but thought amiss,
choosing frankness rather than the open way; by the pattern
of the satirists and their genius. But since that time thou hast
known better, for see how thou hast been taught not by precept
only, but by sad example and experience. Therefore now and at
this time of day remember a reverse of character. Enter again
into true nature (for such is that nice and even bashful modesty),
and embrace also that latter part of this Ἐπισφαλὲς δὲ καὶ τὸ εἰς
αἰσχρολογίαν προελθεῖν—and ἐπίπληξον τῷ προελθόντι ["It
is a dangerous habit also to approach obscene talk—rebuke
the one who begins it if possible; but if not an opportunity to
do so, express your dissatisfaction at least by silence."—*Epict.
Ench.,* c. xxxiii., § 16.] *Grief for another's good, joy for another's
ill.*—See how related; whether one does not imply the other.

See what thou wrotest thyself the other day in thy short
but very advantageous retirement at North.- Han, viz., the
*Pathologia* at the end.—*Jocositas vero, sive risus magnus,
effusus, non cohibilis, laetitia est de turpi externo et alierno,
tanquam bono nobis. Gaudium enim sive laetitia nisi de
bono pulchrove vero vel opinato non est. Et quia risus talis
non appetitio est, non aversatio, non dolor, sed gaudium sive
laetitia, sequitur necessario ut objectum ejus (viz., ridiculum
illud et malum alienum) quasi bonum vel pulchrum nostrum
spectetur. Ex invidentia ergo et odio proficiscitur risus talis,
et est malitiae seu malignitatis species.*

The Hebrew philosopher, *Eccles.* xxi., v. 20—"A fool lifteth
up his voice with laughter, but a wise man doth scarce smile a
little."

See what was written so long since on this same subject upon
joy. The same here as to mirth, as to laughter. The test news,
how if ill news in the midst? how surprised! how sillily look
(as they say)! how mute! Wouldst thou not have wished thyself
to have been otherwise taken? Go not therefore out of
the true measure and tone of character, and then thou

canst never be wrong taken, or at unawares. This is security, peace, constancy, magnanimity; the other cowardice, falsehood, treachery.

*C.* ENTERTAINMENTS.—" Fix your attention." Ἐντετάσθω σοι ἡ προσοχὴ [Stretch (apply) your attention.—*Epict., Ench.,* XXVIII., § 6], which answers to Συνπαρεκτείνειν τὴν νόησιν τοῖς λεγομένοις [Direct your attention to what is said.—*Mar. Aurel., Med.* VII., § 30], and τὰ ἡγεμόνια αὐτῶν διάβλεπε [Examine men's ruling principles.—*Ibid.,* IV., § 3].

Pierce into the bottom-work of their minds; the dark chambers and corners of their heart; their principles of judgment; their decisive determining thoughts and rules of action ; their spring, source, origin of affection, hatreds, loves, appetitions, aversations; their genuine fancies, imaginations, opinions, Δόγματα, decrees, judgments; not those they set out to show before others. Penetrate, to dive and search into their ways, minds, dispositions, humours, feelings : a work just contrary to that other diving, sifting, fishing (as it is called), and mysterious searching into their affairs and circumstances. Let there be no divining, guessing (if possible) their thoughts, and studying to prevent by humouring, pleasing, hitting their fancies, endeavouring thereby to make one's self acceptable and mighty amongst them, and capable of managing them thus in an outward way.—Have nothing of this; nothing to do with secrets, their family or state secrets, their secret tales, projects, interests, amours, or any other secrecies ; but disclose by their good leave (or whether they gave leave or no) the secret and hidden mystery of all their life and action. Look into their breasts laid open, reveal the mystery of their mysteries, and behold how poor, how low, how shallow. See whence these other mysteries not worth the looking into, the bottom of all this, the motive, end, where the *fines bonorum et malorum,* the οὐσία ἀγαθοῦ—καὶ λοιπὸν προσέχω τοῖς ανθρώποις, τίνα φασί, πῶς κινοῦνται [And for the rest I am attentive to other men ; what they say, and how they are moved.— *Epict. Disc.,* Bk. IV., c. iv., § 7.]

Be these thy entertainments and discourses with thyself (though in company), these thy tables, when needs there must be tables and discourse of that kind ; this thy table-talk within, with self, and let alone that other, no matter how it succeeds, or what it is.—Lead it, look after it who will : be it kept up or let it fall : thou canst not err in having no part in it, for there is no necessity thou shouldst have any.  But if thou hast any part in the discourse of that kind, and this discourse and reason go not along with it and strictly accompany it, thou shalt be sure to err and to repent.

D. EXERCISE ("Ἄσκησις).—Κἂν ἀσκῆσαί ποτε πρὸς πόνον θέλῃς, σεαυτῷ καὶ μὴ τοῖς ἔξω—διψῶν ποτε σφοδρῶς ἐπίσπασαι, &c., καὶ μηδενὶ εἴπῃς [If ever you wish to exercise yourself in labour and endurance do it for yourself and not for others—if you are very thirsty take a draught of cold water and spit it out, and tell no man.—*Epict. Ench.*, c. xlvii.].

Τὸ Γυμνάσιον—ὅτι κρεῖσσόν ἐστι πάσης περιπορφύρου [Diogenes says that to be naked is better than a purple robe.— *Epict. Disc.*, Bk. I., c. xxiv., § 7]. Thus the old poet—"the flinty couch of war," and "my thrice-driven bed of down."

And in this thy field, why not the same ? Is the thing itself less generous, less great, less triumphant ? If there be any real triumph : if there be anything magnanimous, anything heroic, any virtue, any praise.

Away with these other fields, laurels, trophies : the Alexanders, the Cæsars, the modern fighters of Badens, the Eugens.  What are these ? and what, τὰ ἡγεμονικὰ αὐτῶν ? [their ruling principles.—*Mar. Aurel., Med.*, Bk. VIII., § 3].

Think of thy own work ; thy own conquests : ἔκβαλε ἀντὶ Προκρούστου καὶ Σκίρωνος λύπην, φόβον, ἐπιθυμίαν [Instead of Procrustes and Suron, grief, expel fear, desire.—*Epict. Disc.*, Bk. II., c. xvi., § 45].

Awake ! Up ! Rise ! Or art thou weary of this work ? Is it ever to cease ? is it ever to *relax* ? Why shrink then ? why draw back ? what effeminacy is this !

# ATTENTION AND RELAXATION.

Let experience at least teach thee what it is to wander abroad, and to suspend for ever so short a time the superintendency and care of self. Ἐάν ποτέ σοι γένηται ἔξω στραφῆναι, . . ἴσθι ὅτι ἀπώλεσας τὴν ἔνστασιν [If it should ever happen to you to be turned to externals, you must know that you have lost your purpose in life.—*Epict. Ench.*, c. xxiii.]. Whether it be to please or gratify others; to gain or retain others; to reform or to restrain others: or whether it be through any of these thoughts ἐὰν ἀμελήσω τῶν ἐμῶν, . οὐχ ἔξω διατροχάς [If I neglect my affairs I shall not have the means of living.—*Ench.*, c. xii.]; or that other, 'ἀλλ' ἡ πατρίς, ὅσον ἐπ' ἐμοί', φησίν, 'ἀβοήθητος ἔσται' ["but my country, you say, as far as it depends on me, will be without my help."—*Ibid.*, c. xxiv., § 4].

See the effect of this, and how the thing proceeds. In the first place attention (that fixed attention towards the scope and end) immediately is lost. The good habits which were incumbent on the mind, and which as faithful guards watched over it, are taken off. The good * affections, † inclinations, and declamations, are by disuse relaxed and their vigour transferred to a contrary kind. The sentiments, thoughts, motions, feelings, meditations, the right modification of appearances, and the use and management of objects: all these and whatever else is proper to a state of health, are by this suspension lost, or become heavy, languid, dull, and spiritless. Solitude is a burden, and the power of self-entertainment is come to nothing; hence a greater propensity than before to amusements and wrong exercise. Then the next engagement is stronger and more intense than the first; and so onward, till all be lost and what was a relaxation only, becomes at length a total dissolution.

What folly, rashness, and madness is it, to attend to other things in such a manner as to lose attention to that which is principal; and for the sake of outward economy, to quit that

* ὄρεξις.    † ἔκκλισις.

231

which is inward? How wrong and injudicious it is to be drawn from this, on account of that which we call *doing good*? How wretched and mean, to faint in this work and to seek for relaxation? This is a plain betraying of the whole and is the part of an apostate and deserter.

But *reason* is to be defended, the *right*, the *truth*, τά προαιρετά οὐκ ἐφ’ ἡμῖν, the concern of others, the fault theirs, the mischief theirs. My own concern is for truth, reason, and right *within myself*; and how maintain this? Not whilst the aim or ὄρεξις [desire] is towards another truth and the establishment of reason abroad, not whilst reformations are dreamt of, new people and a new world. Hence ensues impatience, heat, eagerness, debate. *Shall I let this pass? shall I see truth betrayed?*—What truth? Consider, where is now simplicity? where is patience, meekness, benignity, tranquillity? where is that right affection of complacency towards men and resignation to Deity? This is *truth*. This is the great, the only, concern; and when this is yielded or given up, then it is that truth is betrayed.

Remember how often thou hast proved, and by what repeated experience, that the beginning of all miscarriage, the chief and in a manner only cause of failure, is that which happens in conversation and company, contrary to the precept and to what is so positively enjoined in the rules belonging to this place. For, thus it is. The mind, which at first seemed to be on its guard, strong, resolute, and able to hold out, is through attention given to those other subjects, at last tempted by some seeming fair occasion to make a small step outwards, supposing it to be only for once, on this particular occasion, and thinking to retreat again safely within itself.—" If I say but this word I shall set the matter right. If I allow myself but this small complaisance, I shall keep myself well in his opinion. If I indulge but in this one thing, it is enough. I shall be thought passable and not altogether morose, and changed from what I was. Right. This is well, now I am applauded, now I am saluted and congratulated, now I am felt."—Here is the corruption : here the breaking in. But remember : whatsoever causes joy and satisfaction when present, causes grief * and

* *Epict. Disc.*, Bk. IV., c. 1., § 84.

disturbance when absent; whatsoever is the subject of joy or sorrow with respect to the present, must be the subject of appetition and aversion with respect to the future. Hast thou, then, forgotten these rules ? If not, consider what must necessarily follow. The mind being elevated ever so little by this success, is instantly drawn into a new desire, a new appetition. The * ὄρεξις [desire] grows; and a contrary ἔκκλισις [aversion] and declining is in that instant immediately produced or begotten. The ground thus gained (as having now become a matter of consideration) is to be kept: and this with no small earnestness and concern. Nor can the matter rest here, but more must be added, more must be grasped at, more procured to make this good, and to secure and fortify what is acquired. Hence further excursions, other sallies, other attempts: till at last, we come again into the same field, fighting, as before, with the same arms and for the same things as when we were in the depth of idiotism.

Thus we leave our harbour and put to sea again, so that in a few moments we lose sight of land; or if we turn our eyes back to view anything in that region which we have quitted, everything appears so faint and dim, everything of that sort is contracted into so narrow a size, that it is scarce discernible or knowable.

Endeavour now at this season and in the midst of this to recall any of those principal rules, anything that relates to human kind and the condition of life, anything of Deity, anything belonging to the virtues. Apply that sovereign δόγμα of *what is ours, what not.* See how this is looked upon: mind how it affects, and whether it be not merely as a dream or some antiquated story. What to do in this miserable state ? how move or turn ourselves ? Wilt thou never remember of what nature this is and how this is brought about ? Art thou not henceforward at the mercy of the winds and weather ? Art thou not delivered up to another train and set of fancies ? And then when retired again and with thyself alone, how dost thou find matters ? what reception at the time ? how are the fancies and imaginations disposed, and in what order, what course ? How do

* *Epict. Disc.*, Bk. IV., c. iv., § 35, and *Mar. Aurel. Med.*, Bk. VII., § 27.

they run, how lead, introduce, and follow one another? What method, use, management, correction, regulation? Is it not all hurry, chance, confusion, anarchy? Do they not range high and low, carry all before them and with them, elevate, transport, depress, deject? Here hope, there doubt and consternation: and here hope again.—" Was not that well managed? was not that turn dexterous? No, but that other thing was unfortunate, that lost me. What will they say or think? how shall I get out of that affair? what apology? what excuse? "—Is it come to this then at last? are these the thoughts? this what we aspire to and affect? the sum of all our wishes? our highest ambition and hope?

Remember this:—How certain and inevitable these consequences are; and that in this state, and whilst this habit and constitution lasts, the only safety is in retirement from all this sort of converse; and if at any time unhappily unwarily engaged in it, to see that it continue * not long, that it do not grow customary and begin to gain and be familiarised. For even where a guard is kept, and the particular rules observed, yet by a long-continued attention (though ever so reserved) towards the matters of discourse, towards the common reasoning and ideas, it must necessarily follow (in such a mind as thine) that the other attention must of course be lost. And if complaisance, imitation, and flattery be added; if smiles, countenance, and approbation be joined; and an outward sort of harmony be kept: things will be yet worse, and thou wilt soon find that thou dost begin to harmonise *within*. At least all harmony of another sort will be lost; the other measures and numbers broken and disordered. Touch any spring whatever, and mind what sound! Is not all dead? is there any more use or virtue in the instrument? is not the art perished? How recall this? in what way renew it? where take it up again? The work itself feels heavy and tedious; all within is become unapt, and the disposition turned another way. See what a crowd of other ideas: impertinent, idle, monstrous, imaginations, and wild fancies rushing in, making havoc, uproar, confusion; rejoicing as it were at their new admittance, and revenging their former exclusion.

* cf. *Mar. Aurel Med.*, Bk. VI., § 11.

These are the hurricanes and tempests. Such is the ravage they commit—*et terras turbine perflant* [and sweep the earth with a whirlwind—*Virgil, Aeneid*, Bk. I., line 83]. When are we to expect a calm again? when return again to our harbour? when are those halcyon days to be restored? is it not more likely to be chaos and night? whither does this tend? what does it bode? Remember what Epictetus says "the pilot neglecting his duty discovers how little is wanting to over-set the bark." *

All depends on a certain succession, series, or train of fancies, and on that faculty or power which controls, manages, and uses them. If this be once interrupted, it is chance that governs. And thus it is a chance whether reason be ever regained.

If there be no end, no measure, no rule, all is madness. If there be, then, whatsoever is acted without it must be madness. If I throw away my rule, if I lose my end, what power, what faculty, can I reserve whereby to be sure of resuming this again when I think fit. If this be impossible, then at any time when I act thus and have consented to suspend attention, I do not *suspend*, but in effect *renounce* it wholly, since it no longer depends on me to renew what I have broken off. If so, then this is not temporary and voluntary madness; but real and absolute, since I myself know not certainly when it shall cease, or whether it shall ever cease at all.

RELAXATION.—'Οὐκ αἰσθάνῃ, ὅτι, ἐπειδὰν ἀφῇς τὴν γνώμην, οὐκ ἔτι ἐπὶ σοί ἐστιν ἀνακαλέσασθαι αὐτήν, οὐκ ἐπὶ τὸ εὔσχημον, οὐκ ἐπὶ τὸ αἰδῆμον, οὐκ ἐπὶ τὸ κατεσταλμένον; ["Do you not see that when you let your mind loose it is no longer in your power to recall it, either to propriety, or to modesty, or to moderation?" *Epict., Disc.*, Bk. IV., c. xii., § 6].

Πρόσεχε οὖν ταῖς φαντασίαις, ἐπαγρύπνει. οὐ γὰρ μικρὸν τὸ τηρούμενον, ἀλλ᾽ αἰδὼς καὶ πίστις καὶ εὐστάθεια ["Attend, therefore, to the appearance of things to watch over them, for that which you have to preserve is no small matter, but it is modesty and fidelity and constancy."—*Ibid.*, IV., c. iii., § 7.]

Is this right? Is this really so? Or had it best be again a relaxation? another trial?—What has come of it? How

---

* *Epictetus, Discourses*, Bk. IV., c. iii., § 5.

relaxation? It is not relaxation here as in other things (unbending, strengthening); not as the common misapplied verse, *Neque semper arcum tendit Apollo* [Nor does Apollo always keep his bow bent].

In this place the bow is the worse, and returns worse to its bent. Every moment an injury, a weakening, with danger, too, of breaking if it stays long. Nor is this all; for in the use of the other bow the objects (such as the mark, butt, target, or whatever else) remain the same, being passive and as fair for exercise when the bow is resumed as when it was laid down. But here far otherwise. The objects, indeed, in a strict sense are as passive as those others. τὰ πράγματα ἔξω θυτρῶν ἔστηκεν [Things stand passively out of doors.—*Mar. Aurel., Med.,* Bk. IX., § 15].

But there are other bows that are bending all the while that this is unbent. Counter-machines are raising; the *balistae tormenta* and all the engines of a certain kind, playing from another side with new force and, as it were, from a higher ground. But when on this side things stand fixed and bent, the other fall of course, without battery or labour, and the combat is little or nothing. No struggle, no force, all is easy, smooth, and manageable without difficulty; so that one would wonder and say, "Where was this mighty enemy? what was this we feared so much?" But in the other way, how soon will those contrary voices be heard, "Alas! where are the helps? where are now the rules? and what do these avail? τί μοι ἐμπαίζεις; [why do you mock me] and ἀρκεῖ ἐμοὶ τὰ ἐμὰ κακά" [my own evils are enough for me. —*Epict. Disc.,* Bk. II., c. xix., § 18, 19].

Therefore, no flattery of this kind. Never un-bent, for when unbent know what is then on the contrary, bent, strenuous, vigorous. Deceive not thyself. There is no relaxation, no remission, no unbending, no relieving, resting, recreating, reposing. Deceitful names! proper, indeed, as to other works and labours, but which have no place as to the work within. This will ever be going on, either in the right or wrong way, ever advancing and pressing on, even when most unseen. It is ever growing imperceptibly, ripening, coming to a head either as good fruit or as the fungus; for neither is the natural plant ever at a stand, nor is this plant. The workman may lie down and rest, but never nature, till at last once for all. The work of the heart and this other work will keep pace. The χρῆσις φαντασιῶν [use of appearances] will be, whilst the συστολή [contracting] and διαστολή [expanding] exist. As in one engine, so in the other : as with the materials of one, so of the other. Blood good or bad, appearances good or bad, motion, exercise regular or irregular, in measure or out of measure; it must go on still. Something must be doing, and strongly doing. Some pulse or another, some energy or another, either with nature or against nature, either a struggle or a free course, either convulsion, fever, hurry, uproar, chaos : or natural motion, order, uniformity, and design.—What is relaxation, then ? How relax ? how rest ? Bid the heart rest, bid the heart relax, the lungs take a remission. And shall I say a jot more reasonably to that other part, take thy ease and be relaxed. "Mind, be contented. Let the *Visa* alone, or leave them to themselves; use none, or mind not how thou usest them."

What is this to say but "Mind! Be contented, and be no mind. Mind! be nothing or worse than nothing: a madman's mind." Learn, therefore, to speak properly, and when thou sayest to thyself "Relax, take thy ease," explain and say, "Mind and governing part! have done; and let the ungoverned take their turn. Let the fancies, ungovernable amongst themselves, govern thee. Be thou their subject : not they thine. Let them model thee : not thou them. Let the ground thou hast gained on them be gained now again upon thee. As the work was strong that way, so let it be now as strong this way."— For so it must be; this is the nature of the thing. This is the only relaxation : change from one work to another; from this thou hast taken up with, as the only happiness and good, to that which is directly contrary or the cause of all misery and ill : from this vital healing, restoring operation, to that deadly, fatal, and destructive one.

This is the relaxation. This the unbending : unbent, that another bent may be the stronger; relaxed, that something else may become the more intense.

What palls, heaviness, lassitude from want, disuse, or but

remission of the Προσοχή [attention] ? This is what Marcus Aurelius speaks of, when the application to outward things and attention that way are beyond a certain proportionable time and degree, so that this necessarily follows.

But this not the worst yet. What impossibility of taking it up again at pleasure! Therefore, not lost only for the present; but lost absolutely, and depending on chance and circumstances for recovery. What is this but *madness ?*—This wretched state of disability, helplessness, how oft experienced in voyages, journeys, intervals, in business and affairs, in breaking off, lazy hours, garden, and how much worse still in any time of pain, sickness, or the like ?—But if the contrary attention must, therefore, so rigidly be kept, how deal with the world ? how engage ? how company ? sociable acts and offices of a civil life ?—So to what was said long since.

Remember that this is for one who is yet more than προκόπτων [progressing]; not one who is less, and in such circumstances, in such an age of mankind and with such sores (p. 123). But being truly προκόπτων [improving], how possibly powerful, eloquent, apt both here and there ? how watch that enemy and *this enemy ?* how learn this fight and discipline and that other with crafty men, a cabinet, senate, or a field ? how these stratagems, this art, this multiplicity of invention, this readiness of mind, turn of thought, with capacity, ingenuity, and withal that other ?

# IMPROVEMENT.[1]

## (Προκοπή.)

Ἀεὶ γὰρ πρὸς ὃ ἂν ἡ τελειότης τινὸς καθάπαξ ἄγῃ πρὸς αὐτὸ ἡ προκοπὴ συνεγγισμός ἐστι [For it is always true that, to whatever point the perfecting of anything brings us, progress is an approach towards it.—*Epict. Disc.*, Bk. I., c. iv., § 4].

Remember, therefore, ποῦ τὴν προκοπήν; [where seek improvement? &c.—ὅπου σου τὸ ἔργον; [where lies your work]—the ἀλτῆρες [weights], the ἀσκήματα [exercises].—*Ibid.*, Bk. III., c. xxvi., § 39. To what end? and for what all this? τί θέλει με ποιεῖν ὁ θεὸς νῦν, τί οὐ θέλει; πρὸ ὀλίγου χρόνου ἤθελέν σε σχολάζειν, σαυτῷ λαλεῖν, γράφειν [What is the will of God I should do now? what is not His will? A little while ago it was His will you should be at leisure, should talk with yourself, write about those things, read, hear, prepare yourself.—*Ibid.*, Bk. IV., c. iv., § 29]. And now what? ἀπ᾽ αὐτῶν πεφθέντων τὰ ἔργα [Show the acts which come from their digestion.—*Ibid.*, *Ench.*, xlvi.]. Be it so then, and in very deed (ἔργα), nothing less, nothing more. Not a word, not a syllable besides: but all within thyself, and to thyself alone, and this to be as sacred with thee, never to be transgressed. But πρῶτον αὐτὸ πέψον [First digest it], otherwise what but πρᾶγμα ἀκάθαρτον καὶ ἄβρωτον? [It will be a thing impure, and unfit for nourishment.—*Ibid.*, Bk. III., c. xxi., § 2].

Ever remembering this, premising this, carrying this still along with thee, at all times—hereafter, now, this moment, in what thou art now doing, writing, exercising, studying; that it may be real studying, real exercise: not a cheat to abuse thyself, not a show, not fine thoughts to improve in conversation, not the wretched pomp and *fucus* of meditations, even with self, much less for others, or with a thought towards others, as seeking a discharge, evacuation, vent.—What a dis-

[1] *Holland*, 1703-04.

temper is this ? what a habit ?—Vile ! vile !—This would be to degenerate again, as a while ago. For then was this truly that vile thing, that bile, crudity, vomit, phlegm. Take care thou return no more to this vomit, this odious habit of mind. The animal impurity is not half so vile.

Remember, then, and good reason : for what are these but memorandums ? what is this but to be thy own remembrancer ? —conviction past, demonstrations sound, rules expeditious ; the application is all, all but to remember.

Memorandums—for what ? about what ? a small concern perhaps, a trifle : for what else can it be ? Neither estate, nor money matters, nor policy, nor history, nor learning, nor private affairs, nor public. These are great things. In these are great improvements. How many memorandums, how many commonplace books about these. Who would think of any other memorandums ? Would one dream of making any for *life ?* Would one think that this were a business to improve in ? What if this should be the thing of all others chosen out for a pocket-book and memorandums ?—But so it is. Remember, then, the memorandums as truly such, and for such use, as memorandums only, to this purpose, this end.

Improvement. Advancement.—In what ? whither ? as how ? Is there such a thing belonging to this place ? is there study or art here. Bethink thyself. Is there then really such a science ? And is the faculty, mystery, skill real ? If so, how is it in other arts, where improvement is looked for, advancement aimed at ? How if a mathematician ? how if an accountant ? how if a student in language, in rhetoric, aiming at mastery in writing or in speaking; a manner; a style ? And is this style ? are these words or letters merely. Is the improvement here ? the advancement hitherwards ?—Away ?

'Ὡς γὰρ τέκτονος ὕλη τὰ ξύλα, &c.,—οὕτως τῆς περὶ βίον τέχνης ὕλη ὁ βίος αὐτοῦ ἑκάστου [For as the material of the carpenter is wood—so the material of the art of living is each man's own life.—*Epict. Disc.*, Bk. I., c. xv., § 2]. This is the subject, and accordingly in this must be the improvement. Begin, therefore, and work upon this subject—collect, digest, methodise, abstract. How many codes, how many volumes, lexicons, how much labour, and what compiling in the study of other laws ? But in the law of life, how ?—Think, therefore, at what time of day, think how late thou began it. How many times left off; and how this last time, after such an advance, how long renewing, with what pain, and how so followed; supinely, heavily, neglectfully, wretchedly. Or is this easier learnt and retained ? a matter of less trouble and thought ? of less moment and concern ?

Begin then. Not (as before) to leave off; again, anon, beg pardon for awhile, lie down and rest—from what, thou wretch ? from food ? from rest itself ? Wouldst thou be restored in peace to those innocent, calm, gentle passions that will be sure to give thee rest, having given it thee so long; as thou hast (it seems) but too cheaply experienced ? Or is it that thou art already perfect, or like to be so very soon, in this way ? Or if so, may this art, like other arts or trades, be intermitted without prejudice ? or be quitted wholly when something offers better to live upon ? What better ? what to succeed ? and what to do. What are other trades for ? and what this ? is it one and the same ? and will this like others bear a relaxation, or but a respite ? How is it with other arts when out of use ? and what art shall bring this into use again when once out ?

Now, therefore, begin anew; truly anew; and not as before : not μετρίως κεκινημένον [laying hold with small effort.—*Epict. Ench.*, c. i., § 4]; not κατὰ ψυχρὰν ἐπιθυμίαν [with half-hearted zeal.—*Epict. Disc.*, Bk. III., c. xv., § 7]. Know thy work, know thy subject, matter, instruments, rules. Has the carpenter so many ? is there so much closet-work, paper-work, so much study, writing, figuring, practising there; and not in the same manner here ? Why writing ? why this flourishing, drawing, figuring, over and over, the same still ? what for ?—What, but for the art ? Not for show; but for exercise, practice, improvement.—Writing and then burning. Drawing and rubbing out. Chalk a wall, board, anything that comes to hand.—Mind, then. See how it is with these practitioners. Or shall thy industry come behind ? thy attention, application, fervour be less ?— Apply, therefore, exercise, write, compose, cast the sums, chalk out the design, lineaments, proportions; scan, practise, prove. Be always on some rule, some demonstration, some draught, some scheme or another : and let other schemes alone. Be

s

sharpening, steeling, and pointing the counter *visa*, hardening, moulding, casting, and polishing the Δόγματα and right images * σιδηρῖα [knives], ὄργανα [instruments], ἐλχειρίδια [hand - books], ready; the instruments, weapons, arms, according to art and discipline; redress, convert, invert, provoke (for trial and practice), challenge, incite. —This by such and such a rule; from such a theorem, problem. This by such a demonstration, axiom, postulation. This by the golden rule: not that of arithmetic. This by the third, fourth, fifth proposition: not of that Euclid, but of this other: the teacher not of those lines and figures, but of these other lines, the figures, proportions, and symmetry of life; without which science all is confusion — appetitions, aversations frustrated: moral relations broken: fancy wild — madness and distraction all.

Go on, then: exercise and write, but remember ἀλλα πως [but how?—*Epict.*, *Disc.*, Bk. III., c. xvii.], and σεαυτῷ καὶ μὴ τοῖς ἔξω [for yourself and not for others.—*Epict. Ench.*, c. xlvii.], else τὰ λογάρια, καὶ πλέον οὐδὲ ἕν [trifling talk and nothing more.—*Ibid.*, *Disc.*, Bk. II., c. xviii., § 26]. Let the rules look as odd or ridiculous as they will; what is that to thee, whose business is only to improve by these, not publish them, profess, or teach them? What are the rules in mathematics, grammar, or music to the vulgar and those unversed? What but sport? And are these specious countenances any other than vulgar, commonality people, mere people, and if nearly looked into the very dregs too of the people, however they may appear outwardly? For how are they as to life? They who seek not any rule here, nor think there is any rule, what are they better than vulgar? Unless perhaps they are the mightier and more to be admired, for sporting with these things and despising what they understand not; whilst others, understanding themselves as little, are less persuaded of their understanding.

What, therefore, can they make of this but sport? what is the divine man to his commentator of this age? What is his follower to both his? Or if not constantly, yet by starts and

* *Mar. Aurelius, Med.* III., § 13.

fits when frightened by too home-truth, a plain word, or a strong light ; yet these the most favourable of moderns. To the rest sport or pity. For what else ? what better to be expected ? Take care, however, not by thy own fault to give occasion to this pity or this sport by exposing anything (as it must be exposed, if discovered and directly owned), for this indeed would be ridiculous, harsh, odious, pitiful.

Enough then. Remember Maxim A, § 6, κἂν περ θεωρήματος, &c. [If any conversation arise among the uninstructed persons about philosophical principles generally, be silent.—*Epict. Ench.*, c. xlvi., § 2], and what resembles this in discourse about morals, philosophy, nowadays, when it so happens. Here double the watch, strengthen the guard, be alarmed, awake, doubly strict to the law, for double reason.— Silence ! for thy own sake, for the thing's sake, and detest this prostitution.

# THE BEAUTIFUL.

## (Tὸ Kαλόν.)[1]

In things *inanimate, animate, mixed.*

*Inanimate.*—Beginning from those figures with which we are delighted, to the proportions of architecture. The same in sounds.

*Animate.*—From animals (and their several natures) to men, and from single persons of men—their humours, dispositions, tempers, characters, manners—to communities, societies, commonwealths.

*Mixed.*—As in a single person (a body and mind): Love.— And thus in communities; a territory, land, culture, structures and the ornaments of a city, mixed and making up (in conjunction) that idea of a native country. *Patria,* and the love of that sort.

> *Dulce et decorum est pro patria mori.*
> [" 'Tis sweet for native land to die."
>
> *Hor.,* Ode III., 2, 13.]

In things inanimate, nature before the arts, and thus from stones, diamonds, rock, minerals; to vegetables, woods, aggregate parts of the world, as sea, rivers, hills, vales. The globe, celestial bodies and their order; the great architecture of Nature —Nature itself.

In things animate, from flocks, herds, to men and other orders of intelligences, to the supreme intelligence—God.

Tὰ πλεῖστα, ὧν ἡ πληθὺς θαυμάζει εἰς γενικώτατα ἀνάγεται, &c., and τὰ ἐπιγινόμενα τοῖς φύσει γινομένοις [ "Most of the things which the multitude admire are referred to objects of the most general kind, those which are held together by cohesion or natural organisation, such as stones, wood, fig-trees, vines, olives." —*Mar. Aur. Med.,* Bk. VI., § 14]; and [ "Even the things which

---

[1] Naples, 1712.

244

follow after the things which are produced according to nature contain something pleasing and attractive."—*Ibid.*, Bk. III., § 21].

Decorum, Honestum, Pulchrum.
*Le Beau, Le Grand, Le Majesteux, Le je ne sais quoi.*
The goodly, fair, becoming, handsome, noble.
In person : in manners.

Carriage, inward, outward.—The coming into a room, saluting, looking round, viewing, accosting—a generous part in company, in a family, in the public, upon a journey with strangers; civility, courtesy, affability, good breeding. What gracefulness! what winningness! and this too even with the vulgar, for to what do we with more emphasis apply the word handsome ?

What search, what running after, what pursuit of this appearance in all the subjects, except the true ! What study, application, charm ! See with what spirits, ardour, and vehemence the young man, forgetting his own species, seeks this in those objects of his love: a horse, a hound ! What doating on these beauties ! What admiration of the kind itself ! and of the particular ! What care, idolatry, consecration, when the beast beloved is (as oft happens) set apart even from use, and only kept to gaze on !

See in another youth not so forgetful of his species ; but remembering it in a wrong way. A lover of the beautiful (φιλό-καλος) of another kind. Xenophon's brave friend Episthenes. A Chaerea: *elegans formarum spectator.* See as to music, how See poetry, rhetoric, and the numbers of this sort; what study and politeness !

See as to other beauties where there is no possession, no enjoyment or reward, but seeing and admiring only. Pictures and designing, statues, architecture, the rapture and enthusiasm of the lovers of this kind. The beauty of gardens, the inward ornaments of houses, apartments, furniture, the ranging, order disposition of these matters. What pains ! what study ! judgment ! science !

See yet in persons of a different kind who go not so far out of themselves to seek this universally attractive species, but having unhappily feigned to themselves a wrong self, bestow their pains and culture on a body and its ornaments. And here, what study of gracefulness and the decorum! What care of every motion, station, attitude! Voice, gesture, looks, apparel! See the effeminate, the affected, and their character distinct from the sordidly sensual and mere voluptuous.

The tendency and aim of all this—rejoicings, sighings, faint imperfect endeavours and impotent reaches after the τὸ καλόν.

Νεανίσκε, τίνα θέλεις καλὸν ποιεῖν; γνῶθι πρῶτον τίς εἶ, καὶ οὕτω κόσμει σεαυτόν . . τὸ λογικὸν ἔχεις ἐξαίρετον, τοῦτο κόσμει καὶ καλλώπιζε· ["Who is it, young man, whom you would render beautiful? Know first who you are, and then adorn yourself accordingly.—The excellence lies in the rational part. Adorn and beautify this."—*Epict. Disc.*, Bk. III., c. i., § 24, 26.]

The transition easy. So, *Epict. Disc.*, Bk. IV., c. xi., § 26, τὸ καλὸν ζητεῖς, καὶ εὖ ποιεῖς. ἴσθι οὖν, ὅτι ἐκεῖ φύεται, ὅπου τὸν λόγον ἔχεις, &c. ["You seek beauty, and you do well. Be assured, then, that it springs from the rational part of you"]. O that this were known! O that thou thyself wouldst but know (truly know) this!

The disposition and order of one of their finer sort of gardens or villas: the kind of harmony to the eye from the various shapes and colours agreeably mixed and ranged in lines intercrossing without confusion and fortunately coincident; a parterre, cypresses, grove, wilderness, walks; statues here and there of virtue, fortitude, temperance, heroes, busts, philosophers' heads, with architecture, mottoes and inscriptions of this kind. Solemn representation of things deeply natural; as grottos, urns, obelisks in retired places and at certain distances and points of sight, with all those symmetries that silently express such order, peace, and sweetness.

\* But what is there like to this in the minds of those who walk here, and are the possessors of all this? What peace?

---

\* The same of the other orders of the τὸ καλὸν: as in music, painting, and what else of this kind is celebrated amongst the great and creates the passion of *virtuosos*. But they themselves, who? what?—Such are their works; such the composition; such the pieces they admire. But what is there like to this in the minds of these musicians, painters, lovers of art, &c.?

What harmony ?—None, for if there were, there would be no
need of this exterior sort: no admiration: no search of order
here: no passion towards this beauty, or any beauty of this sort.

Therefore, remember ever the garden and groves within.
There build, there erect what statues, what virtues, what ornaments or orders of architecture thou thinkest noblest. There
walk at leisure and in peace; contemplate, regulate, dispose: and
for this, a bare field or common walk will serve full as well; and,
to say truth, much better.—The worship of virtue ($\tau\grave{a}$ $\check{o}\rho\gamma\iota a$ $\tau\hat{\eta}s$
$\grave{a}\rho\epsilon\tau\hat{\eta}s$.—*Mar. Aur. Med.*, III., 7), and these inward walks and
avenues. *Compositum jus fasque animo, sanctosque recessus
Mentis.* [Duty to God and man well blended in the mind,
purity in the shrine of the heart.—*Persius*, Sat. II., 73, 74.]

$\theta\acute{\epsilon}\lambda\eta\sigma o\nu$ $\kappa a\lambda\grave{o}s$ $\phi a\nu\hat{\eta}\nu a\iota$ $\tau\hat{\omega}$ $\theta\epsilon\hat{\omega}\cdot$ $\grave{\epsilon}\pi\iota\theta\acute{\upsilon}\mu\eta\sigma o\nu$ $\kappa a\theta a\rho\grave{o}s$ $\mu\epsilon\tau\grave{a}$
$\kappa a\theta a\rho o\hat{\upsilon}$ $\sigma a\upsilon\tau o\hat{\upsilon}$ $\gamma\epsilon\nu\acute{\epsilon}\sigma\theta a\iota$ ["Be willing to appear beautiful in
the sight of God; desire to be in purity with your own pure
self !"—*Epict. Disc.*, Bk. II., c. 18, § 19].

These are the models, platforms, plans. This is that order,
and striking beauty, faintly shadowed out in those shapes and
rangings of things which strike the sense, and are the entertainment of the vulgar great.

Remember, withal, the gardens and ordering of another
kind, — grotesque, antiques, satyrs, goats, bacchanals. The
measures, proportions, music, dance, &c., that matches this.
Such is thy mind in a certain state, when certain thoughts are
not incumbent, certain views not present; in short, whenever
for the sake of these other beauties, beauty itself, the $\tau\grave{o}$ $\kappa a\lambda\acute{o}\nu$,
$\tau\grave{o}$ $\theta\epsilon\hat{\iota}o\nu$ is lost, out of sight, or faintly appearing. Such are
perpetually their minds (and such are the gardens that befit
them) who, seeming to have a different gusto, a fancy more
refined, make for themselves those other better proportioned
works, seats, gardens, and all those other charming, romantic
places; but which suit them not one bit, there being nothing but
what is Gothic or grotesque *within*.

On one side, Gothic architecture, Dutch pictures, Italian
farce, Indian music; on the other side, Attic numbers, Ionic and
Corinthian orders, and the Greek models in every kind—Phidias,
Appelles, Homer, and Hemskerk, Scarron, Tom D'Urfey.

Compare with the two orders of life—the rake and vicious,

the orderly and good.   Or are there no measures, no numbers, or
proportion here ?  nothing like this in life ?

Harmony, melody, symmetry.—The music of the lyre, the
pleasant matching of colours, the agreeable mixture and ranging
of parts, figures, lines, striking proportions, degrees, forms,
attitudes, beauty and grace.   What is all this ? and whence ?
whither ?—With what does it suit and match ?   What manners,
tempers, affections, and order of life best correspond, pair, and go
in tune with this ?

Take it in the finest descriptions of vice ; take a Petronius.
Try.  Is this it ?  does this do ?  Is it the life of an Encolpius or
an Ascyltos ?  Is it the ship of a Tryphon ?—See but how this
is in the most debauched authors that copy after nature, that
write naturally and ingeniously.   Away with these other
romances, the women-authors, French gallantry and amours,
the modern plays and novels ; where there is neither nature nor
anything natural so much as lewdness : as those who are wittily
lewd see well enough.   For, polite as they are (even in the way
of politeness), they secretly laugh at all this and stick to nature
—as much as there is or can be of nature in vice.   But for the
very real, true nature, and what is according to that nature
truly graceful, proportionable, harmonious, and of the higher
virtuoso kind ; what can it be but virtue itself ?

Or can riot, corruption, and perfidiousness suit with this
idea ?  And what is vice but corruption and perfidiousness ?—
Strange ! that there should be such skill, such art and nicety
in judging of these other beauties, and so little or none at all in
this which is the chief of beauty, the root and ground, too, of all
that other beauty !  For if thou wantest to be convinced of this,
consider but of those lines or features of a face together with the
whole person and outward carriage of one of those finer beauties
that are most taking with the polite sort of lovers, and that are
aptest to create a notable passion of that kind.   See whether
this be not all of it, though in different ways, one and the same
expression or delineation of an ingenious mind, sweet temper,
good soul, generous passions, and affections—in short, of virtue
itself ; and whether those attitudes and motions which have such
an astonishing effect mean anything in the world less, or suit
less to anything, than to that work and those postures which

follow when another passion has got ground and leads where it lists.

A palace and buildings—a theatre and ladies—fine shows—wit—humour, and that which is taking of this kind—sweet, pretty, delicate!—or wonderful! mighty! prodigious!—What are these and such like extollings? and of *what?*—Why allow thyself anything of this kind, or that so much as borders upon this, unless thou wouldst betray thyself wholly; forsake the shadows of truth, excellence, real beauties, and go over, as a deserter, to other colours?

Do so then, ὅλος ἀπόκλινον ἐπὶ τἀναντία—καὶ ἀναπηδῶν ἐπικραύγαζε τῷ ὀρχηστῇ, ["Incline with your whole force the contrary way. Jump up in the theatre, too, and cry out in praise of the dancer."—*Epict. Disc.*, Book IV., c. ii., § 9]. A virtuoso to propose poetry, music, dance, picture, architecture, garden, and so on; extol, commend, be in raptures.—A female or other beauty? follow the passion, love, enjoy, make songs, extol the fair one, the object of thy love. If this be beauty, if this be thy virtuosoship, follow this, admire, commend.

> *Si, Mimnermus uti censet, sine amore jocisque,*
> *Nil est jucundum vivas in amore jocisque.*
> ["If, as Mimnermus tells you, life is flat,
> With naught to love, devote yourself to that."
> *Hor.*, Epist. I., vi., 65-6.]

But if thou refusest this, and wilt have to do with another kind of beauty, what is all this gaying, looking, and wandering abroad at this time of day? What are thy praises, commendations, likings, but vile, awkward, fulsome things? What is the *euge!* and *belle!*—sweet? pretty? delicate? In whose mouth does this sound well? What is sweet? what pretty? And as how? for whom? for thee? (is this thy business?) for such as thee? such a lost, buried thing?—Pedant! philosopher! moralist! corrupter of pleasure! intruder! Thou animal of another species! thing out of season! instrument out of tune! —amphibious creature, Æsop's bat, not bird, nor beast: and the consequence? What, but to be odious both ways, to others and to thyself? Unfortunate both ways, contemptible, miserable? ἀμβολιεργὸς ἀνήρ [the dilatory man.—*Epict. Disc.*, Bk. III., c.

xii., § 32], and ὁ ἐπαμφοτερισμὸς ἑκάτερόν σοι ποιήσει, οὔτε προκόψεις κατ᾽ ἀξίαν οὔτ᾽ ἐκείνων τεύξῃ ὧν πρότερον ἐτύγχανες [and wavering will cause both results; you will neither improve nor have former enjoyment.—*Ibid.*, Bk. IV., c. ii., § 5-6].

If the τὸ καλόν, therefore, be here, where they lead, it cannot be where those of another kind lead. If these are heroes, those were puny wretches. But if there be a cause such as thou hast imagined, if that be indeed a right cause, then is this but imposture and deceit. Declare for one or other. The question. Vote.—But I have voted.—And art thou still at, "oh, pretty!— sweet, pretty, delicate!"—Is not this voting and un-voting? Why give a hearing to these things? why so much as an ear? much less a heart or tongue? But if even an ear be allowed, if the least uncautious attention or seeming assent be given (see!), the heart straight will follow. Hast thou not tried this?—Enough!

Fly-traps, pretty inventions!—A vista in a garden,—a machine in a play,—a lady in a new dress. Is it not charming, rare, excellent? Who would not willingly be thus trapanned? But what is the vista or perspective?—A few sticks, a daubed wall, a cheat. What is the machine?—Cords and sweaty porters pulling at them. And the lady?—See: if thou hast eyes; if not, follow example, commend everything, swear 'tis all heavenly.

If that be beauty which is pointed to, which every finger can show, and every eye see, why this inward search of things invisible?—Man! use thy legs. Travel up and down, run the balls, run the playhouses, the churches, parks; run whole countries and over seas, and all to see sights.—*See! See!*—this is all. And in a child, what else? Is it not the same passion? Novelty, surprise, colours, squares, rounds, triangles, the bustle of children and the business about these things, their architecture, their models, and buildings, and their pleasure of showing this to others.—See! See!

If this, then, be the thing, be thou also one of the children: take the materials and the bricks, the mortar and the earth: make terraces, great houses and little houses, grassplots, knots, and all other delightful ingenious things: and cry, See! But if the thing be not here nor anywhere hereabouts, no nor anywhere abroad or without, but within, within only; then what is this *See! See!* Hast thou not said this and heard it said enough?

Hast thou not shown enough and seen enough? Enough, and but too much?—Enough then, and neither show any more, nor mind when these things are shown, else there is an end of other sights and of that beauty thou hast hopes of knowing.

Ὦ, φίλε Πάν τε καὶ ἄλλοι, ὅσοι τῇδε θεοὶ, δοίητε μοι καλῷ γένεσθαι. [O dear Pan and all the gods grant to me that I be beautiful.—*Plato, Phaedrus*, 279, 6.]

Look! see!—What? where?—I can look into my mind and see finer things by much. But if these outward things are fine with me, the others will be lost that are truly fine, and that make me so, in the better sense; or will a fine suit, a fine garden, or house, make thee fine?—a fine man indeed! Thus whilst I am in search of fineness, hunting beauty, and adding (as I imagine) great beauty to myself in these ways, I really and in effect grow deformed and monstrous, sacrificing all internal proportions, all intrinsic, real beauty and worth for the sake of these things, which are neither the world's beauty, nor the public's, nor society's, nor my own in particular, nor anybody's besides. What beauty then? how beauty? how ornaments? and of what? What is it I would beautify and adorn?

A sight!—what sight?—abroad, out of myself? in things outward? in matter, paste or dough?—No, but in gravel, cockle-shell.—In dirt or clay?—No, but in brick and stone.— What are gardens, what are houses of show?—What are those the children make? what are dirt-pies? or where lies the difference? in the matter or in the minds thus employed? Is it not the same ardour and passion? the same eagerness and concern? the same falling out and in? angry, and friends again, in humour and out of humour, crying to get; then weary and then crying again, when the same thing is parted with or the time comes to leave the play. But those are but rattles and little playthings.—Right: and these are great ones. What is a rattle?—a figure, colours, noise? And what are other noises? what are other figures and colours?—a coach, liveries, parterre and knolls? cascades, *jetts d'eau*?—How many rattles?

What is the whole circumstance put together? the pedigree, coronet, seat, garden, name, title? What is it but as they say themselves (jestingly, but with a pleasure which they plainly enough express) to make a rattle? in earnest, what else?

Again then, a sight !—what sight ?—Anything that is truly a sight and worth contemplating ? Such an one, indeed, there is, and such thou art admitted to (thanks to the author and introducer), such thou mayst perfectly enjoy, nor wilt thou ever satiate of the spectacle. But as for these petty sights and fancies, these baby structures, house ornaments, or ornaments of an estate or of a family, a name, a character in the world, or whichever of the subjects where thou hast a fancy to build and do great matters; wait but a moment or two, and see how it will be. Come but a small change in inward or outward disposition, and immediately, " O wretched ! what is all this ? " What indeed ?—But had this never been but what it should be, had these things passed for what they ought to pass, it would not have been " O wretched ! " Had neither these nor other of the false sights taken place, amused and thus infatuated, no change in outwards, no variation abroad, had made any variation, any revolution or concussion here; but the inward disposition had been right and well.

How these sights and withal vacate to another spectacle ? And not only how vacate ? but how apt ? how fitted ? how a right disposition ? how peace ? How simplicity, for that view, that object, which is of all the simplest, the divinest, only divine?

# LIFE.

Life what ?    To whom in common ? volatiles, reptiles, aquatics and the amphibious kind, flocks, herds, and the herd of mankind.    What is it in the fœtus ? what in a worm ? what in the vegetables ?    *Filii terræ emancipati.*    Those with their mouths upwards catching nourishment here and there ; these with their mouths downwards, fixed to a place, and sucking their nourishment from the earth—what difference in the anatomy ?    Where is there any art of curiosity in the one more than in the other ?    Pipes and juices ; and in that other sort, a more subtle juice ; spirits that agitate to and fro, and move the strings and wires that move the engine.

If life be anything better than this work, this architecture, this fabrication of the visa ; if this imagery, work, and statuary, art of moulding, casting, re-casting, framing, shaping, proportioning, modelling, polishing, with the rest of this kind, displease, quit it, or see what is better.    Throw the hammers and tools away.    See what will come of it, and whether the work will stand or no.    But if not, if it be still imagery-work, only of a worse kind ; if the tools thus flung away should be taken up against thyself, and thou shouldst begin to be hammered in thy turn ; if such be the nature of the thing, that no sooner one work is left off but that the other begins ; then methinks it were better to lay these matters anew upon the anvil, go again to the forge, set up the pedestals, and to work again with the same tools, rather than that thou shouldst mount the pedestal thyself, be wrought upon, and become the handiwork of these unhandy masters.

Consider of true life and false.    A false vegetable life, as when the root is cut ; a false animal life, as in a syncope, or when the great nerve is cut ; a false rational life, as when something else is cut, that is to say, with the vulgar, when only the δύναμις χρηστική [power of service] or simply παρακολουθητική [the understanding] is cut ; but with the truly knowing, when

the real παρακολουθητική [understanding] suffers or is lost;
when the τὸ ἐντρεπτικὸν καὶ αἰδῆμον [the sense of shame and
modesty] is cut off; when this course is intercepted, this energy
ceases, and that ἀπολίθωσις [petrification] is made, which is
spoken of by Epictetus (*Discourses*, Bk. I., c. v., § 3).

True life is when that which should be active is active; that
which should be passive, passive only. True animal life is when
animal spirits with all under them are subject to the will, as
mere will or fancy. True rational life (which with man is only
true life) is when the will, mere will or fancy, is subject to
reason. In the two contraries, it is contrary; in the first of
which (viz., in the animal, false), the spirits obey not, but act of
themselves and cause involuntary motion; in the second (viz.,
rational, false), the appearances and the fancies in the same
manner lead and govern, are not led and governed. Thus uppermost is undermost: active, passive; inversing, crossing, and
confusion.

Upon the whole, remember what is true life and what false;
and that as all life is fancy, or a certain motion, course, and
process of fancies, the business is to know what kind of course,
what exercise this is; whether a regular march and orderly
procedure in time, measure, and proportion, as when the fancies
are led and governed by a rule; or whether it be a jumble and
hubbub, as when the fancies lead and govern without rule; a
mind and will making these to be its subjects, or these a mind
and will; a man governing fancies or fancies a man. One of
these two is necessary; either that a man exercise these, or
these him; either the mind working upon the fancies, or fancies
governing the work of the mind, and (as people say) making
work with it.

*Strenua nos exercet inertia.*
[Restless idleness wears us out.—*Hor.*, Epist. I., xi., 28.]
*Invidia vel a more vigil torquebere.*
[Sleepless thou wilt be racked by envy or by love.—*Ib.*, I., 2, 37.]

That which is within thee must be either ὁ ἐν σοὶ θεὸς ἔστω
προστάτης[1] [the deity presiding within] νοῦν καὶ δαίμονα[2] [intellect
and the daemon], an Æsculapius, a Hermes, a Mulciber, or

[1] *Marcus Aurelius Meditations*, Bk. III,, § 5.  [2] *Ibid.*, Bk. III., § 7.

wretched matter, clay, metal, drugs in the hands of wretched chemists, or merciless Cyclops.

The δαίμων and τὸ δαιμόνιον ; the τὸ ἡγεμονικόν [the ruling faculty] and τὸ θεῖον [Deity]. Copy and original; the same here in the microcosm as in the τὸ πᾶν [the whole]. Either atoms or Deity. No medium. That multiplicity or this simplicity. No compromise—anarchy, or monarchy.

That which is governed is here wholly for the sake of that which governs, and that which governs is of a different species, far nobler than that which is governed, and this is according to order.

Come on, then. Again, what are we ?—Minds. What are minds ?—Intelligences, reasons.—Yes, to what purpose ? What good for ? Of what use ?—To get estates, make fortunes.—What are estates ? what are fortunes ?—Coaches, dishes, wine, lechery, toys.—Say then rightly what it is we are. For those minds we talk of are but appurtenances or means. These are the real things. τὰ ὄντως ὄντα. In another sense, what have we our minds for ?—For these.—Where are our interests ?—In these.—Where are our thoughts and employment ?—In these.

In short, where lies the whole of the matter : life, happiness, misery ?—In these ? These are our concerns, from hence we have our characters, and here we have our very true and genuine selves. Why, therefore, should we not denominate ourselves from these ? So lords from their land. This is their name. Are they not proud of it ?

A man, who ? one belonging to such a piece of ground.—So here—a man, who ? what creature ? what thing ?—a mind—how so ? by what title ? how is a mind belonging to him or he to a mind ?—What shall we say then ? who ? what ?—a human figure and voice; one belonging to a live-body; to a piece of flesh of such a feeling; to certain members and senses. For what is principal ? what guides ? what is the rudder ?

This is that he, that reason, mind, or rather thinking appurtenances—understanding ? intelligence ? as how ? what ?— a little craft, an animal power, or use of fancy, with the help of a cunning sort of a language, articulate sounds to the imagery of fancy.—And is this all ? Notable compound ! pretty device to cater (as a good man says) for a body. A good convenient mind and serviceable reason : the humble handmaid, servant, drudge, or (to speak broader) the band and pomp to these principal parts and essentialities of life. *Cibus, somnus, libido, per hunc circulum curritur.* Consider the excellency of this work; what life is, and how to be prized whilst it is thus. And know withal that if it be in earnest prized, it is beautiful it is thus, and no better; for when it ceases to be thus and becomes an honest, good life, it will no longer be prized at this rate, but perfectly indifferent, readily resigned, and of the two rather more freely parted with than kept.

[1]'Ἀειπάθεια.—From one pulsation (as in a water engine) to another; from one draught and remission of air to another! from repletion to exoneration; and from exoneration to repletion; from toil and labour to rest; and from dreams of one sort to dreams and delusions of another.

This is life—recruiting, repairing, feeding, cleansing, purging; aliments, rags, excrements, dregs. Which of all these sensations is it for which life is eligible? Where is the day or hour in which we can say we live upon the present, and that our happiness is not still future and in promise? Which part of our past life would we desire to live over again? or for the diversions of that age which next succeeded? If for neither, what is it, then, that we call *sweet* in life? Where can any future pleasures or joys (if it is by these that we reckon, equal the vigour and liveliness of those past and of an age when the sensations of that kind are exquisitest? Where, therefore, lies the charm and temptation? The past and present are nothing; and the future is all. Now, what can this produce? Everything wastes and is perishing; everything hastens to its dissolution; already thou thyself art come to a perfect growth; and now thy body is in decline, and faster and faster must corrupt. Mortalities must every day be expected—friends dropping off, accidents and calamities impending, diseases, lamenesses, deafness, loss of sight, of memory, of parts. Few persons in the world grow better, and many grow worse every day, so as to lose the natural good dispositions they once had. All is misery, disappointment, and regret. In vain we endeavour to drive away those thoughts; in vain we strive by humour and diversion to raise ourselves;

[1] Rott., 1698.

which is but to fall the lower. He and he only is in any degree happy, who can confront these things; who can steadily look on them without turning away his sight; and who, knowing the sum and conclusion of all, waits for the finishing of his part, his only care in the meanwhile being to act that part as becomes him and to preserve his mind entire and sound, unshaken and uncorrupt; in friendship with mankind, and in unity with that original mind with respect to which nothing either does or can happen but what is most agreeable and conducing, and what is of universal good.

Consider the number of animals that live and draw their breath, and to whom belongs that which we call *life*, for which we are so much concerned; beasts, insects, the swarm of mankind sticking to this earth, the number of males and females in copulation, the number of females in delivery, and the number of both sexes in this one and the same instant expiring and at their last gasp; the shrieks, cries, voices of pleasure, shoutings, groans, and the mixed noise of all these together. Think of the number of those that died before thou wert or since; how many of those that came into the world at the same time and since; and of those now alive, what alteration. Consider the faces of those of thy acquaintance as thou sawest them some years since; how changed since then! how macerated and decayed! All is corruption and rottenness; nothing at a stay, but continued changes; and changes renew the face of the world.

If every life be liveable, then is a dog's, or, what is worse, a cunning flattering man's. What is a silly bird's? a bee's? a cricket's? A merry one (as they say)? a simple-hearted, innocent one? a busy one? a famous and (as they count) an important one? What are all these?

But do thou remember what life and the *law of life* is (Τίς ὁ βιωτικὸς νόμος—*Epict. Disc.*, Bk. I., c. xxvi.), and, therefore, as is shown here, on every occasion to conform to nature (ἐν παντὶ στοχαστέον—*Ibid.*, Bk. I., c. xxvi., § 2), otherwise the life not liveable; and, being below thy species and what thou wert born to, is better and more generously quitted. Καλλίω θάνατον σκεψάμενος ἀπαλλάττου τοῦ βίου ["Acknowledge death to be better than life, and depart hence."—*Plato*, Laws, ix., 854 c.]. Either one or the other, see which, and do honestly as is best.

T

If life be no such precious thing; if every life be not indeed worth living, not even in the most vulgar opinion (since even the vulgar can despise it on certain terms); if only, then, such a certain life be to a man eligible, worth living, worth preserving and cherishing, with that necessary pain and labour the life requires; then consider on every comparison of thy own with other lives that thou seest are lived, whether by men or beasts, that which is no way valuable. Parts can no way be so in the whole. What is this, therefore, that we call *pleasure* for which we would live?

The pleasures of the debauch, amours with women; the basking of a fowl on a dung-hill; the crowing and victory of the cocks; the State victories; the campaign victories. Would I live this life? Would I live a dog? would I be a wolf, a sheep, a goat? Then say at such a time, "Am I not this or that creature?" — Eating (as loving eating), venery (as taking with venery), playing (as minding play, delighted with play) —What is all this? what is all play? what is jest and then earnest? Have I known anything better? have I been a man? If so, is not this a real metamorphosis, transformation; and is not this always made and in being in every part of life that is not led after a certain rule and with a certain consciousness?

Life is as those that live it. What are those? What are we? *Nos numerus sumus et fruges consumere nati.*[1] Tolerable carrion; fit to be let live. Honest poor rascals not so bad as when they say "scarce worth the hanging." Life-worthy persons, if a bare liveable life. But say, what are we? What do we make of ourselves? How esteem ourselves? Warm flesh, with feelings, aches, and appetites. The puppet—play of fancies.—O the solemn, the grave, the ponderous business.— Complex ideas, dreams, hobby-horses, houses of cards, steeples and cupolas.—The serious play of life.—Shows, spectacles, rites, formalities, processions; children playing at bugbears, frighting one another through masks. The herald, priests, cryer. The trump of fame; the squeaking trumpet and cat-call; the gowns! habits! robes! How underneath? How in the nightcaps,

[1] "We are a mere number, and born to consume the fruits of the earth."—*Hor.*, Epist. I., 2, 27.

between the curtains and sleeps ? How anon in the family with wife, servants, children, or where even none of these must see ? Private pleasures, other privacies ? the closet and bed-chamber, parlours, dining-rooms, dressing-rooms, and other rooms. In sickness, in lazy hours, in wines, in lechery ? taking in, letting out.—O the august assembly; each of you, such as you are apart !

What is life to the very vulgar in a certain aspect ?—How at these seasons and on those occasions when they consider life as mere life—the same in one creature as in another ? Hogs, dogs, worms, insects, dray-horse, the shambles and slaughter-houses, the common soldiery.

This is that thing so sad to part with, so precious to retain. This is that catastrophe ! The bottom of the tragedy ! Is not this all ? Do not the vulgar see this ? Why else is that of the tragedian hearkened to and received so well ? " To be or not to be," &c.—" A consummation devoutly to be wished."

The buffoon on the stage. We are all but spans and candle-ends. But this is a jest. Is it so ? Bring me a Caligula ; 'twill be quickly earnest. The comedy of the Gallo-Greeks. Excellent play. Admirable comedian. Nothing more instructive. Who could better make this out ? Who ever saw this ridicule better or showed it more perfect ? But this was horrid ! Was it so ? When the jest is turned, it seems it is earnest and not to be laughed at.

*Temporibus dives*—words ! words ! How is it in a sickness time ? a fire ? an earthquake ? Are not these the same as the tyrant ? Do they not do more work ? What is nature doing every day ? Where is the tyranny ? Where the tragedy ? Why tragedise ? Does not this make out the spans ? Or what are we, forsooth—ells, fathoms ; not spans, long-lasting papers, nor snuffs and candle-ends.

*Majores nostri praeterierunt, nos abimus, posteri sequentur; quid istuc quaeso ? quid istuc est ? Nihil ita crebro ut mortem vident. Nihil ita obliviscuntur ut mortem.* [Our ancestors have passed away, we are passing, our descendants will follow ; what is this, pray ? what ? Men see nothing so often as death. They forget nothing so often] as a wild, modern scholastic has it. Or a late preacher in : Our very graves were once living. We dig through our forefathers to bury our friends, and shall soon become earth ourselves to bury our posterity.

O the bustle; a day or year, more or less; what a business *usque!*

Wish for noon; then for evening; then for to-morrow; then for next day. A week hence and I shall receive such a letter. In a fortnight afterwards I shall be satisfied about such an affair. Next month I shall see an end of this and what the issue of the other. One year more and I shall see how this matter in the public is like to go; and how that other in my own family. And when all this is come about, what then? Will things be all settled and fixed when they are come thither? Will the sun and moon stop their course? or, which is all one, will those changes, successions, or revolutions of things be stopped, or but suspended or stayed? Must not corruptions, decays, and deaths carry on the course of the world? Are not particular men and societies of men, families, and nations included in this great circulation? Are not relations, friends, thy country, self, included? And are not all things continually changing state?—What state of affairs is it that thou waitest for? What wouldst thou see brought about, in thy family or country? Are they flourishing or but in a tolerable way now at the present? Wait but a little and thou shalt see it otherwise. Mortalities will come; corruptions, public and private. Friends falling off by degrees and carried away; some by death, others before death: a new face of things; new revolutions. Or wouldst thou live and grow older and yet expect to see no deaths, no changes, no disorders, no decays? If this be senseless, what is it to wait for events, to look out for new settlements and regulations, to build, and rear, and prop that which can never stand, and is still mouldering away faster and faster? Why look beyond this day? Why live still for to-morrow and not the present?—But when I have seen an end of this, this shall be the last time.— And so every time. How long has it been thus? How often deceived? To what an age art thou now come since this was determined? And see where thou findst thyself! Is it not at the same place, meditating the same things, and in the same manner?

When, therefore, wilt thou begin to *live*? How long shall thy life be thus imperfect and broken? How long ere thou

rememberest that thou art not to live to-morrow, but to-day?
And that thou dost not live to-day, unless to-morrow be as it
were set out and appointed for death?

As oft as thou sayst to-morrow, remember that to-morrow is
for death and not for life; otherwise thou art dead already; and
dead still in a worse sense, if what is said here be not
thoroughly felt.

Remember that life is this present moment, and that it is
ridiculous to live *ill* now, in order to live *well* at any time hence.
And yet how oft is this the case?

Remember that the best preparation against the *future* is to
mind the *present*.

One ten years more, and then another ten; and then even
in a vulgar way death is to be thought on, and thoughts turned
that way. Who shall succeed? Who inherit? And is it not
truly vulgar to stay till then? and either now, or then, to be
concerned for more than this present?

Will it be any otherwise than it has been? Was it not
to-day as it was yesterday? and yesterday as the day before?
Think about yesterday as the day before. Think what *yesterday*
was, and how far thou wouldst esteem it an advantage to live it
over again, and so again and again. Who would bear it? Yet
what is life else? Why need another yesterday? How often
wouldst thou live it over again? To what further time wouldst
thou live? Hast thou seen enough? Is not *once seeing* enough?
How often wouldst thou be spectator? how long a guest?
Where is the modesty of this? where the respect, the observance,
duty, gratitude towards the master of the feast? Enough, then.
Rise and give thanks.—Pass on, move. You have seen. Let
others see.

At night always thus. I have been admitted to the
spectacle, I have seen, I have applauded. It is enough. Thanks
to Him who introduced me, who gave me this privilege, this
advantage.

In the morning am I to see anew? am I to be present yet
longer and content? I am not weary nor ever can be of such a
spectacle, such a theatre, such a presence; nor of acting whatsoever part such a master assigns me. Be it ever so long, I stay
and am willing to see on whilst my sight continue sound; whilst

I can be a spectator, such as I ought to be; whilst I can see reverently, justly, with understanding and applause. And when I can see no more I retire, not disdainfully, but in reverence to the spectacle and master, giving thanks, τῷ κεκληκότι σε ἐπ' αὐτά, τῷ ἄξιον τῆς χώρας ταύτης κεκρικότι. [To Him who hath called one to them and judged one worthy a part.— *Epict. Disc.*, Bk. II., c. i., § 39].

To die the death—of what? of a dog? a hog or sheep? No, but of a man. How go to slaughter like a man? What is slaughter (see the bugbear word)? What is fever? the stone? the gout? Is not this slaughter? What tyrant? what Caligula? What knives? Are not these knives? or a sword, or axe, anything more? Does it make longer work? Is it not a human lot, a common exit, and as incident to honest man as any other bye-way?—as the falling of a horse, or the falling into a ditch? Die in a ditch! No, by no means; but in a feather bed, which is much softer; and to be choked by a quinsy or imposthume, far better than by so much puddle.—Or is the bed of honour so much better?—There it is now again the ditch water may serve, provided it be the town-ditch, when the place is stormed, or if the battle be at some canal or muddy ford.—Excellent, noble! for this surely is a manly work, this a human and generous death: to die pursuing, wounding, killing, not wild beasts, foxes, or hares, but men, of the same blood and kind with us.—To be buried by a mine, to be blown up, or drowned, be it earth, air, water, anything, any place, any manner, it is one and the same, alike honourable, indifferent; so it be but in the field, so it be the general's command. Wretch! What general? what field? who gives the command? Under whom art thou enlisted? who brought thee into the field of action? What is honour? what valour, fortitude, magnanimity? Is there a cause? is there a leader? If none, what are those other causes and this ado about a public and a world? But if there be a real cause, what is it but that supreme one and that which he commands? And then, what death is there that should concern us?—What but that one sort, viz., that it be a ready one, a free one, a noble one? Why talk to us of a ditch or knife? why of a scaffold? If it be his command, it is honourable; and the less it seems so to others, the more honourable still in itself, the more disinterested the part, the more generously hard and soldier-like. For how is it that the good soldier is tried ? and what is it they call part of honour ? and for whom ? What part would the women in all likelihood have assigned them were women also to be in the fight ? Who are they that in a sea engagement are sent down into the hold ?—Wouldst thou be thus taken care of ? Wouldst thou be insured from fire, water, and a ditch, that thou shouldst not die by any of these, though by chance thou dropped into them, nor by the iron, nor the cord (if the occasion were), nor after any of these ways they call ends ?—How sad ! Is it not necessary then thou shouldst be sad ? Why not as well as merry ? Why not as well an instant or an hour before death as twenty hours or a hundred times twenty (for some certain number thou must count) ? Why not as well before this sort of death (suppose) now coming as any other sort of death by and bye to come ?—But this is an ignominious one, this is shameful.— In respect of what ? of whom ? of the laws of the universe ? or of these idle tales, the play and talk of children ? Say truth then, and confess thyself one of these children. Confess that thou either knowest no such universe, nor laws, nor chief; or that such as He is, thou art ashamed of Him ; as being ashamed of His Administration and Providence.

To die any death is natural, for one door is the same as another. The natural or unnatural is the going out. How this is done: with what mind. For if with a right mind, this is all that the nature of a rational creature requires or needs. He has all he wants. It is a consummation. All the numbers are full ; the measures perfect ; the harmony complete.

To die, when over, is to do *nothing ;* when not over, it is to *live.* It is in life, therefore, or nowhere, that death is. It is death indeed to fear death. It is death to live and dream. See that thou dost not truly live this death; and it is no matter what death thou diest.

How many deaths in such a life as this ? What else is death ? What hideous, what ghastly, but this alone ? What skeleton or corpse but this ? What spectre beside these sad spectres, heavy dreams and haunting visions ? The nightmare, agony, endeavours and efforts to awake.

To go to death !—Right, whither else wouldst thou go ?

Wouldst thou be carried, perhaps, or drawn? Is this the right way of going? Wouldst thou thus go? or not go at all? What is life but going? What is passing away time, diverting, sleeping, playing, planting, building, dining, supping, and to bed, but going? What is this that thou art at present doing but going? For, even if improving (if, happily, this be so), what is it else but going and having to go?

To draw to an end!—Right, what wouldst thou draw to else? Wouldst thou draw to thy beginning and be so much nearer to thy birthday? If not then to thy death day. So take it and be content. What else wert thou born for? What did thy birth signify? What betoken or portend? Immutability? Duration? Perpetuity?

To go to death.—Dost thou not go every night? Or are dreams life? Such dreams, too, as are thine as yet? Often impure, seldom composed, seldom restraint, correction, or redress. How when waking? What if little better then? —Is this life? Are these the dreams so heavily parted with? Is this the thing—*to die?*

To go to death. To go from life.—To go from eating and drinking. Dost thou not go from them, rise from them every day? But I would go again. I have not gone often enough.— How many times more? Away, man! rise, wipe thy mouth; throw up thy napkin and have done. A bellyful (they say) is as good as a feast. Enough of these fillings and emptyings. Up, once for all, and make not such a business of meals, which are just as satisfactory when over, and the sooner over (except to a hog, or worse creature than a hog) the better.

Death (they say) is a debt to nature. Why not, rather, life that debt, and this happily over, the debt paid and the account discharged?

Nature debtor to life. Life the credit side of the account. Death the balance due, always ready. Does the trade displease? Take the balance and the account, or why complain? Either trade honestly, or leave off. But make not these wrong charges and ridiculous articles. What does it signify? Who will be cheated by it? On whom is the house like to fall?

If life be indeed such a gain, such a prize as made of, then have I indeed a debt to pay. But if otherwise I am now paying, and being come to die, it is I that am paid; it is I that have been creditor, and nature justly and kindly gives me back my debt.

The more worth the less valued: the more valued the less worth. And this with justice, for what is there worth valuing in life besides the actions that depend on this very indifference? for, as for the other actions, what are they?

[1]Consider that even with the truly wise, the truly happy man, life still is but indifferent. How, therefore, with thee? Can it be so much as indifferent? If *there* no gain, *here* what loss? and how dear may it cost ere it is over.

On one side sure of no harm: on the other side sure of no good; but perhaps harm. How is this condition equal? See what thou fearest when thou fearest death.

It is but for once.—Comfort thyself—for what? for death? No, but for life, for this is the thing more rightly.—It is but for once.—Right.—Once only such a body, such senses, such offices about a body and matters belonging. A moment or two, and all will be well; and why not even this moment, if all within be well, as it should be?

By virtue all is made well; for now, if for now only; for hereafter, if for hereafter.

If more life after this, will it not be the better still for what I am doing? If no more, is it not well that I do as I do?

All who have denied order and a God have denied a future state, for we never hear yet of a future state and no God, though of a God and no future state. If, therefore, there be a future state, how can all be but well? If nothing future this is all the ill. And why ill? why not all well? If so, why not stay? If otherwise, go; who hinders?—Is not this well?

[2] The several stages, and the last stage.—The travelling by the messenger, the procáccio in Italy. After a long journey, many events, many hardships, many escapes, at last welcome to Florence, Rome, Naples, or the place desired, the harbour, the end of the voyage.

So of life. The end, the upshot, harbour, and port. All was but to get well hither, all but to this end. What fatigues by the

---

[1] St. Giles, May, 1705.    [2] Probably Naples, 1712.

way; what hazards? In what company? Wherein the satisfaction of travelling for travelling's sake?—But art thou come safe? and hast thou wrought of a safe mind? Is all well and sound? Then welcome! and why not as well when sooner as when later? Why not the rather, when sooner? But be it sooner or later it well deserves the welcome and usual compliments of the procáccio.

The same in any disturbance of life. Remember the usual comfort upon the road. "It will soon be over. We shall soon be at the place."

Why make a business of so little? The play is short. Be not morose, but sit it out. Two acts are over; there is no fear of a fourth or a fifth, and in all likelihood thou shalt be acquitted for less than even the second, which is yet unspent.

Whether the rub be in the passage or thyself?—Where indeed but in thyself? For what passage in nature is gentler, smoother, easier? Unless perhaps thou art frighted at the convulsions and pulling of the things, when even sense is in a manner gone. Does pain increase as senses decrease? Are these the agonies. Is this the passing? the hard thing? Is it not easier still the nearer it approaches? Is it not (as the buffoon said) all down at hill? What road is plainer or better beaten? What path more flowery, if rightly taken? Where is the gulf (as they say) to be shot?—Shooting of the gulf!—Is not this story and that of the vulgar much alike?

What passage or thoroughfare, transmission or change, more natural than the passing of this animation, breath, or spirit from this channel or rivulet into that other? as that common description of the poet's, a river disemboguing itself into the sea: at first perhaps from rocks and through steep countries.

*Non sine montium*
*Clamore vicinaeque silvae.*

[Not without noise of mountains and of the neighbouring wood.— *Hor.*, Odes III., 29, 38-9.]

But at last gliding with gentleness into the bosom of a Thetis.

*Cum pace delabentis Etruscum*
*In mare.*

[Peacefully gliding to the Etruscan sea.—*Ibid.*, line 36.]

# PHILOSOPHY.

What specious exercise is found in those which are called
" Philosophical Speculations [1] ? " The formation of ideas, their
compositions, comparisons, agreement and disagreement ! What
is to the purpose ? what can have a better appearance ? what
can bid fairer for genuine and true philosophy ? It is well. But
let me look a while within myself. Let me observe there
whether or no there be connections and consistency, agreement or
disagreement ; whether that which I approve this hour I do not
disapprove the next ; but keep my opinion, liking, and esteem
of things the same. If otherwise, to what purpose is all this
reasoning and acuteness ?

[2]To-day things have succeeded well with me, consequently
my hopes and opinions are raised. " It is a fine world ! All is
glorious ! Everything delightful ! Mankind, conversation, company, society. What can be more desirable ?" To-morrow comes
disappointment, crosses, disgrace. And what follows ? " O
miserable mankind ! wretched state ! Who would live out of
solitude ? who would engage in the public or serve mankind ?"
Where is truth, certainty, evidence, so much talked of ? It is
here that they are to be maintained if anywhere. [3]Again, what
are my ideas of the world of pleasure, riches, fame, life ? What
judgment am I to make of mankind and human affairs ? What
sentiments am I to frame ? what opinions ? or maxims ? If
none at all, why do I concern myself for anything, or study
anything with such nicety of distinction ? What is it to me, for
instance, to know what kind of ideas I can have of space ?
The three angles of a triangle are equal to two right angles,
of this I have clear ideas ; this I can be certain of. What is this
to me ? What am I the wiser or better ? Let me hear concerning what is of some use to me. Let me hear (for instance)
concerning *life*, what the right notions, and what I am to stand

---

[1] See *Characteristics*, I., p. 299.     [2] *Ibid.*, 300.     [3] *Ibid.*, 301.

to that I may, when the spleen comes, not cry " vanity," and at
the same time complain that " time is short and passing." For
why so *short*, if not found *sweet ?*    Why do I complain both
ways ?    Is vanity, mere vanity a happiness ?    Or can misery
pass away too soon ?    This is of moment to me to examine.
This is what is worth my while.    If I cannot find the agreement
or disagreement of my ideas in this place ; if I can come to
nothing *certain* here; what is all the rest to me ?    What signifies
it how I come by my ideas, or how I compound them ; which
are simple and which complex ?    If I have a right idea of *life*
now at this moment, that I think slightly of it, and resolve with
myself that it may easily be laid down on any honourable
occasion of service to my friends or country, teach me how
I shall remain in this opinion ; what it is that changes ; and how
this disturbance happens ; by what innovation, what composition,
what intervention of other ideas.    If this be the subject of the
*philosophical art*, I readily apply to it and study it.    If there
be nothing of this in the case I have no occasion for the sort of
learning, and am no more desirous of knowing how I form or
compound those ideas which are distinguished by words,
than I have of knowing how and by what motions of my
mouth I form those articulate sounds, which I can full
as well pronounce and use without any such science or
speculation.

But it is necessary I should examine my ideas.—But what
ideas ?    The ideas of space, extension, solidity ?    What is it to me
whether a vacuum or a plenitude ? whether matter be divisible
*ad infinitum* or not divisible ?    What have I to do with the
examination of those ideas which I may be the best versed in
of any man in the world, and yet of all men be the farthest
from tranquillity ?

The cataract in the eye and the many other cures in physic.
In mathematics how ? in astronomy ?    The world moving : sun
standing still.    Say this to the vulgar and hear what they will
reply.    Thus even in trade and politics (subjects vulgar enough
and such as interest causes to be well examined), consider the
two propositions : " an ounce of silver worth an ounce of silver,"
and " dominion founded in property."    Easy maxims, plain,
certain, yet how hard !    What a mystery and how unintelligible

to the greater part of professors in this kind! Consider now of the ὄρεξις [desire], the ἔκκλισις [aversion], how easy! No τὰ εφ' ἡμῖν and οὐκ ἐφ' ἡμῖν [the things which and the things which are not in our power], the προαίρετα [the will], and the ἀπροαίρετα [the absence of will]. How easy and yet—

To solve the phenomena in a true sense: not the phenomena of the skies or meteors: not those in mathematics, mechanics, physics; not those which, by solving or unfolding ever so skilfully, one is neither better, nor happier, nor wiser, nor more a man of sense or worth; of a more open, free understanding, liberal disposition; a more enlarged mind or a generous heart: but those which, being not unfolded nor well resolved, contract and narrow a man's genius, cause a real poorness in the understanding, disturb, distract, amaze, confound, perplex, lead away like those dancing fires of the *ignis fatuus*, plunge into abysses and cast into endless labyrinths. Who would not be learned and expert in this art? and yet who is?—But be thou, since thou mayest be. For what is there easier? or costs less? Hast thou not tried?—Enough then, Μελέτα ἐπιλέγειν ὅτι ᾽φαντασία εἶ καὶ οὐ πάντως τὸ φαινόμενον᾽. ["Practise saying 'You are an appearance, and in no manner what you appear.'"—*Epict. Ench.*, c. i., § 5.] Let this be thy philosophy and leave the other phenomena for others.

Either that which I call philosophy is so from the subtlety and niceness of the speculation (and then mathematics, physics, and all of that kind is philosophy), or from its being the superior and judge of all the others, as that which teaches happiness and gives the rule of life. Again, if the study of happiness be philosophy, and that happiness be in outward things, then the study of those outward things in which happiness consists, and how to attain these outward things, is philosophy; and the study of wealth, preferment, or some other such thing, must be that which we call philosophy. Whereas if happiness be not in outward things, but in a mind, then the way to happiness must be to correct and amend those opinions which we commonly have of outward things; and thus the work of philosophy is to fortify a mind, to learn how to be secure against avarice, ambition, intemperance; how to throw off cowardice and effeminacy; how to cure disquiet, restlessness, anxiety, and to find that which may satisfy and content us, since riches, honours, &c., neither can, nor if they could, are such as to be counted on, as durable or certain. Here therefore lies philosophy (if philosophy be anything), and this every one sees is a matter of practice. What have I to do, therefore, with those speculations which relate not to my own amendment? But it is necessary I should examine my ideas.— But what ideas? The ideas of space, extension, solidity? What is it to me whether a vacuum or a plenitude? whether matter be divisible *ad infinitum* or not divisible? What have I to do with the examination of those ideas which I may be the best versed in of any in the world, and yet of all men be the farthest from tranquillity?

[1] Why wonder at philosophy? If philosophy be (as defined) the study of happiness, what does every one but in some manner or another, either skilfully or unskilfully, philosophise? For, either happiness is in outward things, or from self and outward things together, or from self alone and not from outward things. If from outward things alone, then show us that all men are equally happy in proportion to these; and that no one is ever miserable by his own fault.

But this nobody pretends to show, but all confess the contrary. It remains, therefore, that happiness is either from self alone, or from outward things and self. If from self alone, what should I do but study self. If partly from outward things, partly from self, then each must be considered, and some price or other set to those matters of an inward kind and that depend on self alone. If so, and that I consider in what and how these are to be preferred, how they are to take place, or how yield; what is this but to *philosophise*?

For, what must I do in this case; since something there is which depends on myself? How is that *self* to be governed? How far, and in what, am I to be concerned? If any way at all, it must be thus: how to free myself from those contradictory pursuits and opposite passions which make me inconsistent with myself and own resolutions; how to extinguish that which is the occasion of repentance; how to calm my anger; how to quell resentment and revenge; how to contain in matter

[1] *Characteristics*, II., pp. 438-439.

of venery, so as not to fall into extravagant loves, or be entangled in any passion of that sort from whence I may not easily get free; how to keep out luxury and hinder effeminacy, laziness, and those other sorts of passions from gaining ground; how to stand out against ambition, prevent avarice and immoderate appetites; how to bear with accidents and support the common chances of the world.—But if I study this, and turn philosopher after this manner, I shall be of no consideration in the world; I shall lose other advantages.—Right.   And therefore this still is philosophy, this is the thing itself, [1] to inquire where and in what we are losers; which are the greatest gains; [2]whether I shall find my account in letting these inward matters run as they please; or whether I shall be better secure against fortune, by settling matters within, than by acquiring first one great friend and then another; or by adding still more and more to my estate or quality.   Begin, then, and set the bounds; let us hear how far are we to go and no further? what is a moderate fortune, a competency, and those other degrees commonly talked of ?   Where is my anger to stop ? or how high to rise ?   How far may I engage in amours and love ? how far give way to ambition ? how far to other appetites? Or am I to set all loose? are all these passions to take their swing and no application to be given to these; but all to the outward things they aim at ?   Or if any application be requisite, say how much to the one and how much to the other ? How far are the appetites to be minded, and how far outward things ?   Give us the measure and rule ; see whether this be not to *philosophise*, and whether willingly or unwillingly every one does not do as much.—Where, then, is the difference ? who is it that philosophises *well*, who *ill* ?—Weigh and consider.—

But the examination is troublesome, and I had better be without it.—Who says this ?—Reason.—Hast thou, therefore, polished thy reason, bestowed pains upon it, and exercised it in this subject ?   Or, is it likely to pronounce fully as well when unexercised as when exercised ?   Whose reason is truest in mathematics ?   His whose is exercised, or whose is un-exercised ? Whose in policy and civil affairs ? whose in physic, or any other

[1]*Characteristics*, II., p. 439.      [2]*Ibid.*, p. 440-1.

subject whatsoever ?  How comes morality and life to be alone excepted ?

Thus is philosophy established for, as every one reasons, and cannot but of necessity reason concerning his own happiness, concerning what is his good, what his ill ; so the question here is only who reasons best.  For, even he who rejects this reasoning or deliberating part, does it from a certain reason, and from a persuasion that this is best.

# LETTERS.

## TO JOHN LOCKE.[1]

PARIS, *December 1st,* 1687.

DEAR SIR,—Though I expect now a letter from you very soon, yet the concern I have lest the trouble you gave yourself about me has made you ill, make me not neglect this post; nor am I willing to hazard the prolonging of it to one letter only. I am removed since that and come into a pension, where now you may direct your letters to me. It is an Château vieux dans la rue de St. Andre des Arts.

I have yet pitched on no masters of exercise. Till I have done that I can prefix myself no hours to study, nor have I yet bought any but French books.

These plays here are very ordinary either to read or see. Their opera I have not seen yet, but shall to-morrow. I am afraid I shall like that but too well, for I am a perfect slave to fine music. I find I can conform better to their dirt here than their manners. I have hitherto had no disturbance from our own countrymen. Here are not, as I am told, by half so many as there were last winter.

Sir John is this moment beginning his French and his master at his ventilabria, which divert me from what I am doing. Though truly I have no more to say now, but how much and

[1] John Locke was living in Holland at this time on account of the part he had played in English political affairs through his relations to the First Earl of Shaftesbury. Lord Ashley (afterwards the First Earl of Shaftesbury) visited him at Rotterdam at the beginning of his tour on the Continent, after leaving the school at Winchester. He then proceeded to Paris, where he wrote to Locke the first of those letters which have here been obtained from the Lovelace Collection.

with how great sincerity I am your obliged friend and humble
servant,                                                A. ASHLEY.

Sir John[1] desires me to give his humble service and Mr.
Denoun[2] presents his to you.

[Address] : For Mr. Locke, to be left with Mr. Benjamin Furly,
Op. de Schipmakers' Haven, tot Rotterdam, Holland.

---

### TO JOHN LOCKE.

PARIS, *December* 22*nd,* 1687.

DEAR SIR,—But that I am not ashamed to reveal my
greatest frailties to you, I would not make you the confession
I am going, of having deferred until now the answering of yours
(though received the day before yesterday). But I hope the
ingenuity of this declaration will merit your belief, when I tell
you that it was the effect of my desire only to do it in better
order, and when I had time enough to myself to be some hours
alone with you, though in absence, whereby I hoped to give
myself as well as you more satisfaction. But since I could not
and have not yet obtained that wish, I must content myself (as
not the first time) with what I can get, and make the best use of
it. The reason of this has been that I am just now surprised by
a message from the envoy with a journey to Versailles to-morrow
at six o'clock, with whom we were engaged to go the next time
he went thither.

It is unnecessary here to speak of my concern at your not
receiving mine, mixed with the joy for the danger I escaped by
writing my second. But I must needs tell you I am not satisfied
that you speak nothing particularly of your health as I desired
you. And this is no manner of customary or ceremonious
question in me, but what I desire earnestly to be resolved me,
as I find by myself, that that friendly expression so often used
by Tully, *cura ut valeas* [take care of your health], is
not ill-grounded, for I find your health of such concern to me
that I cannot but use that expression to you here, and truly

---

[1] Sir John Cropley.     [2] Lord Ashley's tutor

I have a reason more incumbent on me, for that I fear I have been the cause of some bad to you, as I need not wonder, when you would use so many hazards, so much against my will, on my account.

To thank you for the advice I have received in your letters, as well as from your mouth, would be a subject too big for this paper, or indeed for my tongue, and is what I shall never attempt, or at least never pretend to speak of as it deserves. So that I resolve to lay all that aside and beg to be dealt by as I do, and I flatter myself that if it were only to satisfy me, Mr. Locke would quit everything that might be a hindrance to speaking his mind to me freely, and that might be so many clouds to that light I receive.

It is now pretty late, and I can only let you know that for my exercises I have begun none, nor shall I until the holidays are over, for it will be but losing so much money. Lord Salisbury's new convert is here, come since I, but has nor will hardly receive any visit from me : which I find he resents. He has with him two more English converts, one Hales is one, besides some priests whom he carries with him. Sir John Cropley desires me to give you his humble service, and Mr. Denoun gives you his. If you can read this I shall have my intent, which is only to do better than to lose to-morrow and stay till next post.

Believe me, that I am, with all sincerity, your most obliged friend and servant.

---

### TO HIS FATHER. [1]

HAMBURG, *May 3rd (Old Style)*, 1689.

MY LORD,—The hardships I have suffered in a terrible German journey of almost two months, with the respite of only a few days, might have been much more tolerable if in that time I could have had occasions to have eased myself by that satisfaction and real pleasure which, in my assurance that by every

[1] This letter is of importance, as it gives us for the first time an account of a considerable part of Lord Ashley's early journey abroad, after leaving the school at Winchester.

letter I create it to your lordship and my mother, I receive myself in so great measure when I write. But nothing that was ever can be more justly called intolerable than the condition during all that time I was in; when so entirely cut off from all correspondence that I had not left me an active part in it. Nor could I more know how to give your lordship and my mother news of myself than I knew how to get it of yourselves, although at Vienna I wrote, being told I had a chance. But I fear it is almost as impossible that a letter should go thence, as it is absolutely that it should go from any other of the parts of Germany I passed through, without the help of a correspondent in Holland or Flanders to receive them there, such as your lordship knows by my former letters has been unprovided, having no other but him in France, through whose hands was the only way thought of for the convenience of letters, when these late revolutions were unexpected, and when only I did not dream of the passage of France being blocked up for me in my return. It should have been the cause of my visiting another, and so large a portion of Europe, and by the necessity I should find myself in of going back through a great part of Germany, I should have been engaged to have made a journey through the heart of that country. A journey so frightful in the very idea that, as greatly as my curiosity is raised, and my desires grown towards my improvement in the knowledge of mankind, of the variety of nature in its other works, and of more of the countries of these nearer parts of our world, yet I confess I was often so daunted at the object (such as it was set out to me by those whom by my experience I could now justify to have spoken without hyperbole), voluntarily I believe, indeed, I should have hardly embraced the resolution, not though the reward that was before my eyes for what I should undergo were the sight of more of the most famous cities, the seats of the great actions of the late ages, of countries productive of so many rarities, of that empire whose constitution has made it formerly in the united force of its princes so formidable, and of more courts, and those the most considerable of Europe. But now, thank heavens, first for the cause of this last and greatest piece of my travel, our late purge from those promoters of the interest that was to have enslaved us to the horridest of all religions and to the service of the usurpations and treacheries of that neighbouring crown that has aimed so long at the subjection of all Europe. I would have gone as far as round the world out of my way (although to have been without the profit of it) to have found at my return my country freed from such a distemper that had so long hung about it and had got so fast hold. In the next place am I pleased that since by this happy occasion that made France too hot for us, the intended course of my return by Marseilles and Toulon along the southern parts of that country, and so up the river Loire, was cut off, and that my way home was through Germany, that I made a bold sally into the body of the country, with the resolution not to go so far through it as I should have been obliged without seeing what was of worth in it. So making my compass but a little wider, I saw of Germany what ought to be seen. If your lordship has received my letter from Vienna, you have heard of my journey from Venice thither, and what remarks I could give your lordship in such a piece of paper. I was very happy in the advantage I had to be there just before the opening of the campaigns, when all the great men and officers in the Emperor's service were there met from all parts to advise and to receive instructions for the management of the war, the separation of their commands, and the division of the forces between Hungary and the Rhine. I stayed there two days more than the time I had allotted for that court, and except for the mourning that I was forced to make, in which they were there very deep, the civilities I had there would have tempted me to have stayed longer. There is no need one finds of the language of the country, French and Latin being so much known and used, but especially the first, and Italian is spoken from the Emperor down to the guards. I left Vienna the 19th of April, new style; since then I have passed through a long tract of countries that have afforded me such variety of scenes that I will not attempt to make your lordship any description of here, especially since I hope so soon to be with you. I will content myself to tell your lordship only that I passed through the rest of Austria, and also through Moravia, a fine country, but that bears such marks of a friend as one would hardly distinguish from those that an enemy leaves behind him, and even as bad a one as the Turk or Tartar, but it seems there is little difference 'twixt them and the Poles whether a country has them as friend or enemy if they but come within it. Here it was that the Polish army passed and repassed in their return from the succour of Vienna, where they did no other service but to help off with the biggest part of the plunder, and then quarrel that they got no more. We partook in the sufferance of these poor people, whom they spared nothing to but their lives on their return, for from linen, bedding, and bedsteads to knives and trenchers there was nothing (since they spoiled or carried off all) left renewed in all that country that bears resemblance of any such thing. As for bedding or linen, most of the other countries we passed afterwards were never so happy as to have had them. And, indeed, for our lying we had been pretty well weaned from beds before we got to Vienna, but afterwards clean straw grew a delicacy, and we were contented in a seven or eight days' journey every night to lie promiscuously among the rest of the creation, the tame beasts of cottage; and I assure my lord, when a barn or a cock-loft was found for our night's lodging, we thought ourselves fortunate that night. Out of Moravia we went into the kingdom of Bohemia, and stayed at Prague two days. This is one of the biggest cities I ever saw. The country is a mighty fine one, a rich soil and full of silver and copper mines, some of which they still work, but with pains and expense little more than equivalent. I need not describe to your lordship how miserable the people are, after I tell you the number of Jesuits that are amongst them. In Prague they reckon about 2000. I leave your lordship to reflect on the condition of this poor place under this swarm of such vermin, by the trial we have had lately of a few of them only amongst us. Your lordship may imagine, perhaps, the ill-condition we had been in if fallen into their hands, for this country was their conquest from an established strict profession of the pure Protestant religion. From Bohemia we went to Dresden, but the Elector of Saxony's court having come from thence (where its chief residence is) to Derplitz, a little town within the Emperor's dominions in Bohemia, where the Elector had come to take the waters and baths, we went thither first, and from thence we came to Dresden, in Saxony, which belongs to that Elector, and one of the prettiest towns I ever saw, in the fineness of its situation and the gentleness of its building. The palace afforded me noble sights. But it is for Berlin, the Elector of Brandenburg's Court, that since I have spoken of places I should, speaking rather but a word on all the rest, have reserved a side for this, where greatness and goodness meet to such a degree in the persons of the Elector and his Princess, where, with so much policy, power, martial discipline, and temper, and amidst such splendour and magnificence, there reigns so much justice, sincerity, and virtue, in a manner I thought unknown at a Court. It may very well, indeed, come into competition with any Court of Europe after Versailles for state and majesty ; for the extent of his dominions and the number of his forces are as great as those of some crowned heads. The countries that the Emperor possessed were esteemed not more considerable than his before these late conquests in Hungary. The troops of the Elector are certainly the best soldiers in the Empire. Nor was it without malice that they were so exposed at the siege of Buda ; and there was more in it than the common politics of throwing the greatest dangers on allies. These were Protestants and such as now they find zealous for the interest of their fellows. They have been instrumental in our delivery by their union with our King when Prince of Orange, who had in his service some of their best men, that were lent him for the glorious expedition. They have generously broken with the French without hearing of any propositions for their private interest and advantage. They have already this year had an encounter, in which they cut off handsomely eight or nine hundred, a beginning that I hope will soon be followed by more considerable advantages when England is able to do its part on the common enemy. The Elector was extremely kind to me. He had me at his table with him the three days which he kept me there above the single day I had designed for that place, because resolved to redouble my pace. This was because our reports were that there would be a dispute yet on our continent, which I should be sorry to be absent from now so near home if it should happen, as God prevent, and which I am now satisfied will not be, nor the dispute so long in Ireland, till I arrive in my country, as I am coming with all speed, and hope to be there in twelve days. I was persuaded to wait here one post by the assurance that I should hear it then confirmed that a convoy of two or three men-of-war were set sail for this place, which I should have embraced as a happy occasion : and might have set me in four or five days from hence in England with safety, through the seas that are not yet cleared of the French pirates.

To-morrow I go for Amsterdam. It will be, in spite of my teeth, an eight days' journey. When I am there I have but a little arm of sea to cross and I am with your lordship. I am forced, notwithstanding the leisure I have had to write this long letter, to end abruptly, for my time has betrayed me. So let me only entreat your lordship and my mother, with my usual fervency, to believe that still, with all love, sincerity, and affection, I am, and must be to my last breath, your dutiful son,

A. ASHLEY.

My love from your lordship's own mouth and my mother's to my brothers and sisters, with your interests in them to persuade them that I am their kind affectionate brother.

I will beg your lordship leave to present here my services to Mr. Williams. I had intended him a letter of the same size with your lordship's here, but I am surprised with the post hour that hurries me away with this.

———

TO HIS FATHER.

ST. JONE.'S, *July*, 1689.

In my brother Maurice's concern I am to tell your lordship, that the result of my continual search, inquiry, and farther study, and of my advising with those able men that were mentioned in your hearing, and of others in the same capacity, is to confirm me in my own sentiments on this occasion, which I, in short, did explain before your lordship and my mother. And since I shall be here obliged to reduce it into a little order, I will beg your lordship's attention.

Here is a young man (which title only his stature and growth would give him), come to that age that should be called his years of discretion. To make him a scholar he has been entirely committed to the breeding of a school. For the sake of this, all other advantages have been quitted or waived, except those that prepare and fit for company and conversation, and that of the outward carriage—the arts both of body and mind that are necessary to admittance amongst the better rank of people, and such improvements as were not practically to be given him at that college, or could be expected should grow up with him there. Yet, indeed, to such a measure are they here lost, and into such a contrary extreme do we find him fallen, as would make one hesitate, whether so dearly one would have even purchased what was expected. But then, all that which is called good breeding is not only totally lost in him, but the end for which these advantages have been has advisedly been neglected; that part, that main part, I should call it, of his education, for which all the rest have been purposely omitted, this is failed and has come as yet to nothing. The seven improving years of his life have been sacrificed at Winchester, and all given up for Latin and Greek, and he is so far from understanding the first that he can neither make nor construct a sentence; besides that, in any other sort of reading he has no manner of tincture, sure, nor, as your lordship saw, can he be brought to relish so much as a piece of Sir Walter Raleigh, or your English Chronicle, a life in Plutarch, or any such pleasant and easy story. Why, then, your lordship sees that from all that is necessary, so everything that may be called a want in a young gentleman's education, all is entirely lost in him, and he is utterly a stranger thereto. There is nothing left to be lost in him, unless he were to be brought to lose some ill qualities that have grown up in the void that others have left, for here has been an acquisition indeed. It is impossible but some example should lead him; a very young life is formed after it, and there is but the good and the bad, so if the first be forsaken, the consequence you know. Besides that, at Winchester[1] I can tell your lordship it is only those that study and are diligent, and scarcely they, too, that escape that mother vice of drinking —the predominant of the place; where the punishment of it would be worse than insignificant among the scholars unless the reformation were made, or began at least, amongst the

[1] This description of the school at Winchester by Lord Ashley has an increased interest because he had himself previously attended it.

reformers, for whilst the example remains amongst the superiors, I leave any one to judge of what efforts the correction of it is likely to prove amongst the youth. However, I should not desire to speak this out to your lordship, for I should be loth to draw Winchester College about my ears for telling these tales out of school, but your lordship has heard, I believe, what that so much esteemed Bishop of Oxford said of their sister, New College—that Palmer was the only sober man of it; though, for my own part, I think his lordship might have spared his reflection, for I believe the numbers were little more than proportionable through most of the other colleges.

But not to go from my matter, I will tell your lordship that as to my brother, my fears are that all the evil he has acquired in his conversation is not only clownishness, nor a practice of idleness, that worst habitude he has contracted. Without examining him too severely, or relating what particularly I have observed or have been informed of, I would only offer to your lordship to reflect on the change of his temper from what it was a year or two ago. Whether that perfect good nature, that trusty sincere plain dealing, disinterest and without craft, and that benign bookish temper, whether all this has continued in him. Where are all the marks of those mighty improvements that must have been produced in him, if it had continued but in any measure ? Whether or not your lordship finds that there be now in his temper some contraries too observable; something of a surliness and a rugged conversation, not so open, free, or true-hearted, or so free from design, pique, and little equivocation and trick ; and whether all the bookish inclinations have not had a severe check in him. When one sees now these years that by the computation of the time were to have produced such a different one, so great a change of nature as this cannot have been worked but with the corruption of his mind, and by untoward notions that have got into him by the means of his idle company, that have been able to get such a victory over a natural temper. This is the briefest account I can make your lordship of my brother Maurice's condition. If it be a just one, and that by what pains I have given myself I conceive it rightly, I should then be capacitated to give a right judgment of what remains in this case to be done for his good. If a physician be able to advise when he thoroughly understands the nature of the distemper, I could wish truly it were in this case that is now my employment, as the proverb makes it in theirs, that a disease once known is half cured, as then, I will venture to say, I should have made a very fair progress before this time.

The first distinction one would make in the education of a younger brother in respect of his fortune in this world is by what must serve to one of the two distinctions of gownsman or swordsman. Under the first denomination come all that have a dependence on or relation to either law or divinity; under the other all that have the same regard to the court or camp. The latter have so near a relation to one another that whatever need the first stands in, so of the other, as in the camp there is little success to be expected in matters of advancement, but by the means of the Court; and a good soldier shall do but little in the raising himself if he be a bad courtier.

The sea-breeding I bring not in here, for if I were to do it I must enlarge upon my distinctions; and that of a merchant will not come under this, as I have set it, being neither properly a gownsman nor swordsman, nor has any education necessary to prepare him for his trade but a good hand and arithmetic, for languages he learns with his trade in his apprenticeship. The expensive education of an academic is just for that of a swordsman for court or camp, and destructive and ruinous in regard of all other education I have named. Schools, first, and then Universities and Inns of Court, are the beaten roads of those advancements that belong to the second part of the division. And for Latin, besides the accomplishment of gentlemen, it is absolutely necessary to every considerable station and almost every office (except within the camp), as well in the pulpit, as on the Bench. This one single, easy, pleasant language has been the stumbling block in my brother's fortunes, and this must be got over by my brother Maurice, or he must do as my brother John, and apply either to sea-serving or to merchant's affairs.

Now, till he has his Latin, neither the University nor Inns of Court are for him. How to do then for this Latin. Try him at the old place? Let him in for his other seven years? Or,

which would be just as profitable, set him to another school, as
my brother John was when just in his circumstances ? At home
with a governor to himself or a whole college of them, if he
were to have them, would be still worse than all this. Then
here comes the difficulty—whither will you send him ? And to
state more than a difficulty (for I look upon it as an impossibility), how will you then order it, with good assurance of his
advantage and safety, to place him out without the expense of
one person to himself, that must overlook and must be able to
give an account of every hour of his diversions as well as of
his studies ? Without which I shall apprehend him to be but
slightly prepared against the dangers that threaten him, and
shall conceive but faintly how this Latin is likely to be got down
with him. I must own to your lordship I think this but
exposing him to a quicker and more certain ruin to send him
anywhere from you into the world, but under the guard of one
that you can confide in and one that has a capacity and industry
to get him the quickest over his Latin into the other parts of
learning that but by this he is not capable of. There is no
course you can put him in that you can have any hopes of his
doing well in, or that one can dare advisedly trust him to,
without this. Therefore, that which came originally and purely
from your lordship, and what I have since so maturely considered, I cannot but applaud our happiness ; that a person
should be immediately offered, one of whose integrity and worth
I can say more of than of any man's, as I know him better than
I can say I know any man, and one in whom that character
above required is so fully verified, and one that I can now
oblige to undertake this work that so nearly concerns both me
and my family.

There remains now the determination of what place you
will send him to, where Mr. Denoune [1] may be helped by the
greatest advantage and freed from the greatest obstacles in this
work. I have already named beyond sea to your lordship, so

---

[1] Mr. Daniel Denoune, whom Lord Ashley here recommends as a
tutor for his brother Maurice, had been his own companion in the Con-
tinental travel from which he had so recently returned. He was a
Scotchman, and is described by the Fourth Earl as a " very ingenious,
honest person."

that I need not cautiously prepare you to receive the thing without surprise. But I will tell in short only: that there a governor's authority over him, his power and influence on him, will be much greater than it is possible it should be here. He has him there in a world where he can only follow him as he leads, and begins with ¡him upon a new bottom. There he will be removed from the danger of his flatterers, his companions equally (in age, I mean, far have they been from that in quality), his familiars and all that sort of gang, the efforts of which kind of society, as they are usually, so they will be in him: an aversion to his learning, a pleasure and a habitude in idleness, which is soon followed by things that are worse; then a disregard of his true interest and improvement, and a contempt of his influence and his precepts.

To this I will add that at Utrecht, which is the place I would for the present send him, they will live cheaper than they can in England, and, besides, the neatness and pleasantness and healthiness of the place; the better degree of the people are very gentle. It has also one of the finest universities that is, where he will have before his eyes another example than is at either of ours, and here at this University Mr. Denoune was and hath taken his doctor's degree. But I have spent my spirits as well as my paper, and have only enough left of such to tell your lordship and my mother that I am your dutiful son,

A. ASHLEY.

---

## TO MR. TAYLOR, OF WEYMOUTH.

ST. G.'s, *February 16th*, 1689-90.

Sir,—After my acknowledgments and thanks to Sir John M. for the concern he showed for my interest on the report of my standing, I think myself particularly obliged to pay them in no small measure to yourself, Sir John having imparted to me the considerations you had for me.

I think I may say, and doubt not but it will appear within some time, that it was not on ill grounded reasons that I took the resolution which I owned at the first news of the Parliament's

Dissolution,[1] not to stand for this next; though at present I can do nothing more than protest to you and those other of my friends who designed me for one of their representatives, that it has been grounded on considerations and principles far opposite to the want of zeal in my country's service, whatever may be otherwise thought of me by some who know me not well, nor will yet a while know my reasons. When the message came to me hither from you I was then gone into Wiltshire to prevent some gentlemen, who were able to have promoted my interest there towards being a member of this Parliament, supposing my intentions had been to have stood for it. And since, by having been absent at that time, I lost that occasion of returning my acknowledgments, I will desire the favour of you to acquit me to the Mayor and those other of the Corporation who have so voluntarily obliged me, and to assure them from me that had not I before taken and declared my resolution, I should now meet their offers with greater satisfaction than any others whatsoever, and as indeed they are a greater invitation to me than anything besides; so I repine more on this account that I am so necessarily obliged not to stand at all for this Parliament. But that, however, I live in no small hopes of showing them (at some time) the desire I have, and the preference I give to their particular service as well as that of being not unworthy of the esteem they have shown to have for me.

I ought to reserve something yet more particular for yourself in respect of your worthy sentiments for our family, through the memory of my grandfather, which has been a thing so almost universally ungratefully dealt with in this nation that I mark the vindication of it in any one more as a noble instance of generosity than of kindness to myself. But as for this, I only hope that by Sir John M.'s means, or some other way, I may ere

[1] Parliament was dissolved on the 27th January, 1690, and a new one was summoned to meet on the 20th of March. Although Lord Ashley was still a minor, he would have been eligible to a seat in the House of Commons, as it was not until 1696 that an Act (7 and 8 William III, c. 25, § 8) was passed disqualifying minors from election. He preferred, however, to devote several years to private study, and did not therefore enter Parliament until 1695, when he was returned as a member for Poole.

long have the occasion to be well acquainted with you, at which time I doubt not but to show you fully what I now assure you of, that I am, sir, your most obliged friend and humble servant,

A. A.

———

TO JOHN LOCKE.

St. Jones's, *January the* 21*st*, 1692.

Mr. Locke,—I write to you in a cover purposely, that you may be assured I mean not this as a letter, or give it to you for such; therefore I could find in my heart to take no notice at all that I had received any letter from you, as I did a post ago.

Indeed, were I now otherwise in every respect well fitted to write, I should by this one thing be hindered from saying anything either agreeable or diverting, or in any measure answerable to the least part of what you have written. You may know that that which is here meant is the matter enclosed, of which I spoke to you when last with you, and some time before.

The subject of it you may allow to me to be a melancholy one, therefore I beg you excuse me here for anything farther, only let me have your advice the soonest you can, and about his[1] and my brother's[2] coming over, each of them on their several accounts—the one that of his health, the other that of his education. You know all the circumstances that relate to each, and without troubling you to give your reasons, I should be glad to hear only your determination in that point particularly.

I beg I may be remembered to my lady,[3] as one who has all the respect for her in the world.—Dear Mr. Locke, I am entirely yours, Ashley.

[Address: To Mr. Locke, at Sir Francis Masham's, at Oates.]

———

[1] Mr. Denoune, the tutor.     [2] Maurice Ashley.

[3] Lady Francis Masham was the brilliant and devoted friend of John Locke. She was a daughter of Dr. Ralph Cudworth, the Cambridge theologian and moralist, and the second wife of Sir Francis Masham, a country gentleman, who resided at Oates, in Essex. In their home Locke lived from 1691 until his death in 1714.

## TO JOHN LOCKE.

*3rd March,* 1692.

Do not expect, sir, that I should thank you for all your compliments to me on my coming of age.[1] It was no more than what I needed to make me relish the pleasure of that circumstance at that time, as I should do, and so as a man in reason should be supposed to have the means to do, if he have not hard luck indeed. I tell you I could not have abated you one ace of a compliment, since only those of your fashioning, amongst so many others as I have had, are only able to give me the least liking of myself. The rest, as extraordinary as I can assure you they have been, have not yet been able so much as to make me not repine at the having left behind me three such lovely years as are counted by our young men from eighteen to this age, and by the women a little under at the same proportion from sixteen to the confines of twenty, which begins to sound sadly, and which is a kind of a summer solstice where motion is stopped, or at least rendered imperceptible for some while. But to tell you a plainer reason yet than this why I do not think myself obliged to you for your compliments, it is because they were due to me. And on what score, think you ? I'll tell you instantly. But in the meantime now, were I but to know the truth, what a fine turn should I see here on a sudden in your opinion ! What pretty things are you thinking of this vain creature that devours compliments at a rate that never was heard of ! Say seriously, do you not begin to wish you had given them slower and with a little more deliberation ? I warrant you yes. . . . But not to frighten you more than is convenient, nor to punish your rashness too dreadfully, I'll tell you then in what sense it is that I say all these compliments were no more than due to me. Thus it is. You forsooth had forestalled all my happiness and anticipated all the joy that I was to have conceived by right in the day of my manhood. You used me like one that should tell me the plot of a play, or the latter end of a romance, in the middle of it, and so spoil the conclusion, where the pleasure is to be. You were used to treat me

[1] Lord Ashley was born February 26th, 1671, and consequently became of age in February, 1692.

at that rate, dealt with me so like a friend in every strictest relation, seemed to seek my company for my company's sake, and conferred with me upon subjects as though you were really better for not being alone. Now, all this from one like you, from a man so unvulgar as you, I leave anybody of good sense to judge if it were not enough to put any young fellow beside himself, who had his vanity turned the way that mine ever was; and if this were not fully enough to make him miscount himself a man before his time. Thus had you seasoned me so as to leave me not the least matter to raise joy out of; but enough to have answered any of my congratulations with the least feature of gladness, or with any mark of satisfaction on my side. But that in consideration I suppose of the wrong you had done me, this letter of yours came most seasonably, and just made amends by giving me some additional pleasure at that time above what was ordinary; which otherwise I could not have had upon my own score, and by giving me some good thoughts of myself that I never had before. For I think I might say that if other people by their compliments could have made me apprehend myself something that was above a mere boy; you by yours could make me imagine myself something beyond a common man such as now pass in the world for such. So, ending with the same continued air of vanity with which I began, in which, however, you have the chief hand, I rest just as I was, for if I could be, I would be more, your constant friend and faithful servant,

ASHLEY.

Monr. La Treille has come out of Mr. Vain's family some time, and is now with us here in town, where I never fail to see him once a day. I have room now to say none of those compliments you pretend, only my plain humble service to my lady. Sir John Cropley is yours. I know not how to send for the puppy. Let me know.

---

## TO JOHN LOCKE.

LONDON, *March the 26th,* 1691 [2].

MR. LOCKE,—I am sorry that my brother's arrival with poor Mr. Denoun should have given me such business as has hindered me writing to you the last post or two upon the subject

W

you wrote me; and that my sudden journey into the country with him and the business I have now to despatch should here hinder me from writing what I would do and from speaking my sentiments on this head as distinctly as I would do had I more time. I should have done very ill indeed to have left you in suspense ever so little a while; but that I did not, for Mr. Clerk assured me he would inform you again more particularly what were my thoughts and resolution, and what my power was in the matter. All that I shall here say is, that I desire you, as to what relates to me, to think that in the honour (I mean the fidelity and justice) of the family, you have now a full assurance of whatever you could have assurance of before, and that your security is as good for whatever my grandfather,[1] in the name of his family, has signified a promise of. During my life, therefore, and whilst I am master of any proportion of what was his, you have that to your interest that is equivalent to what you could have were he (as I wish him) alive. And for what is to come after my life, I shall take all the care you can expect, and that you now propose, that you may have security yet farther. I can now indeed do nothing, for I have nothing; and I, who hold all by bounty and courtesy, cannot plead or ask a stronger tie for another's interest than that which I must be contented with for my own. So that if there be a danger for you should all pass into the hands of him that is next to me without stopping ever any part of it in mine, it is a danger which all my power cannot divert from you, for I can do no more hereafter than now or heretofore, if I come never to possess or hold anything from my godfather more than I do now or have heretofore.

I need not say I wish for you, after what I have said, because it is plainly no more than wishing for myself, as much at least as that by the order of nature I may enjoy a heritage after those who had place and were born before me, and before those who are after and were born since me. I can say that this occasion has taught me to go farther in wishing than I used to do: for considering myself only, those matters are so indifferent to me that I never make any wish at all about them.

[1] The First Earl of Shaftesbury had bestowed upon Locke in 1674 an annuity of £100 a year for life.

In concluding, I only tell you that I hope you will be so far from doubting of me in what honour would call me to perform, that you will rather expect from me much more yet in all concerns than what that merely would oblige me to in your behalf. Since you are sure of such a place in my friendship (if I may use such a big-looked phrase) as I think scarce any can have besides yourself, which may make you compute always with a right estimate how much and after what rate I am your friend and servant, ASHLEY.

In deep earnest I here warn you that if (as you threaten) you renounce a certain office that you some time since assumed for me and acquitted yourself faithfully of (viz., that of the conveyance of my respects and services to Lady Masham), I solemnly renounce all friendly offices for you and all the fine things I ever said. Therefore pray do something extraordinary this time to atone.

### TO JOHN LOCKE.

RICHMOND, 7*th July*, 1692.

MR. LOCKE,—The giving characters of people is, in my opinion, not only a very dangerous undertaking, but a task, too, of some labour and hardship, when besides the strict consideration of the person spoken of, so much must be had in relation to the persons addressed, and that after one has formed one's own judgment with much pains, there is still so much remaining in the nicety that there must be in delivering of it to others, who perhaps have such different notions and understand even the same things so differently from what one's self does. But I have not this part of the trouble with you which I should have with others, and since you desire of me to write you of Mr. La Treille's [1] character, I can say well enough what is necessary in the little time that I have here allowed me, since it is you that inquire.

You well know what it is that reconciles me to the acquaintance and friendship of such as I chance to meet with in the world: when I find in any one a concern for somewhat

---

[1] A tutor evidently desired by Mr. Locke for young Masham.

more in nature than what is merely called oneself, or has
immediate relation to it; and that they carry their reason
free and open, with no excepted places, which endure no
examination and that will not bear the calling in question;
the first is good nature, the other is good sense.   It being
my luck to find as much as this in the gentleman now mentioned,
with that which I esteemed a good insight into what should
or did employ mankind, and a good understanding (as I thought)
in what was best and most satisfactory of all that (by which
I understand that which frames and polishes society).   By this
means I grew into his acquaintance and gained that habit of
conferring reason with him, and looking together often into
those things that molested or benefited mankind and ourselves;
that from this commerce he became to me one of those whom
I most acceptably saw and loved chiefly to converse with in
writing or discourse, which I have almost constantly done with
him this year or two as hardly with any so besides.   How
far this may be a bias in my judgment of him in other parts
and in relation to other things, I cannot say myself; but would
wish you to view as narrowly as possible, that if I deceive
myself I may not at least deceive you, or others by you.

As to his being a governor for a young man, all I can say is
that I have thought him so much the fittest of any I knew (and
you know what a general acquaintance I have had occasion
to have in that form of men), that when I expected my ,brother
should have been left without a governor, by the loss of poor
Mr. Denoun (my long acquaintance and former fellow-traveller),
I then designed Mr. La Treille, if he had been free, for that place,
not balancing at all between him and any other.   He is extremely
well versed in humanity, and is in my opinion an extremely
good judge in all polite learning and in the politer manners and
customs of the world, though I understand not by that the
particular way that some men have of setting themselves off,
which depends not so much on experience or insight, as in a
happy constitution that breeds assurance, the possession or want
of which does more than can be imagined almost in the opinion
we beget of ourselves in others.   I know not what disadvantage
it may be reckoned to Mr. La Treille, the having left him the
perfect use but of one eye.   I did not myself reckon upon it

more than as a danger to himself, he having nothing for reserve, and the running double the risk of becoming blind by any accident that another man runs, who has both eyes well and has another in store if any mischance happen to one. For with what he has at present he does things (and even those that require greatest accuracy of sight, as in writing and reading) more perfectly than I can do with what I have got of sight more than he. Having told you these particulars, you, or indeed any one, may draw my judgment of what remains as to his integrity, temper, and all of that kind. For how should I stand thus with him, if I were not persuaded myself that he had of that kind what was better than was ordinarily met with? So I need say no more, only I should add indeed that I never knew any such success, above once or twice in my life, in the teaching of a young body as I have known in Mr. La Treille: and for the matter of overcoming that mighty giant language, with youth, the Latin. Nor is there any great mystery there to wonder at, when a man has diligence and good humour, and only dares but to contradict the precepts of some, whose trade is teaching, by postponing certain abstract notions those gentlemen have framed on language, not very aptly calculated, I imagine, to young heads, till such a time as they are a more natural and speedier way made masters of the language they learn: at which time it is easy for them in one fortnight to understand (as much as they are ever to be understood) all the parts of that science.

I do not speak this without living instance myself; for this you know was what, after eight years in a free school (and that one of the best, too—Winchester), recovered a brother of mine in two years afterwards from knowing hardly anything at all of any language but his country's, to be master completely of more than one language, besides other things that took up much time in the while. But I have run on here I know not how. How shall I excuse myself? 'Tis to Mr. Locke I write. That is truly a very natural excuse, for it is the real reason; and there is nothing surer than that I should have served nobody else so. But is not this very injurious, that when you know how little guilty I am of long letters to other people, you should be the single person for whom I become tedious?—I here say nothing for myself, but that I am very much yours,          ASHLEY.

## TO JOHN LOCKE.

LONDON, *the 6th*, 1693.

MR. LOCKE,—I have stayed now, this night, to the utmost hour of the post that I might give you, if I could, a positive assurance of my coming by Tuesday's coach. But having had no answer yet from those whom I expected this night in town to end my business, and there being therefore yet no places taken, I cannot possibly conclude as I would. However, that you may see what concern I take in this affair, I resolve to pronounce it now to you, *that I will come;* and unless by a messenger on purpose you hear on Monday that something has made it impossible, Mr. Popple and I shall be ready on Tuesday to be taken up by you where the coach sets us down.

I have no time to say anything farther. You will have no reason to remind me more of my word. I am sure already I have acted beyond it. Not only an extraordinary regard and service for you, but a zeal somewhere else, inspires me to do things beyond what I am only obliged to by a promise. Let that be the chief part of the return you make me, to represent that zeal as well as you think it deserves. And if you let my Lady Masham know with what respect I always think of her, it will be the way to make me, if possible, with farther obligation than I have, your sincere friend and humble servant,

A. ASHLEY.

If Sir Francis Masham be at Oates, I beg my very humble service.

---

## TO JOHN LOCKE.

ST. GILES'S, 28*th May*, 1694.

I ought to be extremely satisfied with anything that I have done, or any accident happening, that should be the occasion to me of receiving any letter from you more than I should have done. And I ought to be more than ordinarily satisfied with any such thing at this time; since, as my concerns have disposed of me, I am not likely for a long time to receive any pleasure or advantage of an acquaintance that I know so well how to value, except only what is of this kind. I have too little hopes of seeing you here, ever to talk of them, till I have better encouragement from you, or fresh ground from my own circumstances to press you upon it. And without this I have nothing else to depend upon but the hearing from you, since I shall hardly now be able to see you, I know not when, in town, and far less at a certain place [1] besides that I have been at, which, though not so big, is worth a thousand such towns. I wish I deserved the character you give me, and could willingly flatter myself upon what you say of me; but that I should make your opinion of me yet more groundless, and have no sort of worth at all, if, for as much as lay in me, I suffered you to continue so much deceived. And were it not that I should only look affected in what I said, and so give you occasion to say more of a kind that I am apt to like too well, I would honestly show you that I was not, nor could be, of that consideration or worth in the world which you make me to be. If, such as I am, I prove to be yet rather better than several of our *patrician blood*, I am sorry for them, and for the commonwealth I live in, that it should be so bad with them. The comparison indeed seems to give me some advantage: but what it can amount to, I very well know is only, not as if I should do more good, but a little less mischief in the world than might be expected from one of that number I make.

I could wish too (for I find you have set me a-wishing) that in this absence my letters were able to give you that satisfaction you seek in them, and could be worth the esteem you place upon them. For my own part, I know myself to be, in this province of society (if I may use such an expression), so very unapt a creature, and so little able to sustain a part, that I should be ashamed to invite any ordinary person, and much less you, to come into so unfair, so unequal a party; nor could I be pleased with myself that I had designedly engaged you in a commerce where there would be nothing reciprocal, and oftenest a mere load and trouble sent in exchange for an advantage and an entertainment. Indeed in another sort of commerce I never apprehended so much as this. In free conversation, by the advantages of being face to face, the suiting and timing of

[1] Oates.

things, and a great many helps besides, one may be, with a little plain sense and a good deal of honesty, not only of some use, but entertaining enough in the way of friendship. But I, who am never very well satisfied with what I speak, should be very sorry to be obliged, for an agreeable present made me, to return so bad a one as a bundle of such thought as mine, and an essay of my own, of such a genius, such invention, such a style as mine.— I find, if I go on, I shall do as bad as what I pretend to be displeased with. I will only say one thing more, which I am but seldom displeased with saying, and never but pleased with solidly showing, that I am your sincere friend and humble servant,

A. ASHLEY.

## TO JOHN LOCKE.

ST. GILES'S, *September 8th*, 1694.

MR. LOCKE, — Neither my business, nor diversions, nor studies, which you mention, are, or can be, such as hinder me from reflecting often, and as I ought, on the advantage I have in being thought of, as you tell me I am, at Oates. My businesses and diversions do not take me up as they were used; nor are they followed by me with that heat which with other people they generally are; nor am I any one hour so much in them as not to have my mind much more elsewhere than upon them, having got a business into my head which by nobody else is looked upon *as a business,* but with me is instead of all other business and diversion, *that of learning how to be an honest man and a friend.* Other people may be born to these qualities. It is my misfortune to be such as that I cannot but esteem thought, exercise, and a continual application to be necessary in this case for me.

You may imagine that I can hardly be so much as I speak of employed in this, and not have those people in my thoughts whom I am forced to distinguish from the rest of the world whenever I think upon the subjects of friendship, worth, and love of virtue and of mankind. As for my studies, since they all lie towards this business that I speak of, all that I learn by them, or chiefly strive to learn, is, what mankind has been heretofore in former ages, and under former revolutions, that

I may guess the better at what they are, and may be expected to be, in such a turn of an age and time as is this present one. The poor stock of knowledge which I pick up is all about this single matter. Other notions than what are of this odd kind I have not to communicate to you, which you desire of me, as if I could have any that were of any worth to you. And as for what my notions are, which in this way I gain, I must beg your pardon for not communicating them. I might whisper them in your ear, perhaps, or I might venture to trust another person [1] near you with the impertinence of them, but they are not at all fit for writing, nor to come in the way of other people. They are either too ridiculously absurd, or too odiously true.

We have a refined, polite, and a delicious age; whatever opposes what is established here is rude, barbarous, deformed; and whatever has a contrary taste is contemptible. The standard of good sense, of manners, pleasure, virtue, everything is here. I acquiesce, being very safe in this: that whatsoever is thought, or not thought, concerning me in this adored age, and by the adored people in it, is likely to give me no great disturbance, which saves a man a great deal of pains, if one considers what employment this gives to other people. I would not have you think that this, which I have said so perfectly by chance, was said to place a mark of distinction upon the concern I show for your friendship and good opinion, nor to give an advantage to my way of receiving the favours of another person, which I pretend to know so well how to value.

Whether I think little or think much of what is or ever may be said of me, in a city or a court, amongst great people or a crowd, this I am certain of: that I think very much upon how I am and how I may be thought of at Oates, and it is no small part of the aim and business of my present life to keep and deserve that esteem I have got there, and to be more and more that which I am taken for, when I am well looked upon by those that are there. It is not, as you imagine, so new a thing to me, or what I want so much to be acquainted with, how I am several times thought of and in the good opinion of the lady of the house. I have vanity enough to keep alive the remem-

[1] Lady Masham.

brance of what was once made to appear to me of that kind, and
to count upon it. I hardly need any new intimation of it,
though I can never hear of it so often as not to receive pleasure
every time. The marks I have already had of that esteem long
since has put it out of my power to doubt of it, because I am so
well persuaded that whatever that person would seem to be, they
really are; and that any other part is unnatural to them, as
much as it is with other people not to say, upon every occasion
of that kind, much more than they think, which is one of the
chief reasons why I so much value everything in them, and
receive everything from thence with that regard. Though any
other body in my place would find out many more reasons that
would make a greater show than mine, and I am even satisfied
that in the real judgment of the world I should undervalue
my Lady Masham with my respect if I should say fully in what
manner it was grounded. Goodness and sincerity, and a great
many other things of that kind, would sound just as well as
good nature and simplicity; and I am afraid if I should speak
about a value for religion, and such thoughts about it and about
the liberty of mankind as I have known in my Lady Masham,
I should hardly be able to give it any turn that would make me
excusable to this age for commending a lady in that manner.
See what a hardship I am placed under, in my respect for one
that I can never think I show enough for, when at any time
I would endeavour to show a part!

But I have another more just exclamation to make, which
is: how horridly tedious I grow! This is a fault my pen has,
worse yet a great deal than ever I discovered of my tongue,
and therefore I am forced to use it more slenderly. I beg you
to excuse me this time, and wish that of all this you were to
read no more than that I present my humble service to my
Lady Masham, and that I am, with a great deal of sincerity,
your friend and humble servant,				A. ASHLEY.

My father[1] is in a very good way of recovery, though he
yet keeps his bed. My brother[2] presents you with his very
humble service. I should be extremely glad if you would
send the book which my Lady Masham has given me to

---

[1] The second Earl of Shaftesbury.		[2] Maurice Ashley.

Wheelock,[1] in town, that he may send it to me hither, for I earnestly desire it as soon as possible.

I write this post to Wheelock, who is in town, to be sure to have that ready which you spoke for. I hope soon to be in that method that you shall never need to give yourself again the trouble of speaking or writing a word on that account.

---

### TO JOHN LOCKE.

LONDON, *November* 29*th*, 1694.

MR. LOCKE,—I know not whether it will be possible for me to wait on my Lady Masham and visit you this season; but this I am sure of, I cannot possibly have more desire to do it than I already have. I needed nothing to convince me that what good I was able to do in the world, was better and more worthily bestowed in serving a person or two, like some that live but in a corner of Essex, than in serving a crowd of such people as are now making the great ado that is made in the world, and whom I am now in the midst of, as my ill fortune has ordered it. The greatest part of what I do in the world is not because I hope anything, but because I think I must be doing. I can assure you I do not act out of any friendship to the age, or to mankind, such as they are at present. Were there no principle to engage me to serve them, besides their own merit, besides their characters, besides the opinion I had of them, and the esteem I bore them, upon my word it would fare ill with them for anything I were ever likely to do in their behalf, though in ever so pressing an occasion. I fancy that I am not apt to make to myself too flattering a picture of the world. And I believe that whatever this public that you talk of is like to have of my service, it will never have over much of my respect; nor shall I be apt to fall into any gross errors on that account. All I know is, that there are some whom I have a real respect for; and if I were now at liberty to do what respect and inclination most led me to, I should quickly show my forwardness to accept of the invitation that is made me.

[1] John Wheelock, steward at St. Giles's.

If you believe my sincerity in this, you will make my excuse for me; if otherwise, all I can say besides will signify nothing whilst I am kept here, and can do no more than write. But I have more confidence in you than this comes to, for if you know this it is enough (and that I cannot doubt of) that I am, very sincerely, your real friend and humble servant,

A. ASHLEY.

## TO THOMAS STRINGER.[1]

LONDON, *February the 15th,* 1695 [*N.S.* 1696].

I will not trouble you any farther now, nor, indeed, have I time. We have got a bill to be engrossed, which lays an incapacity on the elector (as the late-passed Act does on the elected) in case of corruption, meat, drink, &c., and which obliges the Knights of the shire to have £500 a year, or the inheritance of it, as freehold within the county, and a Burgess £200 a year somewhere at least in England on the same terms. You could, I believe, scarcely imagine with yourself who these are in the world, or who they are in the House, who oppose this, and all other such bills as this, might and main; and who they are that are condemned for flying in the face of the Government, as they call it, by being for such things as these are, and pressing such hard things on the prerogative or court. In short, you would hardly believe that your poor friend that now writes to you has sentence (and bitter sentence too) every day passing upon him for going, as you may be sure he goes, and ever will go, on such occasions as these, whatever party it be that is in or out at Court, that is in possession of the places, and afraid of losing their daily bread by not being servile enough, or that are out of places, and think, by crossing the Court and siding with good and popular things against it, to get into those places of profit and management. No more. My kind service to Mrs. Stringer, and my service too to your son.—I am, your sincere friend, &c.,

A. ASHLEY.

[1] " His zeal in defence of liberty may be seen from his letter to Thomas Stringer, Esq., a gentleman who had held office [as attorney and secretary] under the Lord Chancellor Shaftesbury."—Birch.

## TO HIS MOTHER.[1]

*Beginning of* 1696.

MADAM,—Had it been my misfortune to have been led into a behaviour ever so unbecoming me, or to have given you never so just an occasion of offence, yet the consideration of that early time my faults must have been committed in, when I knew myself so little, and was of an age so little able either to judge or to act right; this, and the proofs your ladyship has since had of my entire submission and willingness to do anything that may regain me your favour, my earnest desire to mend whatever has been amiss, and to atone for whatever you may have judged me guilty of, or that I have failed—in all this, together with the application that has been made for me by all those here whom I have the happiness to be related to through you, and who have had the goodness all of them to plead my cause for me—this, I say, I might have expected would have been of sufficient weight to have inclined your ladyship towards me, and have gained for me, if not kindness and forgiveness, at least something in answer to that sincerely dutiful and humblest application I have been so long making to your ladyship.

But when I am as yet not conscious to myself of any one action, purely my own, and which I myself am answerable for, by which I have ever given your ladyship just offence, or knowingly committed anything against my duty, or that may have deservedly lost me anything of that exceeding great kindness and affection you were once pleased to show and profess for me—when I reflect on this, and find that after all I have done and what has been done on my behalf, you continue still the same to me, and your anger not at all lessened, so as to have either more charity towards me or more regard to my submission—this I confess is astonishing, but I must submit to what God pleases. I thank Him that he has been so merciful as to make me sensible of what it is to be a son, and what I am to do as such. I trust in Him that He may one day also give you the heart of a mother, and restore me to the good will

[1] Born Dorothy Manners, daughter of John, eighth Earl of Rutland.

and blessing of a parent. In the meantime, give me leave to renew again my offers of paying my duty and attendance with that submission I intend. If I may have permission, since there is nothing that I would not do, nor no private interest I would not sacrifice willingly to convince your ladyship, and to show all the world how much I am your ladyship's most humble, dutiful, and obedient Son.

## TO LORD RUTLAND. [1]

To my Uncle Rutland.                    *April,* 1696.

MY LORD,—I have been so long sensible of my unhappiness in lying under your lordship's ill opinion, that though I constantly endeavoured to make the best application I could to your lordship, in the offer of the most respectful duty and service, which I have continually preserved, yet I had not any encouragement at all to hazard the making my application this way to your lordship, or to hope that any letter might be favourably received. But now lately I have learned from some of your lordship's relations, that your lordship is inclined to have more favourable thoughts of me, and though I was refused when I made the offer of paying my duty the last year in waiting upon you and my mother, I have now hopes of renewing that offer, to be more kindly accepted.

If I had ever justly offended my mother, and had not atoned for and repented of so ill an action, I might well deserve this or any mark of your lordship's displeasure. But I solemnly protest and can call God to witness that I know not as to that in what I have erred, and if I have erred, nobody can more sincerely repent of it and be willing to do more to deserve a pardon. Your lordship knows the application I have made to her, both by letter and otherwise, both myself and by relations, and your lordship knows how unsuccessful it has been with me. I must say I have done all I can do, till your lordship is pleased to tell me what more, for the rest of my mother's relations (whose direction I constantly follow) can tell me nothing further. It is hard for a son to

[1] John, 9th Earl of Rutland, born May 29th, 1638, created Duke, 29th March, 1703; and died 10th January, 1711.

answer for whatever happens of difference betwixt a father and a mother. I were unnatural if I did not do my utmost to reconcile it. But I can no more be responsible for my father towards my mother, than for my mother to my father, nor is one more under my power than the other. God forbid I should be able to say that either were subject to me. But in the most favourable sense I am far from deserving that that should be said for me as to my father, though it be not my business here to complain. But this I am sure of, that before my mother declared herself so incensed against me, I had more of that influence over her than ever I had, or can pretend to have, over my father. All that I can say is that I am not only ready to do but will rejoicingly do anything that can be told me, and shall count myself obliged for any such advice or assistance given me. Whatever I have in the world (and it is but lately that I could say I had anything) is at her service and always shall be; whilst I have anything she may command it, and where I have any power she may command me in anything. If nothing from me is able to prevail with her to think of her family, yet the case of my sisters I should hope might, who as to their coming up in the world, and what is necessary in that respect, are destitute of all manner of assistance and support, and can only receive it from my mother or some of her relations. I, for my own part, having no other service in my power to do for them besides what relates to their fortunes, in which I have done and shall do my best. I beg your lordship's pardon for this long trouble, and am with all respect your lordship's most

---

## TO HIS MOTHER.

*October* 10*th*, 1696.

Madam,—Though I have hitherto had so little success, yet I can never cease repeating what I have done so often before; nor can anything discourage me from making my application to your ladyship with the greatest humility. I can only say what I have done before; but what I shall now do with greater zeal if possible. If there be anything by which I may ever merit your favourable thought, or even regain your kindness, I humbly beg of you that you would let me know it. There is nothing upon earth that I can give, nothing that I can part with, nor nothing I can do which I shall repine at if it be a means to me to obtain that happiness. It is long since that I have said that I would no longer stand upon my justification in anything. If I have formerly done it, I beg you would forgive me that too, as well as whatever in my youth I may have offended in before I came to years of discretion, or to that sense of my duty to you which I thank God I now have. Had I had formerly at those years the same serious sense which I now have of what that duty is, I am confident I should have prevented your falling into displeasure with me, and never have given you the least of those occasions. They are now what I heartily mourn for, and call God to witness that if ever I become so happy as once again to be restored to your favour and affection, I shall count it above all I can gain in this world. And I doubt not but that if you could any way know my sentiments at this time, and know how great a change is in me, you would not only allow me what I so earnestly beg for (the leave to present myself to you and to appear before you), but you would receive me with the indulgence of a mother, and no longer think me an ill son, which I am sure I no longer am to you, whatever I may have been at any time before. It may I hope be some proof of this to tell your ladyship that I have done all I am able with my father, and have constantly spoken with all the earnestness that becomes me in your interest. I now know and am satisfied that there is no servant nor anything of that nature which he would not part with on the account of seeing you. I obtained it from him yesterday that he would give me leave to write to your ladyship and present his love and service with my own duty. It is this that has made me trouble your ladyship at this time, that I am now obliged to be going from hence immediately because of the Parliament.

If I may hope to hear in one line from your ladyship, or but in any letter to any of my aunts or relations in town, I shall be extremely thankful. I just hear you have been ill, but are better. I sincerely thank God for your recovery, and am with the greatest sincerity (and in the deepest sense of that misfortune I lie under), your ladyship's, &c.

## TO HIS MOTHER.

*November 14th,* 1696.

MADAM,—I have not only had the satisfaction of hearing from the report of some of my friends that your ladyship had more favourable thoughts of me, but I have now lately had the happiness to have an instance of it under your own hand in a letter which my Lady Chaworth was so kind as to communicate to me.

I do assure your ladyship that notwithstanding it may seem but little what your ladyship is pleased to show and allow in favour of me, yet I value and esteem it as abundant, and am abundantly thankful, and shall ever be so though I never receive more, which yet I hope to live to deserve, and until I do deserve will never ask. I shall never while I live attempt to justify myself on anything that has been formerly, and shall never claim the least regard from you but on the account of that entire submission which I profess, and of what I may hereafter perform.

I beg leave again and again to repeat this, that there is nothing in the world which I would not do to demonstrate the sincerity of that duty I profess, and that whatever I may have ignorantly done, or been led to do, at any time when I had little sense of anything, and at years in which I neither had nor could be said to have discretion, I have now another sense of what duty is, and of what becomes a son. There is no interest of mine anywhere which I shall not make submit to this, nor anything which I will not show you I am ready to do for the sake of this.

I return your ladyship my thanks, with all humility and grateful acknowledgment, that you are pleased to condescend to see me and suffer me to wait on you where you are. I had prevented my letter and waited on you that instant, but on the account of what holds me here and my obligation at this time to the service of the public. The first hour I can obtain leave and can get a discharge from hence I shall immediately pay that duty which I have so long zealously desired to do, and shall have the honour at the same time of waiting on my Lord Rutland and of paying that respect I owe.—I am, your, &c.

x

## TO JOHN LOCKE.

LONDON, *April 9th,* 1698.

You have been extremely kind in the trouble you have put yourself to on my account, for a Plutarch, which I have not yet received, but expect from Mr. Pauling, who has promised me to send it. I wish I could say I have had great need of it, and that I had been of late more conversant with the ancients and less with the people of this age. I am sure it had been better for myself, and for anything that I or any mere honest man is able to do in public affairs in such a generation as this. I think it would have been altogether as well for my country and mankind, if I had done nothing, so fruitless have my endeavours been, and so little profit arisen from those years I have entirely given from myself to the public, whilst in the main I myself grow good for nothing, but rather grow liker and liker to that sort whom I act with and converse amongst.

Neither is it without cause that a man may fear such an alteration in himself, when one sees such shipwrecks around one, and that many an honest man that has held out in former times, and endured storms, has been cast away in these happy times, when we expected virtue and honesty should have succeeded better than ever.

However, this is not by way of excuse for myself, or as preparing you for some new turn, for I hope I am still honest and shall keep so, which it may be I should not if I had followed even the very best examples and the advices of the very best friends. But if I have any honesty left, I owe to your good friend and mine, old Horace, and when I have heard of the wonderful things to be done for the public by coming into the court (as they call it), his words have sounded in my ear—

[1] Quia me vestigia terrent,
Omnia te adversum spectantia, nulla retrorsum.
[Because the footprints frighten me,
They all point towards you, none away from you.
—*Hor.,* Ep. II., 1, 7.]

But no more of this. I hope the time is not long ere I shall change the unprofitable and ungrateful study of these moderns of ours for a hearty application to the ancients, and then you shall, as you desire, hear enough from me concerning those.

My servant Wheelock went into the country for a fortnight, and left not money in town, or had it not. But I write to him this post to despatch it, and send me returns. I am glad to hear my Lady Masham is in town, that I may have the happiness to wait on her, and I am glad to find you keep where you are, though I lose your company yet a while.—I am, your sincere, humble servant, A. Ashley.

——

### TO MONS. PIERRE DESMAIZEAUX.[1]

St. Giles's, *August 5th*, 1701.

I received yours, which I had answered without delay but for the agreeable entertainment I had in reading your translation communicated to me. I take it extreme kindly of you to be in this or any other work of your leisure, and I shall be glad to give you all the assistance and encouragement I am able.

I have a general acquaintance (as you very well know) with most of our modern authors and free writers, several of whom I have a particular influence over. If the author of your translated treatise be one of these (as I verily believe he is), I can give you assurance of that assistance you require, and which will be a great addition by making the translation in effect another original.

In the meantime I cannot but exhort you to continue your work begun; which, by what I have seen hitherto, is indeed beyond any expectation I could have of a thing of like nature, and your own thought of sending it as a present to Mr. Bayle (to whom I cannot but fancy it will be agreeable) is a further

——

[1] Pierre Desmaizeaux (1673?—11 July, 1745) was a French Protestant, who took refuge on the revocation of the Edict of Nantes in Switzerland, and afterwards went to Holland. He became known to Bayle, who introduced him to Shaftesbury, whom in 1699 he accompanied to England. Here he engaged in diverse kinds of literary work. He published numerous books. Among those of a philosophical character he edited "A collection of several pieces of Locke" (1720), and a "Recueil de diverses pièces sur la philosophie, la religion naturelle," &c., par Leibnitz, Clarke, Newton (1720).

inducement to me to be urgent with you in this matter against your own modesty.

One thing I have to add to you, as a serious and earnest request, and in which you will infinitely oblige me, that on the first occasion you have of writing to Mr. Bayle you would tell him how ashamed and troubled I am for having been so long in his debt as I have been, having never once written to him since his kind and obliging letter I received by you, and in which I have an additional obligation to him, by the acquaintance he has given me of one so deserving as yourself, which is a favour I shall always own to him, and show that I am not unworthy of by approving myself your sincere and hearty friend,

SHAFTESBURY.

TO MR. BENNETT.

*November 15th,* 1701.

MR. BENNETT,—I return you and my worthy friends of Shaftesbury[1] my most hearty thanks for your kind expression of friendship to me in that notice you have taken of my services to the public and to your town, and for whatever services I or my family have rendered to either. I think this to be the greatest return of gratitude and the highest token of your favour that you are pleased to repose so great a trust in me as to desire a friend of mine for your representative in Parliament. I shall not offer one to you but whom I can answer for equally as for myself, this being a trust of the highest importance. And as I am in this respect tender of the public, so I cannot but be the like of my friend in deferring to use a person's name till I learn from yourself and my other good friends, whether you insist on my acceptance of this kind offer, so as to make no breach amongst those I so heartily wish united for the public's sake, and for the service of the town. To it I of all persons am the most bound in particular on account of yourself and the rest of these my worthy friends, to whom I shall ever acknowledge this great obligation, by approving myself your ever faithful friend and humble servant.

[1] Parliament had been dissolved on November 11th, 1701.

## TO  BENJAMIN  FURLY.[1]

CHELSEA, *December* 29*th*, 1701.

Mr. FURLY,—I believe you hardly wonder at my silence this last month, when you consider how great a scene has opened for the public, in which I was called to be so great an actor, having strongly obliged myself to be so ; for as, on one hand, you know well I was determined to retire absolutely from all public affairs, and never to have stirred out of my privacy in the country, had the King persisted in the resolution of keeping the last Parliament and ministry ; so, on the other hand, having been at one time almost the single man alive that peremptorily insisted on a dissolution, and having tried all along both by my friends here and in Holland to evince the necessity of it, and to bring it to effect, in which perhaps I may have been some instrument, I had the strongest obligation on earth upon me to act with vigour, as I have done since the opportunity the king has most happily given us, and it has pleased Providence to bless me with great success,[2] for having my province, and that a very hard one, in two counties long in the hands of the most inveterate of the adverse party, I notwithstanding carried all that I attempted in both. In one of them, viz., Wilts, which my brother[3] and his friend represent, instead of two inveterate Tories, we have there mended the elections by eight, which is a majority of sixteen in Parliament, and in Dorsetshire, my own county, we have gained also considerably—my friend Mr. Trenchard being in the room of a constant ill vote for the county, and my friend Sir John Cropley being also brought in by me at the place of my name, Shaftesbury, which was ever entirely in their hands since my grandfather's death, but which I have now entirely recovered,

[1] Mr. Benjamin Furly (born 13th April, 1636), an English merchant of literary tastes, at Rotterdam, was the friend of Locke, Sidney, and Shaftesbury. A volume of their "Original Letters" to him, in which this one is included (pp. 162-4), was published by his descendant, Th. Foster, in 1830. His three sons, Benjohan (born 6th January, 1681), John, and Arent, also corresponded with Shaftesbury.

[2] The fourth Earl says his father turned the scales in this election.

[3] Hon. Maurice Ashley.

and made zealous. And as a token that the King himself is right, as we would wish, he yesterday gave me most hearty thanks for my zeal and good services on this occasion, and this before much company, which is a sufficient declaration against Sir Edward Seymour [1] and that party, to whom my opposition was personal, and who himself in person, and by his relations, opposed me everywhere in the elections, though, I thank God, were everywhere defeated.

I have thoroughly, and as a friend, considered of the concern of your son Arent, and though I could have given you but little encouragement before, I think I may give it you now, depending on this happy turn of the King and Administration, which being as it formerly was and seemed likely to continue, what hope could there be for any of us or our friends ? I will advise further about it with mine and your friends, for you may trust me that I am not indifferently, your friend,

SHAFTESBURY.

My kind respects to all yours, and to friends, particularly Mr. Van Twedde, for whom I truly grieve.

———

## TO LORD MARLBOROUGH. [2]

*April* 10*th,* 1702.

MY LORD,—Before the King had given you regiments I had his promise that in case Colonel Farrington had a regiment, the place he held in the Stamp Office should be for my friend Mr. Micklethwayt. [3] When Colonel Farrington had the regiment,

---

[1] "The ablest man of his party," says Burnet, "was Seymour, who was the first Speaker of the House of Commons that was not bred to the law."

[2] John Churchill, First Duke of Marlborough (1650-1722) was the most powerful personage at Court during the reign of Queen Anne. In his campaigns on the Continent he, moreover, added fresh lustre to the British name by the victories of Blenheim, Ramillies, and Malplaquet.

[3] Robert and Thomas Micklethwayte were two brothers whom Shaftesbury befriended. For Robert he obtained a position in the army, and for Thomas an office in the civil service. It was Thomas Micklethwayte who carried the second edition of the *Characteristics* through the press.

I waited on the King, who confirmed his promise to me, and afterwards I carried Mr. Micklethwayt to kiss the King's hand upon it, which he did, and I returned the King my thanks.

If by your lordship's favour in representing this to the Queen she has such goodness as to allow my friend the benefit of the King's[1] promise, it will be the highest obligation on your lordship's most obedient, humble servant, SHAFTESBURY.

[*Upon the back of this letter to Lord Marlborough is written the following comment, of which a copy, with the omission of the first paragraph, also appears on another memorandum dated July 9th, 1703.*]

By the enclosed letter to my Lord Marlborough (delivered to him soon after the King's death), I put in my claim for my friend upon the foundation of what the Queen had publicly declared, that she would make good what the King had absolutely promised. But my lord has been pleased to take no notice of this ever since.

My zeal for the Revolution, and for that principle which effected it, made me active for the support of the Government, and for the establishment of the Protestant succession, and it was my good fortune to have my services well thought of by the King, and acknowledged by him with great favour.

I had the honour of many offers from the King, but thinking that for my own part I could best serve him and my country in a disinterested station, I resolved absolutely against making any advantage from the public, either to myself or family, by taking any employment at Court. The only favour I asked of the King was a small office of two or three hundred pounds a year for my friend Mr. M——te, who had been serviceable to me in serving him. He kindly granted it, but presently after his promise fell ill and died. And as this was the only favour I ever asked of the King, so it is the only one I shall ever ask of those after him, who I know have just regard to his memory, and whose wisdom will show them that their happy succession has been owing to that Prince, his cause and friends. And it will be of the greatest satisfaction to me to be thus obliged by those whom I am by principle obliged to serve and will serve still with the hazard of all I have in the world. SHAFTESBURY.

[1] King William, who died on the 8th March, 1702, was succeeded by Queen Anne.

### TO BENJAMIN FURLY.

ST. GILES, *November 4th*, 1702.[1]

MR. FURLY,—I hope that before this reaches you, your son Benjamin will be safely arrived : who brings some letters from me to you and other friends.

My letter to yourself was but short ; since your son, who came so lately from me, and was so kind as to stay some time with me longer than he first designed, was able to tell you all my thoughts of our public affairs, from which I am now much withdrawn, and must be more so, not only because of this season, in which it is not so proper for such as I am to act; but in truth because my efforts in time of extremity, for this last year or two, have been so much beyond my strength in every respect, that not only for my mind's sake (which is not a little to one that loves retirement as I do), but for my health's sake, and on the account of my private circumstances, I am obliged to give myself a recess, which will have this agreeable in it, besides the retirement which I love, that I shall promise myself the happiness of seeing you in Holland ; since you have been so long a-coming to us, but are still so far from it, by what I can guess.

I have received yours of the 7th, your style, enclosed in your son's, who wrote me he was then about his journey to Harwich for the next pacquet. I was mightily pleased to read in yours of the generous offer of a certain great lord [2] to you for the preferring of some young man of your recommendation to his service in his great employment, nor was I less pleased to see how the young lads received it when you read it to them, and methought I saw, as if I were present, their honest ambition and friendly emulation : but it is Harry's duty to waive his part, and I really think, by what I can judge by this first view, that in prudence, and according to best advice for their common interest,

---

[1] cf Original Letters, pp. 133-6.

[2] Charles Mordaunt, third Earl of Peterborough (1658-1735), who was about to take command of the English forces in the warfare with Spain, had applied to Mr. Furly for a secretary. The choice lay between Henry Wilkinson, the protegé of Shaftesbury, and Furly's son Arent, the "foster-child" of Locke. Arent Furly received the appointment, and continued in the service of the Earl until his death, which occurred during the campaign in Spain, in 1705.

and the interest of each in particular, it is better that this favour should be for Mr. Arent; since being your own son, a kind of foster-child too to Mr. Locke, my lord's great friend, he can enjoy the fruits of your recommendation and carry the force of your own and friend's interest with my lord much better than a stranger can do, or one whom I am, as perhaps may seem, but remotely concerned for. Besides that, as for any interest that I have myself with my lord, it is what I cannot much count upon, since this last year or two that he threw himself so eagerly into the Tory interest, and prosecuted both the impeachments and all those other fatal, obstructive, and unjust measures, with so much violence. He has now smarted for it, having been barbarously treated by that party he went over to, who sacrificed him last year in the House of Commons, where his son, though my good friend and pupil, never gave us a vote till about that time. My lord is now come back to his original friends and principles, and those sores are all healed up, but how it may stand between myself and him I know not, as to his part, for great men are not so forgiving as we that are of a lower genius and meeker spirits; and, indeed, as much as I honour him now and congratulate his advancement, which I do more heartily perhaps than any friend he has in the world, yet at that time I opposed him earnestly, and told him the treatment he would infallibly meet with at last from his new friends whom he then joined with.

I was going to have written more, but I just received notice that my Lord Portland,[1] being going through our country, is just coming hither to stay with me this night, so I shall not have time to add further. . . .

<hr>

## TO MONS. PIERRE DESMAIZEAÜX.

[2] ROTTERDAM, *2nd November*, 1703.

SIR,—I am obliged to you for yours, which I communicated to Mr. Bayle. I am sorry you were not present with Mons. St. Evremond at his death. However, the mark he has placed

[1] William, first Earl of Portland and father of the first Duke.

[2] "It appears by my father's private account book that he left England and embarked for Holland August 9th, 1703. He returned from Holland and arrived at Chelsea August 26th, 1704, having been set on shore the 22nd at Alborough, in Suffolk."—From Memoranda by the fourth Earl of certain events in his father's life.

on you of his esteem and friendship will, I hope, be of advantage to you in helping to make you known and valued.

I perceive you have not done anything further in the affair of Lord Buckhurst, my Lord Dorset's son. But whether you think fit to solicit that business or no, I could wish you to remember to wait on Mrs. Lundy, who, though she has been placed by fortune in circumstances not suitable to her birth or merit, is well worth making court to. She has qualities that give her an interest with those who are not won by ill or indifferent ones, and if you are so fortunate as to improve that beginning of an acquaintance which I gave you, you will find it, I believe, as agreeable as it may be useful to you and service-able in your affairs, for she is a sincere friend, and indefatigable in serving those she esteems so.

I am sorry Sir John Cropley knows nothing of that comedy you lent me, and which, at your desire, I lent him. I remember I saw it afterwards in his own chamber at my house at Chelsea, but whether he took it thence to London, or has left it there, I cannot tell, but have written to my servant-maid at Chelsea to see if it be in his apartment, or anywhere else in my little house.

If you give yourself the trouble of writing again to me at any time, you need not trouble Mons. Bayle by enclosing to him, but either let it be given in at Chelsea or direct it yourself for me to be left with Mr. Benjamin Furly, merchant, in Rotterdam, and it will be conveyed to your constant friend to serve you,

SHAFTESBURY.

I could wish Mr. Stephens's second part were well trans-lated into French, as it would be if either by you or the same hand that did it first. It would be a very small trouble, and would sell well here with a new edition.

---

## TO JOHN WHEELOCK.[1]

ROTTERDAM, *November* 6 [1703].

I thought you had not been in the world, it was so long since I heard from you. Just now I have yours on your return to St. Giles's.

---

[1] Mr. John Wheelock was the auditor and head steward of Shaftesbury's estate at St. Giles's. He enjoyed the utmost confidence and genuine esteem of Shaftesbury.

I am sorry to hear all things are so low and tenants so disheartened. The greater must be my frugality and care to repair the great wounds I have made in my estate. I shall keep in my compass of £200 for the year that I stay here, and if this does not do it shall be yet less, and the time longer, for I will never return to be as I was of late *richly poor ;* that is to say, to live with the part of a rich man, a family and house such as I have, and yet in debt and unable to do any charity or bestow money in any degree.

If I find my house at St. Giles's and rank greater than I can sustain with my estate, the rather give up my family and sell all, so that I may have something to do good with, than bestow all in supporting such a vast house and appurtenances. I wrote you much (in a letter some time since the death of my poor sister Gertrude) about this very matter, the charge of my house, &c., and of the alteration of the kitchen, and so as to bring that and the passage to the cellar under my own and housekeeper's eye through the public court, which if anything will contribute to ease my charge and make me live within compass at St. Giles's. But if this cannot be done without adding more roof to St. Giles's, I can never consent to its doing. But I believe you may find a place for the wardrobe elsewhere, and not add any such room, as you once proposed, to the new kitchen.

Pray be more constant in writing to me. I have written this post to my brother and to my brother Hooper, and to Sir John, Mr. Micklethwayt, and others, so cannot write but this short and confused note at present.

My kind love to brother and sister Hooper. I wrote to my sister but a few posts since. Remembrances to my family, Mrs. Cooper especially, and recommend to her the care of my sister Hooper now her lying-in is near.

I thank God I recover very much, and find this air and retirement the same relief to me as I expected and found once before.

---

## TO JOHN WHEELOCK.

ROTTERDAM, *November* 16*th*, 1703.

I wrote you word that I had heard from you in one short letter since your return to St. Giles's; but have yet heard nothing in answer to anything I have written since my sister Gertrude's[1] death. I enclose you herein a letter for sister Hooper[2], to whom, as well as to Mr. Hooper also, I wrote some time since, but have not yet heard. My sister's time I know must needs be near by this time. Pray go over sometimes to Boveridge and desire earnestly of my sister that she would take due care of herself and not be sparing in sending for Dr. Pitt, and having all advice and assistance on every occasion. I know she is but of a tender constitution, and by my late loss I am made more and more apprehensive; so that if my sister has any regard to my satisfaction she will take more care and be better helped than I know she has been on these occasions. Pray desire Mrs. Cooper[3] too (to whom my kind remembrances) to go over sometimes.

I say nothing of my family till I hear from you in answer to much that I have written.

Your last before my sister's death was very satisfactory to me. I approved of everything you did and proposed to do, excepting only the addition of something to the old wardrobe-roof. Far from adding anything to St. Giles's, I would to God I could in any way contract.

I hope by your good management for me I may be able (if I live) to support myself at St. Giles's, but it must be after a very different way of living. I should have been glad to have lived in the way that is called hospitable in my country, but experience has but too well shown me that I cannot do it. Nor will I ever live again as I have done and spend to the full of my estate in house and a table. I must have wherewithal to do good out of my estate, as well as feed a family, maintain a set of idle servants entailed upon me, and a great mass of building yet more expensive. If my estate cannot, besides my house and rank, yield me five or six hundred pounds a year to do good with (as that rank requires), my house and rank may both go together, come what will of them, or let the world say what they will, they shall both to ruin for me, for I shall never think of

---

[1] Gertrude, who was unmarried, died (as here appears) in 1703.

[2] Dorothy, who married Edward Hooper, of Hern Court, Hants.

[3] Elizabeth Cooper, housekeeper at the estate of St. Giles.

supporting them since I have not wherewithal to do it and that which is more necessary. And if ever I hope to live to return again and keep a family, it must be after another rate, and by your help I hope to regulate matters otherwise.

As to what you have proposed of setting up the Bull Inn again in a little credit and tolerable condition for reception, 'tis what I extremely wish. And it is now chiefly in my absence that this must be begun and the custom established even for my own servants. Your example will be able to effect it, and an absolute shutting up of St. Giles's house stables, not to be opened again by the trick that was served me a little before my coming away. If you are now able to deal with these people and these ways, all the service you can do me in this kind will avail. But I hope you will be resolute and peremptory by my authority to prevent these breakings in upon my economy, which if they proceed and so get the better of you, the consequence will be great indeed, when I tell you that I shall at last give over family and house, and all, and determine never more to see St. Giles's, nor keep up the house, but let it sink, discharge all my servants, let it to a farm, and so farewell. This is very serious and true. I would not have you think I am trifling; it is now past that time of my life. I do not reckon upon many years of life, but those that are remaining I will not pass in making myself a slave to a great house and family, striving to make an estate hold out which is not big enough. If my brother will marry he may take all and leave me only a hundred pound or two a year. If he will not, it is his fault, not mine. My health and constitution is gone, and spent in public services and troubles of my family.

By next I shall send you a paper to be sealed up under your seal, together with my will, of which I left a duplicate in your hands. Love to brother and sister Hooper. Dues to friends. God be with you. Pray write a little oftener.

## TO LORD SUNDERLAND.[1]

ROTTERDAM, *November 9th,* 1703.

MY LORD,—I have ever esteemed it as the greatest of honours that you were pleased to distinguish me so early in

[1] Robert Spencer, second Earl of Sunderland (1640—1702), was

your life by such particular marks of your friendship and esteem, and it cannot be but the greatest satisfaction to me to see that your lordship preserves still the same regard for me, with that opinion which you have ever had of my love to my country. I have served it hitherto very diligently (how successfully I know not), and given my earliest years to that service as I would do my latest, did not my constitution fail me. I remember a time when I feared more for your lordship than for myself, but I rejoice for my country's sake that that turned otherwise. Your lordship recovered, I soon afterwards sunk under it, and was forced to retire hither into this country, to an air which was never found good except by very bad lungs. It set me up, and I returned to the same service in my country till the time that I had the honour of serving again your lordship in another house. But I was unable to go through this last winter, and I am now got into the same retirement, by which I am a little recovered. How I should be able to cross the sea again so soon, and in the winter time, I cannot tell; but I have no hopes of being able to go by this convoy which brings the King of Spain, and I know not how soon we may expect another. Whatever becomes of me, or wherever I am, I hope your lordship will always believe that I have ever been, and shall be to my last, your lordship's most sincere and faithful humble servant, SHAFTESBURY.

---

TO SIR ROWLAND GWINN, AT HANOVER.

ROTTERDAM, *January* 23rd, 1704.

SIR,—I am extremely obliged to you for yours, and the kind thoughts of me which you express in it. What you have heard of me as to my being much retired and having left public affairs is true.

I kept in them as long as I was able; but by a constitution unfitted for the fatigue of business, I had long since been forced to quit, but that I chose to suffer anything rather than not come

in the Halifax Ministry under James II., whose cause he abandoned, and went to Holland. He returned to power under William III., but was compelled to resign in 1697.

in heartily and with all my strength at that last hour when I apprehended not my country only, but mankind, was sinking, had not the Prince,[1] then alive, been supported, a war entered into, and an English Protestant Succession established.

I have lived to see the chiefest of those ends compassed, and those good laws passed for the establishment of our constitution, which I wished for at the Revolution; but which were afterwards got with so much envy, struggle, and pain, as I cannot remember but with regret, for that Prince's sake, whose memory, however, with all true Englishmen, I must still honour and love. I hope the remainder of this good work will be perfected, and the war for common liberty carried on with vigour; it lying wholly now in the *power* of our English Court, where I hope the *will* is not wanting; and I rejoice to hear such noble maxims from an English Throne as we have lately had from thence.

If those persons of your Court are such as you describe, there are yet treasures of happiness in store for England and the world. I can rely on your judgment sooner than on most persons living, but cannot help in myself a natural diffidence of courts, after having been deceived so much in one I so early loved, and had such thoughts of as to believe it no less than impossible to have seen it sacrifice its best friends and lay itself at last so low by such repeated acts, and by losing even that degree of faith and gratitude which attends common policy and interest. Everything in nature seems to demonstrate this truth, that things are to be maintained and advanced by the principles on which they were founded. But courts are super-natural things and subservient to none of these rules. All is miraculous there, and out of the order of common human policy, or at least seems to be so, to retired and speculative people such as myself.

But I have troubled you enough, having no better or other subject for a correspondence, which otherwise I would with the greatest willingness embrace, but that the terms are so unequal between one in a principal court of Europe and one living out of the world, and knowing little of what passes till long after it has passed and is no longer news.

[1] Prince William of Orange.

Though I am not now in Parliament myself, where I never was of much service, and for the future can be of little or none, yet I cannot but regret the loss we have of you, whom I have ever esteemed one the most fitted and most useful.

If anything can make amends, it is your being where you are to give that good advice you are so capable of, in which station, as one of the greatest importance to us, I am necessitated to think you of any Englishman the most fitted. I am conscious, too, of the services you did me at a former court (our then presumptive successor's), where I first knew you, and where, as an omen of my being for ever a bad courtier, I made choice of you (an Englishman and Whig), instead of any other to present me, which is a circumstance it's likely you may ere this have forgotten. I am glad, however, of this occasion of remembering it, though at such a distance of time, that I might thus show you with what early obligation, and by what ties of private friendship as well as public principles, I am and must be your most real and faithful, humble servant,

SHAFTESBURY.

## TO THE BISHOP OF SARUM.[1]

ROTTERDAM, *February 5th,* 1704.

MY LORD,—I am very much concerned to find your lordship should have had trouble given you, from a concern of my family, especially so unhappy a one, and in which I am so little able to give your lordship the satisfaction I earnestly wish.

I would willing take up as little more of your time as is possible, and, therefore, beg your lordship to believe what I say here is the utmost I can ever say.

Whether the gentleman[2] that has still thoughts of my sister[3] has in any respect ill used either her or myself or made any ill return to my friendship shown him, I will not enter into or judge of ; but, be it of what nature soever, if there be anything of that kind I willing pass it over, and as much as in me lies forgive it him. Nor shall I any more oppose his pretensions to

---

[1] Gilbert Burnet was Bishop of Salisbury (Old Sarum) from 1689 to 1715. He was one of the earliest of Broad Churchmen.

[2] Francis Stonehouse, Esq.      [3] His sister Frances.

my sister, or dis-serve him by using my authority or credit (if I have any) with my sister, to turn her from her present thoughts. I shall be no way a hindrance to the match, though for reasons I would by no means give your lordship the trouble of hearing, I can never be for it, or in the least concerned in it.

It may be against my opinion and against my judgment (for that I cannot help), but it shall not be against my will, for your lordship thinking favourable of it, and it being my sister's desire, I acquiesce and would give a formal consent too, if that were necessary, but it is not so. My sister is of age, and at her liberty may dispose of herself and fortune, and I am willing she should do so; as she likes best and thinks most for her happiness, which I shall always wish her.

I am ashamed of this trouble your lordship has had, and will add no more to it, besides assuring you that nobody can be with more sincere respect than I am, my lord, your most faithful and humble servant.

P.S.—The trouble I am in makes me doubtful whether I have expressed myself as clearly as I ought when speaking to your lordship of my consent, which relates only to my readiness to pay my sister, without controversy or delay, that fortune which she has in reality, independent of me, by Act of Parliament. If I have besides determined any additional fortune for my sisters, it is where they dispose of themselves to my satisfaction; not as this sister is like to do, to my affliction, in which, however, I submit.

## TO HIS SISTER FRANCES.

HOLLAND, 18*th March*, 1704.

SISTER FRANCES,—I received yours, and am glad to hear from you that you take kindly anything that I have written, though in answer to others, where you were silent yourself.

My leave [1] which you speak of, is what you have never wanted for anything since of age. My advice I have been ready enough to give you, and if you follow it not there is no offence, nor shall I complain; my desire having been that you

---

[1] To marry Francis Stonehouse, Esq.

Y

should be free and independent on me, as I made you and your sister long since by Act of Parliament.

Whatever place or circumstance you are in (for that I know not) I wish you happiness, all that your choice can afford you, and whatever you may be towards me shall always be towards yourself, suitably to my relation and the bond of nature, your loving brother,                    SHAFTESBURY.

---

## TO SIR ROWLAND GWINN.

ROTTERDAM, *April* 19*th*, 1704.

It is hardly possible for me to receive anything with more satisfaction than I have done yours.

The marks of your friendship are what I shall always esteem amongst the greatest advantages that can come to me on my private account, and on the public's share, there could have been nothing so satisfactory and rejoicing to me as to be assured by you (as I fully am) how excellent and deserving those persons are on whom the future happiness of England and the world depends.

The undeserved regard which the Electrice [1] is pleased to express for me, with the notice taken of me by the Queen of Prussia,[2] and the letter from her which you have communicated to me is so great an honour that I cannot pretend to make any return myself, but must for this rely upon your friendship and good offices in my behalf, that as little worthy as I may be of such an honour in every respect besides, I may not however appear wholly unworthy, by want of a due acknowledgment and grateful sense.

It is not a mere aversion to courts that hinders me accepting so obliging an offer and invitation from such who were they even private persons I should yet have the highest esteem for in

[1] The Electress Sophia, of Hanover, mother of George I., King of England.

[2] Sophia Charlotte, daughter of the Electress Sophia, and grandmother of Frederic the Great. She was a brilliant woman, and a patron of learning. The philsopher Leibnitz was her revered friend and teacher.

the world, and for whose sakes, as great a lover as I am of free climates, I could be contented to breathe despotic air and quit retirement to visit once again a court. But I am now obliged to think of returning into England, and my stay can be but short on this side.

Wherever I am, I beg you to believe that I esteem myself under great obligations.—Your faithful friend and affectionate humble servant,                                    SHAFTESBURY.

----

TO JOHN LOCKE.

CHELSEA, *September 7th,* 1704.

If I had been in a condition to have written a line, I should not have sent you Mr. Furly's without something from myself, and were I now so well as to undertake a journey, I should be thinking of seeing you in the first place before any other of my friends, especially hearing (as I do with great trouble) that you are of late worse [1] than you used to be.

My own distemper (which was an ill fever got at sea after having been three weeks a ship-board) is, I hope, quite off, though I am yet very weak.

When perfectly recovered (if it so please God) my first thoughts will be of a journey to you. Meanwhile, pray believe me (as I hope you ever did and will), your faithful friend and humble servant,                                    SHAFTESBURY.

Pray present my humble service to Sir Francis and my lady. Being obliged now ere long to set about a work long delayed—a monument for my grandfather, as enjoined me by my grandmother—I should be extremely glad that you would so far remember my grandfather as to let me have some lines from you for an inscription, in Latin and English.

[Address]: For Mr. Locke, at Sir Francis Masham's, in Oates, near Bishops Stafford, Essex.

----

[1] This was Locke's last illness, as he died on the 28th of October, 1704.

## TO DR. BURGESS.

### ST. GILES'S, *January*, 1704 (5).

SIR,—Your letting me know the report of my restraining my brother[1] from standing for Wilts was a great favour and obligation in giving me the opportunity of doing myself justice in a very sensible part. It has pleased God to render my life in prospect very useless to my country through an unhappy constitution unable to bear the town air, and much broken of late years by my strict attendance of Parliaments there, and other public services such as I was able to undergo. I began early and served heartily, perhaps beyond my strength, and not contented to serve alone, I did my best to qualify a brother, in other respects as well as with a good estate, to serve with me, which I thank God he did, in very trying and urgent times, with as much integrity and zeal as my heart could wish.

What particular circumstances should make him at present decline the service I cannot enter into; but by my own behaviour and life, as well as for what I have done for him, I can hardly think my friends can suppose it other than the greatest pleasure and satisfaction I can enjoy to see him active in the public, either with me or in my stead, and as much as I know of his modesty and unambitious temper, which restrain him perhaps in stricter moral bounds than ordinary, I cannot think it possible he should refuse (as you express it) to serve his country, though elected without his interposition. I should readily expostulate with him on this subject : but as the obligations I have laid on him were never so intended by me as to take from him the condition of a *free man,* so in this particular, as well as in others, I have promised to leave him to his perfect liberty, and must do so whate'er it cost me.

I owe an infinite debt of gratitude to that great man you mention, both on my own and brother's account, if I may call that infinite which I count never sufficiently to be acknowledged by me. But the noble principles espoused by him, and the love of mankind, his country, and the best of causes, will assure him

---

[1] Maurice Ashley.

of a recompense above what a thousand such as I am can make, though I shall ever be devotedly his.

With hearty thanks to you for this, your good wishes and prayers, I remain, your affectionate humble servant.

---

### TO PETER KING.[1]

ST. GILES'S, *January,* 1704 (5).

SIR,—My ill health, which has been my hindrance in many things, has done me the most sensible injury in making me fail so long in my acknowledgment to so good a friend as yourself, particularly after so great a demonstration of your friendship. The few sheets or lines, however imperfect, which our deceased friend, Mr. Locke, has left on the subject of my grandfather,[2] are to me, at least, very precious remains, and, if nothing more, are, however, the kindest pledges of his love to the memory and family of his great friend. How happy for me, and for the public, perhaps, no less, that he had lived to perfect them. But who so fit to perfect this, or any other thing he left, as the person whom he has left to succeed him, and who, as nearest related to him in blood, is the nearest so in genius, parts, and principles? And methinks at leisure hours it would be no unpleasant task for one who so nobly asserted the rights of the people to vindicate the much-injured memory of one who a champion in that cause, and must make no small a part of the history of those times when the foundation was laying for the present glorious ones, and for the happy Revolution that gave birth to them. The noble progress of this cause in those latter days has often made me wish a historian worthy of it, and if this, or any other occasion, ever so slight, could be able to turn your thoughts towards a matter of so great weight. I should think it very happy, for it is not a single man's life, but the history of our own age, that I am wishing for, not for the patriot's sake, but for the cause.

[1] Peter King (1669-1734), the Lord Chancellor, was a relative and protegé of John Locke, and received from him a bequest of all his manuscripts, now known as the Lovelace Collection.

[2] The first Earl of Shaftesbury, with whose family Locke held such intimate relations for many years.—See p. 329.

But be this as your better genius may direct you, I scarce could allow myself to hint such a thing to you, being thus interested, as I confess myself, and being already so much indebted to you, and by several obligations, Sir, yours, &c.

P.S.—I must confess I have naturally a great impatience to see the sheets, but being not willing to venture the original by any carriage, I should be extremely glad of having a copy by the post as soon as you can get them written out for me.

Since what I have written to you I have received an earnest letter from Mons. Le Clerc, in Holland, to send him what I possibly can of Mr. Locke's life, particularly the former part whilst he lived with my grandfather, designing, as he tells me, to write on that subject, and expressing great zeal for the cause as well as for the persons. But this is for foreigners, and requires haste, having promised that the account which he is to give of Mr. Locke and his writings should come out soon. I will engage to send him what I can and let him know I have consulted you, that whatever I send may pass through your hands to be corrected and improved. This has given me greater assurance in sending this letter to you, with what I have ventured to propose, and might have served for my excuse had it come sooner, but I hope you are friend enough to forgive my weakness, if there be any, in my concern for the memory of such relation, joined as it is closely with that of our friend.

## TO JEAN LE CLERC.[1]

ST. GILES's, 13*th January,* 1705.

SIR,—I have great pleasure in receiving your commands. It is enough for me to know that I can serve you in anything,

[1] Jean Le Clerc (1657—1736) was of Swiss origin, but occupied for many years the chair of Philosophy, Belles Lettres, and Hebrew in the College of Remonstrants at Amsterdam. He was an eminent critic and divine. His literary labours were extensive and varied. The large influence he exercised in Europe was, however, chiefly due to his periodical publications, the "Bibliothèque Universelle," 26 vols., Amst., 1686—1693; "Bibliothèque Choisie," 28 vols., Amst., 1703—1713; and the Bibliothèque Ancienne et Moderne, 28 vols.,

for no one would do it more readily or heartily, but when you add to this the interest of our friend's memory, it lays the greatest obligation on me, and I must own and what I am apt to be the most concerned for is the vindication of that relation's memory,[1] that is so kindly joined by you, as indeed it naturally is, with that of our common friend.[2] My misfortune is to be retired at present in the country, for my recovery from a sickness I got by ill weather and a long fatigue at sea, on my coming away from you in Holland.[3] This has made your letter long in coming to me, and must make me longer in consulting my relations and those old people of my family in town who can remember far back. But I will make all possible despatch in sending you those particulars of our friend's life (since his coming into my family), which I could with pleasure give you a large account of, excepting only the precise dates required. How happy should I be to enjoy for a while your conversation on this particular subject particularly; though on every subject it is the most desirable and what I am the most covetous of. I should not have lost so late an opportunity of enjoying it, but had made a second journey this last summer to Amsterdam, had I not heard of your intending to visit Rotterdam, where I was then staying for a convoy which brought me away in haste. You shall hear from me again as soon as possible, and since you have honoured our nation in many respects besides in learning of our language, I shall continue to write thus to you in English, for I think it not to be esteemed a compliment merely to say that by having won so great a man as yourself to an esteem of our sense

Amst., 1714—1727. He published in " The Bibliothéque Choisie " for 1705, an " Eloge Historique de feu M. Locke," which has been the foundation of many subsequent biographies of Locke. In its prepara-tion he sought information of Shaftesbury. Indeed, this celebrated Eloge consists largely of a translation of two letters, one of which, dated 12th January, 1705, Le Clerc received from Lady Damaris Masham, at whose house Locke resided from 1691, until his death in 1704, and the other, which here immediately follows in the text, under the date of the 8th February, 1705, contained a sketch of Locke's life, written for him by Shaftesbury.

[1] The First Earl of Shaftesbury.        John Locke.
[3] Shaftesbury returned from Holland in August, 1704.

and writings, we have gained as much honour in letters as lately in the field by arms. I am satisfied in no nation you have more friends that honour and esteem you, and I intreat you to depend on myself as one who have long been and am now like to be with the greater obligation, your faithful friend and humble servant.

P.S.—I have written Mr. King,[1] Mr. Locke's nearest relation, and heir, and who inherits many of his qualities, and is at present the greatest young man we have, both in our laws and in the Parliament. Mr. Locke has left his books and writings to another young man[2] of great worth and of a good estate, of whom you will have a better account from Oates, I having not the honour of being so particularly well acquainted with him as that family is to whom he is a neighbour ; but I hear there are many of Mr. Locke's manuscripts in his hands designed for the Press, of which you might easily be informed if you would allow yourself a little time.

---

## TO JEAN LE CLERC.[3]

### St. Giles's, in Dorset, *8th February*, 1705.

Mons. Le Clerc,—Having once written to you in my own language, I continue to use the same privilege. I am sorry that I am in no better a condition to acquit myself of my promise to you. My recovery has been so slow that I am scarce yet got up and have been unable to hold any correspondence with my friends in town. Mr. King promised to send me the papers I mentioned to you of Mr. Locke's, who it seems had begun some Memoirs[4] of his own relating to my grandfather. Those, however imperfect, yet as being Mr. Locke's own, I should have been glad to have sent you with what supplement I could

[1] Peter King, Lord Chancellor.

[2] Frances Cudworth Masham, to whom Locke left half his books. The other half and all his manuscripts were, however, bequeathed to Peter Lord King.

[3] cf *Notes and Queries*, Vol. III., Feb. 8th, 1851, pp. 97-99.

[4] The "Memoirs relating to the Life of Anthony, first Earl of Shaftesbury" were printed in Locke's Posthumous Works, 1706.

make myself, but Mr. King's engagements in public affairs has made him delay this so long that according to the account you have given me of the shortness of your time, I must wait no longer, but content myself with giving you what I can out of my own head, without other assistance.

" Mr. Locke came into my grandfather's family in the summer of the year 1666, by his friend Mr. Bennett,* of the town of Shaftesbury. The occasion of it was thus : My grandfather had been ill for a great while, after a fall, by which his breast was so bruised that in time it came to an imposthumation within and appeared by a swelling under his stomach. Mr. Locke was at that time a student in physic at Oxford, and my grandfather taking a journey that way to drink the waters (having Mr. Bennett in the coach with him), he had this young physician presented to him, who, though he had never practised physic, yet appeared to my grandfather to be such a genius that he valued him above all his other physicians, the great men in practise of those times. Accordingly by his direction[1] my grandfather underwent an operation which saved his life, and was the most wonderful of the kind that had been heard of till that time. His breast was laid open and the matter discharged, and an orifice ever afterwards kept open by a silver pipe, an instrument famous upon record in the writings of our Popish and Jacobite authors, who never failed to reproach him with this " infirmity." After this cure, Mr. Locke grew so much in esteem with my grandfather, that as great a man as he had experienced him in physic, he looked upon this but as his least part ; he encouraged him to turn his thoughts another way ; nor would he suffer him to practise at all in physic, except in his own family, and as a kindness to some particular friends. He put him upon the study of the religious and civil affairs of the nation, with whatsoever related to the business of a Minister of State, in which he was so successful, that my grandfather began soon to use him as a

* A gentleman of a sound Protestant family, always in great friendship with ours. Both father and son were members of Parliament for that town, and were stewards to my grandfather.

[1] In other MSS., " On his advice, and almost solely by his direction."

friend, and consult with him on all occasions of that kind. He was not only with him in his library and closet, but in company with the great men of those times, the Duke of Buckingham, Lord Halifax, and others, who, being men of wit and learning, were as much taken with him; for together with his serious, respectful, humble character, he had a mixture of pleasantry and a becoming boldness of speech. The liberty he could take with these great men was peculiar to such a genius as his. A pleasant instance of it runs in my mind, though perhaps the relation of it may not be so pleasing to another. At an appointed meeting of two or three of those great men at my grandfather's house more for entertainment and good company than for business, it happened that after a few compliments the cards were called for, and the Court fashion prevailing, they were engaged in play before any conversation was begun. Mr. Locke sat by as a spectator for some time; at last, taking out his table-book, began to write something very busily, till being observed by one of the lords, and asked what he was meditating. My lord (said he), I am improving myself the best I can in your company, for having impatiently waited this honour of being present at such a meeting of the wisest men and greatest wits of this age, I thought I could not do better than to write your conversation, and here I have it in substance, all that has passed for an hour or two. There was no need of Mr. Locke's reciting much of the dialogue. The great men felt the ridicule and took pleasure in improving it. They quitted their play and fell into a conversation becoming them, and so passed the remainder of the day.

When my grandfather, from being Chancellor of the Exchequer, was made High Chancellor, which was in the year 1672, he advanced Mr. Locke to the place of Secretary for the Clergy. And when my grandfather quitted the Court and began to be in danger from it, Mr. Locke now shared with him in dangers as before in honours and advantages. He entrusted him with his secretest negotiations, and made use of his assistant pen in matters that nearly concerned the State, and were fit to be made public to raise that spirit in the nation which was necessary against the prevailing Popish party. It was for something of this kind that got air, and out of great tenderness for Mr. Locke, that my grandfather, in the year 1674, sent him abroad to travel, an improvement which my grandfather was glad to add to those he had already given him. His health served as a very just excuse, he being consumptive as early in his life as that was, so that having travelled through France he went to * Montpelier, and there stayed for some time. He returned again to my grandfather in the year 1678, and remained in his family till the year 1682, which was the year my grandfather retired into Holland, and there died. Mr. Locke, who was to have soon followed him thither, was not prevented in the voyage by his death, but found it safest for him to retire thither, and there lived at our good friend Mr. Furly's, of Rotterdam, till the happy Revolution of King William, which restored him to his native country and to other public offices of greater note, which by fresh merits he had deserved. Witness his then published books of government, trade, and commerce, by which he had as considerably served the State as he had done the Church and Protestant interest by his defence of toleration and the support of the Revolution principles. But of this part of his life you need no information.

Thus far I have made mention of Mr. Locke as to his station in public affairs under my grandfather. Now as to his services in private affairs, and the concerns of a family which was in every respect so happy in him that he seemed as a good guardian angel sent to bless it.

When Mr. Locke first came into the family, my father was then a youth of about fifteen or sixteen. My grandfather entrusted him wholly to Mr. Locke for what remained of his education. He was an only child, and of no firm health, which induced my grandfather, in concern for his family, to think of marrying him as soon as possible. He was too young to choose a wife for himself, and my grandfather too much in business to choose one for him. The affair was nice, for though my grandfather required not a great fortune, he insisted on good blood, good person and constitution, and above

*It was here he became acquainted with my Lord Pembroke, then a younger brother, who is at present so great an ornament and support of his nation.

all good education and a character as remote as possible from
that of a court or town-bred lady. All this was thrown upon
Mr. Locke, who being already so good a judge of men, my grandfather doubted not of his equal judgment in women. He
departed from him entrusted and sworn as Abraham's head
servant *that ruled over all that he had,* and went into a far
country (the north of England) to seek for his son a wife, whom
he as successfully found. Of her, I and six more of us (brothers
and sisters) were born, in whose education from the earliest
infancy Mr. Locke governed according to his own principles
(since published [1] by him), and with such success that we all of
us came to full years with strong and healthy constitutions. My
own was the worst, which was, however, never faulty till of late.
I was his more peculiar charge, being as eldest son taken by
my grandfather and bred under his immediate care, Mr. Locke
having the absolute direction of my education, and to whom
next my immediate parents, as I must own the greatest obligation, so I have ever preserved the highest gratitude and duty.
I could wish that my time and health would permit me to be
longer in the account of my friend and foster-father, Mr. Locke.
If I add anything as you desire concerning my grandfather
himself it must have a second place. This being a subject more
selfish, and in which I may justly suspect myself of partiality,
of which I would willingly be free, and think I truly am so in
this I now send you. But I fear lest this, such as it is, should
come too late, and therefore hasten to conclude this with
repeated assurances of my being your obliged friend and humble
servant.

P.S.—If, after what I have said, I dare venture a word to you
as to my grandfather's apology for the one and only thing which
I repine at in his whole life (I mean the unhappy words you
mention, *delenda est Carthago*), it would be this, that the public
would not insist on this as so ill and injurious if they considered
the English Constitution and manner of those times, in
which the Prince, more lofty in prerogative and at a greater
distance from his people than now-a-days, used but a few words
to his Parliament and committed the rest to his Keeper or

[1] " Thoughts concerning Education," 1693.

Chancellor, to speak his sense for him (as he expressed it in the conclusion of his own speech). Upon which my grandfather, the then Chancellor, and in his Chancellor's place,* spoke the King's sense as the King's mouth, in the same manner as the Speaker of the House of Peers or Commons speaks the House's sense, as *the House's mouth,* for so he is esteemed and called, whatsoever may be his own private sense, or though he may have delivered his own opinion far contrary.

Such was my grandfather's case: who was far from delivering his vote or opinion in this manner, either as a Councillor or Peer or in his place in Parliament, where he carried on a directly opposite interest, he being already in open enmity with the Duke of York and his party that carried on that war. In so much that he was at that very time suspected of holding a correspondence with Holland in favour of the Commonwealth party in England. However it be, it is no small comfort to me, that that wise Commonwealth of Holland, the parent and nursing mother of liberty, thought him worthy of their protection when he was a sufferer for the common cause of religion and liberty, and he must ever remain as a noble instance of the generosity of that State and of that potent head of it, the City of Amsterdam, where yourself and other great men have met with a reception that will redound to their honour.

My grandfather, turning short upon the Court (as Sir Wm. Temple† expresses it), had only this plain reason for it: that

* This speech as an act of Council was examined beforehand in the Cabinet. Mr. Locke saw the first copy of it, which was very different, and after it was altered in the Cabinet, my grandfather complained to Mr. Locke and a relation of his, whom Mr. Locke introduced into the family. The same has left me a written account of that affair, and so great was my grandfather's concern and trouble, that he, who, of all men, was esteemed the most ready in speaking, was forced to desire Mr. Locke to stand at his elbow, with the written copy, to prompt him in the case of failure in his repetition.

† It is my grandfather's misfortune to have Sir Wm. Temple, a valuable author, very unfavourable to him: there having been a great quarrel between them on a slight occasion of my grandfather's having stopped the gift of plate after his Embassy—a custom which my grandfather, as Chancellor of the Exchequer, thought very prejudicial.

he discovered the King to be a Papist, through that disguise of an *esprit-fort*, which was a character his vices and over fondness of wit made him act very naturally. Whatever compliances my grandfather as a statesman might make before this discovery to gain the King from his brother and the French party, he broke off all when, by the Duke of Buckingham's means, he had gained this secret. For my grandfather's aversion and irreconcilable hatred to Popery was (as fanaticism) confessed by his greatest enemies to be his master passion. Nor was it ever said that the King left him, but he the King; for nothing was omitted afterwards by that Prince to regain him, nor when that was found impossible, nothing to destroy him.—But I must end, lest I fail this post."

---

### TO SIR ROWLAND GWINN, OF HANOVER.

St. GILES's, 24*th February*, 1704 (5).

SIR,—When I received your last but one I was at Rotterdam, waiting a convoy for England, from whence I hoped soon to have written an answer, but after a miserable passage,[1] and being above a month aboard, I got a sickness which has held me this whole winter, and had I not retired hither from the town must have ended me ere now. In this state I thought it not worth troubling you with a letter; otherwise I should never have lost an opportunity of entertaining so agreeable a correspondence, and had I been any ways active in the public as formerly, I should not have failed to prevent you in the thoughts of coming into the next Parliament. It would have been the highest pleasure to me to have endeavoured to have served you in this way. But in my present state and circumstances I am so remote from all concernment in the approaching elections[2] that I know no more of them than by uncertain rumours; nor do I know concerning my nearest relations or friends whether they stand or no, or for what places. So that I am pretty secure against such a censure in a future House of Commons as was designed

---

[1] August, 1704.

[2] Parliament was dissolved on April 5, 1705.

me in the beginning of this by the Tory party, for meddling too much in the affair of elections. Whether the Court would be as ready to join with them now against those of my principle I know not, but there has been no injury or ill usage omitted hitherto that could possibly come from thence, and they have so far either discouraged or disabled us poor Whigs that no doubt but by the power which in these countries they have wholly placed in Tory hands they will obtain such a Parliament[1] as will make all easy to them. But it is not for a retired sick man to reason deep in politics, otherwise I should be still wondering at the hard fate of Whigs at this present time, more than ever since at the very time they are the chiefest support of a Ministry and the only of a Government, they are themselves the only obnoxious people and the farthest off from being considered.

In the midst of our promising successes abroad one has but too many subjects of allay. The death of that wonderful Princess, the Queen of Prussia,[2] had I never known her but from fame, would have been but too melancholy. How much the honour of knowing her and being (as you tell me) remembered by her must add to this you may imagine. I hear this moment of the death of my good Lord Huntingdon,[3] a youth I shall for ever regret, having found in him more valuable qualities and more love of his country than in any of his age and rank.

I know not why I mention this, or how I came to write so long a letter, being indeed unfit to write long as my health is, and having so many melancholy occasions.

The news you write me of the Electrice's[4] bearing the Queen's death is a great comfort; should hers follow we were miserable indeed. Forgive me that I add only my being your obliged friend and humble servant.

[1] In the new Parliament, which met in October, 1705, the Whigs had a majority.

[2] Sophie Charlotte, Queen of Prussia, died 1st February, 1705.

[3] George, eighth Earl of Huntingdon, died February 22nd, 1704-5.

[4] The Electress Sophia of Hanover, mother of the Queen of Prussia.

## TO LORD SOMERS.[1]

CHELSEA, *October* 20*th*, 1705.

To Lord S——s, with "Moralists" (then entitled "The Sociable Enthusiast."[2])

MY LORD,—Enclosed is an odd book, without date, preface, or dedication. It might have been dedicated to you, perhaps, if it had been to be published. But the author has more kindness for you and himself than to call either name in question for meddling with such subjects. You have had a "Tale of a Tub" dedicated[3] to you before now, but a "Tale of Philosophy" would be a coarser present to come publicly upon you as that did. But here you are screened, and if you have any fancy to read, you have privacy sufficient. For so wholly and solely is the book dedicated to you, that nobody has set their eyes on it, nor shall, besides yourself. How do I know that? (you will say), for is it not in your power to show it?

[1] John Somers (1651—1716), Lord High Chancellor of England, may be regarded as the best type of the "Old Whigs," and to him was chiefly due the credit of the Act of Union of England and Scotland. He was a man of great erudition and a patron of learning. He corresponded with Le Clerc, offered aid to Bayle for his Dictionary, and secured pensions for Addison and Swift. Shaftesbury forwarded to him all of his philosophical productions before they were otherwise given to the world, and also accompanied them, as in the present instance, with most interesting letters.

[2] Two copies of this earlier printed work are to be found among the Shaftesbury papers in the Record Office. The one has still its original title-page of "The Sociable Enthusiast: a Philosophical Adventure written to Palemon" (Bundle 24, No. 5); the other has substituted in manuscript the new title of "The Moralists: a Philosophical Rhapsody" (Bundle 24, No. 4). The latter copy is also full of corrections and additions in the handwriting of the third Earl of Shaftesbury, nearly as printed in the "Characteristics," Vol. III. If the date ascribed to this letter be correct, "The Sociable Enthusiast" would belong to the year 1705, whereas "The Moralists" appeared in 1708—9.

[3] The "Tale of the Tub" (1704) was dedicated to John, Lord Somers, by Dean Swift.

—No. There is a certain constraint which a man of your character lives under. You are bound by candour and fairness not to do what you are forbidden by one who has this right over his own gift. You have it free, and are desired to use it as freely. If you have no fancy for it burn it, or despatch it any way. Show it you must not, for it is otherwise enjoined you, and though you are too fair to do this injury to a stranger, how know you, after all, but it may be a friend, and a particular one, whom you may thus disoblige ? But as to this point I am safe, after what I have said. Now a word to the business itself.

There was once a time when statesmen and such as governed in the Senate and in the field thought it no disgrace to them to give many spare hours to philosophy. One might have seen the noble patriots meeting often upon these parties in the country, and at their villas near the town, to debate of these affairs, enquire into the laws of their greater country and discourse of the nature of the universe, the ends of man, and the distinctions of good and ill. The Laliuses and the Scipios, the Ciceros and the Brutuses, are now out of date. Philosophy has not the honour to be owned by men of note or breeding, and the author you have here to deal with has been hard put to it to contrive what persons he should bring in play, upon whom he might father his philosophy. At last he e'en desperately ventured it with the younger men, and laid his scene in the midst of gallantry and pleasure. For gallantry and ladies must have a part in everything that passes for polite in our age. The worse luck for us. It shows our Gothic extract. 'Twas knight errantry made the fair sex the rule of everything. The same zeal that made the priesthood absolute over men's souls, made the sex as powerful over their understandings. Posterity pays for this: for since ladies have had to do out of their chambers, and priests out of their temples, philosophy has gone to wreck, and there has been sad havoc among the men of sense. Reason, wit, and letters are no longer a security to great men's understandings. They betray themselves on every occasion of their private lives, and are no more able to regulate their opinions or conduct or what relates to their happiness than the merest of the vulgar whom they despise. Nobody stands to his own choice in life or death. It is a lottery-chance of our soul.

z

Effeminacy and superstition are twin passions, and philosophy (their common foe) being set aside, they play their tricks alike upon mankind. For as those fops who escape the most dangerous beauties are caught at last by some odd monks, so unhappy bigots, breaking out of the common road of religion, are entangled in by-paths and deeper in the briars than before. To save the invidious examples of time present, I could bring several known instances of a former witty reign, where many of the wits that laughed at common religion were taken up with conjurers, chemists, astrologers, fortune-tellers: and the Monarch himself, too, at the bottom as great a cully in this kind as he was in another. His death crowned all. The whore and confessor closed the scene, and pieced admirably well with the morals that went before.

This is human nature. This is what we must all come to, if we take no more care of ourselves to get better notions of things, a truer taste and more settled opinions than such as are palmed upon us by fashion or authority. It is not wit, pleasantry, or humour that can fence against those spectres of our childhood. Nor can a little brisk thought wed us to the new opinions we are fond of, when we think we become wiser than ordinary. We may think what we will; but neither the former nor the latter of these are our own opinions. A great deal must go to make an opinion *our own* and free it from affectation and dependency. Formalities, pomps, and ceremonies must be broken through, prejudices torn off, and truth stripped as naked as ever she was born. Religion and gallantry have been wonderfully dressed up in latter days. The ancients were very scanty in the first and so impolite as to know nothing of the latter. No wonder indeed since they stuck to simple nature, which has been improved so much since their time. For Christianity is super-natural religion, and gallantry super-natural love. It is a wonderfully hard matter to deal with super-natural things, and therefore we moderns, though in these affairs we so much exceed poor ignorant heathens, yet for certain we have more dangers multiplied upon us, and have reason to take greater care of treading awry. It is as hard to pick out a right creed and be orthodox, as it is to find the point of honour and be the nice lover and well-bred man of the ladies.

Here are rocks we often split upon, which the ancients (bold, blind fellows) could sail through with all ease. Hardly can one find any shipwrecks of this kind in the lives of their great men. Their religion seldom cost them their wits. They could die without superstitious fears, and have mistresses at a better rate than the loss of their fame and fortune.

But who am I that censure thus at my ease? Who am I that pretend to be a guide, and take upon me to write of philosophy and the ancients to one so knowing as yourself? To answer you in the fashion of our days I will tell you a story. There was once at Amsterdam a prodigious thick fog, which came on such a sudden upon the city about exchange time that not a man could see before his feet. Happy was he that had a house nigh at hand; for those who were at a distance knew not how to get home, and many that attempted it were quickly over head and ears in the canals, and by their loud outcries warned others to make a halt. In this distress who, think you, were the only guides that could happily conduct men to their homes? Truly, no other than a poor blind fellow or two, who, being not at all worse-sighted for the mist, and being well used to the streets, could walk them in their slow pace as freely now as at any other time. But now for application of my story. Business is a strange mist, especially public business, which, as the affairs of mankind are at present embroiled, is enough to darken the brightest genius in the world in matters of philosophy and speculation. These mists, as it happens, are no obstacles to me; I have little to do in politics, but in other dark mysteries, where I have been long poking about my way, blind as I am, I may chance lend a hand upon occasion to a discerning man, help him, perhaps, out of the vapours and give him a good night's rest when he may want it. Is it not just that you, who lose so much of your rest for the public, should enjoy all the tranquillity or happiness that philosophy, the muses, or human wit can present you with? He were an ungrateful wretch, who, enjoying his ease and the blessings which these countries owe to a late prince,[1] should have no good witness for the prosperity and happiness of his best Minister, and, I had almost said, his

[1] King William.

only friend, who, had it not been for that ungrateful service,[1] might have enjoyed quiet enough, and at an easy rate, long ere this might have purchased a much fairer fortune, and sat down loaded with wealth, free of envy, and without so much as an enemy in the world. Do not think, however, that I pity you. Who is there that would not wish for such enemies as yours, to be beloved and thought of as you are? A good fame is an advantage to be set against any loss whatever, nor would I wish to see you such a philosopher as to abate one tittle of your passion for that honest fame you are conscious of. All fame is not alike. There is as much difference as between noise and music. Mere fame is a rattle to please children, and the famousest people in the world are famous fools. But the fame that arises from the consent and harmony of wise and good men is music, and a charm irresistible to a heroic soul. The fame of nobility, high stations, warlike feats or conquests, make not a single note in this symphony. What love was ever gained by these? What hearts were ever won in this manner? But where extraordinary abilities in public business and a masterly genius in the chief concerns of a people are joined with a firm adherence to their interest, and accompanied with a modesty, sweetness of temper, and obligingness hardly found in those of the lowest rank; 'tis no wonder, if the sound of such a fame be enchanting; its numbers being thus filled; its force owing to judgment, and its increase to esteem and love. Not to be pleased with such a fame as this, is to have no love for mankind; for where love is greatest, there is always most pleasure in a return. May you still love and enjoy this generous well-born fame. May you grow every day more conscious, and know and feel your strength of this kind, so as not to part with one hair of it for all the deluding *Delilahs* of a court, which once already has so barbarously betrayed you. Or should you deliver yourself up to be bound, let it be with withes only and not ropes, which, like that Jewish Hercules, you may break with ease. May all other bonds and fetters prove as easy to you. For liberty of mind is the highest good a philosophical friend can wish you. And as

[1] Lord Somers was impeached under William III., and also his name was struck off the Commission of Peace on the accession of Anne.

such a one (for so every one in his way) I pray strenuously for you "that the same evenness of temper may attend you which hitherto you have preserved in every state; that the command of passion so advantageous to you in public, and with others, may be of the same use and happiness to you in private with yourself. That you who make every one easy, may have everything sit easy with you, religion, love, honours, greatness. That courts and mistresses, and all charming things, may be yours, and not you theirs; nor any powers have the privilege to call you theirs except reason and your country. For when you are most theirs, you will be most your own."

## TO LADY PETERBOROUGH.[1]

CHELSEA, *October*, 1705.

MADAM,—I never felt the unhappiness of a sickly state so much as now that I am unable to answer the great honour I receive from your ladyship in making me (as a family friend) a sharer with you in your concern for my Lord Mordaunt.[2] I am sensible of the sad impressions his conduct must have made on so excellent a mother, whose early concern and constant cares for a family deserved to have met so much happier success as they have been extraordinary, and almost without example, in those of your rank, and so much justice I must do my Lord Mordaunt, as to own I never saw in a son a truer or perfecter return of natural affection. The sense of gratitude, the duty and veneration he expressed for you on some particular occasions in which he honoured me with his confidence when I last saw him, was one of the most amiable parts I was ever witness to in a young man, and discovered a tenderness and piety seldom joined with so much spirit, gallantry, and bravery, as he has shown to be his character. But the thoughts of Lord

[1] Carey, daughter of Sir Alexander Fraser, of Durris, Kincardineshire.

[2] John, Lord Mordaunt, was the eldest son of the third Earl of Peterborough. His early letters indicate that he made a confidant of Shaftesbury. In political life, however, he is known to have moved the impeachment of Shaftesbury's friend, Lord Somers.

Mordaunt's merit, so agreeable to your ladyship, at other times may perhaps only aggravate your grief for him at present, when you consider the ruin he may have brought upon himself by disobliging his father, whose severity he has so much reason to fear. Forgive me, madam, if I say I esteem it even impossible that my Lord Mordaunt should have cause to fear equally from your ladyship. Each parent has a several part. The very best of fathers must yield in tenderness and affection to a mother. I shall offer little therefore to your ladyship by way of intercession for my Lord Mordaunt, persuaded, as I am, of your great goodness. All that I would willingly add should be, if possible, to comfort you and alleviate the affliction. But this I fear may be in vain, if there be no other prospect than of ruin to Lord Mordaunt, who draws the ruin of his family after him if he falls a sacrifice to his father's resentment. What comfort or what advice to offer your ladyship in this most unhappy circumstance I know not. I am in many respects disabled from interposing in such . . . concerns of relations, and have nothing left me here besides a sad condolence. My friendship with Lord Mordaunt and the concern I have had for him since his very infancy, the honour and respect I have for my lord his father, and the inviolable and profound esteem which I have ever preserved for your ladyship—these surely are sufficient to make me no slight sharer in your family affliction, which I think may justly be esteemed a public one, when I consider what family it is, and not only the past, but the present and immediate services and merits of the persons that are concerned.

I must own that when I think of the glorious services Lord Peterborough [1] has performed, and is carrying on still with so much hazard and disregard to himself; when I think of his two sons, whom he exposes no less than he does himself; and when I think of the wife and mother of these, who has seen and must still see all that is dear to her exposed in this manner to perpetual danger for her country's sake, I cannot at the same time but think that country very unfortunate if it be under a government

[1] Lord Peterborough was at this time conducting a campaign in Spain.

that will not think such a case as this worthy its regard. But surely, Madam, it is far otherwise. We have not only an excellent Sovereign,[1] but one of your own sex, the best of wives and best (the most unfortunate) of mothers. Her hand alone can heal so sad a wound as this. She is a mother of as many families as her nations hold. But she is more particularly so to her nobility, and those in her immediate service. Her great opposite and enemy, the most detestable of princes,[2] thinks himself in policy so much bound to this part that he has long since put himself upon the foot of being a reconciler of breaches in this kind, and a restorer of the particular families of his nobility whom, in general, he has brought to ruin and slavish dependence on his will. Were this accident at the French Court and either of the noble families of such importance and service to the Crown, we should soon see the unhappy breach repaired and the union of the families made perfect by the prince's favour. I would not willingly think that any prince's favour or bounty should be beyond that of our own. Hitherto it has not appeared so, for we have seen bounty extended even to friendship, and merit has justified the choice. But nothing can confirm it more than if the same bounty be seen to extend itself in proportion elsewhere. And that this will happen so I cannot but have some hopes, and I beg your ladyship to count this thought as something, though the suggesting it anywhere else be far out of my sphere.

An unhappy and uncommon distemper in my lungs has banished me from the town these several years, and I am hardly yet recovered of a twelve months' lingering fever, occasioned by asthma, which a few moments of the town smoke constantly throws me into, and which I begin already to suffer under, so as to be forced in a few days to remove some miles farther from it than I now am. This sad account of myself I am forced to add to the rest of my tedious letter, lest my declining to act farther in your ladyship's or your family's service in this particular should be thought anything else than that utter incapacity which leaves me no more than the sincere profession of being. Madam, &c.

[1] Queen Anne.     [2] Louis XIV.

## TO LORD COWPER.[1]

### St. Giles's, *2nd December,* 1705.

My Lord,—I am extremely sorry that at this time especially I should be forced to apply to you on any account by letter, when I long so much both to wait on you and to enjoy the satisfaction of seeing you in a station which no friend of yours or the public's more truly congratulates with you than I do. Nor am I so selfish as to trouble you at this time of day with anything that relates to my interest merely or my family's. But since the only part left me in public service for these late years has been my country interest in these parts, where I am almost single and have to do with a party now more exasperated than ever, it would be an unspeakable mortification if the Court should appoint my brother-in-law, Mr. Hooper, for Sheriff, a young married man newly come to a small estate, his father being alive, who but a few years since underwent the same service, and had the burden of Sheriff upon him. At the same time there stands the first in the list, one Mr. Whitaker, a gentleman many years ago thought fit to serve, and placed upon the list, who, if I or my interest have ever served the Government, has as zealously disserved it, having been, next the Papists and Nonjurors, one of the fiercest opposers of that interest which the Government has now owned and countenanced. And at this happy time of distinction, it would be doubly unfortunate if one of these (and not the right one) should be taken and the other left. The affair must instantly be decided, and I humbly beg your lordship's assistance and protection.—I am, &c.

---

## TO A FRIEND.

### St. Giles's, *2nd December,* 1704 (5).

23rd August, 1704. . . . "May you live long and happy in the enjoyment of health, freedom, content, and all those

William Cowper (1642—    ), the first Earl Cowper, was appointed Lord Keeper on the 11th October, 1705. He was the most prominent person in the negotiations for the union of England and Scotland, and after it was effected, became (4th May, 1707) the first Lord Chancellor of Great Britain.

blessings which Providence has bestowed on you and your virtue entitles you to. I know you loved me living, and will preserve my memory now I am dead. All the use to be made of it is that this life is a scene of vanity, that soon passes away, and affords no solid satisfaction but in the consciousness of doing well, and in hopes of another life. This is what I can say upon experience, and what you will find when you come to make up the account. Adieu. I leave my best wishes with you." [John Locke to Anthony Collins.[1]]

The piece of a letter you sent me savours of the good and Christian. It puts me in mind of one of those dying speeches which come out under the title of a Christian warning piece. I should never have guessed it to have been of a dying philosopher. *Consciousness* is, indeed, a high term, but those who can be conscious of doing no good, but what they are frighted or bribed into, can make but a sorry *account* of it, as I imagine. Now it being my turn to say something in a dying way (for so, indeed, I am looked upon), I take upon me to send you, as my disciple, this counter charge.

As for *good wishes*, you have abundance, though without compliments. For loving me or my memory, be that hereafter, as it may prove best for you, or as you can bear it. The use I would have you make of it is, that our life, thank heaven, has been a scene of friendship of long duration, with much and solid satisfaction, founded on the consciousness of doing good for good's sake, without any farther regards, nothing being truly pleasing or satisfactory but what is thus acted disinterestedly, generously, and freely. This is what I can say upon experience, and this you will find sufficient at the last to make all reckonings clear, leaving no terrible account to be made up, nor terrible idea of those who are to account with.

Thus runs my charge to you : something different (as you

[1] Anthony Collins was an intimate friend of Locke, who shortly before his death wrote him a letter (Bk.I., Mus. Add. MSS., No. 4290), of which the closing paragraph is here contained in the context. Upon this farewell message of Locke, in the accompanying letter to a friend who had forwarded, Shaftesbury comments in his most characteristic manner.

see) from the admired one given by our deceased acquaintance. Now a word or two by way of remark.

*Life is vain* ('tis true) to those that make it so. And let those cry *vanity*, for they have reason. For my own part, who never could be in love with riches or the world, nor ever made any great matter of life, so as to love it for its own sake, I have therefore no falling out with it, now at last when I can no longer keep it; so without calling names or giving hard words, I can part freely with and give it a good testimony. No harm in it all that I know; *no vanity.* But (if one wills oneself) a fair, honest, sensible thing it is, and not so uncomfortable as it is made. No, nor so over-comfortable as to make one melancholy at the thoughts of parting with it, or as to make one think the time exceeding *short* and *passing.* For why so short if not sound and sweet?[1] Why complain both ways? Is vanity, mere vanity, a happiness? or can misery pass away too soon? But the sweet is living (it seems), mere *living* and doing just the ordinary animal offices of life, which good manners will not allow one to call by plain names. As for other offices more immediately human, and of the rational kind, such as friendship, justice, generosity, acts of love, and such like, the exposing of life, health, or fortune, spending of it, throwing it away, laying it readily down for others—for friends, country, fellow-creatures — these are no happiness ('tis supposed); no solid satisfaction without a reward. Hard, hard duties, if nothing be to follow! Sad conditions at the best, but such as must be complied with for fear of what is worse.— O Philosophy! Philosophy!—I have heard, indeed, of other philosophy heretofore, but the philosophers of our days are hugely given to wealth and bugbears; and philosophy seems at present to be the study of making virtue burdensome and death uneasy. Much good may do those improvers of misery and diminishers of all that is good in life. I am contented that they should cry, *Vanity!* For our part, let us, on the contrary, make the most of life and least of death. The certain way for this being (as I conceive) to do the most good, and that the most freely and generously, throwing aside selfishness,

[1] cf p. 268.

mercenariness, and such servile thoughts as unfit us even for this world, and much more for a better.

This is my best advice; and what I leave with you, as that which I have lived and shall die by. Let every one answer for their own experience, and speak of happiness and good as they find it. Thank heaven I can do good and find heaven in it. I know nothing else that is heavenly. And if this disposition fits me not for heaven, I desire never to be fitted for it, nor come into the place. I ask no reward from heaven for that which is reward itself. Let my being be continued or discontinued, as in the main is best. The author of it best knows, and I trust Him with it. To me it is indifferent, and always shall be so. I have never yet served God or man, but as I loved and liked, having been true to my own and family motto, which is—LOVE, SERVE.

## TO MR. VAN TWEDDE.[1]

St. Giles's, 17th *January*, 1705 (6).

I am sorry I should have delayed so long returning an answer to yours. Yet I have the satisfaction to think I have been answering it in another way, by doing what you generously recommend to me for the coming interest of the two nations, on whose mutual friendship and good correspondence depends not only each other's happiness, but even the happiness and preservation of all mankind. Though I have with great grief beheld the sad effects which the misunderstanding between us this last summer has created : yet I can comfort myself in this otherwise deplorable case by considering that the causes of this are of no force or duration, having no real being in themselves, but like phantoms which a clearer light dispels.

It would imply a mean and unworthy opinion of the councils of either nation to suppose that personal or private matters amongst their officers and ministers, should be the sole occasion of such a misunderstanding as has been breaking out. No interest ever so great can be set in balance with that which

[1] Mr. Van Twedde was one of the friends Shaftesbury made in Holland.

now unites us (even for preservation sake) against a common enemy.[1] If any interest stand in competition, it can be only that of liberty at home; that liberty for which you show so noble and just a jealousy; and may those Argus eyes you speak of be ever open and watchful; never charmed or laid asleep by any magic or power of treacherous natives or ambitious foreigners. I hope I may gain belief with you when I sincerely protest I cannot be less anxiously careful and concerned for your liberties than for those of my own country. Nor have I been ashamed to say it. I had rather see liberty lost here than there, since here it may be recoverable, but there never. We may be serviceable to you indeed (as now and formerly) against a foreign yoke. But against a domestic one, heaven grant we may be never tried. This service can hardly be reciprocal. You may deliver us, but not we you. We are a body that cannot move without our Prince; and princes are not heroes in this kind. The greatest security we have against arbitrary attempts in our own Prince is the despair of success. But when Holland is subjected the work is fair and inviting at home. Liberty loses its sanctuary; the cause of sovereigns sounds instantly in a louder manner through the world, and he must be indeed a divine and god-like Prince who can resist such a confederacy, and to the reproach of other Crowns and absolute Governments remain the single instance of limited authority and popular control. But liberty, which with you is perfect, stands safe, and with us that liberty which we enjoy (and which is all that in nature we are capable of or should aspire at) is most happily established. There is nothing can induce our present Court to any attempts like those heretofore against us. Never was any Prince so justly confided in on this account as is our present Queen. Her interests, measures, the foundations of her title and Government, the bias of her administration, all lie the contrary way, and this current of affairs tends to secure and confirm the same to us for futurity. There may perhaps be a Court interest still kept up against such as are supposed to carry free principles too far. There may be trimming measures which may keep us uneasy here at home, and lose many advantages abroad, whilst we

[1] France.

tamper with a false party that must be ever treacherous to this Government and whatsoever is founded on it; there may be feuds and animosities about courtiers' favourites, and the extravagant gains or supine and insolent behaviour of such as always cost dear to a Court that will protect them. But as long as there is in our English Court no formed design against our liberty (which never can be till there be a formed Tory Ministry), I dare engage there never can be a thought of attempting anything in favour of the Tory interest on your side, never can it enter into their heads or suit itself with their interests to set up either Stadtholder, Governor, or Captain General, or any other form of tyranny. Should any Minister dare meddle in this it would be found his own rashness, not the act of the Court or Ministry, who I verily believe would not fail to give satisfaction upon any discovery of this kind, if any such practice has been or should be for the future.

But notwithstanding I appear to you thus secure as to any formal design in our Ministry or Government, yet I must own still that there are many signs and tokens sufficient to create a jealousy of some design carrying on, whilst the secret negotiations and mysterious behaviour of some great men are attended with the murmurs of people about the divisions which have happened on your side during this last campaign. This has been the occasion of people's penetrating too far and imagining mysteries much greater than in reality they were. The private piques between great men (which turned more upon punctilious ceremonies and little interests of their own than upon any State policies, of their superior courts or governors) came in this manner to make a noise. The murmurs on our side, whilst we attributed all this to the divisions in your State, raised in you the jealousy of a Stadtholder, or some monster of that kind, as a uniting project; and the murmurs on your side, which arose in great measure from this jealousy, raised on our side a jealousy of a peace secretly being carried on, in which if there were any tampering on our side, be sure that it must have been the particular artifice of a private ambition (which will meet with due treatment if once made public), but not the sense or meaning either of our Ministry or nation. There is no need I should tell you that in all our nation the only lovers of Holland are the lovers of liberty, called Whigs. The contrary party (the Tories) are inveterate, and I remember a saying of one of the best and wisest of our latter patriots, who used often to give it for a rule, " that if you would discover a concealed Tory, Jacobite, or Papist, speak but of the Dutch, and you will find him out by his passionate railing." An instance of this you have in a late printed speech of a certain lord, whose first pledge of his conversion to another party was his railing at the Dutch. He was once my particular acquaintance and friend ; but violence of passion and furious animosities against some great men at Court have thrown him into a contrary extreme, and he is become another R——— T———[1]. But to return to my point. Holland being itself free, and joined in interest thus naturally to the free party in England, in opposition to the tyrannical sort who wish its destruction, one would think it impossible that the Whigs here should favour any but those of the same principle with them in Holland, or that the Whigs of Holland should be jealous of the Whigs here. But as for our Whigs the case lies thus. They were delivered, raised, supported by King William, who, whatever he were to you, was in truth to us the very founder of liberty, our good lawgiver, and establisher of our state. What was acted in foreign affairs during the greatest part of his reign was chiefly by himself, without much privity of his Ministers here. Those who were raised under him, and by degrees let into the secret, were of the Whig party, and having no other inlet but by the King and those of his party in Holland, having no acquaintance or correspondence but with his friends and creatures, and having the highest veneration for him and all that he did, how was it possible but they should be led wrong and take all their notions perversely from the very original, whilst they were thus estranged from the Commonwealth party in Holland, and looked upon the Prince of Orange's interest with the same eye in Holland as in England, taking all who were in any degree his enemies to be enemies in the same degree both of the Protestant religion and common cause ?

This is the unhappiness which to this very day we labour under, and I wish the misunderstanding were only on our side.

[1] Probably Sir Richard Temple (1634—1697).

But there is as unhappy, as fatal, as unjust, and as wrong a jealousy on your side which helps to estrange the Commonwealth party from ours, and that is a jealousy of a mere commonwealth in England and the mistrust of an ambitious temper, which is too natural in us, and which would more readily break out under such a form with more advantage against its neighbours. I own it. Truth and the love of mankind forces the confession from me, though to the disadvantage of my country. But then I will aver that imposture itself can produce nothing more false, fulsome, and vain than this insinuation that the Whigs in England think of a commonwealth other than what they enjoy, or that any other is or can be practicable in Britain. Yet is this base insinuation the constant means made use of by our arbitrary party to poison our Prince's ear and hinder him from confiding in his people. But the senseless notion is grown at last so stale and common, after having been so long made use of to serve the purposes of that party that is, indeed, despised by every one amongst us, as I doubt not but it is by yourself and all other good patriots who are as knowing as you are in the common affairs of both nations. The only labour, therefore, will be on our side to inform the heads of the honest party, and let them into a better knowledge of men and things abroad than what they acquired under their great patron when alive, and now, since his death, is transmitted to them by his friends and Ministers, with whom alone they have any correspondence. So that by what I have said, it will be perhaps less a riddle to you to hear it a common expression with our Whigs, *Alas, what will become of Holland without a Stadtholder!* so little do they know what a Stadtholder is, or would prove to their private as well as to the common cause.

I entreat you, therefore, and your friends not to be alarmed, or imagine any mystery from such speeches or discourses of our innocent deluded Whigs, who, as their eyes open, and as they are better informed, will be far enough from giving their voice or helping hand to any such pernicious attempt, by which they would be self-murderers and cut the throat of their own cause. It is said that a disease is half cured when known. I have endeavoured to show you the disease. If in time I discover any worse than I now suspect, you shall not fail to hear of it : nor shall I be tender of our Ministry whenever I discern any foul dealing or tampering in your home affairs. In the meantime, Heaven grant an undisturbed union and mutual good correspondence between our Ministers and generals in the common affairs of both nations, against the common enemy, whom we may now press on all hands with a happy prospect of effectually reducing him if we follow our blow, and stop not our hand after such signal advantages Providence has given us. But if through private jealousies or hopes or flattering prospects of separate advantages and the sweet sound of peace and syren tongues of France (much sharper than their swords), are able to prevail over us, we and our posterity may then deservedly and justly groan for ever under greater miseries and a heavier yoke than any that was ever yet brought upon the world by those universal monarchies which former ages have felt. But this judgment I pray Heaven avert. Nor am I one of the fearful or ill-boding sort, as you know very well. I am full of hopes, especially when I see such spirits as yours and your friends, to whom I beg to be recommended for my hearty affection and acknowledgment of all their favours, and yourself in particular can never want the assurance of my being your, &c.

---

### TO JEAN LE CLERC.

ST. GILES'S, *6th March*, 1705 (6).

To MONS. LE CLERC,—Having received your eighth tome,[1] and read it with great pleasure, I cannot but trouble you with a letter, though only of thanks; for my eyes, which have not recovered so fast as the rest of my health, will not allow me to enlarge as I would willingly do on many particulars, by which you would see how great an impression you have made on me by these last writings, and how much your generous love of truth and liberty procures you true esteem and friendship with those who are far off from you.

[1] Bibliothèque Choisie, 1706.

Your defence of Buchanan [1] will oblige all British men, and can offend no English but such as are slaves, or in slavish principles; and such I reckon can have no property, no country, nor can be called Englishmen, nor indeed *men*. For though I make allowances for that part of mankind who have their education under a tyranny, and know no other law than absolute will; yet for such who have been bred under the government of laws to desert their privileges and give up their native rights, seems to me to be an apostacy from manhood; and such as these scarce deserve indeed to be treated as men. But of such as these (I thank God) we see not many coming up in this age of mankind. There is a mighty light which spreads itself over the world, especially in those two free nations of England and Holland, on whom the affairs of all Europe now turn, and if Heaven sends us soon a peace suitable to the great successes we have had, it is impossible but letters and knowledge must advance in greater proportion than ever. There are indeed inconveniences which for the most part attend all good things, and liberty of thought and writing will produce a sort of libertinism in philosophy, which we must bear with. There were far worse liberties objected to us Protestants at the beginning of the Reformation than any that can be now objected. For as to blasphemous enthusiasts and real fanatics we have few or none very dangerous remaining. And as for Atheists, or such as favour those hypotheses in philosophy, their manner and phrase is both modester and more polite, and as such less dangerous; for I am far from thinking that the cause of Theism will lose anything by fair dispute; I can never (in my opinion) wish better for it than when I wish the establishment of an entire philosophical liberty. It is the profane mocking and scurrilous language that gives the just offence, makes fatal impressions on the vulgar and corrupt men in another manner than by their reason. And as this is the only weapon with which we are not fitted to encounter with such adversaries, so it is the only case in which I would wish the magistrate to interpose on our side. For I am against all other appeals thither, both in religion and philosophy,

---

[1] George Buchanan (1506—1582), historian and scholar, a Scotchman of much learning and literary power.

AA

thinking it a kind of cowardice and mistrust of our cause to call for other help, or do anything which looks like a beginning of *delivering over to the secular arm.*

You must therefore allow me to congratulate with myself on the liberty of these our days, since, notwithstanding it has drawn on you the trouble of defending the common truths, and chiefly that high one of a Deity, yet it is the only occasion that could have given me such a satisfaction as I have had in reading your arguments, and seeing the noble ancients (with their noble follower, our Dr. Cudworth[1]) so happily and usefully revised. Nothing but this could have made me not regret the misfortune of my old acquaintance, Mons. Bayle,[2] engaging as he has done in the matters you mention, out of his sphere. But I am persuaded that your moderation and temper, joined with your abilities and better cause, will not only convince others but advantage even himself. I have not read as yet what he has written.

I must beg you to accept of a book or two more of ours—an Euclid and a Greek Testament, which will shortly come to your hands, and that you will take this, as small as it is, for a token of my being, &c.

### TO MR. STEPHENS. [3]

CHELSEA, *July* 17*th*, 1706.

MR. STEPHENS,—The early apology you made me for your late unfortunate piece of work gave me indeed some sort of satisfaction, which might have lasted, had your public apologies been answerable. As for the book itself, had there been no indirectness, I could easily have overlooked the rest. I must

[1] Ralph Cudworth (1617—1688), who wrote "The True Intellectual System of the Universe ; or, Atheism Confuted " (Lond., 1678), which was the most critical work of his time in English on the history of ancient philosophy.

[2] Pierre Bayle (1647—1766), author of the famous " Historical and Critical Dictionary," and a noted sceptical writer.

[3] Mr. Stephens was a young clergyman, who was aided by Shaftesbury, but who published a pamphlet, that involved his friend.— See letter, 13th December, 1707.

confess, as I am a plain man myself, I am for serving a cause by plain means, and can neither write nor speak but as I think ; but for difference in thought or judgment, no one (I believe) can make larger allowances than myself.

Your going so contrary to any notions you had drawn from my conversations would have given me no disturbance. But since you had so wholly forgot me in your work, you should have remembered me at least in your recantation, and should not have given the world to judge that it was from the conversation of your friends, without distinction, that you received such impressions as those.

As for the great Lord, [1] I never had any obligation to him, though I have done him justice often both at home and abroad, when his character stood otherwise than it does at present. But as for the Commoner, he is my old friend, and in young days was my guide and leader in public affairs ; nor have I ever broken friendship with him, though different judgments in public affairs has long broken all correspondence between us. But were he not or never had been my friend, I have been so much and so remarkably yours, that I· may (though very unjustly) be judged one of those whose too free conversations you have complained of, and by seeing you or living with you now, presently, as I have done heretofore, I may do a great injustice to myself and others without any real service to yourself. So at the present, with my good wishes only, I bid you farewell.

----

TO PIERRE COSTE. [2]

CHELSEA, *October 1st*, 1706.

MR. COSTE,—I have been a little out of order lately, or otherwise you should hardly have had so long a respite as three or four posts after yours, which proved, as most times, so

[1] Probably the Duke of Marlborough.

[2] Pierre Coste (1668—1747), a critical writer and French translator. He was one of the French Protestants who was compelled to take refuge in Holland upon the revocation of the Edict of Nantes in 1685. As tutor of Frank Masham, he resided in England at Oates, from 1697 to the death of Locke, in 1704. He thus became

inextremely agreeable.  You see by that expression of *most times* (which in modern breeding should have been *always*), I am not afraid to use the simplicity which you and I are admirers of, and which I may reckon upon as the chief tie of our acquaintance and friendship.  I am confident I may well call it the beginning and foundation; and believe in conscience there is little or no other security or bond of any friendship or liking. For there is nothing constant but what is simple.  All other relishes are changeable as they are complex and various; and when mutual relish is gone good-bye friendship and acquaintance. It becomes us, therefore, to hold our simplicity, as what we think the only integrity.

I could not but look into Monsieur Dacier[1] out of a kind of insulting malice, to see how he with his Court models of breeding and friendship would relish that place of Horace, which you commend so heartily, and to my heart's wish.  What says he to the *Sanctior paene*?[2]  Nothing truly: or at least nothing to the purpose.  For he is ashamed of it in his heart, and therefore to cover it speciously, he drops this excuse for the ill-bred modification, that it was *pour ne pas offenser la divinité, qui avoit présidé à sa naissance.*  It is very unnatural to Mons. Dacier to assign to Horace any religion at all, after he has represented him as regardless of all religion or religious rites of his country, as to make an open jest of it, and of all things sacred in that pretended mock recantation of Epicureanism, Ode 34, Bk. I., which, in Mons. Dacier's sense, would be the poorest triumph and most affected piece of profaneness in the world, considering the gravity of the ode, and of all those its fellow odes in honour of the gods, and of the religion then established.  But Mons. Dacier knew little of the simplicity of

well acquainted both with Locke and Shaftesbury.  Of Locke's works he published in French Le Christianisme raisonnable (Amst., 1696 —1703), Pensées sur l'éducation des enfants (Amst., 1698), and Essai sur l'entendemant humain (Amst., 1700).  He likewise published Newton's Traité d'optique (Amst., 1720), and Shaftesbury's Essai sur l'usage de la raillerie (Amst., 1710).

[1] Oeuvres d'Horace en latin et en français avec des remarques.— Par Monsieur A. Dacier, Paris, 1681, &c.

[2] Odes IV., XI., 17, 18.

Horace or measure of his irony. For there is so just a measure of his irony that nothing is more simple or honest. There is a due proportion in irony well known to all polite writers, especially Horace, who so well copied that noted Socratic kind. Go but a little further with it, and strain it beyond a certain just measure, and there is nothing so offensive, injurious,* hypocritical, bitter, and contrary to all true simplicity, honesty, or good manners. And such would be Horace's 34th Ode if Mons. Dacier's admired discovery were any discovery at all. But as for his discovery of Horace's religious fit and delicacy of devotion, just in the midst of this pleasant and voluptuous ode, he might, if he had pleased or otherwise known of it, have told us that without regard to any exterior or superior demon, the soul or genius itself (the true demon) committed to every man at his birth, was by the ancients esteemed sacred of itself, as so committed and entrusted by nature, or the supreme universal divinity. And this would have shown him a stronger reason why no man can justly, honestly, or truly pretend to prefer anything else on earth to this genius of his. For this we ought to undergo a thousand deaths, rather than suffer it to be injured, debased, or made miserable; for by death it is not made miserable, nor so much as hurt. If not the better (as they say) it will not be the worse: that is certain in respect of any one who has such due care and concern for it. Horace for all this might easily be ready to sacrifice his life for his country, his friend, or any other cause he liked. He said as much as this to Mæcenas very often, and proved it true at last that he could not survive him, whether trouble and concern were the occasion or whether something voluntary, over and above, joined in the cause of his soon succeeding death. But to tell Mæcenas that his own genius, his own happiness, his own real interest was not of equal concern to him—nay, that it was not more sacred, more solemn, and more a matter of concernment, this would have been as nauseous and silly in those days, and with those persons, as in reality (and according to theirs and our religion) it is impious and profane.

* Hic nigrae sucus lolliginis haec est
Ærugo mera : quod vitium procul afore chartis.
—Sat. I., iv., 100, 101.

But now that I am got again so deep in Horace's character, I must needs try if I can give you any better idea of what I venturously wrote you upon it in that long letter a while ago. Besides, you tell me that you have time before you ; which I am glad of, and will recommend to you, therefore, the reading of some pieces in Horace in a certain order after my fancy, the better to compare times, and things, and passages, but without so much as looking into a commentator or thinking of any that you have ever read.

My notion is that Horace's whole life is clearly and purposely transmitted to us in his writings,* particularly under his apologues. And by this mythology I pretend to reveal to you both his history, chronology, philosophy, divinity, circumstances, and fortune. But before we come to the point of proof, I will lay you down my proof.

I take the life of Horace, therefore, and divide it into three principal states or periods. This is very formal, you see. The first period is that which I call his *orginal free republican state.* His friend and patron during this time was Brutus, who was head of the cause, and who raised him to the command of a legion. His philosophy was suitable thereto ; that of Brutus,†

> * Lucili ritu—
> Ille velut fidis arcana sodalibus olim
> Credebat libris, neque, si male cesserat, usquam
> Decurrens alio, neque, si bene ; quo fit, ut omnis
> Votiva pateat veluti descripta tabella
> Vita senis.—Sequor hunc.—Sat. II.. i., 29—34.

And below

> Quisquis erit vitae scribam color.—l. 60.

And he has been as good as his word, for he has painted himself in true colours through all his succeeding changes of life. For that this satire was none of his latter pieces may be seen by his ardour of writing, which was so well abated afterwards when he wrote Ep. II., Bk. II.

† See the two old writers of Horace's life, as well as Horace himself, S. VI., v. 48, L. I. ; Ep. II., L. II., v. 49 ; also S. I., v. 76, and Ep. XX., v. 23. In both of these last places, in the last most demonstrably, he refers to Brutus and the great commonwealths man with whom he was in war, for after Philippi he made no more campaigns.

the old genuine\* *Academic,* or as Cicero says, in reality, the downright Stoic; that of his uncle Cato; that of Laelius, Scipio, Rutilius, Tubero, and almost all those commonwealths men, as well as of the new ones, Thrasea, Helvedicus, Soranus, and the rest in after times. But for distinction sake, let us, if you will, call this philosophy the Socratic, civil or social. For thus Horace himself distinguishes, Ep. I., v. 16: "Nor were there, indeed, any more than two real distinct philosophies, the one derived from Socrates, and passing into the old Academic, the Peripatetic, and Stoic; the other derived in reality from Democritus, and passing into the Cyrenaic and Epicurean. For as for that mere sceptic, and new Academic, it had no certain precepts, and so was an exercise or sophistry rather than a philosophy. The first, therefore, of these two philosophies recommended action, concernment in civil affairs, religion. The second derided all, and advised inaction and retreat, and with good reason. For the first maintained that society, right,† and wrong was founded in Nature, and that Nature had a meaning, and was herself, that is to say in her wits, well governed and administered by one simple and perfect intelligence. The second again derided this, and made Providence and Dame Nature not so sensible as a doting ‡ old woman. The first, therefore, of these philosophies is to be called the civil, social, Theistic; the second, the contrary.

I assert, therefore, that Horace's first philosophy was suitable to his first patron and cause. Here we have him first studying at Athens, then fighting upon the same principles at Philippi, with what success he tells you in pleasant raillery on himself (Ode the 7th, of Book II.). His military courage and philosophical were much alike. The shield was thrown away, and philosophy after it, as a poor defence against

---

\* Ep. II., L. II., v. 45.

† "Quidve ad amicitias, usus rectumne, trahat nos" was the stated question. See *Hor.*, S. VI. of Book II., v. 75. He was of the latter opinion when he wrote "Oderunt peccare boni virtutis amore," Ep. I., xvi,, 52. But of the former opinion when he wrote S. III., L. I., v. 113, "Nec natura potest justo secernere iniquum."

‡ So the Epicurean in Cicero treats Providence under the name of Εὔνοια. See Tully, de Nat. Deor., Lib. I., S. VIII., page 18. Edit. Davisannus—Fatidica Stoicorum Εὔνοια.

necessity and starving. Here, then, comes Horace's second period or state, for he soon gets to Court, and this I call his debauched, slavish, courtly state. His patron Mæcenas, a suitable one, and his philosophy, too, as suitable, being of the second kind I mentioned. "Naturam expellas furia." Nature is powerful, and will return when she has fair play. Horace could not long hold it. The slavish objects, the servile ties, the abandoned principles and manners, the parasitical tables (as Augustus calls them in his letter to him), all these, into the midst of which he was now got, and in which he had served a more than seven years' apprenticeship, began to work heavily on his nature. And hence arose his third and last period, viz., his *returning, recovering state*, and his recourse to his first philosophy and principles, sorely against Mæcenas and the Court's desire, who would have kept him, and did all they could to do so, but in vain.

Now, therefore, for the distinguishing of these states or periods, I would advise you to begin first by the third satire of the first book, which is the strongest in his new way, and most pointed against the civil and Theistic philosophy. "Cum pro-repserunt" (v. 99), and "Jura inventa metu" (v. 3), are decisive and characteristic. And indeed the first, second, and fifth, seem to be so too, especially that fifth, as you may see in the end. There is no need to read more of it. Nor is that fourth to our purpose, being all critical and not moral. So that the third, the first, and second being only what you are to read entire, you will be pleased to observe, that though the third be the most positive, yet the first and second will negatively show you the same thing, I mean that by the faintness of the philosophy, and the absence of all that strenuous and round dealing with vices, which afterwards in his life you will perceive, it is apparent that the pieces are of that same school and formed upon a Court philosophy, so that the placing of these first satires is apt enough to my purpose. Nor is there any one in all the first book which I assign to Horace's immediate returning state, though the sixth looks very much that way. The first plain one of that kind, though this be but barely a beginning or tendency, is satire sixth of book the second; where you will see Horace begin to sicken, and may easily find which way his pulse beats. But before you come to read this, I would wish you to read epistle the fifth, where he is in his exulting state; and epistle the 15th, especially towards the latter end, where he begins, you will see, to be a little sensible of his case : and then, if you please, Ep. XVII.; where, like a master in that parasitical way, he gives precepts very satisfactorily, and at his ease; but in the immediate following one, the 18th, with more diffidence and mortification, v. 86, "Dulcis inexpertis cultura potentis amici." —For he had now, as we say, *bit upon the bridle*, and had received sufficient check.

Hence, now comes the third and last turn of Horace, viz., his recovering, returning state. In this I consider him (by a subdivision) as beginning and as determined. To his beginning and first entrance I refer this last-mentioned letter, viz., the 18th, together with which I would have you now read that before-mentioned satire, the 6th, of book the 2nd, which piece will begin to give us the first light. For now Horace begins to get light himself. I ought to have promised to you, that as to the first state or period of Horace's life, we have no *writings. For it was, in fact, necessity only and misery, after the fatal day of Philippi, that made him (as he † faithfully and honestly tells you) turn poet for bread. But now he began to see that his bread was too dearly earned; and now comes his conversion or restoration. Here it is that by my fables I pretend to discover Horace, and lay open his secret. As soon as ever Horace comes to fables he is dipt. He dares only tell his mind in fables.

*As for the 7th S. of B. I. the fact related was indeed before the battle of Philippi, but so little before, that by considering only times and circumstances, and Horace's station and character under Brutus, it is easily seen that the relation and farce itself must have been written some time after that revolution in the . . . State, which made such a terrible revolution in Horace. This was one of his first lewd pieces, for so I may call it, not only with respect to its scurrility and buffoonery, but as a reproach and disgrace, was not very becoming in one who was an outlaw himself in the same cause, and the bringing in the brave Brutus's name on this occasion was not so very suitable to his general's and patron's dignity. Rupilius, a Praetor, with the rude Persius, however ridiculous, were no insignificant helpers in the cause. † See Ep. II., Bk. II., v. 51.

All his fable-pieces are of the third period, They are in all seven. Two of them are but slight touches. The rest are formal apologues fully and distinctly told. All mean that same thing. If you have the moral of one, you have it of all. One key serves to all the locks. The first, which is that of the mice in Sat. VI., Bk. II., you have read, I dare say, often enough in your life. But now I pray you read once again. For when formerly you read it you little thought perhaps that ever Mæcenas should have been meant by the city mouse and Horace by the poor frighted country one. But so I will show it to you. Go, therefore, now straight after having read all the rest, as desired of you, in order, and concluded last of all with this epistle and fable of the mice; go, I say, directly to Ep. II., Bk. II., notwithstanding this be a little out of order. For this epistle is one of the last pieces in our subdivisions; and, if I am right, must have been one of the latest of Horace's life. However, that you may see the thing plainer, go to that contrary extremity, and see Horace writing to a friend, not to Mæcenas, nor under that heavy burden of a seeming obligation, but to an indifferent person, to whom, without offence, he could tell his griefs and positive resolution of retirement. Hear, therefore, his second apologue, or story of Lucullus's soldier (which is honest Horace himself), v. 26. The moral and application of which begins at v. 41 and so to v. 54 inclusive, but which is not perfect and declaratory till afterwards, v. 141.: " Nimirum sapere est abjectis utile nugis." For, as Lucullus's soldier has done with fighting, so Horace renounces writing. The cause ceases and the effect is taken away. But what cause ? Horace is at ease. He has got his zona (his estate) again. Ah! many thanks to Mæcenas. And will he leave Mæcenas then ? Will he retire and slight him ? Is not this ungrateful ? Let us hear Horace answering for himself.

And now, therefore, if you please, go to the third and fourth apologue, and read with wondrous care (for this is the most wondrous, nice, and artful piece that perhaps was ever written in the world) the seventh epistle of Book I. Here the apologue of the fox and weasel is first related, and is put with all the force imaginable for Mæcenas against Horace. But by that following story of Vulteius, he sets all right, and shows Mæcenas

that the effect (as I told you) ceases from another cause. His
mind is no longer the same that it was. Had he ever so little
estate he would now retire and philosophise. Though not a
word of philosophy all this while to Mæcenas. It is a paw-word,
as they say, and though he asserts the thing itself thus plainly,
yet he uses other names of liberty and rest, for philosophy
was too shocking, too harsh an idea for the soft Mæcenas. Yet
does not Horace abate one tittle of his right. " If you upbraid
me," says he ; " Mæcenas, if you reproach me for ingratitude
take back your gifts." "Cuncta resigno," v. 34. " Magis apta tibi
tua dona relinquam," v. 43, apt indeed for you a great man, an
Atridas, not apt for poor Ithaca, such a mind as mine, naturally
mean and simple, and now at last returned into so homely and
rough a philosophy, out of which and a tolerable contented state
of poverty, you, Mæcenas, debauched me, as that orator Philip did
Vulteius. For it was not out of mere hunger that I got
cunningly and fox-like into your granaries. I was enticed,
corrupted, and drawn. Nor is it at this time a bellyful and
plenty merely that keeps me from making court to you, as
having got what I wanted. It is not this makes me desire to be
at liberty, as if I only meant a life of indolence through a kind
of surfeit of pleasure, but no real dislike rest and liberty above
either pleasures or riches, or all that the Indies and Arabia can
afford one. If you believe it not, try me, I beseech you, once
again in honest poverty. Leave me but where you found me.
Let me be empty again, lean and hungry as I was, when out of
Court, and see if you can catch me there by the same baits a
second time."

To make this still plainer (if by this time it will not be
plain enough), pray go now to the fifth and sixth apologue in
Ep. X., of Book I. The first is (as I told you) one of the slight
touches, but it is a plain one. Horace has had enough of Court
diet. The *Pontificum coenae*,[1] which he mentions in one of his
odes as so very rich and sumptuous, were at the same time very
surfeiting, it seems. He had served an apprenticeship, and as
the Dutch servants are said to leave their masters for being
forced to eat salmon and other fish, which in midland countries

[1] Ode XIV., Bk. II., l. 28.

are esteemed such rarities, so Horace was now a runaway from the Court delicacies, "Utque sacerdotis fugitivus liba remso," v. 10. After which follows the sixth apologue, a plain one, v. 34, where you may see how uneasy Horace is under his rider, and would gladly be at grass again, and turned wild, stripped and naked, into the wild field, at all adventures, either of starving or being beaten up and down and pestered by the stag, his enemy. For this was but a slight sore, and tolerable in comparison with the royal saddle and management, and all the several airs he was forced to go in this courtly academy under his princely riders. Better it was to labour and search in the old Socratic * academy for truth and wisdom, whatever it cost. Better it was, as Horace now thought, to study quietly for his mind's sake, though he should starve, than for the entertainment of others and to delight the over-dainty and curious † palates of Mæcenas and the Court. Indeed the Court (to come to my seventh and last short fable) may in another respect be well called the lion's den (see Ep. I., Bk. I., v. 73), and which even in our days and in our nation proves we see but too fatal to all good patriots, especially old Whigs such as was Horace.

But I have now made my letter long enough, and have set you (I think) a round task; I hope, however, not of an unpleasant kind, so that if you find nothing at the bottom of what I have written there is no loss, for reading Horace, though ever so often over, can never be a loss.

I had forgotten to tell you that after all this course of reading I have set you, you may do well to read over Sat. VII. of Bk. II., and then Sat. III. of the same book, to see how artfully Horace (as in his first epistle of Bk. I.) covers his rigid philosophy, which ere this he in reality was returned to, but would give it an air of raillery. In both these satires, as also in that short epistle, the eighth to Celsus, you will see Horace painted to the life, as he was in the second period, with all his vices, from which and from his lewd poetry he was now getting free, and shifting the best he could. Here therefore I must desire you in the last place to read over Ep. I. of Bk. I., and note v. 10, "Nunc itaque

* See Ep. II., Bk. II., v. 45.

† Denique non omnes eadem mirantur.—Ep. II., Bk. II., v. 58.

et versus et cetera ludicret pono." Here you will see his struggle
and hard labour to get clear of the Court pleasures. And if the
word pleasures surprise you, see how thoroughly, and as one
may say revengefully and spitefully he treats pleasure (even
love and mirth) in his bitter irony at the end of Ep. VI. of Bk. I.,
which is one of the most puzzling as to philosophy, because it
seems in the beginning to favour the anti-theistical sort, by
speaking against amazement and astonishment about the order
of the heavens, as if it were after the Lucretian or Epicurean
kind. But it is strongly of the other sort, and means quite
another thing, as I could show you at leisure out of Cicero,
Seneca, and those copies of ancient Socratic philosophy, from the
originals of which Horace drew his, when he was either in or
towards this his third period.

And now at last when you have read all this, and undergone this college (as they say in Holland) upon Horace's works
after my peculiar notion, if you think it not merely whimsical,
you will have a full proof from the story and life of Horace, as
well as from his ever visible candour and ingenuity, that he did
not make that solemn ode of his (the 34th, I mean, of Bk. I.)
as a scurrilous mockery of buffoonery against the Socratic
philosophy, against virtue, against religion, or the established
religious rites of his country. But that it was actually a truth,
and a sincere one in his mouth, that he had, to his sorrow,
" Parcus deorum cultor et infrequens," by having fallen from his
first principles, with which he began the world; but that in
process of time, after having experienced all that pleasures
and a Court with looser morals and a more flattering
philosophy could afford him, he did at last " Retrorsum vela
dare atque iterare cursus relictos." Nor was it necessary
that Horace in such a recantation as this should treat religion
any otherwise than according to the vulgar notions. It had
been ridiculous to philosophise profoundly in the ecstasy and
rapture of an ode. Enthusiasm could never be more becoming
than here; and it is in this spirit that this ode is written.
What are all his other religious odes and secular poems? Nor
was it merely as a poet that he had the liberty of being
enthusiastic. Did not the graver philosophers—the Pythagoreans, the Platonicians, and the rest — accommodate their

notions to the vulgar, and treat these matters κατ᾽ οἰκονομίαν, as the term of art was with the Stoics. Who spoke of fortune more than they ? Who apostrophised her more, or treated her more freely and poetically, describing her mutability, inconstancy, and, as it were, triumphing over her ? Yet was not this esteemed as in the least detracting from Providence. The greatest irregularities of fortune were from appointment and a regular control. Fate was in all, and fortune was subordinate to Providence. It was Providence itself, but in another view. Though when these philosophers spoke of fortune more philosophically and scholastically, it then stood indeed as opposite to order and divine appointment, and in that sense they denied there was any such thing in nature as accident, blind chance, or fortune. But if fortune had been understood by the vulgar in an Epicurean sense, as opposite to Providence and rule, how could temples have been erected and worship paid to her as to a deity ? For she could not for her part be an Epicurean idle deity. She was either no deity or an active one, and had her name, notion, and description from activity, and a mind either good or bad, favourable or mischievous. Therefore, for Horace's not solving the phenomena of the winds and of thunder, like a cool philosopher, and for his speaking of fortune in a vulgar way, as he does here in this ode, it need create no difficulty with one who knows ever so little of the ancients. There can be nothing more natural, if we leave it to natural judgment, and not to the learned art of critics, whose only business is to improve difficulties and confound the most ordinary plain sense of authors, in order to say something extraordinary themselves.

## TO TERESIAS.[1]

St. Giles's, *November* 29*th*, 1706.

.  .  . So much for myself and private affairs, temporal and spiritual, as you are friend and father in both senses. Now as to the public and the affairs of Scotland. You ask

---

[1] Evidently a pseudonym borrowed from Teresias of Thebes, the seer in Greek tragedy.

my opinion (father !)—you shall have it, and it will savour more (I fear) of the philosopher than the politician.

It is long since that I spoke to you with so much boldness and assurance in public affairs, even where all mankind almost were doubters, that you may easily take me for one of a very decisive and presumptuous judgment. But as in philosophy so in politics, I am but few removes from mere scepticism, and though I may hold some principles perhaps tenaciously, they are, however, so very few, plain, and simple that they serve to little purpose towards the great speculations in fashion with the world. That there should be a balance of power in the world is one of the plain principles which the world (thank God) is pretty well possessed of in this rising age. That the balance should for the good of mankind be composed not of a few, but as many powers as is possible, is as simple and as just a principle, but not so generally understood, much less when so reduced as to bring these smaller powers or sovereignties within the limits of cities, and those too of no enormous bulk of widely extended territory. Such powers as these, united by confederacy, or standing league (as of old the Grecian cities by the Achaian, and at this day the German circles, Swiss cantons, and Dutch states), are doubtless the most perfect and according to nature; but how ineffectual to preserve a general balance against greater and more unnatural sovereignties when such appear in the world, history and reason will in good measure show us.

When the confederate Greeks had only barbarian powers around them, the vastest of those powers was unable to destroy them ; but when a neighbouring petty Prince by their commerce and practice grew polite, though with a slender proportion of extended dominion, he soon found means to conquer them and lay the foundation of an universal empire, for want of some other power or more such powers to oppose to him.

The Roman Commonwealth by the same means grew, though more slowly (Carthage being the check), yet more fatally on the world ? You may wonder perhaps that I should have such high thoughts of my own country as to believe that should they fall into a Commonwealth, they would immediately tread the same fatal path of greatness. The over-generous spirits infused by

popular government into so vast a body so framed and situated
would soon I fear employ themselves and give disturbance to
Europe. But as we are happily controlled by the nature of our
mixed government, there is little danger from England, or even
from Britain, as formidable as we may fancy ourselves in such
a union.[1] Nothing can be happier for Europe and mankind than
that this island should in respect of government remain as it
is constituted. Should it degenerate into absolute monarchy,
Europe could have no relief from it, but remaining as it is it
will retain the same power as well as interest to preserve the
balance. And in effect it is this power that in two succeeding
ages has broken the two only powers[2] which have bid fair
for universal monarchy since the destruction of the Romans.
To which of these effects, therefore, will this union probably
operate? Not to a Commonwealth, surely? This is the least fear.
And if so, much less will there be fear of our giving disturbance
or jealousies abroad. We shall have employment enough at
home for our high spirits, and mismanagement and disorder
enough to keep us from such an increase of trade and wealth as
to swallow up our neighbours. The Dutch are safe. Let them
beware of getting a Court amongst themselves. A Court here
will be a sure hostage for their trade; whilst luxury and
corruption reigns on our side, frugality and public good on theirs.

But how stands it on the other hand? What danger from
the union as to our monarchy's growing absolute? Here, father,
comes my doubt and scepticism. If disunited, a Continent-war
and standing force; if united, a Parliament faction and standing
pensioners threaten our constitution. But a war[3] I fear we
must have, whichever way it go. Our Court has cast the die.
The Rubicon is past, and whether is it not better for us to
engage with them after union than when disunited? In the
latter case we have injustice, in the former justice, of our side.
In one way should we have success, it would be a conquest, in
the other only a rebellion suppressed; which of these two may
be made the fatal use of is the only consideration remaining.
And humanity, methinks, would incline one's judgment to that

[1] The Union of England and Scotland.          [2] Spain and France.
[3] War with Scotland.

side where least blood is like to be spilt, though more cruelty perhaps exercised, as when a rebellion is suppressed and the conquered treated as traitors, not as enemies.

<hr/>

## TO LORD SUNDERLAND.[1]

### ST. GILES'S, *7th December*, 1706.

MY LORD,—When the public is so happily served, and the highest wish I ever had for my country is fulfilled, in your being of the Ministry, I have no reason to regret my banishment from affairs, except only the loss of so sensible a pleasure as it would be to me to congratulate with you, attend on you, and see you act a part so advantageous to all mankind, and so rejoicing to those in particular who have early bound themselves your friends. For my own part, to whom you have allowed so strong a title to that honour, it is impossible for me to be wholly silent on such an occasion, and though it be my greatest pride that amongst all your lordship's friends you have not any one more disinterested than myself, or that shall trouble you less on account of those favours which that station empowers you to confer; yet as there is one, and only one, concern of that kind which I have had at Court, your lordship must hear it and be troubled with me once for all, for when I have told my story I have done.

Your lordship knows that after I first quitted the public service on account of my ill health, I returned again to it as unfit as I was, and in the last year of the King's reign exerted all the interest and power I had in his service and that of his sinking friends, not without the flattery of having in some measure succeeded. As the greatest service at that time lay in the elections, and as my province was the hardest, though one the most of consequence of any, so it was impossible for me to do all myself, without the help of friends. I had some that had good fortunes of their own, and these I made yoke-fellows with

[1] Lord Sunderland was a prominent Whig and the youngest member of a Whig junta, which included also Lords Somers, Wharton, Halifax, and Orford. On the 3rd December, 1706, he became Secretary of State, thus being the first of the Whigs to receive office under Queen Anne.

me and obliged them to employ those fortunes as I did my own without other regards. But I had, together with these other friends, one young gentleman in particular who had his fortune to make, and had fixed on the army for that purpose.

I turned him from it; having the prospect of the King's favour for him; which I obtained in the promise of a small place, on which he kissed the King's hand just before his death. As sad a time as followed afterwards to all that loved the King's memory or the Queen's real interest, yet being conscious to myself of no ill merit towards Her Majesty, and of much the contrary to my Lord Marlborough himself, I applied to him, and solicited a favour [1] which was allowed to several others in the same circumstances in consideration of the King's promise. But I met with hard usage, not in this respect merely, but in many things of a very public nature,[2] which I have perfectly acquiesced in, and should now think myself even highly recompensed and obliged if I obtained but this promise of old date for my suffering friend. My entreaty to your lordship is only to present a letter from me to my Lord Duke, which I would not offer any other way than as presuming on your friendship. This will be the only trouble I shall give your lordship, for I shall do no more than represent my case. I am not unwilling to be obliged to a Ministry, now your lordship is of it. I know not whether I am worth obliging; but I believe nobody can be obliged at less cost. As much as I am removed from business in the higher part of the world, I have still a little interest in the country where I live; and it happens that the corner where I am confined is a very important one to England, and has often very nearly proved so in a fatal sense. If I do little good, I flatter myself I can prevent some harm, and may one day or other be found useful in this respect, which whilst your lordship is in affairs would be more particularly my happiness, as one who would rejoice to show how much he ever was, my lord, your lordship's most, &c.

[1] The appointment of his protégé, Micklethwayt, to an office.

[2] On the accession of Queen Anne Lord Shaftesbury was deprived of the Vice-Admiralty of Dorset, a small office which had been in the family for three successive generations.

## TO THE DUKE OF MARLBOROUGH.

St. Giles's, *7th December*, 1706.

My Lord,—I should still have looked on myself as too inconsiderable to be remembered by your grace had you not been pleased to mention me with favour when my Lord Somers did me the honour to speak to you of a concern of mine.[1] It was soon after the Queen's coming to the crown that I applied to your grace on behalf of a friend, who just before the King's death[2] had his promise for a small place that was vacant. Others in the same circumstances had benefit of the King's promise, by Her Majesty's great goodness. But it was my misfortune to receive both in this and other respects very distinguishing marks of Her Majesty's displeasure, though conscious of having otherwise deserved. I should, however, at this hour esteem myself highly honoured and obliged in all respects by this small mark of favour, but if there be difficulty I shall press no further on your grace or any other that have the honour to serve the Queen, being easily satisfied of the little value of my services or interest, and that I have only flattered myself in thinking I was worth being remembered by your grace, as having been very early and constantly, my Lord, your grace's most zealous, humble servant.

## TO LORD SOMERS.

St. Giles's, *January*, 1706 (7).

My Lord,—I know you will forgive me if without any apology I continue to communicate every little matter which I think of the least moment to the public, since I think it of the greatest that you should have knowledge of everything. Enclosed therefore is a memorial relating to an affair of which I talked much with your lordship, and had a disagreeable prospect. I own there is nothing so disagreeable to me as what carries with it the least prospect of disunion between Protestant Powers, especially those two great nations on whom the liberty

---

[1] Micklethwayt's appointment.

[2] King William died 8th March, 1702.

and happiness of mankind depends; and your lordship, who is so much the promoter and author of our home union, will ever, I know, be solicitously concerned for that foreign union and correspondence on which the good effect both of that and all other public labours must depend.

The memorial was by some considerable hands given to my Lord Duke of Marlborough at his coming last away.

What notice he may take of it I cannot tell. It is but a random aim. There will be every year stronger endeavours, and if something be not done to give hope from this side, the more impatient provinces will get the better and force that of Holland to consent to such a charge on our corn and other commodities as I dreadfully fear may in time breed ill blood, for our advantages are prodigious by that free import we have there, and were it otherwise, yet when we see (as I hope soon) the glorious day of a British union,[1] we need less insist so hardly with them on the point of trade, when our advantages will be to ourselves and in the eye of Europe so mighty and increasing.

Now, my lord, as to my private concern; with many very sincere acknowledgments for your friendship and kind advice, I have done as you directed me, and shall continue to do; depending absolutely on your guidance and further instruction, and hoping I may deserve this kind treatment by the sense I have of it, and being so sincerely as I am, my lord, your lordship's most faithful and obedient humble servant.

## TO MONS. BASNAGE.[2]

St. Giles's, 21*st January*, 1706 (7).

Sir,—It would be a great satisfaction to me on any terms to have the honour of writing to you, but you have made it satisfactory in the highest degree by the manner of your writing, and the occasions you have given me. I take withal the privilege

---

[1] The Union of England and Scotland took place May 1st, 1707.

A French Protestant who resided in Holland owing to the revocation in 1685 of the Edict of Nantes.

which you allow me of writing in my own language, and esteem it as an honour to my country that you should have given yourself the pains of adding this our language to your store of knowledge and better learning.

I know not whether I should easily give way to my grief for the loss of our common friend, Mons. Bayle,[1] on which you have so kindly condoled with me, but that the subject of public concernment which you have joined with it is an obligation on me not to dwell too long on my private sorrows. For in this case I must own my private loss makes me think less of that which the public has sustained by the death of so great a man. This weakness friendship may excuse, for whatever benefit the world in general may have received from him, I am sure no one in particular owed more to him than I, or knew his merit better. But that I should thus have esteemed him is no wonder. The prejudices raised against him on account of his sentiments in philosophy could not be expected to raise scruples in those who were no ways concerned in religious matters, but that the hard reproaches of the world against him on this account should not have been able to lose him the friendship of so great and worthy an actor in the cause of religion as yourself, this, I must own, is highly generous and noble, and to be acknowledged not only by all lovers of Mons. Bayle, but of truth and philosophical liberty. Nor can anything, in my opinion, more discover the firm trust you have in the merits of your excellent cause, or the thorough consciousness you have of your own sincerity in it, than the being willing thus to do justice to the memory of a friend, who in whatever respect esteemed erroneous, had undeniably such qualities and virtues as might grace the character of the most orthodox of our age. I know very well that it is in religion and philosophy, as in most things, that different opinions usually create not only dislike, but animosity and hatred. It was far otherwise between Mons. Bayle and myself, for whilst we agreed in fundamental rules of moral practice and believed ourselves true to these, the

---

[1] Pierre Bayle died in 1706. As the pioneer of the French enlightenment he was deemed extremely sceptical by his orthodox contemporaries.

continual differences in opinions and the constant disputes that
were between us, served to improve our friendship. I had the
happiness to see that they lost me nothing of his; and I know
my own increasing every day as my advantages increased by
his improving conversation. I may well say *improving* in every
respect, even as to principles in which the enemies of Mons.
Bayle would least of all allow him the character of a promoter.
But if to be confirmed in any good principle be by debate and
argument, after thorough scrutiny, to re-admit what was first
implanted by prevention, I may then say, in truth, that whatever is most valuable to me of this kind has been owing in
great measure to this our friend whom the world called sceptical.
Whatever opinion of mine stood not the test of his piercing
reason, I learned by degrees either to discard as frivolous, or not
to rely on with that boldness as before; but that which bore
the trial I prized as purest gold. And if that philosophy,
whatever it be, which, keeping in bounds of decency, examines
things after this manner, be esteemed injurious to religion or
mankind, and be accordingly banished from the world, I can
foresee nothing but darkness and ignorance that must follow.
I think the world, and in particular the learned world, much
beholden to such proving spirits as these. And for my own
part I even place to Mons. Bayle's account those excellent things
written by other hands in defence of truths which he gave
occasion to re-examine. What injury such a one could do the
world by such a search of truth with so much moderation,
disinterestedness, integrity, and innocency of life I know not;
but what good he did I in particular know and feel, and must
never cease to speak and own. You will forgive me this sally
of zeal in behalf of my deceased friend, since you have in a
manner invited me to it by the generous notice you have
taken of him, and the unexpressible satisfaction you have
given me in the account of his last days, and his philosophical
character, so deserving and in every respect so like himself, as
I expected.

It would be inexcusable in me to be wanting in any
office of private friendship, being excluded so much as I am
from the public service by my ill-health, which will not suffer
me in the winter and chief season of business to live in or

near our capital city, where coal is burnt, so that I am half banished from society and civil life, except when I am abroad in your towns of Holland where turf-fuel is used, which is as medicinal to me as the other is destructive. But happily before I left the neighbourhood of London (which was not till the latter end of November) I received letters from some friends of your nation and our common religion, which both instructed me and put me on the agreeable service of soliciting in this cause.

I represented the concern to those of our great men with whom I had any influence, and I can assure you I found in them all the good disposition that can be wished towards the service of the French Protestants against the time of peace or whensoever any treaty of that kind advances. Our Ministry grows every day more Protestant. All attempts at further separation between Protestant communions are vanished, and the spirit of moderation and union prevails, so that all animosity ceasing, which was kept up against those who conformed not to Episcopacy, there is no handle left of contempt or reproach against our fellow-Protestants abroad, whose interests it will be esteemed as an honour to our Ministry to pursue, and I dare hope they have it in their thoughts to make a merit of it in the end. For as strong as our Ministry is, and as deserving as are the favourites and great men of this reign, they all know that without an honest popularity and good esteem with the generality of Englishmen, no power can support them long in England. Therefore, besides their principles and good inclinations, it is to be hoped their interests, when well considered, will lead them to act honourably in this affair. I could carry this assurance so far, upon these foundations, that supposing the war were only between France and us, and that we were but near an equal match, I am persuaded that, as many heavy years of war as we have had, we should under such a Ministry and so excellent a Queen sustain it joyfully whole years longer, and push it the most hazardously for the sake of that single glorious article of restoring the Protestants in France, which the Bishop of Salisbury with deserved applause on our solemn thanksgiving day before Queen and Parliament gloriously asserted, not speaking (as may be well presumed) on such an occasion without foreknowledge of approbation to that and other terms of peace, which he there recommended and gave hopes of. The sermon indeed is worthy of being read abroad, that it may be seen what noble principles are asserted before crowned heads themselves, which is no less an honour for such free crowns, that are so happy and secure by the common benefit of those laws and that liberty which they enjoy together with the people of whom they are the head. A small encouragement from the Court will make our people contribute their utmost in the cause of religion. Nor is England so cautious or apprehensive of a religious war. They have not the same regards for Catholic allies as the Protestant Powers abroad.

But above all things, and for the sake of that religion itself, which is so dear to us, we are bound to cultivate in the strictest manner our friendship with the States General. Now, though their zeal for religion be equal to ours, yet their views in this respect will be probably very different. Nor do I attribute this to our greater zeal for religion, but to our blindness in policy and interest of State. For as they who are a wise nation know their strength to consist in numbers of people, especially such as are religious and industrious, we for our parts, whether through the jealousy of our Churchmen on account of their Episcopal form, or whether through a natural inhospitality and aversion to strangers, by whom we have formerly more than any nation been infested, whatever it be, we no way care for any foreigners coming to settle amongst us, and for this reason shall in all likelihood be the more forward in the generous part of securing to the French Protestants the possession of their religion in their own country. But if the States General, through better policy, greater caution and foresight, and more necessary regard to their Catholic allies, cannot in this point come up so high as we whom nature by our situation has made so independent, and by our temper so little desirous of advantage, and increase by foreigners ; what then shall be done in this case for the poor French Protestants ? How shall we solicit, or what ask ? For to make war, or continue it so much as one hour, on that single article of *restoration of religion in France,* is hardly with any assurance or hope to be proposed to the great men of the Government where you are. But if nevertheless it be soundly pressed, and enforced and well solicited (since it is no more than just), it may produce some equivalent, or at least some terms or proposals which compassion and shame may inspire: so as that the Protestant interests may not be so absolutely abandoned as at the last place, when it was not so much as thought of. You know it is a maxim somewhere that *more than right should be asked to the end that mere right may be obtained.* But this is no more than *mere right* which is asked, and may therefore be better urged with modesty; and should it produce only such terms for the French Protestants as might gain those who are detained their liberty, and those who are escaped their estates, the United Provinces would have chiefly the benefit of it, and might reap this great advantage without the envy of England, who will be wholly neglectful of its interest in this respect, and do nothing (I fear) either by way of naturalisation or any other encouragement towards so advantageous a settlement. And this I should think might have its force with the great men of your Government. In the meantime you may do well to make use of our zeal for a restoration, and excite others by this example, which I hope we shall give very remarkably whensoever any negotiations or treaties are set on foot.

Nothing, I assure you, shall be wanting in me so far as I am able to press and solicit so pious and glorious a design; as if I had the perfectest hope or assurance of success even in that very degree.

I thank you for the light you have given me as to former negotiations on our part; and I doubt not but by further search you may find other instances of England's like concernment in the Protestant interests abroad, during the reign of Queen Elizabeth especially, who put herself at the head of the Protestant cause, and whose example may very becomingly be applied at any time to our good Queen and her present Ministry, should you have occasion of making any representation or memorial.

These are the best thoughts which in my poor capacity I am able at present to give you. My zealous endeavours shall not be wanting to the utmost of my power in a cause I can never be ashamed of, nor afraid to serve.—I am, with particular respect, Sir, your most humble servant.

## TO JOSEPH MICKLETHWAYT.

### St. Giles's, 11*th January,* 1706 (7).

Dear Jo,—You may wonder to see a letter from me at last, after promising so long to write to you, but not having been able to keep my word. Indeed, ever since my sickness, upon my leaving you in Holland, I have had so ill eyes that I have been forced to break almost all my correspondence except with good Mr. Furly, who is so kind as to accept of an ill-written line or two, and that but seldom, in return to many obliging and full letters, on many subjects. However, I hope your brother has not been wanting to do me justice in letting you know how constantly and kindly I remember you on all occasions. And to say truth, nothing could have hindered me writing to you since my eyes and health have been better, but that lately I have been endeavouring to do your brother a considerable piece of service, on which his coming over to you (as he has designed) has very much depended. And I still have some hopes of effecting my purpose, or else should not be accessory to keeping him away so long from you and his friends, whom he has such desire to see in Holland.

I, therefore, write this to you without so much as telling him of it. And hope I may even surprise him with the good service I have been so long endeavouring for him. Or if I succeed not, I know both he and you will kindly accept of my endeavours, since I am so truly concerned for your interests, and cannot but be so in a particular manner for yours, whom I have taken such care of, as a child or younger brother of my own, so as to have a kind of natural affection for you, and accordingly I ever heartily pray God for your well doing.

Nothing could have more rejoiced me than to hear, as I did this last year, of the character you began to gain for industry and application to business. I am sorry to hear of your master's death, and hope that other advantages proposed will more than repair the disturbance, and help forward in the gaining you such a character, together with such experience and good conversation,

---

[1] A brother of Thomas Micklethwayt for whom Shaftesbury sought to obtain a public office.

as may in a year or two's time fit you for setting out well in the world.

Time runs away. I hope you will not be impatient, but remember that the best fruits must have time for growth, and that you will soon reap the fruit of your labours and patient industry. I pray God prosper you, and hope you remember my good advice and promises you made me, who am your hearty friend,                                                          SHAFTESBURY.

[Address]: For Mr. Joseph Micklethwayt, to be left at Mr. Furly's, merchant, in Rotterdam.

---

### TO JOSEPH MICKLETHWAYT.

ST. GILES'S, *February* 26*th*, 1706 (7).

DEAR JO,—I am resolved you shall hear soon enough from me this time, lest by delaying as I did lately, for one reason or another, I come at last to make you think again that I have forgot you. But as I can assure you I never did, so now more than ever you may depend on my careful thoughts for you, for many reasons added to those I had before. In the first place your kind letter very naturally, and in a way which no art can imitate, assures me that you have a regard to me and count me as in some measure a parent to you and good friend. In the next place, as I am in the deepest manner bound for your good behaviour, having spent so many of my hours in your instruction, and had you so long a little one under my wing, which has engaged some of my friends, and now in particular (as you mention) my worthy friend Mr. Van Tweede himself, to have an opinion of you, what a trouble do you think it would be to me, I do not say if you did amiss, for I am in no fear of that, but if you should not in every respect answer that character and opinion which I have helped to create of you? I must on this occasion, dear Jo, put you in mind of an excellent passage of Scripture, which is, that of those "to whom much is given, much will be required." I have never been afraid to tell you to your face that I thought you had good parts, nor did I ever think that your being a gentleman by family would make you less industrious, civil, humble, and obedient, where it

became you to be obedient; on the contrary, I thought
that a right sense of such advantages would make you exceed
those of meaner extract and education in all kinds of complacency
and ingenuity. I used to comfort you by this prospect, for
whatever other natural defects or disadvantages you had,
representing to you how much the way of trade and in a
foreign country would be the fittest to employ and render you
considerable and useful; for so it had been, although your education had been such as to have taught you nothing else than mere
trade, and ability in that way only. But it has pleased God
from the very beginning of your application this way, to lay
such friends in your way as were able to forward your understanding in many things besides. And now at last you are in
the house and under the guardianship of so wise a man, that
I may say to you as great an advantage as you are likely to
have in the true knowledge of trade above most young men.

Yet trade itself will be one of the least things for you to
learn, if you make the advantage which you may of such excellent
converse and example. Wisdom, prudence, and virtue are above
all other things. And what you want in the knowledge of books
can only be made up to you effectually by being so placed
near the converse of persons so universally knowing. The
knowledge of the affairs of mankind and Europe are advantages
which few young men in your calling could hope to learn, and
for this and many other accomplishments, if I were to think
of a school, it would be the house where you are happily
received. For mere schools there are none, nor can be, for
reason and good sense. They are things that must be *caught*,
not learnt in the common way of instruction. It is a phrase
amongst painters that they must catch a likeness, as when they
have a Prince or some great man's picture to draw they can look
upon only now and then and in passing. So, Jo, I advise you,
you must endeavour to *catch*. You are naturally quick enough,
and the misfortune is, youth is but too apt to *catch*, but always
the wrong way. An ugly face, a wry mouth, or an ill posture is
sport for boys, and they can mimic anything of that kind
presently, but a comely behaviour, a handsome, decent deport-
ment, goes unminded, and makes no impression. Therefore, dear
Jo, if you would learn those handsome, comely qualifications of

prudence, gravity, understanding, and good sense, you must take your eye off from silly things and idle amusements, and see for the likeness and resemblance of reason and good sense, of which you will find many good models where God has placed you, and which if you do not let escape you, of necessity you must become a man of understanding. For if we give virtue and wisdom fair play, and do not shut our eyes against it, whilst at the same time we open them wide upon folly and nonsense, in this case, I tell you, God having given us withal good natural parts, we stand yet fairer towards the good than the bad, and virtue and wisdom may be said to be more catching than vice and impertinence. So may it prove with you, dear Jo, and so it surely will if the endeavours are answered or prayers heard of your good friend, SHAFTESBURY.

---

## TO MICHAEL AINSWORTH.[1]

CHELSEA, *October 3rd,* 1707.

GOOD MICHAEL,—I have just received yours as I am now packing up in haste for St. Giles's, the season being come that I can no longer bear the town neighbourhood.

I had a letter from you some time before, which I took kindly and deferred to answer till I had time to write at leisure. But now I have none at all. You may not only keep Mr. Locke's Essay, but any other book you want you shall have for your use out of my study.

I am glad to find your love of reason and free thought. Your piety and virtue I know you will always keep, especially since your desires and natural inclinations are toward so serious a station in life, which others undertake too slightly and without examining their hearts.

I suppose I shall see you at St. Giles's ere you go where

[1] Michael Ainsworth was one of Shaftesbury's protégés. While in attendance at University College, Oxford, a number of letters were addressed to him by his patron as " Good " or " Honest " Michael, which have been published in a book, entitled " Several Letters written by a Noble Lord to a Young Man at the University, first printed in 1716." Of his early life see letter dated May 23rd, 1710.

you design. Be prudent in keeping secret what I recommend to you for your own sake, and I shall heartily forward your good undertaking, as I promised, and pray God to give you success, being your good friend and well wisher,

SHAFTESBURY.

[Address]: To Mr. Michael Ainsworth, at Mr. Jones's, Corhampton, Hampshire.

––––––

## TO MAURICE ASHLEY.

St. Giles's, *October* 21*st*, 1707.

DEAR BROTHER,—I am sorry I should have lost the favour you intended me of a visit at Chelsea, having so little hope of seeing you elsewhere. My coming away so suddenly was extremely fortunate for myself, the eastern winds having blown ever since. I have been so long a stranger to the affairs of Carolina,[1] having never been informed of them but by the public prints, that I am unable to give you the advice you desire, and which I should gladly do if I were capable. Matters being come to that sad pass you describe, you will do prudently, no doubt, to make the best you can of so desperate a game. I have not been able to discover any writings about Ely lease in all my late search ; nor have I found so much as the original lease itself. But having got (as I told you) a new lease by good fortune, just before the last Bishop's death, I am safe, and consequently you are so, and may be at ease, since nobody but I myself can bring you in danger. And being now grown a more careful man by experience after having been but too careless in matters of interest and fortune, I can both keep and look after things as I should do, and dare trust myself with whatever is proper for me to keep.

Methinks 'tis very long since I had the happiness of seeing you here at St. Giles's. But I forbear to importune you, having been formerly so unfortunate on that subject; so shall leave it ever to your inclination and the time of your convenience, being always your affectionate brother and humble servant.

[1] This refers to the interests of the first Earl in the early settlement of the American colony of Carolina.

## TO MAURICE ASHLEY.

St. Giles's, *November 5th*, 1707.

Dear Brother,—I am sorry for poor Carolina ; being satisfied how matters stand by what you have written.

I hope you are satisfied, too, as to the other affair, and that you think a danger from me to be no danger. Mortality nor accidents cannot hurt you in the case. If I do it, it must be wilfully, and that I hope can never be a fear with you, nor worth my giving myself any trouble with lawyers, which, however, I should be glad of, in a certain family case, whenever you should give the occasion.

But as to these and other matters, both public and private, in which I have been so unfortunate as to urge you too far, I will never, if I know myself, give you occasion to reproach me hereafter. I wish in all respects you may do to your own liking and satisfaction, and shall be officious no farther than in what is necessary to prove myself, your affectionate brother and humble servant.

## TO ROBERT MOLESWORTH.[1]

St. Giles's, 13*th December*, 1707.

Sir,—You will pardon me if I say it was no surprise to me to hear this post how kindly you had acted for me; when, after the common rate of friendships, one in my case might have expected to have been almost forgotten. But I know too well the value of yours, and though my being now accustomed to live so distant from the town and company reconciles me easily to the parting with more than half the acquaintances I have made in the world; yet that which I had the happiness of making so

[1] Robert Molesworth (1656—1725), created first Viscount Molesworth on 10th July, 1719. His early pamphlet, entitled "An Account of Denmark as it was in the year 1692" (Lond., 1694), was warmly approved by both Locke and Shaftesbury for its vigorous utterances of Liberal principles. He became an intimate friend of Shaftesbury, who confided to him the history of his first and unsuccessful love affair in the letters which were published by Toland, in 1721.

early with you has been too well grounded and on too good principles to suffer me to think of ever resigning it.

The affair in which you have so kindly concerned yourself in relation to my solicitations for a friend of mine, and the hard usage I have met with in many respects since the beginning of the Queen's reign, has opened a mystery to me by which I can explain some part of my ill fortune, at least what has been within this year or two past. They were indeed extraordinary officious persons who so charitably made use of my name in behalf of Parson Stephens.[1] But common honesty should have taught them to make use of nobody's charity against their will. And this charitable representation of me was doubly false; because it implied in the first place, that I had forgiven him myself, before I could be supposed to ask forgiveness for him of others. But I neither forgave him, nor perhaps ever shall. The reason is, that this Stephens was one whom I often saw, and having been friendly to him and helped him in some troubles that he had brought upon himself many years ago, I had reason from his own promise and protestations to expect that he would never have meddled with matters out of his sphere, and least of all in public affairs have struck directly at my interest and opinion, for so I esteemed his usage of the Ministry, in particular as to the character of my Lord Duke of Marlborough, which he had often heard from me, and which both at home and abroad, before and after the King's death, I had in a particular manner espoused with a warmth which my friends well know, and with a vanity (which to me was a great one) of acting disinterestedly, and without any obligation but that to truth and merit, and the interest of my country. I confess I could not at first believe Stephens the author of that pamphlet, until I heard of his owning it, and then could not but think the Ministry highly generous in disdaining to take his punishment for satisfaction. From that time to this I cast him off, nor would ever see his face. Though even at this time I can hardly think him such a villain as to have dared use my name in his own behalf. *Who* those were that used it for him I can't judge, but *what* they were I well know.

[1] See letter of July 17th, 1706.

But be this as it will, if notwithstanding the forgery and abuse, my Lord Treasurer[1] or Lord Duke could have thoughts of obliging me in another case, I must own my obligation to be beyond a common one, and I hope to return it by a more than common gratitude. And by representing this for me, now the occasion has offered, you will add to those obligations which have long made me your faithful friend and humble servant.

Mem.—To Mr. Molesworth on his speaking (unknown to me) to the Lord Treasurer about Micklethwayt affair, and about Parson Stephens. The Lord Treasurer took this letter from Mr. Molesworth to show the Duke of Marlborough.

---

### TO MR. DARBY.

St. Giles's, *February 2nd*, 1708.

Mr. Darby,—I shall be glad to receive Mr. Hughes's acceptable present of his Translation of Mons. Fontenelle,[2] and doubt not but I shall have reason to value it for its own sake as well as the translator's.

I thank you and the unknown person, your friend, for the intention of a dedication on the subject of my deceased friend, Mons. Bayle, whose acquaintance and friendship, as I was ever free to own whilst he was alive, so I readily would now he is dead; and would do anything that looked respectful to his memory. Whatever his opinions might be, either in politics or philosophy (for no two ever disagreed more in these than he and I), yet we lived and corresponded as entire friends. And I must do him the justice to say that whatever he might be in speculation, he was in practice one of the best of Christians, and almost the only man I ever knew who, professing

---

[1] Sydney Godolphin (1645—1702), the first Earl of Godolphin, was Lord of the Treasury during various periods in the reigns of James II., William III., and Queen Anne.

[2] Bernard Le Bovier de Fontenelle's Discourse concerning the Antients and Moderns. Translated by Mr. Hughes. It is to be found also in a volume with Fontenelle's "Conversations with a Lady on the Plurality of Worlds." Translated by Mr. Glanvill. London, 1719.

cc

philosophy, lived truly as a *philosopher;* with that innocence, virtue, temperance, humility, and contempt of the world and interest which might be called exemplary. Nor was there ever a fairer reasoner, or a civiler, politer, wittier man in conversation. His learning the world knows enough of by his books. But this I knew of him by a long and intimate acquaintance, and living under one roof with him, which made me a nearer witness as to his integrity and worth, for which he was yet far more valuable to me than for all his wit and learning. But notwithstanding all I have said, and would gladly say of him in all places, and before all the world, I must entreat you to let this matter of dedication pass by me, for there are certain draughts of flattery which essentially belong to that cup, and are too strong for my weak stomach. I never yet could bear the thoughts of it, and being forced by my constitution to live retired as I do, I cannot bear being so public in another way. So that I beg you would excuse me yourself, as well as to the gentleman who designed me the kind favour.

### TO LORD SOMERS.

(With the printed Letter concerning Enthusiasm.)[1]

*July* 12*th,* 1708.

MY LORD,—Your enthusiastic friend, you see, had made his words good as to what he lately wrote your Lordship upon the discovery of his last letter concerning enthusiasm and prophecy.

However concerned he was at first for being discovered in such a manner, he still told your lordship he was sure there was no cowardice in the case; nor would he be ashamed to own publicly whatever he had written your lordship in private as your devoted servant, for you have none more so, or that desires more publicly to appear so, than himself. The only question is whether anything he is capable of writing can be judged of

[1] The "Letter concerning Enthusiasm" was written by Shaftesbury to Lord Somers under date of September, 1707, but was first printed anonymously in 1707-8. It was occasioned by the fanaticism of some of the French Protestants who had taken refuge in England. Excessive enthusiasm, he here maintains, is best overcome by "raillery" and "good-humour."

value enough to make a present of to your lordship. Were he satisfied of this, he could go further and add both your lordship's name and his own, which, however, in spite of him will be guessed at, after what passed, not only in a certain club (as was intimated to your lordship), but elsewhere in the world, the letter having been from that first person communicated also to some of the author's friends who knew him intimately, and could discover his correcting hand. It was mere fortune it came not in print before now, since a printer several months ago had it left in his hands by some of those persons formerly mentioned. Others have done it the honour to copy pieces of it in their letters, which your friend has seen, and have given it the advantage of their own dress, in which it was likely to come abroad soon into the world amongst the writings of those gentlemen who frequently supply the press, and borrow freely of one another or whoever else comes in their way.

However it be, no one besides your lordship can say positively of the letter whose it is or to whom. You are under no obligation of owning it, much less of patronising or defending it. You have neither the piece nor the author to answer for, and this, my lord, is a sufficient saving for your character. His own he values not; for be it treated as it will, it can neither hurt nor benefit the public, whose service he is so unfit for. It is enough for him if he can serve your lordship, though merely by the good example of endeavouring it, and honouring to the utmost of his power the man whom he thinks deserves the best of his country and mankind. He would be glad to raise such an emulation and see it a fashion with authors as well as with men of note to contend for your esteem, and strive who should appear to be what he thinks himself in reality, your most zealous friend, and faithful, humble servant.

———

TO BENJAMIN FURLY,

CHELSEA, *22nd July*, 1708.

MR. FURLY,— . . . I was over and above indebted to you for your succeeding letter which brought such glorious news.[1] Nor

———

[1] Of the victory of Marlborough over the French on the 11th July, 1708, at Oudenarde.

do I wonder that the particulars you gave at first were not so exact; for though there be not in the world one who admires the Prince Eugene[1] more than I, yet I have long observed that both in England and Holland he has many pretended admirers who cry him up to the skies, for no love to himself but hatred to other people. But I will have done with these subjects; having long pleaded in vain with certain persons on your side in the behalf of the sincerity and good designs of our Ministry here at home, and of some great persons who, though I will not justify some infirmities of others, and many misbehaviours in their former lives, yet have given such proofs long since of their fidelity to the interest of Europe and zeal of the common cause, that nothing but a spirit of detraction can call it in question. This was a doctrine I preached from the first coming of our Queen to the crown. I am sure I had no obligation to her Ministry. They were far from being personally my friends, or any way reconciled (as they are now more and more indeed) to that which I esteem the right party in my country. This I had the good fortune to convince Myn Heer Wellant of when I first came into Holland, the first year of the Queen's reign. But great jealousies have grown up since. Myn Heer Wellant is now dead. I have none that seek my opinion (as he then did) and so I am free of the burden of justifying courtiers and great men, which to such a one as I am, is a hard task at best, since great men will have great faults, and when their politics are good their morals will be ill; and their lives give scandal to such a formal liver as I am, who neither aim at riches nor ever admire what the world (especially people of my rank) call pleasure.

I hope we have one truly good and great man[2] coming up in the world, and that is he whom I contributed what lay in my power to place Mr. Arent[3] with this last time. I am sorry to find affairs have no better a prospect on that side. . . .

---

[1] Prince Eugene of Savoy (1663-1736) was one of the greatest generals of his time. Although of French extraction he served under the banners of Austria in the war of the Spanish Succession. His forces were united with those of Marlborough both at Blenheim and Oudenarde.

[2] General James Stanhope.          [3] Arent Furly.

## TO ROBERT MOLESWORTH.[1]

CHELSEA, *September* 30*th*, 1708.

DEAR SIR,—Two reasons have made me delay answering yours : I was in hopes of seeing our great lord, and I depended on Mr. Micklethwayt's presenting you with my services, and informing you of all matters public and private. The Queen is but just come to Kensington, and my lord[2] to town. He promised to send me word, and appoint me a time, when he came. But I should have prevented him, had it been my weather for town-visits. But having owed the recovery of my health to the method I have taken of avoiding the town smoke, I am kept at a distance, and like to be removed even from hence in a little while, though I have a project of staying longer here than my usual time, by removing now and then cross the water, to my friend Sir John Cropley's, in Surrey, where my riding and airing recruits me. I am highly rejoiced, as you may believe, that I can find myself able to do a little more public service than what of late years I have been confined to in my country, and I own the circumstances of a Court were never so inviting to me as they have been since a late view I have had of the best part of our Ministry. It may perhaps have added more of confidence and forwardness in my way of courtship, to be so incapacitated as I am from taking anything there for myself. But I hope I may convince some persons that it is possible to serve disinterestedly, and that obligations already received (though on the account of others) are able to bind as strongly as the ties of self-interest.

I had resolved to stay till I had one conference more with our lord before I wrote to you, but a letter which I have this moment received from Mr. Micklethwayt, on his having waited on you in the country, has made me resolve to write thus hastily (without missing to-night's post) to acknowledge, in the friend-liest and freest manner, the kind and friendly part you have taken in my private interests. If I have ever endured anything for the public, or sacrificed any of my youth, or pleasures, or

[1] cf Letters from Shaftesbury, printed by Toland.
[2] The Earl of Godolphin, then Lord Treasurer.

interests to it, I find it is made up to me in the good opinion of some few; and perhaps one such friendship as yours may counterbalance all the malice of my worst enemies. It is true what I once told you I had determined with myself, never to think of the continuance of a family, or altering the condition of life that was most agreeable to me, whilst I had (as I thought) a just excuse,[1] but that of late I had yielded to my friends, and allowed them to dispose of me if they thought that by this means I could add anything to the power or interest I had to serve them or my country. I was afraid, however, that I should be so heavy and unactive in this affair that my friends would hardly take me to be in earnest. But though it be so lately that I have taken my resolution, and that you were one of the first who knew it, I have on a sudden such an affair thrown across me, that I am confident I have zeal enough raised in me to hinder you from doubting whether I sincerely intend what I profess. There is a lady whom chance has thrown into my neighbourhood, and whom I never saw till the Sunday before last, who is in every respect that very person I had ever framed a picture of from my imagination when I wished the best for my own happiness in such a circumstance. I had heard her character before, and her education, and every circumstance besides suited exactly, all but her fortune. Had she but a ten thousand pounds my modesty would allow me to apply without reserve, where it was proper. And I would it were in my power, without injury to the lady, to have her upon those terms, or lower. I flatter myself too, by all appearance, that the father has long had, and yet retains, some regard for me, and that the disappointments he has had in some higher friendships may make him look as low as on me, and imagine me not wholly unworthy of his relation. But if by any interest I had or could possibly make with the father, I should induce him to bestow his daughter, perhaps with much less fortune (since I would gladly accept her so) than what in other places he would have bestowed, I shall draw a double misfortune on the lady, unless she has goodness enough to think that one who seeks her for what he counts better than a fortune may possibly by his worth

---

[1] In the hope that his brother would marry.

or virtue make her sufficient amends. And were I but encouraged to hope or fancy this, I would begin my offers to-morrow, and should have greater hopes that my disinterestedness would be of some service to me in this place as matters stand.

You see my scruple, and being used to me, and knowing my odd temper (for I well know you believe it no affectation), you may be able to relieve me, and have the means in your hands; for a few words with one who has the honour to be your relation would resolve me in this affair. I cannot stir in it till then, and should be more afraid of my good fortune than my bad, if it should happen to me to prevail with a father, for whom the lady has so true a duty that, even *against her inclination*, she would comply with anything required. I am afraid it will be impossible for you to read or make sense of what I write thus hastily, but I fancy with myself I make you the greater confidence, in trusting to my humour and first thought, without staying till I have so much as formed a reflection. I am sure there is hardly any one besides you I should lay myself thus open to, but I am secure in your friendship, which I rely on (for advice) in this affair. I beg to hear from you in answer by the first post, being with great sincerity, your faithful friend and humble servant.

----

## TO ROBERT MOLESWORTH.[1]

### BEACHWORTH, IN SURREY, *October* 23*rd*, 1708.

DEAR SIR,—You guessed right as to the winds, which are still easterly, and keep me here in winter-quarters, from all public and private affairs. I have neither seen Lord Treasurer, nor been at Chelsea to prosecute my own affair, though as for this latter, as great as my zeal is, I am forced to a stand. I was beforehand told, that as to the Lord, he was in some measure engaged ; and the return I had from him, on my application, seemed to imply as much. On the other side, I have had reason to hope that the lady who had before bemoaned herself for being destined to greatness without virtue had yet

----

[1] cf Toland's letters from Shaftesbury.

her choice to make, and after her escapes sought for nothing so much as sobriety and a strict virtuous character. How much more still this adds to my zeal you may believe, and by all hands I have received the highest character of your relation, who seems to have inspired her with these and other good sentiments, so rare in her sex and degreee. My misfortune is, I have no friend in the world by whom I can in the least engage, or have access to your relation, but only by yourself, and I have no hopes of seeing you soon, or of your having any opportunity to speak of me to her. If a letter could be proper, I should fancy it more so at this time than any other, provided you would found it on the common report which is abroad of my being in treaty for that lady. This might give you an occasion of speaking of me as to that part, which few besides can know so well, I mean *my heart*, which, if she be such as really all people allow, will not displease her to hear so well of, as, perhaps in friendship and from old acquaintance, you may represent. If the person talked of be really my rival,[1] and in favour with the father, I must own my case is next to desperate, not only because I truly think him, as the world goes, likely enough to make a good (at least a civil) husband, but because as my aim is not fortune, as is his, he being an old friend too, I should unwillingly stand between him and an estate, which his liberality has hitherto hindered him from gaining, as great as his advantages have been hitherto in the Government. By what I have said, I believe you may guess who my supposed rival is, or if you want a farther hint, 'tis one of the chief of the Junto, an old friend of yours and mine, whom we long sat with in the House of Commons (not often voted with), but who was afterwards taken up to a higher House, and is as much noted for wit, and gallantry, and magnificence, as for his eloquence and courtier's character. But whether this be so suited to this meek good lady's happiness, I know not. Fear of partiality and self-love makes me not dare determine, but rather mistrust myself, and turn the balance against me. Pray keep this secret, for I got it by chance, and if there be anything in it 'tis a great secret between the two lords themselves. But sometimes I fancy

---

[1] Charles Montague, Earl of Halifax.

it is a nail which will hardly go, though I am pretty certain it has been aimed at by this old acquaintance of ours ever since a disappointment happened from a great lord beyond sea, who was to have had the lady.

Nothing but the sincere friendship you show for me could make me to continue thus to impart my privatest affairs, and in reality, though they seem wholly private and selfish, I will not be ashamed to own the honesty of my heart to you; in professing that the public has much the greatest part in all this bustle I am engaging in. You have lately made me believe, and even proved, too, by experience, that I had some interest in the world, and there, where I least dreamt of it, with great men in power, I had always something of an interest in my country, and with the plain honest people; and sometimes I have experienced, both here at home and abroad, where I have long lived and made acquaintance (in Holland especially), that with a plain character of honesty and disinterestedness I have on some occasions, and in dangerous urgent times of the public, been able to do some good. If the increase of my fortune be the least motive in this affair before me (as sincerely I do not find), I will venture to say it can only be in respect of the increase of my interest, which I may have in my country, in order to serve it.

One who has little notion of magnificence, and less of pleasure and luxury, has not that need of riches which others have, and one who prefers tranquillity and a little study and a few friends to all other advantages of life, and all the flatteries of ambition and fame, is not like to be naturally so very fond of engaging in the circumstances of marriage. I do not go swimmingly to it, I assure you, nor is the great fortune a great bait. Sorry I am that nobody with a less fortune or more daughters has had the wit to order such an education. A very moderate fortune had served my turn, or perhaps quality alone, to have a little justified me and kept me in countenance, had I chose so humbly; but now that which is rich ore, and would have been the most estimable had it been bestowed on me, will be mere dross, and flung away on others, who will pity and despise those very advantages which I prize so much. But this is one of the common-places of exclamation against the distribution of things in this world, and upon my word, whoever brought up the proverb, 'tis no advantageous one for a providence to say *Matches are made in Heaven.* I believe rather in favour of providence, that there is nothing which is so merely fortune, and more committed to the power of blind chance. So I must be contented, and repine the less at my lot if I am disappointed in such an affair. If I satisfy my friends that I am not wanting to myself, it is sufficient. I am sure you know it, by the sound experience of all this trouble I have given and am still like to give you. Though I confess myself, yet even in this too I do but answer friendship, as being so sincerely and affectionately your most faithful friend and humble servant.

## TO LORD SOMERS.

(With the "Moralists.")

*December 10th,* 1708.

MY LORD,—Once again your enthusiastic friend salutes you in his old way and with an old present. Your lordship has here a piece, now published to the world, which formerly was private to yourself. Had it been worthy your lordship's name, how glad would your friend have been of presenting it to you publicly! But what shall one do? A piece that has mischief in it must not be publicly addressed to your lordship; and a piece that treats of religion, and has no mischief, will infallibly be found dull. Such a one is this I enclose to your lordship, and for which I might otherwise perhaps claim your countenance and favour; for hardly will our clergyman find anything here to take offence at. The fear is that the man of wit will rather think the author retained on the priest's side, and will despise him as much for an enthusiast in this piece as the priests have reviled him for an atheist in another.

The title,[1] your lordship sees, is changed, and so is much besides in the book. If it were worth your reading then, I hope it is more worth it now. But that it ever did or can deserve that honour I dare not say. I beg only of your lordship that you would destroy that other imperfect copy, and if you think

[1] The "Moralists" was originally entitled "The Sociable Enthusiast." See p.

this worthy of a place in your library, I shall rejoice to have it serve there but as a remembrance of my being in every capacity, my lord, your lordship's most affectionate and devoted, humble servant.

P.S.—I have sent the book unbound to your lordship in haste, the title page unfinished, lest it should be abroad anywhere before you had it.

---

### TO LORD HALIFAX.[1]

16th *December*, 1708.

MY LORD,—It is three or four years since I promised the bearer (Mons. Desmaizeaux, a French Protestant) to introduce him to your lordship. Being a man of letters, his greatest hope was from your favour, and knowing the honour and esteem I have for your lordship, he persuades himself that a character from me may do him service.

He was earnestly recommended to me many years since by an excellent judge, Mons. Bayle, who esteemed him for his ingenuity and polite learning. If a man of that character, who is versed in the ancient and modern languages, and a master in his own, with a natural good genius, and a sufficient practice and acquaintance with the affairs and men of letters abroad, may be thought of any service, I may perhaps be fortunate in recommending him; if otherwise, I hope your lordship will pardon this trouble I give you in behalf of one of the starving race of scholars. There are so few left, and these so low-spirited, and out of hope, that they can hardly prove troublesome or importunate. Perhaps there might have been none of this sort left among us, had not your lordship, even in your

[1] Charles Montague, Earl of Halifax (1661—1715), was a prominent Whig and Parliamentary orator. He became Chancellor of the Exchequer on 30th April, 1694, having just previously been the chief agent in the formation of the Bank of England. With Lord Somers and others he was impeached (14th April, 1701) by the Tories on the charge of sharing in the Treaty of Partition. On the 10th April, 1706, he was appointed one of the Commissioners to regulate the union with Scotland. He was a life-long friend of Sir Isaac Newton, and a constant patron of learning.

private character, been a patron to them, when they had none left in the public. How they may multiply now your lordship and your friends are coming into Court, I know not; but otherwise a peace (should we have ever so good a one) would hardly mend their circumstances; and my advice to them should be to pray for war, and turn engineers against the next siege.— I am, my lord, your lordship's most faithful and obedient humble servant.

TO PIERRE COSTE.

St. Giles's, *February 19th*, 1708 (9).

Mr. Coste,— . . . One word, however, as to the Muses, with many thanks to you for your entertaining French treatise. I assure it was extremely pleasant, and I found it the only just and sensible work of this kind.

The author seems to have nobler views than he dare show; though I confess towards the latter end he made me a little blush for him (for I was mightily in his interest) when he seemed to give in to the machine and decorations of the theatre. For this is vulgar, miserable, barbarous, and is directly that which corrupted the Roman stage, or rather, made it impossible for them to succeed in their tragedy or opera.

Migravit ab aure voluptas
Omnis ad incertos oculos et gaudia vana.[1]

Read but the passage of Horace to Augustus in his exquisite satire, for it was more than a critique upon the Roman stage—and those sort of spectacles in which (as we know by Suetonius) the monarch, as polite as he pretended to be, had a popular taste. So that Horace had a delicate string to touch in this affair, as delicate almost as if he had been to write to him upon his own *Ajax*, which he had wittily said he *had fallen upon his sword*, and was self-murdered. But perhaps the subtle wit of his friend Horace helped to guide his hand. And here in this epistle to him, though he attacks him not in person, it is more than likely he attacks his relish. He falls upon the whole race

---

[1] All pleasure has passed away from the ear to the restless eyes and empty joys.—*Hor.*, Ep., Bk. II., i., 187-8.

of Latin poets, both modern and ancient (his two friends, Virgil and Varius, for decency-sake excepted), and shows what their genius was from the beginning, and how afterwards, when it should have been refined, it grew rather worse by running into the marvellous, the outrageous, the extreme of things. Yet he owns the Romans had a genius for tragedy, could they have cultivated it, and kept their ear. But they ran all into *eye.* 'Twas no wonder indeed that the Roman people should soon come to the taste of tragedy; for they were free and popular, and had the true foundation of a taste in this kind, which is a relish of the afflictions and misfortunes of those who make the world unfortunate and afflict the people. For tragedy opens the inward scene of the palace, and shows us the misfortunes and miseries of the great; by which the people are not only revenged but comforted and encouraged to endure their equal plain rank when they see the tyranny attended with such disasters, and those seeming happy lords of mankind more galled and troubled by the inward disturbances, which belong naturally to their state of fortune and mind, than the very lowest degree of people that live orderly, and under the restraint and security of equal laws.

And when you have considered of this, you will perhaps find out another reason than that which Horace assigns to his monarch-friend. For indeed the liberty of Rome miscarried quickly; they were hardly got out of barbarism but they fell instantly into slavery.

> Post Punica bella, quietus quaerere coepit
> Quid Sophocles, &c.
> Et placuit sibi natura sublimis et acer ;
> Nam spirat tragicum satis et feliciter audet.[1]

But here Horace is forced to be a little lame. He shuffles off from his subject and gets to comedy, though it is plain he had his thought elsewhere ; and the machines he afterwards

---

[1] For the Roman " after the Punic wars began to inquire what benefits might accrue from reading Sophocles, &c., and gave satisfaction to himself by nature high and daring ; for he possesses a sufficient conception of tragedy, and ventures upon it felicitously."— *Hor.*, Ep., Bk. II., i., 162-6.

speaks of as the corruption of the stage were far more applicable here than there.

Now this is what our French author at last gives into, and for which I was ashamed for him in his last page but one. A little of this false taste again he discovers (page 25) where, speaking of the Italian recitative, he complains of its simplicity, *qu'il est trop simple, trop uni.* Now when I come to speak with you at leisure (since you desire my thoughts on this subject), I will undertake to show you that the Italians are so much in the right in this, that if other causes did but concur, they would for this very reason be in a fair way of restoring the ancient tragedy (the true opera) with its chorus, and all the charms depending on that ancient plan and method. Meanwhile I dare prophesy, that as countries grow more polite, and take after this Italian manner of rendering their recitative more plain and simple, the opera will every day gain more upon the other theatre, and our best tragedy at last melt into opera, which union will be a kind of reviving of the ancient tragedy in all its noble orders of music and continued harmony. But the mock-choruses of the French are the most ridiculous things in the world, and a gross sort of music fit only for the parterre, and in my time constantly sung by the parterre in company with the actors, so that I used to think myself rather at church than at an opera, where all throats at once were let loose to join in this Psalm-music of a confused multitude. And for the *rècitatif* of the French, which, instead of distinguishing from the passionate and moving places (reserved for regular music, and the only subject proper for it), they endeavour equally to adorn, it is a perpetual bar against the success of their opera, as to the tragic part and poem. For let a poet do what he will, the more noble, quick, and strong he makes his action, the parts of that kind, if sung in regular song, will render all ridiculous. Whereas, the more sedately passionate parts or places (if I may so call them) of reflection, such as soliloquies and the real parts of the chorus (who should be *one* and is one in the action, though representing *many*)—these, if reserved for the great art of the musician and attended by the symphonies, would have their due effect upon the audience, and the tragedy would go on peaceably on a plainer foot, just next to common speech, and even below the present recitative of the Italians, which therefore, instead of being too simple (as the author censures it), is in reality not reduced enough to its true ancient simplicity.

But I see, unawares, I have written a whole sheet of hard criticism upon the ingenious author you have sent me. To make him amends I am resolved to copy a whole paragraph which I read with admiration, and can't help applying to higher subjects than those he treats of.

Page 14.—His words are : " Quelquefois vous entendez une tenue contre laquelle les premiers tons de la basse continue font une disonnance qui irrite l'oreille; mais la basse continuant de jouer, revient à cette tenue par de si beaux accords, qu'on voit bien que le musicien n'a fait ces premièrs dissonances, que pour faire sentir, avec plus de plaisir, ces belles cordes où il ramène aussitôt l'harmonie."

You know me for a great enthusiast, at least as the world goes. For to talk of the world as harmony, or of a master of the music, is on every side a mystery. The men of wit believe no such hand at all, and the bigots know not what to do with the dissonances : c'est le diable $\pi \acute{o} \theta \epsilon \nu$ $\tau \grave{o}$ $\kappa \alpha \kappa \acute{o} \nu$. *Graecum est* (as the monk said) *et non potest intelligi.*

You may perhaps understand me, however. If not, I have no more time this bout.

———

## TO LORD TOWNSEND.[1]

CHELSEA, *May* 28*th,* 1709.

MY LORD,—Mr. Furly, of Rotterdam, having desired the honour of being introduced to your lordship and thinking my hand a proper one, I could not refuse to employ the credit he thought I had with your lordship in the service of so old a friend and true an Englishman. His thorough experience in the affairs of Holland, and his zeal for the Protestant religion—the common cause—and the interest of the two nations, are qualities which will make him valued by your lordship,

[1] Charles Townsend (1674—1738) second Viscount Townsend, was a prominent Whig Statesman. In May, 1709, he was sent to the Hague as Plenipotentiary to treat for peace with France.

and may perhaps render him useful to you in the present conjuncture of affairs.

Besides the share I have in the public satisfaction, I have a particular one of my own, in seeing your lordship (whom I so easily honoured) entrusted, as you are, in the affairs of your country and of Europe.

I doubt not but it will be attended with the highest success; and that, besides the concern I have for my country and the common interest of mankind, your lordship will believe my good wishes to be increased by being, with so much respect as I am, your lordship's most humble and most obedient servant.

<hr>

### TO LORD SOMERS.

(To Lord S——s, with the Essay on the Freedom of Wit and Humour.)[1]

B——, *June 2nd*, 1709.

To MY LORD.—Nothing but the height of respect could have kept your friend from addressing the enclosed to you. Had he dared to converse with you in idea, as he did in a former letter, he should have pleased himself and perhaps the public far better in this performance. But his care to remove your lordship from the suspicions of the clergy, who have of late been so horribly alarmed, has made him unwilling to give you publicly the air of a correspondence with a supposed enemy of the Church, for such the author of this essay will infallibly be esteemed, though he names neither *Church* nor *Priest*, nor says anything concerning any mystery of religions, but has kept such measures of decency as may secure him, he hopes, from giving the least offence to any except the merest bigots. All his aim is, in plain sense, to recommend plain honesty, which in the bustle made about religion is fairly dropped. The defenders of religion, as well as its opposers, are contented to make nothing or a mere name of virtue.

The priest (as a trader) makes a bargain of it, as lottery-

[1] Shaftesbury's "Sensus Communis, an Essay on the Freedom of Wit and Humour," appeared anonymously in May, 1709.

adventure with a sure return of a million per cent. and more, if you have the luck to hear good council and choose the right fund. The atheist (a cautious dealer) supposes it a game of interest, a play for fame or fortune. Neither of the two comprehend that honest motto : *prodesse quam conspici.*

Mr. Hobbes would say of your lordship that you understood how to gain fame by seeming to avoid it. What the priest would say in the case is hard to imagine. He might fulsomely, perhaps, extol your secret meaning, and say you despised other advantages, and had an eye only to *the recompense of reward.* But even this would not serve turn, as the case of our salvation is stated to us. For as to the interest of your soul, were this, my lord, the chief concern with you, a private closet would be more suitable than the cabinet of the prince; a college or cloister more beneficial than a Court or Parliament; and texts of Scripture with the holy fathers a properer speculation than the intrigues of State, and the mystery of this kingdom of darkness. For *the children of light* have a magnanimous contempt of this earthly Jerusalem, and pray daily for its destruction, and for the coming of that kingdom which shall put an end to all fleshly power and worldly glories. But for us *worldlings*, who are given to think so gloriously of our country and the prosperity of our nation, and brethren *after the flesh*, it is in reality, my lord, a great happiness for us, and very much our interest, that your soul should be in no better a way than it is. We cannot, however, but be sorry that it should fare the worse hereafter in another world, for having taken so much care of us and our affairs in this. And we cannot but with regret consider the disparity of your lordship's ministry with that of the Holy Church, where the saving of a soul or two will, it is thought, be of more advantage and higher honour to a country curate, than the saving of nations will be to so wise and worthy a statesman as yourself. What souls your lordship may have helped to save for eternity, God knows. It is certain many sinners have been sent without confession or absolution into another world during this bloody war, which, it is confessed, may be too justly laid at your door. And if we allow salvation in the Romish church, it is in vain to plead for your lordship that by this war alone we have been saved from

DD

persecution and dragooning. Besides, who knows whether in such a militant state our church might not have prospered better and been in less danger than in these times of forbearance and moderation. For spiritual interests come not under the same rule with secular affairs ; and a church, though seemingly prosperous and flourishing, may carry mortal symptoms which only its doctors can discover. In the same manner may a church in the eye of the world seem ready to sink when the upholders of it know that its ail is little or nothing, and that its danger can be only from the rash attempt of interposing human means for its deliverance. All that can be said for your lordship and those who have zealously supported the Revolution is, that you meant well to our temporal interest, and that accordingly things indeed have answered well in the end. And now especially we have more assurance, since your lordship is like to have the finishing of what you began, and are now taking care that after a successful war we should not be betrayed by a bad peace.

If your lordship, however, finds but small satisfaction in all this good you have done, and are still doing, if you are unable to taste the pleasure of doing good for good's sake, you are certainly very much to be pitied. For rewards in this world are uncertain, and in the next it is evident that no church, or churchmen, of whatever kind, will allow you to be one jot more a saint for all the good you have done or may do in this kind. In the heathen hell the hottest place, it is true, was for [1] betrayers of their country, as in their elizium the principal seats were for [2] patriots. So that supposing your friend to be such an errant heathen as the priests would make him, your lordship will nevertheless be his saint. For with him good ministers are as guardian angels, and should, in his opinion, be honoured and revered as such. Accordingly your lordship, who is conscious of what part you bear, may judge the affection of your friend, with what sincerity and constancy he is, my lord, your lordship's, &c.

[1] Vendidit hic auro patriam dominumque potentem Imposuit.— *Virg.*, Aen. VI., 621.
[2] — His dantem jura Catonem.— *Virg.*, Aen. VIII., 670.

## TO MICHAEL AINSWORTH.

*June 3rd*, 1709.[1]

HONEST MICHAEL,—I received yours since your recovery, which I am glad to hear of. The new book you have discovered, and the account of it, gave me great satisfaction. Your conjectures of it perhaps are not amiss. Dr. Tindal's principles, whatever they may be as to church government, are, in respect of philosophy and theology, far wide from the authors of the rhapsody.

In general truly it has happened, that all those they call *free writers* now-a-days have espoused those principles which Mr. Hobbes set a-foot in this last age. Mr. Locke, as much as I honour him on account of other writings (viz., on government, policy, trade, coin, education, toleration, &c.), and as well as I knew him, and can answer for his sincerity as a most zealous *Christian* and believer, did, however, go in the self-same tract, and is followed by the Tindals, and all the other ingenious free authors of our time.

It was Mr. Locke that struck the home blow: for Mr. Hobbes's character and base slavish principles in government took off the poison of his philosophy. 'Twas Mr. Locke that struck at all fundamentals, threw all order and virtue out of the world, and made the very ideas of these (which are the same as those of God) *unnatural*, and without foundation in our minds. *Innate* is a word he poorly plays upon; the right word, though less used, is *connatural*. For what has birth or progress of the fœtus out of the womb to do in this case? The question is not about the time the *ideas* entered, or the moment that one body came out of the other, but whether the constitution of man be such that, being adult and grown up, at such or such a time, sooner or later (no matter when), the idea and sense of order, administration, and a God, will not infallibly, inevitably, necessarily spring up in him.

Then comes the credulous Mr. Locke, with his Indian, barbarian stories of wild nations, that have no such idea (as

[1] cf Letters to a young man in the University, Lond., 1716, pp. 38—44.

travellers, learned authors ! and men of truth ! and great philosophers ! have informed him), not considering that is but a negative upon a hearsay, and so circumstantiated that the faith of the Indian danger may be as well questioned as the veracity or judgment of the relater ; who cannot be supposed to know sufficiently the mysteries and secrets of those barbarians : whose language they but imperfectly know ; to whom we good Christians have by our little mercy given sufficient reason to conceal many secrets from us, as we know particularly in respect of simples and vegetables, of which, though, we got the Peruvian bark, and some other noble remedies, yet it is certain, that through the cruelty of the Spaniards, as they have owned themselves, many secrets in medicinal affairs have been suppressed.

But Mr. Locke, who had more faith, and was more learned in modern wonder-writers than in ancient philosophy, gave up an argument for the Deity, which Cicero (though a professed sceptic) would not explode, and which even the chief of the atheistic philosophers anciently acknowledged, and solved only by their " primus in orbe deus fect timor."

Thus virtue, according to Mr. Locke, has no other measure, law, or rule, than fashion and custom ; morality, justice, equity, depend only on law and will, and God indeed is a perfect free agent in his sense ; that is, free to anything, that is however ill : for if He wills it, it will be made good ; virtue may be vice, and vice virtue in its turn, if he pleases. And thus neither right nor wrong, virtue nor vice, are anything in themselves ; nor is there any trace or idea of them naturally imprinted on human minds. Experience and our catechism teach us all ! I suppose 'tis something of like kind which teaches birds their nests, and how to fly the minute they have full feathers. Your Theocles, whom you commend so much, laughs at this, and, as modestly as he can, asks a *Lockist* whether the idea of *woman* (and what is sought after in woman) be not taught also by some catechism, and dictated to the man. Perhaps if we had no schools of Venus, nor such horrid lewd books, or lewd companions, we might have no understanding of this, till we were taught by our parents; and if the tradition should happen to be lost, the race of mankind might perish in a sober nation.—This is very poor philosophy. But the gibberish of the schools for these several centuries has, in these latter days of liberty, made any contrary philosophy of good relish, and highly savoury with all men of wit, such as have been emancipated from that egregious form of intellectual bondage. But I see, good Michael, you are on a better scent.

I can say no more at present, only I would not have you inquire further, as yet, after that book, entitled an *Inquiry*.[1] Because it was an imperfect thing, brought into the world many years since, contrary to the author's design, in his absence beyond sea, and in a disguised, disordered style. It may one day, perhaps, be set righter, since other things have made it to be inquired after. Have patience in the meanwhile. Adieu! God be with you.

[Address]: For Michael Ainsworth, University College, Oxford.

---

## TO JOHN WHEELOCK.

*July 9th,* 1709.

WHEELOCK,—After having waited seven years in hopes of my brother's marrying, and a year or two more in search of such a wife as was suitable to me in my present circumstances of health and way of living, I have now news to tell you, which, I conclude, will be joyful to you, though not surprising. It is that I am now engaged in earnest, and in a week or fortnight you shall be with me, where you shall see the family and the woman herself.

She is well-born on both sides—father's and mother's—and in both senses of a good family, and of worthy, virtuous, and good parents, right to the public, related to me, and long acquainted. But, as particular friends as they are, I have not seen any of them this eight or nine years, since my health changed and I retired from town and business. I have determined on the youngest of the daughters. The eldest was a grown woman when I used to be much with the family. She

---

[1] Shaftesbury's *Inquiry concerning Virtue or Merit* was printed first in the year 1699, by Toland, when its author was in Holland. His corrected edition appeared in 1711 in the *Characteristics.*

has been married since, and proves an excellent wife. The younger girls were then little ones and in a nursery, so I remember them not. Their tempers (by what I can learn) are all of them much alike, and suitable to the education and good example they have had.

I know more of them, as to their character, than I ever can expect to know of any women while I live. They are a healthy, sound breed, and the youngest, they tell me, is the strongest constitution of all, well proportioned, and of a good make. No beauty. More I know not as to her person, for I shall not see her myself till I have determined all else. And for her fortune, I inquire not of it, for that is not my aim or thought, as you well know. By the family estate (which is but a handsome country gentleman's) the daughters' portions, one may believe, cannot be very considerable, especially where there are younger brothers, and sisters besides.

If my health holds tolerable, as it has done this last month, I hope in one more to conclude the affair.—I am in haste this time. Let me hear of what I last wrote to you. God be with you.

### TO JOHN WHEELOCK.

WINDSOR, *August 8th*, Monday night.

WHEELOCK,—I received yours by Tom, but could not answer you the next morning because I took a sudden resolution and came away early that morning hither, so bid him tell you where I was gone, and let Mrs. Skinner know the same, and that I hoped to meet you and her, or one of you at least, at Rygate, on Wednesday or Thursday, depending on your despatch in those affairs which are now so necessary and near at hand. For a room I must have, nor will wait now above ten days after my coming from hence. This will be the pretext, for I shall immediately send to meet Mr. Mead (in Mr. Eyre's absence), at Sutton, to draw a paper of a word or two by way of articles on that single point I told you, and there will be an end of the affair, for settlements there shall be none. I wonder to hear you speak in yours of a *fortune*, when you know it is what I had laid aside the thought of, even in a case before this, and that in this case I have plainly told you there was *none*, or the same as none, nor to be regarded or thought of by me. My family and its preservation, my own preservation and health and ease and content, is enough surely for any friend of mine or my family's to rejoice at after such a sad prospect, and the little hopes was left from my bad state of health and from the moral usage of relations, and those who ought to have been a comfort to me, instead of a load and torment in return of all I had bestowed and done. And in reality, should I not find you (as I do the rest of my friends and well-wishers) heartily delighted and rejoiced with the prospect I have given, it will be very surprising to me. I shall not bid you be merry, I can assure you, if you have not the inclination. But I must needs tell you what I have said before, that I shall distinguish affections towards me at this by the tokens of this kind (whether of joy or heaviness), better than by anything else that has happened, or can ever happen in my life.

Those who have been ungrateful, unworthy, and treacherous friends will be thunderstruck with this account when they hear what they so little expected, believing all my talks of marriage to be only threats or boasts, and that if anything tempted me, it would not be so much my family's preservation and the concern of children, as riches, interest, or at least wit, beauty, or some of those tempting objects which they thought I was by my retirement safe from. So they looked on me as a safe - deceasing bachelor that would leave no issue behind me, nor mind anything but my crabbed books, writings, and philosophy. But they will be surprised by this day or to-morrow seven night, when I shall send them an account of my being the third or ninth after to be married to a *very young* lady, not for love's sake (since I never saw her till the match was resolved on), nor for riches, but for my family's sake only, and my own ease in a private and country life. But I can now tell you (which I could not before) that I have seen the young lady, and I protest that I think she is injured in having been represented to me as *no beauty*, for so I wrote you word before I had seen her. Whether I am partial I cannot say positively, for when one comes as I did to the sight of one whom one had had chosen by character, and had determined to be one's wife, one may be allowed to be a little biassed in judgment as to the person and appearance of the lady one may be supposed to see with *other* eyes than ordinary, and it is fit it should be so. Therefore, with these *other* eyes of mine let me tell you I think I was wrong when I said from common report that she was no beauty. For I think her a very great beauty.

————

TO LADY RUSSELL.

*August* 24*th*, 1709.

MADAM,—After the many proofs of that friendship with which your ladyship has long honoured me, it was no surprising one that you had the goodness some time since to suffer me to speak to you with so much freedom of my private affairs, and of the thoughts I had of marrying to preserve my family. It was my misfortune (your ladyship knows) to be detained this last year or two in the prosecution of an affair in which I have had no success ; though I would gladly have taken the lady without anything, and upon whatever terms her father would have thought fit. When I had the honour to mention these particulars to your ladyship, I assured you at the same time that since I despaired of success in this place I would pursue my intentions for my family's sake without further delay, being resolved in my circumstances of health (which kept me from living in or near the town) to have no other regard in the choice I made, than merely that of a good family, a good character, and such an education as might best suit a lady's temper to my circumstance and way of life. And I presumed withal to assure your ladyship that I should take it for the highest honour to be guided in this by your ladyship's recommendation if any character of that kind should offer to your thoughts. It has been my fortune in the meanwhile to renew an old acquaintance with a sober, good family I formerly knew, and was intimate with. They are of a good extract and good principles, and have educated their children accordingly, with the happiest success. A daughter

---

[1] Mary, daughter of Wm. Russell, the first Duke of Bedford, who married in 1691 Edward Russell, Earl of Orford.

of these I have found of a temper, person, and health as I could wish; so 'that, having all the assurance I could possibly have of her character, from the worth and virtue of her parents (my old friends) as well as from her own carriage and behaviour in every respect, I have determined to make my choice here, where I have nothing deficient but fortune only, and I have taken this freedom to impart my greatest affair to your ladyship, whose friendship I ever esteemed as the highest honour. . . . The lady is youngest daughter to late Mr. Ewer, of Hertfordshire, her mother a Mountague, granddaughter to the old Lord Manchester.

I should be ashamed to trouble your ladyship with further particulars, having already made my letter such a long one. When your ladyship writes at any time to Belvoir, I should think it an honour to have my lord Duke of Rutland hear of my concern at your hand.—I am, with the utmost respect, madam, your ladyship's, &c.

### TO MAURICE ASHLEY.

BEACHWORTH, *August* 24*th*, 1709.

DEAR BROTHER,—What I have long hoped in vain to see you do, I have myself at last resolved on, and for my family's sake have thought of a wife, the likeliest to bring me children. Herself well born, and of good blood on each side, of a fit age, make, and constitution ; modestly bred, in a sober and virtuous family. She is youngest daughter to late Mr. Ewer, of Hertfordshire. Her mother a *Mountague.* The family long known to me, though I have not seen them for some years past till now lately. This I thought fit to acquaint you with before I concluded the affair, and am, dear brother, your affectionate brother and humble servant.

### TO JAMES EYRE.

BEACHWORTH, IN SURREY, *August* 26*th*, 1709.

To MR. SOLICITOR EYRE.

SIR,—Amongst the many inconveniences I suffer by having such a health as will not allow me to live in or near the town, I have never found any greater, as to my own concerns in particular, than the being deprived of your company, and the constant recourse I should have to you for assistance and advice as a friend, as well as counsel in all the affairs of my family.

You have of late shown how truly you are that family friend, and have by the kindest proofs in the world confirmed that personal as well as traditional friendship there is, and ought to be, between us, in assisting me by your interest and friends in my applications, where I began them, when I first turned my thoughts to marriage. It was, I must own, at a late hour, but you better than any one know the reasons, and can answer for me that I did not neglect my family, nor forgot the thoughts of continuing it, when I took such pains for many years to see my brother settled, and had immediately on my father's death, by your assistance, enabled him to marry and come into the world with all the advantages I could bestow on him had he been even my elder son, as I had indeed in a manner made him to me. But many years are since past, and he has given me still less hopes of his marrying to honour and support his family. When at last I took the resolution myself (unwillingly I must needs own), you were the first friend that knew it, and the first who assisted me in an affair which, could it have been successful, might in some measure have made up those losses to my family which an officious care of it, and an over-tenderness for others I depended on, had led me into. But, as was natural to one so little mindful of interest as I am, I had no sooner engaged in courtship to the excellent lady (my Chelsea neighbour) but, rather than lose one whom I had so high an opinion of, I renounced all regards to fortune, and offered my lord her father to take her with nothing, and acquit him of all expectations I might have from him in future, offering him withal to settle all the estate I had, with whatever jointure he would command, for his daughter. This resolution made me continue my pursuit another year, and after having attempted last summer in vain, I came up early this spring from St. Giles's to renew my application, which still proved as unsuccessful. So having resolved to lose no more years, nor attempt any more what was hazardous or doubtful as things stood with me in my state of health; and my great concern being the mere preservation of my family, I firmly determined to choose the first young lady I could meet with, out of a good family, that should be of a person, health, education, and temper suitable to my design, and to my manner and way of living. Such a one I have had the good fortune to find, so as to have nothing in the world that is not suitable to my own or friends' desire; excepting the matter of fortune, which is but very small, and indeed not to be named : three or four thousand pound, and no more. For settlements, therefore, you may believe I shall make none; but reserve the entire power over my estate to make the best advantage during my own life, or in the minority of a son, which may be the best reparation and equivalent for a portion neglected. I have only engaged to make a jointure of six hundred a year, rent-charge to the young lady, and to be released of thirds and dowry, &c., on this account. And thus far I have ventured in your absence; reserving till I see you, and consult at leisure with you, the settlement of all other matters, which you know are so disposed in my will, that should I leave a wife with child of a daughter, my family would not be sunk, and by a power left I can (in a codicil) make provision for a daughter in that case. So that since the honour you have done me in answering my servant Wheelock's letter so kindly, I am in concern lest you should hasten your journey upon my account, and therefore send to prevent your thoughts of that kind. I believe I shall soon finish the affair. The lady's name is *Ewer*, of a good old family and place in Hertfordshire; her mother a *Montague*, Lord Manchester's grand-daughter ; the family long known to me, and related by the mother side.— I am, dear sir, your faithful friend and humble servant.

## TO JEAN LE CLERC.

REIGATE, *November 6th,* 1709.

SIR,—I received the other day a most acceptable present from a most agreeable hand. I mean the fragments of Menander,[1] from yourself. Nothing of that nature could have so delighted

[1] Menander et Philemonis Reliquiae cum notis H. Grotii et J. Clerici. Greek and Latin. Amsterdam, 1709, pp. 375. This work was dedicated to Shaftesbury. The English translation of the dedication may be found among his MSS. in the Record Office.

me, unless it had been possible to have restored the poet entire.
For though I have often with passionate concern regretted the
loss of many authors of antiquity, as among the Romans what is
wanting of Titus, Livius, Tacitus, and some valuable pieces of
Cicero; yet in respect of the Grecians we have been so fortunate
in the number of their books preserved, that (excepting some
works of philosophy, as those of the first and latter academies,
and other chiefs of sects, from whom Cicero has only copied),
I know not any lost authors that I have lamented as I have
done the moral and polite Menander, in whom the manners of
the Greeks, philosophy itself, with truth and nature, appeared
in such inimitable simplicity, and whose translator Terence I
value more than all the original moderns put together.

By this you may easily believe your present will not be
lost upon me, and that I shall hardly content myself with
barely reading the dedication, which is still so much the more
acceptable to me because so unlike a dedication in form.

You know me a lover of *liberty* and *letters,* and as I can
aspire to no honour I think so great, you have done me the
greatest in making me your friend upon such a foot.

To tell any one that he hates flattery is to flatter him. This,
if it be true, should be shown in fact; not told. The servile
manner of dedications has in reality brought things to such a
pass, that in pieces of that kind, the highest compliment to a
character is to be wholly silent on it.

It is long since I have held myself so much indebted to you,
that I earnestly wished for some occasion to acknowledge it by a
particular token of my respect. Nor could I content myself
with the few books I now and then sent you. If I have gone
further at present I can plead an established custom in the case
between authors who are professors in learning and men of the
world who are dignified with titles, so that I gladly lay hold of
the occasion of your dedication to justify me in making you a
present of the enclosed. I might otherwise perhaps have
scrupled the doing it. But I hope by this token, such as it
is, if you are so kind as to accept it, you will believe that as
I am ever ready to serve you with whatever credit or interest I
have, so you may freely command of me whatever at any time
in the way of expense you should have the least occasion for,

κοινὰ γὰρ τὰ τῶν φίλων. [For friends have all things in common.] I am, sir, your obliged friend and humble servant.

P.S.—When you are so kind as to let me hear from you at any time, please to direct your letters to me to be left at Mr. Norcott's, goldsmith, in the Strand, London. By this means, whether I am in my own county or nearer the town (for my health allows me not to live in it), your letters will come to me the sooner.

## TO GENERAL STANHOPE.[1]

REIGATE, *November 7th,* 1709.

DEAR SIR,—Your letter was a most obliging one, and as yours, I may truly say the most obliging in the world.

It would be hard for one who had yet less vanity than myself not to be flattered by the particular friendship of one whom, as a stranger and without the bias of personal acquaintance, they could not help esteeming and honouring above all men. Had it been my fortune to have only known you by character, I might have preferred my disinterestedness, whilst I paid you that natural preference which was due to you from one who pretends to rate men by their virtue and the love they have to the interest of their country and mankind. But you have long since given a check to the vanity I might have of this sort, and have given me such a share in your heart as makes my concern in everything that relates to you to be of a nearer and more selfish kind. If anything remained yet to bind me to you more, it was the turn you have taken in this letter of yours, where you make me the confidant of your philosophy, and are not ashamed to trust me with this secret of your thus employing your leisure hours, in expeditions aboard fleets and with the command of armies. For your comfort you know well enough that though you have few companions

[1] General James Stanhope (1673—1721), afterwards first Earl Stanhope, served in the army with brilliancy and success during the war in Spain, until made prisoner at Baihuega on 9th December, 1710. He entered later upon a political career, and became Chancellor of the Exchequer in the reign of George I.

in this way among the moderns, you have the best of ancient heroes to keep you in countenance, and that these latter were not only used to carry with them the books of philosophers, but their persons too, if they could tempt them abroad. What I know of the matter will be always ready at your command, and I shall rejoice if I can be a kind of exercise to you as a fellow wrestler, though of less strength, in this wholesome kind. For to tell you the real truth I don't only esteem philosophy and letters to be the good nourishment and preservative of the patriot and the statesman, but of the hero, and that there is not, nor ever can be, a truly great man in either way without this diet. It is the peculiar happiness of such as these who mean the good of their country and interest of mankind to have philosophy on their side. For there was never yet any philosophy heard of that allowed of an ambitious part in the public. Philosophers indeed there have been that denied man to have any such instinct as that which led to the good of society or his fellows, and consequently dissuaded him from the public service and from obeying such unnatural motions as these, if he found any such in himself. And this for certain is most true, that if man be not by nature sociable, he is the foolishest creature on earth to make society or the public the least part of his real care or concern. But if when he tries to shake off this principle, he has either no success or makes things worse with him than before, it is a shrewd presumption of what he is *born to.*

As for *innate principles* which you mention, it is, in my opinion, one of the childishest disputes that ever was. Well it is for our friend Mr. Locke, and other modern philosophers of his sire, that they have so poor a spectre as the ghost of Aristotle to fight with. A ghost indeed! since it is not in reality the Stagyrite himself nor the original Peripatetic hypothesis, but the poor secondary tralatitious system of modern and barbarous schoolmen which is the subject of their continual triumph. Tom Hobbes, whom I must confess a genius, and even an original among these latter leaders in philosophy, had already gathered laurels enough, and at an easy rate, from this field. It is the same old contest when rightly stated.

"Natura potest justo secernere iniquum" [Whether nature

is able to discern right and wrong.—*Hor.*, Sat., Bk. I., iii., 113].
"Quidve ad amicitias, usus rectumne, trahat nos" [What is it
which influences us to form friendships?—*Hor.*, Sat., Bk. II., vi., 75.]
Not whether the very philosophical propositions about right
and wrong were innate; but whether the passion or affection
towards society was such : that is to say, whether it was natural
and came of itself, or was taught by art, and was the product of
a lucky hit of some first man who inspired and delivered down
the prejudice. For the opposers of the social hypothesis in
those days were not so over frighted with the consequences as
to deny every idea to be innate, lest this should be proved
to be so.

"Dente lupus, cornu taurus petit; unde nisi intus monstra-
tum." [The wolf attacks with its teeth, the bull with its horns,
for what reason unless from some impulse from within.—*Hor.*, Sat.,
Bk. II., i., 52.] They could allow nature to bestow ideas suitable
and proportionable to the organs, faculties, and powers she had
formed, as the idea of destruction from a precipice to a
quadruped without wings, and the idea of security in the air to
a volatile that had wings even before they were tried (for these
are facts we thoroughly see and know), so in the same manner
the idea of sucking and being sucked to a viviparous creature
that has teats, and to its offspring, which can subsist at first by
no other way, and though deprived of the means, discovers its
endeavour after it.—But all this I must leave to your author
and you after you have considered him with Locke, whose *State
of Nature* he supposes to be chimerical, and less serviceable to
Mr. Locke's own system than to Mr. Hobbes's, that is more of a
piece, as I believe. You will be satisfied more in particular
when you happen to read again what this latter gentleman has
written upon the subject of *liberty and necessity*,[1] and have
compared it with Mr. Locke, as well as Mr. Locke with
himself, I mean his several editions one with another. For
he made great alterations on these points where, though a
*divine* may often waver, a *philosopher*, I think, never can.
For where the consequences of reasoning are not feared, there is
no subject (as I think I could plainly show) so easily brought to

[1] Mr. Hobbes' "Letter about Liberty and Necessity, 1656."

an issue as this last I have named, and which I therefore look upon as the test and touchstone of a genius in philosophy. But so tender the subject is, that none who have a real insight, and withal a tenderness for mankind, will venture to treat formally of a matter which can never be got over by low geniuses, and can never so much as make a difficulty with any who impartially and intrepidly philosophise.

Thus have I ventured to make you the greatest confidence in the world, which is that of my philosophy, even against my old tutor and governor, whose name is so established in the world, but with whom I ever concealed my differences as much as possible. For as ill a builder as he is, and as little able to treat the home-points of philosophy, he is of admirable use against the rubbish of the schools in which most of us have been bred up. But if, instead of the phantom he opposed and had always before his eyes, he had known but ever so little of antiquity, or been tolerably learned in the state of philosophy with the ancients, he had not heaped such loads of words upon us, and for want of a sound logic (in which he shows himself pretty diffident) imposed on himself at every turn by the sound of names and appellations, whilst he is continually giving the alarm, and cautioning others against the deceit. This you will find easily in him upon your reading, if you take but any remarkable word of his, as in particular the word *law;* which leads him into so many labyrinths, and was the reason why, after having found out other sorts of laws, he wanted a law for fashion and opinion. And this according to him was virtue and honesty. As if writing to the Italian or other good masters, or understanders of music, he had said that the *law of harmony was opinion;* or writing to the maker of scholars in statuary or architecture, he had said in general that the *law of design or the law of beauty in these designing arts had been opinion.* Had Mr. Locke been a *virtuoso,* he would not have philosophised thus. For harmony is the beauty, the accord and proportion of sounds; and harmony is harmony *by nature,* let particular ears be ever so bad, or let men judge ever so ill of music. So is architecture and its beauty the same, and founded in nature, let men's fancy be ever so *Gothic;* for there is *a Gothic* architecture which is false, and ever will be so, though we should all turn Goths, and lose our relish. The same is the case of virtue and honesty; the *honestum* and the *decorum* in society, for which you, my friend, can never, I know, lose your relish.

I might make abundance of excuses for what I have written if the subject I have been writing on had not communicated something of the manners that belong to it, and turned me from compliments to plain language. Allow me, then, in that language, and with all the sincerity in the world, to thank you for your kind expressions and services, particularly in young Micklethwayt's concern. Your good friend and mine, Sir John Cropley, is equally obliged with me by this favour you show. I leave to him to write you of the public. I have said so much on speculative matters of another kind, that I am scarce fit to enter upon these subjects. The affairs of the North will try the honesty and courage of our Ministry. The prospect is ill, but they ought not to be frighted by it into a hasty peace, and if right measures are taken to corroborate still more and more our alliance and union with the Dutch, and strengthen the hearts of our people at home, this plunge may redound more to the honour of the two nations and happiness of Europe, by carrying the point of liberty and balance further than first intended, or thought of, so as to bring not Europe only but Asia (which is now concerned), and in a manner the whole world, under one community; or at least to such a correspondence and intercourse of good offices and mutual succour as may render it a more humane world than it was ever known, and carry the interest of human kind to a greater height than ever.—What a fortune is that of our Ministry ! What single man or number of men had ever yet such power in their hands. Such power (and may that be the use they make of it) *of doing good !*—I am, dear sir, your obliged and ever faithful friend and obedient humble servant.

### TO ARENT FURLY.

REIGATE, *November 7th,* 1709.

MR. FURLY,—I received yours with Mr. Stanhope's, to whom the enclosed is an answer; but as it is nothing like business, and only fit for him to read at his leisure, pray for my sake too I desire you give it him not till then after his other letters and

EE

despatches are over, and that he has little or nothing to do. I have not received yours yet by way of Lisbon. I am glad I knew not to what danger Mr. Stanhope would have been exposed till after the danger was over, and the ill-concerted expedition at an end.

These alarms make me wish Mr. Stanhope well at home. For he is not a general merely, but of greater use at home than the greatest of those are abroad, and should the happiest success there cost England his life, it would be dearly bought. I hope he remembers the House of Commons and the home affairs of the good people, as well as the brave troops of Britain, and I hope his interest and esteem with both will grow alike.

I hope and I doubt not but you grow yourself in his esteem and trust, which I am persuaded must make you grow still a worthier man, were it only by considering that the reputation of the greatest and best of men does in a great measure depend on the character and behaviour of those they entrust; and if no other principle (as I know you want none) could make you endeavour to deserve the best, I am satisfied your affection and gratitude of this kind would be sufficient.

I preach to you (you see) as heretofore, and am therefore, as ever, your faithful and affectionate friend.

---

## TO THOMAS WALKER.

REIGATE, *April 23rd,* 1710.

SIR,—I return you the leaf corrected as you desire. If the purpose of your book (which I have never seen) be to treat of the antiquity of families or family-seats, you may read what relates to mine in Camden's Britannia on Dorsetshire; particularly in the notes added to a new edition some years since. And in the same Camden's History of Queen Elizabeth you will find Sir A. Ashley knighted on the taking of Cadiz, in which expedition he served as Secretary of War, with a particular commission from the Queen. If you go to great exactness on the new matches and would mention the family on the lady's side, you may observe that my wife's father (whose Christian name the correction will show you to have been Thomas) was (till a few years since that he purchased Bushy Hall) always written of the Lea, or of Lees Langly, which are estates adjoining, and of the latter, of which the family is still possessed, as they were also of Lees Langly (as I have found by the Herald's Office), in direct descent from Richard Ewer, living 34th of Henry 8th. My wife's mother is a Montague, granddaughter to the Earl of Manchester, and her mother was an heiress of the Baynards, of Wiltshire, from whom the present Mr. Montague has his estate and seat of Lackham, in that county.

Your book must needs have been incorrect, since in two places I have corrected my own name, which you will see right spelt, as I subscribe.— Your humble servant,    SHAFTESBURY.

[Address]: For Mr. Thomas Walker, in London.

---

## TO BISHOP BURNET.

REIGATE, *May* 23*rd*, 1710.

To THE BISHOP OF SARUM,

MY LORD,—The young man[1] who delivers this to your lordship is one who for several years has been preparing himself for the ministry, and in order to it has, I think, completed his time at the University. The occasion of his applying this way was purely from his own inclination. I took him a child from his poor parents, out of a numerous and necessitous family into my own, employing him in nothing servile, and finding his ingenuity, put him abroad to the best schools to qualify him for preferment in a peculiar way. But the serious temper of the lad disposing him (as I found) to the ministry preferably to other advantages, I could not be his hindrance ; though till very lately I gave him no prospect of any encouragement through my interest. But having been at last convinced by his sober and religious carriage, his studious inclination, and meek behaviour, that it was real principle, and not a vanity or conceit, that led him into these thoughts, I am resolved, in case your lordship finds him worthy of the ministry, to procure him a benefice as soon as anything happens in my power, and in the meantime design to keep him as a chaplain in my family.— I am, my lord.

[1] Michael Ainsworth.

## TO LORD SOMERS

(With Soliloquy).[1]

REIGATE, *May* 26*th*, 1710.

MY LORD,—I rejoice that, as things have happened upon the late combustion in the literate world, I can accost your lordship in as cheerful a strain as this of the enclosed print, which will be published in a day or two. Had not your lordship interposed your good offices and interest in behalf of what was formerly addressed to you, I should have been forced perhaps, against any inclination, to have taken a graver tone and justified myself in form. Not that I should be brought to do so in any case, except where I thought there was really need of some public apology and excuse. For your lordship well knows that I had little intention of exposing that good Protestant bishop, or bringing any contempt on our good Reformers of early times. What one writes freely to a friend in private is very different from what one writes for public view. I know what the meaning was of a certain person whom I ever thought your lordship's friend and servant, to act as he did in that affair and expose me in such a manner to so many and such as he did. I hope he never will betray your lordship, nor any friend of yours, in such a manner hereafter. But of his character your lordship knows more and will judge better than I. Though by late sore experience of my own, and the knowledge of his behaviour in other families and secret affairs, I have found what I long suspected, but was unwilling to believe.

As for the former accident which happened by his means, I am very far from being sorry for it, notwithstanding the combustion it had like to cause, since it has led me into a power of doing more good than my weak state of health would let me hope. I am now in no apprehension of what may happen from him or any other in such a way. I have written nothing since, nor shall at any time for the future in such an incautious manner as may give offence to people whom I esteem, or with whom at least I think it my duty to keep fair. Let those whom

[1] Shaftesbury's "Soliloquy or Advice to an Author" was published anonymously in 1710.

I may happen to offend by this enclosed exclaim as they think fit; I shall make no apology for myself, nor think of making them any reparation. As enthusiastic as your friend is, he resolves to be very discreet. So that if there be anything entertaining in what is here presented to you, your lordship may be diverted by it without regard to consequences, or to the interest of one whom your good nature would incline you to be concerned for, knowing how much he is and ever must be, my lord, your lordship's most faithful friend and affectionate humble servant.

## TO MICHAEL AINSWORTH.

REIGATE, *July* 10*th*, 1710.

GOOD MICHAEL,—I believe, indeed, it was you expecting me every day at ———— that prevented your writing, since you received orders from the good Bishop, my lord of Salisbury, who, as he has done more than any man living for the good and honour of the Church of England and the reformed religion, so he now suffers more than any man from the tongues and slander of those ungrateful *Churchmen*, who may well call themselves by that single term of distinction, having no claim to that of Christianity or Protestant, since they have thrown off all the temper of the former and all concern or interest with the latter.

I hope whatever advice the great and good Bishop gave you will sink deeply into your mind. I am willing you should accept of the offer of a curacy under so good a divine and lover of moderation as you describe. I would have you know, however, that I designed taking you into the house this summer at my coming to St. Giles, to give you, as I thought, the more credit on your entering upon orders, not fearing that you would receive any prejudice by it in your modesty and humility, when I took you sometimes to my own table, and you had at all times the convenience of my second table with those of good condition and gentle circumstances. My bounty to you should withal continue by being plentifully furnished with books (for I shall bring my Chelsea library soon to St. Giles's, now I have been forced to part with the house itself and live wholly from the town). You will perhaps much better pursue your study there than elsewhere. However, I charge you to make your judgment of this impartially by yourself, and do accordingly, letting me know, for I shall not set out this week. But by that time I can have received an answer from you to this I am assured that (if it please God no unexpected calamity befalls me) I shall be coming to St. Giles's.

As for the Bishop's articles, they were sent to you long since to place in my library. Should there be any mistake, or should Mrs. Cooper have kept the books packed up, you may show her this part of my letter, and desire her to open the packet or books, that the books may be placed in the library, and that you may lose no moment of time to benefit yourself by study, especially by this which is immediately recommended to you by your good superior, and is so worthy, great, and learned a performance. . . .

I pray God to bless you in your new function with all the true virtue, humility, and moderation, and meekness which becomes it.

---

## TO JEAN LE CLERC.

REIGATE, *July* 19*th,* 1710.

SIR,—It is one of the greatest pleasures I have to hear from you, in common with the public, of what relates to learning and knowledge, which you promote everywhere, and with more advantage to the world (for it is the Protestant and free world alone that I consider) than any other person I know in it besides. But it is a more particular satisfaction still to hear from you in private, and find that you esteem me, as I truly am, your zealous and faithful friend. I am only sorry to find by this affair you have imparted to me that you look upon the malice of some enemy as so considerable and worthy your concern. What you write me in your defence is sufficient against all the charge of this disguised author. Nor could it be expected that you should do more than collect and bring together those fragments of Menander, which was only to give the world a taste. If it relished the kind of literature, and you had found encouragement, you would have bestowed time and have gone farther in the work, when a second edition had been required. This you gave us reason to hope, and in your preface recommended it to the lovers of learning to send you their assistance. Instead of it you are fallen upon with anger and malignity. I do not think this will in any respect hurt your character or diminish the esteem the public and all public-spirited men have for you. The peevish temper of your adversary is sufficiently known, and his judgment and wit as much undervalued as his learning and mere scholarship is esteemed. But the affairs of the learned world are come to that pass that if a man be really a scholar, it is expected he should be a pedant, and partake of that captious, insulting, emulous, and quarrelsome humour for which universities are so famous.

It is strange that the bitterest quarrels should be those of Christians, and that among Christian feuds and animosities the most violent, and those carried on with the least quarter or token of humanity or civility, should be such as are exercised between the men who are set apart to keep the world in peace, by the culture of letters and philosophy. I cannot but think that in this sort of controversy the person who says least and is the most patient, obtains the victory. Sure I am that when an able and wise man, already in possession of the public ear, is turned aside from his great purpose and daily labour of instructing the world and raising the age to greater knowledge, virtue, and liberty, when, I say, such a public benefactor is by provocation drawn aside to encounter minutely and circumstantially with those envious adversaries, who disturb him only on this account, not he only, but the age itself, is a sufferer, and the adversary triumphs over both. But such as yours is (if I mistake him not) will in a short time betray himself very grossly, and save you the trouble of exposing him to the world. He who charges others for entering into parts of learning for which they are not (as he pretends) sufficiently qualified, has ventured upon a work, which, of all others, was the surest rock for him to split on.

His Horace will be the most elaborate monster that the learned world ever saw produced. He has mangled him and torn him in pieces, so as that the author is scarce knowable in his own text. I have seen many of his horrible corrections, and not one of them but had been presumptuous, even in an annota-

# 424 *Letters.*

tion or in the margin. But he has frankly displaced the readings of the manuscripts and all the ancient and new editions, to make room for his own conceptions, which (as I told my Lord Halifax) was, in my opinion, a defacing Horace in the worst manner in the world; especially in so fair an edition and print as was designed for it. This work of his you should (methinks) wait for. You may do the world a kindness by warning it. Such was the intolerable arrogance and rash decision of a very learned man (but ever inexcusable) Daniel Heinsius, who thus abominably treated Horace, and dismembered, dislocated, and inverted him in places of all others the most correct, natural, fluent, and beautiful to those who read Horace in another spirit and relish than that of pedantry. It may be a subject worthy of you, to show the mischief of such managers in the commonwealth of letters, and what hereafter is like to become of ancient authors, if they are thus treated by their editors.

But for personal matters and the controversy of this kind, I hope you will not lose us so much of your time as to engage in it according to those points of honour and notions of returns and satisfactions which have introduced the way of duels among the men of letters, and often force a peaceable and good man to act contrary to the Christian or philosopher's part as well in this way as the other.

I should write more particularly and plainly on these matters had I time. But being obliged to take instantly a journey into the West of England (where my concerns lie), and this chiefly too on the public account, because of the ferment which the seditious High-Churchman (Sacheverell) has raised in those and other parts of the kingdom, I am forced to despatch this with great haste and confusion. So can add no more, but that I am, as you (I hope) believe me, your affectionate friend and humble servant.

P.S.—Since I wrote this I happened to look over a paper which comes out twice a week, and is sometimes very polite and ingenious. If you cast your eye only to the last paragraph you will see your adversary ingeniously reflected on by the name of Poly-glottes.

[Address]: To Mr. Le Clerc, in Amsterdam.

## TO SIR JOHN CROPLEY.

ST. GILES'S, 24*th July*, 1710.

I am sorry to hear the intended dissolution.[1] It will be dreadful to Europe. But if France miscarry in this one stroke (for they have now found our weak side), woe be to the instruments they have employed for this purpose, and double woe to those apostate British men who have pushed this affair so far, that if they do not at once carry all for France and the St. Germain family, are for ever undone.

I value not what Parliament there is. We can have none that will undo what the last has done and pronounced in the cause of liberty and the revolution. All that they can do is to strike at some particular men, who, if they are wise and bold, may defy their enemies and make a quick turn upon them. If they tamper and make terms, let them take their fate for their pains.

Remember how things stood at the time of the Occasional Conformity Bill; how were we then used by the great ones, whose heads are now in such danger ?

Remember when the poor Prince[2] was brought with his asthma-fits into the House of Lords to make a vote for that Bill, and who they were that, a few hours after the King's death, moved in the House of Lords to have the Convocation upon a foot of equal session with the Parliament. They made us suffer sufficiently. It is their turn to feel. Let them not murmur. We are forgiving and are become their friends. But we must and ought to have sound pledges. Let them strike thoroughly and use their interest vigorously on the right side, and for the cause they have espoused and nobly served abroad, and I will engage my head for theirs, and forfeit my reputation of common sense, if this Parliament be not chosen to heart's content. But if they are shy or act by halves with us, or any degree under an entire and absolute resignation, they must take what follows; if Europe be lost, we must all sink together. But if that be

---

[1] Parliament was dissolved 21st September, 1710, the Whigs giving place to the Tories in the elections which followed.

[2] Prince of Denmark.

saved by some good Providence, as it has been already in greater
dangers, then we shall swim, but they sink who have acted
timorously and refused to put their whole interest without
reserve on that party which alone has the power to save them.
In haste, adieu.

P.S.—If you understand not the language I write in, either
of the chief Oak-Lords, but chiefly the first, would be able to
explain it.

---

## TO LORD GODOLPHIN.

REIGATE, *January* 29*th*, 1710 (11).

MY LORD,—In the height of ungrateful times, and in the
midst of those experiences you have had of that kind, I have
assurance enough to believe that, though your lordship has
neither seen nor heard from me for some time, you believe me
one of those whose gratitude on a public account makes them
now more zealously than ever your adherents and real friends.
What thoughts your lordship may have of the worth of mankind
in general I know not. For these are trying times. But as
long as you have in your mind a single reserve, and can believe
there is in your nation one single lover of its interest, you may
safely assure yourself that, though you know not the person,
you have certainly a friend full of zeal and indignation on your
account. You may be sure that such a one does with higher
honour and esteem than ever espouse your interest, which, as it
was proved once by the highest blessings and successes, so now
by the contrary is like to be thoroughly proved the interest both
of prince and country.

In this calamity,[1] my lord, you will have only your single
share. But you have certainly been above all men blessed in
having almost all mankind, and even your enemies, conscious
with you of the good you did, and the benefit the world and
common cause received under your ministry. If envy could

[1] Lord Godolphin was commanded by Queen Anne on the 8th of
August, 1710, to break his staff of Lord Treasurer, which he had held
for ten years, the trial of Dr. Sacheverell having caused an ultra-Tory
reaction.

have place where honesty and a public spirit prevails, your lordship might the soonest of all men be envied by the generous and good. Far am I, for my own part, from condoling with you. Nor could I, on the other side, be so partial to a friend against my country as on this account to congratulate with your lordship, if I might have the honour to treat you on this foot of friendship. I must own it, however, a temptation. For well, methinks, I taste your present quiet, and could sympathise in the ease and comfort of such an honourable recess.

Could you imagine, my lord, that anything but necessity could keep from you so long an humble servant of yours, who has sincerely such sentiments as these he writes? You must think him surely in an ill way, if not already out of the world. Indeed, my lord, you may reasonably think so. I have not at this moment so much strength or breath left me as would serve to speak half what I have here imperfectly written. The winter season has almost killed me, and I have no prospect if I escape to pass another in this climate unless the air of a warmer happens to set me up. I am importuned by my friends to go to Florence or Naples, and I have the vanity to think myself so much yours, and, as such, depended on by your lordship, that I could not take the resolution without informing you; as my friend and your bound servant, who present you this, will be able to do more particularly, and as a witness for me how much I am, my lord, your lordship's most obliged and most faithful, humble servant.

## TO LORD DARTMOUTH.[1]

REIGATE, *January 29th*, 1710 (11).

MY LORD,—The subject of the enclosed petition will be my apology for not waiting on your lordship with it, having not been able since the winter season to stir out of my chamber.

The early acquaintance I had the honour to make with your lordship, and the sense I then had of your merit and obliging

[1] Wm. Legge, first Earl of Dartmouth (1672-1750), became Secretary of State on 15th June, 1710, upon the dismissal by Queen Anne of the Earl of Sunderland.

qualities, gives me the confidence to depend on your good offices, in representing me with favour to Her Majesty, that having been ever full of duty towards her, and thoroughly zealous in the interest of her Government, I may with Her Majesty's leave, and under her protection, obtain my passage through France early this spring, to recover, by the only means remaining, that health, which together with my life, or whatever else I enjoy, would readily be spent in Her Majesty's service, and the support of her honour and interest.—I am, with great respect, my lord, your lordship's obedient, humble servant.

### TO LORD HALIFAX.

REIGATE, *February* 23*rd*, 1710 (11).

MY LORD,—There being a young gentleman newly come into the world,[1] who has the honour of being related to your lordship, both by his father's and mother's side, it is hoped your lordship will not refuse being made a party to the ceremony of giving him a name. When he comes hereafter into the wider world, to learn his part in it, it will be his highest advantage to be bred under you, and become your charge. It is peculiar, my lord, to your character to have a generous concern for the youth in general, and it would be hard if such a youth as this should escape you, who, if ever any was, may be said to be born to liberty, and devoted to the interests of those who are the lovers and defenders of it. For whatever motives *other* parents may have had, *his* (I am sure) had never met but in this view. And it will be satisfaction enough to his father, however short his life may be, if he can flatter himself with the prospect of leaving to his friends and party a successor, who, either by his name, his interest, or his genius (if he should be so blessed), may in the least contribute to their service.

A word more, my lord, I will venture to add in my own person, for by this time I may presume my fatherly affection has betrayed me. It is to beg that, if your lordship grants the favour I have asked for my son, you would remember him

---

[1] Shaftesbury's only child and heir, the fourth Earl, was born on the 9th of February, 1711.

hereafter as your Whig-godson ; and if I am no longer in the world to inspect his education, that you would esteem yourself concerned for him in this public sense. I have known it, my lord, laid roundly to your charge by the gentlemen of certain fatal seminaries that you were a general corrupter of the youth. For my own part, I have no heartier prayer than that my son may strongly take the infection. Whatever his faults or vices may prove, I shall have enough to compensate all, if I can flatter myself with the hope of his inheriting that principle by which he will be inseparable from his country's interest and from those who best support it. And thus I am sure he must ever prove, as his father has long been and is, with the greatest respect, my lord, your lordship's most obedient humble servant.

---

### TO LORD HOWE.[1]

REIGATE, 26*th March*, 1711.

MY LORD,—The honour of your relation, and particular friendship, to which I have had so early and long a claim, assures me of a favour which I have to beg of your lordship, in which I have reason to believe you can easily do me a very particular service. It is only to give my character (which your lordship may more justly do than any one) to a person on whom I must chiefly, if not wholly, rely, for the obtaining my pass through France to Italy, where I am advised to go for my health's sake, having no hopes of recovery but from a hotter climate. As much an Englishman as your lordship knows me to be, you can satisfy your country neighbour (of whose honour I have ever heard very advantageously) that I am one who neither for my religion's, my country's, nor my Prince's sake, would do a dishonourable act, such as that would be in the highest degree, if, obtaining a passage through France, I should make that nation or Prince receive the least injury from the favour granted me. On the contrary, I should surely be grateful to my power as far as honour could carry or permit me. And if

[1] Scrope Howe, 1st Viscount Howe (1648—1712), a staunch Whig.

that great man [1] of the French nation, who, notwithstanding his present misfortunes, has very justly a high credit and influence at that Court, could be apprised of this plain and honest character, which I can boldly claim to be my due, I am confident I need not fear being suspected of any mystery, or any engagement with our Home Ministry or Court, or that I am any way capable of acting a feigned part to serve any cause or Prince on earth, so as to make an unworthy use of a favour, to which, if granted to me, I shall probably owe my life. This is all I think fit to express in paper, committing the rest to your lordship's management in behalf of me.—I am, my lord, your lordship's most faithful, obedient, humble servant.

[To Lord Howe.]

P.S.—Whatever particulars relating to my affair your lordship is willing to be informed of, my worthy friend Sir John Cropley will explain to you in the best manner.

---

TO LORD SOMERS.

REIGATE, *March* 30*th*, 1711.

MY LORD,—The works [2] of your enthusiastic friend (disabled in most other workmanship and service) I presume to send you thus, one volume after another as they come out of the press. For one who is your lordship's friend and the public should manage time for you the best he can. And by this method you may have spare minutes now and then to tumble over what you have read before with what is newly added, to render it complete and of a piece with what remains, the third volume being wholly new.

The whole work should have of right been dedicated to your lordship, you have reason sufficient to conclude, as well as that it would have been the highest satisfaction to the author

[1] Probably James Fitzjames, Duke of Berwick.

[2] Shaftesbury's "Characteristics of Men, Manners, Opinions, Times," appeared in three volumes in 1711.

to sign himself thus publicly your devoted friend and servant. But there are reasons again on the other hand which your lordship well knows for suppressing this ambitious forwardness and zeal; that your lordship may be no further dipt (as our modern phrase is) than as you are already. It would be the highest advantage to a certain party that your lordship should stir a step out of your character, or seem to act against them in any other capacity than that in which you have hitherto moved. For as in a ship that goes with wind and tide and carries us prosperously and to heart's content we hear nothing but steady! steady! so is it with your character, and so would I have it continue; that no noise may be heard from any side but that of steady. Let others tack as occasion or shift their sails as occasion serves. It is joy to me to see you hold the helm as steady as you still do. Even now amidst the storm it is joy to me to remember that there was once a time when *one* pilot alone advised putting off to sea and saved us from riding securely in a calm, upon a coast where, if we had remained ever so little, we must inevitably have perished. How naturally every man loves his pilot when he is himself abroad with all his goods and effects is easily understood. For my own part, I have learnt almost from the moment of my birth to embark myself with the public, and to have no other bottom than that alone. How tender, therefore, I naturally am of my pilot your lordship may easily imagine. And though as an enthusiast I could readily cast myself away, and be a Jonah for the advantage of the ship, yet I can truly boast that I am more sparing of the pilot than any one in the vessel. And for that reason I have, within the space of a twelve month, been strong in my resentment against those of the crew who mutiny because their pilot, taking his proper measures and working in his own way, is not at every turn ready upon the deck to do common drudgery, and expose himself equally in every capacity besides. Whether the mere deck or quarter-deck would have been my own station had I been able to keep my legs, I know not. Sure I am, however, that I should never have spared myself (as I never did when able), though I have many smiling friends (and particularly a late Minister, kinsman, and old companion of mine) to put a query upon this head, and call in doubt a resolution and public zeal which may venture to say is at least a pin higher than their own. But "facile omnes cum valemus rectu consilia grotis damus." I could counsel, too, in my turn where I myself am sound, and others not so thoroughly proof as to bear ordinary raillery. But let who will rail or make slight of me, they shall never suffer by it whilst the public receive any advantage by them.

By this third volume of Chamber-Practice your lordship will find that if my good humour be quite spent, I have courage, however, left to attack and provoke a most malignant party with whom I might easily live on good terms to all the advantage imaginable. Their blessed fountains of virtue and religion were never perhaps thus searched before. The poisonous principles, indeed, which they dispense under a religious appearance have been often exposed, whilst their sovereignty in arts and sciences, their presidents in letters, their alma maters and academies, have been acknowledged and taken for granted. They who treated the poor Presbyterians as impolite, unformed, without rival literature or manners, will perhaps be somewhat moved to find themselves treated in the same way, not as corrupters merely of morals and public principles, but as the very reverse or antipodes to good breeding, scholarship, behaviour, sense, and manners. For should this grow credible, and take either with our growing youth or their grown parents, I hope endowed seminaries might chance to make a much worse figure, and the October Club prove less considerable than at present in that height to which a modern statesman (not of their own kind) has to his country's danger, and perhaps to his own plague hereafter, exalted in our senate.

But this, perhaps, may be an insinuation too advantageous, and savouring of the fatherly love of an author towards his own offspring. When the three volumes are finished (as the next month they probably will be), I shall presume to send your lordship another copy of the whole in better paper and in sheets, that if your lordship thinks it worth binding for your library, you may assign it what place or habit you like best. —I am, my lord, your lordship's most faithful friend and humble servant.

## TO LADY WALDEGRAVE.[1]

REIGATE, *May* 4*th*, 1711.

MADAM,—Had my fortune never allowed me the honour of knowing you otherwise than as your character and your high birth distinguishes you to all, I should have been more surprised with the generous and obliging part I have experienced, and with the extreme goodness and favour by which I am likely to receive even my life itself at your hands. But as I have the happiness to remember an early time when, amidst all the honours that were paid you, you distinguished yourself more by your goodness, condescension, and humility, than by any other princely titles or greatness that belonged to you, you will allow me, who once treated and must ever treat you on the same foot of profound respect and highest honour, to acknowledge still your superior character and highest quality; that of your readiness to do good, and to employ yourself in whatever is generous and worthy of yourself.

I am so sensible, madam, how fully you possess this merit, that I dare flatter myself you will be able to judge my acknowledgments and sense of it; and that as distant as I am, and out of the knowledge of that great and worthy prince (your brother, my Lord Duke of Berwick[2]), I may be represented to him, however, as one not wholly unworthy of the favour which at your desire he has procured me, of passing through France, to the warmer climates where I can alone hope to recover my health, of which I shall henceforward be the more desirous, that I may live in some measure to acknowledge how much I am, with the highest obligation and most profound respect, madam, your most obedient and most humble servant.

[1] Henrietta Fitzjames, the natural daughter of James, Duke of York, afterwards James II., married November 29th, 1683, Baron Henry Waldegrave.

[2] James Fitzjames, Duke of Berwick (1670-1734), the natural son of James II., by Arabella Churchill, sister of the great Duke of Marlborough, was in 1711 Marshal of France.

FF

TO MICHAEL AINSWORTH.

REIGATE, 11*th May*, 1711.

I am glad the time is come that you are to receive full orders, and that you hope it from the hand of our worthy, great, excellent Bishop,[1] my Lord of Salisbury.

This is one of the circumstances I hope may help to insure your steadiness in honesty, good principles, moderation, and true Christianity, now set at nought and at defiance by the far greater part and numbers of that body of clergy called the Church of England, who no more esteem themselves a Protestant church, or in union with those of Protestant communion, though she pretend to the name of Christian, and would have us judge of the spirit of Christianity from theirs, which God prevent, lest good men should in time forsake Christianity through their means. As for my own part of charity and friendship towards you and your poor family in other respects, as well as this of breeding and raising you to this capacity of the sacred office you are to take, I shall be sufficiently recompensed if you prove (as you have ever promised) a virtuous, pious, sober, and studious man, as becomes the solemn charge belonging to you. You have been brought into the world, and come into orders, in the worst time for insolence, riot, pride, and presumption of clergymen that I ever knew or have read of, though I have searched far into the characters of high churchmen from the first centuries that they grew to be dignified with crowns and purple, to the late times of our Reformation and to our present age.

The thorough knowledge you have had of me and of the direction of all my studies and life to the promotion of religion, virtue, and the good of mankind will, I hope, be of some good example to you. At least, it will be a hindrance to your being seduced by infamy and calumnies such as are thrown upon the men called moderate, and in their style indifferent in religion, heterodox, and heretical.

God send you all true Christianity, with that temper, life, and manners which become it. I am your hearty friend,

SHAFTESBURY.

[1] Bishop Burnet.

## TO LORD GODOLPHIN.

REIGATE, *May* 27*th*, 1711.

MY LORD,—Being about to attempt a journey to Italy, to try what a warmer climate (if I am able to reach it) may do towards restoring me a little breath and life, it is impossible for me to stir hence till I have acquitted myself of my respects the best I can to your lordship, to whom alone had I but strength enough to make my compliments, and pay a day's attendance in town, I should think myself sufficiently happy in my weak state of health.

I am indeed, my lord, little able to render services of any kind; nor do I pretend to offer myself in such a capacity to any one except your lordship only. But could I flatter myself that ever I parted hence, or while I passed through France, or stayed in Italy, I could anywhere, in the least trifle, or in the highest concern, render any manner of service to your lordship, I should be proud of such a commission.

Sure I am in what relates to your honour and name (if that can receive ever any advantage from such a hand as mine) your public as well as private merit will not pass unremembered in whatever region or climate I am transferred. No one has a more thorough knowledge in that kind than myself. Nor no one there is who, on this account, has a juster right to profess himself as I shall ever do, with the highest obligation and most constant zeal, my lord, your lordship's most faithful and most obedient, humble servant, SHAFTESBURY.

## TO SIR JOHN CROPLEY.[1]

DOVER, 2*nd July*, 1711.

SIR,—This word only as to Mr. Coste. I beg you that as his friend, for such I know you are, you would remind him of what I strictly left in charge with him as to his own concerns and interest; that by no art or artifice he would be drawn in again, to think of parting with an annuity which I helped to

[1] This letter is the first in Shaftesbury's "Copy Book of Letter from my departure from England in July, 1711, to March 22nd (inclusive), being then in Naples, 1712."

procure for him, and to which I have in kindness to him annexed another of at least equal value to be a security for him against all necessity, or very ill fortune hereafter. This I charged him with, before all our friends at supper, last time at Reigate, with this addition: That I would not have his friends in the world (especially since he had hopes now of having some that were in a way of greatness) pretend on his account that they needed not concern themselves for his interest or fortune, since he was now already provided for and engaged than as he has no better preferment, and that I love him too well to let him be at a loss, or so employed as is unfit for him, or below him.

A good place of any kind, or in any rich family, to travel or otherwise serve in the education of youth would be as much to his advantage as Lord Ashley's hereafter, who in five or six years will claim to be his charge, and receive the benefit of his knowledge and experiences in the affairs of youth and education.

Meanwhile, I shall expect Mr. Coste with me as occasion serves for his journey, if his friends do nothing for him; as for France, I despair of his passing.

---

## TO SIR JOHN CROPLEY.

PARIS, *August* 11th, 1711.

By my last you will hear how I have fared, what strength I have got by my rest here after my sad fatigue and fit of my asthma on the road, and what I am making to get out of this kingdom as fast as my sad health will suffer me. So to-morrow, if I hold tolerable, I set out for Lyons, where I must determine which way to pass the soonest and safest over the mountains, which I am in hopes to do in a litter for my wife and self, and by the shortest way, without going round by Switzerland or Geneva, which might be very severe for me and retard my passage till the ill season came to pass the mountains. By what my wife writes to her sister, and what you will hear by Mrs. Skinners, you will be informed of all little particulars relating to me. I must be forced to be short this post, and would have been contented to have omitted writing this time myself, but for that affair of which I cannot write by any hand but my own. You may believe how it vexed me to find the application which was made (as you tell me) of one of the imaginary *characters* in "Characteristics." By good chance Mr. Crelle had put up the foul unbound copy which had been dirtied in your pocket, a part of the last volume where those *characters* stand. I presently called for them, and read them over to consider what such a turn might produce, and I was more vexed when I considered the thing by the first impression it made on me. Afterwards, when I was more cool, I came to this issue in my own thoughts : that in the first place, if I had hurt a friend, I was, however, conscious to myself of a far contrary intention. And consciousness, according to that author (if he be not an hypocrite and an impostor), is the best comfort and soundest satisfaction in this world when it is honest and has sincerity and innocence on its side. So that let what friend soever be piqued, or what enemy soever more exasperated, if just occasion was never given, let appearances stand as they will, there is no subject of long vexation or trouble. This, however, I must desire of you (and I owe it to the inviolated private friendship and affection I have ever preserved for that honoured person and family under all difficulties, misfortunes, and differences, from my earliest youth to this moment) that you would represent this honest protestation I make to you about this affair, which you may well do, who were the witness to the haste in which that latter part was written, and the liberty which the author gave to himself and to the heat of his imagination in this rapidity of writing, far different from the cooler and more sedate accurate sheets of the preceding volumes, where everything was deliberate and more maturely considered. This, too, you know, that to this very hour I know not the person whom perhaps I may have made an enemy at this rate, by repeating a sentence of a friend of ours upon his behaviour in the House of Commons. You know I guessed the person to have been one now in high employment, but you protested to me it was not he and you would let me know no more. In this case I may honestly say, and without affectation, that justice was blind. The author knew no friend or enemy, no party or side, no Ministry or interest besides the public's, when he wrote in this vein of satirical humour. I take it for granted that the same malicious interpreting wits have assigned other real characters to every imaginary one, and so the characters adjoining (that, I mean, of the old church-patriot [1] gained by Court favour) may be assigned to Lord Rochester,[2] at least I am persuaded it would have been so applied by the same rule, and with the same reason, had he been alive. I am sure if the person I am concerned for considers it in such a view, he may find full as plausible a foundation, and yet I can say it with the sincerest truth, that the thought of such a lord or present Minister never came into my head, as often as you have heard me say that of late I looked upon that great lord indeed to have sacrificed his party and acted that very part described.

Be it as fortune or as the genius of the great man is like to determine of it, whether he thinks me sincere in this, or contrariwise! as the appearances are; this, after all, I will venture to affirm, that let malice do its worst in this case, or let what application soever be made of that character, there is yet room left from that very foundation (considering that it is a philosopher who speaks) to make out as great a character as the greatest statesman of these last ages could ever claim, not excepting even my grandfather, for whose memory I have so partial a zeal.—But I have outwrit my paper and my strength, so, dear friend, adieu !

----

## TO THOMAS MICKLETHWAYT.

PARIS, 11*th August*, 1711 [N.S.]

DEAR COU.,— . . . If the success of certain papers be as you represent, I may hope for power and ability even yet in my life, to render both public and private services at a season of my life and in circumstances in which I despaired of being of further service in the world. For a fame in these cases is all in all. He who is master once of the public ear is in possession of the highest power, if he has wit and

----

[1] " Characteristics" iii., p. 170.

[2] Laurence Hyde, Earl of Rochester (1641-1711), was a member with Godolphin and Sunderland of the first Tory Administration to control under that name English national affairs.

a character on his side. Opinion of power (as a philosopher says) is in this case truly power. I am sorry for the unthought-of sting which is fixed to the tail of one of the characters. But to repair that injury, you will see what I have written to Sir John this post, which I once again leave to his judgment whether to show or not. This, too, I would have him add from me; and would he take my opinion, he should not out of fear (as happened about a year since) decline the freedom and open manner. " That at the worst, allowing the whole world to be possessed of this fancy, and falsely prejudiced in the imagination of such a real intended picture ; yet if the painter's hand can be esteemed and rated so highly by his countrymen as to be thus narrowly scanned and weighed, each casual line or accidental sally of humour or fancy, it is in the power of the same hand not only to do justice to himself where he has been misconstrued and to the great person whom he has seemed to wound, but even to make over and above reparation, and from that very error of the public to take fresh ground and new advantages the more disinterestedly and powerfully to represent one day, both his own private friendship and the particular merit of that friend, who by the effect of his counsels and ability will (as I doubt not) soon prove to all Europe, as well as to England, the different foundation which his Ministry and measures have had from what his enemies represent and what in general the world has been ready to believe."

This, for my part, would I say firmly and boldly were I to speak for myself, or (as I should more properly say) for *you,* since in reality, were it my own case, I should not so much as bestow a thought further than this: "that if a great Minister, who ought to know the worth of my friendship, would take a fancy to lose it for a surmise of fancy, a forced interpretation made on a free pen, let him suffer the loss; his own will be the greater than the honest man's, who loved him better, perhaps, than any one besides, and beyond what he deserved if he were capable to conceive a pique or a disturbance on such a matter."

As for Mr. Coste's concern, you will by this time (if he shows you my letter to him, which I wrote from hence) see my naked and unfeigned regard and concern for him; and that if he understands friendship, he will find enough in it to think he has a real *friend.* My very resolution turned so much on him and on his being with me, that after a fruitless fresh attempt to have leave for him to be with me in France I determined positively for Italy, when I had reason enough (as I still have) to decline the danger of so terrible a journey as that to Italy through armies, wasted countries, and mountains in a doubtful season. For the rains if not the snows will be coming ere I shall (as I fear) be able to pass that way. But all my measures are taken for my journey to-morrow morning to Lyons, instead of Montpelier, which was the only place I thought of on my first arrival here after the sad fit of my asthma I had on the road by those fatigues I suffered. Besides my friendship and real kindness for Mr. Coste, it is my interest as well as his (if I hope anything from him for Lord Ashley hereafter), to have him in employment in the world, if employment worthy of him be found, as I rejoice to hear by him that there is. His improvement, his experiences, and acquisitions of this kind will be Lord Ashley's [1] good hereafter. Mr. Coste wants not men of letters or speculation. Practice of the world and converse and business will be his better scene. My own loss in him will be repaired by this reflection: that I had at last settled everything for his meeting me in Italy. Pray assure him of all this fully, and of my constant friendship, since I cannot write myself by this post to him. Kind dues to the Beachworth family; love and blessing to your brother Jo.[2] Services to the club, all that kindly inquire for me. I grieve to hear of my apostate disciple, Arent, that after ruining his health by vicious courses and raking he should with that sad remainder of life and health have embarked in such a new and contrary service after having got an honest maintenance, and served with such honour under so great a soul as Stanhope, whom in his present ill-fortune [3] he could have nobly complimented by for-

---

[1] Pierre Coste, who had been tutor of Frank Masham until the death of Locke. As he was a French Protestant, it was not possible for him, owing to the revocation of the Edict of Nantes, to accompany Shaftesbury through France. Shaftesbury evidently designed, however, to employ him later as a tutor for Lord Ashley.

[2] Both Joseph Micklethwayt and Arent Furly were with General Stanhope during the Peninsular campaign.

As prisoner of the Spanish.

saking all business for his sake, and till he was restored to what his merits to his country entitle him. I congratulate with Jo that he has so happy an opportunity to express his zeal, tenderness, and love of such a master. God grant this younger disciple of mine may profit by this occasion and example. Adieu.

---

## TO THE DUKE OF BERWICK.[1]

LYONS, 28*th August*, 1711.

MY LORD,—By the kind good offices and friendly regard so noted in your grace's character towards your countrymen, and in so particular a manner experienced by myself, I am at last with much difficulty arrived at a place in France where I have first of all perceived in some degree the advantage of the hot climate, which I have been obliged to seek as the only preservative of a ruinous health. And I now flatter myself that if, by your grace's great favour so kindly offered me in yours to Mr. Furly, I may happily pass the mountains in a good season (so as to get as far southward at least as Rome before the winter comes), there may be still hope for me that I may enlarge my term of life, so as to be able to acknowledge hereafter in a better manner how much I owe it to your grace's favour and friendship. For without this and the encouragement given me by my Lady Walgrave's great goodness and concern in my behalf, I had never attempted, or at least never succeeded in the attempt of such journey as this. At present, my lord, I am forced to remain here at Lyons for a few days to recover strength, which I so much want, and to prepare myself for my further journey by Grenoble, whence your grace is pleased to mention your convoying me to Mount Cenis, or where I may have assurance of safety by a pass from the Duke of Savoy,[2] to which my double passes and leave from both

---

[1] The Duke of Berwick was at this time, as a marshal of France, in command of the French troops on the borders of Piedmont. It was thus necessary for Shaftesbury to be convoyed by him through the French forces in order to reach Italy.

[2] The Duke of Savoy was a British ally, whose Italian dominions Shaftesbury now sought to enter.

Courts may, I presume, entitle me. What application I am to make, your grace will please inform me. I shall wait here your grace's commands, whether to myself directly or by Mons. de Melliant, the Intendant from whom on your grace's account I have already received the greatest favours and civilities.

I humbly beg your grace's pardon for the ill manner of this writing, of which my present weakness and cough is the occasion. I should be sorry my hand should take off from what my heart is so zealous to express, how much I am, with thorough obligation and respect, my lord, your grace's most faithful and most obedient, humble servant.

---

### TO THE DUKE OF BERWICK.

Lyons, *September 5th,* 1711.

My Lord,—Having received the honour of your grace's most obliging letter and pass[1] this morning, with the account of the kind provision you have been at the pains to make for enabling me to pursue my journey in my present weak state, I resolve to come forwards towards your grace in a litter from hence to-morrow morning, that I may the sooner (if at all able) attend your grace, and acknowledge to you personally what I shall endeavour to do, by all possible ways, the great and unspeakable obligations by which I am, and must remain, your grace's most faithful, obedient, and most humble servant.

---

### TO PIERRE COSTE.

Turin, *3rd October,* 1711.

It was about two or three days after I had written my first to you from Paris, that I received your first, of which you have since sent me the copy in your second, which I have received since I came hither. I should have written to you again presently from Paris on the receipt of yours, but being pressed in time, and writing by the next post to our common friend Mr. Micklethwayt, I satisfied myself with letting you know by him the real satis-

[1] The original passport in French accompanies this letter in the MSS.

faction I received in hearing of your advancement in a station befitting and becoming you. Could you doubt my sentiments on this occasion? Has not my whole conduct tended to make you known and be esteemed according to what I esteem your merit?

If all the world had forsaken or forgotten you, think you that you would at last have been less rated, or with less welcome and heartiness received into my obscure retreat and little family? I can assure you I have such thoughts of your friendship that I can easily flatter myself, as sickly and melancholy a state as mine is, you could be well satisfied to bear me company in it, if the want of you abroad, and the claim of other friends whom you might serve in an active sphere, did not make me protest against it, and refuse to take you from what was more your own and a public good. Pray think no more of my friendship for you, on the foot of this last year or two; you know it of longer date. It was stamped and fixed before travelling was thought of, or a wife or a child. These circumstances are apt to raise an ill dust with those who have not very strong eyes in friendship. And *interest, interest* comes in ever and anon, and must seem a kind of key to things with which it has nothing to do.

When I first took you as a friend, I happened, unfortunately (though with good meaning), to have a hand in making a bargain, which afterwards proved no very advantageous one, and had like to have proved much worse had I not, with some friends, supported your interest with some vigour. Your recompense from that family, though a small one, yet to a person in such circumstances as yourself is of more than double or treble the ordinary value. This I often explained to you, and by what I represented and acted for you in that affair, I have engaged you (as you have solemnly promised me) not to part with that small annuity to which you know in what manner I have added, that all future prospects may be easy to you, and a mere dependency may not be your lot. That this is free to you and under no obligation as it comes from me, I hope you believed long since, and accepted so when you knew it.

If my child lives, his guardians, who will know the value I set on you, will make the care and charge of him the greater advantage to you, and would bid higher to gain you (if it stood on interest merely) than any other governor or friend besides. But Lord Ashley, by his good leave, has nothing to do here. Glad I am you saw him, knew him, and early loved him. I hope, too, you will call and see him often. But, as I tell you, these matters were before he was thought of; and the providing for you was my care before I had the thought of being either a husband or a father. If my espousing you as a friend has been any occasion that others have the more warmly espoused your interest or considered you the more, it is a double satisfaction to me and no disappointment that you are taken from me to a good employment in the world; and I must confess the prospect is the more satisfactory, since I find the prospect of my living is so much straitened, and that the passage of the Alps has just brought me to death's door, &c.

[Address] : To Mr. Coste, at London.

## TO JOHN MOLESWORTH.[1]

TURIN, *7th September*, 1711.

SIR,—By that time you receive this letter I shall probably, if alive, be very near the honour of waiting on you at Florence, for I set out in a litter for that place from hence to-morrow morning.

Having been brought last winter almost to death's door by my persecuting distemper (the asthma), to which you have known me long subject, I left England at the pressing desire of all my friends and physicians, who told me nothing could be of service towards my recovery without the benefit of the warmth and air of Montpelier, or some place as southern at least and mild in Italy. I had the Queen's leave to have stopped at Montpelier, or where I pleased in France, and I was civilly offered the favour from the French Court when I passed at Paris. But I was unwilling to owe more to France than merely the favour of a passage through the country. So I ventured to come hither over the Alps, where I suffered so much

[1] John Molesworth (1670—1726), the second Viscount Molesworth and son of Robert, was for many years the English Plenipotentiary in Tuscany.

in my weak state that I have lain almost dying these three weeks at this place, which I had much ado to reach, and though a little recovered within this day or two, can scarce hope to reach Naples, the place assigned me by all that are knowing in my case.

If I can but reach to such a friend as you, I shall think myself happy, particularly in having yet an opportunity of assuring you of the sincere honour and esteem with which I have long held your father's family, and in consequence as well as on account of your particular worth and merit. Your most faithful friend and humble servant.

[Address]: To Mr. Molesworth, at Florence.

----

### TO JOHN WHEELOCK.

ROME, *November 6th,* 1711.

By the blessing of a most happy season during my journey, by the goodness and warmth of the climate, and by the easiness of that usual carriage in this country—a litter, I am come through in the weakest and lowest condition imaginable to this city, and within less than a week's journey more of Naples, my intended resting-place, and that from whence I have my only hopes of recovery, having out of unwillingness to owe so great an obligation to the French Court, refused their offer of wintering or staying as long as I pleased at Montpelier, and there being no air or place of health (in my case) equal to Montpelier, except Naples, to gain which I have gone and am to go so far. But though I die there I shall have much greater satisfaction than to have been obliged to France so much as I should have been, and at last have died there. I must own I had a fairer prospect before the fatigue of this voyage and passage of the mountains (the Alps) in war time and between camps in too late a season, so that Montpelier might have saved my life, and if Naples does it after this, its air may be justly in greater esteem than ever for people in my case. You will have heard by Bryan,[1] from Turin, of my desperate state and weak condition when there, nor had I

----

[1] John Wheelock's nephew, who accompanied Shaftesbury to Italy.

any relief till I reached Florence, where I first perceived some help to my short breath and continued cough, as I have done yet more since I came to this warmer air, which may make me hope still more from the warmer and more balsamic where I am going to settle this winter.

As good a husband as I have been (and my wife surely the best housewife as well as wife, nurse, and friend that ever was known in her whole sex), I have not been able to keep with the expense proposed, but have expended at least a hundred pound a month by Bryan's reckoning, I fear I shall be little able to diminish it. But it will not be, I trust in God (and can surely presume), much beyond this present compass. If I live my family and paternal estate will not (I hope) be prejudiced by this remittance out of it for my subsistence, and if it please God you live too I know my affairs will prosper, and Lord Ashley want no father at home to take care of his concerns and the family to whose principles and public affection, as well as blood, he will (I hope) succeed. I know your affection for that family and for him himself, whom I saw (and since hear by every one) is so winning and engaging a child. I am happy on his account as well as my own in having so faithful a servant as yourself, and whether I live or die am easy in my thoughts, having, together with you, such good friends (though no such relations indeed) to take care of the pledge I shall leave you. For as for more children, should I recover this great illness, it is what I shall hardly expect, at least none of his health and strength, being so severely sunk in my constitution and so much lower than even this last winter when I was at worst. . . . God prosper you. I have not strength to write much at a time or often. I leave the rest to Bryan. Dues as due, &c.

My wife remembers kindly to you. Give kisses from us to Lord Ashley when you come again to him next.

---

### TO MR. CHETWYND.

NAPLES, 17*th November*, 1711.

SIR,—If I had less strength left than I have, I should endeavour still to return you my sincere acknowledgments on my arrival here in an air and climate the only one from whence

I could hope a recovery in my almost desperate state, and where I never could have hoped to arrive but by your kind assistance and friendly services.

If the effect of them be so fortunate as to allow me ever to act or live again in the world, I shall hope for many occasions to acknowledge in a more particular manner the many favours and civilities I received both from yourself and brother at Genoa, whose care in providing me the litter at such a difficult juncture was indeed so happy for me.

It is by the return of the litter-man and the voiturins you helped me to at Turin that I take this opportunity of safely conveying this line of thanks from a very weak hand, being, indeed, but barely alive, and unable to lie down in my bed, where my cough and short breathings keep me still upright, as when I was with you, for I can keep yet in no other posture, and by this token alone you will judge my weakness, and excuse the imperfections of this from your obliged and faithful humble servant.

[Address] : To Mr. Chetwynd at Turin.

----

### TO PIERRE COSTE.

NAPLES, *November* 23rd, 1711.

.   .   .   This I can only say, that from the time I came hither (which is about a week since) I found my cough a little abated.

I know not where this letter may find you, for by this time I judge you may have entered on the station and in the place which I much rejoiced to hear so advantageous to you.   Should it happily bring you into Italy, I should be highly pleased.   For should I be then alive (were it a twelve-month hence) I should be still here.   And if you come with a young nobleman or gentleman into Italy, I take for granted it is impossible you should escape coming to Naples.   Or were your stay at Rome or Florence only, it should go hard with me (if I were in any travelling condition and the season good), but I would see and pass some time with you there.   Wherever you are, I hope I shall hear constantly from you.   You are my only book correspondent; and I am sure you will count it no fatigue to write me now and then a page or two about the matters of the literate world, which is the only one I am concerned in, and which, whether I am sick or well, in a living or a dying way, I am always equally glad to hear of.

I wrote you in my first from Paris, how I found the Abbé Bignon disposed; how civilly he put me off, and how speciously he complimented me so as to avoid seeing me at all, or hearing a request he knew I had to make to him about your coming into France to me. I was so civilly used by Mons. Torey and all the Ministers besides, and so courted to stay in France, that I am satisfied it could be only on this account that the Abbé Bignon served me so; he having shown also sufficient inclination to be civil to me, but that by the agent I employed (as well as by former advices) he had already smelt out my design of asking leave for your stay or passage through France. As you well remember, I feared the case to have stood in the same manner with Mons. Tallard in England by the letters you saw which passed between us, about my family and the persons that accompanied me. Bigotry is higher than ever in France. But I must conclude now. Your sincere and constant friend.

[Address]: A Monsieur Coste à Londres.

## TO THOMAS MICKLETHWAYT.

Having so soon quitted Paris and passed Rome (the two only places for virtuosoship of this kind, I mean drawing and designing for engravery) there is no hopes that I can time enough, get a hand to execute the five draughts besides the already executed draught you have sent me of Mr. Gribelins for "The Moralists." This made me think whether I could reduce the whole six (viz., one for each treatise as first resolved) to three (viz., one for each volume), to stand in the *general* title page (for so I must call it) of each particular volume,[1] so

---

[1] Shaftesbury made in Italy the final changes for the press in the second edition of the " Characteristics," which was published in 1713 shortly after his death. In addition to the corrections much attention was given by him to the designs of the plates that appear for the first time in this edition.

that after this manner the first of the three plates would in the first volume stand next to the first general title-page, and in the other two volumes they would stand the first of all in the same place, as I remember, where stands at present the wooden cut of a pan of coals and fire burning out, which, as I take it, is the ornament Mr. Darby has put to the general title-page of each of the three particular volumes.

But at present, as my weak state is, and in absence of all artists to help me draw out the designs I had in mind for Mr. Gribelin, I have only this expedient, and I think it will be pretty enough. Let the wooden-cut of the pan of coals in each of the three volumes be left out, and exactly in their place (*mutatis mutandis*) let Mr. Gribelin's smaller draught stand engraved. The bigger I confess is mighty fine. But it will be intolerably pretending to make a whole leaf of it, or indeed to make anything to the book beyond a mere flourish.

You will object that this device of the triumph of liberty is peculiar only to one treatise, viz., "The Moralists." But as that piece and that very subject (moral and political) is the hinge and bottom of all three and of the whole work itself, it will well become every title-page, and may well stand three times over, having a small letter or two engraven to refer to the place as thus: Vol. 2, p.—— Grib. sculp.

I have not the second volume, so cannot note the page.

I am quite spent, so adieu. Dues to all.

----

## TO THOMAS MICKLETHWAYT.

NAPLES, *8th December*, 1711.

Your letters are of great comfort to me, speaking as they do of all my friends, the public, and my mental as well as personal offspring. To know one does good, though in the remotest and lowest state, and to have the prospect of doing still more and more, even after life, is a great pleasure to one who stands upon the brink.

It has happened that I have just received your letters on the days that I have been at the worst, and that I had reason to think would be my last, and though I can promise little to you of my recovery, I hope you will not cease writing to me with

GG

the same vigour and alacrity in whatever condition you may
expect your letter shall find me. This, remember, I expect from
you *as a friend*, and that you write oftener than you do, for
methinks the consideration that perhaps you will not have many
more letters to write to me should make you afford me a weekly
letter (since Sir John and you hear weekly from us) whilst you
are conscious that the most agreeable employment of my last
minutes is in hearing thus from you and friends, and of what
relates to the public and our common concern in it. Many
grateful acknowledgments to worthy Mr. Collins [1] for his kind
regard to both my offsprings. Has not Lord H——x [2] been yet
to see his godson ? Has he despised the charge committed to
him ? Or does he count it no public one, but merely private and
selfish ? Little has he to do to praise " Car—cks," [3] or any work
of that author, if he has no honester or more generous thoughts
of his principle and sense. I expect with satisfaction the coming
of the " Bibliothèque Choisie " and pamphlets [4] by sea. You say

[1] Anthony Collins.     [2] Lord Halifax.

[3] The " Characteristics."

[4] *Account of books, pamphlets, &c., sent to the Right Honourable
the Earl of Shaftesbury by the Italian Galley, Henry Alexandre, Master.*

Bentley's Horace, stitched.
States Memorial to the Queen.
  ,,  Letter to the Queen.
Dr. Swift's Letter to the Lord
  Treasurer.
Reflections on Dr. Swift's Letter.
Horatius Reformatus.
Survey of the Distressed Mother.
Two Protests of the Lords.
The Medley, No. 21.
Duke of Marlborough's Case.
Four Parts of John Bull and the
  Key. Dr. Swift.
Bishop Fleetwood, Four Sermons.

First and Second Report of the
  Commission of Accounts.
The Fourth Part of the Defence
  of the Allies.
The Windsor Prophecy. Dr.
  Swift.
Preamble to Baron Masham's
  Patent.
The Commons Representation.
Votes of the 10th June.
Gazette of the 16th February.
Speeches, addresses, *Spectators*,
  and *Examiners.*

Two prints of a large Mosaic pavement lately found in Oxford-
shire, one of them in its proper colours.
Six fine prints, lately done by Mr. Gribelin.
Cole's Dictionary.
Argill's new project, dedicated neither to ye Queen, nor to ye

not by what ship, and speak as if they were to be sent to Florence from Leghorn, which if so (since there can be hardly hand-carriage from Florence hither) they must go back from Florence to Leghorn again. If W——k [1] has forgot to leave the books and things I left with him to be sent after me by the first sea-carriage, I shall be sadly disappointed. Pray remind him of it.

My two first volumes of "Car—cks" noted and marked by me (the duplicates of the set left in your hands), was to be part of this cargo. I only brought the last volume, viz., the Mis——s,[2] in my trunk with me. I would gladly revise all before I die and send you my last corrections before the second edition is begun. In this last volume, which I have with me, I have made many more small corrections (none such as to break the pages), and though I should make few or none to the two former volumes which were written and corrected so much at leisure, yet I have corrected so much in this last that I must lay down my scruple against its being said "*the second edition corrected.*" And, therefore, as soon as you have read this be pleased to turn to the instructions written on the blank leaves at the latter end of your copy (after the Index), and scratch out from the first line (viz., "*In a second edition if there ever,*" &c.) to the paragraph "*If I go to the expense,*" &c. For it must now necessarily be said "*the second edition corrected.*" And the corrections shall in a few posts more be sent to you when Mr. C——e has copied them from my shaking bad hand. Your zeal about the plates or cuts proposed has so encouraged me that if I had the strength I would attempt something further. I mean one, at least, for each volume, according to what I wrote you the 24th of last, which

Lord T——r, nor to ye H——s of P—r—t, but to ye Unbelieving Club at the Grecian.

Two sets of "Characteristics," one of them complete with the corrections exactly made by my clerk from the originals in my hand ; the other set consists of several odd volumes, sent up by Mr. Wheelock from St. Giles's.

A silver watch of a middling size, the whole nicely adjusted or made by Delarder, who is now very famous—price with the chain £12.

[1] John Wheelock, Steward at St. Giles's.

[2] Miscellaneous Reflections.

letter, lest it should miscarry, I will make Mr. C——e [1] write you a copy of, as he shall of part of this by next post, or in a post or two, &c.

---

### TO JOHN MOLESWORTH.

NAPLES, *the* 15*th December*, 1711.

SIR,—As unfit as I am to hold a pen, I can hardly forbear the attempt of writing with my own hand to a friend who is so good as not only to excuse but forbid my doing it. I have indeed been unable of late to write, and have been forced to take that liberty with my friends in England which you so kindly offer me, of using another hand instead of my own. I now therefore comply with your commands and treat you as I do the nearest friend. I can yet say little promising of my health or recovery.

The late public news from England has been very disagreeable.* The article which Mr. Eckersall has copied out of the *Leyden Gazette* looks very dismal; but I hope still there are further mysteries beyond this, and that a certain manager, though he has dark ways, is not preparing us for a real black deed. French Ministers may be served perhaps in their own kind, and overtures made with as great sincerity to them as theirs formerly to us. France, perhaps, at last may be the dupe, and the allies, as well as the people of England, more spirited for the war, after the terror of such a peace in prospect. He who plays alike on both our home parties must try by some bold experiment how high each will bid towards the vastly growing expense. And if he can raise the luke-warm party to act through emulation or aim at popularity, he is sure of the concurrent zeal and warmth of another party which is now undermost, and which by this means he may still keep so, or at least in equal balance with that which he now chiefly espouses. Private piques among the great may be a further cause of these embroils; yet I cannot but believe the case to be as I formerly told, and as I now write you; and that in the issue (when some

[1] Mr. Crelle, his secretary.
* Emperor's Envoy Count Gallus sent away.

matters have been canvassed and well debated), even *this* Parliament[1] will be vigorous in their votes against France, and chase away the spectre of a rumoured peace.—I am, dear sir, your obliged and faithful humble servant.

[Adress]: To John Molesworth, at Florence.

————

### TO SIR JOHN CROPLEY.

NAPLES, 29*th December,* 1711.

Though I am unable yet to write to you with my own hand, you will be glad (I know) after the desperate condition I have been lately in to find that I am able to dictate to Br—n's[2] or Mr. C—l's,[3] whose hands I must be forced to use. The hopes I have of getting up once more to see another summer is from the inexpressible mildness of the winter where I now am, and the conveniences which at last I am come to have about me, particularly as to my medicines, those excepted which my wife wrote to you for. An honest, plain physician whom the Viceroy sends constantly to see me procures me this and other necessaries in my case, and really helps me by his advice, visiting me constantly and without taking any fee, as so commanded by the Viceroy, with whom he is a domestic. I wrote you that Count Gallas's recommendations came lately to the Viceroy. What I procured from Count Wratislau was by my own boldness and assurance in accosting him as I did at Milan. He was surprised to hear of me there. It was on the very day that the whole city was in an uproar, and drawn out in their streets to receive the Emperor; the Count (as first Minister) holding his Court in his great palace, laid up with the gout, with his Princes and grandees attending him. Late at night I sent him my message, which he received so well that being wrapped up in my night-gown, just as I came out of my litter, I was carried in men's arms through his anti-chambers and great company and set close to him, where I had my audience and a very friendly reception.

[1] Parliament met on December 7th, 1711, with a reorganised and strengthened Tory Ministry.

[2] Bryan Wheelock.    [3] Mr. Crell.

Your letters procured to Mr. Chetwynd came just at my leaving Turin. Those to Mr. Molesworth to Leghorn and to the Consuls here came also in good time. But what I would entreat and most earnestly enjoin you is (as I got my wife to write last post to sister Nanny) that you would again, as soon as possible, procure from the same great persons their word of thanks in return to the Viceroy and Count Wratislau for their favours to me. This is an owning of me, and will double the strength and lastingness of the recommendations. And if a new Viceroy is talked of, you must (as you have any regard for my well-doing) be early active in laying out for fresh recommendations directly, or by the same or other German or Austrian hands. My kind thanks, too, and compliments to Mr. Hill, &c.

Your letters which I received last post (too late to answer) were dated October 18th, October 20th, November 2nd, and November 9th. Your great packet of the 26th of October, about Lord Ashley's change of nurses (and for which you talk of having paid four shillings), came a great deal sooner than some of these which you wrote long before it. This I mention that you may yourself learn and make me understand how this matter is. But if you will do nothing as a man of business, nor regard dates, nor file, nor number letters, nor keep memorandums, nor know or correspond with the merchants or parties (such as Mr. Furly, Mr. Molesworth, &c., by whom your letters are conveyed), it is in vain to think of a correspondence, and all your letters will come thus confusedly, dilatorily, and many lost. I doubt not but my cousin Mick, as a man of business, is more observant ; and I am willing the oftener to do as at present, and write to you in his rather than to him in yours. I must reserve some of my strength for him, so bid adieu.

Pray continue your ridings. Use spectacles by all means, such as magnify the least : the clearest glass. Never fail to bathe your eyes a little after meals. Good fair water sufficient. If too cold in the mornings or at other seasons, mix a drop or two of brandy. This is my plain method, and best advice which you ask. Vervine water I found excellent. Garlick, onions, and many such hot things, even tea, coffee, and hot liquors, often very pernicious. So is looking at the fire and writing much by candle-light. My wife and I return kind thanks for your repeated particulars concerning the dear little one. And I myself in particular return you thanks for your agreeable accounts about the spiritual child, as you call it, which pray remember to entertain me with sometimes, whenever you pick up anything or hear remarks. Adieu. Adieu.

P.S.—For what relates to my sorry state of health I must refer you to my wife's—this post to her sister.

---

## TO THOMAS MICKLETHWAITE.

NAPLES, 29*th December*, 1711.

DEAR COUSIN,—I begin with you where I ended with Sir John, about the method and regularity of correspondence, which I know you are so kind as to observe. Accordingly, on my part, I begin by telling you that having by my last of the 8th instant answered yours of the 23rd of October your style (which was the first I received here at Naples), I have since received your following one of the 9th of November. Whether those letters which are enclosed to Ben Furly, and sent directly to Mr. Fleetwood, the consul here, or those which go to Florence to Mr. Molesworth, have the best or quickest conveyance hither I cannot yet resolve you, but desire you would consider. And I shall for the future inform you of the days I receive your several letters here. Your *first*, viz., of the 23rd of October your style, I received this December the 7th of our style here; and your next and latest, viz., of November the 9th, I received this same December 22nd.

In my last I promised you a copy (for fear of miscarriage) of my preceding letter of the 24th of November, in which I in particular answered yours of September the 18th, which brought me the draughts of Mr. Gribelin's, and which I received enclosed from Mr. Molesworth on the road from Florence, October 28th, N.S. I need not now do this, since I have determined to do all *thoroughly* or *nothing* beyond what is already done or drawn by Mr. Gribelin; so that till I can write again to you and have proved the skill and hand of some designers or draughtsmen that may be found here in this city, I would have Mr. Gribelin attempt nothing. This general scheme only and the following fundamental points of instruction I would have you foreknow and consider together with him, and (separately) with Mr. D—y,[1] that I may have their and your answer the soonest possible.

In the first place, on no account let anything be changed in the present device and frontispiece, not only because (as you well observe) it confounds the hieroglyphic, where indeed there is not nor should be the least patch or straw's breadth of work insignificant or idle; but because the round figure has already passed in the world, and will better suit by its variety with the squares and oblongs, which are to follow if I proceed in my work.

And in this case my resolution is (as I hinted to you before) to have three several plates of the same *relievo* marble or lapidary sort, as that which Mr. Closterman drew for me; and Mr. Gribelin has copied and lessened into the true sizes, the least of which must positively be our size for the reasons which I wrote you before. The two borders which Mr. Gribelin has added to the top and the other to the bottom of this little size is excellently invented, and I will make good improvement of it. For whereas these borders of Mr. Gribelin's are at present mere grotesque, and carry no fable or moral with them, the same kind of flourishing and grotesque bordering (distinct from the lapidary kind) shall be still preserved, but withal a real moral device substituted to support the sense of what is in the middle. Were it not for this intended change Mr. Gribelin might go on presently to engrave the little size of this device, which (as I wrote you) might well enough serve for the title-page of each of the three separate volumes : notwithstanding that its direct reference is to that single treatise, the *Moralists*, p. 252 ; but as I resolve, if able to make complete work of it, you must hold your hand till you can hear further of me. In the meanwhile will tell you full out what I design.

The six treatises being parted into three volumes, have accordingly a different genius and spirit each of them. And the pieces joined in one volume are so far of the same genius (as particularly the two first treatises of volume first), that

---

[1] Mr. Darby, the printer of the *Characteristics.*

different devices can very hardly with any justness be given to them. So that to the title-page of each of the three volumes I design only a separate plate of what I call the lapidary kind, with the additional border at top and bottom, as I have described before. And thus the main device both of the first and third volume will nearly resemble or match the triumph device, already lessened and bordered by Mr. Gribelin, which (after the small alteration of the borders) must stand as the main device in the title page of volume second, and serve (as it justly may) at once for the *Inquiry* as well as *Moralists*, both of which come under the title page of volume second, there being nothing in this volume but what is purely moral, or relating to that moral or civil liberty of which the draft expresses the triumph. The spirit of the first volume is far from this gravity or order, and the third volume still more after the comic or satiric way. Accordingly I design the cover (over and above the three main plates for the three title pages) to have six flourishes, viz., one for each of the six treatises, to stand at the top of the first page of the actual print and text, where the wooden flowers or leaf work is at present; but then the very same small plate which serves for the first treatise of volume first must serve again for the second and third treatise of the same volume. And so the small plate which serves for the flourish of the first treatise of volume second must serve again in the same manner for the second treatise of the same volume. The third volume (as you know) has but one treatise, and accordingly will have but one and the same small plate only once stamped. Now these three small plates (which by repetition in the two first volumes will make in all six printings) are to be of the same grotesque kind, moralised or humoured after the same manner as the intended borders of the lapidary plates of the three title pages.

Thus you have the idea of my design, which you may make Mr. Gribelin and Mr. D—y (separately) comprehend. The ornaments will thus be proportionately distributed through the work. The designs will suit the author's purpose, and the workmanship will be as if wholly contrived for ornament, and modelled for the advantage and purpose of the engraver and bookseller in setting off their work. There will be nothing affected or pretending in another kind, and as I wrote you, taking it altogether with the first device already current in the frontispiece, it will have the air only of flourish and embellishment. I shall be at a sad loss if Wheelock's parcel, where are my two first volumes of corrected *Characteristics* (the duplicates of those I left in your hand), should not come with the first parcel of books which you send me by Mr. Bahl's conveyance to Leghorn, but without naming the ship. If this omission has been, I hope it will be repaired, and the books sent me by the next ship-conveyance.

This long letter I have dictated by fits for four several days as my weak condition would permit. The weather, which till this day or two has been perfect June and July English, has since become sharp as our early May season, with the north-east winds. I have been near relapsing by it, but can just hold up, and as it lasts (they all assure me) but for five or six days of the whole winter, I may hope yet to live over a summer, and shall go on now every day in this amusement you have given me and in the correction of *Char——ks*, the only work I am fitted for, and perhaps best fitted in a languishing state. For having never had time to cool since the writing of *Mis——s* (struck out you know and finished at a heat), I have now enough to quell the floridness and warmth of fancy, and can be myself a squeamish critic over myself, so that I hope to make this last sally to be at least as polite and chaste in style as any preceding.

It would be well if you made one of your trusty clerks copy out all this that I now send, or shall after this, in relation to the plates and second edition, that Mr. Gribelin and Mr. D—y may *separately* and *severally* read and comprehend the design, to prevent all mistakes or misunderstandings between us. You may add this memorandum to your copy of what is for their reading out of this letter. . . .

I defer writing to Mr. Coste till I am able to use my own hand. Many thanks to him (I beg you) for his last, with the account of the *Bibliothèque Choisie*. And I again and again return him thanks for the criticism of his ingenious friend (whom he does not name) on page 235 of the *Miscellanies* relating to the Turks, on whom, perhaps, I bear too hard; but I have softened the passage accordingly to the very idea of the worthy critic, and by change of a few words have corrected (I am persuaded) to full satisfaction. I have just strength and time remaining to bid you (in my own hand) a kind adieu.

___

## TO PIERRE COSTE.

NAPLES, 12*th January*, 1712.

I thought to have had the patience by delay answering yours of November the 10th, from London, till I had been able to do it wholly with my own hand, but as I have not been able yet to do as much to any friend, I chose rather to write as I have done to others by an assistant hand without waiting to hear from you in return to mine of the 23rd of November from this place.

The last return of my asthma-fits, with a high fever, soon after my arrival here, and rest after my fatigue of travelling, has brought me so low that I can neither use my legs (which have been much swelled) nor apply to writing without faintness and pain of my eyes, which have very much suffered.

I need not say how agreeable your letter has been, first for its friendliness, abundantly expressed in a few lines, and in the next place for the length of it in what follows after, which is obliging and friendly in the next degree.

It must sound oddly (I know) to thank a friend at once for writing short and long, but I really think that between sound acquaintance and friends declarations of friendship can seldom be too short, nor the trifles or little circumstances that belong to it ever be too full or long. The less thought they are written with the better. I am careful sometimes in writing to a stranger, but I make it my vanity to be exceedingly negligent to a friend, and should be sorry to write or dictate otherwise than at random.

But what I must in a very particular manner thank you for is the concern you have shown for the interest and improvement of the *Ch——cs*, in the overseeing of the proposed translation of Monsieur Le Cl—'s extract,[1] and above all for procuring me the

___

[1] Le Clerc made an Extract of the *Characteristics* for circulation.

criticism (whether your own or friend's) on page 235 of Vol. III. The lower my state of health is, and the more remote I am from doing service or acting in the world, the more I am entertained and obliged by anything of this nature. And as you tell me there is like soon to be occasion for a new edition, I beg you would soon communicate to me whatever occurs in the way of criticism, whether from enemy or friend. Nothing could be more just than this which you have already imparted to me. The author has laid overweight upon the Turkish clergy, and indeed upon the Turks themselves, in their mere religious capacity. For it is more in their military capacity, and kind of Scythian policy (common almost to all barbarous warlike nations), that they are jealous of letters and enemies to arts and sciences, as introducing a contrary administration in government, and different manner from their own. That in this respect they are sufficiently averse to real learning and the polite arts (particularly all painting, sculpture, &c., even on a religious account) I need not justify to you, nor that their priests are their encouragers in this, and in their total neglect of all Greek and Latin literature, as well as of all other language besides their own. The passage itself I have corrected thus : " But so barbarous," &c.

I was mightily delighted to hear by yours that your friend Monsieur Le Motte had so favourable an idea of the treatises from Monsieur Le Clerc's extract. You did a particular kindness in taking from Mr. Micklethwayte a copy for Mr. Leibnitz, of whose judgment I shall be glad to hear.

Your visit to Lord Ashley, you may be sure, was a great pleasure to me to hear of, especially as you were accompanied by Mr. Collins.[1] I have heard no commendations nor received any friendly congratulations that have made me feel a fatherly joy so sensibly as those which have come with such good omens and prognostics from Mr. Collins. I return him, in my own and Lord Ashley's name, many kind acknowledgments, and have no better wish for Lord Ashley than that he may hereafter gain him for a friend, and imitate his virtue, worth, and public spirit, &c.

[1] Anthony Collins.

## TO JOHN MOLESWORTH.

Naples, 19*th January*, 1712.

Sir,—I often think it a considerable compensation in my present lot or fortune in the world, that during the time I had strength and health to act in it I was so happy as to gain those for friends whom I most wished to make such, and whose friendship in reality I could never have so thoroughly experienced as since my loss of health and banishment from affairs; notwithstanding which I have found them equally concerned for me, and constant in their kindness. Mr. Molesworth, your father, is one of those whom I have had the happiness to count upon, and prove as one of this small but precious number. So that the right I had to your friendship was a kind of hereditary one. But you have kindly found out a way to make it original by many acts of friendship, and particularly at this present, turning so much to my advantage the remembrance of a few hours' conversation, and of a few lines which I wrote you since upon the same subject of our public affairs.

It is indeed with the most obliging favour and friendship that you thus congratulate with me on the better prospect of things in England, making me at the same time of necessity to call to mind my own views, which, however odd or wide of the general sentiment, I was ready to hazard and expose to such a friend as yourself.

I am sorry I received no letters this post from England. I should with joy have dwelt upon the circumstances of this first shock a certain party has met with from the true English spirit, which, having often made war, but having never before been advised with or entrusted with a peace, has given occasion to that remarkable censure of historians : " That what advantages we English gained by our bravery in war were lost for us by the negotiations of our Ministers on a peace." But since our next is like to be a Parliamentary peace, I hope, by the still continued blessing of Providence on our army and the constant firmness and resolution of Parliament, *to preserve the Spanish entire to the House of Austria.*[1] We shall see

---

[1] For this purpose war had long been waged.

in the end a peace worthy such a Queen as ours, who so far consults her people; and worthy of that great name which may perhaps be given it of the first Parliamentary treaty and confederate establishment of the liberties of Europe. Let the enemies of liberty endeavour afterwards as artfully as they can to supplant that generous principle in particular nations which Europe in general, and even the absolute princes themselves, are forced to recognise and joyfully embrace under the glorious title of the *common cause.* Surely it can have no small influence upon men, whether under tyrannies or free governments, to see this necessary confession of the common right of mankind, and find that even the great, who deny this right to those who are under their government, are glad, however, to see such an establishment and constitution in Europe itself as may preserve them and their equals in a firm and established free state.

A particular thing which will very much surprise you is that a certain peer whom Mr. Eckerfalls' correspondent will name to him in the cover of this, came zealously into the vote, which was carried only by six in that House, for it was there and not in the House of Commons (as you supposed) that the majority was of that number, there having been a far greater afterwards, but in the contrariwise, in the House of Commons. This I learned luckily by this post (when all my letters from England failed me) from a letter I received directly from Holland of the 25th of last, and of this also Mr. Eckersalls' correspondent will send him the copy, as well as of a pleasant passage out of one of my own English letters, which I received from you the post before, &c.

[Address:] To Mr. Molesworth, at Florence.

---

## TO THOMAS MICKLETHWAYTE.

NAPLES, 19*th January,* 1712.

DEAR COUSIN,—I begin my letter to you, inditing (which is the best I am able to do) without waiting the coming in of the post lest it should go out again before I receive my letters, as it did this last week when I received Sir John's of November the 30th, and your last of November 23rd, for which I could not return you thanks till now. Sir John, however, will have heard of me last post by my wife's letter to her sister, to whom she writes again this post. My last, which was of the 29th of last month, was jointly to Sir John and you, and I now send you a copy of what I then wrote relating to *Philol*[1], Mr. Grib—n and Mr. D—y having left out what I would have you strike out with your pen in those instructions. For whereas I was not then resolved on any more than a single plate of the little flourish kind for the treatises in each volume (repeating the same stamp in the first and second volume, where there are more treatises than one), I have now determined not to stick at so small a matter, but employ my invention for three more of the little sort (that is to say, six little ones in all), since the great trouble and work, as well for me as Mr. Grib—n, will be the three main lapidary plates, as I have termed them, which belong to each separate volume. This your continued encouraging accounts with the relating of *Philol's* great success and your own pressing solicitations have produced. You may be sure our friend's letter from Spain, and his manner of taking the thing, has not a little contributed to raise me on this occasion ; and I hope for his sake, your own, and mine, you will find means handsomely to let him know so in a line or two, with your *knowledge* of my concern for him. And well I may say *your knowledge.* For upon this article you know and can say enough. Let your brother also know how much I love him for his zeal shown for his great master,[2] who will be still far greater hereafter for being depressed now. Besides that this will save him perhaps from the same fate which his two brothers by their over-bravery, or by the envy of foreign generals, have met. Should I live I might hope to see him rise out of his retirement with nobler thoughts and higher estimation of his own time and health than to lavish both after the way of our Whig-grandees. If he pursues such studies as these, and can break out of a certain track of life, he will be in no danger from the fashionable companionships, long suppers, and sittings-up which make

---

[1] The *Characteristics.*

[2] General Stanhope, captured by the Spanish at Brihuega, 9th December, 1710.

English Parliament campaigns to be as dangerous to him as his courage can make either those of Spain or Flanders.

But to my *Philol* again.—I had sent you word something positive this post with relation to my draughtsman here (whom I was beginning to employ), but that he fell ill the day after I had him here with me, and was myself well enough to instruct him in one of the designs which he has just begun. I shall see by one day's work whether he is able to go through. If not, I know not what to do in the case, being at such a distance from Rome, and not like to find a tolerable hand in this place, there being but one good artist, and he superannuated. Arts (as well as husbandry and manufactures, both in this country and in France) decline lamentably. At Rome, Florence, &c., no encouragement nor youth coming up, the Pope himself quitting his virtuoso-genius since he is grown into the cares of a politician. But, whether plates or no plates, my great concern is for the *correctness* of this second edition. For this you know I wholly rely on yourself, and I expect in a solemn manner your discharge of this guardianship and (I may say) public trust, as you have any regard for whatever belongs to me, or any desire to make return for any services or good I have done mankind, my country, or yourself in particular, since I have called myself your friend. You know what a wretch D—y[1] is with whom you will have to do. You know his niggardliness and artifices notwithstanding all the generosity and frankness I have shown towards him. He will be sure to pinch in everything, ink, paper, character, whenever he can save, and never come up to a full price for anything, to have it excellent, notwithstanding his real interest at long run, and what he has already gained. You must begin with him betimes. He must be close stuck to and plied. You understand how to deal with such slippery gentlemen. This will make the edition worthy of my correction and great accuracy (as you will find), as well as of my study and Mr. Grib—n's art, and the whole expense and trouble of the plates, which are to come gratis to this niggard and insensible wretch, both in gratitude and his own true interest. I mightily want my two first volumes, which

---

[1] Darby, printer of the *Characteristics.*

were left with Wheelock, to come with the first things sent after me by sea. I am undone if Sir John and you act not so far in concert with him about my necessary affairs and correspondency as to have let him know of the *Read* galley, the ship which in your last you tell me Sir John's and your things are sent. For if the two volumes mentioned come not by this first conveyance, it may be long ere I send you the corrections, which will be few (I daresay) in these two first; but the business is, I want these for the sake of the last volume, which I cannot well finish (though I have it here with me) unless I have the other two together with it. When I send you the corrections I will send you here and there my note or remark upon them as the reason why I make them, and what the nicety is, for they will be very small and not many. This may make your labour pleasanter, and help you perhaps in the improvement of your style, which in the station you are, and upon the foot you now stand in the world, may be of no small advantage to you, the age running so much into the politeness of this sort.

I am sorry your second thoughts have hindered your sending some pamphlets as part of the cargo. I must beg you to let me have a few of those of both sides which have sold the most. I care not which are the better or the worse written, or how ill or mere Grub Street, or of which party they may be, 'tis what the public has swallowed that I want to see, be it ever so indifferent: as either an Examiner, a Medley, or an Observator; whatever has been much read or bought up, though past and old. And a few of these papers impartially picked from one side as well as the other can be of no ill consequence or trouble for you to choose and send. My old acquaintance Dr. Davenant's[1] new work, be it ever so extraordinary in either way, I must needs have to peruse. So pray remember it with the rest and set it down in your Table-Book. For if I live in the world and can be of no use amongst you I must know what passes, especially in this literate kind.

[1] Charles Davenant (1656—1714) was a political economist. He published "A report on the public accounts of the kingdom" in 1710-12.

HH

I wrote to Mr. Coste last post directed (as he desired) to his friend in Holland, because of the likelihood of his being there with his new charge, my ancient friend Sir Hardy Hobard's son. I sent him the correction of that passage which he or his friend very kindly and justly criticised. I hope, if he was still in England with you, you joined together in putting it down exactly as it ought to be in the copy left in your hands for Mr. D—y.

I must conclude with desiring you to send me punctually whatever criticisms, friendly or hostile, scurrilous or genteel, are made either by word of mouth or writing, either in verse or in prose, on *Char——ks.*

For my health I refer you to my wife's this post to Sir John. I live indeed, but can hardly say I breathe or move. What would become of me at this time in any other place you may judge, when I have much ado to hold up even in this delicious climate and mild wintering; and stir not yet from my bedside and chair, near a fire, which no one besides has need of in this warm suburb of the soft, healing, cherishing, enhanting siren, Parthenope.—I am, &c.

## TO THE REVEREND DOCTOR FAGAN, AT ROME.

### NAPLES, *the* 23*rd of January,* 1711-12.

SIR,—Though I can truly say that the kind services and civilities I received from you in the short stay I made at Rome have ever since run in my mind, with the constant resolution of returning you my hearty thanks and acknowledgments, it has been (as you may imagine) no small discouragement to me to think that, though I could write a line, I had still but little prospect of my recovery so as to have the hopes of seeing you any more. That I have now lately risen so far out of my weak state as to flatter myself I may, after enduring this winter in so healing and mild an air as this, be able ere long to pass some months with you at Rome.

It would be a great pleasure to me to renew those agreeable conversations I had with you. I am persuaded that in most acquaintances there is from the first beginning a kind of sense by which it may easily be foreknown how agreeable or lasting they are like to prove. And if I do not extremely flatter myself, I can with some assurance believe that I had the happiness to share that sympathy with you which naturally makes the prospect of a correspondence very pleasing. I must confess that our present times are such as render that which is commonly called news too nice a subject for a correspondence by letter, so I neither ask you what news, nor pretend to send you any except what may relate to letters, sciences, or arts. And how much these are declining in this place you may judge by this very instance, that now, since the late wars and revolutions, some of the chief university schools and conveniences of the students are turned into stables and quarters for the soldiers.

The academies for painting are in a proportionable state. And I have little hopes of finding a young painter to employ (as I told you I had thoughts) in copying the great masters and drawing things of history, statuary, and the Roman and other antiquities, which would be the most agreeable entertainment to me at present. If you hear of any ingenious artist of this sort, pray be so kind as to write me word. If such a one had a mind to travel as far as Naples, I would willingly bear his charges and keep him with me in my own house a month or two on trial, with whatever reward he could well desire for whatever work I should employ him in. And were he but a sober, civil person, it would be the same to me whatever country or religious persuasion he were of; or though even a *Frenchman*, provided he had come early thence, and been some considerable time in Italy.

If the enquiry into such an affair as this be the least troublesome to you, or out of the way of your conversation, I would not by any means engage you in it; and shall only desire (when I have the happiness to hear from you) to know for what price one may purchase the prints of Trajan's or Antoninus's Pillar, either separate or both together, or what good book of prints there has come out of late years (since Pietro de Bellory's time) relating to the ancient statues, medals, or *basso relievo* of the ancients.

I have written you methinks a long letter, as if I resolved at any rate to cut out work enough for correspondence.

I beg pardon that, being still weak as I am, I have been forced to use a secretary's hand.

I now add only with my own that I am, &c.

***

## TO SIR JOHN CROPLEY.

NAPLES, *the* 16*th February*, 1712.

. . . For my employments and studies, since books are in a manner wholly denied me, I am now (as I have written you word) wholly amused in virtuosoship; and since life would grow very heavy upon my hands, if I did not think I could be still some way profitable to my friends and mankind, I flatter myself that I shall be able so to order it as to make even these lighter studies of some weight and consequence as well as pleasure and entertainment. Especially since you over again so thoroughly confirm what my cousin Mick has written me so often and sanguinely on the prosperity of my *first-born*. My wife (who sends you a thousand thanks for your kind accounts of my *younger one*) wrote you word in her sister's, how I was now taken up and diverted by antiquities, medals, and chiefly drawings, and pictures brought to me every day to see, my acquaintance in these matters beginning now to enlarge, and my discoveries proving more successful. Meanwhile never was such a deadness as to all arts in Italy; and many families sinking here under poverty make pictures a sad drug, though the modern painters are high enough paid for what they do in church for the priests. For of the increase and adorning of churches and monasteries there is no end. My own designs, you know, run all on *moral* emblems and what relates to Ancient Roman and Greek History, Philosophy, and Virtue. Of this the modern painters have but little taste. If anything be stirred or any studies turned this way, it must be I that must set the wheel agoing, and help to raise the spirit.

Pray tell my cousin Mick that I have at last resolved to take his advice, and have sent for a young painter from Rome to be with me here in my house, and, besides this charge, I have actually bespoke a piece of history (after my own fashion and design) of an eminent master in this place, and who is

the best now in Italy. I could not without this have made
any considerable figure among the virtuosos, especially being
confined at home and infirm as I am. But I have now at
command both music and painting of the finest and gravest
sort, in which it is a great pleasure to me that my wife has
such a good relish. My great piece will be of about fourscore
pistoles' charge to me. The first draughts and sketches are
made all in my own chamber, where this famous master often
works and sometimes eats with me ; so you see I am like to be
dipped sufficiently in expense in these affairs, besides the plates
and engravings for *Philol,* which will be over and above,
and of which I am to write to my cousin Mick very largely in
a post or two, if I continue well, and hear from him that he is
still zealous in the affairs ; otherwise, if after he has heated me
he should grow cool himself, I should have a bad time of it.
For your part you are (as I wrote you in my last) in a likelihood of being a good gainer by these studies and charges of
mine here in Italy at this nick of time. For if a sudden peace
comes not, I shall be able to lay out your two hundred pounds
to so much advantage in some pieces of the best hands that you
may wish perhaps your commission had been for as much again.
For my own part, as I dedicate my studies and expenses to the
promotion of science and virtue merely, I shall never purchase
one piece for myself as an ornament or piece of furniture, though
I could even have a Raphael or a Guido for a single pistole.
My charges turn wholly, as you see, towards the raising of art
and the improvement of virtue in the *living* and in posterity to
come. So that whatever I meet with of the deceased masters,
or pictures already painted, be they ever so cheap, or the
occasion ever so favourable, will be either for you or for
nobody. For I shall hardly turn factor for any one besides.
And as a hundred pound or two will go but a little way
in the great pieces of humanity or history of the Carachs,
the Guidos, and such great masters as those ; the next
degree of painting (which is that of nature in perspective
or landskip) will be that which best suits you, and which, I
think, you have the most taken to of late. For, as I remember,
you have, besides the copies of Poussin, a copy of Salvator Rosa,
also by Mr. Closterman, which you told me you could not bring

to Reigate, because of its bigness. Now I could at this instant, for little more than double what you paid for such poor 'prentice-copying, procure an original piece or two of the same Salvator Rosa (a townsman of this very place), equal and even beyond those very fine originals which Mr. Closterman, by the help of his journeymen, took copies of, and sold to you. I believe that before I can hear in answer to this I shall have secured at least one such piece for you. I shall earnestly desire to send them over immediately to you, to hear of your liking and the virtuosos' judgment of them. You may insure them or not, as you fancy, when I let you know of the ship by which I shall send them, or any other I may light upon. If you would have the price a secret you must return your bill by way of advance to myself directly, and entrust me as your steward, otherwise, as I entrust my stewards with every farthing of my expense (which stands in so many particulars in their accounts), they must necessarily be privy to your good or bad pennyworth, however I happen to deal for you.

Here is, you see, a letter full of what I can only write by way of entertainment in return for the many particulars of private and family news (especially from St. Giles's, my gardeners, and plantations) which you are so kind as to write me of so fully, besides what you write to my wife of Lord Ashley and to me of *Philol.*

---

## TO JOHN WHEELOCK.

NAPLES, *February* 23*rd*, 1712.

WHEELOCK,—I am much concerned at not hearing since by Sir John's. I hear you are gone back again to St. Giles's, so I fear your letters and bills of credit (if any) must be miscarried.

I am not yet well enough to write more than my good wishes, and to tell you that not only I want to hear from you, but that I think your nephew Bryan would be happy in receiving more of your good advice, which I saw by chance in one of your letters to him. This is a place and circumstance which, both as to trade manners, languages, and many negotiations and affairs of my own, he may by my help extremely improve himself. But then I must tell you (as I often tell him) that this place is withal the very seat of luxury and pleasure, and ever had, as it has still, the power of creating dissoluteness in all that are not severely on their guard, but especially all youth. The very air inspires indolence and laziness, as the richness of living and fruits of the soil do luxury and a certain over-degree of health. Never were a more ingenious and a more dissolute people both at once. So that when modern times confirm what was in the ancient, a man in health and youth may well need counsellors, since the poets made this the very seat of the sirens and of Circe that corrupted and transformed men. And, in truth, 'twas this very spot that corrupted, in one winter-quartering, the best disciplined army and severest general that was ever in the world, even Hannibal himself.

Therefore after all this learning and philosophy I have written you on your nephew Bryan's subject (and which I assure I think no jest) I hope you will on a double score remember to write to Naples, which soil and climate (as by parity of reason you may judge) is likely, I hope, to be as assistant to me in my state and circumstance as I have represented dangerous to him, if his own sense and your good counsel make him not very strict over himself, and industrious and indefatigable against the siren laziness, the mistress of this place, which from thence receives its Latin name *Parthenope*, the siren.

I hear my sister Hooper and her children have escaped through the dangerous distemper of the measles, so dangerous to children, and soon followed by the small-pox, which I pray God were as safe over with them, and with Lord Ashley, of whom I hear hopefully from all hands.

As low as my state is (for I am yet too weak to stir out of my chamber), I hope to make even my slighter studies not only entertaining to my friends, but of advantage to the public, and to improvement of ingenuity and liberty. My hundred a year pocket money, which I allow myself, will wholly turn this way. I have no other expense, and have a wife who is frugal and managing within doors beyond all example, and indeed to a miracle. If Bryan be the same without doors I am sure we shall come again soon within compass. For we are in the cheapest of places beyond sea, and I have no expenses but what I tell you, my wife being not likely to spend near her own hundred pound; she is so good a huswife; but for me and the house still more than for herself.

God prosper you as you serve and love a family which has been and is devoted to public good and friendship. Let me hear of my affairs, and prospect of farm and stock for payment of my debt. Dues to my relations and friends. My wife sends you her kind remembrance.

## TO THOMAS MICKLETHWAYT.

NAPLES, 23*rd February*, 1712.

. . . So that as to my young draughtsman (who proved a sorry creature) I have been forced, after a good deal of pains and some pistoles that I bestowed, to send at last to my correspondents at Rome (as you see in Sir John's) about a young painter according to your advice and desire. And the person to whom I chiefly address being a friend of Mr. Kent's (a young man whom I think you once named), I do not know but he may happen to be the very person.

Until some such new draughtsman comes to me I am wholly at a stand as to my hieroglyphics, both the lapidary and flourish kind, which are none of them subjects for me to enter upon with a great master, though when they are near finished I shall be sure to join such a one's opinion and hand to my workmanship. In the meanwhile I have a noble virtuoso scheme before me, and design, if I get life this summer, to apply even this great work (the history piece bespoke, and now actually working) to the credit and reputation of *Philol.*

But this is not the only view of service which I ground on this chargeable and high attempt. Our present great Minister, or at least some future one, may possibly have some compassion for the poor arts and virtuoso-sciences which are in a manner buried here abroad and have never yet raised their heads in Britain. It might be well for your joint interest and Sir John's, as friends to one another and to me, if through your hands a present should be made of a glorious piece not only worthy of a Prime Minister but even of the reigning Prince, or of some Prince of the Royal Family to whom the piece itself may be a council and instruction. Pray lay this saying up in your memory, for I should hardly bestow my time and pains, with about fourscore pistoles prime charge and with so many consequent expenses, for the sake of a piece of furniture merely for St. Giles's or as a mere ornament to *Philol.*

I know that by what I have said I must have highly raised your curiosity, which till next post I am unable to satisfy, and then you shall have it all before you by the copy of a little treatise[1] (which Mr. Crell is now actually transcribing from the foul) written, or rather dictated, on this subject of the great piece of history in hand, and which will come within the compass of a sheet of paper. But it being written in French for the painter's use, you cannot have it in its right condition until it be thought over anew and translated into its natural English. It* will be in Mr. Coste's power to make this piece truly *original* as it now is, by touching it up (as the painter's phrase is) and converting it wholly into pure language with his masterly hand and genius. And in this condition I could willingly consent he should carry it or send it over to his friend to be inserted in the very next *Bib. Chois.*[2] of his friend's friend, Mons. Le Clerc. Now, these scholars and great men of learning are (I know) very little given to these virtuoso studies, yet I cannot but fancy that if Mr. Coste gave in to it heartily he could engage them also, and even without using authority or telling names, might introduce the matter into the world, which afterwards might more agreeably and by a gradual discovery come to know the author and that of *Char——cks* to be the same. For by the time that this little treatise could be published a large plate after the great piece would be finished at Rome by an excellent engraver, a disciple with my history painter, and bred with him at Rome under Carlo Marat. And when a dozen or two of the large prints from this plate shall be sent over to you to be given to friends in England and to Holland, to Mr. Coste's and my

[1] " The Judgment of Hercules." * From here in my own hand.
[2] *Bibliothèque Choisie.*

friends there, a little octavo-plate might be made by Mr. Gribelin (as should afterwards be directed) for a companion of another of the same kind and size, to be inserted in that page[1] of the *Moralists*, where mention is made of the ancient moral Socratic pictures, particularly those of Prodicus and Cebes, whose names are mentioned, though not the name of Socrates. For of that name, you know, I am ever very tender.

But all this will depend on Mr. Coste, whether his affairs or humour (for in this kind fancy and humour must govern, even in the best of men) will allow him to mind such a virtuoso-business as this. And in this case you must engage him withal to bring with him from Holland the best edition or two (with Notes) of Cebes' Table,[2] with the ordinary ugly prints (such as there are, of this beautiful Socratic piece, which I shall have time to study at leisure, and fit for a companion to this other Socratic but more simple and (in painting) more exact natural and just piece of Prodicus, now carrying on, and upon which I have composed my little treatise in French from what passed in conversation with my painters, and some other virtuosos with whom I can converse only in that language. So here at last you have my secret out. And if Sir John should in his comical way ask you, " Well, Mick, what do you think my Lord's a-hatching ? I believe it is a young Milo." You may tell him yes ; and that the egg will be sent you ready *peeped* (as the hen housewives say) for you to bring forth, and help the chick into the world. I can assure you a friend of yours said yesterday that the face and air of the young *Milo* was mighty like you, and so I really think, though it has not so much of the *Adonis* (you may believe) as my young hunting gentleman in St. Giles's cedar-room.

Where to write to Mr. Coste, or how to [find] him flying, I cannot tell, having had no news from him but by you since his going to Cambridge, or since his positive engagement with his young gentleman,[3] who happily brings him hither (as I hope) early this summer.

[1] *Characteristics*, Vol. II., p. 254.

[2] The Tabula Cebetis, which is often printed with the Discourses of Epictetus.

[3] John Hobart (1694 ?-1756), first Earl of Buckinghamshire.

As for the main matter of all—viz., my corrections for the next edition of *Char——cks*, you may conclude that I have suspended the sending them to you at present, because of the time you have given me by telling me it will be towards midsummer before Mr. D——y can begin. However, I will immediately despatch the corrections to you when I have received my two first volumes from Wheelock ; and should you hear that the ship by which he sends these has come by any accident, you must forthwith send me a new set of all three, corrected exactly and carefully by the originals in your custody.

## TO SIR JOHN CROPLEY.

NAPLES, *the 1st March*, 1712.

. . . In the little capacity which is now left me of doing good to my friends or mankind, you may believe that such a letter, from such *a man* and such *a friend* as Stanhope, has strengthened me in my purpose of living on, and doing my best to continue this broken, imperfect, half-life, whilst I find myself thus thought of and my labours turned to so good effect. But as for any letter to myself, I have not been so happy as to receive it. It must have been stopped in France. Perhaps the Ministers, who may suspect us for politics, may have stopped it to try whether no secret character or chemical ink may lie hid, so that I may hope at last to receive it after it has undergone its probation. However, pray fail not to write him in your next that my success, whatever I hear of as to the rest of the world, I esteem but as a slight matter in comparison to that which I have had over him. You see I speak with the air of a master. And I hope in this respect at least he will prove my disciple ; that upon his return to his country, as much time as he may give or as I would wish him to give to his friends and to public conversation, he would resolve to redeem himself, his mind, his health, and constitution, as well as his powers, from that gulph of quality-entertainments. I mean the invitation-dinners and suppers of our Whig-grandees or of his fellow generals ; without which, if he can no longer be popular, it were better his country should want his present services, and that he should reserve himself for a time when it may want him more, and receive greater advantage from him, without such sacrifices on his part.

This is a string I touched once in a letter to my Cousin Mick. But whether you or he will think fit to show such strokes as these I know not. It is my part to speak what my genius dictates. This word of counsel to him is my best friendly return and mark of love.

By next post (tell my Cousin Mick) I hope to send him his young Milo, promised in my last. He will have shown you what I wrote about the egg I have been hatching, viz., the picture and little treatise[1] founded on this design. The picture, you have heard, will cost me a good fourscore pistoles, and the little treatise will cost me double trouble, having been forced to write it originally in French for the use of my painter and virtuosos here, and now (what is ridiculous and odd enough) to translate it into my native language—a greater trouble than the other. I shall send the English one, when it is done, to yourself, and shall desire you, if you like it, to give it to the same good friend[2] to whom the *Fable of the Oaks* and all virtuoso matters of mine have been communicated. And in reality this very device and picture, though now promoted on *Philol's* account, was originally started on a conversation some years time at a country house, near which I retired again myself a year after, and in that few days' retirement made a visit or two again, on you know whose account. Now on the same person's account (were nothing of friendship or gratitude to be considered) I cannot but think this gentle intercourse of friendship (supported by you) would be of service hereafter. But you may think my *heart* perhaps better than my *head,* and so conclude me in an error. However, for my heart's sake, and as I love and admire the man and still more and more, I must needs have you communicate even my weaker labours and employments. And should he be really entertained and delighted, and I should find my great picture actually answer my expectation, it may chance to go over to you, as a present to the great man, who may perhaps find it worth a present to a greater hereafter. For

---

[1] "The Judgment of Hercules."  [2] Lord Somers.

this I will boldly say: that if my design be well executed by my workman, my fourscore pistoles will make in time the value of a thousand and produce a picture truly fit for a present to a Prince, especially a young one, who may hereafter govern a great people. For my young *Milo* relates to better achievements than those of a horseman, or a wrestler. But of this enough. Adieu, adieu.

## TO THOMAS MICKLETHWAYTE.

NAPLES, 29*th of March*, 1712.

DEAR COUSIN,—Never will I promise anything hereafter, though but for an hour beforehand, which depends upon such a wretched health as mine. It is now a month since, and in three several letters (viz., of the 23rd of last month to yourself, of the first of this month to Sir John, and of the 15th again to yourself), that I have promised to send you my young Milo in manuscript, with the letter to my old Lord (as a certain lady calls him). But, by what my wife writes this post to Sir John, you will see how I have been prevented. My painter too is now fallen ill, just as the great piece was almost finished, and of which I had very great hopes that it would have proved a very noble picture. Meanwhile my young painter from home is coming to me, and I shall proceed in the lapidary and little grotesque designs. I rejoice to hear the *Phœnix* is come safe to Leghorn, so that as soon as they arrive here (which is commonly pretty tedious) I hope to send you the main concern of all—viz., corrections[1]—and depend on you for this as the great concern of my life, that the corrections may be effectual, and that Mr. D——y performs this with entire fidelity and accuracy, which I well know will never be without your assiduous, watchful, strict, and high hand over him in the whole work.

If I live to see this it will be my sufficient *nunc dimittis*. However, while I live, I shall, as you see, keep my pen and style in exercise, to exert it, if I am urged, in my own, my friends', or country's behalf. But as to the public I bear all, confiding

---

[1] Corrections for the second edition of the *Characteristics*.

in that personal friend, who I hope will some time or other bring light out of this darkness. Were it not for this I could unfold a tale (as the ghost says in Hamlet) which would make some ears in Britain tingle. For sick as I am, I carried eyes with me through France and other countries where I have been; and I have old secrets laid up in my memory, and transactions known to few Englishmen besides myself. But hush :—I am now a virtuoso, no politician. Were my noble and ancient friend the Lord Treasurer[1] a virtuoso also, or a lover or promoter of these arts, I should, perhaps, address myself to him upon these matters, though not just at such a time as this when he is so deeply employed, and sustains so great a weight both of our affairs at home and those of Europe. A certain Lord indeed (your patron and my friend) had, at my coming away, the offer from me of any kind of service I could do for him in the virtuoso or any other kind here abroad. But he answered coldly to the offer. I have but one friend[2] besides of any long standing who is this way given, but in a higher, more bookish, and learned way, and who from the beginning has chiefly attracted my thoughts of this kind. The first fruits of my pen having been for him, as perhaps the last may be, my best thoughts in this way, as I have professed, having been raised in me from the fancy of his agreeable genius and conversation. To him, therefore, I should send these further amusements of mine, immediately and directly; but that Sir John and you, as adopted virtuosos, must and ought to share in passing. Besides that I think it handsome, generous, and just, that the person himself, as an old friend, should not be forgot by either of us, and that such a pleasant remembrance by a trifle (in which neither business nor politics have anything to do) may be of no small use as well as comeliness, decency, and gratitude.

So pray, dear couz, remember, and see that Sir John plays me fair. When certain letters of mine have been suppressed, and my natural steps supplanted, it has not proved so well, as you and he may possibly remember. Honesty and courage are very good ingredients in policy. And I am now at a time of my life when, if I am not complied with in the plain ways of

---

[1] Harley, Earl of Oxford.     [2] Lord Somers.

friendship and the natural compliments, which by instinct I am led to make, I shall be apt to break out in another manner. So pray trust to my good humour, and let things go in the pleasant channel I design. You shall have the work and epistle by next post, if I have but one tolerable day between this and that.

I add a word in my own hand, though not well able to tell you of a commission which, I am sure, will be highly agreeable to you and Sir John. If you have never heard of the great and learned family, the library, collections, and assembly of friends of Don Joseph Valletta, of this city, you may turn over to the Bishop of Salisbury's[1] fourth Letters of Travels, dated the 8th of December, 1685, from Rome. It was but the day before yesterday that these gentlemen made me a kind visit, and to-day they have sent to desire me to transmit some small literary works to their learned acquaintance in England, with whom their correspondence has been a long time interrupted. They know not that Mr. Dodwell[2] was dead, but to the Bishop of Salisbury and Sir Isaac Newton I engaged that whatever they should send should be well recommended and taken care of. The bookseller to whom they address, it seems, is Mr. George Strahan, near the 'Change, and they have made use of the recommendation of one Mr. Thompson, who was here about a year since, and whose letter they have to Mr. Strahan. By next post I may, perhaps, send you their letter and order to this bookseller, after whom I would have you enquire and send me word. In the meantime, when Sir John or yourself can have the opportunity to speak to these gentlemen and their remembrances either to the Bishop of Salisbury or Sir Isaac Newton (by my Lord Halifax's means if you are not directly acquainted with Sir Isaac), I hope you will not neglect it. You may be sure I shall be glad to receive from you as soon as possible any word or compliment, message or letter, from the Bishop or Sir Isaac to these learned gentlemen and great men. I should be glad, for their sake, to engage them in an acquaintance with our worthy friend Mr. Collins. Pray

[1] Bishop Burnet's "Some Letters containing what seemed most remarkable in Switzerland and Italy," &c., Amst., 1686.

[2] Henry Dodwell, the elder (1641—1711), a profound scholar and voluminous theological writer.

let me know if such a correspondence would be agreeable to him.
And when you mention me to him let it be with the highest
respect and friendship, not forgetting my obligations to him for
his kind visit to the little one at Kensington.

—

TO JOHN MOLESWORTH.

NAPLES, 29th March, 1712.

I am indebted to you for two most obliging letters, as well
as for your particular care of my parcels from England, which
by this means I hope soon to receive here entire.

What you communicate from Spain of both your brothers'
safety after the hazard of that glorious action of Cardona, is
a sincere joy to me, and what alone could balance my share
of grief with that greatest and most deserving of men, General
Stanhope, for the loss of his late remaining brother in that
common cause, which he has served the best, and at the dearest
cost man ever did. And as mournfully as things appear in
respect of public affairs, this single life spared by Providence,
with the hope of his release[1] (as from England I am written),
makes me not despond, especially whilst the spirit of our
nobility and in general that of the people seems to run so
differently from that of the present House of Commons. And
as I am willing to draw the best comfort I can out of these sad
circumstances, I cannot help suggesting to you the thought I
have of the wholesome and early experience which the noble
house of our Protestant succession is now making of a certain
party, with which unhappily all our Princes (even the very best)
have been doomed at some time or other of their lives to engage.
It was more than once our good King William's lot. And
Heaven defend her present Majesty.

Meanwhile, if the pretence of high services to a prerogative
and Crown be that which gives this party such high success in
every Prince's ear, it is worth noting what work this loyal
party are at this instant cutting out both for a Crown and
Ministry in future time: whilst the *arcana imperii* and the
inmost springs of State are thus treated, and brought into the

[1] General Stanhope, then prisoner at Saragossa, in Spain.

hands and under the immediate cognisance and debate of our popular grand council.

Thus the gentlemen of the Tory party act the natural part of the Whigs. God grant that when time serves again, these latter may not do the work of the Tories. For I have known when this has been. Though for my own part I am so contented with the present balance of power in our nation, and with the authority and prerogative of the Crown, such as the Tories have reduced it, that I can say from the bottom of my heart, I am as an Englishman the most truly monarchical in my principle, and having really in some measure a jealousy upon me of the injury which may be done our common-weal by the diminution of our monarchical power in some parts of our constitution; which I am absolutely convinced is the freest we are able to bear. I well know the Tory expedient to set all right again and restore at one blow all the loppings they have made of our national monarchy in these two last reigns. But I hope they will be frustrated, and that our good Queen will be awakened ere long when she sees the Restoration coming on so fast before her eyes, and in her own time.

You have Lady Shaftesbury's humble services, with particular thanks for your enquiries after Lord Ashley, who, by what we hear, holds the same character of health, strength, and humour; and receives many encomiums from his visitants, and the company whom he meets every day in his Hyde Park airings.

You have been indeed a true prophet as to my health, from what you observed of this unnatural cold weather. I am much relapsed of late, confined still to my chamber, and scarce able to breathe, having strength only sufficient, by help of another hand, to express with what sincere respect I am your affectionate and humble servant.

[Address:] To Mr. Molesworth, at Florence.

---

### TO SIR JOHN CROPLEY.

NAPLES, *29th March,* 1712.

You have here enclosed my letter long promised and (as you see) long since written to our old Lord.[1] The little treatise[2]

---

[1] Lord Somers.     [2] " Judgment of Hercules."

II

which accompanies it (and which I hope you will deliver or convey carefully, and handsomely sealed up with it) I have also enclosed this post to my cousin Mick.

These are amusements I would not trouble any friend with who was in business, so that the friends (if I have any) who are now in affairs would have no reason to think I passed them by.

When I sent you mine to my Lord Dartmouth, I proposed a letter of thanks and acknowledgments to my Lord Treasurer[1] for his most particular favour and friendship. And, indeed, I can't enough acknowledge my obligation to my old friends T—— and S—— for their constant and kind remembrance.

Mr. Slater's favour to Lord Ashley was an inexpressible delight to me.

I am but in an ill way, so must have done, referring you to what my wife writes this post to her sister.

---

### TO MR. CHETWYND.

NAPLES, *the 5th of April,* 1712.

The spring is but newly felt; I have just got life and breath by it; and I now take my pen (the first time that I have used it) to acknowledge the favour of yours received here in the depth of winter, when I could scarce say I was alive.

We had indeed a glorious season here, both before and after Christmas; but towards the end of February, and afterwards in March, when we concluded the winter to be wholly passed, we had a pull-back of at least a month, so that our mountains (even Vesuvius itself) lay covered with snow. What I should have done in another climate is hard to say, since this warmest of Europe has scarce served to keep me alive. This has quite taken from me the hopes I had of revisiting you this summer at Turin, in order to return home the spring or summer following. I must be contented at this distance, and on these bad terms of an interrupted correspondence, to continue my acknowledgments of your friendship shown me, and to cultivate an acquaintance which was no less agreeable than it was happy to me in the preserving of my life.

[1] Harley, Earl of Oxford.

I can entertain you with little or nothing from such a part of the world as this, where the little conversation I have, and the only news of business stirring, relates to the shows and ceremonies of the place or to the studies of the virtuosi. Politics are not of this sphere. We are glad to hear news, but can send none. And for reflections on what passes, though I am ready enough as an Englishman to speak my thoughts at a venture, as they come across me, I find my circumstances, however, have made me partake something of the Italian spirit and that of the place where I am. In reality I think myself grown wonderfully temperate and cool in politics, after having passed so long a season without the least emotion of the surprising news which post after post we have received from the Courts of France and England ever since I had the happiness of seeing you. But the face of affairs seems to be somewhat changed, and (thanks to Providence) our Queen, our nation, and Europe itself seem to be now in a safer way. The figure which Englishmen were like to make abroad put me in mind of those times before the Revolution, when I travelled[1] here a very young lad, but experimentally sensible of the contempt we were then treated with by almost all other nations. But I hope we shall, all of us, and particularly you gentlemen in business, be able to hold a better countenance, when it appears that we are not like to lose for want of wit and honesty that reputation which we had got by arms and generous councils.

In this sense I think I may congratulate with you, though, obliged as I am to the French Court for my passage and the civilities I received, I should unwillingly insult over them on account of those blows which Providence alone has struck them in the death of their Princes[2] at a time when it is apparent they thought themselves at once healed and secure of all other wounds which had been or could be given them hereafter.

I shall be rejoiced to hear at any time of your health and prosperous affairs, whether you stay abroad or return home. I must entreat you, whenever you write to our worthy friend

[1] In 1687.

[2] The Dauphin, son of Louis XIV., died in 1711, and the Duke of Burgundy, the Dauphin's son, in the spring of 1712.

Mr. Hill, to assure him of my sincere respects and constant good wishes. I will beg the favour, too, that you would present my humble service to your brother, to whom, though unknown, I have been so much obliged.—I am, Sir, your most faithful humble servant.

[Address :] To Mr. Chetwynd, at Turin.

TO THOMAS MICKLETHWAYT.

NAPLES, *the* 12*th of April,* 1712.

DEAR COUSIN,—I have yours of the 29th of February with advice of your receipt of mine of the 2nd of the same month, new style. I return you many thanks for your exactness in all. As for the affair of my life and health, you will know how much it depends on your sudden and early thoughtfulness and inquiry for me since my resolution of not suffering Bryan to lose his footing of a fortune in public office. I say no more of this, because I know, for my wife's sake and mine, I know how impossible it is for you and friends (but particularly yourself) to be unmindful or slow in this affair.

As for my virtuoso studies, my sole employment at this time, you may be sure they go on as fast as my weak state will permit. Mr. French, my young painter, is come to me from Rome, and is with me in my family. I have an engraver also coming from Rome, but upon another foot, he being only for the great plate (of a foot long and more) of my great piece of Hercules, now finished. And earnestly I long (as you may well believe) to hear of the delivery, reception, and success of my epistle and treatise[1] thereto belonging.

I have received Mr. Gribelin's print of the cartoon in your cover, and shall be ready, I hope, in a week or fortnight to send him his plan to begin on some of the devices. But the corrections, which are the principal concern, must take place, if I receive, as I hope shortly, my trunks and books from Rome, where they are now detained.

Of other virtuoso schemes and devices you will hear something by my wife's this post to her sister, so that you may see

[1] " The Judgment of Hercules."

I do not spare expense in this kind. What commissions Sir John will give me I do not know; but though I had his order for a hundred pound or two to lay out for him, I will not lay out a penny of his without his express desire renewed. I have your list of pamphlets as well as of medals to come by the *Neptune* galley. I just hear by old Ben of the arrival of Mr. C[oste], but not a single line all this while from himself. I am mighty glad you did with a good grace and at a good season what you write me in relation to the New Year's gift and first year's annuity, which I had rather should be so implicitly transacted than expressly by order from my own hand. It has given you better scope, and you have used the liberty left you to good purpose, as I believed you would.

The judgment you make of his character left behind him is very just. It is in so far innocent on his side as that no one of his nation in the same circumstance as himself would talk or act otherwise in politics than as he has done, and does.

It is in vain for them to aim at principles. They have none, and never can have any, in government. They may like the Whigs at this or that particular season. But not a Tory in England, not even an Oxford or a Christ Church College proselyte, but in effect, and in real practice, when matters come to an issue, and things press, would be found more true by far to liberty and property and a national constitution than either poor C——[1] or the best that ever was born and bred a Frenchman. This I know, and can pronounce, by good experience of mankind. And were my son on this account to take his principles and sense of community, a constitution, and a public from good Mr. C—— (which will not, nor can ever be the case), I had rather trust him at the foot of Gamaliel, and send him with the Hydes and Finches to our university under the tuition of a Doctor Allderidge[2] or Atterbury.[3] But I return many

[1] Pierre Coste, who had evidently become a recusant to Shaftesbury's political principles.

[2] Henry Aldrich (1647-1710), Dean of Christ Church, Oxford, a High Churchman, and the author of "Artis logicæ compendium," 1691.

[3] Francis Atterbury (1662-1732), Bishop of Rochester, a High Church dignitary favourable to the Jacobite cause.

thanks to Sir John and you for being so indulgent to poor Mr. C——, notwithstanding these natural infirmities and want of manhood in this sense. You know withal his obligations to a new great family, and the power in particular that ladies must needs have over him, as a Frenchman, in that way of politeness which is now esteemed the highest of the world.

———

### TO SIR JOHN CROPLEY.

NAPLES, 12*th April*, 1712.

It is but the last post that I write to you by my wife's hand of what you chiefly desire to know, my state of health and remedies. I am not worse since then, though I had a bad fit of breathing this last night, for which and the rest of this kind I must refer you to my wife's this post to her sister. I have not yet received, nor am like to receive, Mr. Stanhope's letter which I count so great a loss. I am highly obliged to you for your advices about my brain-offspring,[1] though since what you copied to me from Stanhope's letter in praise of it, I am become dead and insensible to any other praise or commendation of my labour in that kind. The fame of it, indeed, may be of service and advantage to me in a narrow sense of private interest as well as to you and couz Mick in our joint friendships, and particularly in his fortune so dependent on the pleasure and humour of the great. But for any real good which it may further do in this present age, or at least in my time, I am very much a doubter. Nor do I hope to hear it ever said again from such another honest heart as Stanhope's that one might grow the better (I mean the better and honester man) for reading it.

The sad account of our killing Prince Eugene's nephew in England by the kindness of our Whig friends, and the high living of our grandees, makes me still revolve in my mind what I wrote both to yourself and couz Mick of what I apprehended so much for our friend Stanhope hereafter on the peace and his release from captivity,[2] which I am afraid will be but one period.

[1] The *Characteristics.*    [2] August, 1712.

I am sorry for the death of my old friend Lord Pelham.[1] As the world goes I have taken him all along for one of the honestest of men, and most true to the interest of the public.

I must now turn myself to couz Mick, thanking you for yours of the 29th of February (the last date), to which I have thus answered, adding only my kind remembrances to all yours and to Mopet a kind adieu.

### TO JOHN WHEELOCK.

*April 26th,* 1712.

This is the copy of what I wrote you April 12th in Bryan's hand, adding a great deal privately to you in my own of which I could not have a copy kept. Let me again and again remind you of my instructions, and not to think me so weak and changeable as to depart from what I resolved when going away so deliberately both with Sir John's, Mr. Micklethwayt's, yours, and other friends' approbation, my wife joining heartily with me also as to her part; so neither as to Lord Ashley or his hired coach or any other circumstance of my family affairs let any change be imagined or hearkened to by you, however my good friend Sir John may in zeal be transported from his good judgment. My instructions in writing were with the foresight of this, and to this very end, so that I wonder to find you hesitate and suppose me still so hesitating and uncertain myself.

It is sad to be left thus in such silence and with so little correspondence on your side. Not a friend's letter besides (among the many weekly of my wife's and mine) has as yet miscarried, and yours (bills and all) are lost. No duplicates sent or coming that I can yet learn. I suffer on all accounts. 'Tis very sad.

I hope you will be able to find the parcels of books, &c., which you should have sent with the tin boxes now safely come to hand by the *Phœnix* galley. There are wanting my precious (though foul) two first volumes of *Char——cks*, corrected and

[1] Thomas Pelham, first Baron Pelham (born 1650), died 23rd February, 1712. He belonged to the Whig party, and was Lord Commissioner of the Treasury during the years from 1689 to 1702.

marked with crosses and ordinarily bound at Reigate by the instrument, and Mrs. Skinner's work. I miss also Coles's *English and Latin Dictionary;* Mr. Coste's corrected translation of *Sensus Communis,* a little French book—the title, *Essai sur la Raillerie*[1]—for the words *Sensus Communis* are not in the French title.

I have a sad winter even here; am in a weak way, but rather hope of recovery. Dues to all; love and wishes to family, &c.

## TO THE ABBE FARELY.

NAPLES, *the 3rd of May,* 1712.

SIR,—Since your obliging letters of the 25th and 28th of January to my own and second self,[2] our debt to you is still increased by the same double favour of the second of March in answer to ours some time before.

Though I have now strength enough to hold a pen, I am hardly got out of my chamber, having tried but one day (and that with ill success) to take the air in a coach. But the warmth of the season, though long a coming (for we have had an extremely cold spring), has abated my cough, and raised me a little from that very weak state to which I was reduced by my cough and asthma, with my fever still hanging on me.

The good nurse, governess, and doctoress, whom you so kindly remember, has much ado to forbear being again *scrittorist** on this occasion : not merely in my behalf, as sparing me a pains which she knows in other respects is so agreeable to me, but that she may herself have the satisfaction of making you her kind returns for the most truly and obliging compliments you have made her. There are none indeed which are so pleasing to her as those of the kind you have made her on my account. We live in hopes still of peaceable times, and seeing you once

---

[1] Essai sur l'usage de la raillerie et de l'enjouement dans les conversations que roulent sur les matières les plus importantes [Signed S. C. S. v., *i.e.,* A. A. Cooper, third Earl of Shaftesbury] Traduit de l'Anglais [by Pierre Coste]. Amst., 1710.

[2] Shaftesbury's wife.  * Secretaress.

again at Paris, in our way home. It is a great satisfaction and honour for us to be remembered, as you mention, by my Lord Duke of Berwick, Mrs. Waldgrave, my Lord Timouth, Lord Fitz-James, or any of that noble family, to whom we beg the return of our most grateful acknowledgments, and most humble services.

A line or two sometimes from yourself, with or without news, will always be highly agreeable; it being itself the most satisfactory news to hear well of the noble good family, and of yourself in particular; who may justly claim the acknowledgment of my being (as Lady Shaftesbury would also have you to esteem her) your sincere friend and humble servant.

P.S.—The Dutch prints which you have been so kind as to send us come to this place (as we find) much sooner than by yours from Paris. But any article of news from Paris itself would be very acceptable, whenever you are so kind as to write to us.

[Address:] A Mons. L'Abbé Farely, à Paris.

---

## TO HENRY WILKINSON.

NAPLES, 10*th of May*, 1712.

HARRY,—I am sorry that by my slow recovery I am still hindered from writing to you as I would sometimes do, and much more fully, with my own hand. Particularly I would wish to do so in answer to yours of the 1st of April, in which you ask advice, &c., with particular bemoanings of your misfortune under your present circumstances, and from the malice of enemies. What enemies you should have made yourself or by what means I cannot conceive, being a single man and employed in no public business or station of difficult conduct, by which enemies are acquired.

I have often told you that ill surmises and apprehensions, as well as want of patience and meek sufferance of some few slights and accidental offences from friends or indifferent persons, is the cause of procuring enemies and sometimes of turning friends also against us. But I hope this is not your case. Interest will always cause struggles and emulation in the way of ordinary business and conversation. But this needs not rise to quarrel and provocation, which a single man, who has only his own conduct to answer for, may easily, by meek behaviour, prevent when he has no public charge or hard duty incumbent on him.

If in other respects your circumstances or credit are low, I fear it will not be the right time for you to think of marriage, unless a very unexpected advantageous offer presents. But to wait or court rich offers is an expectancy I have often known ruinous to young men, and chiefly those in business. If it please God that by your diligence and perseverance in sobriety and industry, you get credit and interest, I should not be sorry to hear you were established by a discreet match; especially with a family of the country where you are, or in any part of Holland, or the Provinces. But for the English nation I fear it will not prove so fortunate for you to apply there; and your thoughts had better be where your education and business have been. Take care of the enclosed. God be with you.

[Address:] To Mr. Wilkinson, at Rotterdam.

---

## TO JOHN MOLESWORTH.

NAPLES, 17th *May*, 1712.

SIR,—The continuance of your favour by each post since the 26th of last month gives me the highest proof of your friendship, as well as the greatest pleasure imaginable in the advice and just remarks which you communicate.

Our common home-concern and the common cause itself is so particularly become the affair of Providence that hardly the worst of Ministries (had we such a one) could with the utmost industry effect our ruin. The death of this last princess (the St. Germain issue) will give such strength to our Protestant House of Hanover, that if they adhere to the noble principles of their memorial they will not only be the means of saving the honour and interest of our good Queen, but secure to their house hereafter a happy and prosperous administration.

What you suggest with just ground as to the Court of Turin will, I hope, soon appear, though things have hitherto looked so ill that way. If he be, as he is esteemed, a wise and able prince,[1] I can now say we are sure of him. The little prospect of issue from the Emperor raises his pretensions and hope so strongly towards the crown of Spain that he too must come in with us, upon the memorial foot, and join in the Whig maxim of *Spain and the Indies to be absolutely taken out of the Bourbon family.* Should our Court and that of France offer him the crown of Lombardy, to buy him off from this prospect and the fair game he has before him, I am satisfied if he be truly able, he will despise it, and choose to receive a crown, as he may easily on better terms, from the same hands and by the same interest as the King of Prussia received his. But if there be anything in that negotiation of the *flying spectre*[2] (of whom you have again written), I fancy it is some intrigue of this kind. The hook must be well baited that catches such a prince. And as good an angler as a certain gentleman is thought to be (especially in troubled waters), I doubt whether he will find success in such an affair. That prince, I conceive, will not easily sacrifice the interest he has made himself in the grand alliance, nor set at defiance three such powers as the Emperor, the States, and the successional house of the Crown of England, so fortified as of late, and between whom and the real English and Protestant party there seems at present so firm a correspondence established. . . .

### TO THE REVEREND DR. FAGAN.

NAPLES, *the* 21*st of May*, 1712.

SIR,—The unaccountable miscarriage of both our letters had made me almost quit the hope of keeping up my correspondence with you otherwise than by the opportunity of persons coming and going between this and Rome. But your last, of the 14th, having come safe and in due time, as well as several others between Mr. Brown and my steward, I resolved to return answer in the same manner and send you my kind thanks for your inquiries after my health, which till very lately has scarce in the least advanced.

[1] Victor Amadeus II., Duke of Savoy.    [2] Earl of Peterborough.

I now find a little comfort in the summer season, which is now advanced after a very unseasonable and unnatural spring. I am not yet able to take the benefit of the air abroad, having tried but once or twice, and that with very ill success, the weather happening ill.

I continue to entertain myself with those amusing studies in which you have assisted me by your correspondence and the recommendation of Mr. French, who will stay with me some time longer, and (I hope) not to his disadvantage.

The world is now in sad confusion even in the courts of Princes themselves, where death reigns as cruelly as in the field. All counsels are perplexed and policy in a manner out of its bias. The ambitious and great may be less envied than ever; and those who by necessity are driven from public affairs and the higher sphere of action may with less reason be lamented.

I should think it a happy improvement in my health if I could but hope soon to bear a journey to Rome, though without partaking in any of the entertainments of the place besides your single conversation and the view sometimes of the ancient works and those few moderns which have followed and approach them.

Enclosed is an answer to our good friend, whose letter you were so kind as to forward, as you have kindly offered to do mine in return.—I am, with particular esteem, Sir, your sincere, humble servant.

[Address:] To the Reverend Dr. Fagan, at Rome.

## TO PIERRE COSTE.

NAPLES, *the 5th June,* 1712.

To MR. COSTE,—I have at last heard from you fully and with great satisfaction concerning that long period of time in which you have entered into new occupations, travelled about England, visited universities, crossed the seas, saluted your old friends in Holland, and received my last with my project in painting, which I earnestly wait to receive back again corrected from you, since you think it really worth correcting.

You enjoin me to speak of my health. It is the subject on which, I confess, I have the least pleasure to write, since I can

give such indifferent hopes of it. By my using thus another
hand (as I have been forced to do almost in every letter since my
last to you), you may readily guess how matters stand with me.
We have had a wretched cold spring. All March and part of
April I lay still extremely ill. This last month I recovered a
little, and was able four or five times to take a little air abroad;
but the last time, being surprised in a thunderstorm, though
closely wrapped and in a close chair, I have been much thrown
back; so very weak I am grown. If pains can be alleviated and
a sick state made easy or tolerable to anything besides a good
mind, well exercised, and inured to hardship, I have had that all
along, and still have, which would soften the hardest affliction.
I mean that companion, nurse, and friend whose fortitude and
strength of mind you heard so justly spoken of by Dr. Hobart.
Methinks, as you have seen one part of this good lady's virtues,
I want you should be witness to this other different part and
change of scene. For of all pictures I think such as these the
finest. And as for my virtuosoship and dealings in those
arts, it has all its reference to such sort of views and beauties,
as you may see sufficiently by what I sent you last. I
must own it would be a particular satisfaction, if the little
specimen,[1] *touched up* (as painters say) by your finishing hand,
could communicate to others any part of that delight which I
myself have found in these amusements thus morally turned, and
with a glance towards manners, honesty, and virtue. And I could
wish you would make the trial of this by communicating the
piece thus corrected and transcribed (if it be worth it) to some
friend or friends, who, having no partiality for the unknown
author, might discover to you the real acceptation it would in
probability find with the polite sort of mankind. And a line
or two giving me an account of the real issue of such an
experiment would be very acceptable.

I rejoice to hear that it is my worthy friend Sir Harry
Hobart's[2] son with whom you are engaged. I hope I am likely
to have the happiness of seeing you with him at Naples soon,

---

[1] "The Judgment of Hercules."

[2] Sir Henry Hobart, fourth baronet, who was killed in a duel
in 1699.

though you say not what time you compute your journey. You will find me, if alive, entertaining myself very busily with drawings, sketches, prints, medals, and antiques, which as well as pictures and other virtuoso-implements are brought often to my chamber and bedside; and sometimes, when able to be up and receive company, I have a virtuoso-friend or two, particularly Don Joseph Valetta's family and friends (so noted for their learning and collections) who are so kind as to visit me upon these unequal terms.

If you could bring with you a good book or two relating to medals, I should be very glad. I can get none here but the Italian; none either in Latin or French.

You may easily believe the satisfaction I had in hearing so fully concerning *Characteristicks*, and particularly of the value set on it by such a Prince as you named to me. As for a translation of the other pieces, it is what I have never thought could be attempted. But could you revise and correct the same translation of the *Letter of Enthusiasm*,[1] with a few notes after the manner of the following letter, viz., *Essai sur la Raillerie*.[2] I might have hopes that by leaving them in your friend's hands at Amsterdam, the booksellers agreeing might publish them together correct. And sure I am that the already published translation of the Essays (with the few after corrections of your pen) is a most perfect and true original, with improvement. You say not how I should address my letters to you, so I am forced to send this at a venture to Mr. La Motte by way of Rotterdam, as I did my last.

The good Lady (my more than *one half*) takes your remembrances very kindly, and remembers you with suitable return, and with great delight, in particular on the favourable account and promising hopes of the little one whom you saw at Kensington.

[1] Shaftesbury's "*Letter Concerning Enthusiasm*," Lond., 1707, was also printed in French at the Hague, as appears by its review in Le Clerc's *Bibliothèque Choisie*, Utrecht, 1710, Vol. XIX., pp. 427—431.

[2] Shaftesbury's *Sensus Communis, an Essay on the Freedom of Wit and Humour*, Lond., 1709, and also in French at the Hague with the title *Essai sur l'Usage de la Raillerie. Ibid*, pp. 431—436.

## TO SIR JOHN CROPLEY.

### NAPLES, *the 7th of June*, 1712.

. . . I was sorry to read such melancholy expressions from you in respect of my ill state of health. Methinks I should from that very ground have greater weight in persuading my friends (those who are so affectionately such) to take the greater care of their own healths and lives. And the kind regard you have for my former and latter issue (for which I have taken so much pains to live) should methinks hearten you more, whilst Providence is so wonderfully favourable to us in this, as by your repeated accounts I still hear with so much satisfaction. Nor need my spouse and I regret the loss of being witness of little one's prettinesses, whilst we have so good a correspondent and such a sharer as yourself.

For my other progeny which you reprove me for speaking more of, and with more seeming affection, you may be sure I can't refrain still talking with you of it. And in particular, I am longing to hear how the Notion[1] and Letter[2] has been received by my *old Lord friend.*[3]

Your *modicum*, as you call it (though I have not received your bills) is already engaged, and will procure you, I hope, the two noble pieces I mentioned to you in mine of February the 16th. They are alone a noble furniture for any moderate room, each being seven or eight foot high and five or six broad, without frames, and are exact beautiful matches for one another, which makes them the more valuable both together. If you continue the resolution of having the copy of what you say is so perfectly my own performance (meaning my piece of Hercules), you shall soon have it with you when it is perfected and dry enough to put up for sending. Nor will it be a copy,

---

[1] "A Notion of the Historical Draught or Tablature of the Judgment of Hercules," which appeared in English in 1713 and was reprinted in the second edition of the *Characteristics* in 1714.

[2] "A Letter concerning the Art or Science of Design," which was first published in the edition of the *Characteristics* issued in 1732.

[3] Lord Somers, to whom the "Letter concerning Design," which accompanied the "Judgment of Hercules," was addressed.

but in reality an original as much as the great piece itself, on which I have bestowed so much of my money, which makes this piece come so much the easier, for a fifth part or little more— viz., twenty pound English or thereabouts. But if you like not this overplus of charge, you shall have the pleasure, however, of seeing it, for it shall be my purchase, and pass through your hands (as the Letter and Notion) to my same old Lord friend, having given him a kind of distant hint of such a small present, as you will have read in the letter itself. Pray write in answer how you will determine this, for on my own side I am determined, and the piece is going on.

Now I must a word to cousin Mick, so bid kind adieu.

––––––––

TO THOMAS MICKLETHWAYTE.

NAPLES, 28*th June*, 1712.

DEAR COUSIN,—It is a great satisfaction to hear thus punctually from you (as by last post and this) since Sir John's being at Beachworth. In this your last of May 16th, I learn the share you take in the tutorage of our little one. Continue it, I conjure you, dear couz., and remember to put them in mind of what my wife and I both wrote a while since, and what my wife now writes to Sister Nanny this post.

I have been dictating as much as I am able to Sir John about what he so earnestly presses me, my health—a sorry subject. By next post, or at furthest the post after, I hope to send you what will be more agreeable, my only amusement and allay of pain—I mean my virtuoso-doings, viz., my instructions for another volume. Frontispiece plate, which will be that of volume third, as full of mischief and shrewd meaning as the other (the Triumph), already sent and now in hand, is innocent and merely philosophical. The last of these three plates which I am to send you will be the first according to their natural order. But you will see the reason why I send you this third and last volume-plate before I send you that of the first volume, which will be easy to comprehend as well as to execute after this third, which I am to send you the next. The remaining single six grotesque plates for the six several treatises (to be placed over each first page of the text) will be easily finished and sent to you post after post, when this great design and long packet of instructions has been despatched, of which I give you and Mr. Gribelin warning so long beforehand, it being such a knotty business, though I hope you will have no little pleasure in it, and be perhaps some improvement.

The *Neptune* galley has come and the things are safe.

I am much puzzled about Sir John's hundred-pound commission, since his strict reducing of me to that sum, and the manner of remitting it me, concerning which I refer you to my letter to him this post.

I was much mortified the other day, when the noble family of Valettas and Dorias visited me again, that I could not by your means return them any compliments either from the Bishop, Sir Isaac, or others, in answer to their application and compliments through me. Though I could get nothing (nor yet can) like either thanks or compliments by Sir John's means to the Viceroy here, yet I hoped by your means, and by my own letters and applications, to have procured some compliments from our learned in England, in return to these considerable inhabitants of a place where I am like to reside, and need so much protection and countenance.

The book you mention, designed by these gentlemen (as I suppose) a present to the Bishop, &c., is of Sig. Doria's writing. He is of that noblest family now in the world from the Doria of Genoa, the only founder of a State among the moderns, and to be numbered with the ancient Publicolas Lycurguses, &c.

Pray how has Monsieur Le Clerc's translated extract gone off? If this lies on hand I shall fear *Philol.* begins to deaden. Pray let me know the truth. I would not waste my time in meditating future improvements and virtuoso embellishments if the public really grows indifferent, and there be no earnest call for another edition. Pray be sincere with me in this, and I shall know how to instruct you to deal with Mr. D—y, if I live.

What you write again this last time about a servant gives me hopes. Some English he must necessarily know, though he be perfect in French; as on the other side he must know

KK

French in some tolerable degree, though he be ever so good an Englishman. Nor after all should I have had any reluctancy to comply with Sir John's petition for Jack Howard had he been but so diligent as to have got the principles of the French language ; and in that case a French valet-de-chambre, taken as a supernumerary and a kind of second steward during my passage or stay merely in France, would have done my business completely, at a small charge.

## TO JOHN WHEELOCK.

NAPLES, *July* 12*th*, 1712 [N.S.].

Bryan has written you of my lingering state. I know not yet what hopes I have of recovering or ever seeing you. Meanwhile I may thank Providence for the time gained and a family saved when I thought it past retrieve. Your accounts of Lord Ashley are very joyful. He is my all, I must expect to leave no more after me. My health is too unpromising for such thoughts. By your care his estate and circumstances I hope will be made up. I hope you are yourself satisfied in what you have done and acted at St. Giles's for his, and mine, and family's sake. What signifies it who besides is dissatisfied with your execution of my orders ? Must not my family take breath awhile ? Has it not sufficiently spent itself for the public, as well as I, my breath, health, and life ?

Be satisfied that I myself am entirely so in all you have done. And I hope you will at last know me for a steady man and firm to my own determinations. I earnestly conjure you never more to relapse into doubts and mistrusts of me. But pursue your instructions. And never mind so much at what even my friend Sir John reports to you contrary to them.

I cannot but be surprised at one thing in your last letter about Bryan. I was expecting that when I heard from you next you would have shown your concern for my acting as I have done with such regard to your nephew and so little to myself, in being content to let him go (rather than lose his station) after such pains as I have taken to fit him not only for my own service but for the world, and for business and mankind at large, by such instruction, advice, council, reproof, exhortation, familiarity, friendship, as if he had not been yours but my own relation.

And now I am to come, God knows, into the hands of strangers, perfect strangers, and foreigners, perhaps Papists, and this in my sick state and with a wife, poor Mr. Crell growing every day less and less capable of anything. What is the meaning of your writing as you do about your nephew, as if it were my choice that he should leave me ? But I will not be his hindrance. Nor could I well expect that he should make me such an offer as to lose his place and fortune for my sake. Had he made the offer I could not indeed have found in my heart to accept; you know how little selfish I am and in such cases how I am apt to act. Meanwhile, if John Howard have really such a kind of affection for me as you intimate, I have need enough of him about me in my sick state, and to ease my poor wife. His business and station will be my chamber, and his habit accordingly gentleman-like, and place creditable. He may be a help to my wife in inspecting the steward or caterer's accounts, and to me in bills, returns, &c., which I shall not willingly let pass through a foreigner's sole management. A little, very little French would make John Howard a seasonable support and frugal addition to my small family, if the fellow's affection stand really towards me as you hint. Pray write your thoughts, but keep them [otherwise] to yourself. God be with you.

---

TO THOMAS MICKLETHWAYTE.
(By my wife's hand.)
NAPLES, 19th *July*, 1712.

DEAR COUSIN,—You see by whose hand I am forced to write to you. My two assistants (Bryan and Mr. Crell) are both down in fevers, of which we have every one felt something, and I myself with much ado got over it, but weakened and fallen away to the utmost degree, kept alive by the fine season and warmth of air by which I breathe, and hope while it lasts to recover some strength.

Yours last received (viz., of the 6th of June), with the copies in that (and in Sir John's of the same date) from our captive friend,[1] has so raised my spirits and thought, that notwithstanding good reasons, public and private, to discourage me in such entertaining and pleasant amusements as the adorning *Char——ks*[2] and other pieces (as yet but embryos) with devices, lapidary, grotesque, and of other kinds, I am now come again to the same agreeable study, and resolve in composition and design of every kind (both pen and pencil) to support, adorn, and recommend as well as I can those tracts which so brave a soul and so excellent a genius believes to be of advantage to mankind, and likely to prove beneficial to my countrymen, and to the cause of liberty and virtue.[3]

Accordingly, whereas I was now resolved once again to stop at the three frontispiece-volumes—plates of the lapidary kind, I now take heart and resolve to proceed with the six little grotesques for each treatise, as I before engaged. And now

[1] General Stanhope.    [2] The *Characteristics.*

[3] Extract of a letter from General Stanhope to Sir John Cropley, of the 26th April, 1712.—I cease not to study *Characteristics,* and find my value and admiration for the author increase daily, nor do I believe anything hath been writ these many ages so likely to be of use to mankind, by improving men's morals as well as their understandings. I can at least affirm of myself that I am the better man for the study I have bestowed on them, and if I mistake not very much, they will occasion a new turn of thinking as well as writing, whereby our English authors may become hereafter more instructive and delighting. I assure you that I often please myself with the thoughts of taking a pilgrimage after the peace to make him a visit if he continues abroad, and should think a journey taken for that purpose may better deserve to be accounted an act of religion and devotion than most pilgrimages are. I am sure it would be a very agreeable one if you would be of the party, and, considering the chief end I propose to myself in it, am apt to believe that you would not need very much persuasion. It would be making our friend but an indifferent compliment to say, that as things are like to be at home, one would choose to be absent oneself from thence some time, not to see what one does not like, nor do I believe that it would be necessary to urge that as an argument to persuade you to such a ramble ; and I protest to you, for myself, that I could with pleasure leave any company and take ever so long a journey purely for a few days' conversations with him.

*Cebes,* &c., may follow in due time, if my life go beyond this summer, and that I live to see the beginning of another.

Meanwhile what a difference there is between the zeal of one who ought, one would think, to have no small share (I mean Mr. C——[1]) and the great man who would go so far out of his way to promote *Philol.*[2] All the hints I can give cannot induce him so much as to revise, correct, and add a few notes to the translation of the first treatise (viz., Letter of Enth.)[3], which, joined to his already translated second treatise (viz., *Sen. Com.*), would make a pretty volume, with a preface and dedication to that great prince[4] who (as Mr. C.—— himself wrote me) took such pains in the midst of these hard times and weight upon him, to have a few scraps of that author translated for him, here and there. Of this I sent you an extract out of Mr. C——'s own letter. But neither that prince's curiosity, or applause, or any other fame besides in the world, could move me like that zeal and opinion expressed by our captive friend.

Thanks, dear Couz., for the letter I expect from the Royal Society and Sir Isaac Newton, to my virtuoso friends here.

I shall be mighty glad to receive that unworthy fellow D——y's sheet of criticisms on *Char——ks*, however pedantic or ignorant any of them may prove. I entreat you to let me have them all; and in answer to his cunning covetous practices with you, remember what I wrote to you in mine of 7th of June, and in the warmth of discourse when you push it home let fall to him, " That the same author has already finished two tracts of a new set of treatises, on subjects which, though wholly different from the former set, will prove the greatest support, reinforcement, and illustration imaginable of what has preceded ; and in a way new, beautiful, virtuoso-like, fashionable, polite, beyond any idea he can have of it; and that the titles, as well as the substance, of those old and of these new will exactly correspond, though the turn and manner of the pieces be so diversified."

Let him chew upon this; and if he prove not tractable, let him know that we have Italy for cuts, designs, and ornaments; and that we have Holland for paper and print. Keep close in

---

[1] Pierre Coste.     [2] The *Characteristics.*
[3] See letter 5th June, 1712, footnote p.     [4] Prince Eugene.

your hands the corrections I shall send you (which will be very considerable), and so tell him you intend to do, till all be fixed with him to your content: and hereupon you may venture to demur, and send me word how the gentleman proceeds, and whether he will not instantly come to terms.

I hope you have received my draughts, last post, of the third volume, lapidary plate, with the instructions enclosed in Sir John's, because of not making one packet too big.

---

### TO PIERRE COSTE.

NAPLES, *the 25th of July,* 1712.

MR. COSTE,—I received yours of the first from Utrecht just at the time I have got strength enough to use a pen myself, and write a line in return. Had yours come to me but a day or two sooner, I had been still unable to write not only by own hand, by anybody's about me ; for, besides my own habitual distemper and weakness, I was scarce out of a fever, which was general through all my little family : my wife and her servant, Mr. Crelle, Bryan Wheelock, and every English servant I had, having been down in the same fever, and Mr. Crelle (who should write for me) still in the weakest condition imaginable. But my wife (thank God), with her excellent constitution, soon got over it. A little matter depresses me, and I am sunk indeed very low ; but the warmth of the climate keeps me alive.

I do not wonder at your complaint of the uncertainty of your rambling life ; but I hope it will contribute to your health, yours being still in a condition to profit by it. And I count it a happiness for a man of letters to be stirred up so, and set a running once in four or five years, to balance the ill effect of study, retirement, and a sedentary life, which are apt to make an untoward revolution in his spirits and humour, as well as on his constitution. You had your share in your almost five years' confinement in the deserts of Chiply, where I am sure you were cohabitant with no mind or understanding but what might be called *desert.*

Though I see the reasons why you could not *touch up* my

little draught of Hercules,[1] &c., I cannot but regret my loss in it, being so kindly importuned as I am by some of my virtuoso friends here for a sight of it, ever since I read some paragraphs to them, and gave it my artist to read in the condition it is for the better carrying on of the great piece, which is now finished to my satisfaction.

In my last (of the 5th of last month) I let fall to you my wishes that after you had corrected this little piece you would let it be seen by some friend who knew not the author, and who would be less partial than your friendship (I am apt to think) may render you in such an affair. If the piece were found valuable I could freely commit it to you; and the author being *for the present* unknown (no matter what happened *afterwards*) should be content to see it abroad in any journal. That of Monsieur Le Clerc's would be too high an honour for it perhaps. The reason why I wish this is because I should, from the effect of this when it was read by people of fashion, be able to judge whether or no it would be worth my while to turn my thoughts (as I am tempted) towards the further study of design and plastic art, both after the ancient and modern foundations, being able (as I myself) to instil by this means some further thoughts of virtue and honesty and the love of liberty and mankind, after a way wholly new and unthought of; at least after a way very entertaining and pleasant to myself, and with the only sort of application or study which my weak health and exceeding low state allow me, nothing being more cheerful and reviving than this amusement of pictures, medals, drawings, and the reading of this sort, which by any other body's help I can enjoy. For whatever language is required a little reading serves; and that so easy that whether it be the lives of the artists themselves, or little stories relating to them, or whatever else out of Pliny or Pausanias, and as well as out of the modern life-writers of late masters, there is no difficulty in lending an ear to such pleasant fragments and things which require no thread of thought or reason, no intention or bent of mind, and which everyone who comprehends the language can read in a natural tone, as comprehending enough of the story and subject. But if I

[1] "The Judgment of Hercules" as first written in French.

barely flatter myself in the imagination of rendering any such subjects agreeable to others as they are to myself, I would fain be resolved, since I should be sorry to throw away time in such little works or compositions, when at the bottom I found they would not (by my pen at least) be rendered so entertaining to the polite sort as to serve instead of an agreeable vehicle for the moral potion, which by itself is become mere *physic* and loathsome to mankind, so as to require a little sweetening to help it down.

I have now to thank you for the most agreeable present you have made me in the transcript of the criticism of the worthy and learned Mr. Leibnitz[1] on *Characteristics*. You may safely in the author's name acknowledge the honour he thinks he has received by it, the satisfaction he finds in the candour and justness of his censure, particularly in what relates to the two great concessions of that author in favour of raillery and the way of humour. Does not the author himself secretly confess as much in his work ? And does he not seem to despise himself in his third and last volume of Miscellanies at the very entrance when, after having passed his principal and main philosophical work in the middle volume, he returns again to his mixed satirical ways of raillery and irony, so fashionable in our nation, which can be hardly brought to attend to any writing, or consider anything as witty, able, or ingenious which has not strongly this turn ? Witness the prevalency and first success of that detestable writing of that most detestable author of the *Tale of a Tub*,[2] whose manners, life, and prostitute pen and tongue are indeed exactly answerable to the irregularity, obscenity, profaneness, and fulsomeness of his false wit and scurrilous style and humour. Yet you know how this extraordinary work pleased even our great philosophers themselves, and how few of those who disliked it dared declare against it. For our author's part I dare declare for him that he takes even

[1] Leibnitz's criticism of the *Characteristics* is to be found in his works (Gerhardt's ed., III., 421-3). An English translation of this review is among the MSS. in the Record Office.

[2] Swift, whose *Tale of the Tub* appeared in 1704, dedicated to Lord Somers.

this censure of Mr. Leibnitz as a real honour done to him, and (what is far more) as a just testimony rendered to truth and virtue. How much must he, therefore, of necessity be raised by the encomiums afforded him from so eminent a hand ?

The vanity you have stirred in me by what you thus communicate from your parts will tempt me to send you, perhaps, by another post some transcripts of like encomiums from another part of Europe, as they were sent to me by certain friends from an illustrious prisoner in Spain,[1] whose passion for certain works has carried him to the thought of employing his studious hours in the attempt even of translating some of the tracts into other languages.

I must confess that these and other approbations from those of the highest merit and best judgment make me conceive so much a higher value than I could have presupposed of those works, and such an opinion of the good they may possibly do in the world, that if Mr. Leibnitz's critical encomium could, with his leave and on account of his great name and just character, be thought worth the being inserted in Mr. Le Clerc's *Bibliothèque Choisie,* I should be very much pleased ; especially since it serves to support Mr. Le Clerc's favourable judgment of that author.

I am too much spent with this which I have written to be able to add more than my own and spouse's kind remembrances to you with all good wishes. Adieu ! Adieu !

P.S.—Upon second thoughts, I find I cannot well send you the copies of that great man's sentiments on *Characteristics,* but reserve them for your inspection, when I am so happy as to see you here in the winter, if I live so long. Pray if you light on any good edition, private or particular remarks, notes, or thoughts on Cebes's Table, pick them up and bring them improved to me by your own reflections, and also the stamp or cut *(taille-douce),* be it ever so indifferent, which is seen annexed to some of the editions of that inestimable little piece.

[1] General Stanhope.

## TO THOMAS MICKLETHWAYTE.

NAPLES, *the* 2*nd of August,* 1712.

DEAR COUSIN,—I have not heard from you this last post. I wrote by the last the 25th of last (not directly indeed, but in my wife's to Sis. N.) in answer to your last of June 13th, about virtuoso matters.

The warm weather continues, which barely supports me, so that I am able to compose, write, and act in my usual way. My wife and family are up again of their fevers, and she herself as well and strong as ever. So it is not my disorder of health or affairs which prevents my sending this post (as I promised) the remaining one of the volume-plates, of which Mr. Grib—[1] has by this time two to work upon; as he shall have the rest of the flourish-works fast enough, I promise him, that he may not exceed the four months in which he has promised to finish. But other subjects have at this instant and for the last fortnight or three weeks filled my head and heart. It becomes me, however, to conquer myself, even in this respect, and for my country's sake (as far as I can be of any use or service in it) to put out of my head the consideration of the political concerns of it. I will master this passion and return to my virtuoso studies. These are my second parts. These are my arms, and in this writing-practice lies my ammunition and artillery, whilst I hold myself in breath and whet my pen for my friends' and country's use, and for their revenge, if I am urged and called to it, by personal ill-treatment.

I may justly congratulate with you, and with myself, that I am under such an incapacity of acting in public affairs, at such a season when the consequence would in all likelihood be a total breach with those old friends, and particularly that great one[2] with whom no power of courts or parties, no private obligations or disobligations to Ministries, could ever make me violate an old friendship which I held from my earliest youth for him and his.

It is now some weeks past since I wrote, after my best fashion, two several letters to a great man on your behalf.

---

[1] Mr. Gribelin.　　　[2] Possibly the Earl of Oxford.

But they are neither of them sent, nor would have been (you may be sure) but through Sir John's and your hands. They were not sneaking. But such as they were I now think it not fit to send them, nor any other until I have better occasion. This is a wicked age and season. God keep you honest. I hope my early advices and written instructions in your table book (when you first entered into a public employ), as well as what I wrote you in a few lines in mine of the 7th of June last, will stick by you. Your prudence, discretion, and reserve will, I hope, nevertheless accompany your integrity. But for a certain liberty which our friend gives himself in writing to me so contrary to his sentiments, though in my own favour, and in order to communicate affairs; it is such a violation of sincerity that were he not my *elder*, and his case (I well know) incurable, I should conjure him to forbear. Content I am, heartily content, to receive no news from you on such terms as these; though I might hear facts without reflections. You are still young, and may keep a virgin heart, though your head grows riper, and can teach you prudence.—For God's sake urge me no more (nor let Sir John) about writing THANKS to *certain persons*, even persons *under* and *below persons, inferior, second persons, and all that*, to speak in Mr. Bays's style.—I know best what style and manner befits me when I write, and what even in prudence and mere policy in your behalf, as well as in respect to my own character, is a proper part for me on this occasion.—Read over, at this moment (I beseech you) what I wrote in my own hand in mine of the 15th of March, from the accidental occasion of Bryan's concern; on which I wrote indeed with some warmth. But your case lay at the bottom. I wrote more coolly afterwards in mine of the 22nd, following in which I spoke of *light out of darkness, Hamlet's ghost*, and recommended *honesty and courage* as *good ingredients in policy;* desiring I might be left to my *good humour:* which I shall endeavour to keep. But for THANKS (I pray!) What *thanks?* To *whom?* For *what?* Am I then that very crane indeed? And has my neck been so deep in throats to such purpose? Am I so mere a worm?—Let me tell you (and I care not who hears me say it), I sit not idle; though far off. I have secrets, a long history, a pen, and something of a name in the world. I can be heard, and in a certain capacity can command the public ear; of which some *late successes* have particularly put me in possession. "I can speak even when I am dead; and shall have that to leave behind me which "may do myself and friends, as well as my country, some kind of right." Let those to whom I still pay the highest respect amuse me, or cast me off if they think fit.—These are my arms —remember.—But for other submissive practices, either in my name or by a countenance, as coming from me, remember I protest against it. And if such a course of insincerity should prevail, and a further siege laid to honesty and virtue, I would throw in such a bomb as would ruin the approaches and sappings of this underground work. My great disciple[1] will, I hope, keep free of this contagion, when he returns. At the same time I most heartily wish him to use prudence and reserve. But I can whisper that in his ear (as far off as I am) which would fire him, if there were occasion.—Therefore, no tampering, I conjure you. — Weigh well this letter and those to which I refer. Remember my strength, my proper arms as well as character.— So to my virtuoso-businesses, and smoother style, and subjects of which you are to hear next post, and which it will be your interest as well as pleasure to promote.—No more of those serious affairs—I have done.—Farewell.

TO JOHN MOLESWORTH.

NAPLES, 2*nd of August*, 1712.

Though besides my ordinary sickness, with the aggravation of a reigning fever, I have had withal a sick family about me for this fortnight or three weeks past (the fever having spared not one of us), I should, however, within that time, or at least by one of these latter posts, have found means to send you a line or two in return to the many you have so constantly obliged me with; but in reality my amazement has been such at the progress of affairs[2] in Britain that I am almost at an end of thinking, much less can I either speak or write of them. In reality matters are now pushed so far that an Englishman, who

---

[1] General Stanhope.
[2] The Whigs dreaded any peace that promised to leave Spain in possession of the House of Bourbon.

is truly such, can hardly make a single reflection which is fit to trust to paper.

I now fear the case of some people is as our old poet Ben Jonson has represented Catiline—"The ills which they have done are not to be atoned but by doing greater." Foundations, however, are not so easily overturned ; and when *all* is struck at there may be more effectual resistance than when pillar after pillar our building was impaired, and the sap carried on with subtilty and underground work. I may well regret that I have no part left me in this unequal correspondence which you are so thoroughly kind as to maintain with me, but only that of condolence. I must still return, however, to that old topic which I must again and again repeat—that if we are not overwhelmed, if we sink not all at once (foundation and all), even this shame and misery may prove our future happiness and safety. For well I know how soon a Court, whatever obligations of gratitude they may lie under, are ready to abandon their best friends in favour of a certain party who can sing in their ear that sweet siren song of *obedience without reserve, absolute power, unlimited monarchy, &c.* But here is a scene now opening, a part of action carrying on, which how tragical it may prove no one can well foresee. But however it ends, the parties who are concerned for our foundation, and have hitherto their successional right acknowledged, will have a full and feeling proof of those men and of those principles which have brought us into this condition.

I should dare go no further had I strength. So you shall have no more from me at present, but my sincere respects, good wishes, and all that must naturally come from one who is so much as I am your faithful humble servant.

P.S.—You have many returns of thanks from Lady Shaftesbury for your remembrances to her and mention of Lord Ashley. I can assure you she partakes so much with me in the present calamities of the public, that she yesterday, on the opening of the letters, applied herself with concern to the public news before she would open her private letters, which, however, brought her afterwards the comfort of hearing that our young gentleman and friends were all well. We both desire to present our humble services to Colonel Molesworth.

[Address:] To Mr. Molesworth at Florence.

## TO SIR JOHN CROPLEY.

### NAPLES, *the 9th of August,* 1712.

SIR JOHN,—The enclosed (as you will soon perceive) is for cousin Mick, to whom and to sister Nanny (who both receive letters from us by this post) I refer you for what relates to us and our concerns; wishing you health, your little charge life and honesty, and our country a name and being, which it may soon lose, as things now appear to me, who never before saw them (as you well know) in a melancholy view.

But I have sealed my lips and chained my pen. I hope at the same time I shall not be personally ill-used, but undergo only the common fate, not of Whigs I mean (for I have long been out of parties), but of Englishmen. Nor did I find even in France that my honest confession of my having been no Frenchman, whilst I was able to act in affairs, was any shame or injury to me even with the Ministers themselves, whose generosity I ought to acknowledge on the account of the great civility and assistance afforded me in my passage through their country.

Glad I am, notwithstanding, that I came hither, over the mountains, though to die here, rather than to have lived there at this time, and spared myself that finishing blow to my ruined health and constitution.

Amidst all you see, I can keep up my spirits as far as they relate to thought and humour. Witness these enclosed instructions for cousin Mick, and the other virtuoso-packet belonging to these instructions, which comes this post in a separate letter to him. Farewell. Dues to all, &c.

## TO BENJAMIN FURLY.

### NAPLES, *the 9th of August,* 1712.

Uncomfortable as things are, and great as the shame and misery is of our poor nation in particular, I must, however, most kindly acknowledge the comfort I receive in hearing from you of news and public affairs, which, though but in a line or two (without over-fatiguing yourself), is of high satisfaction to me. For what greater can I have in these calamities than to hear them by a friend with whom I have jointly spent my life in labouring for the public, and by personal action, advice, study, thought, and the employment of almost all the hours of my life, endeavouring to serve that country and common cause[1] which we now see sinking, if Providence does not wonderfully support the many noble spirits which appear in Holland, and the few which remain in our native country.

Much I rejoice to hear of the increase of your family, though in the female sex; and heartily congratulate with yourself and Mr. Benjohn for so excellent a daughter-in-law, wife, and nurse.

I was glad to receive the blank letter forwarded in your last of July the 15th by the extraordinary conveyance according to the directions formerly given you, but must desire you to superscribe the blank letter which you thus enclose to the great person here. Otherwise it cannot but happen, as has already done, that the seals also of the inward letter must be broken open, there being no superscription or mark to distinguish it. Please, therefore, to superscribe the inward letter directly, *A Monsieur, Monsieur le Comte de Shaftesbury*: for it is only between England and you I need be nice as to my name. Yet I cannot but wonder at what you write me (if I understand it well) concerning a letter of mine coming to you with wax and no impression; for I am careful to use always a fine seal, and that nice way of impression in little, which is of the best sort, and was Mr. Locke's way, as it is now Mr. Micklethwayte's and mine, who seldom, either of us, seal with a whole seal, which is more easily taken off, and set on again without discovery.

[Address :] To Mr. Furly, at Rotterdam.

---

### TO JOHN MOLESWORTH.

NAPLES, *the* 30*th of August,* 1712.

If by some experience in the world, some pains and study, and now last of all by retirement and the free exercise of my thought, I had not learned at least some sort of philosophy

---

[1] The alliance against Louis XIV., from which England had now withdrawn, in view of the approaching peace.

and command over my own temper, I could not even with the
best health and strength propose to myself to write with any
tolerable ease, though to a friend such as yourself, at a time when
all things went so ill abroad and public news, which of late
years have been so bright and promising, are now grown so dark,
and (as you justly represent) in every respect so melancholy and
ill-boding.

It may, perhaps, be only a sort of despair which may render
one however thus easy as I now am, when I not only see that I
am myself precluded from being any way assistant in affairs ;
but when in reality they are become so desperate that I can
foresee no possibility of a remedy but from mere Providence
itself.

We are now at the mercy of one single man[1], who has all
power in his hands, and every secret in his breast. How
Providence may dispose that heart I know not. He has a head,
indeed, but too able. Nor have we had (in my opinion) a genius
equal to oppose to him, besides one whom at last I hear we are
likely to lose, and whom the public prints and private accounts
have given us for dead, or in a languishing state past recovery.
And of this person, I remember, I wrote my mind to you at the
beginning of the year, on the first struggle we made when the
ever memorable memoria (that of Hanover) appeared.

The world does not often produce real able statesmen. And
when it does, there are often great alloys in their character.
Our Whig party, I fear, will soon be a rope of sand. The two
noble lords and worthy Ministers lately fallen were many years
together labouring to break that Whig interest which they now
want. The nation, I believe, will be no more endangered from
what was called a Whig cabal. And we shall only have such
quarter from the opposite party as the superior genius who
controls and manages them thinks fit by his interposition to
afford us. He carries all before him. And were I disposed to
rail at him (as from his schemes, perhaps, I may be), yet should
I hardly think it prudent, even for my country's sake, which
lies so wholly in his hands.

---

[1] Probably reference is here made to Robert Harley,
Earl of Oxford.

You may ask me, perhaps, as a friend, what should one do in such a case? especially one who is a Minister abroad, and personates a Ministry such as it now stands at home?—The question, I confess, is hard to answer. I myself, as private as I am, and out of any public character whatsoever, were I able to go abroad, should scarce know how to demean myself, or what countenance to show. Whoever I met concerned on either side in the affairs of Europe, were he a man of sense and spirit, I could scarcely look him in the face. If an ally, what just reproach!—If a neutral, what censure! What amazement!—If a Frenchman (for this is of all the rest most cruel and hard to bear), what grimace! what half-smiles, feigned compliments, and abusive congratulations!—" Where are now these *English!* those high spirits! those pushing Ministers, generals, parliaments, people!"

Do not, I entreat you, imagine that my meaning is by this to dishearten you from continuing your present public station, from whence, should you at this juncture make yourself be recalled, I am afraid you would do your country and family but ill service. Were it my own case, I will tell you truly how I would do. I would neither act so as to offend the present Ministry and be recalled, to solicit, perhaps, all my life afterwards for my arrears, nor would I act so much to the honour of my own Court and nation as to increase those arrears by my expenses in their behalf or for their credit. On the contrary, since their honour stood as it did, I should think I did them best service by hiding myself and keeping private as a mourner. I should think it even a merit to take shame to myself in my country's case and bear my part in that disgrace it had deserved. Since I could no way make that figure I ought to do, I would resolve to make none at all, but turn economist with all my might. By this means I would soon have the better end of the staff, and make myself be recalled (if in time I should stand so inclined) upon better terms for myself, and with less dependency upon those whose candour I should never count on, and to whose friendship I should unwillingly consent to owe any part of my own or family interest or fortune.

LL

* Looking back on what I have here dictated, I cannot but wonder at myself, how I have run out and given you so long a trouble upon little or no subject. It is a sign that the summer warmth has restored me at least some kind of strength, which I am willing you should have the first fruits of, though ever so coarse and ordinary. Lady Shaftesbury, who joins with me in humble services to you, returns many thanks for your notice of Lord Ashley, who continues prosperous.—I am, dear sir, your very sincere friend and humble servant.

[Address :] To Mr. Molesworth, at Florence.

-----

## TO THOMAS MICKLETHWAYTE.

NAPLES, *August* 30*th*, 1712.

DEAR COUSIN,—I had none from you this last post. Your last was of July the 11th with Mick. Ainsworth's letter. Pray return a favourable answer upon the refusal, and enquire all you can about his character. For I am in great fear for him, and may soon be put to resolve about him in some other case that may happen.

You have two copies enclosed, the first of which to Sir John I entreat you would immediately communicate to Mr. Hooper, in case Sir John happens to be out of town, and that my letters of last post should have miscarried or delayed.

The other† copy is of what you engaged me to write, and what I would never have written to any one in the world but at your entreaty, and on the account of the obligation you have (and I with you) to the father of this *unadvised* young gentleman.—Am I, then, to give advice ? Am I to be the monitor and preceptor ? Am I to thrust myself thus between father[1] and son[2], in private family matters and in public concerns, in which letter,

---

* The rest in my own hand.
† See the letter immediately preceding this [viz., a letter to Mr. Molesworth on politics, dated 30th August].
[1] Robert Molesworth.        [2] John Molesworth, son of Robert.

if I am driven to speak my mind, I am necessitated to speak more than will be liked. And this I must do. Therefore, 'twere far better I were let be silent.—Nor will I hereafter engage in such complicated affair. For as to the public, my scene of action being now over, I will here take my leave of such matters. And (as I have before written you) unless I am urged by personal provocation so as to be in a manner *called* and summoned to it, I will venture to say this is the last formal letter on politics which I shall ever write. But for this young gentleman (to whom I so heartily wish well), his politics as well as his economics run, it seems, at a strange rate. He shows sufficient discontent towards the best, the worthiest, and ablest of that party which is now undermost, and at the same time (as I find, too, by yours) can hardly be brought to keep measures with those who rule. For my own part, as little as I should have liked Pompey and his Junto, I should have heartily sided with him, though there had been no Cato in the case. Catos, God knows, we have none. No, nor yet Pompeys. But setting aside the soldier character (for it is of the statesman alone that I am speaking), I should hardly be so unwise as to desert Pompey and rail at Cæsar. So far from it that, as the event has shown, it had been better to have committed all to Cæsar, when the only heads who were a match for him were taken out of his way.— Now pray hearken but to the conduct of this gentleman. He has not only sent both news and pamphlets of a certain kind to those who will certainly never keep his secret, but has referred the very same persons to me for things of the same nature communicated by himself. So that were I incautious this would be a fine manner of engaging me, as they say, over boots and shoes. Excellent prudence! Rare discretion!

This (dear couz.), this is the conduct which I thoroughly condemn, and would wish you to avoid. But never so as to relax it in other respects, or grow short in zeal and affection for old friends ; never so as to suffer those to grow little in our eyes who were once so *great,* because then in power.

The man who now rules all was for many years as great a man in my eyes as now, with all his outward greatness. And should his turn come to fall he would find that it was more natural and easy to me to express my friendship for him (as I have done before) when he was abandoned and persecuted, than when he governed all without control.

Let me tell you, dear couz., as long as you have been acquainted with me (both Sir John and you), I have reason to fear you know me little. It is not your understanding I accuse. Nor do I think my friend Sir John is wanting in what the world calls ability. But the world is a fine world, I don't say an honest one. I am out of it. I am far off. Nor do I say I think myself out of mind or forgot, but I begin, I fear, to be less and less known by you, as I have been long out of your converse: otherwise my sense in my many late letters would be better taken, and pursued with more confidence and trust. But enough.—Now to virtuoso-matters and my amusements where I am.

I wrote you word last post in mine of the 23rd of August, that the little˚ picture of Hercules was coming to you by the *Liberty*, Captain Haughton commander, who touches at Deal or Dover, where some of your officers or correspondents may, by advice from you, receive it, and take due care, it being so tender a thing. With it I send you a letter, in which I shall give you a particular account of it. It is such a sort of copy (if it may be so called) as has perhaps exceeded the original. 'Twas done almost wholly in my presence, and twice done over as anew to bring it to its present perfection. I have already paid the artist above his hundred ducats (or twenty pounds sterling) first agreed on. But let not this alarm Sir John. The picture, if he pleases, shall be mine, notwithstanding I have the great one. Nor shall Sir John exceed his hundred or hundred and twenty pounds in all. I little dreamt he would have retracted the least from his two hundred pound commission given me by word of mouth in England. I have launched out indeed pretty deep, and am engaged at least a hundred pound over, besides my great piece (which is a hundred more), and I may say again almost another hundred in charge of entertainment and rewards to painters, agents, emissaries, and in correspondences kept up wholly on this account, except only what concerns the little works done for *Characteristicks*, which I in a manner myself designed, and drew; the rest by my draughtsman being but slight work, and what I could have had done for little by any other.

## TO SIR JOHN CROPLEY.

NAPLES, *the* 11*th of October,* 1712.

SIR JOHN,—. . . . It is the same discouragement has turned me from the thought I had of writing to Mr. Stanhope on his safe arrival.[1] You may guess how great a loss I count that of his letter by the poor servant, who by your account should seem to have been lost with it. The polite French can be barbarians enough in such cases as these, and give no quarter or so much as a hearing where the least jealousy is conceived. I have a great deal upon my mind which I could wish you to say from me to Mr. Stanhope concerning my honour and love for him. But as he cannot doubt of his having what is due from me of that kind, whatever there may be extraordinary, I am well enough contented to let sleep, desiring only you would do me justice as his friend and one who claims that name in common with yourself. For my own part, I cannot live to act for him as I once hoped to do. I had but little strength left when I received the first news of his misfortune. After that I had neither power nor means to accomplish my ambitious schemes, if I may call that ambition which had alone in view the raising of another. My own time was already over. Distempers had barred that door, and whatever thoughts I had of greatness, they could run no further than the vanity of contributing towards making him great in the world whom I thought most so in himself. Had I not secretly entertained this ambition, I should hardly have been pushed to make the last vain struggle on our new Parliament. Had that and the dismal news from our friend in Spain arrived but about a year sooner, the Kensington youngster[2] had never been thought of. Nor is it so comfortable a thought to have a posterity, as affairs seem now to tend. A philosopher (as you call me) need not have married for his country's sake on such a prospect. But you were willing I should do what I could to preserve my life, and it is preserved indeed, but by such pains and labour as it is

---

[1] General Stanhope arrived in England on 16th May, 1712, having been a prisoner at Saragossa, in Spain, for nearly two years.

[2] Young Lord Ashley.

hardly worth; not my own pains (for I could never bestow them so), but by my partner's, and such a tender care, such an ability and affection, as hardly I believe is equalled.

Meanwhile, if I have been able to write anything which such a judge as Mr. Stanhope thinks may be of use to mankind or my countrymen in this or in the next age, you may be sure I think it a happiness. But as for my attempting such subjects anew, or offering to write or dictate on anything beyond virtuoso matters, my cousin Mick and you have very ill interpreted my letters to raise such an imagination. Though, if others please to imagine so, there is no harm either for him or you. And as I once told my cousin Mick very emphatically (hoping he would have remembered), 'tis easier to write CHARACTERS than CHAR——KS. But you laugh at this, and say mankind are hardened and value not their fame, present or future. I differ from you in opinion, and think no passion stronger than this, even in our present great men on both sides. But it shall be as you desire. You see quick and understand me. I say no more. My *arms* and *weapons* shall sound no longer. I have dunned your ears too much about them, especially in my late letters to cousin Mick. He shall have quarter as well as you for the future. My trifles of virtuosoship are all I shall entertain you with, and if this prove not entertaining or profiting I have nothing further. My fables of this kind carry (I should hope) some little moral along with them. The mighty treatises which you seem to think me intent upon (according to report from couz. Mick) are barely two such poor tracts as the LETTER and NOTION already sent through your hands to our old lord. Nor have I yet set pen to paper or dictated one word on either of these intended pieces, only noted a few memorandums,[1] that if I should live over the winter I might employ myself a little during the summer following.

Here is a full and true account of my personal state and affairs; as to the crazy part and stories of my sickness and remedy, I leave my poor spouse to write of that, as she naturally

---

[1] Shaftesbury's "Notebook on art painting, ancient and modern masters and works, taste," &c., Naples, 1712, evidently designed as the basis for a treatise, is among his MSS. in the Record Office.

does and will do always to her sister, or when she writes to you herself.  I am weary and spent with what I have done; so with usual affection and wishes adieu, adieu.

Pray let Mick read what I say.  I have at last, after about a month's silence, heard from him, having received his of the 29th of July, with the enclosed remarks [viz., Mr. D—yl first corrections].

TO  BENJAMIN  FURLY.

NAPLES, *the* 18*th of October*, 1712.

The account you write me of the young man who calls your old friend W. P. uncle, is very amazing.  But the most mournful news is what you write me of your great city, which seems to submit.  If so, what becomes of Europe, the English Protestant succession, and themselves, who will rather be the first than last devoured ?

What a certain friend of yours has written you of things being *dark* is true indeed.  But who has helped to breed that darkness ?   Who more than himself ?   I own the ill-usage he once received : and myself resented his ill-treatment more perhaps than any friend he had.  But was it right to sacrifice all to his revenge ?  Nothing was ever darker or blacker than his conduct.

* Again and again I beg and entreat you, *beware*.  You have many seeming obligations and inviting circumstances, which may draw you to openness and trust.  But if you are drawn into it there are many reasons which make it too certain that you will afterwards have cause to be sorry for it.  Were it for nothing else but that your English correspondence might not be discovered and interrupted.  For as to Holland and our friends there, never have they had or can have a closer, bitterer enemy, as his interest now stands, and as his passions have wrought him up.  Neither is there one good or sound man of note in England, to whom he is not now a direct enemy.  Nor can he ever be trusted should any change happen in favour of that common cause, to the destruction of which he has for

* From hence in my own hand.

these two last years employed his whole credit and power; whatever his former merit entitled him to. His art and abilities are great. But I entreat you *remember.*

My kind services to all yours, from him who is as ever, &c. Pray burn this as soon as you have read it. I should write thus to no one besides yourself.

[Address:] To Mr. Benjamin Furly, at Rotterdam.

---

### TO JOHN MOLESWORTH.

NAPLES, *the* 25*th of October,* 1712.

SIR,—Amongst the many happinesses which heaven has afforded to mankind on no other condition, nor by other means than that of liberty alone, we ought, I think, to esteem friendship as the most considerable. I know very well it must be thought hard to deny private friendship to those of a slavish education who prefer private will to public interest and prosperity. But the consequence is inevitable. They who give the public a master, and are willing to serve in common, are impotent in society, and insensible of common good. I can allow strong sympathies and fondnesses to animals, Moors, Persians, and Frenchmen. The gallantries and loves so highly celebrated among these latter I can easily resign to them. But for friendship it has a nature too liberal and just to lodge with a slavish mind, which has either never known, or has apostatised from the principle of common good and public weal. Far different from this latter is the friendship with which you honour me. I have, indeed, pleaded my title, and in my former letters laid claim to it, as descending justly upon me from that genuine friendship of a truly *free* character which I contracted with your worthy father[1], when you were yet not old enough to distinguish between good and evil, liberty or arbitrary power. But you have now by several ways so ratified and confirmed your relation to me in this kind that it is become wholly original and your own proper gift. Had it not been for this freedom and the privilege which such a principle bestows, how could I have

[1] Robert Molesworth.

ventured to appear so pedantic as in my last letter of advice ?
And how could this advice, such as it was in its own nature,
have been accepted by you with so much favour and indulgence,
had not that principle borne me out, which is so well fixed in
you, and upon which the moral of my letter wholly turned ?
If young men of generous spirits, who have fortune at command,
and can be either men of pleasure or men of figure, can at the
same time have such a command over themselves as upon
occasion to live privately and reduce expenses, they are beyond
the power of corruption, and can serve their princes (as long as
they are suffered) with satisfaction and security. And were it
not that Courts and public stations are apt to make impressions
very contrary to what I have suggested, I could heartily wish
that many honest men would be more courteous than they are,
and more willing both to accept of favours and live in all decency
and compliance even under Courts and Ministries which were not
the very soundest one could wish. How soon else should we
lose the usefullest of men in every remote station of the public ?
Let those look to it who have the high steerage. Were I a mate
or inferior officer at sea, I would mind my particular business in
the vessel whilst I was left in it. And if I was commanded on
no duty should not be ashamed of standing idle, whilst I was
still in readiness to act.

As distant as I am from you, it would, methinks, be a kind
of separation, should you return to England. And I might, perhaps, be questioned whether self love had not some share in my
willingness to keep you in the post you hold. But be this as to
your mind and circumstances is most suitable. The times are
coming when we must either sink altogether, or a great change
happen in the course of things. Meanwhile I have only the
receiver's part in what relates to news and intelligence of what
is like to become of us. I have nothing but my line or two of
dry morals in return, with a good wish, a condolence, a con-
gratulation, or somewhat of this kind. The continuance of my
weak state leaves me little more to do in the world, and only
affords a good lady the means of showing herself very good.
For it is by mere nursing that I live. The youngster I owe to
her, and whom you kindly inquire of, continues strong and
sprightly, as we hear every post from England. I beg my kind

remembrances and services to all yours. You have the good lady's, and I am myself, dear sir, affectionately yours.

P.S.—We need be in no fear for our friend Stanhope, whom the honest news-writers, and many on this side the water, give for gone, because of his gracious reception. He is gone a progress : beginning at Bell-Bar, thence to St. Albans, and afterwards as far north as Chatsworth, and returns by Rainham, which is my good Lord Townshend's seat in Norfolk. I doubt not but he will meet other good friends, besides the owners of the houses.

### TO THOMAS MICKLETHWAYTE.

NAPLES, *the* 22*nd of November*, 1712.

DEAR COUSIN,—When you have considered all, and have looked back upon what is passed, you may be convinced, perhaps, that my plain, friendly, and bold ways are the best, at least for my practice and my character. Every man in his humour Nor are my humours, as you will find, so contemptible ; my mere humours. Even when I play only, and divert myself with writing, so vain am I grown (by my friend Stanhope's applause), notwithstanding Sir John's mortifying me by saying how little pen-work signified, and how little my author-character would avail me in other interests or affairs. " For who among the great ever valued their fame now-a-days ? Who minded characters ?" &c. But for whom is it (dear cousin) that I intend all this ? Why would I be thus taken notice of ? Do I want court favour, or popular applause ?—You have not surely lost the clue I gave you. Notwithstanding your long silence, I hope you have put things together, and made something out of my many long letters yet unanswered. Methinks the engines work well : the instruments do theirs. The Gribelins and the rest of that kind, by your help, make a good under-plot (would I could see the finished prints as promised before this), and virtuosoship, methinks, plays its part very aptly, and in good tune. The way lies fair. You have scope for improvement of what is begun. You will find me forward enough upon encouragement, if my prospect hold of getting over another winter : which as yet has come on so wonderfully favourably and mild (excepting a day or two the last week), that I have had thus far the full advantage of a continued summer. And by this and the course of medicines still used, I am able to hold up, and move out of my bed and chair, though not out of my chamber.—Adieu, dear couz.

---

### TO PIERRE COSTE.

NAPLES, *the* 22*nd of November*, 1712.

MR. COSTE,—With extreme satisfaction I have just now received yours of October 21st from the Hague with the account of your and Sir John Hobart's reception and entertainment at Hanover; the honour done to myself in particular by the notice taken of me (which I hope you will take care on occasion sincerely to express in my behalf), and with the three exemplars of the little dissertation[1] in which your admirable judgment and care has made me not a little proud. So that I am in a manner resolved to naturalise it myself and give it to the public Englished at first hand, rather than suffer it to go to Grub Street by help of those Anglo-Gallish translators who generally understand neither the one language nor the other.

But my concern is that in this letter of yours, in which you speak of your sudden journey to France (from whence God send you safe), you say nothing how my letters should be directed to you, or what time you are to stay there, having in your letter before given me hope that we should see you here by Christmas. Now should that not happen until a month or two after it would still be vain for me to hope an answer even to this letter, which going round by Germany will be a month ere it reaches you, though you should still be in Holland, from whence, according to yours, you should be already parted this day, for your letter has been just a month in coming to me, and you say that within a month you are to set out for Paris, having your passport.

How shall I send you therefore my answer concerning the intended quarto edition and the plate proposed? And what encouragement have I (who am so weak in writing in my own

---

[1] The "Judgment of Hercules" in its original French form.

hand) to write to you as I would intimately to a friend on these and other subjects ? The loss of a letter would go deep with me. And I have lost several which I have written to France and which have been written to me from thence. What shall I do till I hear again from you ?

My recovery (if I may call it such) is so slow that I have been few days out of my house even in this fine summer past. And I am now confined to my chamber. But even this is so much better than what was expected in my case, that my spouse and friends are very joyful at it. She in particular sends you her thanks for your kind remembrances, and is herself (she says) self-interested in you as Lord Ashley's future guide and governor.

I beg the return of my humble services to Sir John Hobart[1], and that you would always believe. me your constant and faithful friend.

P.S.—It would be a great pleasure to hear from you now and then, though it were but a line or two from any place in your travels, particularly from Paris and about your friend the Abbé Bignon, of whose politeness I have an high idea, and if he be as good a friend as he is a candid and able critic, I shall be glad for your sake in several respects. I would be glad to know how he happens to like the "Judgment of Hercules." I regret nothing I lost at Paris but the not seeing Abbé Bignon and Madame Dacier, which my ill-health prevented.

---

TO SIR JOHN CROPLEY.

NAPLES, *the* 22*nd of November,* 1712 [N.S.]

To SIR JOHN,—I am forced to look upon myself at present as in a manner cut off from your correspondence. The post before this last, which brought other people their letters of the 7th October from England brought us not a single line ; and this post, by which letters were so earnestly expected, has brought only an account from Holland that the mail, though

[1] Sir John Hobart, first Earl of Buckinghamshire (1694?—1756), son of Sir Henry Hobart. See page

the wind had been long fair, was not yet arrived, which caused many surmises.

Meanwhile, as my far distance and sickly circumstances allay in me all thoughts which might arise on politics and the great turns of State, I easily suspend all reflections. And in this interval shall entertain you only as usually with the amusements of my infirm and painful state of life, which I render this way as cheerful, or at least as easy and tolerable as I well can. But pray see! if amidst all I have not subject enough for vanity? For as useless as I may seem grown of late, I have the fortune to gain the consideration and regard of such a part of the world as I could little expect. You will already perhaps have been surprised, as I myself was the other day, by the prose draught of our young Hercules[1] in the Paris journals printed at Amsterdam. It was no secret indeed, nor could possibly be made one, having been written for the painter's use, and consequently known to the virtuosi here, before you saw it in English. And you may be sure I could not be so conceited as to think I had written it in French in such a manner as not to need correction in the style by a real master in that language. So to our friend Monsieur Coste I sent it without scruple or mystery, and with full liberty to do with it as he thought fit. And see! his answer as I have this post received it from the Hague, omitting other particulars of his return thither from Hanover, &c.

". . . J'ai passé le temps avec beaucoup d'agrément dans cette cour. La Princesse Sophie m'a fait des honnêtetes à quoi je ne 'm attendaes point; et je fus très bien reçu de madame la princesse électorale. Elles m'ont parlé souvent de vous avec des sentments d'une estime toute particulière. Madame la princesse électorale en particulier qui sçut que j'avais l'honneur d'être en commerce de lettres avec vous, me charges expressément de vous témoigner de sa port la considération qu'elle a pour vous. Elle savait que j'avais traduit l'Essai sur la raillerie, et me dit beaucoup de bien de cet ouvrage. Elle croyoit que j'avais traduit la Lettre sur l'Enthousiasme, et un jour que je n'etais pas à la cour elle le disait positivement en présence de Monsieur le

---

[1] The French original of the "Judgment of Hercules."

Chevalier Hobart qui savait le contraire, et qui lui répliqua civilement qu'elle pourrait bien sa méprendre. Le lendemain jallai à la cour ; et devant plusieurs personnes, elle me somma de lui avoner que j'avais traduit cette Lettre aussi bien que l'Essai, &c. Elle jouait au piquet, et comme elle devait bientôt quitter les cartes pour se promener dans la chambre, ja lui dis que dans un moment je la convaimcrais invinciblement que je n'avais point traduit la Lettre sur l'Enthousiasme. En effet dès qu'elle fut levée, elle me fit connoître qu'elle etait bien aise que je l'abordasse, et alors je lui dis que j'étais si éloigné d'avoir traduit cette pièce, que je songeais à la traduire tout de nouveau. Elle m' exhorta à le faire, parce que je lui dis que le premier traducteur a mal representé la pensée de l'auteur en plusieurs endroits. Sur cela elle me fit connaître que elle serait bien aise de lire l'Original en attendant ma traduction, et le même jour je lui envoyai *la Lettre* en anglais, qu'ella me rendait deux jours après. Elle la loua publiquement comme une excellente pièce, où elle ne trouvait rein à reprendre, excepté une petite réflexion sur les premiers prédicateurs de l'Evangile qui lui paraissoit un peu *gaillarde*, quoiqu' innocente dans le fond. Il m' échappa dans une autre conversation de lui parler de la dissertation surle jugement d'Hercule. Elle me témoigna d'abord une grande envie de la lire, &c.

" Je ne vous diron plus rien aujourd'hui parceque je ne veux pas manquer cette poste. J'ajouterais seulement que devant rester encore un mois à la Haye où je suis présentement, je pourrais profiter de vos corrections pour faire riemprimer votre dissertation en plus gros caractère in 4to avec une estampe où serait représenté le tableau de la mainère qu'il a été exécuté à Naples."

Now pray tell me which had I best resolve to do ? Whether leave it to the Grub Street translators and retailers to vend in their own guise, or whether produce the *original translation* (if I may so call it) by itself alone, without that which I count the spirit and life of it, I mean the recommendatory letter[1] to my

---

[1] Shaftesbury's suggestion for an issue of the "Judgment of Hercules" and the "Letter concerning Design" combined was never carried out.

friend-lord, whose property this is, and to whom it is my chief delight to join myself, in these as in former thoughts and contemplations of my retired and leisure hours.

For my own part, should that lord approve the thing, I am resolute enough to send both *Letter* and *Notion* without more ado to Darby (suppressing names only), to be printed in the very same manner and character as the " Letter of Enthusiasm " was. And to that end I will in a post or two send you a title page for him, with the few corrections I may think proper to make. So that if it be thought right you may proceed; if not, the pains will be no loss to me. I can only add in my own hand that I am, as ever, affectionately yours.

———

## TO THOMAS MICKLETHWAYTE.

NAPLES, *the 20th of December*, 1712.

DEAR COUSIN,—I have my pen in my hand once again, though I have reason to say *for the last time*, expecting in a few days to be dismissed by nature, and released from the pains and agonies I endure. For I endure the severest whilst I strive with my disease, and use the utmost efforts as if I were even a coward, to save myself at the entreaty and for sake of my poor deserving spouse, whose goodness and piety, however, is such that I trust in God she is prepared to resign me, and act as becomes her.* Comfort Sir John all you can. You are a *man* in these cases. Sir John is hardly so, through passionate concern for me. Let Mr. Stanhope know my love for him. You know it well, how long it has been such as to deserve his acceptance of the trust and charge I leave him of my family and little one. My other offspring[1] is wholly your trust and charge. You drew me on by kind solicitations and earnest entreaties to engage in these ornaments. And I hope you will not leave me or slacken your own zeal after having moved mine, so effectually as you

* Thus far my Lord in his own hand : the rest in the transcriber's.

[1] The *Characteristics*, the second edition of which was brought out shortly after his death.

will see, by the elaborate papers, instructions, corrections, and six treatise draughts sent by Bryan Wheelock, who is on his way for England.

The nearer I am to my end, and the greater my pains and agonies, the more comfortable it is in my intervals to hear news from you, so that I hope you will not abandon me, but write on to the last until you receive news, not by report but from my *own house*, that I am actually gone. For yesterday, when, together with Sir John's two letters, I received your full and particular one of the last of October, you cannot imagine how agreeable it was to me. And having made Mr. Crell look over Mr. D—y's[1] corrections of second volume, he finds them almost every one ready done to hand in that remaining copy of second volume, which I have here with me, and is to follow the first and third which are coming to you by Bryan Wheelock. This completes the set of originals from whence you are to print. But there being no haste, it seems, in this impression, I join with you in opinion for instantly printing the "Judgment of Hercules,"[2] &c., as I wrote to you and Sir John just before I fell ill, and having presently made my plan you will receive it from Mr. Crell transcribed by the next post that Mr. D—y may instantly proceed. One reflection I have to leave with you concerning the artful gentleman Mr. D—y, and I hope you will not forget it. Let not the plates be entrusted out of sight, but in a faithful hand to be present while the eight hundred or thousand are passing under the rolling-press. For if he has a mind to print several hundred more he may, but without the devices. For I would never consent wholly to spend and wear out the beauty of my plates in one impression. Besides that the gentleman will by this means be kept more under subjection. The plates remaining good still, and safe in your hands.

[1] Mr. Darby, the printer.

[2] Shaftesbury's "Notion of the Historical Draught or Tablature of the Judgment of Hercules" [London], 1713. Cf. Br. Mus., 527, K. 13 (2).

## TO THOMAS MICKLETHWAYTE.

### NAPLES, *the* 27*th of December*, 1712.

As desperate as I am in my condition, I am as good as my word in sending you* what I promised.

Pray forsake me not, but write and act to the last, this last letter of yours, with the three little volume plates and Mr. D—y's third corrections, having been highly pleasant to me and the greatest refreshment. Mr. Gribelin and you have done wonders. Farewell. Sir John and you will hear the rest by my sister Nanny. Last dues and love to Mr. Stanhope, recommending to him Lord Ashley, &c., and all what relates to me with his and our friend Sir John. Adieu.

## TO THOMAS MICKLETHWAYTE.

### NAPLES, *the* 3*rd of January*, 1713.

DEAR COUSIN,—The more painful my hours grow and the fewer I have to expect in life, the faster you see I ply you (and shall continue to do so) with what alone can give me amusement and at the same time advance the principal good which I shall leave behind me, my brain-offspring, so likely to make its way, espoused and honoured as it now is by such judgments and friends appearing in its behalf.

With speed, therefore, my dear cousin, you will, I hope, transmit to me the proofs as I have desired upon the models and instructions here enclosed for Mr. Gribelin and Dárby, whom it will be your concern to animate and unite on this occasion.

For Mr. Gribelin's encouragement I give you liberty to tell him I am so highly satisfied with his masterly execution of the designs, and of his capacity of carrying his hand yet higher, that for six treatise-plates to come (which will be in a manner but half-labour in comparison with three volume-plates already performed) I am willing to give the same sum

*Instructions and scheme for the "Judgment of Hercules," of which a duplicate was put in silk pouch of virtuoso copy book.

MM

which you write me word you had already given him, viz., six pound each plate.

I trust you will not only animate and urge the two artists, but raise the zeal of my two agents, the Wheelocks,[1] by making them sensible (as they cannot be without you) of the importance of the work in which they may be greatly serviceable, the elder in helping you to bear hard upon D—y and keeping him to strict performance; the other by going often between and helping as a sort of corrector when the work comes on, as I hope it will instantly now the new year is come, and that you will so soon receive by him (the younger) the corrected volumes, and after this the additional corrections which I have now completed since Mr. D—y's last received from you.

Having completed also (and here enclosed) my figures of reference from the several devices, you cannot be at a loss to know their meaning, from the printed pages to which they refer and from the manuscript instructions which you have by you.

The FEL. TEM. of the first volume-plate (which is all happiness from the right balance, liberty, and ancient model of religion) is a noted medal-inscription for *felicitas temporum* or *felicia tempora*.

The EN QUO of the last volume-plate (which on the other side is all misery and the modern model) is a poetical ejaculation, as much as to say, " Behold ! whither we are brought ? to what state reduced ?"

There is hardly the least room for criticism on Mr. Gribelin's performance, except in the right-hand corner of third volume-plate, where the just balance and proper harmony of light and shade is somewhat impaired by the over-blackness of the palm tree and river-god, whose crocodile, too, might be a little more enlivened and of a more squat shape, not so high-backed. But pray take care of hurt in touching this. As for the uneven standing of the niche or tribunal, and sitting magistrate between the two ovals of first volume-plate ; the matter is not great, nor worth regretting. I could have wished that the sheaf of corn, which is between Æsculapius's rod and bottle with bubbles in

[1] John Wheelock and his nephew, Bryan.

the upper part of the same first volume-plate, had been neater and shorter-eared, so as not to have appeared so gigantic in respect of its distance. If a little of the darkness of the upper oval of second volume-plate (viz., the land and sky in the perspective with the herd, flock, and fleet) were also taken off, the balance and harmony mentioned would be preserved still more beautiful.

Nothing could be more agreeable to my condition and last minutes than this little imagery, considering the main reference and end.

Adieu, dear cousin. Do for me as you think I have deserved, or may deserve, from you or mankind.

***

### TO SIR JOHN CROPLEY.

NAPLES, *the* 10*th of January*, 1713.

SIR JOHN,—I had no heart to dictate to you (knowing your passionate concern for me) whilst I had no prospect of life so much as from day to day. What remains you will hear by my wife to her sister Nanny. Meanwhile I hope you will not abandon me, but write to the very last of all particulars, public and private, as you have so kindly done hitherto.

Cousin Mick has heard largely from me by both last posts, as I was able by intervals to dictate to Mr. Crell relating to my author-capacity, which I hope you will not contemn, nor he neglect, who has so much forwarded it, and in a manner forced me on my late virtuoso undertakings which he has in his hands.

My *bodily offspring* (the little one) is that in which I doubt not of all your assistances and cares after I am gone. But of my *brain-offspring* I doubt much. Though, methinks, it should be sufficiently rated by you and cousin Mick, since on the strength of it, and by its sole merit, I can have the boldness to claim of our worthy friend Stanhope the acceptance of the joint-charge, trust, and care of little one and my affairs after me.

To this last article you have never answered me, but remember that if I live long enough to receive an answer to this letter, how great a comfort and satisfaction it will be to hear by you from Mr. Stanhope that he kindly accepts of this trust recommended to him from a friend, who so truly loves and honours him.

One thing I have to intreat of you in behalf of Bryan Wheelock, who may suffer by being stopped in his way either by the sickness or quarantine, with which we are just alarmed from the Venetian and German territories where he passed about the middle of last month, finding no passage yet settled through France, nor company or party to join with. Now would you apply beforehand to superiors representing the case, he might escape being turned out should he fail a day or two in the time allowed him, since he took above three months' time to come with all diligence from me to his office as required. His going has been and is a great cause of sufferance to me, and particularly to my poor wife, having no one in my chamber fit to assist me in my sad state. And I must own Wheelock's affection to have shown itself very sincerely in despatching John Howard to me, whose arrival I now expect with earnest desire, as you may be sure my poor wife has reason to do, knowing his strength and handiness about me and fitness to assist in my chamber, where she alone and poor weak Fanny are forced to do everything for me.—Adieu, dear friend.

### TO THOMAS MICKLETHWAYTE.

*[Undated, but that to Sir John is of 10th January, 1713.]*

DEAR COUSIN,—You read what I say to you in Sir John's above. Now will be the time for you to show me how far you love me, as you have professed in prosecuting what you yourself have begun on the foundation of *Char——ks*, &c.

I hope I may soon by the post receive from you the return of the models of the title-pages and, perhaps, the first sheet of the "Judgment of Hercules," if you have resolution enough to print at least the NOTION by itself, to which singly (as I wrote you) the advertisement I first sent (in mine of December 27) may serve as a preface, leaving out only the last words, viz., *in the letter which is here prefixed.*

Meanwhile, let me warn you that as for packets, which are a little bulky, and which I am concerned, therefore, should come safe, it is best to send them to old Ben,[1] to go by the particular way, which is more safe but not so speedy a one. And at the same time I desire that you would, by Sir John or my sister Nanny, give me notice of such a packet coming to me by the same post, else I may not be able to get it so as to make answer by the next return.—Dear cousin, adieu.

## TO JOHN WHEELOCK.[2]

NAPLES, *the* 10*th January*, 1713.

WHEELOCK,—I thought not ever to have been able to so much as to dictate more to you, nor am I now well able. The first days of winter weather (though but five or six in all, and those mild in respect of other climates) brought my cough and asthma to that degree in my worn body that at length it has opened the sluices and become dropsical, my feet and legs swelling upwards, and now above my knees and in other parts of my body, so that my state, indeed, is desperate, and my pains inexpressible.

My comfort in what I leave behind me depends chiefly on your fidelity and the affection I know you have for me and family. My spouse will depend on your advice and counsel in all things. She knows my friendship for you, and that the only reproach I ever had to make you has been your not knowing and trusting sufficiently to that friendship. I now bid you *farewell*, and will here only say to you that, setting aside your services to me and family and my regard for you on that account, I have all along had for you the most sincere affection of a friend, thinking you one of the honestest of men, and the most cordially sympathising with me in the love of honesty, liberty, our country, and mankind.

This (Wheelock!) I hope you will at length believe, and never think hereafter that I mistrusted you, when I have all along so truly and affectionately loved and confided in you.

I will not boast of what a woman I have had from Providence (or have myself made me) of a wife, but I believe

---

[1] Benjamin Furly, in Rotterdam.

[2] This is the last letter dictated by Shaftesbury to be found among his MSS. The long contest with disease approaches its end.

you will say hereafter that for a family (since God has blessed me with a son) I have not chosen or done ill. My other friends I think I may boast of. Sir John is no common one. They will be powerful and considerable, as they are affectionate, though only for the CAUSE'S sake. But it is on you, you (Wheelock!) that I depend both for counsel and service, advice and assistance, in all affairs both for my wife, my son and family, as in my will I have recommended in the strongest manner I was able. Again *farewell.* Continue to write on to me to the last with diligence.

Date your letters; that which I received before your last (which was the fifth of November) had no date besides St. Giles's, the.........1712. You say in yours of no date: "I will return 200 pound before the 25th instant to Sir Henry, to be sent to Leghorn for your lordship, and desire to have your lordship's commands in time enough for what more you want. This is a double way of returning money, as I apprehend. It was my desire indeed at first to have it by bills, but I thought we were at last agreed that as to Sir Henry Furness's channel, it should only be by giving my receipt *here* and your paying in *there* (always beforehand by some hundred pounds), and so settling matters by way of account, remembering how the exchange ran at the time of the payments and receipts. I entreat you to explain this and inform yourself and me exactly of these exchanges and money affairs between us, for it gives me great trouble.

I doubt not but as to expense to keep myself within the bounds I have lately written you several times. Since what Bryan wrote you of the state of my affairs (which was the latter end of September or the beginning of October last) I have taken up by receipt eleven hundred ducats. I shall advertise you still as I go on receiving, that you may keep touch and be beforehand.

You will hear, I hope, from Bryan on the road. Pray God he gets time enough to his day appointed him.

Kind love to friends and family. So God be with you.

P.S.—Pray (Wheelock!) be so kind as to read this over more than once, for my sake. I have heard nothing of John Howard since your last.

## MR. CRELL TO JOHN WHEELOCK.

### NAPLES, *the* 21*st of February,* 1713.

SIR,—I wished my Lady Shaftesbury's affectionate and exemplary attendance on the care of so important a life as my lord's was might have been at present rewarded with success, but it seems there was no effort in art or nature of force enough to preserve so valuable a life and retain a while a soul of the first magnitude, so that it was no other sickness than a perfect decay of body occasioned by so many complicate distempers which carried at last his lordship very easily (as he desired) the 15th of this month, at ten o'clock in the morning, in my lady's and Mrs. Frances's presence.

I notified it immediately to the Viceroy, &c., all regretting the loss of such a lord. His body is embalmed and ready to go by sea. There is Captain Martin, of the *Rebecca* galley. He carries my lord's body and all our goods to Pool, where you will be pleased to receive it.

I send you his lord's papers, last orders, two memorandums according to their dates, so that we shall not stay here a day longer than is absolutely necessary, and consequently I write to Messrs. Furly and Wilkinson about stopping our letters.

I will not write now about my lord's particular esteem he expressed until the very last moment of his life for your personal merit, but I must needs tell you how much I am sensible that, since my first coming to England, all my recreations from the studies were either in your good company or procured by your obliging care. So that if you will be pleased to continue, after my lord's death, the very same friendship, I shall conclude you reckon me, as I am, with the utmost sincerity and respect, your most obedient and obliged humble servant, CRELL.

WILLIAM BYLES AND SONS, PRINTERS,
129 FLEET STREET, LONDON,
AND BRADFORD.

Printed in Great Britain
by Amazon